ABOUT THE AUTHORS

Authors of a number of travel guides on the Mediterranean and United States, Michael Pauls and Dana Facaros lived in Granada for a year researching this book about Spain, visiting its distant corners and seldom frequented villages and trying not to eat too many *Churros.* Their next project is Cadogan's forthcoming *Guide to Italy*, and they were last seen with their two children in Perugia racing up and down the public escalators under the Piazza d'Italia.

CADOGAN GUIDES

Other titles in the Cadogan Guide series:

THE CARIBBEAN
GREEK ISLANDS
INDIA
IRELAND
ITALIAN ISLANDS
SCOTLAND
THE SOUTH OF FRANCE
TURKEY

Forthcoming:

AUSTRALIA
FLORENCE AND TUSCANY
ITALY
JAPAN

CADOGAN GUIDES

SPAIN

DANA FACAROS AND MICHAEL PAULS

Illustrations by Pauline Pears

Series Editors: Rachel Fielding and Janey Morris

CADOGAN BOOKS
LONDON

ACKNOWLEDGEMENTS

This book certainly would not have been possible without the kind assistance of the Spanish National Tourist Offices in London, and in every Spanish city. We would also like to record our appreciation to many others who helped: to all the bus drivers who didn't show Burt Lancaster westerns on the bus television; to Miguel in the stationer's shop on Calle Segovia who's always happy to photocopy a hundred pages of manuscript; to the teenage girls of Granada who came every day to play gin rummy with our small-children, allowing us to get a little work done; to our friends Chris Malumphy and Carolyn Steiner, who came from so far away to cheer us up in our delirium; and finally to the noble vintners of La Mancha, who make some of the best 55c a litre wine on this planet, and never run out.

Cadogan Books Ltd
16 Lower Marsh, London SE1

First published 1987

British Library Cataloguing in Publication Data

Facaros, Dana
Spain.—(Cadogan guide)
1. Spain—Description and travel—1981–
—Guide-books
I. Title II. Pauls, Michael
914.6'0483 DP14

ISBN 0–946313–69–5

Phototypeset in Ehrhardt on a Linotron 202
Printed and bound in Great Britain by Redwood Burn Ltd,
Trowbridge, Wiltshire

CONTENTS

LIST OF MAPS

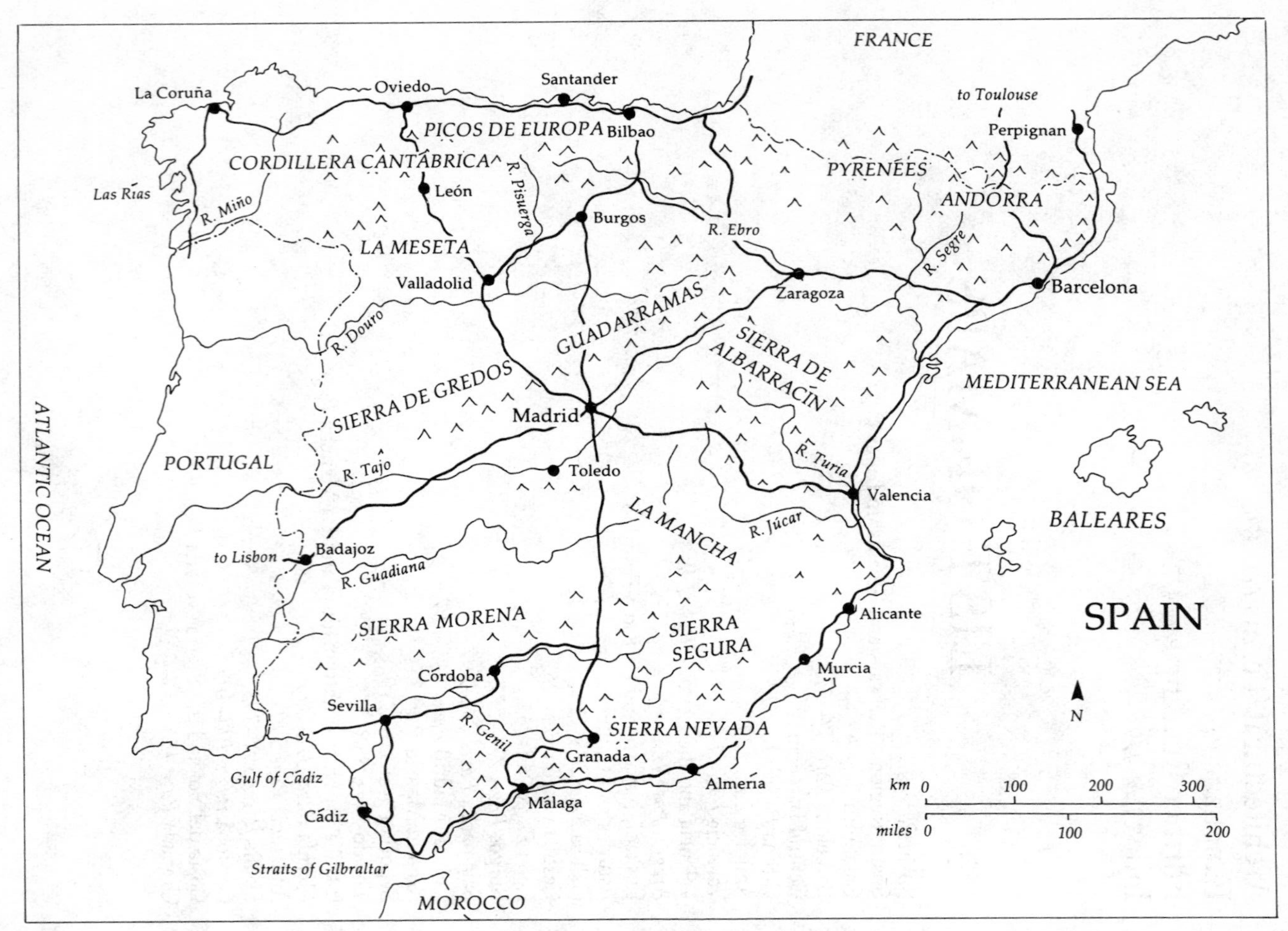
SPAIN
FRANCE
to Toulouse
Perpignan
PYRENEES
ANDORRA
R. Segre
Barcelona
MEDITERRANEAN SEA
BALEARES
La Coruña
Oviedo
Santander
Bilbao
PICOS DE EUROPA
CORDILLERA CANTABRICA
Las Rias
R. Miño
León
R. Pisuerga
Burgos
R. Ebro
LA MESETA
Valladolid
Zaragoza
GUADARRAMAS
R. Douro
SIERRA DE ALBARRACIN
SIERRA DE GREDOS
Madrid
ATLANTIC OCEAN
PORTUGAL
R. Tajo
Toledo
R. Turia
Valencia
LA MANCHA
R. Júcar
to Lisbon
Badajoz
R. Guadiana
SIERRA MORENA
SIERRA SEGURA
Alicante
Murcia
Córdoba
Sevilla
R. Genil
SIERRA NEVADA
Granada
Almería
Málaga
Gulf of Cádiz
Cádiz
Straits of Gilbraltar
MOROCCO
N
km 0 100 200 300
miles 0 100 200

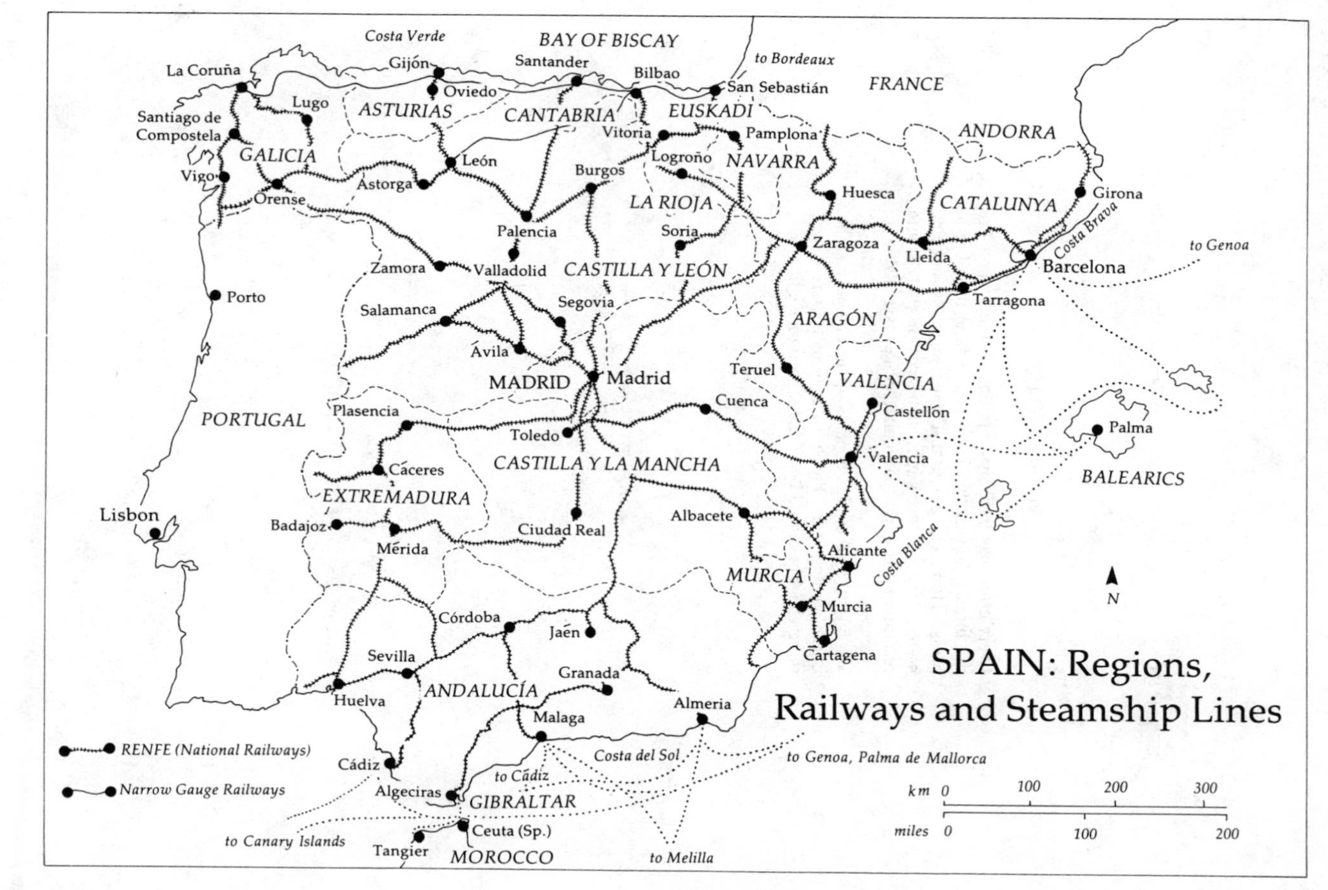

SPAIN: Regions, Railways and Steamship Lines
BAY OF BISCAY
Costa Verde
to Bordeaux
FRANCE
ANDORRA
PORTUGAL
MOROCCO
BALEARICS
GALICIA
ASTURIAS
CANTABRIA
EUSKADI
NAVARRA
LA RIOJA
CATALUNYA
ARAGÓN
CASTILLA Y LEÓN
MADRID
VALENCIA
CASTILLA Y LA MANCHA
EXTREMADURA
MURCIA
ANDALUCÍA
GIBRALTAR
La Coruña
Gijón
Oviedo
Santander
Bilbao
San Sebastián
Lugo
Santiago de Compostela
Vigo
Orense
León
Astorga
Vitoria
Pamplona
Logroño
Burgos
Palencia
Huesca
Girona
Soria
Zaragoza
Lleida
Barcelona
Costa Brava
to Genoa
Tarragona
Zamora
Valladolid
Porto
Salamanca
Segovia
Ávila
Madrid
Teruel
Cuenca
Castellón
Plasencia
Toledo
Palma
Valencia
Cáceres
Lisbon
Badajoz
Mérida
Ciudad Real
Albacete
Alicante
Costa Blanca
N
Murcia
Córdoba
Jaén
Cartagena
Sevilla
Granada
Huelva
Almeria
Malaga
Costa del Sol
to Genoa, Palma de Mallorca
Cádiz
to Cádiz
Algeciras
Ceuta (Sp.)
Tangier
to Canary Islands
to Melilla
RENFE (National Railways)
Narrow Gauge Railways
km 0 100 200 300
miles 0 100 200

PLEASE NOTE

Every effort has been made to ensure the accuracy of the information in this book at the time of going to press. However, practical details such as opening hours, travel information, standards in hotels and restaurants and, in particular, prices are liable to change.

We intend to keep this book as up-to-date as possible in the coming years. Please write to us if there is anything you feel should be included in future editions.

INTRODUCTION

Spain is a vivid country, one that catalyses the imagination. All of us, perhaps, carry around a certain picture of the particular Spain that once caught our fancy. It could be the Spain of blood and sand in the bullring, of medieval crusades and troubadours, or of Moorish gardens full of roses; the seed of it may have been planted by Cervantes or Hemingway, *Gil Blas* or Washington Irving. All of these Spains can be found if sought, but they hardly exhaust the list of treasures of this inexhaustible country. To know Spain you must visit the Galicians and Asturians, the Basques, Aragonese and Catalans. You must see the golden-brown hills of the parched south, and the lush valleys of the Atlantic coast. In between are 3000 castles, great cathedrals, gardens, villages, palaces, and rare works of art.

Another attraction is the Spaniards themselves. A remarkably lucid people, they are friendly, sane and democratic in the widest sense of the word. Not yet as overburdened, overstimulated, and overregulated as many nations we could mention, their openness and considerate good manners make them perfect company for anybody's vacation.

The hotels are fine, and transportation usually easy. The food isn't bad, and it's getting better all the time. The new Spain, in fact, is as relaxed and pleasant a country as you could ask for. Keep your eyes open. Spain is a subtler country than you think, and reveals itself in surprising ways. You may see it in the moon reflected in a pool of the Alhambra, in the face of a Velázquez *infanta*, in a fond medieval jest like the cats and rats chiselled into the cloister in Tarragona, or in a lone eagle coasting over a strong castle in Extremadura. On a train travelling through a sparse southern district in the spring, all at once your glance may take in more colour than you've ever seen: pink and white almond blossoms, oranges on the trees, red poppies and yellow daffodils along the track bed. In a second it will be gone, but you will have seen Spain.

We can't pretend to be opening up new territory. Spain after all is Europe's biggest holiday playground, last year playing host to some 43 million foreign visitors. We suspect that many more who would like to go have been discouraged, thinking the tourist tide has spoiled it all. Nothing could be further from the truth. Spain is not the kind of place that would ever let such a trivial phenomenon make it change its ways.

How this book is organized

Since the restoration of democracy, Spain has become a federal state, dividing itself into 17 autonomous communities. These correspond neatly to the old ethnic and geographical boundaries of this diverse nation, and we've found them a perfect way to divide our book. The exception is in the centre, where we have lumped a number of cities together in a section after Madrid; all can be easily reached from the capital. Note that this book is limited to the Spanish mainland. Both the Balearics and the Canary Islands are worlds in themselves, and separate books on both of them are planned in this series.

INTRODUCTION

Part I

GENERAL INFORMATION

Andalucian village

Getting to Spain

By air

There is an astounding variety of flight options these days to Spain, from North America and especially from the UK; even Spain's national airline, **Iberia**, is getting into the ball game by offering tempting discounts from a variety of American and British cities – there are bargain fly-drive deals, as well as an unlimited domestic flight option for purchasers of regular flight tickets. No matter how you go, you can always save by going off-season (from 15 September–June).

APEX fares, purchased three weeks in advance, and for a minimum stay of seven days and a maximum of 180 days, offer a discount, especially if you're travelling in the middle of the week. Ask, too, about their new 'Moneysaver' fares, their weekend specials (from the UK), and discounts for children under 12. Discounts are also available for domestic flights, especially if you're flying from North America: inquire about the 'Visit Spain' offer.

Iberia offices in the UK and Ireland

London: 130 Regent St, London W1. Reservations: 01-437 5622. Information: 01-437 9822

Birmingham: 15th Floor, The Rotunda Building, New Street, Birmingham B2 4PA. Reservations: 021-643 1953. Information: 021-643 9726

Manchester: Room 2, Level 5, Manchester Airport, M22 5PA. Reservations and

Information: 061-436 6444
Glasgow: Stock Exchange House, 69 St Georges Place, Glasgow 1. Reservations: 041-248 6581. Information: 041-248 6584
Dublin: 54 Dawson St, Dublin 2. Reservations and Information: 0001-779 846

Iberia offices in the US and Canada
New York: 565 Fifth Ave, New York, NY 10022. Tel: (212) 793 5000
Miami: NE Airline Building, 150 South East Second Avenue, Miami, Fla 33131. Tel: (305) 358 8800
Chicago: 180 North Michigan Ave, Chicago, Ill. 60601. Tel: (312) 332 0694
Boston: 20 Providence St, Boston, Mass. 02116. Tel: (617) 426 8335
Washington, DC: 1715 K. Street NW, Washington, 20006. Tel: (202) 293 1453
Dallas: World Trade Center, Suite 145, Dallas, Tx, 75207. Tel: (214) 742 6381
From anywhere in the US, you can use Iberia's toll-free line 800-221 9741
Toronto: 80 Richmond St W, Toronto. Tel: (416) 363 2612
Montreal: 1224 Peel St, 2nd floor. Tel: (514) 861 7211
While most regular flights from the US or Canada are to Madrid or Barcelona, from the UK you can also fly direct from Heathrow to Alicante, Bilbao, Santiago, Málaga, Sevilla or Valencia, or from Manchester direct to Madrid or Barcelona.

Other airlines
British Airways (from the UK) or **TWA** and **Pan Am** from the US offer many of the same services as Iberia. **GBA** (Gibraltar Airways) and **BA** have daily flights from London to Gibraltar. **Air Europe** has begun similar services between London or Manchester and Gibraltar.

Useful Addresses in Spain
British Airways:
Passeig de Gràcia 59, Barcelona. Tel: (93) 215 2112
Serrano 60, Madrid (91) 431 7575
Pan Am: Edificio España, Plaza de España, Madrid. Tel: (91) 241 4200
TWA: Gran Vía 68, Madrid. Tel: (91) 247 420.

Charter flights from the UK
These can be incredibly cheap, in and especially out of season; they offer the added advantage of departing from local airports, perhaps saving you a trip through London. Some of the best deals, however, have return dates limited strictly to one week or two, sometimes four, the maximum allowed by law. In many cases, though, a return charter ticket is a big saving over a one-way regular fare – and although it's illegal to sell the return half of your charter ticket, who's going to put you in jail? In London, check it out at your local economy travel agent or bucket shop, or in your local paper. Charter-flight listings from London are most abundant in *Time Out*. If you're aiming for Galicia, try **Pilgrim-Air**, 44 Goodge St, London W1 (Tel: 01-637 5333).

Charter flights from the US
These require a bit more perseverance to find, though you can save considerably on

the cost of a regular or APEX flight – currently a charter from New York to Madrid is around $530. You may want to weigh this against the current trans-Atlantic fares to London, where in most cases you can get a low-cost flight to Spain departing within a day or two of your arrival. This is an especially cheap way to go in the off season.

Call the major charter companies and compare prices: **Access** (Tel: 800-333 7280) is often the cheapest, even if you end up flying to Málaga via Morocco sometimes; they are also one of the USA's prototype 'bucket shops', offering good last-minute options on empty charter seats. **Spanish Heritage Association** makes use of SPANTAX, a Spanish charter firm. They're in New York, Tel: (212) 520 1300. Also try **TFI** (Tel: 800-223 6363), **DER** (Tel: 800-782 2424), or **CIEE** (Tel: 800-223 7402), all with flights to Spain. The *Sunday New York Times* has the most American listings.

Though it's always advisable to get your ticket as early as possible, with charters be doubly sure of your plans, both in coming and returning, as there are no refunds for missed flights – most travel agencies can sell you traveller's insurances, so that you don't lose all your money if you become ill. You can also expect delays on charters; if you leave on time without any difficulties, you have an especially benevolent guardian angel.

Students and anyone under 26 have the additional option of special discount charters, departing from the UK. Most of the big firms have offices in major cities. In London they are **STA Travel**, 74 Old Brompton Rd, SW7, Tel: 01-581 1022; **WST**, 38 Store St, WC1, Tel: 01-580 7733; and **USIT**, 52 Grosvenor Gardens, SW1, Tel: 01-730 6525.

By ferry

The last sea link between Spain and Great Britain is the **Plymouth–Santander Ferry**, operated by Brittany Ferries. This is a good way to go if you mean to bring your car or bicycle. Prices for passengers are just a bit less than a charter flight; children from 4–13 go for half price, under 4 free. Prices for transporting vehicles vary on size and season – it's most expensive from 22 July–16 September. The 24-hour crossing is made twice a week. For information, contact your travel agent or Brittany Ferries in Plymouth, Milbay Docks, Plymouth PL1 3EF, Tel: 0752 21321. In Santander the address is the Estación Maritima, Tel: (942) 21 4500.

By train

From London to Barcelona it's a full day's trip, changing trains in Paris and at Port Bou in the small hours of the morning. Other alternatives from Paris are to San Sebastian (the same amount of time, changing in Hendaye) or into the Pyrenees via La Tour de Carol and Puigcerdà in Catalunya, or via Toulouse, Pau, and Canfranc in Aragón, this last route involving a couple of changes on the way but saving time if you're aiming for Jaca, Huesca, or Zaragoza.

If you've been a resident in Europe for the past six months, and are under 26 or over 65 years old, you can take advantage of the **InterRail pass**, available at British Rail or any travel agent's, giving you a month's rail travel for £120, as well as half-price discounts on Channel crossings, ferries to the Balearic islands or Morocco, where the pass is also valid. The American **EurRail pass**, which must be purchased before you leave the States, is a good deal only if you plan to use the trains every day in Spain and elsewhere – though it's not valid in Great Britain, Morocco or Eastern Europe. A month of travel is around $300 for those under 26; those over 26 can get a 15-day pass for $260 or a month for $410. Again, it's not much of a deal in Spain – you'll have to pay supplements for any kind of express train. Also note that both InterRail and EurRail passes are not valid on Spain's numerous narrow gauge (FEVE) lines.

If you're under 26, you can save 35 per cent buying BIJ tickets through *Transalpino*. In London their office is at 71-75 Buckingham Palace Road, London SW1 0QL; in the US you can reserve tickets through Campus Holidays, 242 Bellevue Ave, Upper Montclair NJ, 07043 (Tel: (201) 744-8724). Tickets are valid for two months and in that time allow for unlimited stops along the way. BIJ tickets are also available within Spain (see 'Getting Around Spain').

By bus/coach

Two major companies – Supabus (Tel: 01-730 0202) and Euroways (01-730 8235) offer departures several times a week from London to Spain, along the east coast as far as Alicante, or to Algeciras, via San Sebastián, Burgos, Madrid, Córdoba, and Málaga. Buses take a couple of hours longer than the train; the trip all the way to Algeciras takes two days. In the summer the coach is the best bargain for anyone over 26; in the off-season you'll probably find a cheaper charter flight.

Driving

Driving from London you have a choice of routes through France and into Spain. The faster road to Catalunya and the east coast is through Calais, Paris, Bordeaux, and La Jonquera. For western Spain, you may want to try the ferry from Portsmouth to St Malo or from Plymouth to Roscoff and head down the west coast of France. Both routes take an average of a day-and-a-half of steady driving to reach Spain. For the scenery, opt for one of the routes over the Pyrenees, through Puigcerdà and Somport-Canfranc or Andorra; if you're not in hurry, take the classic route through Roncevalles, Vall d'Aran, or through Tarbes and Aragnouet through the tunnel to Parzán.

Passports, customs and visas

Holders of British, Irish, US or Canadian passports can enter Spain for up to three months without a visa; holders of Australian or New Zealand passports need a visa, available from any Spanish consulate. You can also enter Spain with a 'British Visitor's Card'.

If you want to stay in Spain for longer than three months, you should request a *visa de prolongación* (extension visa) when you enter the country. You need one of these to take to the police after you've been in Spain for three months to be updated every three months. This is the new law (as of January 1986), and at the time of writing half the border guards do not appear to have heard of it, and on the French, Andorran, or Portuguese frontiers it's often hard to get them to stamp any visa at all in your passport. The reason behind the law was to crack down on illegal residents and British cons living on the Costa del Sol, who traditionally have renewed their passport visas by stepping over the border once every three months. We hope by the time you arrive they've ironed the kinks out of the system. Also note that the Gibraltar border is now open, so if you fly to Gibraltar you'll have no trouble getting into Spain.

Customs are usually polite and easy to get through – unless you come in through Morocco, where they'll search through everything you own.

Spanish National Tourist Offices

Before you go, you can get maps, brochures and booklets from the national travel offices listed below:
London: 57–58 St James St, London SW1A 1LD. Tel: 01-499 1095
Chicago: 845 North Michigan Ave, Chicago, Ill. 60611. Tel: (312) 944 0215
Houston: 4800 The Galleria, 5085 Westheimer, Houston, Tx, 77056. Tel: (713) 840 7411
New York: 665 Fifth Ave, New York, NY, 10022. Tel: (212) 759-8822
San Augustine: Casa del Hidalgo, Hipolita & St George Sts, St Augustine, Fla, 32084. Tel: (904) 829 6460
Toronto: 60 Bloor St West 201, Toronto, Ont., M4W 388. Tel: (416) 961 3131

Getting Around Spain

By air

Internal flights in Spain are on Iberia or Aviaco. Most flights go through Madrid or Barcelona. Both carriers are nationally run and almost always share the same office in the cities. On the mainland you'll find airports in the following cities: Alicante, Almería. Ampurias (Girona), Asturias (Oviedo), Badajoz, Barcelona, Bilbao, Burgos, Cáceres, Córdoba, Granada, Jerez (Cádiz), La Coruña, Logroño, Madrid, Málaga, Murcia, Puigcerdà, Pamplona, Reus (Tarragona), Salamanca, Santander, Santiago de Compostela, Seu d'Urgell, Sevilla, Valencia, Valladolid, Vigo, Vitoria, and Zaragoza. Other airports are located in Melilla in North Africa, and on most of the Balearic and Canary islands.

Prices are inexpensive compared to most of Europe, and if you shop around and are willing to travel at night on slow days you can pick up some bargains, especially if you're going on a round trip. Also, check out the national charters in Spanish travel agencies. At the time of writing, the cheapest, round-trip flight between Barcelona and Madrid is 12,000 pts (around $90 or £65).

By car

This is probably the most pleasurable way of getting about, though the convenience is balanced by a considerably greater cost; petrol is as expensive in Spain as anywhere else in Europe. In cities, parking is always difficult; another problem is that only a few hotels – the more expensive ones, to be sure – have garages or any sort of parking; you'll usually be forced to take your chance in the street. Spain's highway network is adequate and in good repair. Modern dual carriageways are rare; there are toll roads from Barcelona to Burgos and the Basque country, and down the east coast as far as Cartagena. Elsewhere there are short stretches of highway around Madrid and Sevilla, in Galicia and Euskadi. The government is currently planning to waste trillions of pesetas on a full-scale highway system, but for the time being, the rarely crowded, two-lane roads that blanket the country will do just fine.

To drive in Spain you'll need an **International Driver's Licence**, available through the AA or RAC or any auto club in the US, and a **green card** proving limited liability insurance. Americans should not be intimidated by driving in Europe. Learn the international road-sign system (charts available to members from most auto clubs), brush up on your gear-stick shift technique, and get used to the idea of few signals, and traffic constantly converging from all directions. As in most European countries, people treat driving as a sort of video game, and you'll need to pay a little closer attention than in the States. Seat belts are mandatory.

Renting cars

This is moderately cheaper than elsewhere in Europe. The big international companies are the most expensive; you can do better with ATESA, the government-owned Spanish firm, whose prices for the smallest cars begin at about £80 ($110) per week with unlimited mileage. Small local firms can sometimes offer a better deal, but these should be treated with some caution. Local firms can also be found to rent **mopeds** and **bicycles**, especially in tourist areas. **Hitchhiking** involves a long wait anywhere; few Spaniards ever do it.

Ask your travel agent about the 'Tour Spain' package that offers an inclusive price for ATESA car hire and accommodation in any of Spain's paradores for seven nights or more. The plan is for a minimum of two people or maximum of four in one car; savings are considerable.

By train

Mister Traveler, take the Spanish Train!

RENFE brochure

If you're using public transportation, there is usually an even choice between the bus and train. The slight difference in price usually favours the train, while buses are usually a bit faster.

Democracy in Spain has made the trains run on time, but Western Europe's most eccentric railway, **RENFE**, still has a way to go. The problem isn't the trains themselves; they're almost always clean and comfortable, and do their best to keep to the schedules. Steam engines, country families picnicking on mortadela sandwiches in the aisles, and drunken conductors are now only items for nostalgia, but the new efficient RENFE remains so phenomenally complex it will foul up your plans at least once if you spend much time in Spain.

To start with, there are no fewer than 13 varieties of train, from the luxury **TEE** (Trans-Europe Express) to the excruciating *semidirecto* and *ferrobus*. Watch out for these; they stop at every conceivable hamlet to deliver mail. The best are the **Talgo** trains, speedy and stylish beasts in gleaming stainless steel, designed and built entirely in Spain; the Spaniards are very proud of them. **TER** trains are almost as good. Note that a majority of lines are still, incredibly, single track, so whatever train you take, you'll still have to endure delays for trains coming the other way.

Every variety of train has different services and a different price. RENFE ticket people and conductors can't always get them straight, and confusion is rampant. Prices are never consistent. There are discounts for children (under 4 years old free, 4–12 pay 50 per cent), large families, senior citizens (50 per cent), regular travellers, and 20 per cent discounts on *Dias Azules* ('blue days') for *round-trip tickets only*. 'Blue days' are posted in the RENFE calendars in every station – really almost every day is a 'blue day'. Interpretations of the rules for these discounts differ from one ticket-window to the next, and you may care to undertake protracted negotiations over them like the Spaniards do. There is a discount pass for people under 26, the *tarjeta joven*, and BIGE or BIJ youth fares are available from TIVE offices in the large cities.

Every city has a **RENFE travel office** in the centre, and you can make good use of these for information and tickets. Always buy tickets in advance if you can; one of RENFE's little tricks is to close station ticket-windows 10 minutes before your train arrives, and if you show up at the last minute you could be out of luck. Other stations don't open the ticket-windows until the train is a couple of minutes away, causing panic and confusion. Don't rely on the list of trains posted; always ask at the station or travel office. There may well be an earlier train that makes an obscure connection at some place like Medina del Campo, Bobadilla, or Miranda del Ebro, big junctions where several lines cross. Fares average 350 pts for every 100 km (63 miles) – 520 pts first class – but there are supplements on the faster trains that can raise the price by as much as 80 per cent.

RENFE has plenty of services you'll never hear about – like car transport to all parts of Spain. If you plan to do a lot of riding on the rails, buy the *Guía RENFE*, an indispensable government publication with all the schedules, tariffs, and information, available for a pittance from any station newsagent. It's heavy, but you can tear out the pages you need.

Excursion trains

The *Transcantabrica*, a recent innovation, is a seven-day, 1000 km (625 miles) luxury tour of the prettiest part of the north-western Spain, from León to El Ferrol, with accommodation that 'equals a five-star hotel' on board (the train is stationary during the night), with stops in towns and scenic places like the Picos de Europa and meals in the region's best restaurants. Excursions run once a week from June till October, and currently prices per person (in a double compartment) are 70,000 pts in the low season and 80,000 pts in the high. It is run on the narrow gauge line, *FEVE*, which has tracks all along the north coast of Spain, as well as a few lines on the east coast. Information and reservations on the *Transcantabrica* are available through Spanish travel agents or by calling the information office in Madrid (91)233 70 00. This Spanish *Orient Express* is so popular that a new one has just begun through Andalucía, and there are plans for others. For these, ask at RENFE.

Regular FEVE trips can be fun. The ones on the north coast in particular take in some fine scenery, through Galicia, Asturias, and Cantabria. The Basques have their own lines as well, and one of the most leisurely ways to spend a day in Spain is take the poky old train that goes once a day from León to Bilbao (see **León** for details). It shows off rural Spanish life and scenery at their best. Like RENFE's ferrobus, FEVE is slow, stops everywhere, and costs more than the bus.

By bus

With literally hundreds of companies providing service over Spain, expect confusion. We have included all of the important lines and stations to make things easier. Not all cities have bus stations; in some, like Zaragoza or Bilbao, there may be a dozen little offices spread around town for each firm. Like the trains, buses are cheap by northern European standards but no memorable bargain; if you're travelling on the cheap you'll find that transportation is your biggest expense. Usually, whether you go by train or bus will depend on simple convenience: in some places the train station is far from the centre, in others the bus station is.

Small towns and villages can normally be reached by bus only through their provincial capitals. And in the middle of Spain, it's almost impossible to get from one town to another without going through Madrid. Buses are usually clean and dependable, and there's plenty of room for baggage in the compartment underneath. On the more luxurious buses you even get air-conditioning and a movie (Kung Fu, sappy Spanish flicks from the Franco era or locally-produced rock videos). **Tourist information offices** are the best sources for information. They almost always know every route and schedule.

Left luggage

Since terrorists began leaving bombs in rail stations, RENFE has closed all of its left-luggage facilities; you'll have about an even chance of finding one in a bus station or small bus company office, and sometimes bars near train or bus stations are willing to let you leave your bags. Ask around; the word in Spanish is *consigna.*

City Buses and Taxis

Every Spanish city has a perfectly adequate system of public transportation. You won't need to make much use of it, though, for in almost every city except Madrid and Barcelona, all attractions are within walking distance of each other. City buses usually cost 40 or 50 pts, and if you intend to use them often there are books of tickets called *abonamientos* or *bono-Bus* or *tarjeta* cards to punch on entry, available at reduced rates from tobacco shops. Bus drivers will give change if you don't have the correct amount (within reason, don't give them a 1000 pta note). In many cities, the bus's entire route will be displayed on the signs at each stop (*parada*).

Taxis are still cheap enough for the Spaniards to use them regularly on their shopping trips. The average fare for a ride within a city will be 180–300 pts. Taxis are metered, and the drivers usually quite honest; they are entitled to certain surcharges (for luggage, night or holiday trips, to the train or airport, etc.) and if you cross the city limits they usually can charge double the fare shown. It's rarely hard to hail a cab from the street, and there will always be a few around the stations. If you get stuck where there are none, or in a small village, call information for the number of a radio taxi.

Tourist information

The Spaniards, after receiving millions of tourists each year for the last two decades, are the masters of tourist information. No country has more information offices, or more helpful ones, or more intelligent brochures and detailed maps. Every city will have an office, and about two-thirds of the time you'll find someone who speaks English. Sometimes they'll be less than helpful – especially in the big cities in the summer, when the people at the counter lapse into pixillation from an overdose of strange foreigners. More often, though, you'll be surprised at how well they know the details of accommodation and transportation. Hours for most offices are Mondays–Fridays 10–1 and 4–7, Saturday mornings only and closed on Sundays. Don't mistake tourist offices for the new **consumer information** booths the Socialist government is setting up everywhere. Many large cities also maintain **municipal tourist offices**, though they're not as well equipped as those run by the Ministry of Tourism, better known simply as **Turismo**.

Maps

Cartography, after all, has been a art in Spain since the 12th-century Catalans charted their Mediterranean Empire in Europe's first great school of map-making. The tourist offices hand out beautifully detailed maps of every town; ask for their *Mapa de Communicaciones*, an excellent general map of the country. For serious travellers who want complete town plans as well as highway maps with every back road and village, the best are produced by *Almax Editores*. The best, most up-to-date maps of rail lines – including the FEVE narrow-gauge routes – are in this book.

Money, communications, health and other concerns

Money

Spanish currency comes in notes of 100, 200, 500, 1000, 2000, and 5000 *pesetas*, all in different colours for easy identification, and coins of 1, 5, 25, 50, 100, and 200 pts. Don't be surprised to see Generalísimo Franco's scowling mug staring at you from the older coins – but do watch out for the old ornately decorated notes larger than the standard size. These went out of use in 1986 (except the 1000 and 100 pta note, which will still be good for a while). It wouldn't be inconceivable for someone stuck with one of these to fob it off on a dull-looking tourist. At street markets, and in out-of-the-way places, you may hear prices given in *duros* or *notas*. A *duro* is a 5 pta piece, and a *nota* is a 100 pta, so a little mental arithmetic will see you through.

Exchange rates vary, of course, but until any drastic changes occur it will be helpful to think of it as about 200 pts to the pound, or 135 to the dollar – so those green 1000 pta notes, the most common, are worth about £5.00 or $7.50. Spain's city centres seem to have a bank on every street corner, and most of them will exchange money; look for the CAMBIO or EXCHANGE signs and the little flags. There is a slight difference in the rates, though usually not enough to make shopping around worthwhile. Most banks are open 9 am–2 pm, and Saturdays (sometimes) 9 am–1 pm. You can sometimes change money at travel agencies, fancy hotels, train stations or even restaurants – but the rates may be quite painful. Wiring money from overseas entails no special difficulties; just give yourself two weeks to be on the safe side, and work through one of the larger institutions (Banco Central, Banco de Bilbao, Banco Espanol de Credito, Banco Hispano Americano, Banco de Santander, Banco de Vizcaya). Do it to Madrid if you can. Plastic money will not necessarily be helpful unless you rent cars, fly a lot, or patronize the most expensive hotels and restaurants. If you have credit cards, though, do take them along as they can be lifesavers in emergencies. A Eurocheque card will make your British bank cheques good, though it may not be easy. *Travellers' cheques*, if they are from one of the major companies, will pass at most bank exchanges.

Post Offices

Every city, regardless of size, seems to have one post office (*Correos*) and no more. It will always be crowded, but unless you have packages to mail (a relatively painless undertaking compared to some other Mediterranean countries) you may not need ever to visit one. Most tobacco shops sell stamps (*sellos*) and they'll usually know the correct postage for whatever you're sending. Mailboxes are bright yellow and scarce. Send everything air mail (*por aereo*) and don't send postcards unless you don't care when they arrive. The post offices also handle telegrams, and of course the poste restante (general delivery). In Spain this is called *Lista de Correos*, and it is as chancey as anywhere else. Don't confuse post offices with the *Caja Postal*, the postal savings banks that look just like them.

Telephones

Spain has long had one of the best telephone systems in Europe. During the Civil War it kept running no matter what; commanders used it to keep in touch with their troops, and called towns on the front during offensives to check if they had fallen to the enemy. Today, calls within Spain are ridiculously cheap (5–10 pts for a short local call), and Spain is one of the few countries where you can make an international call conveniently from a phone booth – within Europe at least. In newer phone booths there are complete instructions (in English) and the phone itself has a little slide on top that holds coins; keep it full of 5 and 25 pts pieces – the newer ones also take 100 pts – and you can gab all day like the Spaniards do. This can be done to the USA too, but take at least 3000 pts in change with you in 100s. Britain costs about 200–300 pts a minute, America substantially more. There are central telephone offices (*Telefonicá*) in every big city, where you call from metered booths (and pay a fair percentage more for the comfort); they are indispensable, however, for reversed-charge or collect calls (*Cobro revertido*). Telefonicás are generally open from 9 am–1 pm and 5–10 pm and closed on Sundays; in Barcelona and Madrid there are offices open 24 hours. The national code for Britain is 44, for the US and Canada, 1, and for Spain 34. Expect to pay a big surcharge if you do any telephoning from your hotel.

Official holidays

The Spanish, like the Italians, try to have as many as possible. Everything closes on:

New Year's Day
6 January – Epiphany
Holy Thursday and Good Friday
1 May – Labour Day
Corpus Christi (late May or early June)
25 July – Santiago Apostol (St James' Day)
15 August – Asunción (Assumption)
1 November – Todos los Santos (All Saints' Day)
6 December – Constitution Day
8 December – Immaculate Conception
Christmas

Be aware that every region, town, and village has at least one of its own holidays as well that invariably will close the local banks just when you need one.

Opening hours and museums

Spaniards take their main meal at mid-day, and most shops shut down for two or three hours in the afternoon, usually starting at 1 or 2 pm. In the south, where it's hotter, the siesta can last from 1 to 5 pm. In the evening most establishments stay open until 7 or 8 pm.

Museums and historical sites follow these hours too, though abbreviated in the winter months; nearly all close on Mondays. We have tried to list the hours for the important sights. For seldom-visited ones it can be a problem. Many have a raffish disregard for their official hours, and some others seem to open only when the mood strikes them. Don't be discouraged; bang on doors and ask around. Most of the less-important churches are always closed. Some cities probably have more churches than faithful communicants, and many are unused. If you're determined to see one, it will never be hard to find the sacristan (*sacristán*) or caretaker. Usually they live close by, and would be glad to show you around for a tip. We haven't bothered to list admission prices for museums and sites; usually the sum is trivial. The Alhambra in Granada at 350 pts and the Fundació Miró in Barcelona at 400 pts are the most notable exceptions; hardly anything will cost more than 200 pts, usually much less. Don't be surprised when cathedrals and famous churches charge admission; just consider the costs of keeping up the place.

Embassies and Consulates

US

Madrid: C. Serrano 75 (Tel: 276 36 00); consular office for passports: Paseo de Castellana 52, around the corner.

Barcelona: Via Layetana 33 (Tel: 319 95 50)
Sevilla: Paseo de las Delicias 7 (Tel: 23 18 85)
Fuengirola (Málaga): C. Ramón y Cajál, Edificio El Encla No. 502 (Tel: 47 48 91)
Valencia: C. de Ribera 3 (Tel: 351 69 73)
La Coruña: Canton Grande 16 (Tel: 27 43 00)
Bilbao: Av. del Ejercito 11 (Tel: 435 83 00

Britain
Madrid: Fernando el Santo 16 (Tel: 419 15 28)
Barcelona: Diagonal 477 (Tel: 322 21 51)
Tarragona: C. Satrán 4 (Tel: 20 12 46)
Sevilla: Plaza Nueva 8 (Tel: 22 88 75)
Vigo: Plaza de Compostela 23 (Tel: 43 71 33)
Málaga: Duquesa de Parcent (Tel: 21 75 71)
Alicante: Plaza Calvo Sotelo (Tel: 26 66 00)
Bilbao: Alameda Urguijo (Tel: 415 76 00

Canada
Madrid: Nuñez de Balboa 35 (Tel: 431 43 00)
Barcelona: Vía Augusta 125 (Tel: 319 95 00)
Málaga: Plaza de Toros Vieja 18 (Tel: 21 91 81

Police Business

Crime is not really a big problem in Spain, but the nation is doing its best to catch up with the rest of Europe. As a new phenomenon, Spaniards talk about it perhaps more than is warranted. Pickpocketing and robbing parked cars are the specialities; in Sevilla they like to take the whole car. The big cities are the places to be careful: Madrid, Barcelona, and especially Málaga and Sevilla. Crime is also spreading to the tourist areas, particularly the Costa del Sol. In 1985, the Basque ETA terrorists began a bombing campaign in the Costa del Sol; so far they have been only a minor nuisance, and entirely unsuccessful in scaring away tourists. Even on the Costa, though, you're probably safer in Spain than you would be at home; the crime rate is roughly 1/7th of the British. Note that in Spain less than 8 grams of reefer is legal; anything else may easily earn you the traditional 'six years and a day'.

There are several species of **police**, and their authority varies with the area. Franco's old goon squads, the Policia Armada, have been reformed and relatively demilitarized into the *Policia Nacional*, whom the Spaniards call 'chocolate drops' for their new brown uniforms; their duties largely consist of driving around in cars and drinking coffee. The *Policia Municipal* in some towns do crime control, while in others they are limited to directing traffic. Mostly in rural areas, there's the *Guardia Civil*, with green uniforms and black patent-leather tricorn hats. The 'poison dwarfs of Spain', as Laurie Lee called them, may well be one of the most efficient police forces in the world, but after a century-and-a-half of upholding a sick social order in the volatile countryside, they have few friends. They too are being reformed, now they're most conspicuous as a highway patrol, assisting motorists and handing out tickets (ignoring 'no passing' zones is the best way to get one). Most traffic violations are payable on the spot; the traffic cops have a reputation for upright honesty.

The Basques don't want anything to do with any of these. So far, they are the only community to take advantage of the new autonomy laws and set up their own police. You'll see them looking dapper in their red berets.

Electricity

Current is 220 V, the same as most of Europe. Americans will need converters, and the British will need adapters for the different plugs. If you plan to stay in the less expensive hostels, it may be better to leave your gadgets at home. Some corners of Spain, even some big cities, have pockets of exotic voltage – 150 V for example – guaranteeing a brief display of fireworks. Big hotels always have the standard current.

Photography

Film is quite expensive everywhere; so is developing, but in any city there will be plenty of places – many in optician's shops (*optica*) or big department stores – where you can get processing done in a hurry. Serious photographers must give some consideration to the strong sunlight and high reflectivity of surfaces (pavements and buildings) in towns.

Toilets

Outside bus and train stations, public facilities are rare in Spain. On the other hand, every bar on every corner has a toilet; don't feel uncomfortable using it without purchasing something – the Spaniards do it all the time. Just ask for '*los servicios*'.

Health

Spain has no reciprocal health scheme with any country, so you may want to consider **travel insurance**, available through most travel agents. For a small monthly charge, not only is your health insured, but your bags and money as well, and some even will refund a missed charter flight if you're too ill to catch it. Be sure to save all doctor's receipts (you'll have to pay in cash on the spot), pharmacy receipts, and police documents (if you're reporting a theft). Before resorting to a *médico* (doctor) and his £20 ($28) fee (ask at the tourist office for a list of English-speaking doctors), go to a pharmacy and tell them your woes – though admittedly this can be difficult if you don't speak Spanish. Spanish *farmacistas* are highly skilled and very well may be able to sell the proper remedy after a free consultation; if there's a prescription medicine that you know will cure you, they'll often supply it without a doctor's note. (*El Pais* and the other national newspapers list *farmacias* in each city that stay open all night.)

No inoculations are required to enter Spain, though it never hurts to check that your tetanus jab is up-to-date, as well as some of the more exotic inoculations (typhoid and cholera) if you want to venture on into Morocco. The tap water is safe to drink in Spain, but at the slightest twinge of queasiness, switch to the bottled stuff.

Women and children

On the whole, the horror stories of sexual harassment in Spain are a thing of the past. The younger men are too suave these days to make fools of themselves, but beware the middle-aged cicerone who would carry your bag and show you his pal's nice hotel. Areas with the highest concentration of foreigners are often the worst places for sexual harassment. Up north, in villages and in most cities you'll have few problems, unless you dress provocatively and hang out by the bus station after dark. All Spaniards seem to melt when they see blondes, so if you're fair you're in for a tougher go. If you want to be really inconspicuous wear A-line skirts, a loose blouse and some coloured plastic earrings, and they'll think you're a Spaniard. Even Spanish women sunbathe topless these days at the international costas, but do be discreet elsewhere, especially near small villages.

Spaniards adore children (again, especially if they're blonde) and they'll welcome yours almost everywhere. Baby foods, powdered milk, cereals, disposable nappies (diapers) and so on are widely available. Pack a strong sunscreen for the kids, and don't expect to find babysitters except at the really smart hotels; Spaniards always take their children with them, even if they're up until 4 am. Nor are there many special amusements for children (Barcelona, with its zoo, fun fair and parks, has the most) though these are beginning to spring up with Spain's new prosperity, for better or worse; traditionally Spaniards have never thought of their children as separate little creatures who ought to be amused.

Sports, entertainment, and culture

Football (soccer) is the most popular sport throughout Spain, and the Spaniards play it well: Barcelona (Barca) and Real Madrid are the best teams to watch. **Bullfighting** (see 'Spanish Topics') and **cycling** vie for second place in the Spanish heart and are regularly shown on **television**, which, despite a heavy fare of dubbed American shows, everyone is inordinately fond of watching. Both channels are state run, and the Basques and Catalans each have their own stations in their own languages.

If you want to bring your own **bicycle** to Spain, you can make arrangements by ferry or train; by air, you'll almost always have to dismantle it to some extent and usually pack it in some kind of crate. Each airline seems to have its own policy. The south of Spain would be suicide to bike through in summer, though all right in winter. In summer the best places to cycle are in the Basque Lands, Cantabria, Asturias and Galicia, with their greenery and network of coastal secondary roads.

Spain's sierras attract thousands of **hikers** and **mountaineers**. Los Picos de Europa and the Pyrenees are by far the most popular, though there also some lovely hikes in southern Asturias' Cantabrian mountains, in the Sierra Nevada above Granada, the Serrania de Ronda, in La Sierra of southern Salamanca and Las Hurdes of northern Extremadura, and in El Bierzo of western León and Los Ancares of eastern Galicia.

Shelters or *refugios* in many places offer mountain shelter (write to the tourist office or the Spanish Mountaineering Federation, Alberto Aguilera 3–4°, Madrid-15, Tel: 445 13 82 for a list of these). Hiking boots are essential. In the more popular areas like the Picos you can hire **horses** for mountain excursions.

Many of these same mountains attract **ski** crowds in the winter, especially in the Pyrenees of Catalunya and Aragón, the Guadarramas where the Madrileños make day trips, and here and there in the Cantabrian chain. The Pyrenean installations are the most sophisticated, and attract a sizeable number of foreign skiers who come to beat the high costs in France and Switzerland. We've listed the best-equipped stations, though there are many others without mechanical lifts, as well as a growing number of cross-country courses. For more information and glossy brochures, write to the tourist office or the Spanish Ski Federation, Claudio Coello 32, Madrid 1, Tel: 445 13 82. Once you're in Spain, it's easy to arrange all-inclusive ski packages through a travel agent.

Of course **water sports** are the most popular activities in the summer. You can rent a windsurf board and learn how to use it at almost any Mediterranean resort, while along the Atlantic coast of Euskadi and Cantabria there are several places where the waves are suitable for surfing. If you're bringing your own boat, get the tourist office's literature on marinas before setting out. There's a full calendar of sailing events and races, especially along the north coast, also sailing schools and rentals. A number of Spain's reservoirs have become quite popular as well for sailing, water-skiing and wind-surfing. For more information, write to the Spanish Sailing Federation, J. Vigón 23, Madrid. Underwater activists flock to the Almeria coast in particular for its sparkling water and abundant marine life. Write to the Spanish Sub-Aqua Federation, Santaló 15, Barcelona, Tel: 228 87 96 for more information.

Since the advent of Severiano Ballesteros Spaniards have gone nuts for **golf**, and there are 93 courses around Madrid, Barcelona and the big cities as well as by the costa resorts. You can hire clubs at most courses and green fees are low compared to France. The English built Spain's first course at the Rio Tinto Mines in the 19th century; another English-built course, Puerta de Hierro in Madrid, is probably the best in the country, and there are very good links in San Sebastian and on the Costa del Sol as well. The tourist office can supply names. All resort hotels these days seem to have **tennis courts**, though municipal ones are rare or hard to get to.

Fishing and **hunting** are long-standing Spanish obsessions, and you'll need to get a licence for both. Freshwater fishing permits are issued on a fortnightly basis from the municipal ICONA office: for a listing of the best trout streams (there are many), write to the Spanish Fishing Federation, Navas de Tolosa 3, Madrid-13, Tel: 221 36 33. Deep-sea fishermen need to obtain a five-year licence from the provincial Comandancias de Marina. The Directorate General of Sea Fishing, Subsecretaria de la Marina Mercante, Ministerio de Comercio, C. Ruiz de Alarcón 1, Madrid can supply information on the best areas and boat rentals. Hunters (boar and deer are the big game, with quail, hare, partridges and pigeons, and ducks and geese along the coasts in the winter) are obliged to get a licence as well from the local autonomous community, presenting their passports and record of insurance coverage. The Spanish Hunting Federation, Ortega y Gasset 5, Madrid, Tel: 276 91 84 or the tourist office can supply more information.

Every Spaniard is a gambler, whether it's in the infinite number of lotteries run by the

State (the *Loteriá Deportiva*), the blind, the Red Cross, the church etc., or at the big *frontóns* in Euskadi and Madrid, where the fast action on the jaialai court is matched by the wagering frenzy of the spectators. **Horse-racing** is centred in Madrid, with a summer season at San Sebastian and a winter season in Sevilla. There are 16 **casinos** near the major cities and resorts, and at least one slot machine in every bar.

Bars and cafés collect much of the Spaniards' leisure time. They are wonderful institutions, where you can eat breakfast or linger over a glass of beer until 4 in the morning. Some have music – jazz, rock or *flamenco* (see the Spanish topic 'Flamenco'); some have great snacks, or *tapas*, some have games or pinball machines; in any of them you could see an old sailor delicately sipping his camomile tea next to a young mother, baby under her arm, stopping in for a beer break during her shopping. **Discos, night clubs**, etc. are easily found in the big cities and tourist spots; most tend to be expensive, especially in Madrid and Barcelona. Ask around for the current favourites and the Spaniards will be delighted to tell. Watch out for posters for **concerts, ballets**, and especially for **circuses**. If you grew up on the super-slick acts of Barnum and Bailey, a little travelling Spanish circus with its family acts, tents, tinsel and names like 'The National Circus of Japan' will charm you; they often gravitate to the major fiestas throughout the summer.

El Pais, the Socialists' press, is Spain's biggest and best national **newspaper**, though circulation is painfully low; Spaniards just don't read newspapers (the little magazine with television listings and scandals is by far and away the best-selling periodical). *El Pais* has the best Madrid and regional film listings, where you can see some great films subtitled instead of dubbed; English films are frequently shown on the Costa del Sol and Costa Blanca in the expatriate communities. Films are cheap and Spaniards are some of the world's great cinema-goers, and though half of the great movie places of Madrid have been converted into discos, others are still magnificent. There are also lots of very inexpensive outdoor movie theatres in the summer. Look for new films by Carlos Saura, Spain's brightest cinematic light (*Carmen, Blood Wedding*, etc) or Victor Erice, or most incredibly, Marx Brothers movies dubbed in Spanish.

The other big papers are *Cambio 16* (centrist), *ABC* (conservative, in a bizarre 1960s magazine format), and the *Alcazar* (neo-fascist). You can also get the Spanish translation of *Pravda* and a vast selection of other leftist sheets. Major British papers are available in all tourist areas and big cities; the American *Herald Tribune*, the *Wall Street Journal*, and the awful *USA Today* are readily available where Americans go. Most hit the newstands a day late; issues of *Time* and *Newsweek* often hang about until they find a home. There are also publications in English on the major costas and an English weekly in Madrid that feature local events.

Shopping

There are some delightful tacky tourist wares (Toledo 'daggers', plastic bulls and flamenco dolls ad nauseam) but there are also some excellent buys of quality items like leather (suede coats, shoes and bags) most notably from Córdoba. Ceramic plates, pottery and colourful azulejo tiles are made in various regions of Spain, especially around

Valencia. Lace from Galicia, inlaid wood *taracea* work from Granada (chests, chess boards and music boxes), jewellery from Toledo, woven goods and rugs from nearly every province of Spain are reasonably priced; fine embroidered linens are available everywhere. Good-quality antiques aren't the great finds they once were – Spaniards have learned what they're worth and charge accordingly. Guitars, mandolins and bagpipes, fine wooden furniture and Goya tapestries are some of the bulky, more expensive items you'd like shipped home.

To encourage the nation's craftsmen, the government has organized a kind of co-operative, *Artespaña*, with various outlets selling their work located at:
Madrid: Gran Via 32, Ramon de la Cruz 33, Hermosilla 14, Plaza de las Cortes 3
Sevilla: Rodríguez Jurado 4
Santander: Cádiz 20
Granada: Corral del Carbón
Barcelona: Rambla Catalunya 75
Cáceres: San Antón 17
Oviedo: Uriá 6
Bilbao: Colón de Larreategui
Murcia: Barítono Marcos Redondo 2
Marbella: Ricardo Soriano 54
The major **department store** chains in Spain, El Corte Inglés and the Galerias Preciados, often have good selections of crafts as well. All of the above ship items home. You can also get some good buys at the **weekly markets** where Spaniards do a good deal of their shopping. Local tourist offices will have details.

A little geography for the perplexed

Spain, by European standards, is an enormous chunk of territory, only marginally smaller than France and over twice the size of Great Britain. Americans may consider it as about four Pennsylvanias, with a basketful of Delawares thrown in. The 38 million Spaniards manage the world's 12th-biggest national economy, producing nearly as much as all of India.

The Pyrenees are not as lofty as most people think, but they are difficult to cross; there are only three reliable routes over. They divide the Iberian peninsula authoritatively from the rest of Europe, making it a kind of minor sub-continent, introverted and caught in its own strange destinies. To complete the isolation, more mountains hug the coast on three sides: the Cantabrian chain in the north, the Pénibetic chain in the south, including the Sierra Nevada with the highest peaks in Spain, and a string of low mountains through the regions of Catalunya and Valencia in the east. The ranges guard Spain like a castle wall; inside them is a high tableland, the *meseta*, broken by roughly parallel rivers and mountain ranges. The elevation of this plateau explains the difficult climate of the Spanish interior, chilly in winter and baked and bleached in summer. Madrid, at the centre, is one of the highest capitals of Europe.

Iberia naturally faces the Atlantic – a prime reason for its prominence in the Age of Discovery. Of its great rivers, only the Ebro (from which the Iberian peninsula takes its name) flows into the Mediterranean; the others meet the Atlantic, three of them through Portugal, the Douro, Tajo, and Guadiana.

Spain is a harsh land. Nearly half its soil is unproductive or barren, and the brown, wrinkled hills of the central plateau in summer make a sight unique in Europe. Some parts of the south-east are nearly desert, while others, like the Huerta of Valencia and the Guadalquivir valley, are astoundingly fertile. Along the northern coast, Cantabria, Asuturias, and Galicia display a well-tended countryside of forests and pasturelands as green as Ireland.

Climate

Spain is hot and sunny in the summer, brisk and sunny in the winter, with little variation among the regions except in the matter of rainfall. The northern coast, especially Euskadi and Galicia, fairly drowns all year – that's why it's so green. Rain is scarce nearly everywhere else, and every locality brags in its brochures about so many 'hours of guaranteed sunshine' each year. Statistically, the champion for the best holiday climate is Alicante, with Europe's warmest winter temperatures and hardly any rain, but most of the southern and eastern coasts are nearly as good.

Spring and autumn are the best times to visit, by far; the winter can be pleasant, though damp and chill in the north (you'll probably feel more uncomfortable inside than out; Spanish homes – and hotel rooms – are not made for the winter). Teruel and Soria provinces traditionally have the worst winter climate. The summer can be unbearable in the south, but in the north it's the only time you won't need to carry an umbrella.

The chart below shows the highest and lowest temperatures in °C (°F) you're likely to encounter in each season. It's the best we could find; Spaniards care little for means, medians or averages, but they've always been fond of extremes.

Seasonal Temperatures in °C(°F)

	January		*April*		*July*		*October*	
	High	*Low*	*High*	*Low*	*High*	*Low*	*High*	*Low*
Madrid	17(63)	−8(18)	27(80)	10(52)	39(102)	12(53)	29(84)	0(32)
Barcelona	17(63)	−7(19)	25(77)	7(44)	33(91)	16(61)	24(75)	10(50)
San Sebastián	15(59)	−10(14)	27(80)	5(41)	34(93)	14(57)	24(75)	8(46)
La Coruña	16(60)	−3(27)	25(77)	6(42)	27(80)	14(57)	26(78)	8(46)
Badajóz	19(66)	−5(23)	29(84)	3(37)	41(106)	13(55)	30(87)	6(42)
Alicante	21(71)	2(36)	31(88)	7(44)	34(93)	17(63)	29(84)	6(42)
Sevilla	20(68)	−4(25)	31(88)	4(39)	42(108)	15(59)	31(88)	8(46)

Average monthly rainfall in mm (in.)

	January	*April*	*July*	*October*
Madrid	56 (2)	48 (2)	0 (0)	9 (0)
Barcelona	105 (4)	38 (2)	21 (1)	80 (3)
San Sebastián	142 (6)	84 (3)	92 (4)	142 (6)
La Coruña	125 (5)	78 (3)	35 (1)	135 (5)
Badajóz	103 (4)	88 (3)	2 (0)	72 (3)
Alicante	11 (0)	32 (1)	1 (0)	19 (1)
Sevilla	99 (4)	80 (3)	0 (0)	37 (2)

Where to stay

Hotels in Spain are still bargains – though not as much as they used to be. As in all prices, Spain is gradually catching up with the rest of Europe. One thing you can still count on is a consistent level of quality and service; the Spanish government regulates hotels more intelligently, and more closely, than any country in the Mediterranean. Consequently, the chances of your having a bad experience are slight. Room prices must be posted in the hotel lobbies and in the rooms, and if there's any problem you can ask for the complaint book, or *Libro de Reclamaciones*. No one ever writes anything in these; any written complaint must be passed on to the authorities immediately. It means trouble for the hotel keepers, and they would always rather correct the problem for you.

No government could resist the chance to insert a little bureaucratic confusion, though, and the wide range of accommodation in Spain is classified in a complex system. **Hotels** (H) are rated with from one to five stars, according to the services they offer, not price. These are the most expensive places, and even a one-star hotel will be a comfortable, middle-range establishment. *Hotel Residencias* (HR) are the same, only without a restaurant. Next come *Hostales* (Hs) and *Pensiones* (P), rated with one to three stars. These are more modest places, often a floor in an apartment block; a three-star hostel is roughly equivalent to a one-star hotel. Pensions may require full- or half-board; there aren't many of these establishments, only a few in resort areas. *Hostal Residencias* (HsR), like hotel residencias, do not offer meals except breakfast, and not always that.

The bottom of the scale is occupied by the *fonda* (F) and *casa de huespedes* (CH), little different from a one-star *hostal*, though generally cheaper. Off the scale completely are hundreds of unclassified cheap places, usually rooms in an apartment or over a bar and identified only by a little sign reading *Camas* (beds) or *Habitaciones* (rooms). You can also ask in bars or at the tourist office for unidentified *casas particulares*, private houses with a room or two; in many villages these will be the best you can do, but at least, they're usually clean – Spanish women are manic housekeepers.

Look for the *little blue plaques* next to the doors of all hotels, hostals, etc. that identify its classification and number of stars.

Paradores

The government, in its plan to develop tourism in the 1950s, started this nationwide chain of classy hotels to draw some attention to little visited areas. They restored old palaces, castles and monasteries for the purpose, furnished them with antiques and installed fine restaurants featuring local specialities. They did it so well that *paradores* have become attractions in themselves; for many people they are one of the best reasons for visiting Spain.

Not all *paradores* are in historical landmarks; especially in resort areas, some are cleanly-designed modern buildings, usually in a great location with a pool and some sports facilities. With the *paradores'* success has come some increase in prices; in most cases both the rooms and the restaurant will be the most expensive in town. If you can afford them, though, there are no better places to stay. We've mentioned nearly all of them throughout this book. *Paradores* can be booked in advance from the UK through

Keytel International, 402 Edgware Road, London W2 1ED (Tel: 01-402 8182) and in the US through Marketing Ahead, 515 Madison Ave, New York, NY (Tel: 212 750 8682).

Resort accommodation

Almost everything along Spain's coasts has been built in the last 25 years, and anonymous high-rise buildings abound. Lately the trend has turned towards low-rise 'villages' built around a pool, usually on or near the beach. We've tried to include places that stand out in some way, or that are good bargains for their rating. Most hotels in the big resorts cater for package tours, and may not even answer a request for an individual reservation during the peak season.

In almost all resorts, there's a choice of hotels in every price range. The best bargains, though, are usually in the places where foreigners seldom tread – the Costa de la Luz west of Cadiz, or the small resorts west of Almeria, or to a great extent, anywhere on the north coast outside San Sebastián (Spain's most expensive resort) or Santander. Incidentally, no beaches in Spain are allowed to be private property, so you can play (but not camp) wherever you like.

Cheap accommodation

The best are in small towns and villages, and around universities. Occasionally you'll find a room over a bar, run by somebody's grandmother, that is nicer than a four-star hotel – complete with frilly pillows, lovely old furnishings, and a shrine to the Virgin Mary. The worst are inevitably found in industrial cities or dull modern ones (Valencia and Santander spring to mind). It always helps to see the room first. Some places offer as a matter of course, and they'll show you their best. In cities, the best places to look are right in the centre, not around the bus and train stations. Most inexpensive establishments will ask you to pay a day in advance.

Information

If you'll be travelling around a lot, a good investment would be the government publication *Guía de Hoteles*, a great fat book with every classified hotel and *hostal* in Spain, available for only 500 pts in many bookshops. It's a lot to carry, but you can tear out the sections you need. The government also publishes similar guides to holiday flats (*apartmentos turisticos*) and campsites (*campings*). Local tourist information offices can also give you a complete list for their provinces, and some can be very helpful with finding a room when things are tight.

Price ranges (pts) for a double room with bath
(not including 6% VAT)

Hoteles	*high*	*average*	*low*
*****	35,000	13,700	9,500
****	18,000	7,900	5,000
***	9,000	6,000	3,100

**	5,500	4,100	2,200
*	4,200	2,900	1,400

Hostales and Pensiones	*high*	*average*	*low*
***	5,900	3,400	1,900
**	3,500	2,200	1,000
*	2,800	1,700	600

Unlisted Fondas, Casas de Huespedes or camas (without bath)			
	1,600	800	500

Prices for single rooms will average about 60 per cent of a double, while triples or an extra bed are around 35 per cent more. Of course, *hostales, fondas,* etc. with one or two stars will often have rooms without private baths at considerable savings. Within the price ranges shown, the most expensive are likely to be in the big cities (especially Madrid). In resorts, prices will usually be around the average or below it, while the cheapest places are always provincial towns. The Basque lands are by a small margin the most expensive region in Spain, and tourist cities like Toledo cost more, but in general prices throughout Spain are surprisingly consistent.

One thing to remember is that many of the more expensive hotels have some rooms available at prices lower than those listed. They won't tell you, though; you'll have to ask. Many establishments have discounts in the off-season and higher rates during important festivals. These are supposedly regulated, but in practice hotel-keepers charge whatever they can get for spectacles like Sevilla's Holy Week and San Fermin at Pamplona. If you want to attend any of these big events, always book as far in advance as possible.

Paradores are classed as three- or four-star hotels, and their prices for a double room with bath range from 5600 pts in remote provincial towns to 9000 pts for the most popular. All stay open all year and offer substantial off-season discounts.

Alternative accommodation

Youth hostels exist in Spain, but they're usually not worth the trouble. Most are open only in the summer; there are the usual inconveniences and silly rules, and often hostels are in out-of-the-way locations. You'll be better off with the inexpensive *hostales* and *fondas* – sometimes these are even cheaper than youth hostels. Especially in the north, there are **monasteries** that will put you up in rural areas; ask at the local tourist office for these and for rooms that might be available in **university dormitories.**

Camping

Campsites are rated with from one to three stars depending on their facilities, and in addition to the ones listed in the official government handbook there are always others, rather primitive, that are unlisted. Caravans (campers) and trailers converge into all the more developed sites (the Costa Brava, in particular, sometimes resembles a vast trailer park) but if you just want to pitch your little tent or sleep out in some quiet field, ask around in the bars or at likely farms. Camping is forbidden in many forest areas because of fears of fire, as well as on the beaches (though you can often get close to some quieter shores if you're discreet). If you're doing some hiking, bring a sleeping bag and stay in the free **refugios** along the major trails.

Eating out

Read an old guidebook to Spain, and when the author gets around to the local cooking, expressions like 'eggs in a sea of rancid oil' and 'mysterious pork parts' or 'suffered brain damage through garlic excess' pop up with alarming frequency. One traveller in the 18th century fell ill from a local concoction and was given a purge 'known on the comic stage as angelic water. On top of that followed four hundred catholic pills, and a few days later ... they gave me *escordero* water, whose efficacy or devilry is of such double effect that the doctors call it ambidexter. From this I suffered agony.'

You'll fare better; in fact, the chances are you'll eat some of the tastiest food you've ever had at half the price you would have paid for it at home. The massive influx of tourists has had its effect on Spanish kitchens, but so has the Spaniards' own increased prosperity and, perhaps most significantly, the new federalism. Each region, each town even, has come to feel a new interest and pride in the things that set it apart, and food is definitely one of those. The best restaurants are almost always those specializing in regional cuisine. In Castile, where the cuisine is almost medieval, tureen-sized bowls of soup and roast suckling pig (*cochinillo*) or lamb have pride of place; in Valencia the land of rice, you can order one of its famous *paellas* or a dozen other different rice dishes; in Andalucia, it's *gazpacho* (cold tomato, cucumber and onion soup) in several varieties, and *rabo de toro* (bull's tail cooked with sauce); in Asturias it's hake in *sidra* (the local cider) or *fabada*, an enchanting mess of pork and beans. And no regions pride themselves on their own cooking as much as the Basque lands, Catalunya, or Galicia – and rightfully so. Throughout this book we have pointed out some of the best-known local specialities for each community, but it never hurts simply to ask the waiter what's good.

Be careful, though. Spain still has plenty of bad restaurants. The worst offenders are often those with the little flags and ten-language menus in the most touristy areas, and in general you'd do better to buy some bread, Manchego cheese and a bottle of Valdepeñas red and have a picnic, than throw away your pesetas there. If you dine where the locals do you'll be assured of a good deal if not necessarily a good meal. Almost every restaurant offers a *menú del día*, or a *menú turistico*, featuring an appetizer, a main course, dessert, bread and drink at a set price, always a certain percentage lower than if you had ordered the items à la carte. These are always posted outside the restaurant, in the window or on the plywood chef at the door; decide what you want before going in if it's a set-price menu, because these bargains are hardly ever listed on the menu the waiter gives you at the table.

If you're travelling on a budget you may want to eat one of your meals a day at a **tapas bar** or **tasca**. *Tapas* means 'lids', and they started out as little saucers of goodies served on top of a drink. They have evolved over the years to form a main part of the world's greatest snack culture. Bars that specialize in them have platter after platter of delectible tidbits, from shellfish to slices of omelette or mushrooms baked in garlic or vegetables in vinaigrette or stews. All you have to do is pick out what looks best and order a *porción* (an hors d'oeuvre) or a *ración* (a big helping) if it looks really good. It's hard to generalize about prices, but on the average 400 pts of tapas and wine or beer really fill you up. You can always save money in bars by standing up; sit at that charming table on the terrace and prices jump considerably.

Another advantage of tapas is that they're available at what most Americans or Britons would consider normal dining hours. Spaniards are notoriously late diners; in the morning it's a coffee and roll grabbed at the bar, a huge meal at around 2 pm, then after work at 8 pm a few tapas at the bar to hold them over until supper at 10 or 11 pm. After living in Spain for a few months this makes perfect sense, but its exasperating to the average visitor. On the coasts, restaurants tend to open earlier to accommodate foreigners (some as early as 5 pm) but you may as well do as the Spaniards do. Galicians are the early diners of Spain (8 or 9 pm), while Madrileños might think of going for a bite at midnight or 1 am.

Sticklers for absurd bureaucracy and measurement, the Spanish government rates restaurants by forks (this has become a bit of a joke – one restaurant near the Plaza Mayor in Madrid operates at the sign of the broken fork; a car repair shop in Granada has rated itself two wrenches). The forks have nothing to do with the quality of the food, though they hint somewhat at the prices. Unless it's explicitly written on the bill (*la cuenta*), service is *not* included in the total, so tip accordingly.

Between restaurants and tascas are **comedors** (literally, dining-rooms) often tacked onto the backs of bars, where the food and decor are usually drab but cheap, and **cafeterias**, usually those places that feature photographs of their offerings of *platos combinados* (combination plates) to eliminate any language problem. Others are self-service, and most tend to be drab, though cheap. **Asadors** specialize in roast meat or fish; **marisqueras** serve only fish and shellfish. There are also many **Chinese restaurants** in Spain which are fairly good and often inexpensive; **American fast food outlets** in the big cities and resort areas, and while Italian restaurants are 98 per cent dismal in Spain, you can get a good pizza in many places. Moroccan couscous restaurants are a recent fad and often good, as are the Indonesian rijstafel places that have followed the Dutch to the costas. Don't neglect the shacks on the beach – they often serve up roast sardines that are out of this world. (For menu and restaurant vocabulary see language section on p. 475 at the end of the book.)

Drinking

No matter how much other costs have risen in Spain, the **wine** has remained awesomely inexpensive by northern European or American standards; what's more, it's very good and there's enough variety from the various regions of the country for you to try something different every day. A restaurant's *vino del lugar* or *vino de la casa* is always your least expensive option while dining out; it's usually come out of a barrel or glass jug and may be a surprise either way. Some twenty Spanish wine-regions bottle their products under the strict controls, imposed by the National Institute, of *Denominación de Origen* (these almost always have the little maps of their various regions pasted on the back of the bottle). The most famous is La Rioja, from the banks of Ebro, and the others are certainly worth a try. Spain also produces its own champagne, known as *cava*, which is often just as good as the French and notably cheaper.

Best known, however, is the Jerez, or what we in English call sherry. When a Spaniard invites you to have a *copa* (glass) it will nearly always be filled with this Andalucian sunshine. It comes in a wide range of varieties: *Manzanillas* are very dry, *fino* is dry, light and young (the famous *Tio Pepe*); *Amontillados* are a bit sweeter and rich; *olorosos* are very sweet dessert sherries, and can be either brown, cream, or amoroso. Spanish brandy and *anis* (sweet or dry) are also quite popular. *Sangría* is the famous summertime punch of red wine, brandy, mineral water, orange and lemon with ice, but beware – it's rarely made very well. Each region has its wine and liqueur specialities and nearly every monastery in Spain seems to make some kind of herbal potion. The north of Spain, where apples grow better than vines, produces cider, or *sidra*, which comes as a shock to the taste buds. Ground almonds whipped to create *horchata de chufa* is refreshing in the summer.

As good as the wine is, Spaniards prefer **beer**, which is also good though not quite the bargain wine is. Most bars sell it cold in bottles or on tap: try Mahón Five Star if you see it. Imported whisky and other spirits are pretty expensive, though Spain bottles its own, which may come close to your home favourites, so much so that even the bottles look alike (Larios Gin's bottle looks very much like Gordon's, and there's even a third cut-rate imitator called *Lirios* with a third variation of the famous bottle).

Coffee, tea, all the international soft-drink brands and the locally-made *Kas* round out the average cafe fare. Spanish coffee is good and strong and if you want a lot of it order a *doble* in a *vaso*; one of those will keep you awake even through the guided tour of a Bourbon palace.

Fiestas and annual events

One of the most spiritually deadening aspects of Francoism was its banning of many local and regional fiestas. After surviving in suspended animation for decades, these are now once again celebrated with gusto, and if you can arrange your itinerary to include one or two, you'll be guaranteeing an unforgettable holiday. Besides the ones listed below, there are literally thousands of others, and new ones springing up all the time.

The big holidays celebrated throughout Spain are Corpus Christi in late May; Holy Week (*Semana Santa*), the week preceding Easter; 15 August, the Assumption of the Virgin and 25 July, the feast day of Spain's patron, Santiago. No matter where you are there are bound to be fireworks or processions on these dates, especially for Semana Santa and Corpus Christi. Beware that dates for most festivals tend to be fluid, flowing towards the nearest weekend; if the actual date falls on a Thursday or a Tuesday, Spaniards 'bridge' the fiesta with the weekend to create a four-day whoopee. If there's a fiesta you want to attend, check the date at the tourist office in advance.

Many village patronal fiestas feature *romerias* (pilgrimages) up to a venerated shrine. Getting there is half the fun, with everyone in local costume, riding on horseback or driving covered wagons full of picnic supplies. Music, dancing, food, wine and fireworks are all necessary ingredients of a proper fiesta, while the bigger ones often include bullfights, funfairs, circuses and competitions. In Extremadura, and especially in the Basque lands and Navarre, summer fiestas often feature a loose bull or two stampeding through the streets, an *encierro*. 'Giants' and 'fat-heads' (the former invariably 9 m (12 ft) tall dummies of Ferdinand and Isabel and a Moor, while the 'fat-heads' are usually comical or grotesque caricatures) pirouette through the throngs and tease the children.

Semana Santa, especially in Sevilla and the rest of Andalucía, is played up as a major tourist event, but unless you're prepared to fight the crowds to see the *pasos* (ornate floats depicting scenes from the Passion) carried in an excruciating slow march to lugubrious tuba music, accompanied by children and men decked out in costumes later copied by the Ku Klux Klan, you may want to skip it; the real revelry takes place after Easter.

Calendar

January

1–2	**Granada**, commemoration of the city's capture by the Catholic kings.
19–20	**San Sebastián**'s *Tamborrada*, marches of the Basque pipe-and-drum corps; **Igualada**, near Barcelona, Fiesta de San Antonio Abad (actually takes place on the Saturday and Sunday after 17 January).
End of January	**Ituren** and **Zubieta** (Navarre), dances of the Ioaldunak with pointed hats, fur vests, and big bells.

February

First weekend	**Bocairente** near Valencia, mock battles between Moors and Christians, and fireworks; **Almonacio del Marquesado** (Cuenca) celebrates *La Endiablada*, a religious rite of pre-Christian origin featuring day-long dances and processions of 'devils' wearing floral costumes and heavy metal bells; and **Zamarramala** outside Segovia: a very ancient custom where the 'mayoresses', the ladies of the village, take over for a day; folk-dancing and 12th-century costumes.

Carnival usually pops up in mid-February. **Cádiz** has perhaps the best in Spain and certainly the oldest: parades, masquerades, music and fireworks in abundance. Other lively celebrations at **Ciudad Rodrigo**, with lots of bull action, on the nearby ranches, in the city streets and *plazas de toros*, while **Solsona**, near Lleída, features the 'marriage of the mad giant.' On the Sunday of Carnival, there's an antique car ralley from Barcelona to **Sitges**.

During *Lent* there are Passion Play performances at **Ulldecona** (Tarragona), **Cervera** and **Esparraguera** (Barcelona). From the third Saturday in Lent until the fourth Sunday, **Castellón de la Plana** celebrates the *Fiestas de la Magdalena* with parades, night processions, and pilgrimages.

March

12–19	**Valencia**'s *Las Fallas*, one of Spain's great fiestas, with the world's gaudiest bonfires and the best fireworks west of China (see p. **147**). Saturday before Palm Sunday, **Vic**'s *Mercat del Ram*, where palm

fronds are sold and contests, demonstrations and the choosing of a palm queen.

Semana Santa: the most important celebrations are in **Sevilla**, with over 100 processions, broken by the singing of *saetas* (weird laments); **Cuenca**'s comes with a week-long festival of religious music; **Murcia**has the most charming *pasos*, **Valladolid** the most excruciating; **Málaga**, **Lorca Granada** and **Cartagena** put on major dos, while **Zamora**'s is the most ascetic. On the Saturday of Semana Santa, **Chinchón** (soiuth of Madrid) puts on a dramatic re-enactment of the Passion in the village's Plaza Mayor. Good Friday is celebrated with stark processions in **Bercianos de Aliste** (Zamora); Holy Thursday, by the medieval Dance of Death in **Verges** (Girona).

Easter Week: Festivities continue in **Murcia** with Tuesday's *Bando de la Huerta* (a procession of floats dedicated to local agricultural products), jazz concerts, and on Saturday, the *Entierro de la Sardina* (the Burial of the Sardine) and great fireworks displays. In **Avilés** (Asturias) Easter and Easter Monday are celebrated with the *Fiesta del Bollo*, with folklore groups, cake eating and regattas

April First Sunday after Easter **San Vincente de Barquera**'s *La Folia*, where the sailors transport an image of the Virgin in an illuminated maritime procession. Dancing.

23 **Barcelona**, St Jordi's day, exchange of books and roses. Around the same time **Alcoy** (Valencia) has the best of the 'battles' between Moors and Christians with pageantry, fireworks and great costumes, celebrating St George's miraculous intervention in battle.

Last week **Sevilla**'s *April Feria*, originally a horse-fair, now grown into the greatest festival of Andalucía. Costumed parades of the gentry in fine carriages, lots of flamenco, bullfights, and drinking; **Andujar** (Jaen) the *Romeria of the Virgin de la Cabeza*. Pilgrimage from all over Andalucía the procession to the sanctuary nearby in the Sierra Morena.

End of April beginning of May: **Caravaca de la Cruz**, *Fiestas de la Santisimo Vera-Cruz*, said to be a living memory of Templar rites.

May

First week **Jerez de la Frontera**, much like the April Fair in Sevilla; first Friday, **Jaca** re-enacts victory over the Moors by local women; **Figueras, Badajoz** and **Granada** have *Fiestas de la Santa Cruz*.

mid-May **Madrid**, *St Isidro*, with two weeks of entertainment, the best bullfights, parades and scores of free events.

Pentecost (seventh Sunday after Easter) **El Rocio** (Huelva): the biggest 'romeria' in Spain. Pilgrims converge on this tiny spot in Las Marismas south of Sevilla, in gaily decorated wagons for a week of wild carrying-on. The religious aspect is completely secondary; **San Feliu de Pallarols** (Girona), *Fiesta Mayor* with ancient dances and giants.

Corpus Christi usually falls at the end of May (Thursday after Trinity Sunday), initiating four days of festivities, especially at **Toledo, Sitges** (where the streets are covered with flower carpets), **Berga** (Barcelona), **Zahara de la Sierra** (Cádiz), **Zamora, Cáceres** and **Puenteareas** (Pontevedra)

June

First Sunday **Calella** (Barcelona), *Aplec de la Sardana*, Catalan dance and music contests.

15–July 15 **Granada**, *Festival International de Música y Danza* attracts some big names from around the world; classical music, jazz and ballet; also flamenco competitions in odd-numbered years.

2nd week **Marbella**, *Feria de San Bernabe*, with big-name events.

23–24 **San Juan de Alicante** celebrates St John's day better than any with a huge Fallas bonfire similar to Valencia's; more celebrations at **Prats de Lluçanes** (Barcelona), **Coria** (Cáceres) with bulls in the streets; **Segovia**, with floats; **San Pedro Manrique** (Soria) with bonfires and walks on hot coals; **León** (with parties and bullfights).

End of June *Soria*, 13th-century, five-day celebration of St John, with bulls in the street; **Baños de Cerrato** (Palencia) celebrates a Mozarab-Visigothic mass with ancient music on Sunday after 24 June; **Haro** (La Rioja) pilgrimage and drunken 'wine battles'. **Cudillero** (Asturias), *La Amuravela*, satirical poems on the year's events in the local dialect and lots of drink.

29 **Burgos**, *San Pedro*, beginning of two weeks of International folklore feria.

30 **Hita**, near Guadalajara, Festival of Medieval Theatre. Not only plays, but medieval food, dance, bullfights and falconry, all to the music of flutes and bagpipes.

July

July–August **Hecho** (Aragón), International Symposium of Contemporary Art and Sculpture, with art work all over the mountain sides; **Santander** holds its International Music Festival, jazz in August.

First Sunday **Vivero** (Lugo), *Rapa das Bestas*, Galician wild horse round-up; **Córdoba**, International Guitar Festival – classical, flamenco and Latino. **Zumaya** (Euskadi), Basque sports and dancing by the sea; **San Lorenzo de Sabucedo – La Estrada** (Pontevedra), another *Rapa das Bestas*, with big festivities from Saturday till Monday.

6–14 **Pamplona**, the famous running of the bulls and mad party for San Fermin.

2nd Sunday **Olot**, near Girona, *Aplec de la Sardana*, big Catalan dance festival; **Teruel** begins 10-day fiesta de *Vaquilla del Angel*, with Aragonese jotas, other dances and more.

Mid-July–August	**Cadaques** (Girona), International Music and Art Festival.
15	**Comillas** (Cantabria), catch the goose and other country fair-type festivities and humour.
2nd week	**Valencia**, *Feria*, lots of entertainment and the Valencian speciality, fireworks; **Segovia** has a Chamber Musical festival; **Avilés** has dances, entertainment, and bullfights.
16	**Sort** (Lleída), canoe races and festivities on the Río Noguera, Pallaresa; **San Pedro del Pinatar**, marine pilgrimage on the Mar Menor.
Last ten days of July	**San Sebastián**, International Jazz Festival.
22	**Anguiano** (La Rioja), fiesta with the dance of the *Zancos*, down the streets and steps on stilts; **Bermeo** (Euskadi), boat races, Basque sports and dancing.
24	Lloret de Mar (Girona), the Costa Brava's biggest resort puts on a charming traditional fiesta, ancient Moorish dances.
25	**Santiago de Compostela**, great pagan celebrations for Santiago – national offering to the saint, the swinging of the *Botafumeiro*, burning of a cardboard replica of Córdoba's Mezquita, great fireworks and more; **Tudela** (Navarre), music and dancing for a week for Santa Ana; **Cangas de Onis** (Asturias), shepherds' festival; **Villajoyosa** (Alicante), a week of mock battles between Christians and Moors.
29	**Luarca** (Asturias), Vaqueiro festival, mock wedding and dances; **Santa Maria de Ribarteme** (Pontevedra), pilgrimage made in coffins by people who narrowly escaped death the year before.
End of July	**Jaca**, on odd-numbered years, celebrates the International Folklore festival of the Pyrenees; in even numbered years it takes place at Oloron-Ste Marie in France. **Almería** festival, including jazz concerts.

August

3–9	**Estella** (Navarre), ancient fiesta, with giants and the only encierro where women can run with the bulls.
First Saturday	**Arriondas-Ribadesella** (Asturias), great kayak race on the Rio Sella.
First Sunday	**Gíjon**, Asturias Day celebrations, with lots of folklore.
5–10	**Vitoria**, giants, music, bonfires and more for the Virgen Blanca; on 5 August, **Trevelez** (Granada) has a midnight pilgrimage up Mulhacen, Spain's highest mountain.
9–11	**Foz** (Lugo), San Lorenzo festivities, folklore and kayaking.
11–15	**Elche**, performances of 13th-century mystery play in the Basilica of Santa Maria, beautiful poetry and music.
Second Sunday	**Cabezon de la Sal** (Cantabria), Mountain Day folklore, song contests; **Carballino** (Orense), Octopus festival and bagpipe music.

15–16 **Assumption** of the Virgin and San Roque festivities at **La Alberca** (Salamanca), a very ancient festival; **Sada** (La Coruña) with a big sardine roast; **Amer** (Girona), with Sardana dancing; **Llanes** (Asturias), bagpipes and ancient dances; **Bilbao**, Basque sports and races; **San Sebastián**, International Fireworks contest; **Vejar** (Cádiz) with flamenco; **Chinchón** with an encierro; other festivals in **Coca** (Segovia) and **El Burgo de Osma** (Soria)

Third week **La Unión** (Murcia), festival of *Cante de Las Mines*, flamenco competition, specializing in miners' songs; **Jumilla** (Murcia), *La Vendimia* wine festival.

Last Sunday **Cuellar**, near Valldolid, music, dancing and an encierro; **Vivero** (Lugo), pilgrimage and music, **Ontentinete** (Valencia), four-day Christian and Moor battles

Last week **Sanlucar de la Barrameda** (Cádiz), exaltation of the Río Guadalquivir and major flamenco events; **Toro**, Fiesta de San Augustine, bulls and a 'fountain of wine'; **Medinaceli** (Soria), Medieval Music week.

30 **Villafranca del Penedés** (Tarragona), human towers, Sardana dances, etc.

31 **Loyola** (Euskadi), St Ignatius de Loyola Day.

September

First week **Almagro** (Ciudad Real), Spanish Drama Festival in historic theatre; **Aranjuez** (Madrid), concerts and dancing; **San Sebastián** Basque food festival; **Jerez** and **Valdepeñas** *Vendimia* wine festivals; **Lequeito** (Euskadi), Basque festival, including contest to pull the head off a goose with a greased neck.

8 Virgin's Birthday with celebrations in many places, especially **Salamanca**, **Algemesi** (Valencia), **Tordesillas**. Around this date **Ronda** puts on an 18th-century-style bullfight in its historic ring; ceremonies at **Montserrat**.

11 **Sueca** (Valencia), festival of rice with paella contests.

12 **Graus** (Aragón), big folklore event, with dances and ancient songs.

2nd week **San Sebastián**, International Film Festival; **Murcia**, International Mediterranean Music Festival; **Cardona** (Barcelona), dancing, bulls and Catalan fun and games; **Zarauz** (Euskadi), Basque fun and games.

19 **Oviedo**, big Americas Day celebration, with floats and bands from all over Latin America; **Logroño** has the *Vendimia* wine festival of La Rioja.

24 **Barcelona** has music, human towers and tons of other entertainments for its patroness, the Virgen de la Merced.

October

8–16 **Zaragoza**, festivities for the Virgen del Pilar, with huge floral offering.

2nd week	**Aviles** has an equally big party for Santa Teresa.
14 or so	**El Grove** (Pontevedra), shellfish festival.
18–20	**Mondoñedo** (Lugo), *As San Lucas*, big horse fair dating from the Middle Ages.
Last week	**Girona**, fireworks and more for San Narcis; **Sitges** has an International Festival of Vanguard Theatre and Fantasy and Terror Films, extending into November.
28	**Consuegra** (Toledo), Fiesta of the Saffron Rose.

Best of Spain

This is admittedly subjective, but may give you a start in planning your holiday. They're in no particular order.

Scenery: Picos de Europa, Pyrenees, Costa Brava, Upper and Lower Rías of Galicia, around Ronda, the Alpujarras (Granada), Cantabrian mountains of Asturias and León.

Cities: Sevilla, Cádiz, Segovia, Toledo, Ronda, Ubeda, Santiago de Compostela, Barcelona, Girona, Tarragona, Pontevedra, Cáceres, Granada, Córdoba.

Villages: Santillana del Mar (Cantabria), Albarraicin (Teruel), Arcos and the White Villages of Andalucía, Cazorla and Baeza (both near Ubeda), Burgo de Osma (Soria), Almagro (Ciudad Real), Viella (Lleída), La Alberca (Salamanca), Morella (Castellón), Estella (Navarre).

Parks and Gardens: Generalife in Granada, several in Sevilla, at the palaces of La Granja and Aranjuez, and in Barcelona, the parks of Montjuïc, Horta, and the unique Park Guëll.

Bullrings: Ronda and Sevilla.

Wild country: Sierra Nevada and Alpujarras (Granada), Las Marismas and Coto Donaña National Park (near Huelva), Sierra de Cazorla (near Ubeda), Sierra de las Ancares (Lugo), Ordesa National Park (Huesca), Aigues-Tortes National Park, (Lleída), Las Hurdes (Cáceres), El Bierzo (León), Somiedo Reserve and the Picos de Europa (Asturias).

Zoo: Barcelona, but the pandas are in Madrid.

Castles: Alhambra (Granada), Belmonte (near Toledo), Coca and Peñafie (Valladolid), Loarre (Huesca), Olite (Navarre) Alcazar (Segovia), Almería.

Market building: Valencia.

Monasteries: Montserrat (Barcelona), Poblet (Tarragona), Guadalupe (Cáceres), Las Huelgas and Miraflores (Burgos) and derelict San Pere de Roda (Girona).

Bodegas you can tour: Jerez de la Frontera, La Rioja, Tarragona province.

Lagoon: Albufera (Valencia).

Quiet undeveloped beaches: many on the Costa de Luz, in Almería and Murcia; innumerable wide sweeps of sand and lovely coves in the north in Cantabria and Galicia especially, though the season's obviously much shorter.

Skiing: Aragonese Pyrenees.

Fireworks: Las Fallas in Valencia, Santiago day in Compostela, International Fireworks festival in San Sebastián.

Curiosities: El Escorial, Gibraltar, Salvador Dalí Museum in Figueras, Maragatos of

Astorgas, Mar Menor (Murcia), cave dwellings in Guadix, mini-Hollywood in Almería, Cataluña in miniature (Barcelona), erotic Romanesque church in Cervatos (Cantabria), Las Dueñas cloister (Salamanca), Holy Grail in Valencia, triple-spiral stair at Santo Domingo (Santiago de Compostela), live chickens in the cathedral at Santo Domingo de Calzada (Logroño), megalithic altar at San Miguel de Arretxinaga (Vitoria), Cristo de Burgos, in Burgos Cathedral.
Forest: Muniellos, in Asturias.
English bookstore: Turner's, in Madrid.
Blanco y negros: Cafe Central, across from the post office in Granada.

Architecture and Art – and where to see it

Pre-Roman

The Celts and Iberians were not great builders. Their remains are mostly curiosities, like the three huge dolmen-chambers in **Antequera**, and the stone bulls and boars called *verracos* left all over Avila province. Galicia and Asturias are rich in dolmens and the foundations of Celtic *castros*, the best-preserved in **La Guardia**. The most interesting ancient works of art can be found in the archaeological museums of **Córdoba, Sevilla** and above all **Madrid**, where you can see the finest of all Iberian sculpture, the famous 'Lady of Elche'.

Roman and Visigothic

Considering the literary figures Spain gave the Roman world, it's surprising that Roman Spain comes up so short in art. In the museums of **Madrid, Córdoba, Mérida** and **Barcelona** you'll see the usual copies of Greek sculpture, statues of Emperors, and mosaics not quite up to the level of other lands around the Mediterranean. Among Roman cities **Mérida** is by far the best preserved and **Tarragona** has a number of interesting remains. The aqueduct of **Segovia**, still intact, is the largest engineering work left from antiquity, and the **Alcantará** bridge in Cáceres province is also impressive. Other Roman ruins may be seen at **Italica** near Sevilla; there's also a reconstructed temple in **Córdoba** and the great walls at **Lugo**.

Visigothic art, derivative of the Roman, is best seen in the Archaeological Museum of **Madrid** (the 'Treasure of Gurrazar') and the Museum of the Councils in **Toledo**. A few of their churches survive with the characteristic horseshoe-arch later adopted by the Moors.

Moorish

The renaissance of culture in Islamic Spain, beginning in the 9th century, left great monuments all over Andalucía. **Sevilla** with its La Giralda Tower and Torre de Oro (12th century), **Córdoba** with its incomparable Mezquita (10th century), and **Granada**'s even more spectacular Alhambra (14th century) are the three places to visit. Much Moorish work was wantonly destroyed, but many castles remain, notably the

Alcazabas in **Málaga** and **Almería**. In the north, the Cristo de la Luz church (a former mosque) in **Toledo** and the Aljaferia in **Zaragoza** are the outstanding buildings. Moorish art – ceramics, woodworking, and metalwork, mostly – has its best collections in the Museums of **Granada** and **Córdoba.**

Early Spanish Christian Art.

At the same time (9th century) as the Moors in the south were beginning their golden age, the small Christian principalities of the north were developing an architecture much more sophisticated than elsewhere in Western Europe. The greatest monuments are the Asturian churches in **Oviedo** and the Asturian hinterland, precursors of the Romanesque, as well as interesting Moorish-influenced or 'Mozarabic' churches in the villages of **Soria** province, **León, Navarre, Aragón**, and especially at **Melque**, near Toledo

Romanesque

The often underestimated Spanish Romanesque was influenced by France along the pilgrimage route to Santiago, along which you can see scores of examples: the Pantheon of St Isidore **(León)**, Eunate, Sangüesa and Estella near **Pamplona, Jaca** cathedral, **Sahagún** and ultimately, the great cathedral of **Santiago** itself. The Catalans in particular took to the style: **Ripoll, San Cugat**, and nearly every village in the Pyrenees has a Romanesque church, and in **Barcelona**, the Museum of Catalan Art contains a magnificent collection of the period's art. The best examples in the centre are Santo Domingo in **Soria**, San Vincente in **Avila**, which also still retains its 11th-century walls, and several distinctive churches in **Segovia**. Eccentric variations of the style may be seen in the cathedrals of **Toro, Zamora**, and in the old cathedral of **Salamanca**.

Gothic

The increasingly bitterness of the *Reconquista* broke off many cultural relations between Christian and Moorish Spain; one result was that Moorish influences in architecture ended in Castile and León, allowing the growth of a Gothic aesthetic highly dependent on French originals. The three greatest Gothic cathedrals in Spain are in **León, Burgos**, and **Toledo**; nearly as impressive is the style known as 'Catalan Gothic' with more emphasis on width than height, the best examples of which are the Cathedral and Santa María del Mar in **Barcelona**, the cathedral of **Girona** and that of **Tarragona**. Barcelona also has an entire neighbourhood of secular Gothic architecture and some of the period's finest art in the Museum of Catalan Art and Federic Marés Museum. Like Romanesque, the Gothic style lingered in Spain longer than the rest of Europe, and the last cathedrals ever built in the style may be seen at **Salamanca** and **Segovia**. Plateresque and Isabelline Gothic, Spain's ornate contributions to the style, correspond roughly to the French Flamboyant or English Perpendicular. The best Plateresque is all over **Salamanca**, at the University in **Alcalá de Henares** and San Gregorio in **Valladolid**. The more elegantly serene Isabelline Gothic is best seen at San Juan de los

Reyes in **Toledo** and the Capilla Real in **Granada**. Exquisite Gothic sculpture can be seen at the tombs in the Miraflores convent in **Burgos**; the choir of **Zamora** Cathedral, and at **Sigüenza** cathedral.

Mudejár

In areas where Moorish influence and Moorish artisans survived, a new form was developed around the 13th century. One critic has called Mudejár the 'national style of Spain', combining the best of Moorish decorative arts – brickwork and azulejo tiles – and their love of elaborate geometric patterns with elements from Romanesque and Gothic. **Toledo** has the best collection: several parish churches, town gates, and two lovely synagogues. Perhaps the grandest Mudejár works are the four great church towers of **Teruel**. Many other towns in southern Aragón – **Zaragoza, Calatayud**, and **Tarazona** also have good examples. In the south, the Alcazar in **Sevilla**, built for Peter the Cruel, is Mudejár at its most extravagant. Mudejár elements, especially beautifully carved wooden *artesonado* ceilings, can be seen all over Spain.

Renaissance and the 'Golden Age'

Spain after 1500 allowed Mudejár and other native elements to be swept aside by imitation of Italian renaissance styles, producing some fine buildings but also some very ugly ones. The best are the many works of Andrés de Vandelvira in **Ubeda**, and Juan de Herrera's great **El Escorial** near Madrid. Herrera's cold, tidy 'estilo desornimentado' achieved a great but temporary popularity, evolving into a classically Spanish style of rectangular building with four corner towers and slate-roof spires modelled on El Escorial. The Ayuntamientos of **Madrid** and **Toledo** are two of the best examples.

Spanish painting developed greatly in this period (16th century), notably in the various painters of the **Sevillian** school (best seen in the city's Museum of Fine Arts), and for El Greco (d. 1614; works in the Prado, **Madrid**, and various museums of **Toledo**), and Pedro Berruguete.

Paradoxically, 17th-century Spain, at its greatest age of painting, produced little in the way of architecture. Among the painters the clarity and perfection of Velázquez stands out (large collection in the Prado) and next to him the restrained spirituality of Zurbarán, d. 1664 (museums of **Cádiz, Sevilla**, and the Prado and the cathedral of **Guadalupe**). Other painters limited themselves to orthodox religious commissions, either grim and disquieting (Ribalta, d. 1628, Ribera, d. 1652 and the outrageous Valdez Leal, d. 1690), or saccharine mariolatry with floating angels (Murillo, d. 1682; many works in **Sevilla**, and Alonso Cano, d. 1667, of **Granada**).

Baroque

A bad age for art, as it was for life in Spain. Good Spanish painting died suddenly and completely after the 1660s. Baroque architecture took on some of its most extravagant forms in Spain, in a wildly ornate style called the 'Churrigueresque' after the sculptor and architect Jose Churriguera (d. 1723). Its finest creation is the Plaza Mayor in **Salamanca**; the rest of its energy went mainly into huge retablos that adorn half the cathedrals in Spain. Other Baroque excesses can be seen at the Cartuja in **Granada**, churches in **Priego de Córdoba**, the Convento de Merced in **Córdoba**, the new façade of the cathedral at **Santiago de Compostela**, and the 'Transparente' in **Toledo** cathedral. The Bourbon kings imported foreign architects for their many palaces, of which the best are at **Aranjuez, La Granja** near Segovia, and the Royal Palace in **Madrid**.

19th and 20th centuries

In painting, there is only Goya (d. 1828), but he ranks with Velázquez as one of Spain's greatest (in **Madrid**, the Prado and Goya Pantheon). After him Spanish painting shows little originality, but the works of Fortuny, de Madrazo, Zuloaga and Sorolla fill the museums of **Madrid** and **Barcelona**. Similarly in architecture, the 'ecletic' fashion took hold, resulting in neo-Moorish bullrings and Roman-style public buildings. With the 20th century, Spain unexpectedly exploded into creativity, with painters like Picasso (d. 1973; *Guernica* in **Madrid** and Picasso Museum in **Barcelona**), Juan Gris (d. 1927), Joan Miró, d. 1983, Fundació Miró in **Barcelona**) and the irascible Salvador Dalí (Dalí Theatre-Museum in **Figueres**).

The rebirth of architecture occurred somewhat earlier, in the specifically Catalán Modernista style crowned by Antoni Gaudí (d. 1926, most works in **Barcelona**) and his fellows, Domènech i Montaner and Puig i Cadafalch. The great ceramic artist, Xavier Nogués, Josep Sert the muralist and Gaudí's co-worker Jujol supplied many of the decorative touches.

The coming of the Civil War and Franco put a quick end to Spain's new-found prominence in the arts; despite the restoration of democracy there seems to have been no recovery yet. Apart from a couple of early works by Ricard Bofill in **Barcelona**, there are hardly any good modern buildings in all of Spain, and the painters' meagre works can be seen at the Museums of Contemporary Art in **Cuenca, Madrid** and in the Fundació Miró in **Barcelona**. Still, one cannot visit Spain without thinking that new talents and forms could appear at any time.

Part II

SPANISH TOPICS

El Cid

Air and Light

We can tell you everything about cathedrals and palaces, cities and resorts, but setting the scene for them will prove somewhat harder. One of the delights of all the Mediterranean lands is the endless variety of qualities and colour in the sea and sky. Nowhere, perhaps, will you be aware of these things as much as in Spain.

On the high central plains, where the air is thin, the sun becomes a manifest power. At noon, even on a cool day, it can seem like some diabolical ray, probing deep inside your brain. Always, it illuminates Spain with a merciless brilliance; Spanish writers recall it when trying to explain their country's literature and history. 'Spain', according to one 'is a country where things can be seen all too clearly.' Spanish art could not be what it is without this light. In the Prado, you'll look at rooms of Goya paintings set under an impossibly lovely pale blue sky with clouds like the breath of angels. You'll probably blame the artist for picturesque excess – and then walk outside to find that same Castilian sky, and those same clouds, reproduced over your head.

The winds, too, will make you take notice. Even more than in other parts of the Mediterranean, each has its name and characteristics and when the less gracious of them visit they seize the land like a conquering army. Andalucía and the south annually endure the African *sirocco*; walking into it is like opening the oven door. The *tramontana*, when it's angry, roars over the Pyrenees and knocks the Catalans' houses down. And springtime in Cádiz is sometimes plagued with an utterly bizarre wind called the *solano* that gets under your skin like a scalpel. The effect it has on the female population is legend: in the old days, they would converge on the beach en masse when the solano hit, taking off their clothes and jumping in the sea for relief while the local cavalry regiment stood guard. Today, ask the ladies of Cádiz about it and they'll just laugh.

Bats

Fine country for bats, Spain is. Almost everywhere in the country (but especially in Aragón and around Granada) you'll see clouds of them cavorting in the twilight, zooming noiselessly past your ears and doing their best to ensure you get a good night's sleep by gobbling up all the mosquitoes they can. Spaniards don't mind them a bit, and the medieval kings of Aragón even went so far as to make them a dynastic emblem, derived from a Muslim Sufi symbol.

Lots of bats, of course, presumes lots of caves, and Spain has more than its share. The famous grottoes of Nerja, Aracena, and Valporquero (near León) are only a few of the places where you can see colossal displays of tinted, aesthetically draped stalactites. Hundreds were decorated in one way or another by Paleolithic man; even though the most famous, at Altamira, are closed to the public, you can still see some cave art by asking around for a guide in Albarraicin in Aragón, in the villages west of Cuenca, at Puente Viesgo near Santander, or around Velez Rubio west of Murcia. This last area, from Velez as far west as Granada, actually has a huge population still living in caves – quite cosily fitted out these days – and in Granada itself you can visit the 'gypsy caves' for a little histrionic flamenco and diluted sherry.

Bullfights

In Spanish newspapers, you will not find accounts of the bullfight on the sports page. Look in the 'arts and culture' section; that is how Spain has always thought of this singular spectacle. Bullfighting combines elements of ballet with the primal finality of Greek tragedy. To the Spaniards it is a ritual without a religion, and it divides the nation irreconcilably between those who find it brutal and demeaning, an echo of the old Spain best forgotten, and those who couldn't live without it. Its origins are obscure. Some claim it to be a descendant of Roman circus games; others say it started with the Moors. In the Middle Ages it took the form of bull versus a mounted knight with a lance.

Modern bullfighting, however, has its beginnings in Ronda, about 1800, when Francisco Romero developed the basic pattern of the *corrida* and some of the moves and passes still in use today. The first royal aficianado was Fernando VII, the reactionary post-Napoleonic monarch who also brought back the Inquisition. He founded the Royal School of Bullfighting in Sevilla, and promoted the spectacle across the land as a circus for a discontented populace. Since the Civil War, bullfighting has gone through a period of troubles similar to boxing in the US. Crooked promoters control it, and massive publicity for their favourites by paid-off reporters often keeps the best performers in obscurity. Scandals of weak bulls, doped-up bulls, and bulls with the points of their horns shaved have been frequent. Attempts at reform have been made, and all the problems seem to have decreased bullfighting's popularity only slightly.

A *corrida* begins with the colourful entry of the *cuadrillas* (teams of *toreros*) and the *alguaciles*, officials dressed in 17th-century costume, who salute the 'president' of the fight. Usually three teams fight two bulls apiece, the whole taking only about two hours.

Each of the six fights is a self contained drama in four acts. First, upon the entry of the bull, the members of the *cuadrilla* tease him a bit, and the *matador*, the team leader, plays him with the cape to test his qualities. Next comes the turn of the *picadores*, on padded horses, who wound the bull in the neck with a short lance or *pica*, and the *bandilleros* who agilely plant sharp darts in the bull's back while avoiding the sweep of the horns. These wounds weaken the bull and force it to keep its head lower for the third and most artistic stage, where the lone matador conducts his pas-de-deux with the doomed animal, leading him in deft passes and finally crushing his spirit with a tiny cape called a *muleta*. Now the defeated bull is ready for the 'moment of truth'. The kill must be clean and quick, a sword thrust to the heart.

More often than not the job is botched. Most bullfights, in fact, are a disappointment, but to the aficionado the chance to see one or all of the stages perfectly done makes it worthwhile. When the matador is good, the band plays and hats and handkerchiefs fly; an excellent performance earns the reward from the president of one of the bull's ears, or both, or both ears and the tail.

You'll be lucky to see a bullfight at all; there are only about 500 each year in all Spain, mostly coinciding with a town's fiesta. Madrid and Barcelona are the most likely spots; other cities with more than ten *corridas* a year are Sevilla, Valencia, Zaragoza, Málaga, and Puerto Santa Marisa near Cádiz. Tickets can be hard to get, scalpers sometimes buy them out. Get them in advance if you can, from the office in the ring (*plaza de toros*) itself to avoid commission charges. Tickets range from 200 pts for the cheap seats in the sun to 5000 pts and more, depending on the event, for front-row seats (*barreras*) in the shade. Most *corridas* are held in the late spring and early summer.

Castrum

In laying out their military camps, as in anything else, the Romans liked to go by the book. From Britain to Babylonia, they established hundreds of permanent forts (*castrum* in Latin) all seemingly stamped out of the same press, with a neatly rectangular circuit of walls, and two straight streets, the *cardo* and *decumanus*, crossing in the middle. Many of these grew into towns – any place in Britain, for example, that ends in -chester or -caster.

In Spain, where the Roman wars of conquest went on for 200 years, there are perhaps more of these than anywhere else, and it's interesting to try and trace out the outlines of the Roman castrum while you're exploring Spanish cities. In Barcelona's Barri Gotic, the plan is obvious, and in Avila and Cáceres the streets and walls have hardly changed since Roman times. With a little practice and a good map, you can find the castra hiding inside Córdoba, Mérida, Léon, Zaragoza, Tarragona, Lugo and a score of other towns.

Churros

As James Michener wrote: 'Any nation that can eat churros and chocolate for breakfast is not required to demonstrate its courage in other ways.' These long, fluted wads of fried dough, looking like some exotic variety of garden slug, are an essential part of the Spanish experience, sooner or later every serious traveller will have to step into a *chur-*

reria and face up to them. Properly made they're as greasy as a crankcase and drowned in sugar. The hot chocolate that comes with them should be quite thick to offer some small degree of protection by coating the stomach lining. Spaniards down several billions of them each year.

Pablo Picasso, who as a small boy in Málaga had trouble learning how to count because he could not believe a 7 was not an upside-down nose, recalled that churros always fascinated him, and were the first thing he ever tried to draw – which proves that churros are just as subversive aesthetically as they are in your stomach.

The Cid

In the Spanish pantheon the Cid Campeador comes in a close second to Santiago himself, though like St James his apotheosis owes much to propaganda, especially in the *Poem of the Cid*, written around the year 1200 and the dullest of medieval Europe's epics. And yet unlike the other heroes of Romance, the Cid, Rodrigo Díaz de Vivar (1043–99) was entirely flesh and blood. His title is derived from the Arabic *sayyidi* ('my lord'), while Campeador translates as 'Battler', and his fame spread so widely among both Moors and Christians (in his career he served both sides) that even before his death poems were composed on his prowess. The most famous event of his life, the capture of Valencia, took place when he was already 50 years old.

Through modern eyes, Rodrigo was little better than an outlaw, but for the Castilian warrior-class of the Reconquista, he embodied their greatest values: fearlessness, an exaggerated sense of honour (that famous Spanish *pundonor*), devout Catholicism (he made the pilgrimage to Santiago) and especially his utter pragmatism; he was also generous, paid his debts, was devoted to his family, and always kept his word. He was the perfect man of his time, living in the tolerant frontier society of Christians, Moors and Jews, where a king's powers were strictly limited, and the main issues of the day were the simple pleasures of turf and booty.

Dr Fleming

Ask a Spaniard to name one famous Canadian, and if you get anything more than a blank stare, it will likely be a mention of the inventor of penicillin. To the Spaniards he is one of the titans of science; there is a street named for him in almost every large town. Fleming has also become a sort of patron saint for two special groups in Spanish society. There are two monuments to the good doctor in Spain: one in front of the Ventas bullring in Madrid, and another in the Barrio Chino, the red-light district of Barcelona.

Flamenco and Anti-Flamenco

For many people, flamenco is the soul of Spain, like bullfighting an essential part of its culture that sets it apart from the rest of the world. Good flamenco, with that ineffable quality of *duende*, has a primitive, ecstatic allure that draws in its listeners until they feel as if their very hearts were pounding in time with its relentless rhythms, their emotions seared by its ululating Moorish wails and sheer drama of the dance. Few modern experiences can be more cathartic.

As folklore goes, however, flamenco is newborn. It began in the 18th century in Andalucía, where its originators, the gypsies, called one another 'flamencos' – an old derogatory term from the days when Charles V's Flemish (*Flamenco*) courtiers bled Spain dry. Its songs of oppression, lament and bitter romance soon caught on among the downtrodden of Andalucía, and it spread throughout Spain in this century as they migrated in search of jobs. Like American country music, flamenco was long looked down upon in the more sophisticated north, but is currently enjoying a great revival among Spaniards of all origins.

Travelling through Spain you'll have a number of chances to see flamenco. Beware the touristy places; in an attempt to please all the result is inevitably ghastly, and there are few things more painful than watching a talented performer do a fandago to a juiced-up recording of the *Barber of Seville*. The best way to find the real thing is by asking around in the hole-in-the-wall bars of Sevilla, Córdoba, or Málaga, or by chancing on a festival in an Andalucían village that hasn't been declared 'Of Tourist Interest' by the government – or in a more cultural setting, at the competitions and performances at the International Festival in Granada.

If all this leaves you cold, Spain has excelled in many other varieties of music. The classical greats – Manuel de Falla, Rodrigo, Albéniz, Granados, Casals – and the great guitarists, Andrés Segovia and Carlos Montoyo are well known and medieval music buffs know that Alfonso the Wise composed some lovely tunes. Spain has produced brilliant opera singers but no composers, though it did develop a unique, light melodramatic opera of its own, the *zarzuela*, the Spanish version of Gilbert and Sullivan. This hasn't enjoyed the same revival as flamenco but is still put on with some regularity in Madrid, and is fun to see, even if you can't make out a word.

In Celtic Galicia, the bagpipe (*gaita*) and its Breton-like tunes are still immensely popular. The Basques have their own music, in its symmetry comparable to ancient music from Anatolia; they and the Catalans, are very fond of choral groups, always singing in their own languages when they can. Of all the Spaniards, the Catalans take music the most seriously, and Barcelona is the best place to hear it, from grand opera to flamenco to jazz to the 'New Catalan Song' that sprang up after Franco, and some recent experiments in flamenco-jazz or Galician rock 'n' roll.

Gaudí

The most compelling reason to visit Spain is to see the works of Europe's most innovative architect, Antoní Gaudí i Cornet (1852–1926). This is almost as easily done as said because all of his major works (several of which have been included in UNESCO's list of World Trust properties) are in Barcelona, which is quickly awakening to their appeal to pilgrims from distant lands; you can take an all-Gaudí tour, purchase a box full of Gaudí books, or even build your own little Casa Battló from a paper kit. Ennui with the International style may well be behind this revival of interest in the Catalan master, whose imagination in form, structure, and colour rivalled nature herself. In his hands, stone became organically sensuous, wrought iron was spun into new, marvellous shapes and patterns, the almost impossible parabolic arch, last seen with the Hittites, was reinvented to create a hundred wonderful rhythms and old decorative elements like bricks, tiles, mosaics and ceramic collages became as integral to the structure as its walls or roof. Although always classed as *Modernista* (the peculiarly Catalan school of art nouveau), Gaudí's creation of new forms went far beyond anything built by his colleagues.

A perfectionist, obsessed with and constantly revising every detail of his projects, Gaudí wrote almost nothing and received little attention outside Barcelona during his life, which ended abruptly under a streetcar. His fellow Catalans, however, have always respected his work. George Orwell, writing of the church burnings during the Civil War, wondered that there was one, a peculiar one with spires shaped like bottles, that the mobs always spared: the Sagrada Familia, Gaudí's masterpiece.

The Inquisition

What a day, what a day
for an *auto-da-fé*!
Bernstein's *Candide*

Besides bullfighting and flamenco, it's one of the things Spain is most famous for, an essential part of the 'Black Legend' of the dark days of Philip II.There's nothing to debunk and no need for a historical re-examination; the Inquisition was just as bloody and stupid and horrible as the Protestant propagandists of the day said it was. But what made them do it? Surprisingly, the original motives were largely political. Ferdinand and Isabel introduced the Inquisition in 1480 as an institution entirely under the control of the crown, and they used it as a means to suppress and discourage dissent; with their powers strictly limited under the secular laws, they turned to the Church courts as a way to get at their enemies. Originally, under the direction of a passionate ascetic, the famous Torquemada, the Inquisition's victims were nearly all *conversos*, baptized Jews with wealth or important positions in government or Church. Any of them found guilty of backsliding in the faith would have their property confiscated – if they weren't burned at the stake. It is said that much of this booty went to finance the wars against the Moors of Granada.

In the decades that followed, though, the Inquisition took on a life of its own. From the 1530s on, with the Catholic powers in a panic over the onset of the Reformation, a succession of Inquisitors much worse than Torquemada expanded the Holy Office to every city, with a corps of secret agents and investigators estimated at 20,000. Though terror of it spread to every household, application was crazily inconsistent; the Inquisition saw nothing wrong with the opinions of Copernicus, but sent hundreds of poor souls to the stake for reading the Bible in Spanish instead of Latin.

Despite a cumbersome bureaucracy and a great pretence of legalism, the Inquisition was little better than a kangaroo court. Anyone denounced (even if it were by playful children) had a good chance of spending several years in solitary confinement while the Holy Office decided his or her case. Few were ever cleared. Torture was almost universal – as everywhere else in Europe in that grim age – and after it the accused would be lucky to get let off with a public recantation, a flogging and the loss of all his property. *Autos-de-fé* ('works of faith') were colourful public spectacles, preceded by much pageantry and preaching, where sentences were given out, there the unlucky ones, dressed in capes decorated with flames and devils and bearing signboards explaining their crimes, were led off to the stake. The last, and biggest, was a 14-hour affair with

120 victims personally staged in Madrid's Plaza Mayor in 1680 by the insane Charles II.

Names

Politicians these days complain too much about bad publicity. Medieval rulers, especially the bad ones, were shown no mercy either by their subjects or the chroniclers. Spanish history is full of characters, and we terribly regret not being able to discuss more fully the careers of Wilfred the Hairy, Sancho the Fat, Bermudo the Gouty, Pedro of the Dagger, Enrique the Sufferer, Sancho the Fierce, and of course, that last king of independent León, Alfonso the Slobberer.

Names of Spanish towns are even better. Places like Madrigal of the High Towers, Mirambel, and Gargantiel fairly drip with medieval romance – which dissipates immediately should you ever travel to them – and every city in Andalucía save Huelva and Jaen has had an American or Spanish car named after it. Village names often exhibit the kind of piquant humility you'd expect in Arkansas or Tennessee. In the dusty nowheres of Spain you can seek out towns that translate to Fathead, Chaos, Black Eye, Bucket, Gypsum Pit, Vinegar Mary, Welcome, Onion, Chicken Inn, Cow Head, Slavery, and Snake's Flattery. West of Murcia, you can watch the Reliable River flow beneath the cliffs of Mount Lies, and the really adventurous can take their chances in Pueblonuevo del Terrible ('new village of the ill-tempered') or in any of the four Spanish hamlets called Wrong Turn.

Names of Streets

Franco and his cohorts were a tawdry lot; one of the first things they did after taking over Spain was to rename all the streets after themselves – Paseo del Generalísimo, Avenida José Antonio Primo de Rivera, Plaza General Mola. These are the most common, along with petty hoodlums like Queipo de Llano, General Varela, Colonel Moscardó, General Yagüe, Calvo Sotelo, and others. Almost immediately after the restoration of democracy, Spanish cities began the process of weeding these out. It's been done slowly and discreetly, and one of the major sources of confusion for visitors is that streets and plazas will still be listed in brochures and maps under their old Francoist names; this book has the changes current up to 1986. Some towns, most in Old Castile, haven't changed them at all, and looking at the street signs is a handy indicator to the state of local politics wherever you go.

Santiago

No saint on the calendar has as many names as Spain's patron – Iago, Diego, Jaime, Jacques, Jacobus, or Santiago. English speakers know him as James the Greater, the fisherman, one of the first disciples chosen by Jesus, who called him *Boanerges*, the 'son of thunder'. In the year 44, Herod Agrippa had him beheaded in Caesarea, and in the official histories, his story ends there.

But Spain had another task in store for James: no less than rising up to lead a 700-year crusade against the peninsula's infidels. How it came about that the fisherman James of the Bible became the fierce Santiago Matamoros ('the Moor-slayer'), often appearing in person on the battlefield to kill a few thousand Moors, is downright miraculous or a stunning propaganda coup. The legend begins in the year 812, when a monk in western Galicia 'rediscovered' the bones of St James. An ancient Spanish tradition already had the apostle in Zaragoza while alive, so it seemed plausible that when he died his followers would bring his body back to Spain – sailing with it from Egypt in a stone boat in a week, no less. By 844 Santiago Matamoros had made his debut at the legendary Battle of Clavijo, fighting at the side of Ramiro I of Asturias. In 950 the first French pilgrims had blazed the trail to his tomb.

The pilgrimage to Santiago de Compostela was one of the great acts of faith in the Middle Ages. When it reached its peak of popularity in the 12th and 13th centuries, half-a-million people a year made their way to the shrine, the majority of them French (hence the route is known as the 'French Road'), but some from as far away as Poland, Scandinavia, and the Near East. Pilgrims who made the dangerous journey (if they began, as many did, at the Tour de St Jacques in Paris, it was an 800-mile trek) were rewarded with an indulgence worth half their time in Purgatory, embodied in a certificate called a *Compostela*, which scalpers sold a few hundred miles up the road from Santiago to cheaters. Many of these who went had been sentenced to make the pilgrimage by the courts as an alternative to prison.

Along with their faith, the pilgrims brought new ideas into Spain, including the Romanesque and Gothic architecture that still embellishes the routes they walked, in the form of churches, monasteries, and charitable hostels and hospitals. The *Codex Calixtinus*, the world's first tour guide, written in 1130 by a French monk, Aymery de Picaud, offered advice on where not to drink the water, where to find the best lodgings, and where to be on guard against 'false pilgrims' who came not to atone for crimes but to commit them along the Road. Despite travelling in large bands and benefiting from the police work of the chivalrous orders (the Templars, Hospitalers and Knights of Santiago, founded exclusively to aid pilgrims), many died on the way. Those who returned home brought back wonderful stories and the seeds of European unity from their shared experience.

Although few people these days walk to Santiago, it's becoming increasingly popular to drive along the old pilgrimage routes; the National Tourist Office has even published a special booklet that points out all the service stations along the way. Others, marginally closer to the medieval spirit, take the bus. If you care to follow the great French road through the pages of this book, begin at Roncevalles in the Pyrenees of Navarre. At Puente de Reina, also in Navarre, the road joined the other routes out of the east to form the 'Universal Road', which passes on its way east through Logroño, and the provinces of Old Castile (Burgos, Palencia and León) before arriving in Galicia.

If you can't find a copy of the *Codex Calixtinus* to read on your pilgrimage, good books to get are Edwin Mullins' *The Road to Compostela* or *The Mystery of Compostela* by Louis Charpentier.

Spain and Britain

Where would the English be without Spain? Where would they get their brussels sprouts in January, or canaries, or Seville oranges for marmalade? Long ago the ancient Iberians colonized Cornwall (of course historians can be found who say they arrived in

Spain *from* Britain), and ever since, these two lands have been bound by the oddest of crossed destinies, either as the closest of allies, as in the Hundred Years' War, or the most implacable of enemies.

Strange little connections would fill a book. Morris dancing, or *Moorish* dancing if you like, is said to have come up with John of Gaunt after his unsuccessful campaign to snatch the throne of Castile. One of Her Majesty's biggest crown jewels was a gift from Pedro the Cruel to the Black Prince; Pedro had murdered an ambassador from Muslim Granada to get it off his turban. In politics, we can thank Spain for words like *propaganda, Fifth Column* (both from the Civil War), and *liberal* (from the 1820s), and among the Jews expelled by Ferdinand and Isabel in 1492 were the ancestors of Disraeli.

In Spain, the Welsh may feel right at home in the green mining country of Asturias, and the Irish can honour the memory of the 19th-century Spanish prime minister O'Donnell, the famous governor of Cadiz, Conde O'Reilly, or the thousands of their countrymen who escaped persecution to settle in Galicia in the 16th century. The true Scotsman will make a pilgrimage to the Vega of Granada to look for the heart of Robert the Bruce, hero of the Battle of Bannockburn. In 1329, Sir James Douglas was taking the Bruce's heart to be buried in the Holy Land, when crusading zeal side-tracked him to Spain. In battle against the Moors of Granada, Douglas and his knights became surrounded beyond hope of rescue. Spurring his horse for a last attack, Douglas flung the Bruce's heart into the enemy ranks, crying 'Go ye first, as always!'

Templars

One of the most provocative chapters of medieval history was written by the Order of the Knights Templar, founded during the First Crusade in 1118 by Hugues de Paynes. The 'Temple' of the knights, generally believed to be the Temple of Solomon, was actually the octagonal Temple of the Dome of the Rock, rebuilt by the Muslims in the 10th century – an octagonal design the Templars recalled in the construction of their own temples in London and in Spain, where the Order spread within a few years of its foundation.

The Order was both religious and military, and assisted the crusades, in Spain as well as in the Holy Land. They soon grew more powerful than the kings and popes they ostensibly served, and in 1307, France's King Philip the Fair and Pope Clement V conspired to dissolve the troublesome Order, Clement declaring it heretical and Philip coordinating the secret orders sent throughout Europe for all the Templars to be seized simultaneously at midnight on a certain date – a necessary ploy to ensure the defeat of the powerful knights. The conspiracy succeeded, the Templars were captured unawares, imprisoned and made to face trumped-up charges of sorcery, black masses, orgies and sodomy. Some recanted to save their skins, but many, including the Grand Master, remained silent and were burned at the stake. Their immense worldly goods naturally were inherited by their enemies as well by the newer Order of the Knights of St John.

The Templars were indeed powerful, but their dissolution was a great loss for Spain, where they did their most important work, attempting a kind of syncretism between the peninsula's three great religions. In return for military services performed for the various kingdoms of Spain, the Templars would request castles and land, nearly always in the *juderias* (Jewish quarters) or among the Moriscos, to gain wisdom from their ancient traditions and to defend them from grabby Christians. Their other land requests frequently corresponded with holy sites connected to the peninsula's oldest religions, and their castles and churches that have survived are often fascinating for their mysterious symbolism and hints of the initiation rites they once held.

The Spaniards have long been fascinated by the Templars, and there exists a vast body of scholarly works written about them in Spanish, especially in the 1970s and 1980s. In several places in Spain neo-Templar organizations have sprung up, reoccupying their castles and houses. A new popular guide to Templar sites in Spain, available in nearly every bookstore, is Juan G. Atienza's *Guía de La España Templaria* (Editorial Arín, Barcelona 1985); if you can read Spanish and are curious, it's a good investment.

Unity versus Localism

Spanish history has its pageant of kings and crusaders, rebels and pretenders, saints and heretics. The underlying motives, though, have remained unusually constant over the centuries. In the most culturally diverse nation of Europe, the mainspring of history has always been the issue of unity versus localism. Keep this in mind when looking at Spain's ups and downs, and much that was murky will become clear.

In the Middle Ages, political realities made diversity something taken for granted. In a vast area, divided by mountain chains, lived Christians, Moslems and Jews, and an enormous number of pagans in out-of-the way rural districts, giving rise to the scores of heresies and fascinating survivals of ancient beliefs mentioned throughout this book. Among the nations, the peninsula counted the Celts, Basques, Catalans, Astures, Arabs, and Berbers, as well as the descendants of Iberians, Phoenicians, Romans and Goths. Most of these people lived on the periphery, leaving the inhospitable central plateau as a kind of permanent battle zone.

As it happened, a new force filled this central vacuum. The Kingdom of Castile, with its crusading tradition, became the greatest and eventually the only power on the peninsula, and tried for the first time to impose unity – both political and religious – on everyone. When Ferdinand married Isabel in 1476, it would seem that this unity was achieved – but this was hardly the case. Spain's constitutional history is a fascinating subject; in the Middle Ages regions, cities and even some tiny villages developed elaborated codes of *fueros* ('exclusions') – rights and privileges every monarch pledged to uphold. If Spaniards had heard of the Magna Carta in 1212, they would probably have wondered why it took the backward English so long to do it. Most of these *fueros* survived until the arrival of the Bourbons; before that, despite the unity of the crowns, Castile, Aragón, and Navarre lived practically as separate states, with their own laws and parliaments. Ferdinand and Isabel and the Habsburg kings who followed them became obsessed with the idea of unity, and their monomania contributed more than any other factor to the ruin of Spain.

Aragón and Catalunya finally lost their privileges in 1716, for supporting the wrong side in the War of the Spanish Succession. After that, the Bourbons made Spain into a centralized state on the French model, another attempt to impose unity by force that contributed much to Spain's political instability in the next two centuries. By the 1900s demonstrators in the streets of Bilbao and Barcelona were shouting 'Down with Spain!'

The Francoists, with their imperial dreams, hated these contentious minorities. Franco's slogan was '*Spain – One, Great, Free*', but like the Bourbons before him he was content to settle for one out of three.

The coming of regional autonomy with the new constitution was probably as profound a change as the restoration of democracy itself. To Spain's new leaders goes the credit for finally putting the dream of Castilian-dominated unity to rest. All Spain's peripheral regions grabbed at the chance to set up regional governments, except Castile and León, who had it imposed on them. Already some interesting new experiments in government, education, and regional development have appeared, and a modest renaissance of regional cultures seems to have already begun.

Urbanización

Our dictionary translates this blandly as 'urbanization' but to the Spaniards, perhaps the most consciously urban nation in Europe, it encompasses a whole range of meanings. Especially in Castile, history, climate and economy have conspired to make Spain a land of city-dwellers, and they have contributed more to the art of city-building and city-living than is generally acknowledged.

When the Moors reigned in Al-Andalus, and Córdoba was the largest and finest city in Europe after Constantinople, they set a pattern that would influence the cities of Spain for centuries. Enclosure was the key word: a great mosque and its walled courtyard at the centre, near a palace and its walled gardens. Along with the markets and baths, these were located in the *medina*, and locked up behind its walls each night. The residential quarters that surrounded the medina were islands in themselves, a maze of narrow streets where the houses, rich or poor, locked inwards into open patios while turning a blank wall to the street. Today the great mosques have been replaced by cathedrals, but their courtyards remain; in the cities of the south, famous for their decorated patios and winding lanes, much of this peculiar cellular quality of the Moorish towns survives.

Medieval Spain's most characteristic contribution to urban design is the *Plaza Mayor*. In its classical form, as seen in Madrid or Salamanca, this is an enclosed, rectangular plaza, surrounded by arcaded walks under buildings of an even height. Often the four sides are alike, as if they were walls of a single structure, giving the impression of a building turned inside-out. Such a square counts much more than just a knot in the web of streets; it is like a stage in the theatre, where public life can be acted out with the proper Spanish dignity and decorum. The analogy with the stage is no accident, for theatres in the great age of Calderón and Lope de Vega, such as the Corral de Comedias in Almagro, were perfect little Plaza Mayors in form, with balconies all around and the proscenium at the narrow end. Often in Spanish cities the Plaza Mayor will be replaced, or accompanied by, a *Calle Mayor* (though the name may be different). This is a long central street, arcaded on both sides; a good example survives in Alcalá de Henares. This form can trace its inspiration to the Moors, who learned it from the Romans.

Modern Spain, even in the worst of times, never lost its talent for city-building. The world's planners honour the memory of Arturo Soria, who in the 19th century proposed the *Ciudad Lineal* as a new form for the industrial age, a dense ribbon of city, three blocks wide but stretching for miles, where everyone would be a block or two from open countryside, and transportation to any point made easy and quick by a parallel railway line. A Ciudad Lineal was actually begun north-east of Madrid, though it has long since been swallowed up by the expanding suburbs. No city in Europe has made the transition to a modern, industrial metropolis with more creativity and panache than Barcelona; when the old dry stream-bed in the centre of town was filled in it became the *Ramblas*, a sort of linear park that has been called (and not only by Catalans) the 'most beautiful street in the world'. Other Spanish cities have since copied the form, notably Palma de Mallorca and Granada. Much of the distinctiveness of modern Barcelona comes from Ildefons Cerdá's plan for the 1890s extension of the city, a grid of almost heroic proportions, made of octagonal blocks called *chaflâns*.

During the last 30 years, the time of Spain's 'take-off' into a full-fledged industrial economy, *urbanización* has continued at a furious pace – in all senses of the word. As migrants streamed into the cities during the 1960s, endless blocks of high-rise suburban developments grew up, ugly but unavoidable. To the people who moved into them from poor villages or ancient tenements, they must have represented an exciting new way of life. The name for these is *urbanizaciones* and the Spanish also use the word for their big seaside vacation developments, where they package northerners into urbanized holidays on the beach.

Part III
HISTORY

Visigothic Crown, Archaeology Museum, Madrid

Pre-history

Evidences of culture in Spain go back to the remotest antiquity. Some 50,000 years ago, when Spain was a cooler, more forested place and glaciers coated the Pyrenees, **Neanderthal man** was minding his business in these mountains and in the caves around Gibraltar. Surprisingly, none of his low-brow skulls have been found inbetween. The next players on the Iberian stage arrive about 25,000 BC, in the **Paleolithic age**, at this time the peninsula's many caves began to fill up with Paleospaniards, living well enough off herds of bison and deer to create impressive works of art on cave walls all across Spain and southern France. The accounts are confusing in the extreme, but scholars generally divide these people into the earlier **Aurignacian** and later **Magdalenian** cultures. The latter reached their height around 15,000 BC, and created some of the stone age's finest art, notably in the caves of Altamira in Cantabria.

The Neolithic era, the age of settled agriculture, begins in the Iberian peninsula at an uncertain date. The people known as the **Iberians** may have arrived as early as 7000 BC. They are generally believed to have come from North Africa, and physical and linguistic clues lead to the possibility that they may be the precursors of the Basques, the oldest nation of Western Europe. These people had little to show for themselves until around 2500 BC, and even then, the anonymous culture that built the big dolmen burial chambers at Antequera, north of Málaga, are an exception to the rule.

Indeed, so little is known about these millennia that speculation is useless. Many linguists believe the language of the Iberians to be related to modern Basque. They have over 500 inscriptions to work with from all over the peninsula, and have so far been able to decipher only 11 letters, let alone a whole message. Ancient Greek and Roman writers hint at close links between Iberia and Greece, and also the British Isles; Iberians at some time invaded and colonized parts of Ireland and south-west Britain, and the Irish bards claimed to have learned their alphabet by way of Spain. Surprisingly, while their cousins in the Balearic Islands were building *talayot* fortresses and trading across the Mediterranean, the Iberians of the mainland produced little in the way of architecture or art. About 800 BC, the Iberians are joined by other peoples, notably the **Celts** from over the Pyrenees. These got along well enough with the Iberians; in many cases they gradually merged with some tribes, creating a new people, the **Celtiberians**, who occupied much of the centre of the country.

We have little information on how these people lived. Later Roman writers would describe great differences among the variety of tribes – some as stoic, hard-nosed nomads, turning slightly berserk when moved to war, others happy and settled, good dancers and drinkers. The great mystery of this era is the fabled kingdom of **Tartessos**, roughly modern Andalucía, the only place where the anarchistic Iberians ever founded a state. Phoenecian records mention it, and in the Book of Kings it appears as 'Tarshish', its great navy bringing wares of Spain and Africa to trade with King Solomon. Archaeologists are still looking for the city of Tartessos; some place it near modern Cádiz, others somewhere on the coast further east.

1100 BC–AD 50: Phoenicians, Greeks and, inevitably, Romans

If the Iberians, Celts and Basques were unwilling to coalesce into states and empires, others were happy to do it for them. In this period, when trade boomed all across the Mediterranean, we can think of Spain as, in modern terms, an 'undeveloped' country where foreigners with ambitions and superior technology came first as traders, then as conquerors. The **Phoenician** merchant capital of Tyre 'discovered' Spain about 1100 BC, founding Gades (Cádiz), perhaps the oldest city in Western Europe. They were after Spain's mineral resources – copper, tin, gold, silver and mercury, all things the Middle East was running short of at this time – and their successful exploitation of Spain made the Phoenicians the economic masters of the Mediterranean. Their rivals, the **Greeks**, arrived on the scene somewhat later; expanding from the colony of Massilia (Marseilles) they founded trading towns on Spain's eastern coast, notably Saguntum, Emporion, and Dianion (Denia), in the 7th and 6th centuries.

By this time, Tyre was in decline, and **Carthage**, its western branch office, was building an empire out of their occupied coasts in Spain and North Africa. About 500 BC, the Carthaginians gobbled up the remains of Tartessos and stopped the Greek infiltration. The Carthaginians contributed little to Spain, but they maintained the status quo until 264–41 BC, when Rome drubbed them in the **First Punic War**. The loss of much of its commercial empire made Carthage heavily dependent on Spanish men and resources. The famous Carthaginan leaders, Hamilcar Barca, his son-in-law Hasdrubal, and his son Hannibal, spent most of their careers consolidating their Spanish lands, and when the **Second Punic War** came in 218, in a dispute over Saguntum, it was a largely Spanish army that Hannibal took over the Alps to ravage Italy. The Romans couldn't beat him, but they kept him at bay long enough for their legions to conquer

Spain (210) in his absence. The total defeat of Carthage in 204 made Rome unquestioned master of Spain and all the western Mediterranean.

Unlike their predecessors, the Romans were never content to hold just a part of Spain. Relentlessly, they slogged over the peninsula, subjugating one Celtic or Iberian tribe after another. It was never easy; the most familiar episode of this era is the siege of Numancia, a Celtiberian town near Soria, whose defenders escaped the dishonour of defeat only by burning their town with themselves inside it, after beating off Roman attacks for 19 years. Rome had to send its best – Cato, Pompey, Julius Caesar and Augustus were all commanders in the Spanish conquest – and the job was not finished in the north-west until about AD 50.

AD 50–406: Roman Hispania

For all the trouble they caused Rome at first, the inhabitants of Spain soon became some of the Empire's most useful citizens. Especially in the more civilized south, they assumed the Romans' language, religion and customs in short order. New cities grew up to join Cádiz, Saguntum and New Carthage (Cartagena). Of these the most important were Hispalis (Sevilla), Corduba (Córdoba), Tarraco (Tarragona), Augusta Emerita (Mérida) and Caesar Augusta (Zaragoza). The latter two were among the many towns founded specifically for the purpose of settling pensioned-off Roman veterans, an important part of the policy of Romanization. Another new element in the population was the **Jews**. Rome settled them here in numbers in the Diaspora, and they were to play a constructive role in Spanish life for the next 1500 years.

Roman **Hispania**, like Gaul, was divided into three parts: **Lusitania** included modern Portugal and Galicia, where the vanquished Celts lived quietly on, building their dolmens and gathering mistletoe; **Baetica** (named for the Baetis, or the Guadalquivir) occupied roughly all of Andalucía, the richest and most cultured Roman province west of Tunisia, all the rest was gathered into the big, sparsely settled province of **Tarraconensis**. Rome gave Spain bridges and aqueducts, roads and theatres, landlords and tax collectors, and Spain in turn contributed soldiers, metals, wheat and oil, Andalucían dancing girls and fish guts (don't laugh – we don't know exactly what fish *garum* was concocted from, but it was the most prized gourmet delicacy in the empire, and an important export for Baetica). Spain also gave Rome four of its best emperors: Trajan, Hadrian, Marcus Aurelius and Theodosius, as well as almost all of the great figures of the 'silver age' of Latin literature – Lucan, both Senecas, Martial and Quintilian.

Spaniards today tend to overestimate wildly both the importance and prosperity of Roman Hispania, but there's no denying that while the peninsula lagged far behind the eastern half of the empire in both wealth and level of civilization, it outdistanced Gaul, Britain, Africa and eventually, in the last days of the empire, even Italy itself.

406–711: Roman twilight and the Visigoths

Even before the western frontiers of the empire crumbled in the fatal year of 406, civilization in Spain and western Europe was in a bad way. In 264, Franks and Alemanni devasted the peninsula in a decade of raids. After their repulse, the crushing burden of maintaining the defence budget and the government bureaucracy sent Spain's economy into a permanent regression. Cities declined, and in the countryside the great landowners of the senatorial class took advantage of the situation by squeezing the majority of the population into serfdom or outright slavery. Thus, when the bloody, anarchic **Vandals** arrived in the 5th century, they found plenty of bands of rural guerrillas, or *bagandae*, to help them in smashing up the remnants of the Roman system. The Vandals moved on to Africa in 428, leaving nothing behind but the name Andalucía (originally *Vandalusia*) for their southern playground.

Here once more Spain's history becomes tremendously complicated. Up north, the Basques and Asturians achieved independence. The southern regions were occupied intermittently by imperial troops who took their orders from Byzantium. The **Visigoths** came down from Gaul in 412 to occupy the centre, a military aristocracy of semi-Romanized Teutons who claimed authority from a Western Roman Empire that was by now little more than a name. Roving bands of Suebi, Alans, and Vandals marauded at will, not so much tribes as mobile protection rackets.

The Visigoths were illiterate, selfish and bloody-minded, but persistent enough to endure. There weren't many of them; probably only in the region between Burgos and Toledo did they form any substantial percentage of the population. For their support they depended on the landowners, who by now had made the slow but logical transition from Roman *senatores* to feudal lords. Visigothic princes were capable of knifing each other in the back at the slightest pretence, and when dynastic intrigue failed there was always the issue of religion to keep the pot boiling. The Visigoths were Arian Christians, while most of the old Roman elite were orthodox in the faith; as far as we can tell the vast majority of the population hadn't converted at all, and they probably looked on in bewildered amusement while the two factions anathematized and ambushed each other.

The Visigoths ruled from Toledo, maintaining only a provisional authority in the rest of the peninsula. Despite all the troubles, Andalucía at least seems to have been doing well – probably better than anywhere else in Western Europe – and there was even a modest revival of learning in the 6th century, the age of St Isidore, famous scholar of Sevilla. This helped to improve the Visigothic overlords somewhat. King Leovigild (573–86) was an able leader; his son Reccared converted to orthodox Christianity in 589; both brought their state to the height of its power as much by internal reform as military victories. Allowing the Church a share of power, however, proved fatal to the Visigoths. As the clerics grew wealthy, they found it in their interest to join with the old Roman nobility in checking the power of the kings. Their depredations against the populace, and their persecutions of Jews and heretics made the Visigoths as many enemies within as they ever had across their borders.

711–756: the Muslim Conquest

The great wave of Muslim Arab expansion that began in Muhammed's lifetime was bound to wash up on Spain's shores sooner or later. One of the unlikely protagonists of the Muslim conquest was a certain Count Julian of Ceuta, lonely ruler of the westernmost bastion of the Byzantine Empire, nominally cooperating with the Visigoths.

Legend states that Julian's daughter had been violated by the last Visigothic king, Roderick; whatever his reasons, the Count ferried a small Arab force over to Spain in 710, led by a certain Tarif, who gave his name to today's Tarifa on the straits. Tarif came back to tell the tale of a rich land, in disarray and ripe for the plucking, and in the following year Julian assisted in taking over a larger army – still only about 7000 men – under Tariq ibn-Ziyad who quickly defeated the Visigoths near Zarbate. Within three years, the Arabs had conquered most of the peninsula, driving northwards as far as Narbonne in France.

The ease of the conquest is not difficult to explain. The majority of the population was delighted to welcome the Arabs and their Berber allies. The persecuted Jews supported them from the first, and for the country people, the final extinction of Roman law made free men of nearly all of them. Religious tolerance was guaranteed under the Muslims from the start; some historians have suggested that their campaign was more a financial speculation than a holy war, and since the largest share of taxes fell on non-believers, the Arabs were happy to refrain from seeking converts.

This conquest, however, was never completed. In 718, a legendary prince named Pelayo in the tiny kingdom of Asturias defeated the Muslims at an obscure skirmish the Spaniards call the Battle of Covadonga, opening the way for Alfonso I of Asturias to recover much of north-western Iberia. The Arabs barely noticed; they were busy elsewhere. By 732 their armies had penetrated as far as Poitou in northern France, where Charles Martel whipped them so soundly that their advance was halted permanently. Muslim control of most of Spain was solid, but hampered by dissension almost from the start between the haughty Arabs and the neglected Berbers, and between the various tribes of the Arabs themselves.

756–1031: the Emirate of Al-Andalus

Far away in Damascus, the political struggles of the Caliphate were being resolved by a general massacre of the princes of the Umayyad dynasty, the successors of Muhammad, as the rival tribe of Abbasids replaced them on the throne. One Umayyad escaped – Abd ar-Rahman; he fled to Córdoba, well beyond the reach of the usurping Caliphs, and managed to establish himself there as the first leader of an independent **Emirate of Al-Andalus**.

Under this new government, Muslim Spain grew strong and prosperous. Political unity was maintained only with great difficulty, but trade, urban life and culture flourished. Though their domains stretched as far as the Pyrenees, the Umayyad emirs referred to it all as *Al-Andalus*. Andalucía was its heartland and Córdoba, Sevilla, and Málaga its greatest cities, unmatched by any others in western Europe. Toledo and Zaragoza in the north prospered greatly as well.

Much nonsense has been written about the history of 'Moorish' Spain. Whether glorifying or disparaging it, too often the age has been approached as if it were a foreign occupation. It cannot be emphasized too strongly that Al-Andalus was a *Spanish* culture. Somehow the arrival of Islam, Islamic art and Arab poetry energized the intact, though slumbering culture of Roman Andalucía. Spaniards, Arabs, Berbers and Jews all made their contributions; here, however, they lived in relative harmony, and it would be impossible to disentangle them even if there were reason to try. For its wealth and sophistication, its poetry and scholarship, and its art and architecture, all far in advance of anything else Europe had to offer, we may take medieval Al-Andalus as the height of Spanish civilization.

The political foundation for this achievement was provided by Abd ar-Rahman III, who turned the emirate into the **Caliphate of Córdoba** in 929. When the boy Caliph Hisam II came to the throne in 976, effective power was seized by his chamberlain Muhammad ben abd-Allah, better known as *Al-Mansur* ('the victorious'), who recaptured León, Pamplona and Barcelona from the Christians, and even raided Compostela, stealing its bells to hang up as trophies in the Great Mosque of Córdoba. Throughout this century, the military superiority of the Moors was great enough for them to have finally erased the Christian kingdoms had they cared to do so. If lack of determination was one flaw, another, more serious one was an anarchic inability to create a modern state. Directly upon Al-Mansur's death in 1002, the Caliphate entered a fatal period of factional struggles and civil war. By 1301 the central authority had vanished for ever, and Al-Andalus broke up into a patchwork of petty kingdoms called the *taifas*.

The Christian states of the north were better organized, and despite their relative weakness, it was in this period that they laid the foundations of reconquest. Three small states in particular appeared, and each would one day be an important Christian kingdom. Under Alfonso I ('the Catholic', d. 757) and Alfonso II ('the Chaste', d. 842) little Asturias grew into the **Kingdom of León**. The Basques, independent for centuries already, developed the **Kingdom of Navarre**, reaching its height under Sancho the Great (d. 1035). The north-eastern corner of the peninsula, the 'Spanish march' of Charlemagne's empire that today is Catalunya, attained its independence as the **County of Barcelona**, and began its career as a mercantile power in the Mediterranean under Ramón Berenguer II (d. 1131).

1031–1284: the Reconquista

With Al-Andalus hopelessly divided, these Christian kingdoms had their chance. A son of Sancho the Great gained possession of the border county of Castile in 1037 and made of it a kingdom, installing himself as Fernando I, later annexing León and making the Muslim states of Toledo and Zaragoza his vassals. Almost from the beginning, this new state of **Castile and León** was the scene of permanent civil war, but it was still strong enough to advance when it had a strong leader. Alfonso VI, with the help of the legendary warrior El Cid, captured Toledo in 1085. The loss of this key fortress-city, opening all central Spain to Christian raids, alarmed the kings of the *taifas* enough for them to invite in the Almoravids from North Africa, fanatical Muslim Berbers who had recently established an empire stretching from Morocco to Senegal. The Almoravid leader Yusuf crossed the straits and defeated Alfonso in 1086. Yusuf liked Al-Andalus so much he decided to keep it, and Almoravid domination lasted until 1147, when it was replaced by that of the Almohades, a nearly identical military state also from Africa, that grew up around the reforming fundamentalist zeal of a mystic named ibn-Tumart.

Like the Almoravids, the Almohades went quickly through the cycle of conquest, decadence and decay. The end for them, and for Al-Andalus, came with the Battle of Navas de Tolosa in 1212, when an army from all Christian Spain (and newly independent Portugal) under Alfonso VII destroyed the Almohad power forever. Alfonso's son, Fernando III, reunited Castile and León for the last time, captured Córdoba (1236) and Sevilla (1248), and was made a saint for his trouble. Alfonso X 'the Wise', noted for his poetry and the brilliance of his court, completed the conquest of western Andalucía in the 1270s and 1280s, leaving the newly-formed **Nasrid Kingdom of Karnattah** (Granada) as the only Muslim state in Spain. While all this was happening, the growing **Kingdom of Aragón**, incorporating the County of Barcelona, was completing the Reconquista in the east. Alfonso I 'the Battler' had taken Zaragoza as early as 1118, but it was left to the greatest Aragonese ruler, Jaume I ('the Conqueror', d. 1276) to expand Aragón's rule to Valencia, the Balearic Islands and Alicante.

It would be a mistake to see the early days of the Reconquista as a simple crusade; that was a myth invented in the reign of Isabel and Ferdinand. The age is as fascinating as it is complex. Before the coming of the fanatical Almoravids and Almohads, and the growth of the crusading idea in the Christian Church, Spanish Christian, and Muslims usually had too much respect for each other to lapse into the kind of bigotry of an Isabel or Philip II. Intermarriage was common; all the Castilian and Aragonese kings had some Moorish blood, and the mother of Abd ar-Rahman III was a Basque. Alfonso the Wise and many of the kings of Aragón were just as much at home in Arabic as in their own language, and a warrior like the Cid was just as happy serving the Moslem Emir of Zaragoza as Alfonso VI.

Above all, it was a great age for culture. León and Toledo were beginning their cathedrals at about the same time as the Almohades were building La Giralda in Sevilla.

1284–1476: Aragón and Castile

These two states came to dominate the new Christian Spain. **Aragón**'s career was perhaps the most spectacular. Out of Barcelona's navy and trade connections, it built an empire that included Sicily, Sardinia and even parts of Greece. As a formidable rival to Genoa, Pisa and Venice, Barcelona dominated the Western Mediterranean until a long stretch of bad luck after 1330 – plagues, bank collapses, and class strife directed against the big merchants – sent the city into a long economic decline that enabled Castile to gain the upper hand on the peninsula.

Castile itself, having swallowed up León, Galicia, and most of the reconquered lands, was an aggressive society of ever-greater importance in European affairs. The civil wars between Pedro I 'the Cruel' (d. 1369) and his brother Enrique de Trastamara brought in foreign intervention. Pedro had the support of the English, Enrique the French, and the Black Prince and Bertrand du Guesclin carried out a side-show to the Hundred Years' War on Spanish soil. Such dynastic feuds were still common, though none seriously damaged the kingdom. Castile based its prosperity on the *Mesta*, an enormous crown-chartered cooperative of sheep farmers that supplied Europe with much of its wool; the annual trade fairs at Medina del Campo were the busiest on the continent. Because of the experience of the Reconquista, when new hands were always needed to settle newly conquered lands, economic feudalism ended in Castile long before anywhere else in Western Europe. Still, the nobility flourished, exempt from taxes and loaded with privilege. The Reconquista had seen the creation of three new knightly orders, those of Santiago, Calatrava, and Alcántara, created to replace the heretical Templars who were dissolved in 1312. The new orders, cooperating with an increasingly arrogant and worldly Church, gained great power and wealth in this period.

On the whole, the experience of the Reconquista seems to have had a negative effect on both kingdoms, particularly Castile. Religious bigotry became widespread in the 13th and 14th centuries. The first general pogroms against the Jews occurred in 1391, instigated by the Church. Above all, the years of constant warfare coarsened Castile, creating a pirate ethos where honest labour was scorned, and wealth and honour were things to be snatched at the expense of one's neighbours. In 1474, yet another civil war broke out upon the death of Enrique IV 'the Impotent', this time between the partisans of his (likely) daughter Juana 'le Baltraneja' and his sister Isabel.

1476–1516: the Catholic Kings

Isabel had already married Ferdinand, heir to the throne of Aragón, and when Ferdinand defeated Juana and her Portuguese allies in the 1476 Battle of Toro, the way was open for the unification of the two realms. They reigned together, collaborating in every decision; both were capable and intelligent, though Isabel, representing the stronger kingdom, had the final say. Ferdinand, a subtle statesman and excellent campaigner, did all the work. Under these two, the new Spain reached the height of its glory. In the unforgettable year of 1492, Columbus initiated the Age of Discovery by reaching Hispañola and Ferdinand conquered Muslim Granada, finally completing the Reconquista. Later in their reign Ferdinand would annex Navarre, and the great general Gonzalo de Córdoba 'El Gran Capitan', would conquer Naples and make Spain for the first time a lead player in European affairs.

Also in 1492, the Catholic Kings expelled the Jews from Spain, some 150,000 of them. Soon afterwards, they created the Inquisition, in an age when most European countries were disbanding it. They also broke the agreements they had made with the Moors of Granada, instituting a policy that was little better than genocide. Ferdinand and Isabel's fierce bigotry was popular enough in the nation as a whole – there was plenty of confiscated property to be handed out to loyal supporters – and it set the tone for Spain's grisly history in the next two centuries.

1516–1700: the Age of Rapacity

Or, as historians once called it, Spain's 'Golden Age'. Modern historians entertain fewer illusions, and remind us that any golden age is in the eye of the beholder. In the 16th century Spain fought for hegemony over three continents, and succeeded only in destroying itself.

In an effort to build up their alliances against France, Ferdinand and Isabel had married their daughter Juana to the Habsburg Archduke Philip, son of the Holy Roman Emperor. The death of their other two children made Juana and Philip heirs to the throne, but Philip (called 'the Handsome') soon died, and Juana became deranged with grief. Whether she actually was permanently insane we do not know. Her son Charles arrived from Flanders in 1517, visited her just long enough to force her to sign papers of abdication, and then locked her up in a windowless cell for the next 40 years.

Spain in its long history had suffered invasions and civil wars, plagues and famines, but never had it been forced to bear anything like the **Habsburgs**. This family had the good fortune to marry into half the thrones of Europe, and it was Charles' luck to inherit them all – Spain and its colonies, the Netherlands, Austria, half of Italy and a smattering of German principalities. To top it off, he bought himself election as Holy Roman Emperor, making him the most powerful ruler in Europe since Charlemagne (in Spain he is Charles I, though we know him better under his imperial title, Charles V).

To the rest of Europe, Charles meant unending war, serving both his megalomaniac ambitions and his opposition to Protestantism. To Spain, a country he had never seen, Charles meant economic ruin. Almost immediately upon arriving he and his Flemish minions emptied the royal treasury and shipped it overseas to bribe the German electors. This and other outrages occasioned the Comunero Revolt of 1520–1, in which the cities of Old Castile rose to defend their liberties – and their purses – but were eventually crushed by Charles' foreign troops. It was the beginning of Castile's decline, and 36 more years of expensive Habsburg imperialism ended all hope for recovery. Charles' wars came to nothing, and in 1556 he chucked it all for a pleasant retirement at the monastery of Yuste in Extremadura.

The mess was inherited by his intelligent, pious and grandly neurotic son, Philip II, whose reign began in 1566 with a national bankruptcy, the first of three. Silver from America kept Spain afloat, though almost none of it stayed in Spain long enough to do any good. Philip had his successes, notably the great naval victory of Philip's brother Don John over the Turks at Lepanto in 1571, but mostly the news was bad. The continuing revolt in the Netherlands eventually resulted in Dutch independence, and the failure of the Great Armada against England in 1588 finally put an end to Habsburg designs in the north.

At home, too, things were going very wrong. Philip's religious mania turned Spain into the very picture of a modern totalitarian state. The Inquisition, with a vast network of spies and informers, securely shut down the country's intellectual life. Book-burnings (as parodied in *Don Quixote*) became common, and Spaniards were forbidden to study overseas. The national movement towards *limpieza de sangre* ('pureness of blood') resulted in a national manhunt for clerics and officials with the taint of Jewish ancestry, and oppression of the remaining Moors reached new heights of ferocity. Spanish behaviour in the New World was even more brutal; in the 16th century 80 per cent of the native population of Mexico and Peru died off from disease and overwork in the fields and mines.

One family tradition of the Habsburgs was incest. Philip's fourth wife, Anne of Austria, was at once his niece and the daughter of his first cousin. Not surprisingly, their son Philip III was an imbecile, entirely under the influence of a favourite, the Duke of Lerma. His reign was distinguished by the final expulsion of the Moors in 1609. Most of them lived in Valencia, perhaps the most prosperous region in Spain at the time; the departure of its most skilled farmers ruined it. Philip III married another cousin, and the result was Philip IV. Not quite an idiot, this Philip also had a better choice of favourite. The Conde Duque de Olivares was a flamboyant, tireless and confident reformer, but 20 years of hard work (1621–43) brought not a single noteworthy accomplishment. The opposition of the Catalans and the nobility, along with national exhaustion and lethargy, made reform impossible. In 1640, Catalunya and Portugal (annexed by Philip II in 1580) revolted. The Portuguese eventually secured their independence, and crushing defeats at the hands of the Dutch, English and French (notably at Rocroi in 1643, during the Thirty Years' War) put an end to the age when Spain was taken seriously as a European power. Olivares went mad and died soon after.

Spain was dying with him. Under the Habsburgs, Spaniards had made contributions to European culture despite the terror of the times. The last great generation of Spanish artists, poets and dramatists, including Velázquez, Calderón, and Lope de Vega, were contemporaries of Philip IV, but when they died there were no more to replace them. Economically, a wasteland had appeared. Spain's agriculture had been ruined, its mountains deforested, its manufactures bankrupted. In the Middle Ages the plains of Castile had been the most densely populated part of Spain. By 1650 they had become as lonely and empty as you see them today, and their once thriving cities were reduced to relics of the past.

We cannot credit the Habsburgs with all the blame. They could not have wrecked Spain so thoroughly without the help of a grasping, ignorant Church and nobility. Both found ample opportunity to enrich themselves in every Spanish reverse, while contributing less than nothing to the national life. These institutions had once combined to create the expansive, crusading ethos of medieval Castile; later, ironically, they conspired to assist in a national suicide.

To close the book on the Habsburgs, there's drooling, staring Charles II, whose mother was also his first cousin, and who spent much of his reign playing in the crypt of El Escorial or planning *autos-de-fe*. He may have had only a dim idea he was king, but he lasted 35 years. He spent the last few in trances and convulsions, while the police combed the back alleys of Madrid to find the 'sorceress' who a priest said had enchanted him. Surrounded by a cabal of exorcists, clairvoyants and witch-doctors, Charles passed on in 1700, fortunately childless.

1700–1931: Bourbons, on the rocks

A vacant throne attracted suitors, and prostrate Spain watched while they fought over it. The Austrian Archduke Charles had the support of England, while the French schemed for Philip of Anjou, a Bourbon, and the result was a general European commotion, the War of the Spanish Succession. The English agitated madly, and the Duke of Marlborough won great victories; in the end, though, they abandoned their Spanish and Austrian allies for possession of Gibraltar (seized in 1704), and the promise that the Spanish and French thrones would never be united. The new king, Philip V, was put out at not being able to live in Paris, but he knew what Spain needed most – more palaces. He and his successors spent most of Spain's revenues in constructing a dozen mock-Versailles around Castile, and beyond that did their best never to offend the grandees or the Church.

The one bright exception was Charles III, who came to the throne in 1759. Charles and his ministers, Floridablanca and Jovellanos, tried to reform everything, colonizing the wastelands of Castile, undertaking new navigation schemes, expelling the dreadful Jesuits, promoting industries and even assisting the Americans in the Revolutionary War. Most of his efforts went down the drain with the succession of his son Charles IV, as useless and stupid as any Habsburg; he and his evil wife Maria Luisa are best remembered for the incredible indignities they suffered at the hand of their court painter, Goya.

The disruptions of the French Revolution interrupted the Bourbons' Rococo daydream. Napoleon first threatened Spain, then enticed it into cooperating in his campaigns. The result was the 1805 Battle of Trafalgar, where nearly the entire Spanish fleet was destroyed under incompetent French leadership. Every Spaniard did his duty though, and today, with their invincible concept of personal honour, the Spaniards still take it as a kind of victory. Napoleon finessed Charles V into abdication in 1808, and when French troops attempted to kidnap the heirs to the throne in Madrid, the citizens responded with the famous revolt of the Dos de Mayo, brutally surpressed by General Murat.

In the Peninsula War that followed, French troops occupied all of Spain, and distinguished themselves by stealing as much gold and art as they could carry, and blowing up castles and historical buildings just for sport. British forces under Moore and later the Duke of Wellington arrived in 1809, won most of their battles, and conducted themselves generally disgracefully towards the population. The Spanish themselves recovered some self-respect by heroically resisting the French, notably at the siege of Zaragoza under Palafox in 1809. In 1812, a group of Spanish liberals met in Cádiz to declare a Constitution, and under this the Spanish fitfully conducted what they call their War of Independence.

Victory came with the restoration of the **Bourbons** in 1814. The new king, Ferdinand IV, turned out to be more of a black-hearted reactionary than anyone thought possible, even restoring the Inquisition and inviting back the Jesuits. A successful revolt against him in 1820 was suppressed, strangely enough, by the French, who sent an army over the Pyrenees with Britain's blessing in 1823. In this decade most of Spain's American colonies achieved their independence – the mother country could do little to stop them. Ferdinand's death in 1833 occasioned the First Carlist War, where liberals supporting the rights of the Infanta, Isabel II, fought the Church, reactionaries and the Basques under Pretender Don Carlos. The liberals won, but their succeeding dictatorships under Generals Espartero and O'Donnell accomplished little of value apart from the expropriation of the monasteries and the final extinction of the Inquisition.

Spain, by now, had become a sort of banana monarchy, where any ambitious general could issue a *pronunciamento* and strive for power. Under a Catalan, General Prim, the First Republic was declared in 1874, but it soon succumbed to anarchy in Andalucía and a Second Carlist War as futile as the first. A *pronunciamento* by General Martinez Campos restored the Bourbons in 1876, and liberal and conservative politicians cut a cynical deal under which they would alternate in power. Political frustrations with this arrangement helped the growth of new left-wing groups: Communists, Socialists, and the Anarchist CNT.

The outstanding feature of Spanish life in the late 19th century was the economic and spiritual blossoming of Catalunya. While the long-oppressed Catalans were rediscovering their language and culture, Barcelona attained the position of Spain's biggest and most modern city, its artistic leader and the great stronghold of Anarchism. The heavily industrialized Basque provinces began to assert themselves, too, and even Andalucía, where Anarchism was also strong, began to feel the winds of change. Once more regionalism became a political issue, as thriving peripheral areas began to challenge the moribund Castilian centre.

A crisis for Spanish life came with the embarrassing defeat in the 1898 Spanish–American War, and the loss of Spain's last important colonies. An informal group of truculent intellectuals, the 'Generation of '98', whose most famous members were Miguel de Unamuno and Ortega y Gasset, began to closely examine their country's curious destiny. At the same time, Spain was once more becoming a force in European culture, producing Picasso, Gaudí, and a host of lesser figures. After a long hibernation, the juices were flowing once more.

Spain stayed neutral in World War I, and afterwards King Alfonso XIII entrusted the government to a genial, though rather repressive dictator, Miguel Primo de Rivera, who did much to bring the country's economy into the modern world in the optimistic decade of the 1920s. A newly-confident Spain demanded better; Primo de Rivera was dismissed with the onset of the Depression and when municipal elections in 1931 showed an overwhelming victory for parties favouring a republic, Alfonso agreed to abdicate.

1931–9: The Second Republic and Civil War

In the beginning, the **Republic** was greeted with general euphoria, but the reforms of the leftist government under Manuel Azaña served only to bring the underlying conflicts of Spanish politics to the surface. To the reactionary upper classes, any reform was 'Bolshevik', while the Marxists and Anarchists saw the new government only as a prelude to revolution. Political violence ranged from an attempted coup by General Sanjurjo in Sevilla in 1932, to a series of peasant revolts and land seizures in the poorest areas of Andalucía. Basques and Catalans took advantage of the government's weakness to declare their autonomy. Reaction came when the abstention of many leftists in the 1933 elections brought the radical right into power. Moderate leaders like Azaña found themselves temporarily in jail, and an epic miners' revolt in Asturias was crushed with incredible brutality in 1934.

The alarmed Left formed a Popular Front to regain power in 1936, but street fighting and assassinations were becoming daily occurrences, and the new government seemed powerless to halt the slide into anarchy. Most of the trouble was caused by rightist provocateurs, especially the violent new Fascist party, the Falange Española, led by José Antonio Primo de Rivera, son of the former dictator. The Left responded in kind, seizing the property of aristocrats, burning churches and forming armed militias. At this point the army decided to step in.

Spain's creaky military, with one officer for every six soldiers, had a long tradition of interfering in politics, dating from the scores of *pronunciamentos* (coups) of the 19th century. On 17 July 1936, simultaneous risings occurred across Spain, orchestrated by Generals Francisco Franco and Emiliano Mola. The government was panicked into action, but workers' militias took control of the situation in many areas. Also, a substantial part of the army remained loyal to the Republic, and instead of the quick coup they had expected the generals got a Spain divided into two armed camps. In the early stages of the war, the balance was swung by the Army of Africa, the only effective fighting force, made up of mercenary Moors who had campaigned in Spain's colonial wars in its

North Moroccan protectorate. They quickly captured eastern Andalucía and Extremadura, and their presence made their commander, Franco, first among equals (Mola died in a car crash soon afterwards). The insurgents' hope for an early victory was thwarted by the militia's heroic defence of Madrid.

Almost from the beginning the Civil War became an international affair. Fascist Italy, Portugal, and Germany sent hundreds of aeroplanes and some 200,000 troops. Only Russia helped the Republic (all arms to be paid for in cash, of course; the Fascists were a little more liberal to Franco). The Communists also organized the famous **International Brigade**, though these were only a handful. The list of famous foreigners who participated in the war in one way or another is endless: Hemingway and George Orwell came as war-tourists, André Malraux organized an air squadron and Willy Brandt helped keep peace among the leftist factions while reporting for a Norwegian newspaper. Among the Communists, arrangements for volunteers were handled from Paris by Josep Broz (Marshal Tito), while future national Communist leaders like Walter Ulbricht of East Germany and Togliatti of Italy were agents in Spain.

The great imbalance in foreign help favouring Franco probably decided the war. British governments pursued a policy of appeasement and set up a 'Non-Intervention Committee', pressured the French into going along and ignored German and Italian intervention, while doing their best to keep any aid from reaching the Republic. Dissension among the Republicans themselves did not help. Communists, Socialists and Anarchists often fought each other, and troops from Valencia (where the Republican government had fled in 1936) had to suppress a brief war-within-the-war in Anarchist-run Barcelona in May 1937. With Russia the sole arms supplier, and Communist-run divisions the best disciplined troops, the Communists dominated the government in later stages. In late 1937 the Republic finally found a capable leader in Dr Juan Negrin, but it was already too late.

Franco's slow and careful tactics probably dragged the war on longer than was necessary. The first serious Republican reverse was the fall of Málaga in February 1937, losing them Andalucía once and for all. Spaniards on both sides chuckled when the Italian attempt to mount a blitzkrieg on Guadalajara in the same month lost them most of a division as prisoners. The Germans introduced terror bombing at Guernica, in April, in a campaign where Franco took the Basque provinces and Asturias. In December, the Republicans mounted an offensive in southern Aragón, around Teruel, and another in July 1938 across the Ebro, where the Nationalists had reached the sea to cut the Republican zone in two. Both failed for lack of artillery and air support. After these last efforts, the Republic was through; Franco conquered Catalunya in January 1939, and only token resistance continued in the centre. Madrid surrendered in March.

1939–75: Franco's Dictatorship

Some 500,000 Spaniards died in the war, more in mass killings behind the lines than in battle. When it was over, Franco proved more interested in revenge than reconciliation; even moderate Republican supporters found themselves in jail or forced labour camps. Franco by now was calling himself *Caudillo* (leader) and dressing in full Fascist regalia at public functions. By no means, though, did he convert Spain into a genuine Fascist state. Since the death of José Antonio in a Republican jail in 1936, the Falangists were leaderless, though they greatly increased their numbers during and after the war. Franco manipulated them carefully, letting them organize Fascist-style vertical trade unions and 'syndicates', but they were gradually excluded from power when Franco guessed the Fascists would lose World War II. Franco's relations with the Axis were difficult from the start. Hitler came down from a 1941 meeting at Hendaye, intending to bully Spain into the war, but afterwards stated he would 'rather have his teeth pulled' than ever again talk to such a stubborn character. Still, he gained control over the Basque iron industry, and Franco sent him troops to fight on the Russian front (you'll still see streets names for the *Division Azul* in Spain).

Even had Franco been more willing, Spain was capable of little help. Industry and communications were in ruins, and the country knew famine several times in the dark 1940s. Conditions did not improve until after 1953, when Franco signed a treaty with the United States, exchanging military bases for a measure of international respectability and a huge transfusion of dollars. To please his new friends and at the same time avoid bankruptcy, Franco dismantled the cumbersome Fascist organization of the economy and encouraged a new generation of technocrats (many of them members of the secret Catholic society *Opus Dei*). Their reforms and the American loans began to pay off in the 1960s, when Spain experienced an industrial take-off that gave it the highest economic growth rate in the world – really just catching up for lost time. The growth of tourism and remittances from half a million Spaniards working abroad helped as much as any new industry.

Economic advance, of course, meant social changes. Possibly the greatest was the mass migration of rural people from the south to the industrial cities, resulting for a time in huge growths of shantytowns around Madrid and Barcelona. Between their experience in the cities and the influx of the tourists, millions of Spaniards were exposed to foreign ideas and influences for the first time. Such things are usually trouble for dictators, but Franco proved stubborn enough to resist all pressure for change. As always, his regime depended entirely on Spain's three evil stepsisters, the Church, the Army and the landowners. All legal political factions, Falangists, Carlists and Monarchists were combined in the toothless Movimiento Nacional, but what Franco really wanted was to eliminate politics for ever.

The Spaniards had other ideas. All the leftist groups had maintained clandestine organizations, even organizing a network of underground trade unions. Most groups were simply waiting for the old man finally to die; an exception was the Basques, who evolved the terrorist ETA. These first became prominent in 1973, when their master blasters assassinated Admiral Carrero Blanco, blowing his limousine over the roof of a Madrid church where he was coming to attend mass. Carrero Blanco had been the ageing dictator's strong man and best hope for the continuity of the regime. Franco found no one hard enough to replace him.

1975 to the present: the Restoration of Democracy

Franco was a monarchist at heart, and back in 1969 he had declared Juan Carlos I, grandson of Alfonso XIII, to be his successor. In doing so he passed over Juan Carlos' democratically-minded father Don Juan; Juan Carlos seemed a pliable enough young man, and both Franco and the opposition expected him to carry on the old order. Franco died in 1975, and for a while the new King did nothing to excite anyone's suspicions.

Those who underestimated Juan Carlos, however, received a big surprise when he began confidently and adroitly to move Spain back to democracy. His choice for Prime Minister, Adolfo Suarez, initiated a political reform bill that would establish a democratically elected *Cortes*. On the night of 18 November 1977, the nation watched spellbound on television while the disorganized Francoists in the old *Cortes* committed political suicide by approving it. In the months that followed, the trade unions and the Socialist and Communist parties were legalized, and the Francoist Moviemiento disbanded. Press censorship was ended, and the first free elections in 32 years held, returning Suarez and his centralist party, the UCD, to power. The speed and orderliness of the transition astounded the world. The support of Juan Carlos was of course indispensable, but also, somehow, the long years of Franco's grey dictatorship had created a new maturity among the vast majority who desired democracy. They had been waiting for this opportunity for years, and no one did anything to ruin it. In the words of one perceptive foreign correspondent, Spain was 'a country whose society was open and democratic long before its institutions were'.

A new Constitution followed, one of the most liberal in Europe. Even more remarkably, the long heritage of Castilian centralism was undone once and for all by measures creating **regional autonomy**, making Spain a federal state like West Germany or the US. The new democracy easily survived the old guards' last hurrah, when Civil Guards under Colonel Antonio Tejero attempted a coup by occupying the *Cortes* in February 1981. Elements in the army were behind it, but they backed down when ordered to do so by the King. In 1982, the real transition came when general elections were won overwhelmingly by the Socialists under Felipe Gonzalez, a charmer from Sevilla with a chipmunk smile who has been called the 'best politician in Europe'.

Today, Spanish politics are contended among three major parties, Gonzalez' PSOE, Suarez' new party, the CDS, and the Alianza Popular, a union of conservatives and former Francoists, under a former Franco minister, Manuel Fraga. On the fringes are the Communist PCE, which dwindles with every election, and the tiny neo-Fascist Fuerza Nueva, lately discovered to be in the pay of Colonel Gaddafi. Felipe Gonzalez has maintained his popularity by staying as close as possible to the centre. In 1986, he overcame all the opposition by steering Spain into the European Community, winning a national referendum over NATO membership (something he had opposed four years earlier), and keeping his majority in the latest general elections. Spain has its problems – an incredible 22 per-cent unemployment heading the list – but the self-destructive passions of its past political life appear to be gone for ever. The commitment to upholding democracy seems total, and few Spaniards would dispute that their country is better governed now than at any time in the last 500 years.

Part IV

CATALUNYA

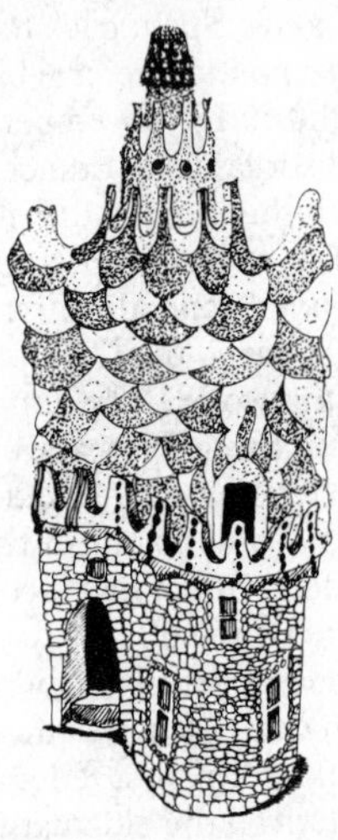

Pavillion in the Parc Güell–Gaudí

On the map Catalunya (in Castilian Spanish, Cataluña; in English Catalonia) occupied a tidy triangle wedged between France, the Mediterranean and the rest of Spain, but that's where the tidiness ends. To the north the mighty Pyrenees stretch down to dip their crooked toes in the sea, forming the fabled Costa Brava; to the south the flat sandy strands of the Costa Dorada peter out at the soggy morasses of the Ebro Delta. In between, dead volcanoes and mountains shaped like pipe-organs squat inscrutably over a landscape littered with Iberian, Greek, Roman and Romanesque monuments. Enough monsters adorn Catalunya's medieval cloisters to fill Carnegie Hall. Nowhere else in Spain has early 20th-century architecture (Modernista, as the Spaniards call it) bloomed so furiously, from Gaudí's Barcelona to wine cooperatives in the tiniest village. A mere glance at the map will convince you that Catalunya is something out of the ordinary; where else in the world can you go from Bot to Flix, from Urtx to Oix, or make a wide sweep from Colera to Coma to Miami Beach, or take in a museum designed by Salvador Dalí, where you can water the plants by feeding pesetas into a Cadillac?

Spaniards and Hispanophiles tend to warn first-time visitors to Spain away from Catalunya; it's too heady, too 'fizzy', lacking the austere *sol y sombra* of the 'real Spain', whatever that may be. But to visit Spain and miss Barcelona, its best city, would be to miss the most exciting and dynamic spirit of post-Franco Spain, the vanguard of modern Spanish culture.

In the old days the Spaniards kept Catalunya under an iron heel. Today, they worry that Barcelona's busy entrepreneurs and intellectuals are transforming the nation into Greater Catalunya. 10 years ago, flying the Catalan flag was a criminal offence; today it

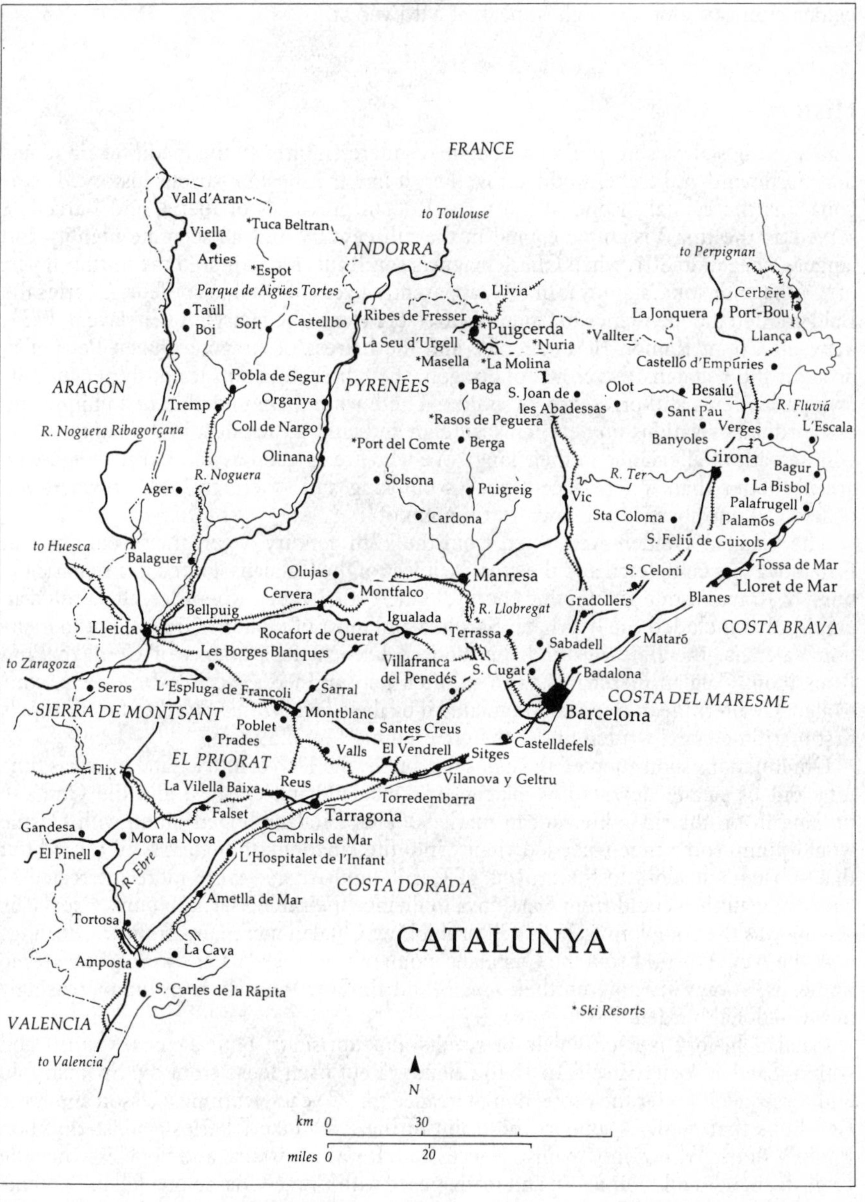
FRANCE
Vall d'Aran
*Tuca Beltran
Viella
Arties
*Espot
to Toulouse
ANDORRA
to Perpignan
Parque de Aigües Tortes
Llivia
Cerbère
Port-Bou
La Jonquera
Taüll
Boi
Sort
Castellbo
Ribes de Fresser
*Puigcerda
*Vallter
Llança
La Seu d'Urgell
*Nuria
*Masella
*La Molina
Castelló d'Empúries
Pobla de Segur
PYRENÉES
Baga
S. Joan de les Abadessas
Olot
Besalú
ARAGÓN
Tremp
Organya
Sant Pau
R. Fluviá
*Rasos de Peguera
Verges
L'Escala
R. Noguera Ribagorçana
Coll de Nargo
Banyoles
*Port del Comte
Berga
Olinana
Girona
R. Noguera
R. Ter
Bagur
Solsona
La Bisbol
Ager
Puigreig
Vic
Palafrugell
Cardona
Sta Coloma
Palamós
to Huesca
S. Feliú de Guixols
Balaguer
Tossa de Mar
Olujas
Manresa
S. Celoni
Lloret de Mar
Cervera
Montfalco
Gradollers
Blanes
Bellpuig
R. Llobregat
Igualada
Lleida
Rocafort de Querat
Terrassa
Mataró
COSTA BRAVA
Les Borges Blanques
Sabadell
Villafranca del Penedés
to Zaragoza
S. Cugat
Badalona
Seros
L'Espluga de Francoli
Sarral
COSTA DEL MARESME
SIERRA DE MONTSANT
Montblanc
Barcelona
Poblet
Santes Creus
Prades
Castelldefels
Valls
El Vendrell
Sitges
EL PRIORAT
Flix
La Vilella Baixa
Reus
Vilanova y Geltru
Torredembarra
Falset
Tarragona
Gandesa
Mora la Nova
Cambrils de Mar
El Pinell
L'Hospitalet de l'Infant
R. Ebre
COSTA DORADA
Amettla de Mar
Tortosa
CATALUNYA
La Cava
Amposta
S. Carles de la Rápita
* Ski Resorts
VALENCIA
to Valencia
N
km 0 30
miles 0 20

waves proudly over the Catalan Generalitat and also, thanks to an intrepid band of Barcelona alpinists, atop the highest peak of Mt Everest.

History

Catalunya has always been a round peg in a square empire; all the medieval kingdoms that Ferdinand and Isabel wedded together, it had the most illustrious history. Tarragona was the capital of one of the three Roman provinces of Iberia, and Barcelona served as the first Visigothic capital in the 5th century, but its separate identity and language began in 801, when Charlemagne's son Louis reconquered the northern part of 'Gothalanda' or Catalunya. In 874, apparently a year of notable coiffeur, Charles the Bald granted independence to Count Wilfred el Peloso (the Hairy). A marriage in 1137, between Count Ramón Berenguer IV and the heiress of Aragón, Queen Petronilla, brought the Catalans the crown of Aragón, though each nation jealously retained its own parliaments and privileges, or *usatges*. These were the foundation of a unique and extraordinary relationship between sovereign and citizen, manifest in the famous Aragónese oath of allegiance to their king: 'We who are as good as you swear to you who are no better than we, to accept you as our king and sovereign lord, provided you observe all our liberties and laws; but if not, not.'

The Catalan Golden Age lasted from the 12th century, when the Reconquest of Catalunya was completed and the creative juices of the Catalans ignited in a remarkable burst of Romanesque and Gothic energy, to the 14th century, when Barcelona ruled an empire that included Sicily, Malta, Sardinia and most of modern Greece, not to mention Valencia, the Balearics and the modern French departments of Cerdagne and Roussillon. Catalan merchants, who so often pop up in Boccaccio's *Decameron*, controlled Mediterranean trade and regulated it by the *Llibre del Consolat del Mar*, Europe's first maritime code, written under the great Jaume I in 1259.

Other nations soon adopted the Consolat, but by the 15th century Catalunya was running out of steam, devasted by plague, spectacular bank crashes, and the Genoese homing in on their Mediterranean markets. The Catalans hoped union with Castile would pump some much-needed vitality into the kingdom, though it soon turned out that subsequent heirs to the crowns of Castile and Aragón were more interested in squeezing all they could from Catalunya to finance their imperial ambitions. Especially grating was the codicil in Isabel's will prohibiting Catalan merchants from any dealings with the New World. From the Castilians' point of view the Catalans were troublesome hotheads, always insisting on their *usatges* and shirking their share of the increasingly heavy national burden.

Catalan history is a chronicle of revolts and uprisings, both against Madrid and within Catalan society itself. In 1640 Catalunya cut itself loose from the Spanish fold and threw itself under the protection of France for 12 years, learning a lesson about the Bourbons that made it support the claim of the Archduke Charles against Bourbon Philip V in the War of the Spanish Succession. It was a mistake, and hopeless once the English abandoned their cause and made peace with France. Barcelona fell in September 1714, and with it all of Catalunya's privileges and autonomous government.

Castilianization proceeded apace, especially among the upper classes who were busy making Catalunya Spain's leading industrial region. In the 1830s, however, the Romantic movement reached Catalunya just as Catalan was in danger of sinking into oblivion. The Catalan Renaixança, or Renaissance, was a literary crusade led by such poets as Jacinto Verdaguer (1843–1902) and Joan Maragall (1860–1911) which helped bridge the Catalan of the troubadour poets and the everyday language of the people. A Catalan is a Catalan because he speaks Catalan, so it's hardly surprising that concurrent with the Renaixança there arose a fervent nationalist movement embraced by all the parties of the political spectrum and nearly every influential Catalan, from Antoni Gaudí to Pau Casals.

Just as Catalan culture began to revive, so did the workers' movements. Anarchism took root in Catalunya's industrial centres as it did nowhere else in the world, and manifested itself in such diverse passions as vegetarianism, free love, violent strikes, progressive schools, temperance and terrorism. Anti-clerical riots and church-burnings – 'Mediterranean fetishism', according to Ortega y Gasset – rocked Barcelona in 1835, 1909 and throughout the 1920s. The city was fondly known as 'Anarchism's rose of fire' and was certainly the most radical in Europe; in 1901 it became the first in Spain to dump its *cacique* (political boss) under the leadership of the bizarre Alejandro Lerroux, who gained international notoriety for his exhortations to 'the young barbarians of today' to 'tear aside the veils of novices and elevate them to the category of mothers'.

In 1931, as soon as Alfonso XIII had left the country, Catalunya declared itself an independent republic in the Federation of Iberia. Since no such thing existed, the nationalists renamed their government the Generalitat and as the Republic wilted, took on in increasing autonomy.

Catalunya was the Republicans' major stronghold throughout the Civil War, and when Valencia fell, Barcelona served as the government's last capital. Orwell's *Homage to Catalonia* brilliantly evokes the war in and around Barcelona through the eyes of a member of the International Brigades. At the end of the war thousands of Catalans fled over the border to France and Andorra.

Franco dissolved the last remnants of Catalan autonomy, prohibited the public use of Catalan, books in Catalan, and the Catalans' most joyful expression of national unity, a circle dance called the *sardana*. The denizens of Barcelona society put their suits and ties back on – a risky manoeuvre in the heyday of the Republic – and went back to business, but try as Franco might Catalan nationalism refused to die. Migrants had been flocking to Barcelona's industrial jobs since the turn of the century, and Franco did nothing to discourage them, hoping a tidal wave of poor Andalucians would dilute Catalanism into a harmless eccentricity.

Absorbing the migrants was and still is the biggest stumbling-block for Catalan nationalists, who nevertheless had many of their dearest aspirations come true while Franco was still warm in the grave. The Generalitat has been restored, Catalan is taught in the schools and broadcast on Catalunya's own TV station; in 1985 alone 17,000 books were published in Catalan, and several times a week businessmen, students and just plain folk gather in the public squares of Barcelona to dance a *sardana* that has yet to lose its momentum. Unlike certain Basques, however, they have few illusions about an independent Catalunya. Common sense and clear-headed pragmatism, what the Catalans call *seny*, is among their most exalted virtues when they're not tearing up the place. Instead of leaving Spain, modern Catalans seem more bent on reforming it, realizing that their differences with the rest of the country have diminished to the level of 'You like tomatoes, and I like tomah-tahs...'

Catalan language

Actually, the linguistic difference is a fair bit wider than that. Catalan is its own proper language, spoken by some 6 million people; the classic faux pas of the foreigner is to call it a dialect of Spanish. Catalan is most closely related to Southern French Provençal, and if you know some French or Spanish you'll be able to figure out the signs – but just try to understand spoken Catalan, which sounds deceptively like Portuguese. Pronunciation is different from Spanish: j's and g's are sounded as in French, x sounds like sh, ch is k, ll is a pure y sound, and -ig at the end of a word is -tch, such as in '*puig*' (mountain) which is pronounced 'pootch'. You can usually warm the cockles of a Catalan's heart or make them giggle by pointing and saying '*Com es diu això en català*?' ('How do you say that in Catalan?'). Free classes are offered in Barcelona – part of the effort to assimilate the Andalucians – but beware, the grammar is impossible. Since streets signs and sights are increasingly marked only in Catalan (though Catalunya is officially bilingual), we have tried, where possible, to use Catalan in this book.

The main sights

Besides Barcelona, Catalunya has two fine provincial capitals, Tarragona with its interesting Roman ruins and Girona with its evocative medieval quarter. Spain's best Greek ruins are at L'Escala on the Costa Brava, which is Spain's prettiest coast – if you have magic spectacles that can see through some of the worst speculative *urbanizaciònes* anywhere. The Costa Dorada south of Barcelona isn't half as built up or half as pretty. Inland, the Pyrenees are the highlight, especially majestic in Aigües Tortes National Park and the secluded Vall d'Aran and even more secluded Vall de Boí. Fantastically situated Montserrat is perhaps Spain's best-known monastery; Poblet near Tarragona is architecturally exciting. For something a bit different, tour the wine regions in the south with memorable wine and unusual modernista bodegas in sleepy medieval villages.

Besides tripping the *sardana*, Catalans love to stack themselves up in towers, especially during fiestas. For the past two centuries otherwise normal men and boys called *castellers* climb on each others' shoulders to the eerie music of the '*grolla*', the best groups attaining eight tiers. The best *casteller* societies come from Valls and El Vendrell, and they can be seen throughout Catalunya at special events.

Catalan cuisine

Like the Basque kitchen, the Catalan has enjoyed considerable influence from beyond the Pyrenees and is rated one of the best in Spain. Not surprisingly, seafood is a main ingredient, in such well-known dishes as *zarzuela*, a mixed fish stew; lobster with chicken; fish *suquet*, (fricassée of fish, usually grouper); any fish with *romesco* sauce (toasted hazelnuts, wine, nutmeg, paprika, garlic and olive oil) or *xapada*, with dried eels from the Ebro delta. *Botifarra* – pork sausage, black or white, with beans – is a staple, as is a hearty stew, *escudella*. In the autumn a Catalan's mouth waters for partridge with grapes, or Brussels sprouts, or rabbit cooked with almonds or garlic sauce. Near Tarragona in the very early spring outdoor *calçotada* feasts are the rage, featuring lamb cutlets, sausage, bread, wine and, the star ingredient, tender baby shallots grilled over the fire, which Catalans, discarding their usual dignity, slurp down, dressed in aprons and bibs. Excellent red wine and *cava* (champagne) are produced in Catalunya; 1978 and 1981 were exceptional in all four regions – Ampurdan, Tarragona, Penedes and Priorato.

BARCELONA

> Barcelona, the treasure house of courtesy, the refuge of strangers ... unique in its position and its beauty. And although the adventures that befell me there occasioned me no great pleasure, but rather much grief, I bore them the better for having seen that city.'
>
> *Don Quixote*, Part II

And so are we all the better for having seen Barcelona, a city that tempts one to dip deep into the well of superlatives. Forty years of Franco's white bread have made the rest of the world forget that culturally it is one of the liveliest cities anywhere, a magnet for new art and progressive ideas; it is a great Mediterranean sea-port, the nerve centre of Spanish industry, and with 3,200,000 people, the capital of Catalunya, which it has always governed as a kind of ancient Greek city-state. With its art nouveau, or Modernista, architecture, its ambitious immigrants and lively arts, its avant-garde tastes and position as the major publishing centre in the Spanish language, Barcelona tends to remind people of New York – and in many ways it is the only really successful modern city in Europe. Nor is it shy about saying so. A compulsive exhibitionist, Barcelona held two great international expositions in 1888 and 1929, which have bequeathed a holiday spirit to the Spanish urge to monumentality with huge, coloured fountains, palaces, flamboyant monuments and an aerial cable car. Now the city is making fervent preparations to host the 1992 summer Olympics.

The Face of Barcelona

Old Catalans may have bewailed their eclipse during the days of Imperial Spain, but moderns may be thankful that the lack of prosperity left the narrow alleys and gothic palaces of Barcelona's medieval quarter, the **Barri Gòtic**, untouched. When the city was finally ready to expand in a big way in the 1850s, it tore down its old walls and sponsored a competition for the new street plan of the extension, or **Eixample**, as it's still called. The winner was an engineer named Ildefons Cerdà, who designed a functional but elegant grid, with grand boulevards and corners cut out of the intersections, forming distinctive octagons. With the 'Pla Cerdà' Barcelona quintupled in size over the next 50 years, a period that fortuitously coincided with the genius of Antoni Gaudí (see p. 39) and his Modernista colleagues. Beyond the Eixample are once independent towns like **Gràcia** and **Sarria** that have maintained their individual character; by the sea **Bar-**

celoneta, the fisherman's quarter, is a planned neighbourhood from the 18th century.

Barcelona is delightfully situated on a plain in an amphitheatre of hills and mountains. At the south end of the harbour rises the smooth-humped **Montjuic**, once key to the city's defence, and now its pleasure dome; on the landward side, the highest peak in the **Sierra de Collserola** is **Tibidabo**, with its priceless views and amusements. Between the mountains and the sea, Barcelona enjoys a mild climate, protected from the north winds and tempered by the summer breeze off the sea.

A good map puts all this into perspective. Free ones are on offer at the tourist offices, but you need microscopic vision to read them. Consider purchasing a large one if you mean to be in the city a few days, but make sure it's up-to-date and has all the Metro stops.

GETTING TO AND AROUND BARCELONA

By Air

Barcelona's international airport is El Prat de Llobregat, 14 km (8.8 miles) from the city. Trains link it every 20 minutes from 6.30 am to 11.10 pm, departing from the central station Barcelona-Sants (at Infanta Carlota and Numància). For flight information, call 325 43 40.

By Train

Besides Barcelona-Sants the city has two other RENFE stations: Apeadero de Gràcia (in the Eixample at Psg. de Gràcia and Aragó) and the Estació de França, also known as Terminus, on Avda. Marquès d'Argentera, near the Parc de la Ciutadella. If you're coming from the north, your train will stop here; other trains usually call at all three. For RENFE information, telephone 310 72 00, or call in at their ticket office on Psg. de Gràcia 13.

Ferrocarrils de la Generalitat de Catalunya (FGC) has lines through Barcelona to the suburbs and beyond, departing from under the Plaça de Catalunya (for Sant Cugat and Terrassa, at least one every hour) and from under the Plaça d'Espanya (to Montserrat). For information on the FGC, call 205 15 15.

By Sea

Barcelona's Estació Maritimo is a main port for Mallorca and Ibiza (daily departures) and Menorca (six times a week). For information, contact Transmediterránea on Vía Laietana 2, Tel: 319 96 12.

By Bus

The main bus station is the Estació del Norte, on Avda. Vilanova, near the Arc de Triomf. More frequent departures for the Costa Brava, however, are on the Empresa Sarfa, departing from Psg. de Colóm 3, Tel: 231 79 46. Buses for Andorra, Seu d'Urgell, Vall d'Aran and Lleida depart from the Alsina Graells station at Ronda Universitat 4, Tel: 222 11 63.

Gaudí (and other) tours are offered by Pullmantur (Gran Vía 635, Tel: 218 02 41) and Juliá (Ronda Universitat 5, Tel: 317 64 54); Juliá also has a daily bus to Montserrat, departing at 9 am and returning at 7 pm.

Within the City

Within the city, buses run until 10.30 pm – the main lines run later – and at each stop their routes and timetables are posted to make them an easy means of transport. Fares are 60 pts (65 on Sundays). The city also has four underground (Metro) lines and a fifth operated by the FGC out of the Plaça Catalunya. As stylish as Barcelona is, its Metro is not, and recent attempts to dress up its long dingy corridors with dismal urban art makes it even more unpleasant. But it is certainly fast and cheap: trains run until 11 pm, or 1 am at weekends, and cost 45 pts (50 at weekends). For either the city buses or Metro you can save money and the hassle of digging for change by purchasing a 10-trip *tarjeta*. The Metro one is 275 pts, and includes the Tranvia Blau (the streetcar to the Tibidabo funicular) and the Montjuïc funicular.

Taxis are omnipresent and reasonable. If you can't find one, though, call 218 42 12.

The Barri Gòtic

Between the 19th-century Vía Laietana and the curving street of Banys Nous de la Palla lies the Barri Gòtic, or Gothic Quarter, sometimes known as Barcelona's 'acropolis'. Here the great governmental and religious institutions of medieval Catalunya rose over the ruins of their Roman predecessors. The quarter sits on the summit of a gentle hill, the **Mons Taber**, where the Iberians built their city of Laye and where Hamilcar Barca, father of Hannibal, founded a Carthaginian colony named *Barcino* in his honour. The Romans, after their conquest in 133 BC, made it officially the *Colonia Favencia Julia Augusta Paterna Barcino* – a mouthful that over the years became simply Barcelona. In the 4th century, the Romans enclosed their colony in the walls that stand to this day; impressive as they are, they couldn't keep out Ataulf, who captured and made the city the Visigothic capital in 415. Towards the end of the 16th century, the city's power gravitated towards the port, leaving a time-capsule behind on Mons Taber. Today the Barri Gòtic is Barcelona's choice district for cheap restaurants and pensions, but slowly and surely the antique shops and art galleries are moving in and changing its face.

The traditional tour of the Barri Gòtic begins in the **Plaça Nova**, or New Square, with its picturesque hodgepodge of centuries. Two Roman towers, renovated in the 12th century, guard the ancient entrance to the city next to the Baroque Episcopal Palace. Across the square the **Collegi d'Arquitectes** celebrates the new with a frieze of dancing Catalans by Picasso and paintings by Miró beneath the windows.

The Cathedral

From the Plaça Nova the great octagonal towers and spires of the cathedral are a guide to the **Plaça de la Seu**, a small square in front of the cathedral, where every Sunday from 10 am to 12 noon and Wednesday evening from 7 to 9 local aficianados toss their coats, briefcases and shopping-bags in a pile and dance a *sardana* around them.

The great **cathedral** forms a wonderful backdrop. This is the third one to stand on the site. Nothing remains of the first, which was destroyed in Al-Mansur's raid on the city in 985; of the second, Romanesque, temple built by Count Ramón Berenguer I, only two doorways remain. The current model, one of the marvels of Catalan Gothic,

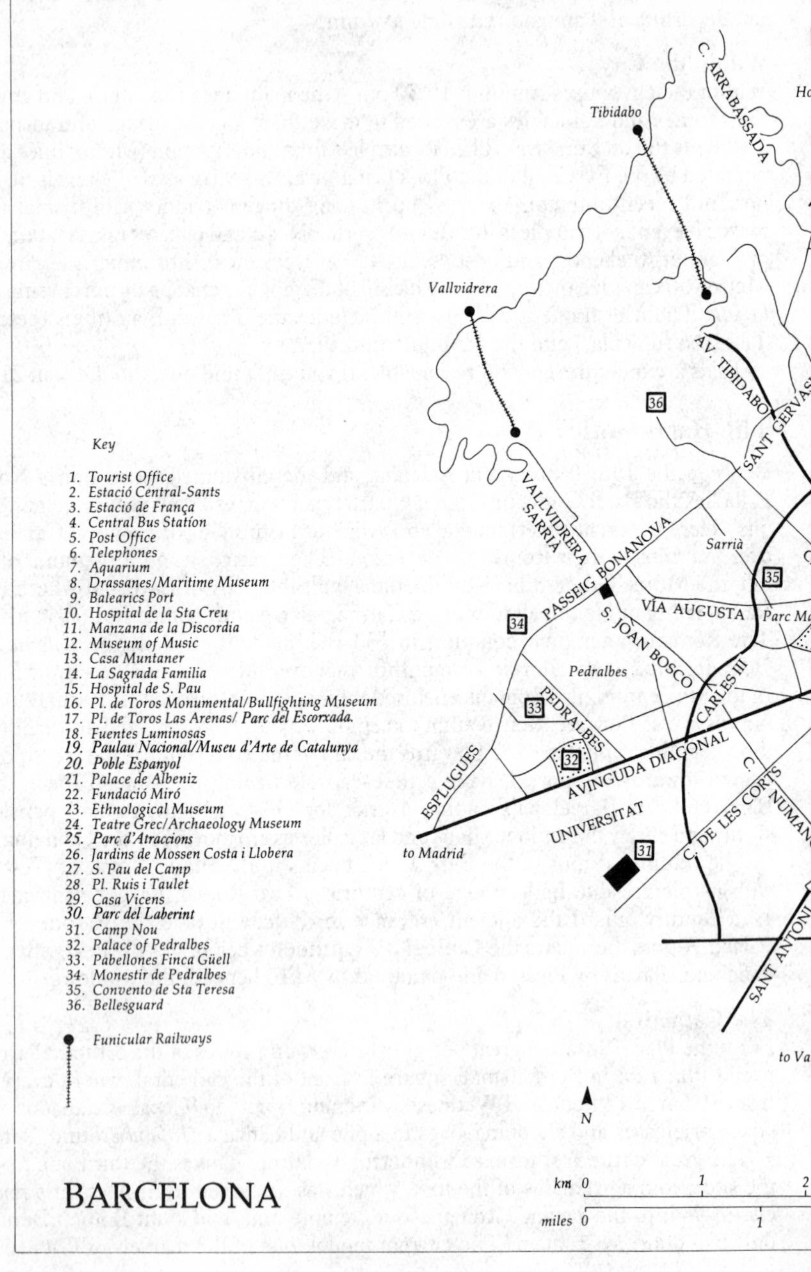

Key
1. Tourist Office
2. Estació Central-Sants
3. Estació de França
4. Central Bus Station
5. Post Office
6. Telephones
7. Aquarium
8. Drassanes/Maritime Museum
9. Balearics Port
10. Hospital de la Sta Creu
11. Manzana de la Discordia
12. Museum of Music
13. Casa Muntaner
14. La Sagrada Familia
15. Hospital de S. Pau
16. Pl. de Toros Monumental/Bullfighting Museum
17. Pl. de Toros Las Arenas/ Parc del Escorxada.
18. Fuentes Luminosas
19. Paulau Nacional/Museu d'Arte de Catalunya
20. Poble Espanyol
21. Palace de Albeniz
22. Fundació Miró
23. Ethnological Museum
24. Teatre Grec/Archaeology Museum
25. Parc d'Atraccions
26. Jardins de Mossen Costa i Llobera
27. S. Pau del Camp
28. Pl. Ruis i Taulet
29. Casa Vicens
30. Parc del Laberint
31. Camp Nou
32. Palace of Pedralbes
33. Pabellones Finca Güell
34. Monestir de Pedralbes
35. Convento de Sta Teresa
36. Bellesguard
Funicular Railways
Tibidabo
C. ARRABASSADA
Vallvidrera
AV. TIBIDABO
SANT GERVASI
36
VALLVIDRERA SARRIA
PASSEIG BONANOVA
Sarrià
35
VIA AUGUSTA
34
S. JOAN BOSCO
Pedralbes
33
PEDRALBES
CARLES III
32
ESPLUGUES
AVINGUDA DIAGONAL
C. NUMANC
UNIVERSITAT
C. DE LES CORTS
31
to Madrid
SANT ANTONI
N
BARCELONA
km 0 1 2
miles 0 1

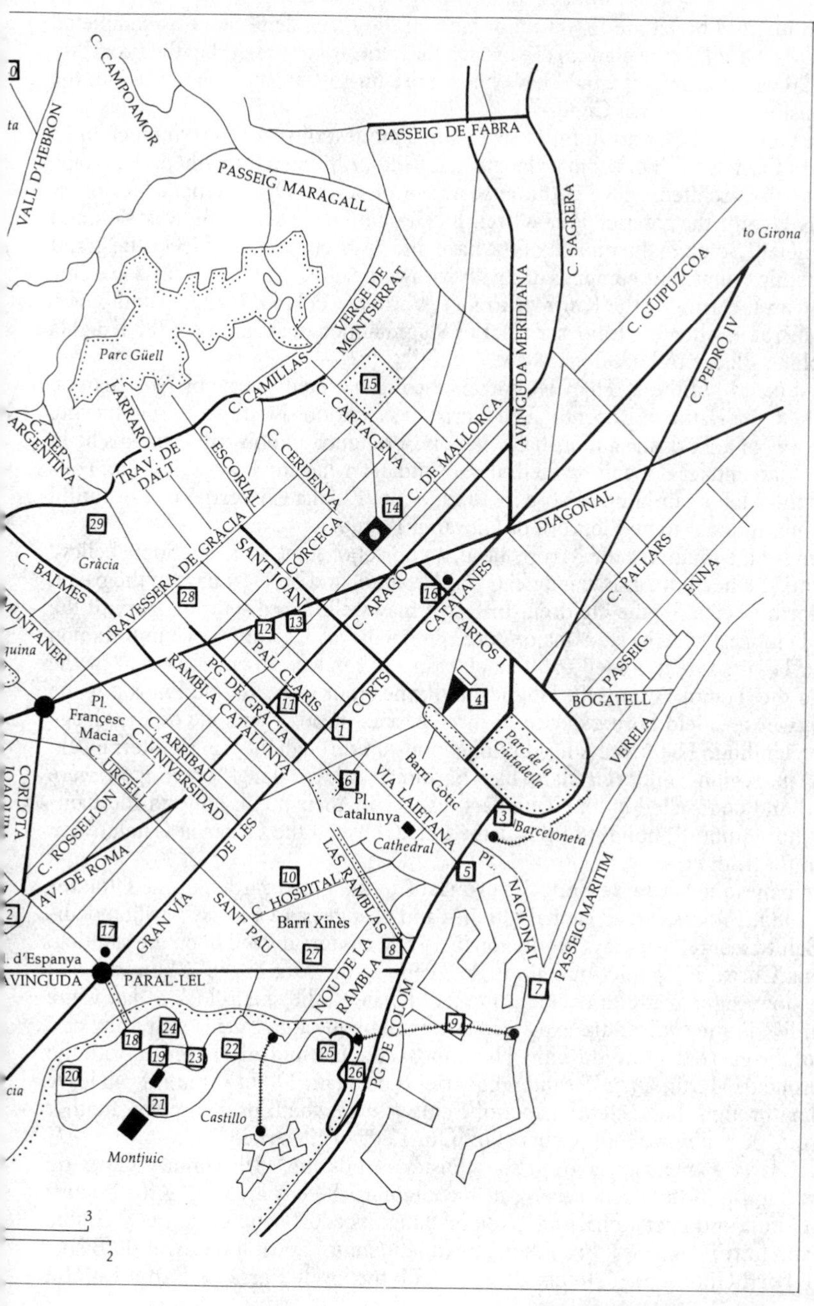

C. CAMPOAMOR
VALL D'HEBRON
PASSEIG DE FABRA
PASSEIG MARAGALL
C. SAGRERA
to Girona
C. GÜIPUZCOA
AVINGUDA MERIDIANA
VERGE DE MONTSERRAT
Parc Güell
C. CAMILLAS
C. CARTAGENA
C. DE MALLORCA
C. PEDRO IV
LARRARO
C. REP. ARGENTINA
TRAV. DE DALT
C. ESCORIAL
C. CERDENYA
DIAGONAL
CORCEGA
Gràcia
C. BALMES
TRAVESSERA DE GRÀCIA
SANT JOAN
C. ARAGO
CATALANES
C. PALLARS
ENNA
CARLOS I
MUNTANER
PAU CLARIS
PG DE GRÀCIA
RAMBLA CATALUNYA
CORTS
PASSEIG
BOGATELL
Pl. Françesc Macia
C. ARRIBAU
C. UNIVERSIDAD
C. URGELL
Parc de la Ciutadella
VERELA
Barri Gòtic
VIA LAIETANA
Pl. Catalunya
C. ROSSELLON
CORLOTA
DE LES
Barceloneta
Cathedral
LAS RAMBLAS
PL. NACIONAL
AV. DE ROMA
C. HOSPITAL
PASSEIG MARITIM
SANT PAU
Barrí Xinès
GRAN VÍA
NOU DE LA RAMBLA
PG DE COLOM
PARAL-LEL
Castillo
Montjuic
1
2
3
4
5
6
7
8
9
10
11
12
13
14
15
16
17
18
19
20
21
22
23
24
25
26
27
28
29

was begun in 1298 by Jaume II, yet the façade on the Plaça de la Seu was completed only in 1892 – based on the plans of the French master Carli (1408). (Had the Progressives of 1820 had their way it would have been more up-to-date and engraved with the entire Constitution and Civil Code!)

Catalan Gothic is best known for its awesome conquest of space, not so much in its height, as in French Gothic, but in its length and width. Although the cathedral has only three aisles the architects gave it the appearance of seven. Once remarkable for its mysterious gloom, the interior is now well lit, the better to take in the vastness and wealth of detail. Stuck in the middle of the nave, the 15th-century *coro* blocks the grand view to the high altar, but compensates with its own beauty. The upper seats are emblazoned with the arms of the Kings of France, Portugal, Poland, Hungary and others dating from 1514, when the Emperor Charles V summoned the Chapter of the Knights of the Golden Fleece to Barcelona.

The first (south) of the 29 chapels contains the lucky crucifix borne by Don Juan on his flagship at the Battle of Lepanto. The Christ has a curious twist to it – from moving out of the way of a Turkish cannon-ball! Ramòn Berenguer and his wife Almodis lie in the painted sarcophagi along the cathedral wall, and in an elegant, low-vaulted crypt designed by the Mallorcan Jaume Fabre in 1339, Santa Eulalia is interred in a beautiful marble tomb, thought to be the work of Giovanni Pisano.

Look under the organ for the Moor's head, an object of some mystery. Some believe it represents the head of Ali Baba, defeated at Lepanto, and on feast days in the past it vomited forth sweets for the children. In fact it may well be a distant memory of the Knights Templar, who were a major force in medieval Catalunya. Count Ramòn Berenguer IV, the Great, joined the Templars in 1131 before an emissary sent by the founder of the Templars himself, Hugues de Paynes (our own Hug de Pinós, say the Catalans), whose shield bore a device of three Moors' heads, symbolic of knowledge and understanding. The Moor's head symbol pops up throughout the Mediterranean, especially in regions once Catalan, like Sardinia. All the kings of Aragón were influenced and counselled by the Templars (especially their pupil, Jaume I the Conqueror), until Jaume II, builder of this cathedral, abolished the Order in Catalunya at the end of the 13th century.

The Romanesque **Porta de Sant Severo** leads to the green garden of the **Cloister** begun in 1385, with its carved capitals, arches and chapels, and a lovely pavilion dedicated to Saint George, who slays his dragon in a 15th-century depiction on the vaulting. On Corpus Christi its gothic fountain is the scene of the 'egg dance' (*l'òu com balla*) when a hollow egg is made to dance in the jet of water. The small flock of fat, white geese that live in the cloister are explained as a symbol of Santa Eulalia's virginity or a memory of the geese that saved Rome. Here, too, is the **Cathedral Museum**, with the golden throne of Martin I, *retablos* and reliquaries (open daily 11 am–1 pm). If you leave the cloister through the ancient chapel of Santa Llúcia, you'll pass through another Romanesque portal by way of the chapel of 'Our Lady of Electricity'!

Across Carrer Santa Llúcia from the cloister stands the 11th-century **Casa de l'Ardiaca** (House of the Archdeacon), now containing the city archives. An attractive blend of Gothic and later Renaissance remodelling, its court contains a pretty Gothic fountain and lofty palm trees. From here, head left (south) down the Carrer de Bisbe, one of the Barri Gòtic's finer streets, adorned with the lovely **Porta de Santa Eulàlia** (another gate to the cloisters) and a neo-gothic bridge (1928) that links the 16th-century **Casa de los Canónigos** to the Generalitat.

The Generalitat and Plaça de Sant Jaume

The Palau de la Generalitat, the shrine of Catalan liberties, was begun in the 15th century to house the representatives of the three Estates (Church, military, and civilian) of the Catalan cortes. Founded by Jaume I, the Generalitat assumed fiscal responsibility of the realm in 1359, acting as the first parliamentary government in Western Europe since Roman times. When Philip V abolished the Generalitat, the palace served as seat of the Real Audencia; from its balcony in 1931 Francesc Macià proclaimed the Catalan Republic, and during the Republic it was the home of the autonomous government. Since 1977 it has regained its original function as seat of the new Generalitat, and is open *only* Sunday mornings from 10 am and 2 pm – but definitely worth the extra planning. It turns its oldest and fairest face towards the Carrer Bisbe, a facade built in 1416 by Marc Safont with its human gargoyles and Catalunya's patron, St George, portrayed on the medallion over the door.

Passing under St George you enter a courtyard, also by Marc Safont, with a perfectly proportioned **Gothic stair** ascending to an exquisite Upper Gallery. On St George's Day (23 April) Barcelona celebrates its festival of the Book and the Rose with a ceremony in this courtyard, a holiday created by the Generalitat in 1456, when Catalan men give their true love a flower and receive a book in exchange from their ladies. A door in the upper gallery leads to Marc Safont's **Capilla de Sant Jordi**, a florid Gothic gem, and to the **Patio de los Naranjos** completed in 1532 and adorned with gargoyles and orange trees. Off the patio, the **Saló Dorado** served as the old audience chamber, while another chamber off the gallery, the more classically ornate **Saló de Sant Jordi** is decorated with art work from the 1920s that Barcelonians love to hate.

The main Renaissance façade is on the **Plaça de Sant Jaume**, cut out of the neighbourhood in the 1840s, where the two main streets of the Roman town used to intersect. It has long been the heart of civic Barcelona; across from the Generalitat stands the **Ajuntament** (city hall) from where the Counsel of a Hundred ruled the city from 1372 to 1714 in the manner of an Italian Republic. The Ajuntament's classical façade, added in the 1840s, is as exciting as mashed potatoes, but the **Gothic Façade** around on the Carrer de la Ciutat, has a charm all its own. The oldest part of the Ajuntament, the **Saló de Cent**, is on top of a black marble stair, but like the other chambers was remodelled at the beginning of this century. Especially notable are the **Alcadía**, where the humourous Xavier Nogués in 1929 painted a vision of 19th-century Barcelona society, complete with the nouveau riche Americano and thrifty Catalan shopkeeper 'Senyor Esteve', and the **Saló de las Crónicas** with golden paintings by the great muralist Josep Sert (1928) depicting the 14th-century Catalan Expedition led by Roger de Flor, when the Catalan Grand Company captured the acropolis of Athens and made Greece a Catalan duchy, and rendered the Ottoman Turks invaluable service by ferrying them across the Bosphorus into Europe, where the Turks formed an Empire far greater than Barcelona ever dreamed of.

From the Plaça Sant Jaume, take the alley north to Paradise (parallel to Carrer Bisbe), for such is the name of the summit of Mons Taber, marked by an ancient millstone in the pavement. Nearby, in the Centre Excursionista, four Corinthian columns from the Roman **Temple of Augustus** remain in place. Paradise alley continues to the Cathedral apse and the **Palau del Lloctinent** (Viceroy's palace), built by Antoni Carbonell in 1557, now housing the Archives of the Crown of Aragón, one of the world's greatest collections of medieval documents, dating back to 844. Step into the courtyard to see the magnificent coffered ceiling over the stair.

Close by, on the Carrer de les Comtes is the entrance to the **Museu Marés** part of the collection donated to the city by the sculptor Frederic Marés, who was also one of Spain's greatest pack rats, gathering the sublime and ridiculous in awesome quantities. The museum is beautifully arranged: 12th–14th-century polychrome wood sculptures – sweet-faced Virgins and stylized crucifixes on the ground floor; on the first, art from the Middle Ages to the 19th century (when the Baby Jesuses start having real hair and dolly faces), with some real masterpieces, a display on the Danse Macabre (a popular theme in plague-ridden Catalunya, where the grinning figure of Death is depicted playfully cavorting with people from all walks of life), and a room devoted to Montserrat memorabilia; the upper floors are packed with every imaginable collectable, from scissors to fans, giant cigars to little lead Moors and Christians for the children (open Tuesday–Saturday 8 am–2 pm and 4–7 pm, Sundays 9 am–2 pm).

The Plaça del Rei

Backtrack around the Palau del Lloctinent, which has a façade on one of Spain's finest architectural ensembles, the little Plaça del Rei. Much of this square is filled by the **Palau Reial Major**, residence of the Counts of Barcelona and later the Kings of Aragón, beginning with the twins, Ramón Berenguer II and Berenguer Ramón, who ruled alternately; the only way to tell them apart was that the first was surnamed the Towhead and the second the Fratricide (so you can guess what finally happened). Readers of epics will recall that the latter was twice captured by the Cid, and in a comic interlude forced to dine to the Cid's satisfaction to regain his freedom.

The palace encompasses the **Chapel of St Agata** on the right side of the plaça, as well as the unique '16th-century skyscraper' – actually five storeys of galleries called the **Mirador del Re Martín** by Antoni Carbonell, and the magnificent **Saló de Tinell** entered via a fan-shaped stair and great arch in the corner of the Romanesque-Gothic facade. Here Ferdinand the Catholic narrowly escaped an assassination attempt by a disgruntled peasant, and in the Saló itself, according to tradition, he and Isabel received Columbus after his first voyage. The story lacks historical support, but a hall as grand as this one deserves a good tale. Built by Pedro the Ceremonious in 1362 and designed by Guillem Carbonell, its six huge rainbow arches cross a span of 17 m (55.3 ft), with wooden beams filling in the ceiling between. Viewed from the corner of the hall, the arches appear to radiate from a single point. A fresco (c. 1300) from a wall predating the hall is now in the antechamber, portraying a procession led by the king and bishop.

From the hall you can pass through to the apse of St Agata's (which has its own entrance on the square). Also known as the Capilla Palatina, it was built by Jaume II and his queen Blanche of Anjou to house the royal relics, the most precious of which is the stone where the breasts of Saint Agatha were laid when she suffered martyrdom in

Sicily. Far more pleasant is the masterpiece of Jaume Huguet, the *Retablo del Condestable*, painted in 1466.

The Plaça del Rei is closed by a Gothic palace moved to this site from elsewhere in the quarter to house the **Museu d'Historia de la Ciutat** (city museum), entered on B. Llibreteria. Here are maps and memorabilia of Barcelona's guilds, Roman finds and art salvaged from ruined churches, the *Llibre Verd* – the 14th-century compilation of Barcelona's privileges by Arnau de la Pena, and the giant clockworks from the cathedral. Your ticket also entitles you to a unique subterranean stroll through ancient Barcelona; archaeologists have uncovered the city's Roman and Visigothic streets directly beneath the modern Carrer de los Comtes, as well as the ruins of a 4th-century Visigothic church (open Tuesday–Saturday 9 am–2 pm and 4–8.30 pm, Sundays 9 am–2 pm).

Impressive views of the **Roman walls and towers** (some 14.2 m (46 ft) high) and of the Capilla de St Agata with its octagonal tower may be had from the Vía Laietana and the **Plaça de Ramón Berenguer el Gran**, with an equestrian statue of the Templar count. Another good section of walls, pierced with Romanesque windows, lies just to the south, along the Carrer Sosts-tinent Navarro. One of the mighty towers here was uncovered only in 1968, as part of the city's plan to restore as much of the Roman circuit as possible as the buildings around them are demolished.

El Call

In the Middle Ages, Barcelona's Jewish quarter (*El Call* in Catalan) lay to the west of Carrer Bisbe and Plaça Sant Jaume. In the 11th and 12th centuries it was the cultural and intellectual centre of Catalunya, with its finest school, as well as home to doctors, translators, several renowned poets, astronomers and philosophers. In 1243 Jaume I ordered El Call set apart from the rest of the city, and that its residents wear special hats. Still, when the Jews were expelled from other territories they were made welcome here, and El Call enjoyed so much royal favour as to provoke envy. In 1391, some Castilians residing in Barcelona spread the rumour that the Black Death had been brought by the Jews, inciting riots in the quarter that led to 300 deaths. King Joan I had the 22 instigators put to death, but could not halt the growing tide of anti-Semitism, and in 1424 the Jews were expelled from El Call, the stones of their synagogues and cemeteries quarried for the construction of the Generalitat and other structures. On tiny Carrer de Marlet, off Carrer de Sant Domènec del Call, one of these stones remains, inscribed with Hebrew letters: 'Sacred foundation of Rabbi Samuel Hassareri, of everlasting life. Year 692.'

Today El Call has a number of antique shops, especially along Carrer de la Palla and Banys Nous, streets that follow the line of the ancient walls.

East of Plaça Sant Jaume

From the north (Gothic) side of the Ajuntament, the Carrer de Hércules (recalling the city's mythological founder) leads to the **Plazuela de Sant Just** and two palaces, **Moxió** and **Palamòs**, the latter now housing the Gallery of Illustrious Catalans. In the Middle Ages this was the grandest private address in Barcelona, built in the 13th century atop the Roman wall, with a fine Romanesque patio. In the mid-15th century it was the home of the Viceroy Don Galcaran de Requesens, who played a major role in the city's first great class struggle, between the party of the Biga (the urban oligarchy) and the Busca (small merchants and guildsmen). Requesens supported the Busca in the name of the monarchy and set off a conflagration, known as the Catalan civil war, that pitted the nobles against the king and the commons (1462–72). Also in the square is the **Church of Les Sants Just i Pastor**, according to tradition founded by Charlemagne's son, Louis the Pious in 801, and used as the parish church of the kings of Aragón. It is the last church in Spain to preserve its ancient privilege of 'Testimentos Sacramentales' bestowed by the founder himself, a privilege which gives an oath said before the altar of San Félix the power of notary, or writ. The 16th-century *retablo* in the Chapel of San Félix is by the Portuguese Pero Nunyes. Note the Visigothic capitals, pressed into service as Holy Water fonts; one bears an anagram of Barcelona in Greek letters.

In 1893 Joan Miró was born and for many years had his first studio in the arcade called **Pasaje de Crédit**, between Carrer de Ferran and the Palau Centelles (1514), on Baixade de Sant Miquel. The arcade, inspired by Parisian ironworks, was built in 1879. It's also interesting to note that several old palaces on the Carrer de Avinyó, at the end of Baixade de Sant Miquel, were converted into brothels around the turn of the century; the ladies of one inspired young Pablo Picasso's *Les Demoiselles d'Avignon* – the painting that gave birth to Cubism. If you walk along Avinyó, note the fine *esgrafiados* on the houses at nos. 26 and 30.

Santa María del Mar

Between the Barri Gótic and the Parc de la Ciutadella lies the **Barri Santa María del Mar**, one of three medieval suburbs (*vilanovas*) that grew up along the main road, Carrer Argenteria, from the walled city to the port. As Catalan maritime interests became more important, so did the quarter, and in the 13th century Jaume I surrounded it with its own wall. **Carrer Argenteria** – the old street of the silver-smiths – cuts across the quarter from the Plaça Angel (the old maritime gate) to the star attraction, the lovely **Church of Santa María del Mar**, perhaps the most perfect expression of the Catalan Gothic style.

The history of the church is bound up with Catalunya's maritime conquests. When Jaume I conquered Mallorca he promised a temple to the patroness of his sailors, though his promise remained unfulfilled until Alfonso the Benign took Sardinia, the last Catalan territorial gain, and laid the first stone of the church in 1329. Santa María became the parish church not only of Barcelona's sailors, but of its successful merchants who built their palaces in this quarter. In 1714 its interior was damaged during the French and Spanish bombardment, and its baroque fittings went up in flames in 1936. However lavish they may have been the present simplicity enhances the sublime proportions designed by Berenguer de Montagut, perhaps with the assistance of the Mallorcan master, Jaume Fabre.

In Santa María del Mar you can see all the features that best characterize Catalan Gothic which was inspired as much by Roman basilicas as it was by the great French cathedrals: the emphasis on the horizontal, the external simplicity and restrained façade (on the Plaça Santa María) with a large rose window (15th century) and octagonal towers topped with terraces. In the interior there's an immense feeling of spaciousness, achieved with minimal interior supports; its simple octagonal piers are some 13.2

m (43 ft) apart – a space unsurpassed in any other medieval building. The central nave is twice as wide as the two aisles, which, however, have the same height, making them appear very long and narrow. Some of the 15th-century windows are beautiful, especially those of the Ascension and Last Judgement. In the Plaça in front of the church, there's a columned **Gothic fountain** with a garden on top.

Carrer de Montcada

Behind Santa Maria del Mar, in the Plaça del Born begins the Carrer de Montcada, one of Barcelona's most atmospheric streets, graced with the 15th–17th-century palaces of Catalunya's rich merchants and nobles. Outstanding individual addresses are no. 20, the **Palau Dalmases** (17th century) with fine sculptures adorning the patio and stair, nos. 23 and 25, both from the 15th century, and no. 12, the Palau de Lió (16th century), with another attractive courtyard and the fine and extensive **Colecciōn Rocamora**, a museum of Spanish costume (open Tuesday–Saturday 9 am–2 pm and 4.30–7 pm, Sundays 9 am–2 pm).

The loveliest palace on Montcada is no. 12, the **Palau Aguilar**, a 15th-century seignorial mansion with a patio by Marc Sanfont. Ind 1963 the palace was completely restored and fitted to house the **Picasso Museum**, the best place in Spain to see the works of a Spaniard generally acclaimed as the greatest artist of our century. Picasso (1881–1973) spent 1895 to 1904 in Barcelona studying and painting the works of his 'Blue Period'. What makes this museum particularly interesting for his fans is that it chronicles his career, from the drawings of an 8-year-old child in Málaga, to his first major painting, *Science and Charity*, a number of works done in Barcelona, including a menu for Els Quatre Gats (1900) in a Toulouse-Lautrec style, the *Portrait of his sister Lola*, *Desemparats* and *The Madman*. Picasso donated many of the works to the museum, most notably 58 studies on Velázquez's *Las Meninas* (1957). The museum is open daily 9.30 am–1.30 pm and 4.30–8 pm, closed Monday am).

Parc de la Ciutadella

The year 1714 is a bitter date in the annals of Barcelona. In that year, after an extraordinary eleven-month resistance, the besieged city fell at last to the troops of Philip V. To punish the city the Bourbon king moved its university to Cervera and demanded the evacuation (without any compensation) of an entire quarter of the city to construct, at Barcelona's expense, the Ciutadella, one of most massive fortifications ever built in Europe. The only purpose the Ciutadella ever had was to intimidate the Catalans; the French captured it by surprise in 1808. When the good Catalan General Prim, took power in 1869, he gave the mastadon to the city, which immediately razed the hated symbol to the ground and made it into a park.

In 1888, Barcelona's progressive mayor Ruis i Taulet, used the new park as the site of the Universal Exposition, which city historians believe saved the city from sliding into provincial backwardness. It also, as all good expositions do, served as a stage for architectural innovation, playing the role of midwife to the modernista style. If you enter the park by its main entrance on Passeig Lluis Companys, you can still see one of the relics from the great fair: the **Arc de Triomf**, by Josep Vailaseca, a peculiar piece of

Mudejár-style brickwork that manifests, if nothing else, the Catalan longing to be different – a longing shared by several other buildings around the Passeig, like the elephantine **Palau de Justicia**, with a façade made entirely of stone from Montjuïc, the **Grupo Escolar Pere Vila**, with its ceramic reliefs, and behind it the idiosyncratic **Compañia de Gas y Electricidad** of 1897.

The park itself is well used, especially at weekends when families come to paddle in the little boats under the **Cascada**, a monumental pile of rocks and mythological allusions by Josep Fonserè, who was assisted by Gaüdí, a young student at the time. Gaudí is credited with the arrangement of the boulders and some of the decorative elements, as well as the graceful ironwork at the park's second gate, on Avinguda Marqués de l'Argentera. East of the lake was the fortress' **Plaça d'Armes**, now a formal garden with the only remaining structures from the Ciutadella: a chapel, the Governor's Palace and the Arsenal, now housing the Catalan parliament and also the **Museu d'Art Modern**, featuring a fine collection of 19th- and 20th-century Catalan paintings, sculpture and decorative arts by such lights as Mariano Fortuny, Isidre Nonell and Santiago Russinyol. One of the newest works is Josep Guinavart Bertram's 1979 work *Contorn–Entorn* – a forest of sinister shapes and mobiles reminiscent of the great cactus garden on Montjuïc (open 9 am–2 pm and Mondays 2–7.30 pm).

Ciutadella also contains Spain's finest **zoo**, with an aquarium, an arena with dolphin and orca-whale shows, a serpentarium, and several albinos – peacocks, a camel, and the world's only white gorilla, Floc de Neu ('Snowflake') who will convince you that apes are more handsome in black. Near the aquarium stands the fountain of the '*Senyoreta del paraigua*' (the lady with the umbrella) the symbol adopted by the city from the 1888 Exposition (zoo hours are daily, 9.30 am–7.30 pm).

Other survivors of the Universal Exposition may be found along the park's Passeig Tilers, a linden-lined avenue with the great brick **Castell dels Tres Dragons**, originally a restaurant by Domenèch i Montaner, one of the best Modernista architects, now housing a **Museum of Zoology**, the pretty **Umbráculo** (greenhouse for shade plants), and the iron and glass **Invernadero** (winter greenhouse), both by Josep Amargós. In between these is neo-Pompeyan **Museu Martorell**, with a geological and paleontological collection (open Tuesday–Sunday 9 am–2 pm).

Barceloneta

Barcelona has always looked towards the sea, and all of its waterfront is devoted to port activities, except for the seaside quarter of Barceloneta, separated from the Parc de la Ciutadella and the port by the Estació de Francia. After the destruction of some 2000 homes to build La Ciutadella, a French military engineer, Prospero de Verboom, designed on this small triangle of land a neighbourhood to replace it, following the most progressive urban-planning ideas of the 18th century. The streets were laid out in a grid, with long, narrow blocks of houses, permitting every room to have a window, and as all houses were allowed only one floor, all had access to sunlight. Verboom's height prohibition was modified in 1837, so that most houses in Barceloneta now have two floors.

Now inhabited by sailors and fishermen, Barceloneta is a lively place, especially in the summer evenings when the city crowds into its numerous permanent and temporary seafood restaurants and cools off at the municipal beach (the sand is nice but the sea none too clean). There's an **aquarium** with 44 tanks of Mediterranean sealife on the Passeig Nacional, the main street into Barceloneta (open daily 10 am–2 pm and 4–8 pm); for a fine view of Barcelona head out along the breakwater that extends from the Club de Natació with its swimming pools. You can catch a *gondolina*, or water bus, from the breakwater to the Columbus monument, or if it's working, go to Montjuïc on the aerial cable car.

Along the seafront

In the **Plaça del Palau**, on the other side of the train station from Barceloneta, the neo-Classical **Aduana Vella** (old customs house), now occupied by the Guardia Civil, shelters a series of interesting murals in the Sala de Actos, portraying the reign of Carlos III, life in commercial Barcelona, and the sad adventures that befell Don Quixote in the city – where he was unhorsed and forced to give up his knightly profession. Diagonally across the square stands **La Llotja**, or stock exchange. In the mercantile empire of the Catalans, such exchanges received the best civil architecture of the day, in accordance with the place commerce held in society. Barcelona's was built by King Pedro the Ceremonious in 1380. In the 18th century it was decided the building needed a neo-Classical facelift, though fortunately the great **Gothic Exchange** inside was left untouched and can be visited – it still serves as Barcelona's stock exchange.

The next large square, the **Plaça d'Antoni Lopez**, has the city's central post office, and nearby, at no. 2 Passeig de Colom, is the house that a tradition claims lodged Cervantes when in Barcelona – which, by his writings, one would guess was his favourite city. The **Cervantes House** has been remodelled over the centuries, though some of its 16th-century elements still adorn the façade.

Two blocks behind the seaside Passeig de Colom runs the Carrer Ample (also called Calle Anche) which for several centuries was the city's most aristocratic address. The Emperor Charles V lived here when in town, as did kings of Hungary and Bohemia, and in later years they were followed by the great merchants. The residents of the street worshipped at the **Basilica de La Mercè** – Our Lady of Mercy, the patroness of Barcelona, who appeared in a vision to Jaume I, asking him to found a monastic order devoted to the deliverance of Christian captives held by Barbary pirates. The first church on the site dates from 1267, but has since often been altered and rebuilt; its Gothic façade was actually transferred here from a church that had to be destroyed to make way for the Ajutament's annex. The fittings are basically Baroque, but there's a fine statue of the Virgin, carved in 1361 by Pere Moragues. Although the monks left in 1836, the cult remains extremely popular. In September Barcelona holds a great fiesta de la Mercè, and when a football team from the city wins an important match, it sings a hymn of thanks to the Virgin.

Towering over the port in the Porta de la Pau is another souvenir of 1888, the **Columbus Monument**, which has the admiral high atop a 51 m (165 ft) iron column, pointing out to sea. Every great city seems to have a large, overdone 19th-century monument, subject now to jests from local wags, and this would be Barcelona's if it weren't for the fervent belief that Columbus was really a Catalan a thesis several Catalan scholar have proved in their books. Catalan or no, during the Spanish–American

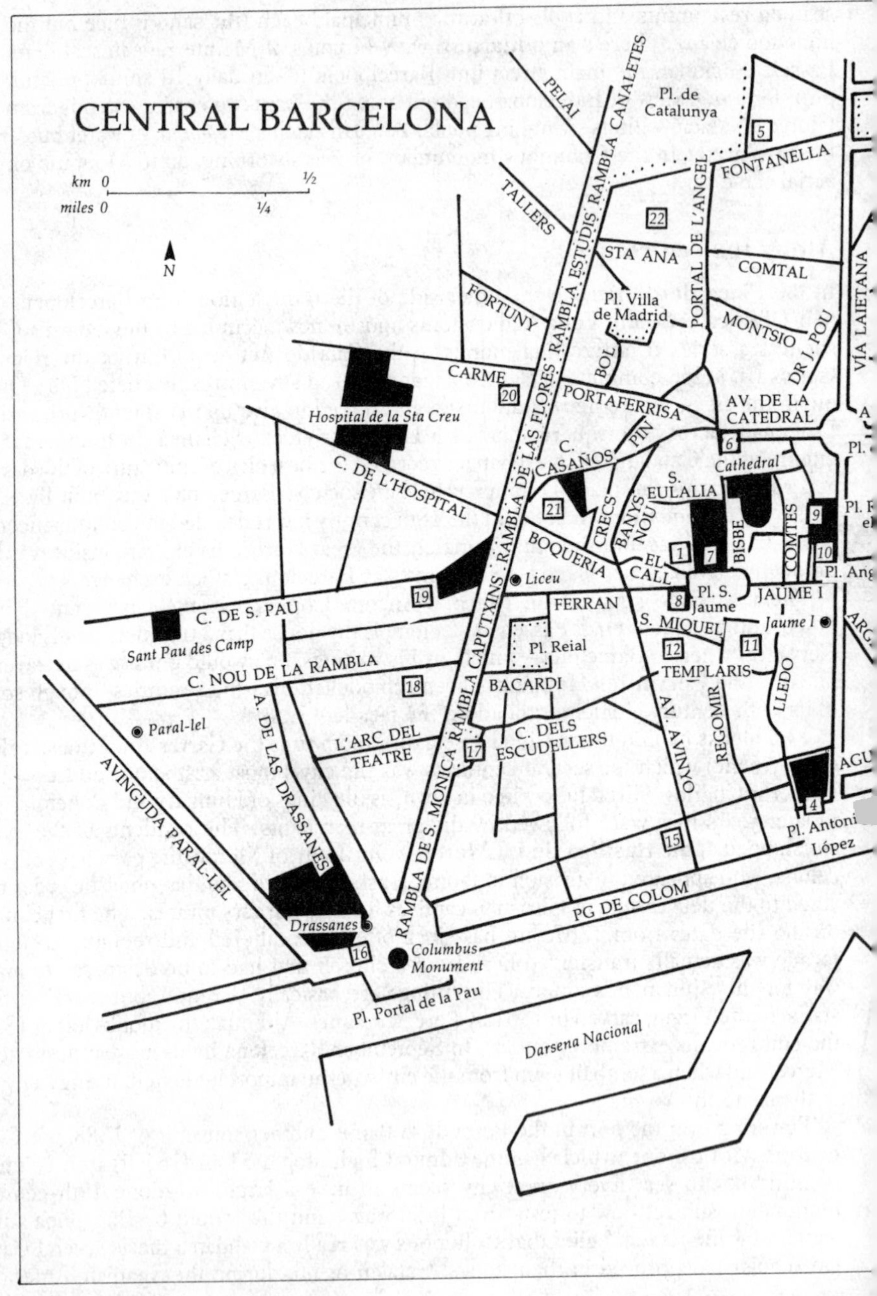
CENTRAL BARCELONA
km 0 1/2
miles 0 1/4
N
PELAI
Pl. de Catalunya
5
FONTANELLA
TALLERS
RAMBLA CANALETES
RAMBLA ESTUDIS
RAMBLA DE LAS FLORES
RAMBLA CAPUTXINS
RAMBLA DE S. MONICA
22
STA ANA
PORTAL DE L'ANGEL
COMTAL
VÍA LAIETANA
FORTUNY
Pl. Villa de Madrid
MONTSIO
DR J. POU
BOL
CARME
20
Hospital de la Sta Creu
PORTAFERRISA
AV. DE LA CATEDRAL
6
PIN
C. CASAÑOS
Cathedral
C. DE L'HOSPITAL
S. EULALIA
CRECS
BANYS NOU
21
BOQUERIA
EL CALL
1
7
BISBE
COMTES
9
10
Liceu
19
Pl. S. Jaume
8
JAUME I
FERRAN
C. DE S. PAU
S. MIQUEL
Jaume I
Pl. Reial
12
11
Sant Pau des Camp
C. NOU DE LA RAMBLA
TEMPLARIS
18
BACARDI
LLEDO
REGOMIR
Paral-lel
A. DE LAS DRASSANES
L'ARC DEL TEATRE
17
C. DELS ESCUDELLERS
AV. AVINYO
AVINGUDA PARAL-LEL
4
15
Pl. Antoni López
PG DE COLOM
Drassanes
16
Columbus Monument
Pl. Portal de la Pau
Darsena Nacional

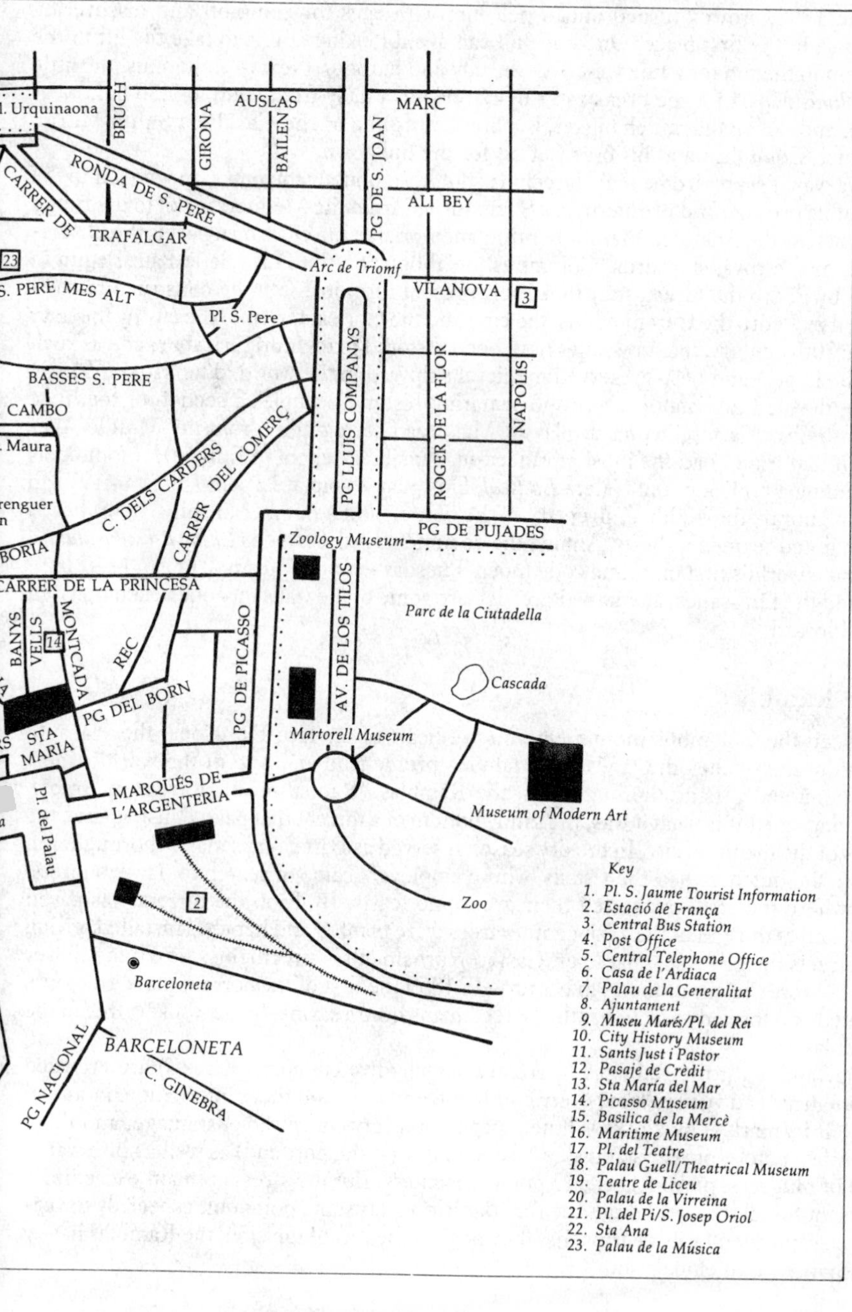

l. Urquinaona
BRUCH
GIRONA
AUSLAS
BAILEN
PG DE S. JOAN
MARC
RONDA DE S. PERE
CARRER DE
TRAFALGAR
ALI BEY
23
Arc de Triomf
S. PERE MES ALT
VILANOVA
3
Pl. S. Pere
BASSES S. PERE
PG LLUIS COMPANYS
ROGER DE LA FLOR
NAPOLIS
. CAMBO
. Maura
C. DELS CARDERS
CARRER DEL COMERÇ
renguer
n
BORIA
PG DE PUJADES
Zoology Museum
CARRER DE LA PRINCESA
AV. DE LOS TILOS
Parc de la Ciutadella
BANYS
VELLS
14
MONTCADA
REC
PG DE PICASSO
Cascada
PG DEL BORN
STA MARIA
Martorell Museum
MARQUÉS DE L'ARGENTERIA
Pl. del Palau
Museum of Modern Art
2
Zoo
Barceloneta
BARCELONETA
PG NACIONAL
C. GINEBRA
Key
1. Pl. S. Jaume Tourist Information
2. Estació de França
3. Central Bus Station
4. Post Office
5. Central Telephone Office
6. Casa de l'Ardiaca
7. Palau de la Generalitat
8. Ajuntament
9. Museu Marés/Pl. del Rei
10. City History Museum
11. Sants Just i Pastor
12. Pasaje de Crèdit
13. Sta María del Mar
14. Picasso Museum
15. Basilica de la Mercè
16. Maritime Museum
17. Pl. del Teatre
18. Palau Guell/Theatrical Museum
19. Teatre de Liceu
20. Palau de la Virreina
21. Pl. del Pi/S. Josep Oriol
22. Sta Ana
23. Palau de la Música

war in 1898, crowds turned out to pelt him with eggs for going off and discovering America in the first place. One way you can avoid looking at it is to take the lift in the column to the top for a fine view over the city and harbour. Next to Columbus, the little *gondolinas* depart for the breakwater by Barceloneta daily from 9 am to 9.30 pm. Near them, and not all that much bigger, is a lifesize **replica of the Carabela Santa María**, in which Columbus and his crew set off for the unknown.

In a way it's a bit ironic that Barcelona should so honour the one man who led to the loss of its prestige and prosperity, as Spain turned from the Mediterranean to the riches from across the Atlantic. A far more fitting memorial to the city's own past is the **Drassanes**, or the royal shipyards, Columbus' neighbour on the Porta de la Pau. Begun in 1255 by Pedro the Great, they took their present form in 1388, the construction costs shared by Pedro the Ceremonious, the city, and the Cortes. Given to the city by the navy in the 20th century, the Drassanes have been restored to their original state, and as such are the largest and best-preserved medieval shipyard in the world. The **Museu Marítimo**, devoted to Catalunya's proud seafaring history, occupies a section of the huge structure, with a fascinating display of Mallorcan cartography from the Middle Ages (when that island had the most advanced map-making school in Europe), ship models (including a replica of the Galera *La Real*, Don Juan's ship at Lepanto, built in 1971 to commemorate the 400th anniversary of the battle), and a number of ships' figureheads and painted seamen's chests. Among the documents is the famous *Llibro del Consulat del Mar*, the world's first maritime code (open Tuesday–Sunday 10 am–2 pm and 4–7 pm). Behind the Drassanes, along the Parel-lel, are some of the walls that once encompassed the shipyard.

The Ramblas

Between the Columbus monument and the heart of modern Barcelona, the Plaça de Catalunya, stretches the city's most famous promenade and one of the world's most charming and urbane thoroughfares, the Ramblas. 'Ramla' means torrent in Arabic, and long ago this is what it was, the sandy bottom of a torrent that passed just outside the walls of the medieval city. In the dry season it served as Barcelona's major thoroughfare, where the butchers had their stalls, where employers came in search of day-labourers, and where the gallows awaited their gruesome feasts. By 1366 the torrent was paved over, and at the end of the 18th century trees were planted and benches installed, giving the streets their present character. Cast iron ornaments – streetlights, kiosks and flower stalls – were the gift of the 19th century. In 1859 the first of the current plane trees was planted and thrived so well that the Barcelonians have a saying, 'to grow like a tree in the Ramblas'.

Day and night the Ramblas (there are actually five connected streets) are crowded with natives and visitors from every continent, and here and there international tourism has left its mark. The kiosks sell newspapers in every conceivable language, and there are cafes, hotels, burger stands, and 'sexy shops' (at the port end) as well as dire warnings of muggers, pickpockets and purse-snatchers. But the streets remain exceedingly pleasant for all that, and if not the real Barcelona, (as some point out, especially to visitors so captivated by its charms that they neglect the rest of the city), the Ramblas have a big share of Barcelona's soul.

The first section, nearest the port, *La Rambla de Santa Monica* has endured the most from pop culture and the tastes of sailors. Yet in the 15th–18th centuries the area was a major producer of artillery, most notably of a colossal 161–quintal cannon called 'Santa Eulàlia' of 1463, that blew up when fired for the first time. Charles V in his endless warfare so heavily patronized the 12 foundries here that they were called his 'twelve apostles'. The foundries have since been supplanted by a typical **wax museum** with inflated prices.

The next **Rambla dels Caputxins** defines the heart of Barcelona's old theatre district, of which the forlorn **Teatro Principal** is the sole survivor. The first theatre on this site belonged to the Hospital de la Santa Creu, to which Philip II granted the privilege of building a theatre to raise revenue. Built in 1603, rebuilt and burned and remodelled several times since (lastly in 1933), it awaits the kiss of a Prince Charming to bring it back to life. In the **Plaça del Teatre** stands a monument to an earlier Prince Charming, Serafi Pitarra, the father of modern Catalan theatre, which you can learn all about in the **Theatrical Museum** in the nearby Carrer Nou de Ramblas 3. A major reason to go is to see the building it's housed in, Gaudí's **Palau Güell**, built in 1888 for Gaudí's great patron, the financier Eusebi Güell, to coincide with the Universal Exposition. Even if Catalan theatre leaves you lukewarm (although there are interesting sections devoted to playbills, posters, the opera and marionettes) this is the only building by Gaudí that you can get into, where you can see his favourite elements – the parabolic arch, the fantastic chimneys and ornate steeple, and a wealth of sinuous, organic detail. The cupola over the main salon is a honeycombed beehive pierced with beams of light (open weekdays except Monday, 10 am–1 pm and 5–7 pm).

Another slight detour off the Rambla, this time on the Carrer de Colom, to the right, leads to the **Plaça Reial**, occupying the site of the former Capuchin monastery, one of many religious institutions that lined the Ramblas until their suppression in 1835. Enclosed by a harmonious neo-Classical ensemble of buildings and arcades, planted with palms, and adorned with the fountain of the Three Graces and streetlamps designed by a young Gaudí, it is a charming oasis, reminiscent of Madrid's Plaza Mayor, and like it, holding a stamp and coin market on Sunday mornings. Some of the shops under the arcades and on the Carrer de Ferran look the same as they did 150 years ago. The church of **Sant Jaume** on Carrer de Ferran was a synagogue, reconsecrated as a church in 1393 by a group of Conversos, although only the door remains from the period.

At the head of the Rambla dels Caputxins stands an institution that Barcelona is specially proud of, the 3500-seat **Gran Teatre de Liceu** (1860), Spain's only opera house presenting a regular season (from November to March) of grand opera, often featuring such homegrown virtuosi as Montserrat Caballe and Josep Carrers (José Carreras). Its rather plain exterior hides one of Europe's largest and most sumptuous auditoriums, with five huge, semicircular balconies; for a look around without attending a show, free tours are offered, Mondays and Fridays at 11.30 am and 12.15 pm. A little further up to the right a swirling Modernista dragon guards an old umbrella shop.

The Rambla de Sant Josep, the next segment, is better known as the **Flower Rambla**; the promenade overflows with the colour and scent of rows of flower stands. If you prefer fruit and vegetables, try the Ramblas century-old market of **Sant Josep**. From the elegant **Plaça de Sant Josep**, the Carrer de l'Hospital leads to the ancient

Hospital de la Santa Creu, founded in 1024 and relocated to the suburbs in 1926, leaving behind its fine Gothic buildings, now home to various cultural institutions. The central hospital surrounds a very lovely 15th-century courtyard. Upstairs, under huge Gothic arches, is the Library of Catalunya, Barcelona's largest, with a million volumes, and across the patio lies the **Casa de Convalecencia** with another fine patio. The vestibule is richly adorned with magnificent 17th-century *azulejos* by Llorenç Pasoles; others can be seen on the stair leading to the chapel. Across the lane is the 18th-century Surgery College, now the **Real Academia de Cirugía y Medicina**, the highlight of which is the elliptical amphitheatre where anatomy lessons took place, with the original marble dissection table in the centre.

From the hospital, the Carrer de Carme returns to the Ramblas and the **Palau de la Virreina**, an ivory-coloured confection from 1778, now home to the **Museum of Decorative Arts** and the **Cambó Collection**, the first containing ceramics, tapestries (a good 16th-century one from Brussels depicting the siege of Rhodes) clocks and glassware from around the world; in the Cambó you'll find a large collection of non-famous works by famous Renaissance and Baroque artists. The palace also has a postal museum (all open 9 am–2 pm and 4–8 pm, free).

Across the Rambla, and separating it from the Barri Gòtic is the **Barri del Pi**, another of the medieval *vilanovas* (new towns) that grew up outside the ancient walls. The spiritual centre of the quarter, the **Iglesia del Pi** – named for a giant pine tree, since replanted on the Plaça del Pi – may be reached via Carrer Casañas. Founded in the 10th century, the present structure dates from 1322 and has octagonal towers and a mighty rose window in its western façade, facing the Plaça del Pi. The north portal, on Plaça S. Josep Oriol, is the oldest, from the 13th century. The interior, with its single nave, is typical Catalan, broad and sober of decor.

The next Rambla, the **Rambla Estudis**, was named for L'Estudi General, or University, that once stood here, founded by Martin I and suppressed by Philip V. The promenade here is a permanent bird and small animal market, lined with a wall of cages. Monuments on this segment include the 18th-century **Iglesia de Belén**, and opposite, the **Palau de Moya**, from the same century, with its arcade. The last little piece of the Ramblas, the **Rambla de les Canaletas** is named for the famous fountain, (if you drink from it, they say, you'll never leave Barcelona), since the 19th century dispensed beneath a pretty four-headed street light. A right on to Carrer Canuda leads to the **Plaça de Madrid**, with its 2nd-century AD **Roman tombs** that once lined the road into the city.

Around the Plaça de Catalunya

Vast and brimming with life, this great square is the nerve centre of Barcelona, lying in between the old city and the Eixample, a major transport hub, and the address of the city's major banks and department stores. In the centre are two illuminated fountains and among the tulip beds a wistful sculpture by Barcelona's own Josep Clará called *The Goddess*.

Behind the Banca d'España on Carrer de Rivudadeneyra, is the **church and monastery of Santa Ana**, where the Cortes were held under Ferdinand the Catholic. The church is in a simple Romanesque style, while the cloister, with its two storeys, is typical of Catalan Gothic with its two floors. Near here (take Carrer S. Ana to Avinguda Portal de l'Angel to Carrer Montsio, no. 3 bis) is the renowned **Els Quatre Gats** (the four cats) built in 1900 in Gothic-Moderne by Puig i Cadafalch. At the turn of the century this café attracted all the leading artists in Barcelona. Picasso's first show was held here, and in later years the 'Cercle Artistic de Sant Lluc', which counted Gaudí among its members, met here. A new Els Quatre Gats has opened across the street, with frequent jazz and other entertainment.

Continue down Carrer Monstió, take a left onto Vía Laietana and then right onto Sant Pere mes Alt for Catalan modernism in its most delightful extreme: Domènech i Montaner's **Palau de la Música Catalana** (1908) undulating, polychromatic, adorned with floral and musical motifs in tiles and mosaics, its colourful interior a brilliant epiphany of the style. There's an old joke: one Catalan starts a business, two start a corporation, and three start a choral society. The Palau was originally built for one of them, the 'Orfeó Català', but now serves as Barcelona's principal concert hall. Next to it stands the lavish 18th-century *esgrafiado* façade of the **Casa del Gremio de los Veleros** (sailmakers' guild).

The Eixample

Parisians have their Right and Left Banks, but Barcelona has its Right and Left Eixample, divided by the delightful **Rambla de Catalunya**, lined with linden trees and *horchaterias* (almond milk bars). The Right Eixample, with its numerous modernista works, is by far the most interesting of the two sides.

Barcelona's widest street, the Gran Vía de les Corts Catalanes, or just **Gran Vía**, intersects the Rambla de Catalunya just beyond the Plaça de Catalunya. Near the corner is the **Cine Colesium**, a grand celluloid palace, and on the next block, the **University**, built between 1861 and 1889 in the Catalan-Romantic style.

Parallel to the Rambla de Catalunya is the elegant commercial and residential boulevard of the Eixample, the **Passeig de Gràcia**, leading up to the old town of Gràcia. Gaudí admirers should take the first right from the Passeig de Gràcia to Carrer de Casp, where at no. 48, stands the **Casa Calvet** (1898), Gaudí's first apartment building – some of the ironwork details, the two crosses, and the decorative elements at the entrance and lift pressage his two works on the Passeig de Gràcia.

Manzana de la Discordia

In the Passeig de Gràcia, in the block between Carrers Consell de Cent and Aragó, are the three Modernista beauties of the **Manzana de la Discordia** – a pun on the Spanish word *manzana*, which means both 'apple' and 'block', before which every passer-by can play the role of the Trojan Paris and award his or her prize to the fairest. On the corner stands the **Casa Lleó Morera** by Domènech i Montaner; its floral loveliness was unfortunately disfigured by a later proprietor, who moved the cupola and altered the shop windows. Next, three doors down, is the neo-Gothic **Casa Ametller** by Puig i Cadafalch, with its stepped gable wall glittering with coloured ceramics, and next to it, Gaudí's **Casa Batlló**. Here Gaudí took a typical residential building of the Eixample and transformed its flat façade into a rippling 'skin' with different shades of blue ceramics (done by his collaborator Josep Jujol i Gilbert) and added one of his characteristic pinnacles to solve the difference in height with the Casa Ametller. The iron balconies have bony forms; for a taste of the interior take the lift to the top and walk down the stair. Near here, to the right at Carrer València 302 is the **Casa Elizalde**, which dispenses information and holds exhibitions on the Eixample.

In the Casa Batlló Gaudí put new clothes on an old building; a few blocks further up the Passeig de Gràcia in the Casa Milà, better known as **La Pedrera** 'the stone quarry' he worked once more with Jujol to carry his ideas a step further. This is Gaudí's final statement in secular architecture (1910), and in the field is as extraordinary as the Sagrada Familia is in the sacred. The entire stone façade undulates around the bevelled corner of the block without a hint of a corner or straight line, a cliff sculpted by waves of wind, with spiralling guardians of stone and tile peering over the roof – surely the world's most fanciful chimneys and vents. Within are two circular patios open to the sky which you can get in to see, though you'll need to get permission from the Cátedra Gaudí to take a stroll on the roof – what a modern critic might call a totally abstract environment. The attic just below is a great tunnel of Gaudí's favourite parabolic arches.

Just beyond La Pedrera, the important **Avinguda Diagonal** boldly slices across the neat squares of the Eixample. If in the Manzana de la Discordia you preferred Puig i Cadafalch, two of his principal works may be seen just to the right, the **Edificio Vidal-Quadras** (no. 373) now the **Museu de Música**, with a fascinating collection of antique and exotic instruments, including one of Adophe Sax's original saxophones (open Tuesday–Sunday, 10 am–2 pm); and the **Casa de les Punxes** (no. 416), a massive neo-Gothic work in stone and brick, its name referring to its pointy pinnacles. If you gave your apple to Domènech i Montaner, turn to the Carrer Mallorca, cutting between the Passeig de Gràcia and the Diagonal, where the **Casa Montaner** (no. 278) is reminiscent of the architect's Palau de la Música with its colourful ceramic façade; it's now the seat of the provincial government of Barcelona. At no. 291, in the **Casa Thomas** you can visit Domènech i Montaner's experiment in neo-Gothic.

The Sagrada Familia

Gaudí's masterpiece is a 'must see' in Barcelona – one literally cannot avoid the sight of its distinctive 108 m (350 ft) 'bottle' towers looming over the skyline. Occupying an entire block of the Cerdá plan with its own Metro station (or you could simply continue up Carrer Mallorca from the Casa Thomas), the 'Templo Expiatorio de la Sagrada Familia' is surely the most compelling, controversial, ambitious and imaginative – and most unfinished – piece of 20th-century sacred architecture in the world.

The temple was begun in 1882, the brainchild of Josep M. Bocabella, founder of a society dedicated to Saint Joseph, who originally hired another architect, del Villar. Del Villar planned a neo-Gothic church and got as far as the crypt when disagreements with Bocabella led to his replacement by Gaudí (in 1891, at the age of 31). Gaudí finished the crypt and then spent much of his remaining 43 years on the project, which became an obsession – for his last 15 years he accepted no other commissions, and actually lived in a hut on the construction site, spending his free time soliciting funds to continue the work. He concentrated on one façade the Façana del Naixement, but was hit by a streetcar before he ever saw it completed.

His followers completed the façade according to his models, but between 1936 and 1954 nothing more was attempted. Since then, a group of architects, using Gaudí's

The Sagrada Familia

models as their basis, have been working on the Façade of the Passion, erecting its four great towers. Their work has offended certain purists, who believe the temple is best left as it was when Gaudí died, as a memorial to his unique genius; they also point out that Gaudí never even followed his own models, but was ever changing and revising. But it's doubtful whether Gaudí himself would have wished the construction stopped. As master builder he has bequeathed a tremendous challenge to the future; like the great medieval cathedrals the Sagrada Familia has irresistibly taken on a life of its own, far beyond a mere lifespan – for it is a work of the human spirit. Even the scruffiest young backpackers understand this, and it's an amazing sight to see them (who have probably never donated anything to their religious institutions back home) dropping 1000 pts notes into the boxes marked 'For the Work'.

Gaudí's design is based on Christian symbolism, with three façades dedicated to the Birth (Naixement), Passion and the Glory; each façade would have four towers, symbolizing the twelve Apostles. Four higher towers would be dedicated to the four Evangelists, and between them, a truly colossal tower symbolizing the Saviour, with a large tower to the Virgin on the side.

The construction site, entered through the new Façana de la Passío on Carrer Sardenya, is open daily from 9 am–6 pm or 8 am–8 pm in the summer, and offers the opportunity to view Gaudí's **Façana del Naixement** in all its allegorical glory, with its three doors dedicated to Faith, Hope and Charity. For a small fee you can take the lift up to the top of one of the towers, for a dreamlike ramble over the main bridge high over the city. A slide show offers an overview of Gaudí's work, and there are large models of the finished cathedral and a display of scale diagrams comparing it to other great churches. In the museum there's a collection of Gaudí's plaster models, which he used to translate his ideas into form and to work out the numerous and very complex structural problems in the building. The apse, also finished by the master, has many lovely natural motifs; from here, steps lead down into the crypt, where Gaudí is buried.

One of the best perspectives of the Sagrada Familia is from the recently inaugurated **Avinguda Gaudí** (at a diagonal from the Façana de Naixement), beautified by the city with the great neo-Gothic street lamps transferred here from the Passeig de Grècia. If you continue up this street, through a neighbourhood called Camp de l'Arpa ('Field of the Dolmen' recalling a long-lost megalith), you'll reach another gargantuan modernista work, Domènech i Montaner's **Hospital de Sant Pau** (1900) covering over 100,000 sq. m (117,000 sq. yds) and richly adorned with mosaics and ceramics.

Walking in the other direction from the Sagrada Familia, you'll find a modernista bullring, the **Plaza de Toros Monumental** (1911), whose three towers support huge yellow, white and blue dinosaur eggs. This is Barcelona's largest ring and also the home of the memorabilia-filled **Bullfighting Museum**, open daily during the bull season from 10 am–1 pm and 5.30–7 pm.

Montjuïc

Gently sloping up 215 m (700 ft) between the city and the sea, Montjuïc has been Barcelona's showcase ever since the 1929 International Exposition. The origins of its peculiar name are much disputed, some claiming it derives from 'Mons Jovis' – the mountain of Jupiter – while others cite the large Jewish cemetery that used to be there, hence 'mountain of the Jews'.

After centuries of serving a defensive role, the city's green thumbs gradually began to claim it as their own, and in 1914 Barcelona made the entire north slope into Montjuïc Park, beautifully landscaped by Jean-Claude Forestier and N. M. Rubió i Tuduri. Its loveliness inspired the city fathers to hold the International Exposition to show it off, unfortunately just in time for the Depression. Style had evolved as well since the Universal Exposition initiated the modernista movement; in 1929 Barcelona was in a period of neo-Mormonism. If you like Salt Lake City, you'll feel at home on Montjuïc.

GETTING AROUND MONTJUÏC

Buses 101 and 61 from the Plaça d'Espanya take in most of the park, taking a great loop from the Palacio Nacional to the amusement park. From the Paral-lel Metro station, you can take a funicular up to the amusement park, and from there a second funicular ascends to the castle of Montjuïc. If the aerial cable car is working, you can travel to Miramar, near the cactus gardens, from the port of Barceloneta.

Plaça d'Espanya

The show begins in the round Plaça d'Espanya, sporting the city's smaller, older bullring, **Las Arenas** on one side. If you like Miró, walk around the ring to the **Parc del Escorxada**, home of his colourful monolith *Dona i ocell* ('Lady and bird'). On the plaça's other side, the tall **Tuscan Towers** frame the grand view of the main exhibition palaces, all the way up to the neo-Mormon Palau Nacional. Various trade fairs occupy the buildings throughout the year. In between them are the **Fuentes Luminosas** – illuminated fountains, the work of engineer Carlos Buigas. At weekends (and on Thursdays as well in the summer) these perform an intricate aquatic ballet of colour and light, while blue searchlights radiate a peacock's tail of beams from the illuminated Palacio

Nacional for a total effect that took their breath away in 1929. For the schmaltzy musical accompaniment, come at 10 pm in the summer, or 9 pm in the winter.

From the fountains, a never-ending stair leads up to the Palacio Nacional, which houses the remarkable **Museu d'Art de Catalunya**, one of the world's foremost collections of medieval art, nicknamed 'The Prado of the Romanesque'. Many of the beautiful frescoes were rescued from decaying chapels in the remote Pyrenees including the three finest, all from the 12th century: *Santa María de Taüll*, *Sant Climent de Taüll*, and *Sant Joan de Boí*, with jugglers and graffiti of a medieval battle scene. There is an outstanding collection of *retablos* and sculpture, including the unusual *Majestat Battló* – a typical Catalan crucifix, where the Christ is portrayed, not in the exquisite agony favoured in the rest of Spain, but dressed like a king, open-eyed and serene, in a beautiful tunic adorned with richly coloured Islamic motifs. The Gothic is equally well represented, with the 13th-century murals of the Siege of Mallorca, fine works by the master Jaume Huget, and the lovely, refined *retablo, Verge dels Consellers* by Lluís Dalmau. There are also later works, like El Greco's SS Peter and Paul, and paintings by Velázquez, Ribera and Zurbarán. Sharing the palace, the **Ceramics Museum** displays a fine collection gathered from the major ceramic centres in the Crown of Aragon – Paterna, Teruel, Manises, Barcelona, as well as 13th-century Arabic–Catalan works from Mallorca (open 9 am–2 pm, except Monday).

Another relic of the 1929 fair is that tour-bus super-magnet, the **Poble Espanyol**, just west of the Palau Nacional. Conceived as an anthology of famous or characteristic architecture from all the regions of Spain, the replicas of the 'Spanish village' were cunningly arranged – though the Disneyland air hangs thick, especially in the overpriced souvenir stalls that occupy every other building. Within the village are two museums: **Artes e Industrias Populares**, with Spanish folklore and ethnographic exhibits, and the **Museo del Libro y de las Artes Graficas**, with books, printing presses, etc (all open daily 9 am–7 pm). Just beyond the Poble Espanyol, at the **Mirador del Llobregat** stands a fine statue by Josep Llimona of St George, looking weary from his exploits.

Around the Palau Nacional

Montjuïc's other attractions lie on the other side of the Palau Nacional. Just behind it are the new formal gardens of the **Palacete Albéniz**, named for the great Catalan composer and formerly the Exposition's Royal Pavilion, now used to lodge visiting VIPs. Further up, off the Avinguda de l'Estadi, is the 72,000-seat stadium from the fair, where the city had hoped to hold the '36 Olympics (but lost out to Berlin) and is currently remodelling for 1992.

This road continues to the **Fundació Miró**, the newest star in the city's cultural galaxy. Designed by the Catalan Josep Lluís Sert and completed in 1975, this pure white, highly acclaimed structure is a gift from Joan Miró and contains a small permanent collection of his works as well as sponsoring exhibits and cultural events of contemporary art (open daily 11 am–8 pm). Descending from here on the Passeig Santa Madrona, you soon run into a second contemporary building, the **Museu d'Etnologia**, with an intriguing collection from Morocco, Japan, Australia, Africa and especially Latin America – Amazonian shrunken heads with serious expressions, laughing, hot-pink skeleton dolls from Mexico, a Peruvian head deformer, and much more (open daily 9 am–8.30 pm, Monday 4–8.30 pm). Below this, take the right-hand stair down to the oldest gardens of Montjuïc, **La Roselada** with the Font del Gat ('cat fountain'), a popular Sunday rendezvous in the last century, then up another set of steps to the very lovely **Jardin Laribal** and down another flight to the **Jardin Amargós**, with its white columns and the **Theatre Grec**, built for the Exposition and used now for summer performances of drama and music.

Near here, in the 1929 Graphic Arts Palace is the **Museu Arqueológic** with an especially interesting collection from the Balearics – megalithic models and Carthiginian sculpture from Ibiza, finds from the colony of Empúries, founded by the Greeks on the Costa Brava in 550 BC, Iberian vases and Roman mosaics of chariot races (open 10 am–2 pm and 5–7 pm closed Monday).

Eastern Montjuïc

To the east, beyond the Fundació Miró, are the newly landscaped **Jardins Mossen Cinto Verdaguer** with a sculpture commemorating the *sardana*, and the neighbouring **Parc d'Atraccions**, with a fun ferris-wheel, roller-coaster, 'Crazy Rat', and the cable car up to the **Castle of Montjuïc**. The first real castle on this site was thrown up in 30 days during the Catalan Rebellion in 1640, when the defenders won a stirring victory over the Castilian forces of Philip IV in the Battle of Montjuïc. Since then the citadel has played a singularly unhappy role in Barcelona's history. In 1808, the French, disguised as allies, were admitted only to take over both fortress and city; in 1909 the Anarchist founder of Barcelona's secular Modern Schools, Francesc Ferrer, was executed here following the 'Tragic Week', which began as a general strike in Catalunya against Maura's call for a draft, and ended up as an orgy of church burnings. Ferrer's role in the affair was dubious, and his death caused a storm of protest throughout Europe. During the infamous La Canadiense Strike of 1919 – Spain's worst and bloodiest, that put the lights out in Barcelona, caused severe food shortages, and shut down 70 per cent of its industry – 3000 workers were imprisoned in the castle. In October 1940, the President of the Generalitat, Lluís Companys, was captured by the Gestapo in France and handed over to Franco, who had him secretly taken to the castle and shot; a stone marks the spot where he fell. In 1960 the military ceded the castle to the city, which has used it to install Frederic Marés' weapon collections, and an interesting series of models of Catalan castles (open daily 10 am–2 pm and 4–7 pm).

Below, near the aerial cable-car station on the Avinguda de Miramar, is **Miramar**, where you can enjoy an especially fine view over the city and port over a glass of beer. Next to the bar, and incongruously over the bustling city docks, are the superb **Jardins de Mossen Costa i Llobera**, one of the world's outstanding collections of succulents, including a towering cactus Manhattan and exotic specimens that look as if they have dropped in from another planet.

The Paral-lel

This wide boulevard below Montjuïc, cutting through the Plaça d'Espanya to the sea, has had a number of official names in its career, but has been known simply as the 'Paral-lel' ever since 1794, when it was discovered to lie exactly on the 41°44′ parallel –

fascinating to the Barcelonians, whose city otherwise refuses to square with the compass. During the first half of this century, the Paral-lel was known as 'the Montmartre of Barcelona' for its music halls and night clubs, several of which have survived as local institutions, like the Moalin Rouge of 1929, now called the Molino.

Between the Paral-lel and the south Ramblas region is the piquant **Barri Xinès** (Barrio Chino in Castilian), 'Chinatown' where locals and visitors gravitate to 'kick the gong around', as they say. For the most part it fails to live up to its notoriety – prostitutes, hustlers, and drug-dealers lurk about the bars at night, but the majority of its residents are newly arrived Andalucian immigrants trying to make a go of it. On summer nights the narrow streets are full of the mournful wail of *canto hondo* – the 'deep song' of Andalucía.

Between the Barri Xinès and the Plaça d'Espanya, just off the Paral-lel on Carrer de Sant Pau is the venerable Romanesque **Sant Pau del Camp**. Of the 12th century, but misused for many years as a barracks, the church has since been restored; the tiny cloister, with its paired columns and triple-lobed arches and garden is especially charming.

Parc Güell

'Toto,' (said Dorothy), 'I feel I'm not in Kansas anymore.'

The Wizard of Oz

It is a characteristic paradox of Spain for it to contain within its borders both our century's greatest monument to Death – Franco's Valle de los Caidos – and its greatest evocation of the infinite variety and magic of life – the Parc Güell. Here Gaudí was able to create a total environment without restrictions; when Eusebi Güell donated the land to the city for a planned garden suburb, it was with the stipulation that his favourite architect should have a free hand in its embellishment. Although only two houses of the development were ever built, the park Gaudí left Barcelona is a living testament to his inexhaustible imagination, a joyous wedding of form and colour with nature.

The Parc Güell is located on one of Barcelona's great balconies, the Montanya Pelada (to get there, take the Metro to Lesseps station, walk 0.4 km (0.3 mile) up the Travessera de Dalt, then turn left up the Carrer Labrand). After trudging through a typically dull *urbanización*, you suddenly come upon the park's entrance, flanked by two enchanted pavilions, crowned by sloping roofs of swirling coloured mosaic, cupolas, and Gaudí's signature steeple. The grand stair swoops past a brightly coloured dragon on its way to the Sala Hipóstila, better known as the **Hall of a Hundred Columns**, with pillars inspired by Karnak and a ceiling adorned with beautiful ceramic medallions by Jujol. The scalloped roof of the hall is lined with a brilliantly coloured ceramic collage (a concept invented by Gaudí), that also serves as the back of a fantastic serpentine bench on the terrace above. Great care went into the apparently disordered patterns of colour, creating new harmonies with each change of perspective. The several levels of the park are defined by porticoes, with unique columns made of stone found on the site, fitted together to form wonderfully sinuous passageways. No two columns are alike; one is a Caryatid à la Carmen Miranda, with rocks on her head instead of fruit salad.

Gaudí lived for some 20 years in one of the houses in the park, located near the park's second entrance at Carrer del Carmelo. Designed by his associate Francesc

Berenguer, it is now the **Gaudi Museum**, open Sundays and holidays from 10 am–2 pm and 4–7 pm.

Gràcia and Horta

Parc Güell lies between two formerly independent towns, Gràcia and Horta. **Gràcia**, bisected by the Travessera de Dalt and the Carrer Major de Gràcia, was throughout the 19th century a vortex for all liberal and progressive ideas: workers, anarchists, feminists, vegetarians, Protestants and ardent Republicans flourished here, formed societies and movements, and published an astounding number of periodicals (there was even one in Esperanto). The **Plaça Rius i Taulet** is the spiritual heart of Gràcia (to get there, take Carrer Goya off the Carrer Major) with its 30 m (100 ft) bell-tower adorned with symbols of the zodiac, invoked frequently as the town's symbol of liberty. Further up, near the Metro station Fontana, is Gaudí's first house, the **Casa Vicens** (1883), on Carrer de les Carolines 18–24. Islamic in inspiration, its façade is adorned with checkerboard patterns of *azulejos* and brickwork; the iron gate and fence of date-palm fronds is exceptionally attractive.

Horta, on the far side of the Parc Güell, nestled between the Muntanya Pelada and the Collserola, has maintained much of its 19th-century serenity. Among the old estates on the Passeig del Valle de Hebrón you'll find the **Parc del Laberint**, formerly the country house of the Marqúes de Alfarràs. In the late 18th century, the Italian architect Domenico Bagutti laid out the gardens, which include a lake, canals, an arbour and a great **labyrinth** of cypress, adorned with fountains and statues of mythological deities, all in the best neo-Classical tradition. To get there, take bus 26, 27 or 73 from the Plaça Catalunya.

Sarrià and Pedralbes

These fashionable former towns lie to the west of the Eixample and north of Diagonal. Barcelona's finest private schools are in Sarrià; one of them, the **Convent of Santa Teresa**, Carrer de Ganduxer 41, was built by Gaudí in 1890. Although constrained by finances and the need to build quickly and functionally he endowed the building with a distinctive rhythm of parobolic arches along the upper floor, and defined the corners with his favourite cross-crowned steeples. On the first floor are magically lit corridors of parabolic arches – a Modernista vision of the medieval cloister. The convent is open only during the school year on Saturday am, by appointment (Tel: 247 62 52).

Sarrià is also the Barcelonians' favourite neighbourhood to play the country squire, although no one's castle can better another Gaudí creation, **Torre Bellesguard**, at Carrer Bellesguard 46, built at the foot of the Collserola on the site of the summer residence of King Martin I. Gaudí restored the medieval walls and built a tall, neo-Gothic villa on the site (1900) – a farewell nod to the past, which Gaudí henceforth abandoned.

Pedralbes lies further out along the Diagonal, where, at no. 686, is the **Palace of Pedralbes** (bus 75 or 7, or Metro Palau Reial), given to the city by the Güells, used briefly by Alfonso XIII, and by Negrín as his headquarters during the last stages of the Civil War – from which, one imagines, he watched the city turn out, along the Diagonal in 1938 to bid farewell to the International Brigades. These days the palace houses a museum with tapestries, furniture, carriages, etc (open Tuesday–Friday 10 am–1 pm and 4–6 pm, weekends 10 am–2 pm). The park around the palace contains some fine ancient trees; on Passeig Manuel Girona nearby there is, all lost by itself, a **fence and gate by Gaudí** (1901), his first work without any historical reference. A more extensive work by the master may be seen on Avinguda de Pedralbes 7, near the intersection of Passeig Manuel Girona - the **Pabellones Finca Güell** (1887), originally built as a porter's lodge and stables for the Güell estate. Even on such utilitarian structures, Gaudí bestowed his minute attention to detail, in the texture of the walls, the diffusion of light through the arches of the stable and, most wonderfully, in the swirling iron dragon with sharp teeth that guards the gate. The old stable now lodges the Cátedra Gaudí, an organization dedicated to the study of his works.

At the head of the Avinguda de Pedralbes are the **Jardines Reina Elisenda**, commemorating the fourth wife of Jaume II, foundress of the glorious Gothic **Monestir de Pedralbes** in 1326. The monastery is unusual in that it was built very quickly and has scarcely been altered since, and as such is considered the epitome of 14th-century Catalan architecture, elegantly simple and based on geometric forms. The single-naved church contains some lovely choir-stalls, the alabaster tomb of Elisenda and stained glass by Mestre Gil, and in the **Capilla de Sant Miquel** murals by a pupil of Giotto, Ferrer Bassa (1343), located near the museum in the Sala Capitular (open Tuesday–Sunday 9 am–2 pm). If you're in Barcelona on the first or third Sunday of the month, come between the hours of 12 noon and 2 pm, when the nuns open their lovely, three-storeyed cloister to the public.

Tibidabo

For an incomparable view over Barcelona, ascend the highest peak of the Collserola, the 550 m (1789 ft) Tibidabo, just west of the city. Its name, peculiar even by Catalan standards, comes from the Gospel of St Matthew, who quotes the devil, 'Haec omnia tibi dabo si cadens adoraberis me' ('All this I will give to you if you fall down and worship me'). Purists might claim the incident really took place somewhere in the Sinai, but a Catalan would counter 'What's so tempting about a rocky desert?' Whereas the view from here, encompassing Barcelona, Monserrat, the Pyrenees and, on a clear day, Mallorca is a tempting offer indeed.

To get to Tibidabo, take the Metro to Av. de Tibidabo, and from there the Tranvia Azul (the little blue streetcar), which goes to the Peu del Funicular, and the Funicular railway to the summit (6.50 am–8.40 pm). The best time to go is in the late afternoon, as dusk falls and the lights begin to twinkle in the great city below. On the summit stands Enrique Sagnier's **Templo Expiatorio del Sagrado Corazón** in the neo-Mormon style – also restaurants, a hotel and an amusement park, offering one of the most panoramic ferris-wheel rides imaginable. Within the park there's the **Mechanical Doll Museum**, which is also fun, with grinning wooden fortune-tellers from bygone days (open Wednesday–Friday 12 noon–2 pm and 3–5.45 pm, weekends 12 noon–3 pm and 4–8.45 pm).

TOURIST INFORMATION

Gran Vía 658, Tel: 301 74 43 (Monday–Friday 9 am–1.30 pm and 4–7 pm).

Central Station-Sants, Tel: 250 25 94 (daily 7.30 am–10.30 pm).

Terminus Station, Tel: 319 27 91 (Monday–Saturday 9 am–9 pm).
Airport, Tel: 325 58 29 (Monday–Saturday 8 am–8 pm, Sunday 8 am–3 pm).
Columbus Monument, Tel: 302 52 34 (Tuesday–Sunday 9.30 am–1.30 pm and 4.30–8.30 pm).
Plaça Sant Jaume, Tel: 318 25 25 (Monday–Friday 9 am–9 pm; Saturday 9 am–2 pm).

Other addresses
American Express: 101 Psg. de Gràcia, Tel: 217 00 70 (weekdays 9.30 am–6 pm, Saturdays 10 am–12 noon).
Central Post Office: Plaça d'Antoni López (at the end of Vía Laietana), Tel: 318 38 31.
Central telephone office: 4 C. de Fontanella (just off Plaça Catalunya) open Monday–Saturday 9 am–1 pm and 5–9 pm, closed holidays. Another office is at Avda. de Roma 73–91 (open 24 hours).
Medical: Emergencies, call 310 50 50. Two hospitals are Clinico; Casanova 143, Tel: 233 80 00 and Santa Creu i Sant Pau; Avda. Sant Antoni Maria Claret 167, Tel: 236 41 20.
Police: Via Laietana 43, Tel: 301 6666.
English books may be found at the Librería Francesa, Psg. de Gràcia 91 and York House, Freixa 45.

WHERE TO STAY

Barcelona is well-endowed with hotels of every price range. On the whole those in the Barri Gòtic, in older buildings, are cheaper than those in the Eixample and beyond. The sentimental visitor will want to stay in the Ramblas, for centuries Barcelona's best hotel address. The choice hotels are now up around the Plaça Catalunya, but for colour and ambiance, you can't beat 'the world's most beautiful street'.

In the Barri Gòtic

Hotel Colón****, Av. Catedral 7, Tel: 301 14 04, is the one upmarket hotel in the quarter, ideally located in a historic building. There are some fine views of the cathedral, a garage, air-conditioning and other amenities; doubles 8340 pts. **Hotel Suizo*****, Plaça Angel 12, Tel: 315 41 11, is another good choice. Relatively small, with a carefully cultivated 19th-century ambiance, it has comfortable rooms and a beautiful bar. Doubles are 5850 pts. **Hotel Rialto***, C. Ferrán 40 y 42, Tel: 318 52 12, is exceptionally comfortable and near the Ramblas. Doubles 5850 pts, all with complete bath.

Hostal Levante*, Baixada de San Miguel 2, Tel: 317 95 65, is the pick of the cheapies: quiet, in the heart of the quarter, and pleasant, with very good views. Doubles, without bath, but hot shower in the hall are 1200 pts. **Hostal Layetana***, Plaça Ramón Berenguer el Gran 2, Tel: 319 20 12, is also fairly quiet and has a good view of the old city wall. Located in an attractive, 19th-century building, doubles are 1325 pts (without bath), but only 1100 pts from September to June. **Pensión Fernando**. C. Ferrán 31, Tel: 301 79 93 is friendly, has showers, and beds for 800 pts a person.

In the Ramblas

Hotel Orient***, Ramblas 45 y 47, Tel: 302 25 58 is on the Rambla dels Caputxins. In its structure it preserves one of the street's oldest buildings, the former monastery and cloister of the Colegio de San Bonaventura, built in 1670. The cloister now serves as the hotel ballroom. Doubles are 5400 pts. **Hostal Cuatro Naciones*****, Ramblas 40, Tel: 317 36 24, is nearby. The Cuatro Naciones opened its doors at the beginning of the 19th century and for the next 100 years was Barcelona's best hotel; it's not so bad nowadays, either, with bath, TV and individual air-conditioning; doubles in the summer are 4700 pts, 4000 pts otherwise. **Hostal Continental*****, Rambla de la Canaletas 136, Tel: 301 25 08, is at the upper end of the street, upstairs. Try and get a room with a balcony; all are quite nice and have private bath. Doubles are 3850 pts. **Hostal Ambos Mundos*****, Plaça Reial 10, Tel: 318 79 70, located just off the Ramblas in Barcelona's front parlour, offers good rooms, all with bath, and some with views of the square from 1900–2500 pts.

Hostal Roma**, Plaça Reial 11, Tel: 302 03 66, is next door to the above and simpler, but boasts one of the city's good cheap eateries as well. Doubles with bath 1600–1900 pts, with basin 1200 pts. **Hostal Tirol***, Rambla de las Flores 85, Tel: 318 15 38, is the best economy pick on the loveliest section of the Ramblas, with fairly good refurbished rooms. Doubles with bath 1600 pts, without bath 1200 pts.

Around the Plaça Catalunya and the Eixample

Ritz*****, Gran Vía 668, Tel: 318 52 00, is Barcelona's grand, elegant old hotel that lives up to its plush name. It also has plush, expense account prices, with its doubles going for 19,500 pts. **Avenida Palace*******, Gran Vía 605, Tel: 301 96 00, has as many stars in its constellation but is definitely more New World-elegant; it is one of the city's favourite hotels. Doubles here are 13,000 pts. **Hotel Gran Vía*****, Gran Vía 642, Tel: 318 19 00 is a charmer that has resisted the urge to remodel, preserving a touch of 19th-century grace from its courtyard to its lounge and the antique furnishings in the rooms. Doubles, all with bath, are from 4950 to 5300 pts.

Hostal Palacios**, Gran Vía 629bis, Tel: 301 37 92 is across the street from the tourist office and a good bargain, with pleasant doubles for 2100 pts, without bath 1600 pts. **Hostal Oliva***, Psg. de Gràcia 32, Tel: 317 50 87, has 16 large rooms, on the street that Gaudí made famous. Doubles go for 2250 pts.

Barcelona's Youth Hostel is on the Passeig Pujades 29, Tel: 300 31 04, near the main entrance of the Parc de la Ciutadella (Metro: Arc de Triomf). 700 pts a head, breakfast 100 pts, no card required.

EATING OUT

In Barcelona you can dine on the finest of Catalan cuisine or chow down on a genuine Mexican tortilla. The pastries and cakes are the best in Spain. Again, look for bargains around the Barri Gòtic.

Vía Veneto, on Ganduxer 10 y 12 (FGC Metro:La Bonanova) has won several gourmet prizes for its exquisite and innovative Catalan dishes. Highly recommended are the *pequeños calabacines en flor en salso de higado de oca* (tiny flowering zucchini in goose liver sauce). Prices vary widely depending on what you order: between 2000–4000 pts. **Eldorado Petit**, on Dolores Monserdá 51 in Sarrià (FGC Metro: Sarrià) is another prize-winning restaurant and generally considered one of the top ten in Spain. Located in a lovely turn-of-the-century building, it has an elegant bar and a menu that changes daily, according to market availability and the chef's refined muse. Full meals here are around 3500 pts. Closed Sundays. **Jaume de Provenca**, C. Provença (Metro: Hospital Clinic) offers Catalan cuisine at its most elaborate – a typical dish is fillet of turbot with saffroned lobster. Closed Sunday night, Mondays, and August (approximately 3000 pts). **Azulete**, Via Augusta 281 (FGC Metro: Bonanova) is Barcelona's most beautiful restaurant and has loyal adherents among the international set – and the King of Spain. The food is good, too – full meals are from 3000–4000 pts. Closed Sunday.

Can Solé, San Carlos 4 (Metro: Barceloneta) is one of the best and oldest seafood restaurants in that quarter of seafood restaurants, Barceloneta. Closed Sundays and Saturday night: full meals from 1300–2000 pts. **Los Caracoles**, Escudillers 14 (Metro: Drassanes). Walk up the Ramblas and turn right at the Plaça Teatre for Barcelona's best-known restaurant. Snails, chicken, and roast meats served outdoors in the summer. Very touristy but very good, around 1800 pts. **Casa Culleretes**, C. Quintana 5 (off C. Ferran, Metro: Liceu) is Barcelona's oldest restaurant, founded in 1786 and still preserving many of its original features, except for its once famous *azulejos* by Xavier Nogués. Still, it is wonderfully antique, and its roast chicken and *zarzuelas* delicious (1500–2000 pts). **Font del Gat**, Psg. Sta. Madrona, on Montjuïc (Metro: Plaça Espanya) serves solid Catalan cuisine in a bucolic setting, in La Roselada garden; the restaurant itself was designed by Puig i Cadafalch; meals between 1000–1500 pts. **L'Olivé**, Mutaner 171 (Metro: Hospital Clinic). Very good Catalan food emphasizing fish and fresh market ingredients; full meals around 1200 pts. **La Rueda**, Rosellón 266 (Metro: Psg. de Gràcia) is an excellent corner of Argentine cuisine, with excellent grilled meats (1200–1500 pts). **La Parrilla/Grill Room**, Escudillers 8 (Metro: Drassanes) is another institution on this lively street done up with a touch of Modernista in the decor. A four-course menu of good Spanish food: 1000 pts.

Kasbah, Víla Vilá 82 (Metro: Parel-lel) has French and Middle Eastern cusine at popular prices, for example: vegetable couscous for 500 pts and crepès suzettes 350 pts. **Peru**, Psg. Nacional 9 (Metro: Barceloneta) is on Barceloneta's main seafood drag and offers good cooking, big portions and low prices. Set menu for 800 pts. **Pizzeria-Restaurant Cantonata**, corner of Ribes and Ausias Marc (Metro: Arc de Triomf) is a popular neighbourhood eatery with flowers on the table and simple but filling food. Menu: 350 pts, pizzas 350–500 pts. **Casa José**, Plaça Sant Josep Oriol 10 (Metro: Liceu) is almost as famous as Los Caricoles for being the one place in town where it's cheaper to eat out than stay at home – a hard-core group of habitués dines there every day except Saturday, when it's closed. You may have to wait for a table, the waiters may be surly, but you can have a four-course dinner for 300 pts.

BARCELONA AT NIGHT

There is always something to do in Barcelona in the evening, from watching the illuminated fountains and taking in the Funfair at Montjuïc (if you've brought the kids) to a slumming excursion in the Barrí Xinès (if you've left them at home). In November Barcelona hosts an international jazz festival; in the summer the city puts on concerts, theatre and dance in its 'Grec' season at the open-air Teatre Grec and in the Plaça del

Rei. Pick up a copy of *Barcelona* magazine, a monthly with detailed listings of events and performances.

Opera and ballet are the staples at the **Teatre del Liceu**, while chamber music, choral groups (especially popular in Catalunya) and guest soloists are the main fare at the **Palau de la Música**, itself sponsoring an international music festival in October. A little more low-brow are the old-fashioned music hall reviews put on at **El Molino**, Barcelona's version of the Moulin Rouge at Vilá Vilá 93, with shows at 5.30 pm (500 pts) and 10.45 pm (1200 pts). Another institution on the scene, the **Bodega Bohemia** at Lancaster 2, is Catalonia's answer to New Orleans' Preservation Hall minus the jazz but with all your favourite tunes of yesteryear, sung by the stars of yesteryear; entrance and first drink, 500 pts. More up-to-date musical reviews, dancing and dining are the fare at the **Scala Barcelona** Plaça Sant Joan 47, with dinner shows beginning at 8.15 pm for 3600 pts; at 12.45 am drinks, dance and show for 1700 pts.

Live jazz is excellent at **Zeleste**, Platería 65 and also at **La Cova del Drac** on Tuset 30. The very popular **La Paloma**, Tigre 27, is a fun, campy place with a variety of live contemporary music. Flamenco tablos are usually good in Barcelona; with all of its Andalucian immigrants, it considers itself the one city in the north that really understands the 'art'. Good places to watch are **Los Tarantos**, at Plaça Real 17 (shows at 10 pm and midnight, entrance and first drink 1800 pts) and **El Patio Andaluz** at Aribáu 242, with a dinner show from 9 pm–3 am.

Discotheques in Barcelona are not cheap. Some popular ones include **Password** at Cta. de Esplugas 47, with art and photography expositions, two terraces and satellite TV; **Studio 54**, Paral-lel 54, does its crazy best to live up to its New York namesake; **Ebano**, Roger de Flor 114, dances to an African beat. **Don Chufo**, Diagonal 618 in the Edificio Beethovan is a bit more sedate, with a disco and late-night cabaret.

Good streets for bars and tapas are Aribau and Montcada. Barcelona's very popular xampanyerias, where you can sip Spanish champagne, **cava**, and munch on elegant titbits from bitter chocolate to raw oysters are worth an evening. Two that offer a large number of different labels are **La Xampanyeria**, Provença 236 and **La Cava del Palau**, near the Palau de la Música.

The renowned Fútbol Club Barcelona (Barça) plays in the 120,000-seat Camp Nou stadium on the Travesseria de les Corts. Under Terry Venables they dominate Spanish football and are always exciting to watch.

The **Gran Casino de Barcelona** is in Sant Pere de Ribes, near Sitges, open 6 pm to 5 am, with a restaurant and shows on Friday nights.

Finally, if you understand Spanish or are just curious, Barcelona's four big companies – the Lliure, Joglars, Comediants, and Centro Dramático de la Generalitat – offer some of the most innovative and exciting theatre in the Spanish language anywhere. Just make sure the performance you choose isn't in Catalan.

Around Barcelona

GETTING AROUND

Sant Cugat and Terrassa are easiest reached on FGC trains from the station under Barcelona's Plaça Catalunya; there are trains at least once an hour, and they take 30 minutes to Sant Cugat, and an hour to Terrassa.

From Barcelona, there's a daily Juliá bus to Montserrat (departures at 9 am, return 7 pm) leaving from Ronda Universitat 5 or, more thrillingly, on FGC trains from the station under the Plaça d'Espanya, with departures at 9.10 and 11.10 am, 3.10 and 5.10 pm – get off at the station Aeri de Montserrat, where you link up with the teleferico that ascends to the monastery (included in the 700 pts return ticket). Trains return to Barcelona at 1.20, 3.20, 5.20 and 7.40 pm.

Sant Cugat and Terrassa

On the other side of the scenic, pine-clad Collserola from Barcelona lies **Sant Cugat del Vallès** (the Roman *Castrum Octavianum*), built around the ancient **Abbey de Sant Cugat**, believed to have been founded either by Charlemagne or his son Louis the Pious. The church itself is as austere as Barcelona's Sant Pi, with its great rose window and tower, but it's the cloister that makes the trip worthwhile, a Romanesque masterpiece, with 144 carved capitals depicting scenes from the New and Old Testaments, carved at the end of the 12th century by the monk Arnal Gatell. Another Catalan masterpiece, the *Retablo of all the Saints* by Pere Serra (1395) is in the small museum in the Chapter house, portraying the Virgin and Child in the centre with an angelic sextet, surrounded by most of the saints on the calendar.

Terrassa, Catalunya's third-largest city and one of its major industrial centres, was, along with Sabadell, Spain's earliest textile manufacturer. Cloth was the mainstay of the Catalans' medieval trading empire, and early examples from Terrassa and the rest of the world are displayed in the **Museu Textil**, across from the **Cartuja de Vallparadís**. The Cartuja, originally a 12th-century castle, was converted to a Carthusian monastery in 1344. The city has restored it, planted a garden, and installed a municipal museum of art.

Across the torrent from the Cartuja is a rare and picturesque ensemble of three churches founded by the Visigoths, when Terrassa was the seat of the diocese of Egara. In the 6th century it was common for the various functions of an episcopal church to be divided between three separate buildings, now known as **San Pedro** (with an unusual 16th-century triple apse and 10th-century stone *retablo*), **Sant Miquel** (reconstructed in the 9th century, but incorporating Roman columns and capitals, as well as a sarcophagus used as a baptismal font – the Visigoths used this church as a baptistry as well), and the monumental **Santa María**, consecrated in 1112, but incorporating the Visigothic apse, has several excellent Gothic *retablos*, and 12th-century murals, most curiously one portraying the murder of St Thomas of Canterbury (1170) a few years after the fact.

Montserrat

Montserrat, the spiritual heart of Catalunya, the symbol of Catalan nationalism, and one of the world's most unusual mountains, lies 50 km (31.3 miles) from Barcelona, up the River Llobregat. Even before the 5th century, hermits were attracted by Montserrat's strange, mystical appearance – a jagged jumble of conical pinnacles, stalactites rising precipitously over deep gorges, domes and shallow terraces, so different from the surrounding countryside that it seemed as if heaven itself had placed it there as proof that all things are possible. In one of its caves, legend claims, St Peter hid an image of the Virgin carved by St Luke; in another, the good knight Parsifal discovered the Holy Grail – a legend utilized by Wagner for his opera.

Not long after the reconquest of the region, in 880, the dark-faced image of the Virgin (apparently hidden by someone, if not St Peter, before the advance of the Moors) was discovered on the mountain, and as is so often the case, it refused to budge beyond a certain spot. A chapel was immediately built on the site, and in 976 this was given to the Benedictines of Ripoll, who added the monastery. In the Middle Ages in Spain Montserrat was second only to Compostela as a pilgrimage shrine; for Spaniards a visit to the shrine was essential before any major undertaking. Ignacio Loyola kept a vigil before the altar, consecrating his sword to the Virgin and becoming her knight prior to founding the Jesuits in 1522. Independent and incredibly wealthy, Montserrat was especially favoured by the Emperor Charles, and his son Philip II rebuilt the church. During the Peninsular War, Catalan guerrillas fortified it as a base, and in reprisal the French looted and sacked the monastery (1811).

Montserrat

As the Catalan Renaixença gathered steam, Montserrat took on a new focus. Verdaguer, Gaudí and Pau Casals were all fervent devotees of the Virgin. Under Franco, Montserrat was the only church permitted to celebrate mass in Catalan, and thousands of couples ascended the mountain to be married in their own language. Even today Montserrat for Spaniards evokes the same image as Niagara Falls does for Americans as a traditional honeymoon destination; they go to receive the blessing of the **Moreneta** ('the little brown one') as the Virgin is affectionately called, before undertaking the adventure of marriage, and to ride up and down on the funiculars.

Spanish pilgrims and picnickers have since been joined by day-trippers from the Costa Brava and by mountaineers who look at Montserrat as a physical instead of a spiritual challenge. To get a real feel for the place, stay overnight, but be sure to bring a sweater or coat, as it can get quite cold on the mountain even in the summer.

The monastery and the church try to compete with their fantastic surroundings by sheer bulk. Only one side of the Gothic cloister remains intact, and Philip's basilica lost most of its sumptuous furnishings to the French in 1811 – though new gifts have managed to fill nearly every corner of the church. The image of the **Virgin of Montserrat** presides over the high altar, and her worshippers file up the stair behind the altar to pay their homage, especially on the big pilgrimage dates – 27 April (all-night vespers on the eve) and 8 September. The famous **boys' choir** of Montserrat, founded in the 13th century and still singing in the same style, performs a *virrolei* and *salve* daily at 1 and 6.45 pm, except during the month of July.

The **Museu de Montserrat** has two sections of gifts given to the monastery by the faithful. On the main square there's a mild selection of Old Masters (El Greco and Caravaggio the big names) and archaeological finds; and in other buildings, in front of the monastery, a collection of 19th-century painting, especially by Catalans of the Renaixença movement (open Tuesday–Saturday 10 am–1.30 pm and 4–7 pm).

Best of all, though, are the walks around the mountain, to its various caves and ruined hermitages. An easy walk, **Los Degotalls**, takes in a wonderful view of the Pyrenees. Funiculars ascend to the **Hermitage of Sant Joan** (every 20 minutes from 10 am to 7 pm), from where you can take a spectacular walk in just over an hour up to the **Hermitage of Sant Jeroni**, the loftiest hermitage – traditionally the one given to the youngest and spryest hermit. You can also get there by teleferico, this departing from the station 2.4 km (1.5 miles) below the monastery (every half hour from 11.30 am–2 pm and 2–5 pm). From the hermitage a short path rises to the highest peak in the range (1253 m: 4072 ft), offering a bird's eye view of the holy mountain itself, across to the Pyrenees, and over the sea to Mallorca when the weather's clear. Before leaving Montserrat, try a glass of the monks' *aromas de Montserrat* – a liquour distilled from the mountain's herbs.

TOURIST INFORMATION

Sant Cugat: Plaça de Barcelona 17, Tel: 674 09 50.

There's also an information booth at Montserrat, on the street leading up to the monastery.

WHERE TO STAY AND EAT

The monks at Montserrat operate two hotels: the **Abat Cisneros*****, the honeymooners' special, with very comfortable rooms, private baths, and doubles only for 4400 pts; and the **Hostal El Monastir****, open April to October, with simpler rooms, and doubles 2800 pts with bath, 1900 pts without. Both have the same telephone 835 02 01, and you'd do well to book ahead. There's also a campsite near the monastery, and a **youth hostel** below the Sant Jeroni teleferico base station, housed in a 10th-century monastery; rooms are 500 pts a person; for reservations call 835 00 35.

Food is mediocre and overpriced at Montserrat, so you may want to bring your own picnic or purchase the makings at the morning market in the monastery's square. Otherwise, the self-service is your best bet.

South to Sitges

GETTING AROUND

Sitges and Castelldefels are very well served by RENFE, with trains from Barcelona's Estació de Sants departing every half hour (it takes just under an hour to reach Sitges). Catalunya en Miniatura is easiest reached by car (just off Autopista A–2, exit 3) or you can take the FGC train from the Plaça Espanya to Sant Vicenç dels Horts and walk 1.6 km (1 mile).

WHAT TO SEE

Wedged between the Garraf massif and a lovely long crescent of sand, **Sitges** is Barcelona's favourite resort. The Modernistas who flocked here at the turn of the century helped make it fashionable, if they failed to turn it into an artist colony, they left their mark among the typical whitewashed houses along the narrow streets. Santiago Rusiñol also left his summerhouse, **Cau Ferrat** (Carrer Fonollar 25), where the Modernistas held their famous revels. Nowadays it's a museum, with two paintings by El Greco, some lovely ironwork, from as far back as the 13th century, and drawings and paintings by a number of turn-of-the-century artists. Adjacent, the **Museu Maricel**, adorned with Gothic windows and door, contains an eclectic collection of medieval to modern art, including a mural of World War I by Josep Maria Sert (both open Tuesday–Sunday 10 am–1.30 pm and 4.30–6.30 pm). Another museum, the **Museu Romantico** conjures up the elegance of the 19th century and its love of gadgets – not to be missed by music-box fans (on Carrer San Jose, same hours).

Sitges is no longer the exclusive summer retreat of the Barcelonians; half of Europe's yuppies, and new hotels to accommodate them, have changed for ever the scene (though the new buildings are fortunately located back from the old town). Yet Sitges retains two of its old traditions, an antique car rally to Barcelona is held on Carnival Sunday, and on Corpus Christi the streets of the old town are turned into stunning carpets of flowers. The new Sitges sponsors the international festivals of Theatre of the Vanguard and of 'Cine Fantástico y de Terror' in October and November; it also has two nude beaches just to the south, the first for straights and the second for gays. On the Greek island of Mykonos similar beaches are called 'Paradise' and 'Super Paradise' but here they're known as the **Playas del Muerto** – 'the beaches of the dead'.

If you'd prefer more beach than swank, **Castelldefels** has a good stretch of sand halfway between Barcelona and Sitges.

Also south of Barcelona, in little Torrelles de Llobregat, a lost fragment of roadside Americana known as **Catalunya en Miniatura** asks the visitor: Why go up and down the principality when you can see the best Catalunya can offer in the space of a few acres, from the perspective of a Gulliver? Here are scale-models of Montserrat, complete with its teleferico, a mini-Ramblas, an airport for Tom Thumb and endless photo opportunities on the order of 'the day we devoured the Sagrada Familia' (open daily 9 am–9 pm).

TOURIST INFORMATION

Sitges: Plaça d'Eduard Maristany, Tel: 894 12 30.

Castelldefels: Plaça Rosa dels Vent, Tel: 664 23 01.

WHERE TO STAY

Sitges isn't for the economy-minded, but if you arrive early in the day you may be able to scare up a room over a bar for around 1000 pts a person. The biggest hotel on the beach, **Terramar****** is well-located on the Psg. Maritimo, Tel: 894 00 50, comfortable and up-to-date, offering its guests tennis, golf, a nice pool and garden. Open May–October, doubles are from 5550–8550 pts. More atmospheric, consisting of three 19th-century villas linked together, is the **Hotel Romantic***, San Isidro 23, Tel: 894 06 43, open April–October. Centrally located, close to the beach, and a romantic garden adds to its charms. Doubles are as high as 3800 pts. with bath, as low as 2900 pts without.

EATING OUT

The best place to eat in Sitges is the long-established **Mare Nostrum**, at Psg. de Ribera 60, serving a wide variety of fish and crustaceans prepared in a wide variety of styles. It also has a good wine list and pretty seaside location (1600–2000 pts).

The Costa Brava

The Costa Brava ('Rugged Coast') officially begins at Blanes and winds its serpentine way up to the French border. The 72 km (45 miles) between Barcelona and Blanes have been dubbed the **Costa del Maresme**, which totally lacks the scenic grandeur of its famous neighbour, though it has some fine beaches, especially at **Arenys de Mar** and **Calella de la Costa**, both well-equipped with hotels. But the real holiday madness lies further north.

Those fortunate enough to have visited the Costa Brava 30 years ago invariably have fits when they contemplate what speculator-man has wrought on the 'Spanish Riviera'. For her part, Mother Nature was lavish, tipsy even, as she sculpted out one scenic cove after another beneath pine-crowned cliffs, tucking lovely sandy beaches among strange boulder formations and rocky wind sculptures, where 30 years ago fishermen parked their boats. At the turn of the century, the Costa Brava, especially around Figueras, was the centre of the world cork industry, and until the 1890s and the spread of the dire phylloxera, the wine to go under all those corks was abundantly produced; even today the abandoned terraces of the old vineyards are a common sight. Castles and ruined walls recall the days when the Spanish Marches were a major battleground.

The Costa Brava is within reasonable driving distance of most of Western Europe, which has fallen for it in a big way. To keep up with burgeoning demand, accelerated by scores of package holiday companies, hotels have been tossed up on the shore in a tidal wave of speculation that shows few signs of abating – but just try to get a room in season without a reservation. After the Costa del Sol, the Costa Brava is Spain's most visited, but all of its trade is shoehorned into a much briefer season (mid-June to mid-September). If you're just passing through in the summer, consider staying in Girona or

Figueras just off the coast, where accommodation is easier to find and bus connections to the beaches frequent.

Blanes to Pals

GETTING AROUND

Blanes is easiest reached by train from Barcelona's Estació de Francia. From Blanes, buses make the 8 km (5 mile) trip to Lloret; you can also take a SARFA bus direct to Lloret from Barcelona (Passeig de Colom 3, near the Post Office). Another SARFA bus from Barcelona passes through Tossá del Mar and the other coastal villages as far as Palafrugell. From Girona there are four buses a day from the bus station to Lloret and the coast; SARFA buses from Girona depart from the Plaça de Canalejas 4. The best way to reach the more remote beaches and villages is the 'Lancha Litoral', the sea bus that meanders up the coast from Lloret to Port Bou. It's slow, but it stops nearly everywhere and takes in some lovely scenery without the hassle of traffic or bus schedules.

WHAT TO SEE

Semi-industrial and an important fishing port, **Blanes**, where it all begins, has one of the coast's longest beaches and is especially popular with campers. It has a pretty botanical garden, **Mar i Murtra** on the way to its most picturesque cove, **Sant Francesc**. Most visitors, however, descend on **Lloret de Mar**, the jam-packed, half-looney fun-house of the Costa Brava, boasting an even longer beach and the coast's greatest concentration of hotels, all brimful of packaged people, most of whom come to drink something a mite stronger than 'Tea just like your Mum makes it' as one Lloret café proclaims – by now it must be Spain's most famous sign. It sums Lloret up beautifully.

13 km (8 miles) north of Lloret, **Tossá de Mar** is one of the prettiest towns on the Costa Brava. Its **Vila Vella** – a maze of alleys, stone and whitewashed houses, embraced by a 12th-century crenellated wall and towers – is a National Historical Monument. Besides the three village beaches, intimate pine and cork-shaded coves are within easy reach. The next town north, **Sant Feliú de Guixols**, once a major cork exporter, now prides itself on its pretty Passeig Maritimo and the 11th-century **Porta Ferrada**, a Mozarabic remnant of a long-vanished monastery. You can get a fine panorama of the nearby coast from the **Hermitage of Sant Elm**, and there's a good beach nearby at Sant Pol, 2.4 km (1.5 miles) distant. Inland, at Romanyà de la Selva, stands one of Catalunya's most impressive megaliths, the **Cova d'en Daina**.

Brash and modern, the **Platja d'Aro-S'Agaro** has little to recommend it beyond its fine beach. **Palamós** fares better in charm, with its fishing fleet and excellent sailing facilities; its Platja de la Fosca beach is safe for the smallest child. Further north, **Palafrugell** provides a good base for a number of beaches and lovely coves, as well as the fishing villages of **Calella de Palafrugell**, **Llafranc** and **Tamaríu**, the latter enveloped in fragrant pine-woods.

Palafrugell is also convenient for visiting **La Bisbal**, a medieval market town (on Friday these days) and ceramics centre. La Bisbal's Romanesque castle belonged to the Bishop of Girona, and it claims to have Catalunya's finest *sardana* dance band, the 'Cobla Principal'. A bevy of medieval hamlets surround La Bisbal. The oldest of these is **Ullastret**, former Iberian settlement and Greek colony, of which the Cyclopean walls remain well intact. A small museum in a 14th-century hermitage houses local artefacts. More recent walls, from the Middle Ages, completely surround nearby **Peratallada**.

Up on its hill, **Pals**, another attractive medieval ensemble (with a pine-shaded golf course) is near enough the sea to have its own beach, framed by a great tree-topped chunk of rock. Near here, Bagur (or Begur) is known for the intense azure blueness of its coves, especially **Aiguafreda** and **Aiguablava**.

TOURIST INFORMATION

Blanes, Psg. de Dintre, Tel: 33 03 48.
Lloret de Mar: Pl. de la Vila, Tel: 36 47 35.
Tossa de Mar: Cruce Cts. Lloret, Tel: 34 01 08.
San Feliú de Guixols, Pl. Espanya 1, Tel: 32 03 80.
Palamos: Psg. de Mar 8, Tel: 31 43 90.
Palafrugell: Avda. Josep Pla, 2. Tel: 30 02 20.

WHERE TO STAY

Not only does the Costa Brava have hundreds of hotels, but it has more camping sites per square foot than anywhere in Spain. Most of the hotels in the big resort towns are block booked by February, but if you come in May or September, you should have no trouble finding a room on a walk-in basis. Otherwise – reserve as early as possible.

Blanes has more inexpensive rooms than anywhere on the coast. The big modern **Par Blanes*****, on the Platja S'Abanell, Tel: 33 03 50, is a great family hotel, with a pool and playground for the children, tennis, a pool and a garden. Doubles are 6250 pts in the peak period, 4800 pts in May and September. A good budget choice in Blanes, **Hotel Rosa***, S. Pedro Martin 42, Tel: 33 04 80, has the same in more modest surroundings; open May to mid-October, doubles are 1500–2050 pts. In between, the **Hostal Patacano***, on the sea at Psg. del Mar 12, Tel: 33 00 02, has six pleasant doubles open all year round for 2500–3500 pts, as well as the best restaurant in Blanes, with meals based on seafood and fresh vegetables (1500–2000 pts).

In Lloret the star luxury hotel is the plush **Santa María****** on the Playa Santa Cristina, Tel: 36 49 04, adding a pool, pretty garden, tennis courts and a very good restaurant to its attractive seafront location. Open from April to October, doubles in high season soar to 12,000 pts, and sink to 7000 pts otherwise. Near the main beach, the **Residencia Reina Isabel*** (Venecia 11, Tel: 36 47 67) is rare in that it stays open all year and offers rooms with more character than most in Lloret for 2000 pts double with bath, 1700 pts without. Another good bet without a restaurant is down the street: **Roca y Mar**, Venecia 49, Tel: 36 50 13, open May–October, with doubles 2800 pts in peak season, 1400 pts otherwise, all with bath.

In Tossá del Mar the most charming place to stay is the **Diana****, on the seaside promenade (Plaça d'Espanya 10 y 12, Tel: 34 03 04), its 21 rooms in an old-fashioned villa with a pretty courtyard. Open May–September, doubles with bath range from 2000–3000 pts. In a more tranquil corner on the Passeig del Mar is the stone-built **Hotel Cap d'Or***, Tel: 34 00 81, with a fine sea view and doubles for 2480–2950 pts, all with bath, open May–September. To get into either of these, do reserve very early. Less well-known, but also offering more atmosphere than the typical Costa Brava hotel is **Sant Pere***, located on the edge of Tossá on the Crta. San Feliú, Tel: 34 03 71, with a garden and doubles with bath for 2000–2400 pts.

In Palafrugell, where prices tend to be lower, there are a couple of good choices: the **Hostal Costa Brava***, S. Sebastián 10, Tel: 30 05 58, open all year with a garden and friendly management; doubles with bath 2625 pts in peak season, 2100 pts otherwise, and the **Hostal Cypsele***, Ancha 30, Tel: 30 01 92, with eight rooms, all with bath (open all year), for 2500 pts.

Palafrugell's coves, Calella and Llanfranc and Tamaríu each have a handful of hotels. In Llanfranc, the **Hotel Llevante*****, Francesc de Blanes 5, Tel: 30 03 66, is open all year; small and smart, it has a very good restaurant and doubles for 5390 pts in season, 3800 pts otherwise. More reasonable, and with air-conditioned rooms, is the **Marinada***, Francesc de Blanes 42, Tel: 30 12 46, open April–September, doubles with bath 3000 pts.

Near Bagur, in Aiguablava, there's the modern and magnificently sited **Parador Nacional de la Costa Brava*****, Tel: 62 21 62, where guests – either of the hotel or just the bar – can enjoy one of the finest views on the entire coast. There's also a pool, and a charming beach just below; doubles from 6500–8500 pts (open all year). In Bagur itself, the **Hotel Bagur****, De Come y Ros 8, Tel: 62 22 07, is located in the centre of town in a pretty building, with comfortable doubles for 3200–4000 pts (open Arpil–September).

EATING OUT

Besides a wide selection of fish and chip shops in Lloret, there's good seafood at **El Trull** at Cala Canyelles, 2 km (1.3 miles) from Lloret, in a pretty garden setting (2000 pts). Those with large appetites in Lloret, can dress up and go to the casino, where on Friday and Saturday nights there's an all-you-can-eat buffet for 1500 pts.

For good seafood and *sopa de mero* (grouper), Tossá's **Bahía** on the Psg. del Mar is the place to go (1400–1800 pts). For live jazz in the summer, it's **La Tortuga**, a bar on San Raimundo de Penafort.

The **Hostal Cypsele** in Palafrugell has a good, Catalan restaurant (1000 pts). Also good in Palafrugell, and featuring that Catalan favourite, lobster with chicken, is the slightly more expensive **Reig**, on Torres Jonama 53.

The gourmet's choice in Aiguablava is **Sa Punta**, on the Platja de Pals, with a very imaginative kitchen, based on the specialities of the north Catalan region of Ampurdán, with exotic specialities like leg of lamb with stuffed plums, and a dazzling dessert cart (2200–2800 pts, closed Mondays).

Torroella de Montgri to Figueras

GETTING AROUND

All trains between Barcelona to France stop in Figueras, which is the centre of the bus network to the upper Costa Brava (though there are connections from Girona four times daily to Estartit and L'Escala); SARFA buses run five or six times a day from Figueras to Rasas and Cadaqués. Port Bou and Llança are easiest reached by trains to France. The seabus Lancha Litoral also serves the coast.

WHAT TO SEE

The coastal road veers inland from Pals to the castle-crowned **Torroella de Montgrí**, with its rambling lanes lined with medieval and Renaissance buildings. A major port in the Middle Ages, it now lies some 4.8 km (3 miles) inland. Its resort satellite, **L'Estarit** is a haven for underwater enthusiasts, who can check out the sea creatures around the tiny offshore **Medas islets**. Once more the road turns inland, by way of **Verges**, where on Holy Thursday night adults and children don skeleton costumes and cardboard skulls to perform the 'Dança de la Mort', their Hallowe'en caperings a memory of the Black Death of the 14th century.

La Escala, on the south shore of the Gulf of Roses, lies 2 km (1.3 miles) from **Empúries**, settled by the Greeks from Marseilles some time around 600 BC. It was an important Roman port, captured by Scipio in the second Punic War, and inhabited after that until the 9th century and the end of the Visigoths. Empúries can be visited daily from 10 am–2 pm and 3–7 pm, and is as pleasant to visit for the site as for the visible remains. Closest to shore stood the Greek colony, with its market (*agora*), streets, cisterns and temples. Further back, in the partially excavated Roman town, two grand villas have been discovered with fine mosaics; a small museum on the site explains how things used to be.

Roses, on the north end of the gulf, has nice long beaches and modern development spread along them. Far more intimate and scenic (and conscious of the fact) is **Cadaqúes**, refuge of artists and writers – Salvador Dalí's home is nearby Port Lligat. More than the other resorts on the Costa Brava, Cadaqués had preserved the atmosphere that began to attract people in the first place – primarily because it's tough to reach by public transport, and if you're driving there's no place to park. The jewel-like beaches of Cadaqués are also too small to hold a coachload of tourists very comfortably. Still, people come, especially in July and August for the International Painting and Music festivals.

Cadaqués lies at the tip of Cape Creus, where the Pyrenees meet the sea, and here, at this geographical crossroad, 9th-century Catalans founded one of their most important monasteries, **Sant Pere de Roda** over the ruins of a Temple dedicated to Venus Pirenaica, in an area thick with dolmens and menhirs – long a holy place. According to legend, when Rome was threatened by an invasion of infidels, Pope Boniface IV decided to send some of the Church's holiest relics, including the head of St Peter, out of the city for safe-keeping. The relics were brought to Cape Creus and hidden in a grotto on the Sierra de Roda. However, when the emissaries who undertook the task returned to Rome, the threat had passed, and they were sent back to retrieve the precious things – only to discover that the grotto had vanished. The monastery was constructed on the site, dedicated to St Peter. Today it is a fortress-like ruin and magically picturesque, and as a National Monument is slowly undergoing restoration. What remains dates from 1022, an early date that has led scholars to call it 'the cradle of the Romanesque'. The views from the monastery over the coast are stunning. To get there, walk up from **Llança**, which along with **El Port de la Selva** and **Port Bou** are clustered near the border of France, in a region called Alto (High) Ampurdán. One of the high things about it is the wind, the Tramontana, which rages through here, mainly in the winter – Port Bou has one of the more protected beaches if it kicks up while you're around.

Figueras

Figueras is the capital of Alto Ampurdán and transport hub for the northern Costa Brava, but is best known these days as the birthplace of Salvador Dalí (in 1904), most surreal of the Surrealists and surely the country's most flamboyant, inscrutable and funny characters; during the Civil War he wanted to go to Barcelona and run a Department for the Irrational Organization of Daily Life (only to be told thanks anyway, it already exists). From his revolutionary early works on canvas and film (notably *Un Chien Andalou*, on which he collaborated with Luis Buñuel, Spain's greatest film-maker), he went on to paint Christian kitsch, but in 1974 he created the wonderful **Dalí Museum** in his home town (on Pujada Castell, the road to the castle). Located in the former municipal theatre, this temple of Surrealism, or as Dalí himself proclaimed, 'the spiritual centre of Europe', is great fun. Nothing is sacred and all is delightfully absurd or grotesque. As its centrepiece there's the former stage with a set by Dalí, accompanied by a full orchestra of mannikins. The museum's catalogue, according to the artist, is intended to misinform. One of Spain's most visited museums, it is open Tuesday–Sunday 10.30 am–1 pm and 3.30–7 pm.

Next to the museum, Figueras, in the spirit of the ancient Greeks who called their terrible Furies the Eumenides ('the kind ones'), has erected a **monument to the wind Tramontana**, depicting a woman about to be blown away. The Pujada Castell continues up to **Sant Fernand Castle**, an 18th-century work of Fernando VII, awesome for its size—its star-shaped walls have a perimeter of 5 km (3.1 miles). During the Civil War it was the main transit centre of volunteers for the International Brigades. On 1 February 1939, the Republican Government, on the run from Barcelona, met here one last time before the bitter end.

TOURIST INFORMATION

Estartit: Rocamaura 29, Tel: 75 89 10.
L'Escala: Pl. Escoles 1, Tel: 77 06 03.
Rosas: Avda. Rodas, Tel: 25 73 31.
Cadaqués: Cotxe 2A, Tel: 25 83 15.
Figueras: Pl. del Sol, Tel: 50 31 55.

WHERE TO STAY

The northern part of the Costa Brava is slightly less developed. In Estartit, the **Panorama***, Av. de Grecia, Tel: 75 80 92, is a good place to bring the whole family without breaking the bank. It has a nice location on the beach, a pool and a garden. Doubles are 1680–3180 pts (open May–September). In La Escala, the **Nieves Mar*****, Psg. Marítimo 8, Tel: 77 03 00, open from February until November, offers tennis, children's activities, and a pool in modern surroundings; doubles go for 4550 pts. Near the Greek ruins, the **Hotel Ampurdán*** on Afueras (no number), Tel: 77 02 07, is isolated and tranquil and on the beach. Open April–October, doubles are 2360 pts with bath, 1720 pts without.

In Roses, there's the self-contained **Almadraba Park******, on the Playa de Almadraba, Tel: 25 65 50, the most chic and sleek on the upper coast (open end of April–October). An air-conditioned room, heated pool, sauna, tennis courts and plush rooms can all be yours for 4800–6500 pts a double. Less expensive and centrally located on the Platja Salata, is the contemporary **Mediterraneo****, Tel: 25 63 00, with typical, pleasant doubles for 2200–3100 pts (open May–mid October). It too has a swimming-pool and one for the children as well.

In Cadaqués there's the smallish **Llane Petit******, a modern and very comfortable hotel with a garden on the beach of the same name, Tel: 25 80 50, open April–September; its doubles range from 6000 pts down to 3500 pts (no restaurant, continental breakfast 275 pts). Older, the **Port Lligat*** has fine views over Cadaqués and Port Lligat, Tel: 25 81 62, open all year, with a children's playground and pool; its doubles are 2550–3350 pts. In the heart of Cadaqués an inexpensive alternative is the **Hostal Ubaldo****, Unión 13, Tel: 25 81 25, open June–September, with doubles for 2650 pts with bath, or 2100 pts without.

In Figueras the **Hotel Durán*****, in town on Lasanca 5, Tel: 50 12 50, has cosy pleasant rooms for 3630–4840 pts (open all year), and is the best place to stay if you'd like to be over one of the best and oldest restaurants in Catalunya. For something a bit more modest in Figueras, the **Hostal España**, La Juncquera 26, Tel: 50 08 69, is also open all year and has quite adequate doubles for 1930 pts with bath, 1735 pts without.

EATING OUT

Roses can lay claim to one of Spain's finest restaurants: **Hacienda El Bulli**, located on a promontory over the lovely Cala Montjoi, where you can moor your yacht while dining. El Bulli has created many of its own recipes, prepared by a perfectionist chef whose menu varies according to season. This famous mecca for gourmets is closed Monday and Tuesday afternoons, and from 15 January to 15 March (4500 pts).

Currently the most fashionable restaurant in Cadaqués is **La Galiota**, with good seafood and soufflés (1800 pts), and if it's packed, as it often is in the summer, try **Don Quijote**, 6 Av. Caridad Serinána just outside Cadaqués, with a nice atmosphere and set menu with typical Spanish dishes for 950 pts. In the evening, **L'Hostal** in the main square often has good music.

People drive in from miles around Figueras for one of the tables in the huge dining-room of the **Hotal Duran** for meals like *zarzuela con langosta* (fish stew with lobster) for very remarkable prices (full meals 1800–2200 pts). A bit more of a deal but equally renowned is the **Ampurdán** on Highway N–11, a mile north of Figueras, famed for its adaptations of regional specialities to the modern palate. Game dishes are a speciality, as are its mint salads and *taps de Cadaqués* – an incendiary rum cake. Prices for a full dinner are around 2500 pts.

Girona

Between the Costa Brava and the highest Pyrenees, the heart of the province of Girona is surprisingly untouristed, despite the hordes that descend on the Costa Brava and its ski resorts, bypassing its oasis of rolling green hills and occasional geological oddities. Yet it is tourism, more than anything, that has brought the province its new status as the wealthiest in all Spain.

Spread over a tumble of hills at the confluence of the Onyar and Ter Rivers, the capital **Girona** (ancient *Gerunda*) is one of Catalunya's most interesting and atmospheric towns. Its position has brought it a history tormented with sieges, most famously in 1809, when the city's inhabitants withstood a siege by 35,000 French troops for seven months, giving up only when their supplies were utterly exhausted. Few of its embattled walls remain, however; like so many cities in Spain Girona has burst its buttons in the last few decades.

GETTING AROUND

Girona's bus and train stations are side-by-side on the Plaça d'Espanya in the Eixample; all trains between France and Barcelona stop here. Girona's airport received domestic flights and international charters, but has no public transport linking it to the city itself. Banyoles, Olot and Besalú can be reached by bus (Tiesa Line) several times a day.

Girona Town

Fortunately, the **Old Town** has been lovingly neglected. Its dim, narrow streets and passages, its steep stairs, little plazas, archways, and solid stone buildings offer any number of elegant urban views. Across the Onyar from the old town is Girona's Eixample – a miniature version of Barcelona's, complete with a handful of minor modernista buildings. Cross between the two on the bridge called the **Pont de les Peixateries** for the much-photographed view of the houses built up directly over the river.

The main street of medieval Girona, the **Carrer de la Força** follows the Roman *via Augusta*, the road of conquest. Narrow and winding, it seems to have changed little since the day when Girona's famous Jewish quarter, **El Call**, was defined by its southernmost reaches, around the steep alleys of Sant Llorenç and Cúndaro. Like the *calls* of Barcelona and Tarragona, the quarter came under the direct authority and protection of the king, enjoying total autonomy from the municipal council, the **Jurats** – a situation designed to exacerbate tension, for the kings not only regarded the Jewish communities as a national resource and favoured them at the expense of others, but made use of these enclaves to meddle in city affairs. But before the decline into the 15th century, when the Jurats, egged on by a fanatical clergy and jealous debtors managed to isolate the *call* into a ghetto with only one entrance, Girona's Jews had founded an important school of Jewish mysticism, the *Cabalistas de Girona*, most notably under Moses Ben Nahman, or Nahmanides, born in Girona in 1194, who was influential in the diffusion of Cabalistic studies throughout Europe. The old school of the Cabala, **Isaac el Cec** is on Sant Llorenç, and just as the Muslims are building a new mosque in Granada, there are plans to refound the school.

Carrer de la Força continues past the **City Museum** (with changing exhibits on the subject of cities) to the lovely **Plaça de la Catedral**, framed by the 18th-century **Casa Pastors** (law courts) and the stately Gothic **Pia Almoina** along the grandiose monumental **stair** to the cathedral.

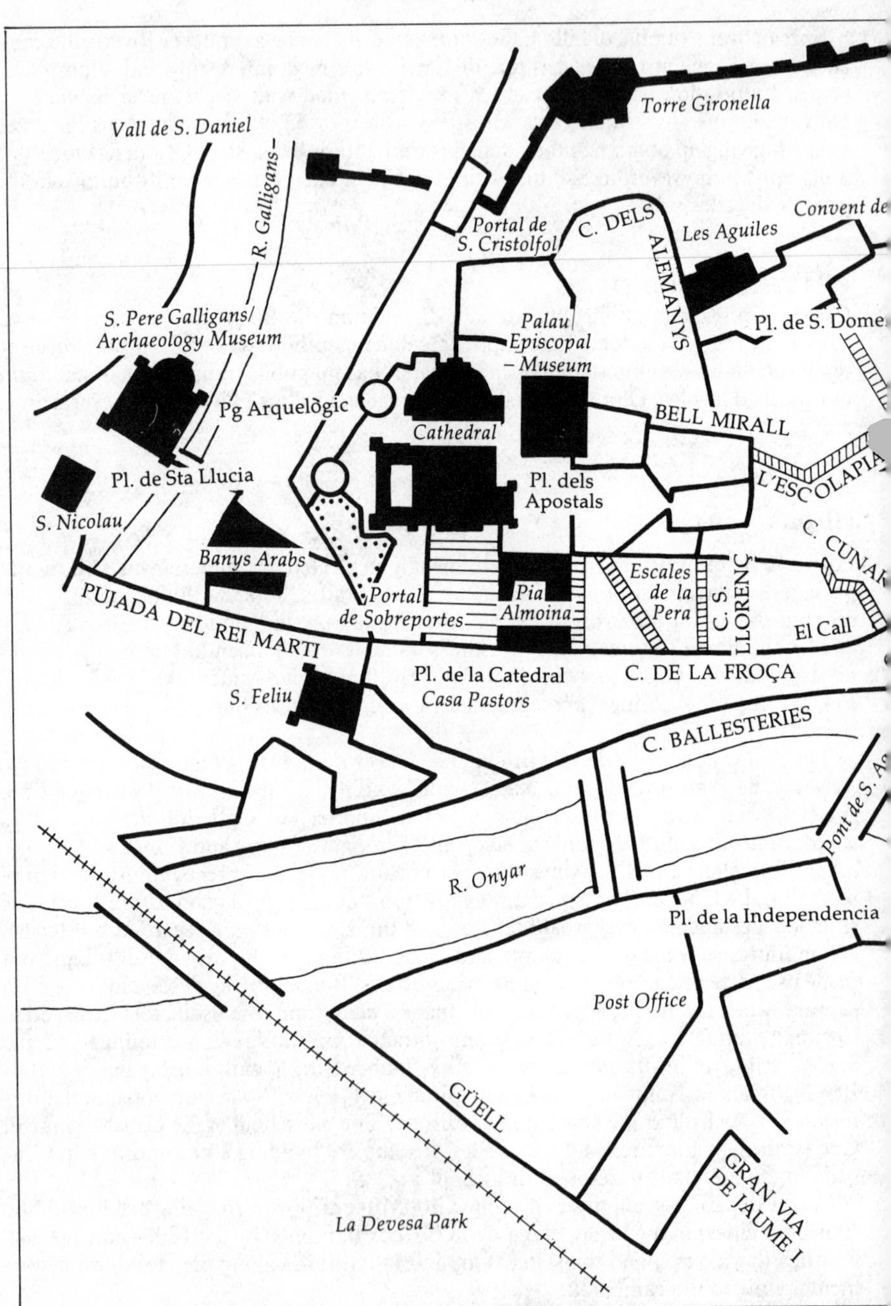
Torre Gironella
Vall de S. Daniel
R. Galligans
Portal de S. Cristolfol
C. DELS ALEMANYS
Les Aguiles
Convent de
S. Pere Galligans/ Archaeology Museum
Palau Episcopal – Museum
Pl. de S. Dome
Pg Arquelògic
Cathedral
BELL MIRALL
Pl. de Sta Llucia
Pl. dels Apostals
L'ESCOLAPIA
S. Nicolau
C. CUNA
Banys Arabs
Escales de la Pera
C. S. LLORENÇ
Portal de Sobreportes
Pia Almoina
PUJADA DEL REI MARTI
El Call
Pl. de la Catedral
Casa Pastors
C. DE LA FROÇA
S. Feliu
C. BALLESTERIES
Pont de S. A
R. Onyar
Pl. de la Independencia
Post Office
GÜELL
GRAN VIA DE JAUME I
La Devesa Park

City Walls
Domenç
C. JOSEP CALLELA
alau dels Aguillana
Pl. de Oli
Pl. de S. Josep
City History Museum
APATIERA
C. CIUTADANS
FERRERIES
VELLES
VOLTES D'EN ROSES
CORT
REIAL
ARGENTERIA
Tourist Office
Municipal Theatre
Pl. del Vi
Pont de les Peixateries
RAMBLA DE LA LLIBERTAT
Pont de Pedra
Pl. Catalunya
STA CLARA
N
GIRONA
C. NOU
C. S. FRANCESC
PL. DE L'HOSPITAL
to Telephones
to Train/Bus Station
0
km
½
0
miles
¼

The Cathedral

The Cathedral of Girona, one of the masterpieces of Catalunya, surpasses the grandeur of the stair with the widest single nave in all Christiandom – 22.5 m (73 ft) across. Originally it was planned as a typical three-aisled nave, when work began in the beginning of the 14th century, but 100 years later the master architect Guillem Bofill (ancestor of Ricardo Bofill, Catalunya's current architectural innovator) suggested an aesthetic and money-saving improvement – simply to add a single great nave to the already completed apse. His proposal was so radical that all the leading architects of Catalunya were summoned to a council to solicit their opinions as to whether or not such a cathedral would stand. The majority said no, but Girona let Bofill do it anyway.

Within the church there are a number of fine details, but it's the colossal Gothic vault, supported by its interior buttresses, that steals the show. The stained glass is recent, the heads of all the saints reduced to simple black ovals – a haunting effect. The *retablo* over the High Altar is a 14th-century masterpiece of silverwork, surmounted by an equally remarkable silver-plated canopy, or baldachin. A ticket will get you into a small but exceptional **museum**, featuring the unique *Tapestry of Creation*, an 11th-century view of Genesis, with the Creator surrounded by sea monsters, the four windbags, the seasons, and Eve popping out of Adam's side; the *Código del Beatus*, is a 974 illuminated commentary on the Apocalypse, with richly coloured miniatures in Mozarabic style. The ticket also admits you into the trapezoidal Romanesque **Cloister**, with exquisitely carved capitals – look for the giant rabbit menacing a man.

More medieval delights await in the **Art Museum**, next to the Cathedral in old Episcopal Palace. Among the exhibits there's a beam from 1200, carved with funny-faced monks lined up like a chorus line, a beautiful 15th-century catalogue of martyrs and a *Calvary* by Mestre Bartomeu (13th century), portraying a serenely smiling Christ with a face like Shiva, ready to dance off the Cross. Upstairs, there are rooms of 19th and 20th-century Catalan paintings (open 10 am–1 pm and 4.30–7 pm, closed Monday).

Portal de Sobreportas

Back down the ninety steps to the Plaça de Catedral, turn left and pass through the **Portal de Sobreportas** and its two round towers, and huge stones of their bases predating the Romans, with a niche hollowed out for the image of 'Our Lady of Good Death' invoked by the unfortunates led through the gate on their way to execution.

To the left stands Girona's most important temple, the 13th-century **Sant Feliú** at the head of its own flight of stairs. It has a curious spire, amputated by lightning, and is believed to have been built over an early Christian cemetery, where the city's patron saint Narcís suffered martyrdom (he is celebrated with a huge fireworks show at the end of October). Inside the church are two Roman and six Paleo-Christian sarcophagi with fine carvings.

Turning right after the Portal de Sobreportas, a door in a plain wall leads to the 13th-century **Banys Arabs** (Arab baths), a Romanesque version of the ancient Roman hammams, illuminated within by an elegant eight-sided oculus on white colums (open 10 am–1 pm and 4.30–7 pm).

Down the Pujada del Rei Marti and across the Galligans river, stand two attractive 12th-century works – tiny **Sant Nicolau** with its three apses, and the former **Monastery of Sant Pere Galligants**, now the **Archaeology Museum**, with an extensive collection of medieval Jewish headstones and a cloister that makes an interesting comparison with the cathedral's (open 10 am–1 pm and 4.30–7 pm, closed Monday).

From here the **Passeig Arqueológic** offers a garden-like stroll along the walls, with fine views over the pretty Vall de Sant Daniel from the ruins of the Roman **Torre Gironella**. Through the Portal de Sant Cristolfol you can make your way back to the cathedral or take Carrer dels Alemanys to the Plaça de Sant Domènec, with Girona's best-preserved ancient walls and all that remains of the city's old university, the Renaissance **Les Àguiles**, adorned with two eagles. Down the steps from this square is the beautiful **Palau dels Aguillana**, with its low arch spanning the junction of two stairs. From here, Carrer Ciutadans returns to the Plaça del Vi, with the tourist office and the 19th-century **Municipal Theatre**, where two Catalan gegants (giants) stand vigil in the courtyard, waiting for a holiday, when they're allowed to sally forth and menace the children.

Around Girona: Banyoles

No one thinks of lakes when they think of Spain, but there's a pretty one just north of Girona in the Garrotxa mountains called Banyoles, with a pleasant hamlet of the same name near its shore. Banyoles town has a 13th-century porticoed square, and a Neanderthal jawbone in its **Regional Archaeological Museum**, in the Gothic Pia Almoina. A few lodgings cater for carp fishermen and Spanish waterskiers, but they offer a serene alternative to the Costa Brava. On the other side of the lake, the tiny village of **Porqueres** has a gem of a Romanesque church, **Santa María** (1182), and prehistoric cave paintings in nearby **Serinyà** (ask in Girona about opening hours).

Olot

Between Banyoles and Olot there's an odd landscape pitted by 40 extinct volcanoes. The largest crater, **Santa Margarida**, is 350 m (1138 ft) across and lush with greenery, while another, **Sant Pau**, is barren and lunar. There are also a number of pretty woods in the region, like the beech grove near Santa Margarida, **La Fageda dén Jordà**, a great place for a picnic. The fine scenery inspired innumerable Catalan landscape painters, and Olot, on the River Fluviá, surrounded by its dead volcanoes, has been the centre of a small art colony since the founding of the School of Fine Arts in the 18th century. The **Museu d'Art Modern**, in the Park de la Ciutat, has many works done in the region. One of the more scenic villages around, **Castellfollit de la Roca** is just down the Fluvia, high atop a basalt escarpment.

Besalú

On down the Fluviá (and 14 km (8.8 miles) north of Banyoles) is one of Catalunya's purest medieval ensembles, Besalú. For one brief, shining hour, after its reconquest by Louis le Deboinair in 800, it ruled an independent county, eventually absorbed by the House of Barcelona in 1020. Today it is mainly visited for its 12th-century **fortified**

bridge, built at an unusual angle over the river, with a tower at the bend, and eight arches of irregular shape and size.

On the far side of the bridge, where the Jewish **call** once stood, a Romanesque **Mikwah** (a ritual lavaratory connected to a synagogue) was recently discovered and restored. It is the only one ever found in Spain, and one of only three in Europe. More good Catalan Romanesque can be seen in the **Plaça Major**, with its arcades, the old Cathedral (from 1018–20) of **Santa María**, a picturesque ruin at the end of Carrer Tallaferro, **Sant Vincenç** and the **Sant Pere Monastery**, with its lions and carved capitals, all from the 12th century.

TOURIST INFORMATION

Girona: Plaça del Vi 1, Tel: 20 20 79.

Olot: Mulleres, Plaça del Mercat, Tel: 26 01 41.

Besalú: Plaça de la Llibertat 1, Tel: 59 02 25.

WHERE TO STAY

In Girona the best choice is the **Hostal Bellmirall***, C. Bellmirall 3, Tel. 20 40 09, a pleasant little charmer in the old town, near the Cathedral, which has the best breakfast in Girona. Doubles with bath are 2300 pts, without bath 1900 pts (open all year). Also located in the old town and open all year round, the **Hostal Reyma****, Pujada Del Rei Marti 15, Tel: 20 02 28 is pleasant and tranquil; doubles here are 2500 pts with bath, 1800 pts without. If these are full, the best choice in the new part of town is the **Condal***, Joan Maragall 10, Tel: 20 44 62, not far from the train station, with comfortable modern doubles for 2300 pts, all with bath.

In Banyoles, the best place to stay near the lake is the **Hostal L'Ast***, Psg. Dalmáu 63–89, Tel: 57 04 14, open all year, with a pool and adequate restaurant; 3000 pts for double with bath, 2200 pts without. Less expensive, but also pleasant and near the lake, **Del Lago****, Psg. Mariano Vidal, Tel: 57 04 14, with a garden, children's nursery and playground; open June–September, doubles are 2250 pts with bath, 1500 pts without.

EATING OUT

Hearty Catalan specialities like *cannelonis* are the mainstay at **Cal Ros**, Cort Real 9 in the new part of Girona (1500 pts). Near the Cathedral, around the corner from the Bellmirall *hostal*, **Can Lluis** offers good pizzas for around 450 pts.

The Catalan Pyrenees

When the Bourbon Philip V ascended to the Spanish throne, his grandfather Louis XIV haughtily declared (according to Voltaire): 'Il n'y a plus de Pyrenées!' History, of course, proved him sadly deluded, though these great mountains have suffered of late a good deal of mental erosion as Spain takes its place as an equal partner in Europe. For the Catalans and Basques, who live on either side of the Pyrenees, the mountains have never been all that high, and when Madrid made things hot, it was customary to slip over the border to visit one's French cousin. Yet the difference between the French and

Spanish Pyrenees is striking. The former are rugged and often forbidding and even at the beginning of May can be a blinding whiteout of snow, while to the south green valleys bask in the sun. The mountains are gentler, more benign in Spain.

Spain divides its Pyrenees into three sectors: the Catalan, the Aragonese, and the Navarrese. Of the three, the Catalan Pyrenees have the easiest access and are the most visited, though innumerable tiny villages remain tucked away in the mountain folds on the banks of sparkling streams. Because of their near inaccessibility, smugglers as late as the 1920s were spiriting away the masterpieces of their tiny Romanesque chapels – a practice halted by their removal to Barcelona's Museum of Catalan Art. Some of Spain's best ski resorts are in Catalunya, as is the lovely national park, Aigües Torts.

En route to the Pyrenees: Vic and Cardona

GETTING AROUND

Vic, Ripoll, Ribes de Freser and Puigcerdà are linked by RENFE with Barcelona eight times a day. Cardona is easiest reached by train from Barcelona to Manresa and then bus; Sant Joan is connected by buses running between Olot and Ripoll.

The hour-long rack railway ride from Ribes to Núria runs five times daily, connecting with the train from Barcelona. Return fare: 1000 pts.

WHAT TO SEE

Vic, in the foothills of the Pyrenees, is an ancient town that served as the capital of the Ausetani Iberians and has been mildly important ever since; among its sights are the **cella** of a 2nd-century Roman temple, the picturesque **Plaça del Mercadal**, where markets have been held once a week since the 10th century, and a collection of Baroque houses and churches. In 1781 Vic saw fit to knock down its Romanesque cathedral and replace it with a neo-Classical pile, mainly interesting for its **golden murals** painted by Josep María Sert in 1930. Vic does preserve, however, a major collection of medieval art in the **Museu Episcopal**, north of the Cathedral on Plaça del Obispo Oliba, with beautiful works by Jaume Huget, Ferrer Bassa, Jaume Ferrer and Ramón de Mur and, most famously, the wonderfully stylized, wooden *Descent from the Cross* of Erill la Vall (open Tuesday–Sunday 10 am–2 pm and 5–7 pm). If you're driving, head out along the road to Manresa for the best view of the extraordinary mountain of Montserrat.

Cardona, to the west, is midway between Barcelona and Andorra. Spaniards know it as the Capital of Salt, for its nearby, unearthly **Salí**, a mountain of pure salt 80 m (260 ft) high and five km (3.1 miles) around the perimeter. On a hill high over the town itself is the attractive ensemble of a **medieval castle** of the powerful Dukes of Cardona (now a parador) and the Romanesque church of **Sant Vincenç**.

Ripoll and Sant Joan

One Romanesque masterpiece the smugglers couldn't cart off is in the Benedictine monastery in the otherwise dreary town of Ripoll, to the north of Vic. Founded by Count Wilifred the Hairy in 888, **Santa María de Ripoll** held a prominent position in early medieval Catalunya and was one of the great diffusers of Arab learning to the West, its vast library containing many translations of classical texts. When the Monastery at Montserrat was founded, it seemed natural to give it to Ripoll. The church was begun in the 12th century, suffered a devasting fire in 1835 and was rebuilt. Surviving intact, however, is the great **West Portal**, the most mature expression of Catalan Romanesque art, called 'the Stone Bible', for it encompasses nearly the whole Book, with the zodiac and some monsters thrown in. The north wing of the two storeyed **cloister** survived as well, with its elaborate capitals. Next to the monastery, in the 14th-century **Sant Pere**, the **Arxiu-Museu Folkloric** contains many of the firearms manufactured in Ripoll beginning in the 16th century, arms that were prized throughout Europe (open Tuesday–Sunday 9 am–1 pm and 3–7 pm).

Just east of Ripoll, **Sant Joan de les Abadesses** on the River Ter is a pleasant medieval town, named for the **collegiate church** also founded by Wilifred the Hairy, in 887, and likewise gloriously embellished in the 12th century. Aquitaine exerted a strong influence over Catalan builders, nowhere more so than on Sant Joan. In one of the chapels stands the church's most curious treasure, a wooden 15th-century Deposition nicknamed 'Las Brujas' – the witches – for the weirdness of its figures. More traditional is the lovely 14th-century alabaster **Retablo de Santa María la Blanca** and a fine Gothic cloister. Also in town, the dilapidated 12th-century **Sant Pol** is worth a look for its carved tympanum, and there's a pretty **bridge** over the trout-filled Ter dating from 1140 and recently restored.

Núria, Llívia and Puigcerdà

Up the River Freser from Ripoll is the small spa of **Ribes de Freser**, not much in itself, but the departure point for **Núria**, a lofty mountain valley and sanctuary (1270 m: 4128 ft), and like Montserrat a popular name given to Catalan girls. The journey up to Núria on a small, privately owned rack railway, built in 1931, is extraordinary. In the valley there are a number of lovely hikes to make in the summer, and pistes to ski down in the winter; the fine 11th-century cult image in the sanctuary, **La Mare de Deu de Núria**, has recently been proclaimed the official Patroness of Winter Sport!

The high plain to the west, **La Cerdanya**, was divided between Spain and France by the Treaty of the Pyrenees in 1659, bestowing on France all the villages of Upper Cerdanya – but not the towns. Hence the anomaly of **Llívia**, an islet of Spanish territory 3.2 km (2 miles) into France. Ancient *Julia Lybica*, a main town on the Roman highway *Strata Ceretana*, Llívia was the capital of La Cerdanya, but now is visited primarily for curiosity's sake (a neutral road links it to La Cerdanya's current capital, Puigcerdà) and to visit its **Pharmacy**, said to be the oldest in Europe – dating from 1420 – and now part of a museum. Nearly every town in Spain has a palatial pharmacy with fancy woodwork, painted ceilings and antique jars – and this is the mother of them all. The medicines are stored not in cabinets, but ornate shrines, veritable *retablos* of drugs.

Puigcerdà, opposite Llívia, is a typical frontier town except in the winter when the skiiers pile in; it's also the capital of Spanish ice hockey. There's a pretty lake with swans and paddle boats for hire, and the mildly interesting **Sant Domènec** from the 13th century.

Some 32 km (20 miles) south of Puigcerdà, on the upper end of the new **Tunnel of Cadi** (Spain's longest, opened in 1984) is the tiny town of **Bagá**, one of the cradles of Catalan nationalism. Near the centre stands a statue of the knight Calcerán de Pinós, who was rescued from a Moorish prison in Almería by the miraculous intervention of a silver Byzantine cross in the 14th-century church **San Esteban**, a cross reputedly brought over from the First Crusade. Catalans assert it was Calcerán's ancestor, Hug de Pinos, the baron of the region, who brought back the cross from Jerusalem and founded the Knights Templar. In the medieval walls there's the family coat-of-arms, with a pine cone (the *piña* of 'Pinos') and the Fleur de Lis, originally a Templar symbol.

TOURIST INFORMATION

Vic: Ciutat 1, Tel: 866 20 91.

Cardona: Plaça de la Fira 1, Tel: 869 10 00.

Ripoll: Plaça Abad Oliba, Tel: 70 11 09.

Sant Joan de les Abadesses: Comte Guifré i Beat Miró 8, Tel: 72 00 92.

Puigcerdà: Querol (baixos Ajuntament) Tel: 88 05 42.

WHERE TO STAY

14.4 km (9 miles) outside Vic, there's the **Parador Nacional de Vic******, Tel: 888 72 11, a charming idealization of a Catalan *masia*, or country-house, located in a pine-grove and overlooking a reservoir. Pool and tennis and a good restaurant – and doubles for 5500–6500 pts. More centrally located, **Hotel Colón***, Rambla Passeig 1, Tel: 886 02 20, has everyday doubles year round for 1850 pts with bath.

The **Parador Nacional Duques de Cardona******, Tel: 869 12 75 makes a stop in Cardona worthwhile. High over the town, it is part of the castle founded in 789 by Louis the Pious. The Romanesque courtyard and chapel are a museum, and the restaurant offers well-prepared Catalan specialities in a lovely setting. The rooms are furnished with Catalan antiques; doubles are 5500 pts.

In Ripoll the most pleasant place to stay is just outside town, on the Barcelona road: **Solana del Ter**, Tel: 70 10 62, a little resort unto itself with rooms, a campground, tennis court, pool and children's playground in a pleasant park-like setting (open all year round; doubles 2600–3300 pts).

There are three one-star *hostales* in Sant Joan, the nicest of which is **Ter**, Vista Alegre 1, Tel: 72 00 05, with the best location. Open all year, it also has a good restaurant: doubles (without bath) 1600 pts.

Up at Núria there are campsites and one *hostal*, the **Núria***, Tel: 73 03 26, with simple doubles for 2500–3000 pts (open all year).

In Puigcerdà there's a wide selection, including the **Chalet del Golf*****, on the Seu d'Urgell road just out of town, Tel: 88 09 63, a cosy little spot by garden and the links, doubles are 5200 pts. In town, **Hotel Del Lago****, Avda. Dr. Piguillen, Tel: 88 10 00, has pretty views of lake and mountains, and doubles with bath from 2800–3200 pts. There are also many inexpensive *hostales* by the train station and throughout town. Best of these is the **Hostal Sala***, C. Alfonso, Tel: 88 01 04, with pleasant rooms and good breakfasts and doubles for 2150 pts.

Llívia has one hotel, the **Llívia*****, Tel: 89 60 00, with a pool and tennis courts and very comfortable doubles for 2900–4100 pts.

EATING OUT

Solana del Ter has Ripoll's best restaurant, featuring Catalan cuisine (1200–1500 pts).

In Puigcerdà you can dine abundantly at the **Kennedy** on Carrer Espanya, with a filling set menu for 800 pts, though if you're driving, head up to the pretty Pyrenean village of Meranges and the best restaurant in La Cerdanya: **Can Borrel**, at C. Regresso 3 (closed Mondays, and from January to Semana Santa), with an imaginative menu of local specialities like rabbit with turnips for 1300 pts. Can Borrel also rent rooms: phone (Tel: 88 00 33) to see what's available.

Llívia's restaurant, **Can Ventura** on Plaça Major is worth working up an appetite for, if you walk over from Puigcerdà, featuring Cerdanya delights for 1500–2000 pts.

WHERE TO SKI

The six major ski installations west of Andorra are among Spain's most sophisticated and among the easiest to reach by public transport.

Vallter 2000, in Setcases near the French border, has 17 pistes, a slalom course, eight different lifts and night illumination on some of the pistes, Tel: 74 05 77. There are five *hostales* in Setcases and four in nearby Camprodron. **Núria**, has six pistes – a couple over 4 km (2.5 miles) long, and two teleskis. Besides the *hostal* at Núria (see above) there are many more down in Ribes, Tel: 73 03 26. **La Molina**, near the village of Plandas south of Puigcerdà, has 26 pistes (three very difficult), a 5 km (3.1 miles), cross-country course, five jump ramps, and 19 lifts. There are nine *hostales* (four- to one-star) on the site; Tel: 89 21 76. **Masella**, also south and accessible from Puigcerdà, in Alp, is one of Spain's best, with a wide variety of pistes – 89 altogether, and five hotels on the site; Tel: 89 01 06. **Rasos de Peguera**, Barcelona's favourite resort – 125 km (78 miles) from the big city – is further south, near Berga in Castellar del Riu-Montmajor. It has 14 pistes, two cross-country trails (5 and 10 km: 3.1 and 6.3 miles) and five lifts. There are nine hotels in Berga; Tel: 821 13 08. **Port del Comte** is at La Coma, near Coll de Nargo to the west, with 34 pistes in excellent condition (four very difficult), slalom, and four artificial slopes, two with grass for summer skiing. There are two hotels on the site; Tel: 811 09 50.

Andorra

West of Cerdanya, the little **Principat de les Valles de Andorra**, as it's officially known, is an independent historical oddity in the style of Grand Fenwick and the Marx Brothers' Fredonia, a little mountainous chunk of Catalunya that has managed to steer clear of the French and Spanish since its foundation by Charlemagne. Its name is apparently a legacy of the Moors, derived from the Arabic Al-gandûra – 'the wanton woman', though unfortunately the story behind the name has been forgotten.

Andorra has two 'co-princes', the President of France and the Bishop of Seu d'Urgell, and according to an agreement spelled out in 1278, in odd-numbered years the French co-prince is sent 1920 francs in tribute, while in even numbered years, the Spanish co-prince receives 900 pesetas, twelve chickens, six hams and twelve cheeses. Napoleon thought it was quaint and left it alone he said, as a living museum of feudalism.

Being Catalan, the Andorrans were always most adamant about preserving their local privileges, which they did through the **Consell de la Terra**, founded in 1419, and considered one of Europe's oldest continuous parliaments. The citizens also claim to be the only people in the world who have avoided warfare for 800 years (surely a claim for small is beautiful), though there was a close call in 1934, when a White Russian count proclaimed himself King Boris I of Andorra and declared war on the Bishop at Seu – a war the Bishop put an end to by sending four Guardia Civils, who escorted the king of two weeks to Barcelona and thence out of Spain.

Until the 1940s Andorra remained more-or-less unchanged, isolated from the world and relying on dairy-farming, tobacco-growing, printing stamps for collectors, and more than a little smuggling. This peaceful Ruritania began to change with the Spanish Civil War, with an influx of refugees and a new popular sport called alpine skiing. And then came the great revelation: why bother smuggling when you can get the consumer to come to you? For many Andorrans, it's simply been too much of a good thing; their traditional society, already swamped by emigrants (25,000 Spaniards and 3000 French and only 7500 native Andorrans) has now all but disappeared under a wave of 6 million visitors a year, most of whom are only passing through to purchase tax-free petrol, booze and smokes. Andorra has a nasty reputation as Europe's highest parking lot, so congested are the principality's roads in the summer. Enough wealth passes through its 462 sq. km (180 sq. miles) to give it Common Market status equivalent to Switzerland.

Outside the summer and peak ski seasons, however, Andorra slows down considerably; even in the summer a stout pair of walking shoes and a reasonable amount of energy can take you far away from the congestion, highrise hotels and discos to some breathtaking scenery, a storybook land of green meadows and azure lakes, waterfalls and minute hamlets with stone houses drying tobacco on their south walls, clustered below a Romanesque church, with the mountains towering overhead in all their grandeur, the silence broken only by the tinkling of cow bells.

GETTING TO AND AROUND

There's a small airport near Seu d'Urgell, 23 km (14.4 miles) from Andorra la Vella, especially used by ski charters. Weather, however, is unpredictable, and there are plans to initiate regular helicopter services between Barcelona, Andorra and Toulouse.

The nearest RENFE station is in Puigcerdà, which is linked by Alsina Graells bus to Seu d'Urgell; from there La Hispano-Andorrana bus goes to Andorra la Vella eight times a day. Alsina Graells also has two buses to Seu and Andorra twice a day from Barcelona (6 hours).

From France, the trip is more dramatic. The closest train station is Hospitalet-Près-l'Andorre on the Toulouse line, with connections from there by SFAT bus (7.35 am) and SALT bus (10 am in the summer). SFAT buses also go to Andorra from Ax-les-Thermes, and SALT buses all year round go from Toulouse to Andorra at 6.25 am. From Perpignan you can catch the Villefranche train at 7.58 am, which links up with the narrow gauge *Petit Train Jaune* ('the little yellow train') which passes through some awesome mountain scenery on its way to La-Tour-de-Carol, where a Pujol Huguet bus meets it at 1.35 pm to go to Andorra, through the **Port d'Envalira**, the highest pass in the Pyrenees.

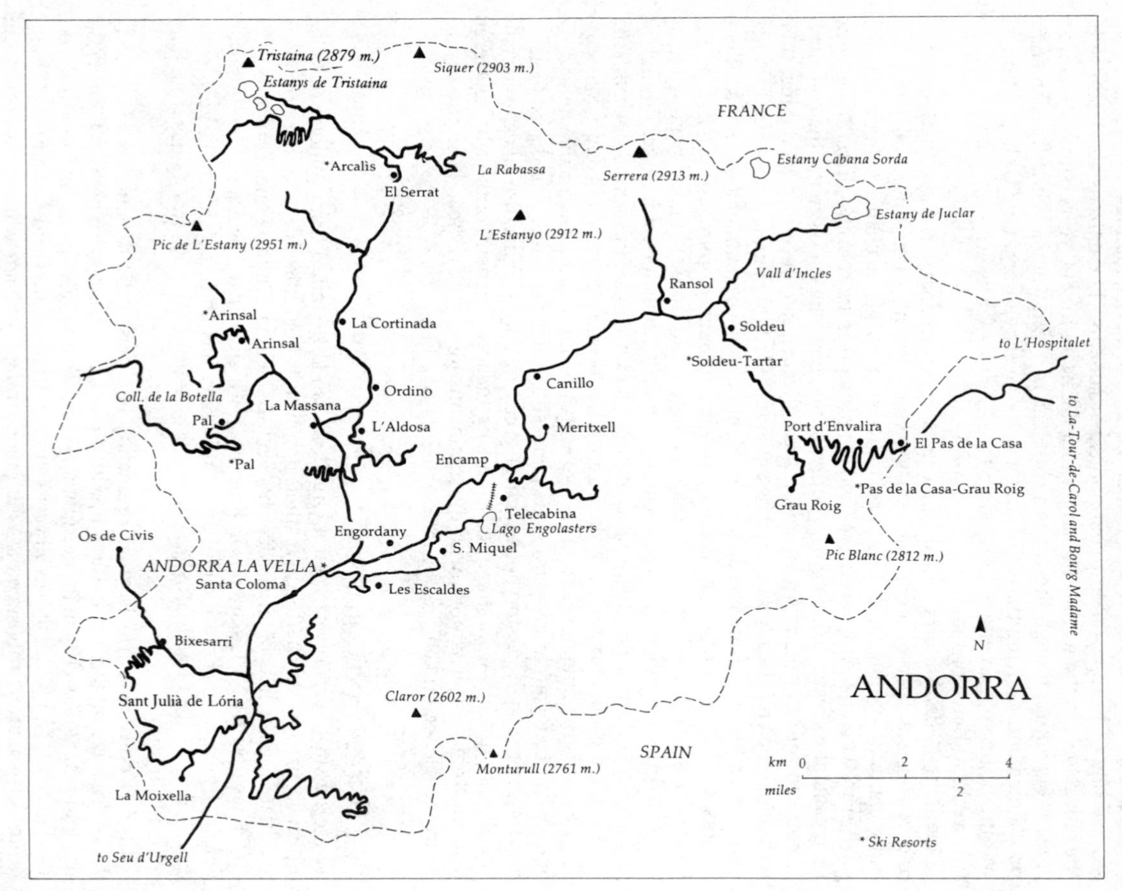
Tristaina (2879 m.)
Siquer (2903 m.)
Estanys de Tristaina
FRANCE
*Arcalis
La Rabassa
Serrera (2913 m.)
Estany Cabana Sorda
El Serrat
Estany de Juclar
Pic de L'Estany (2951 m.)
L'Estanyo (2912 m.)
Ransol
Vall d'Incles
*Arinsal
La Cortinada
Soldeu
Arinsal
to L'Hospitalet
*Soldeu-Tartar
Canillo
Coll. de la Botella
Ordino
La Massana
Pal
L'Aldosa
Meritxell
Port d'Envalira
El Pas de la Casa
*Pal
Encamp
to La-Tour-de-Carol and Bourg Madame
*Pas de la Casa-Grau Roig
Grau Roig
Telecabina
Lago Engolasters
Os de Civis
Engordany
S. Miquel
Pic Blanc (2812 m.)
ANDORRA LA VELLA*
Santa Coloma
Les Escaldes
N
Bixesarri
ANDORRA
Claror (2602 m.)
Sant Julià de Lória
SPAIN
Monturull (2761 m.)
km 0 2 4
miles 2
La Moixella
to Seu d'Urgell
* Ski Resorts

Andorra La Vella

Andorra La Vella ('Europe's Highest Capital') and the former villages of **Les Escaldes–Engordany** have melded into a vast arena of conspicuous consuming. Worth a visit, however, is the old stone **Casa de la Vall**, the seat of the Counsell de la Terra since 1580, and home of the famous **Cabinet of the Seven Keys**, containing Andorra's most precious documents, and only accessible when representatives from each of the country's seven parishes are present. A folklore museum is due to be installed on the top floor (10 am–1 pm when it's free, 3.30–6.30 pm with guide). Just south of Andorra la Vella it's a 40-minute walk to the principality's best known church, **Santa Coloma**, with a unique, round bell-tower and Visigothic arches, dating from the 11th century. A winding road from Escaldes (or ride on the tele-cabina from Encamp to the north) ascends to the isolated 11th-century **Chapel of Sant Miquel d'Engolasters**. Its frescoes, now in the museum in Barcelona, have been replaced by copies, and its three-storey campanile, as often in Andorra, totally dwarfs the church. Beyond the chapel lies a forest and the pretty **Lago d'Engolasters** ('lake swallow-stars') into which, an old tradition states, all the stars in the Universe will one day fall.

Exploring the hidden corners of old Andorra can be difficult if you're not up to hiking or have a car to zigzag up the narrow mountain roads. Buses ply the two main roads through Andorra every couple of hours towards El Serrat (C.G. 3), and more frequently towards Soldeu (C.G. 2). **La Cortinada**, en route to Soldeu, is a good tranquil base, with only one hotel, excellent scenery, and some of Andorra's oldest houses. In a 1967 restoration of its parish church, **Sant Martí**, some of the original Romanesque frescoes were uncovered. **El Serrat** is more touristy but worth a visit in the summer for the gorgeous panorama of snow-clad peaks from the **Abarstar de Arcalís** (via the ski resort). Another branch of the road from El Serrat leads to the three stunning mountain lakes of **Tristaina** in Andorra's north-west corner. There are plans to convert this region, Andorra's loveliest and least developed, into a national park.

Another destination reached by bus (on the Soldeu road) is **Meritxell**, its access road 1.6 km (1 mile) south of the village of Canillo. In Meritxell you'll find the national sanctuary of Andorra – an old Romanesque church standing in ruins since a devastating fire in 1972, and next to it, the new sanctuary inaugurated in 1976 by Ricardo Bofill. The Andorrans aren't sure about this hybrid of their traditional architecture with the modern. Inside there's a copy of the 11th-century Virgen de Meritxell that burned with the old church. **Sant Joan de Caselles** (12th century) according to many Andorra's finest church, is scenically located on a hillside 1.6 km (1 mile) north of Canillo, its interior adorned with a Gothic *retablo*, painted wooden ceiling, and Romanesque paintings; the bell-tower has fine mullioned windows in the Lombard style.

Seu d'Urgell

La Seu d'Urgell, 9 km (5.6 miles) south of Andorra and a good base for visiting the principality, is named for its cathedral (Seu), founded in the 8th century. The present two-towered structure was completed in 1184 and has a fine version of the Romanesque cloister, minus one side. The **Diocesian Museum**'s prize exhibit is a copy of Beatus de Liebbana's *Apocalypse*. The rest of Seu isn't much, though there's some lovely scenery to the south, through the **Garganta de Organyà**, a narrow, 615 m (2000 ft) walled gorge formed by the River Segre, now dammed up to form a long lake.

PRACTICAL INFORMATION

Although Catalan is the official language of Andorra, French and Spanish (especially the latter) are well understood. French francs and Spanish pesetas are the currencies, and prices are always given in both (though if you plan to make some big purchases, you'll get a better exchange rate in pesetas). Entrance formalities are a breeze; the traffic tie-ups occur when you leave, and the Spanish and French police bring out their fine-toothed combs to make sure you're not carrying more than 200 cigarettes, two litres of wine, and a litre of spirits. Note: if you're dialling an Andorran number from Spain, the prefix is 9738, from France, 16078.

TOURIST INFORMATION

In Andorra la Vella: Syndicat d'Initiative, Pl. del Poble, Tel: 202 14.

Andorra Delegation Tourist Office: 63 Westover Rd, London SW 18, Tel: 01–874 4806.

Seu d'Urgell: Psg. Brodieur, Tel: 35 09 91.

The Syndicat d'Initiative sells a map of Andorra's campsites and mountain refuges (*refugios* and *cabanas*). Two trails (*sentiers de grande randonnée*) pass through Andorra: GR 7 and GR 75. Several companies offer excursions in special mountain terrain vehicles to such beauty spots as Claror and Rabassa. A good one is Lito, Av. Meritxell, Tel: 20 000, in Andorra la Vella.

WHERE TO STAY

Andorra now has some 300 hotels, the vast majority of them spanking new. One of the most glamorous, the recently remodelled **Roc Blanc****** (Plaça Coprinceps 5, Escaldes, Tel: 214 86) has a five-storey atrium lobby and a glass elevator, sauna and a thermal spa with a number of treatment programmes offered, including two weeks of magneto therapy to realign your electrons (doubles, 6000 pts). The Roc Blanc's restaurant, **El Pi**, features a very good selection of French and Spanish dishes (2500 pts). Less expensive and centrally located in Escaldes is the **Hostal Marfany*** (Av. Carlemany 99, Tel. 259 57), long-established and comfortable, though only a few of the rooms have baths (doubles 2400 pts). For half that, try the **Pensío La Rosa** in Andorra la Vella (Antic C. Major, 16 bis, Tel: 218 10) with small but clean rooms without bath.

Outside the capital hub there are numerous alternatives, which are especially convenient for skiers. In La Cortinada, the simple **Hotel La Cortinada**, Tel: 351 51, is open all year and has a restaurant; doubles with bath are 1600 pts.

In Seu d'Urgell, in what's left of the town's old quarter, there the recently built **Parador Nacional Seu d'Urgell*****, C. S. Domingo, Tel: 35 20 00, with a heated pool, air-conditioned rooms, and modern, comfortable doubles for 5000 pts. All paradors are very good, but Seu's is topped by **El Castell******, just outside town on the road to Lleida, located in an old castle (Tel: 35 07 04). It also has a pool, air-conditioning, and TV in each room (doubles 5500–7000 pts) as well as Seu's best restaurant, the very elegant *D'En Jaume*, with specialities like lobster tails in puff pastry to simple grilled meat dishes; delicious home-made ice cream tops the dessert list (2600–3000 pts). A cheaper

Saint Miquel d'Engolasters, Andorra

alternative in Seu is the small **Hotel Andria***, Psg. Brundieu 24, Tel: 35 03 00, centrally located and offering comfortable rooms with bath for 2200–2800 pts, without bath 1825–2300 pts.

EATING OUT

The best restaurants in Andorra tend to be French. Best known for its Gallic dishes is the **Molí dels Fanals**, C. Dr. Vilanova in Andorra la Vella, located in an old mill with a garden terrace, with a menu for 2050 pts (closed in June and July). Roast boar and apple pie and traditional French food are also served up at **Versalles**, on Cap. del Carrer 1, in Andorra la Vella (2000 pts). The **Lleida**, Av. Meritxell 70, serves up an Andorran treat – trout – for 780 pts. Outside of the capital, **La Borda de l'Avi** on the Arinsal road, offers typical Andorran meals roasted in front of you on a wood fire (2400 pts).

WHERE TO SKI

Andorra has abundant snow from November to May, combined with clear, sunny skies – a skier's heaven. It has five major installations: **Pas de la Casa-Grau Roig**, just within the border from France, is the oldest (1952) and has 17 pistes, a slalom course, and several slopes for beginners as well as the advanced; 17 lifts, and 28 hotels; Tel: 318 16. **Ordino Arcalìs**, near El Serrat, is perhaps the most dramatically beautiful. Opened in 1984, it has seven pistes and four lifts, and four hotels in El Serrat, Tel: 261 36. **Soldeu-El Tarter**, near Canillo is the biggest complex, with 23 slopes (some especially for children), 16 lifts, 12 km (7.5 miles) cross-country course, 20 hotels and three self-catering apartment blocks; Tel: 511 51. **Pal**, near La Massana has 14 pistes and a slalom course in a splendid forest setting. Partially owned by the government, it is dedicated to preserving as much of the natural environment as possible. There are 11 lifts (two especially for the children's slopes), Tel: 362 36. There is one hotel in Pals, and a number of others along the main road nearby. **Arinsal**, next to the village of the same name, has 12 slopes, and 12 lifts. There are four hotels in Arinsal and many others nearby; Tel: 214 92.

West of Andorra

GETTING AROUND

The nearest RENFE station is in Pobla de Segur, linked four times daily with the provincial capital of Lleida. From Pobla there are two buses to the Vall d'Aran; on the whole it's best to take one of the several direct buses from Lleida to Espot and the Vall d'Aran. There is also a direct bus to the Vall d'Aran from Barcelona at 7.30 am from the main terminal (10 hours). Transport into the Vall de Boí is plagued with uncertainties; it's best if you can drive.

WHAT TO SEE

For beautiful mountain scenery without the tax-free merchandise, head west to the heart of the Pyrenees and the **Parque Nacional de Aigües Tortes y del Lago de San Mauricio**, created in 1955 and encompassing 230 sq km (90 sq. miles) of forests, meadows, lakes and jagged snow-capped peaks, including the pristine **Sierra dels Encantants** ('the enchanted mountains') and the lofty Comoloformo, at 3030 m (9848 ft) the highest mountain in the park. The loveliest spot is the Lake San Mauricio (Sant Maurici in Catalan), completely encircled by trees and mountains. There are several well-marked trails of varying difficulty – especially pretty and none too difficult is the hike from Espot to the refuge in the Encantants, with views over the lake. **Espot** with its hotels is the major gateway into the park; an information booth at the entrance has information on trails, compsites (permits required), refuges and half- and full-day jeep excursions into the park.

The **Vall de Boí**, west of the park, is lovely and secluded, dotted with remote villages whose 12th-century Romanesque churches provided the masterpieces in Barcelona's Museum of Catalan Art. Recently the exteriors of these churches and their square, tower-like campaniles with storeys of mullioned windows (a style believed to have been imported from Lombardy) have been restored: most notable are **Santa Eulalia** in **Erill-la-Vall** and **Sant Joan de Boí**, and the curious **Santa María de Taüll** with its leaning tower, and best of all **Santa Climent de Taüll**, with its six-storey bell-tower. The western entrance to Aigües Tortes park is through **Caldes de Boí**, the most developed village in the quiet valley; from here it's a lovely walk to the **Lago de Cavallers**.

The Vall d'Aran

North of the park and Vall de Boí, the western and eastern Pyreneean massifs join in a rugged embrace, enfolding the verdant 48 km (30 miles) long **Vall d'Arán** in isolated splendour. Almost inaccessible, it was first linked by road with the outside world in 1924. For most of its history it was in practice independent, like Andorra, until Napoleon annexed it to France; it became officially part of Spain a few years later. Some of the older inhabitants still speak *Aranés*, a dialect not of Catalan, but Gascon, which intrigues linguists. The valley's rubble houses are also unique, with their stepped gables, dormers, slate roofs, and carved wooden balconies. Many of them may be seen in the principal village of the valley, **Viella**, gathered in the shadow of its giant Romanesque-Gothic church and its octagonal tower. The inside is worth a look, especially for its 12th-century Christ that originally belonged to the once-mighty monastery of Mitg-Arán, of which only the **chapel** remains, across the River Garonne from Viella. A mysterious monolith nearby suggests the site has long been sacred. The Vall d'Aran contains a number of other charming villages and great opportunities for walks, especially around **Casau** and **Gausac**.

TOURIST INFORMATION

Viella: Sarriulera 9, Tel: 64 09 79.

WHERE TO STAY AND EAT

In Espot there are three modest *hostales*: the **Hostal Roya***, S. Mauricio 1, Tel: 62 60 22, is a good bet, open all year in a scenic location; doubles are 2500 pts with bath, 2200 pts without, and there's an adequate restaurant. In Boí, there's the **Hostal Beneria***, on the Plaça Trayo, Tel: 69 60 30, a pleasant enough lodging open all year, with doubles with bath for 2160 pts, and one of Boí's few restaurants (800–1100 pts) for simple but filling meals.

In Viella there's a fortress of a *parador*, the **Parador Nacional Valle de Arán*****, on the tunnel road, Tel: 64 01 00, prettily located on a mountain side in a dense forest. It has a pool and a good restaurant serving Aranese specialities; doubles are 7000 pts. In Arties, there's the more intimate **Parador Nacional Don Gaspar de Portola******, Tel: 64 08 01, located in one of the more charming corners of the Vall d'Arán and close to the skiing at Bequeira Beret. Doubles here are also 7000 pts. Also in Arties there's the very pleasant **Hostal Valarties****, Major 3, Tel: 64 09 00, especially cosy in the winter, with its fireplaces (doubles 2200–2700 pts with bath, 1800–2200 pts without). It also has a fine restaurant, **Casa Irene**, featuring dishes like duck with truffles for 2200 pts.

Other, less expensive accommodation in Viella includes the small **Delavall****, Bonaigua 40, Tel: 64 02 00, located near the centre of town; open all year, its doubles range from 2200–2700 pts, all with bath. The **Hostal Internacional****, Generalísimo 11, Tel. 64 00 14, is larger and more geared to skiers. Open all year and located near the heart of Viella, its plain but adequate doubles go for 2400–2700 pts with bath, 2000–2200 pts without.

EATING OUT

In the village of Escanyau, in the Vall d'Arán, you can try hearty Aranese dishes at the **Casa Turnay** in the Plaça Major. One of the valley's best restaurants, it unfortunately closes between May and July (1200–2000 pts).

WHERE TO SKI

Baqueira-Beret, just above Viella, is one of Spain's most brilliant installations, scenically located over the Vall d'Arán and boasting 41 pistes (three very difficult), 19 lifts, two slalom courses, and helicopter service to the peaks for new thrills. There are five hotels on the site; Tel: 64 50 25. **Tuca-Betran** is also easily accessible from Viella, offering a wide diversity of pistes (18 altogether, six very difficult), served by nine lifts. There is one four-star hotel at the station, Tel: 64 08 55. **Super Espot**, near Aigües Tortes National Park, offers 10 pistes (two very difficult), four lifts, and modest lodgings in the town of Espot: Tel: 63 50 70. **Sant Joan de L'Erm** is 20 km (12.5 miles) west of Seu d'Urgell at Montferrer Castellbo, and concentrates on cross-country (Nordic) skiing with some very pretty courses, Tel: 35 21 62.

Lleida

GETTING AROUND

Lleida, Bellpuig, and Cervera are linked by most trains between Barcelona and Madrid. Buses from the Pyrenees usually terminate in Lleida: the bus station (left luggage counter downstairs) is on the Avda. de Blondel. The RENFE station is on Avda. Francesca Macia and Rambla Ferran.

WHAT TO SEE

Lleida, or Lérida on Castilian maps, lies along the River Segre in the midst of Catalunya's most extensive plain, or *huerta*. Its Celtic founders called it *Illizurda*, and against the Carthaginians they fought perhaps the first of many battles that scar the city's history. During one war – the Spanish Succession – the defenders saw fit to convert the beautiful cathedral, now called the **Seo Vella**, into a barracks, leaving the town to build a new, far less imposing edifice in the town below.

The Seo Vella is mightily positioned, within the walls of the Moorish-built fortress, **La Zuda**, that still dominates the vast plain. Begun in 1203, the Seo was built under Templar influence and is considered a prime example of the Transitional (from Romanesque to Gothic) style. Major restoration work began in the 1940s: machine gun targets had to be removed from the nave, an upper floor of dormitories taken down from the aisles, and the ugly walls of the barracks' kitchen carefully disassembled to reveal a Gothic cloister of exceptional grace, its 12 arches woven with stone tracery like snowflakes; no two are alike. From the outer arches the view stretches for miles. Long-shorn of its religious regalia, the interior of the cathedral has the curious air of having just been built. Before and after photos in the side chapels give an idea of the task faced by the restorers. The Seo is open Tuesday–Saturday 10 am–2 pm and 3.30–6 pm, and on Sundays from 9 am–2 pm and 4–8 pm. The best of the three portals is the south, called dels Fillols, a 14th-century Flemish work. The colossal octagonal tower can be seen from all corners of the plain.

The rest of Lleida isn't much, though you may want to take a stroll down the Calle Mayor, where you'll find the dull new Cathedral and the fine old **Hospital de Santa María** (1512) right across the street and, just off the Calle Mayor, the 13th-century **Paheria**, or town hall, with a museum of archaeology and local history. Just to the south-west is the **Castel de Gardeny**, the seat of the first territory granted the Knights Templar in Spain (1149) and its Romanesque chapel of Santa María.

Lleida was the birthplace of Enrique Granados (1868–1916), composer of those delicate Spanish dances popularized by Alicia de Larrocha. Unfortunately it's the coarser spirit of Muzak that fills the streets of Lleida these days, pumped through outdoor speakers at every corner, but of course only during shopping hours.

Between Lleida and Barcelona

There are a couple of seldom visited sights along the main road and railway line. **Bellpuig**, some 48 km (30 miles) east of Lleida, contains in its parish church a marvellous Italian Renaissance marble, the **tomb of Ramón Folch de Cardona, Viceroy of Sicily** by Giovanni di Nola. Ramón's armoured effigy rests its head on a helmet, while the sarcophagus below is decorated with a robust pagan scene.

In the Middle Ages Lleida was famous for its university, but like Barcelona's it was closed by a vengeful Philip V, who combined the two institutions to create a third, Bourbon, university in between the two at **Cervera**. This lasted until 1841, when the university returned to Barcelona, leaving behind a monumental university ghost town, now partly used as a cultural centre. Besides the strange forlorn buildings, there are three churches worth a visit: **Santo Domingo** for its cloister, the Romanesque **Santa María** with fine Catalan artwork, and the mysterious round **San Pere le Gros** (1079), thought by some to have served as a funerary chapel/pilgrim initiatory temple.

In the environs of Cervera there are a number of medieval hamlets, like **Biosca**, **Olujas** and an hour's walk from Olujas, **Montfalcó Murrallat**, with a baker's dozen houses encompassed by a vast wall and a ruined Moorish castle.

TOURIST INFORMATION

Lleida: Arc del Pont, Tel: 27 20 85; and Avda. de Blondel 1.

Cervera: Psg. Balmes 4, Tel: 531359

Bellpuig: Homenaje à la Vejez 6.

WHERE TO STAY

Near the centre of Lleida there's the fairly large and pleasant **Hotel Ramón Berenguer** IV*, Plaça Ramón Berenguer IV, 3, Tel: 23 73 45; doubles with bath are 2600 pts, without 1900 pts. Near the bus station there's the adequate **Hotel Rexi***, Avda. Blondel 56, Tel: 22 21 48. The rooms are nothing special, but the showers are good and hot. A double with bath is 1450 pts, without bath 1300 pts. For something even cheaper, check out the *hostales* in the Plaça Sant Joan. There are a couple of cheap *fondas* in Cervera and the central **Hotel Conciller****, Psg. Balmes 2, Tel: 53 13 50, the local Ritz, with a good restaurant and doubles with bath for 4200 pts.

EATING OUT

Lleida is fortunate to enjoy one of Catalunya's best restaurants, the **Forn de Nastasi** on Salmerón 10, which offers an extensive four-part menu including very good seafood, charcoal grills, and house specialities (2300–2800 pts.) Also good and less expensive are **El Trullo**, P. Palma 23, featuring Catalan cooking and a delicious set menu for 1000 pts, and **La Huerta**, next to the market (just below the Seo Vella), specializing in provincial dishes and using local ingredients as much as possible (1500 pts).

Tarragona and the Costa Dorada

Tarragona

Tarragona is one of Spain's oldest cities and one of the best sited, crowning a 61.5 m (200 ft) hill like a great rampart overlooking the sea. The Iberians fortified it so well that many of the later Roman and medieval buildings rise from bases of their huge, rough-hewn blocks as if shedding an old skin. The Romans were quite fond of Tarraco, as they called it, and lavished on it the entire province of Tarraconensis, or Hispana Citerior. Over the years, they made it the most elegant city on the Iberian peninsula; the poets Martial and Pliny praised its superb climate, fertile fields and delicious wines. Augustus relaxed here after his 26 BC campaign in the north of Spain. By the 2nd century AD it had 30,000 inhabitants.

A much-discounted but much-believed legend has St Paul preaching in Tarragona, and the Visigoths made it one of Spain's leading bishoprics in the 5th century; St Hermenegild, a devotee of the Roman ritual, led the city in a revolt against the Arian heresies of his father King Leovigild and was martyred. During Moorish rule, Tarragona is said to have been almost entirely Jewish, to the extent that when it was retaken by Ramón Berenguer IV, the new cathedral was built by Jewish architects. After peaking in the 14th century, the city declined into a backwater.

Modern Tarragona has spread far beyond the walled enclosure on the hill; it owes its revival to the export of wine and the growing popularity of the Costa Dorada.

GETTING AROUND

Tarragona is frequently linked with Barcelona and Valencia by rail, as well as with Madrid, Zaragoza and Lleida, several times a day. The RENFE station is just below the Balcó del Mediteranéo, and there's a RENFE ticket office at Rambla Nova 40. Buses depart from the vicinity of the Plaça Ponent, near the Municipal Forum. For the Aqueduct, take the El Salvador bus (every 20 minutes from Prat de La Riba). Nearly any bus going up the coast will let you off at Tamarit Castle and beach.

Upper Tarragona

Like Barcelona, its main promenades are called the Ramblas – the old (*vélla*) and the New (*nova*). The **Rambla Nova** divides old (Upper Tarragona) from the new and begins at the **Balcó del Mediterráneo**, overlooking the sea and Tarragona's beautiful beach. Looking the other way is a statue of King Pedro III's great admiral-privateer Roger of Llauria: below the Balcó, in a garden setting, are the ruins of the **Roman Amphitheatre** and 6th-century Visigothic church, built to commemorate an early bishop martyred within.

Continuing up and around the Balcó, the **Plaça del Rei** and the **Praetorium** lie up to the left. Popularly called the Castle of Pilate (like Sevilla, Tarragona likes to claim Pontius Pilate) but really the one-time residence of Augustus and Hadrian, and later the Kings of Aragón, the Praetorium dates from the 1st century AD. The French destroyed a good part of it, but left the tower that has just (1986) been opened as the **Museu d'Historia de Tarragona**, devoted to the understanding of the city's evolution. On the lowest level you can wander through the tunnels that led directly to the circus (this now hidden by modern buildings), which served as prisons during the Civil War; on each succeeding floor you can learn about the Visigoths, Moors and the medieval city, and from the top of the tower enjoy a fine view over the old town. Although much of the museum consists of photographs, models and articles in Catalan (a synopsis in Castilian is available at the door), a beautiful 3rd-century AD Roman sarcophagus discovered off Tarragona's coast, a 10th-century *mihrab* from Córdoba, and medieval art merit a visit (open Tuesday–Saturday 10 am–2 pm and 4–7 pm, Sundays 10 am–2 pm).

Next to the Praetorium, the **Archaeology Museum** (same hours) has an especially fine array of Roman mosaics, including one devoted to seafood, a terracotta mask that looks like the Roman Kilroy, an erotic oil lamp and more.

What remains of Tarragona's **Jewish quarter** is near the museum, in the narrow arched lanes around the Plazuela Angels, where the synagogue once stood. Passing through this – one of the city's most picturesque corners – you'll find the Plaça del Forum and the remains of the north-east corner of the tremendous (200 by 300 m: 650 by 975 ft) Roman **Provincial Forum**. This square gives on to the lovely 14th-century arcaded **Carrer Merceria**; where this intersects with the Carrer Major, the city has restored the fine, 17th-century **Casa Consistorial** as a museum and information office.

The Cathedral

A stair from the Carrer Major ascends to Tarragona's most famous monument, the Cathedral, a masterpiece of the Transitional (Romanesque to Gothic), begun in the 12th century and completed in the 15th. The principal façade, shut in by the surrounding streets and lacking the pinnacles planned for it, presents a certain mastadonic aspect, compensated for by a magnificent rose window and fine 13th-century statues of saints, bishops and martyrs.

To enter, follow the signs around to the side entrance. More than the other great Catalan cathedrals, Tarragona has preserved its mystical gloom – which makes it difficult to see the magnificent marble *retablo* in the Capilla Mayor, a 15th-century work adorned with minute details (look for the spider and butterflies), a fine 16th-century organ, and the 14th-century **Chapel of Santa María de los Sastres** (of the tailors – a humble profession in the Middle Ages, but wealthy enough here to endow the Cathedral's finest chapel). Next to it, a door leads into the **Cloister**, its sculpture (12th century) alone worth a trip to Tarragona. The scenes over the door are especially lovely, and among the capitals – where monkish fancy was traditionally allowed to run free – those just to the right as you enter are quite brilliant. Best known is the one depicting two scenes from an old Spanish fable of the cat feigning death to outsmart the clever mice who have taken to hiding in the rafters. The jubilant mice descend to put kitty on a bier for the funeral, only to face an unpleasant, unexpected resurrection. The highlight of the **Museu Diocesano** off the cloister is a 15th-century tapestry of medieval life, *La Bon Vida* (all open Monday–Saturday 10 am–12 pm and 4–7 pm Sundays 4–7 pm).

To the Passeig Arquelògic

Returning down the Carrer Major, take a left turn on to the aristocratic Carrer Cavallers. At no. 14, the Gothic **Casa Castellarnau** has been restored and opened as a museum; like the seignorial palaces in Barcelona, the courtyard and stair are the most charming features. Near the end of Carrer Cavallers is the picturesque **Plaça del Pallol**, where Gothic buildings were built over more ruins of the Provincial Forum. In the walls by the square, the **Portal del Roser** is one of six megalithic gates; note the double axes and Iberian letters carved into the Cyclopean blocks (ancient mason's marks?). Just outside the Portal del Roser begins the **Passeig Arquelògic**, the other star attraction of Tarragona, where through a manicured garden you can get the best view of the walls – rugged Iberian blocks at their base, tidy Roman stone on top, surrounded by walls put up by the English during the War of the Spanish Succession. The best part of the Passeig is near the **Minerva Tower**, where a bronze statue of Augustus, donated by the Italians in 1936, looks on authoritatively. The walk is open Tuesday–Saturday 10 am–1 pm and 4–7 pm, Sundays 10 am–1 pm; entrance Vía de L'Imperi Roma.

Lower Tarragona

Near the Rambla Vella (at the end of Vía de L'Imperi Roma) the **Plaça de la Font** occupies much of the ancient circus; in the houses on surrounding streets big pieces of it are embedded in the walls. On the other side of the Rambla Nova (take Carrer Canyelles down to Lleida) are the columns and foundations of Tarraca's smaller, **Municipal Forum**, the porticoed courtyard where city business was transacted (open Tuesday–Saturday 10 am–1 pm and 4–7 pm, Sunday 10 am–1 pm). Further down, on the banks of the River Francoli (from the Rambla Nova take the Avinguda Ramon i Cajal) a huge **Roman-Paleo-Christian Necropolis** was unearthed during the building of a tobacco factory. Used from the 3rd to 5th centuries, it's the finest example ever found in Spain, producing a large number of funerary monuments, utensils and mosaics, from the pagan Romans to the Visigoths. A couple of interesting crypts remain *in situ*, while the best artefacts are in the adjacent **Paleo-Christian Museum**. Notable are the strange Lions' Sarcophagus, an ivory doll from the 4th century, and the mosaic of Optimus (open 10 am–1 pm and 4.30–8 pm, Sunday 10 am–2 pm).

Environs of Tarragona

The best Paleo-Christian monument, however, lies 7 km (4.4 miles) from town in the village of Constanti: the **Mausoleo Romano de Centcellas**, a substantial Roman villa converted in the 4th century to a Basilica dedicated to St Bartholomew. The basilica, which also appears to have served as a mortuary chapel, consists of two square buildings joined together, but circular within. In 1877 the cupola in one was discovered to be covered with beautiful mosaics, damaged since, of Old and New Testament scenes and a hunt. The stone benches in the apses were probably the scene of **Agape** feasts (open Tuesday–Saturday 10 am–1 pm and 3–6 pm, Sunday 10 am–1 pm).

Also north of Tarragona, just off the main road to Valls in the village of El Salvador, is the spectacular 123 m (400 ft) **Roman Aqueduct**, perhaps better known as the *Pont del Diablo*, 'the devil's bridge', that brought the city its water from the Gayà River. Second only to Segovia's, Tarragona's aqueduct, graceful and golden, enchants in its rural setting.

Up the coast along the ancient **Vía Augusta** (as it's still known) are three other Roman monuments. At 6 km (3.8 miles) stands the impressive 9.2 m (30 ft) **Torre de los Escipiones**, thought to be a funerary monument to two brothers, Generals Publius and Gnaeus Scipio killed fighting the Carthaginians in 212 BC; the figures in relief represent military dieties. At 8 km (5 miles) a monolith marks the centre of the Roman stone quarry, the **Cantara del Médol**; at 20 km (12.5 miles) the **Arco de Berá**, a triumphal arch, spans the ancient road, erected in the 2nd century AD.

Tarragona has one of the finest beaches of the Costa Dorada, the **Platja del Miracle**, and another good one that's usually less crowded at **La Rabassada**, 1.6 km (1 mile) to the north. Tarragona also has a lively fishermen's quarter, **El Serrallo**, a 20-minute walk down from the Rambla Nova and the place to go for good seafood and tapas.

TOURIST INFORMATION

Provincial Office, Carrer de Fortuny, Tel: 23 34 15.

Municipal: Carrer Mayor 39, Tel: 23 89 22. In the summer, there's also a booth in the Rambla Nova.

WHERE TO STAY

Tarragona's hotels fill up quickly in the summer, so book or start searching early in the day – or make a day-trip from Barcelona.

Hotel Imperial Tarraco****, Rambla Vella 2, Tel: 23 30 40, is Tarragona's finest hotel, pleasantly located in the old town, but offering such amenities as a pool and air-conditioning throughout. Open all year, doubles are 7500 pts, with a considerable off-season discount. **Hotel Astari*****, 97 Vía Augusta, Tel: 23 69 11, is near the sea, but open only from May to October. The style is typical resort – with a pool, tennis, garden and terraces, the balconied doubles 3800 pts in the summer, only 2500 pts in the spring or autumn. **Residencia España***, Rambla Nova 49, Tel: 23 27 12, has very nice modern rooms on Tarragona's favourite promenade. All rooms have baths; doubles from 2500–2900 pts.

A good place to look for the cheapest *fondas* and *hostales* is Plaça de la Font or Rambla Vella; if you want to be near the beach there are a few inexpensive choices like **El Callejón***, Vía Augusta 213, Tel: 23 63 80, open June–September, its bathless doubles from 1300–1600 pts. There's also a very pleasant youth hostel, **Sant Jordi**, in the new part of town on Marques de Gaud-El-Jelu, Tel: 21 01 95 (500 pts a person, card required).

EATING OUT

The area's most famous restaurant, **Sol Ric** is a 20-minute walk from the Rambla Nova, on Vía Augusta 227. Seafood is the speciality, from the simple to the elaborate – for something different, try a dish with *Romesco* sauce (a mixture of hazelnuts and

Priorat wine). Sol Ric has a great wine list and outdoor dining in a lovely garden in the summer. There's a set menu for 1600 pts.

In the Rambla Nova, **La Galeria** (No. 16) does very good seafood as well as Catalan dishes in an intimate atmosphere (2000 pts). For more variety – and lower prices – spend an evening in the bars in El Serallo: **La Suda** and **La Ancora** both make excellent seafood tapas.

Two good land-food haunts are just off the Rambla Nova: **Les Coques**, on C. Nueva del Patriarca, with Catalan specialities like rabbit à la Catalán for 800 pts; and the less expensive **Pizzeria Can Faune**, C. Girona 11, with a good curry (and other) pizzas for 395 pts, as well as omelettes, pasta, and a long dessert menu.

Tarragona Province

GETTING AROUND

The six trains a day between Lleida and Tarragona/Barcelona stop at Espluga de Francolí, Montblanc and Valls; another train, three times a day, goes to Falset and Mora la Nova (for Miravet, Gandesa and El Pinell), on the route between Tarragona and Zaragoza. The bus from Tarragona (departs at 12 noon from the Plaça Fomet) stops at Poblet and returns at 5 pm. Other destinations are served by provincial buses out of Tarragona; the tourist office has schedules.

WHAT TO SEE

Tarragona province encompasses three of Spain's greatest wine-growing areas: Tarragones, El Priorat, and Penedés. **Penedés** is famed for its white wines and *cavas* (Spanish champagnes); one town, **San Sandurí de Noya**, is the Jerez of cava, a town packed full of bodegas of the bubbly. Two of the town's largest, **Freixenet** and **Codorniu**, welcome visitors who just drop in. Codorniu is said to be the world's largest producer of sparkling wines with almost 16 km (10 miles) of underground cellars, some so old they're national monuments. Another town in the region, **Villafranca del Penedés**, is the home base of Spain's greatest winemaking family, the Torres, and has a wine Museum, the **Museu del Vi**, just one of six specialized museums in the complex on Plaça Jaume I, housed in a pretty 12th-century palace; others include art, geology, ornithology and archaeology (Villafranca is within walking distance of the Ibero-Roman–Medieval ruins of **Olèrdola**, with its great 2nd-century BC walls). The museums are open 10 am–2 pm and 4.30–7.30 pm, closed Monday). Notable churches in town include the Romanesque **Sant Joan** and the Gothic **Sant Francesc**, housing some fine medieval tombs and an excellent *retablo* by Lluís Borrassá.

El Priorat

El Priorat is red-wine country, producing some of the world's most potent vintages – up to 24° proof. These formidable vineyards were first cultivated by the monks at the Carthusian priory **Scala Dei**, in the heart of the region. Now a picturesque ruin in front of the looming Sierra de Montsany, Scala Dei was Spain's first Carthusian monastery, sounded by Alfonso of Aragón in 1162. It served as the architectural model for subsequent Iberian **Cartujas** and wielded considerable power into the 17th century. It never recovered after the dissolution of the monasteries in 1831 and has been gracefully falling apart ever since.

Falset, the modern capital of El Priorat, has, like so many of the region's villages, one of the world's loveliest bodegas, done in the Modernista style by a disciple of Gaudí, César Martinell (1888–1973). Martinell combined several of his master's dearest principles to create functional cathedrals of wine; Falset's **Bodega Cooperativa** dates from 1919. Other bodegas by Martinell may also be seen in **Rocafort de Queralt** (with an interior reminiscent of the Sagrada Familia), **Sarral**, **Barbara de la Conca** (which also has a good Templar castle), **Montblanc** (see below), and across the Ebro in **Gandesa** and the cliff-top **El Pinell** (Martinell's masterpiece, adorned with *azulejos* by the jovial Xavier Nogúes). Another Modernista, Pere Domènech, built the bodega in **Espluga de Francoli**.

Poblet

From medieval Espluga de Francoli, it's a lovely 40-minute walk to the famous Cistercian **Monastery of Santa María de Poblet**, founded by Berenguer IV in 1151 to commemorate the end of the Reconquista in Catalunya. Poblet was for centuries the principality's most powerful and privileged monastery. Montserrat was and still is Catalunya's spiritual heart, but Poblet and its regal abbots were more concerned with earthly power and politics. This is 'Catalunya's Escorial', final resting-place of many of the Kings of Aragón; it possessed seven baronies, thoroughly oppressed the peasantry and disgraced its women. In later years Poblet was openly dissipated and corrupt, and so despised that when the monks were suspected of harbouring Carlist sympathies in 1835, the local Catalans had the excuse they needed to revenge centuries of maltreatment. In their fury they wrenched apart the buildings, smashed its monuments, and fed its famous library to the flames.

The ruins of Poblet stood overgrown with wild flowers until the 1940s, when a band of Italian Cistercians reclaimed the monastery and set about its restoration. They offer guided tours of their splendid efforts. Within the castle-like walls you can see the huge **wine cellar**, a lovely, evocative **Cloister** in the late Romanesque style, the fine Gothic **Chapter House**, **Refectory** and **Kitchen**. In the great, cathedral-like church are the **tombs of the kings of Aragón**, wonderfully restored by sculptor-collector Frederic Marès; among those interred here are Alfonso I el Battallador (died 1134), Jaume I the Conqueror (died 1276) and his son Pedro III (died 1285). Equally impressive is the **Dormitory**, a great vaulted hall 87.1 m (283 ft) long. Poblet is open daily 10 am–1 pm and 3–6 pm.

Montblanc

Near Poblet and Espluga de Francoli, Montblanc is an enchanting medieval village with finely preserved 14th-century walls and a river spanned by a Gothic bridge. At the main gate a map points out the sites; the best are the Catalan Gothic parish church **Santa María**, with a Plateresque façade stuck on for effect and the Romanesque **Sant Miquel**; between the two stood Montblanc's Jewish quarter. Like the capital, Tarragona province had a majority Jewish and Morisco population in the early Middle Ages; in this region especially the Morisco farmers enjoyed considerable prestige and protection, having made the land bloom with a system of irrigation that Christians regarded as well-nigh magical, digging miles and miles of underground tunnels similar to the *foggaras* of the Sahara.

South on Montblanc's Carrer Major, just outside the town walls, stands the ruined **Convent of Sant Francesc**, with its large 14th-century church – until recently used as a winemaker's warehouse. Yet this monastery produced one of Catalunya's medieval geniuses, Ansèlm Turmeda (1352–1425), who as a young friar left his Order, moved to Tunis, and converted to Islam with the new name abd'Allah al-Turguman el Mayurqui- 'the Mallorcan', for like Catalunya's greatest mystic, Ramon Llull, Turmeda was a native of Mallorca, and like Llull was greatly attracted by the Islamic and Sufi thought that lingered in Spain with the Moriscos. Turmeda took Llull's 'heresies' a step further by actually converting, but his books commanded such respect (among them, *La Tuhfa* in Arabic, *The Dispute with an Ass* in Catalan, and a book of moral parables called *El Fransèlm*, long-used as a text in Catalan schools) that the Church refrained from condemning him, and instead tried very hard to earn propaganda points by luring him back to the fold. It failed, and abd'Allah al-Turguman died a good Muslim and was buried in a holy tomb just outside the Sekkajin Market in Tunis, where he is worshipped as a Sufi saint.

Prades

Between Poblet and Scala Dei is Prades, another fine, walled medieval town in the mountains. In the centre, in the pretty, arcaded **Plaça Major**, stands the unusual spherical **Fountain of Prades** (if it gives you feelings of déjà vu, you've seen a copy in Barcelona's Poble Espanyol). The source of the fountain is unknown, but it has never in known memory, run dry. **Siurana de Prades**, on the road to Cornudell, is even more romantic, with its Arab castle perched atop a cliff known as 'the Balcony of El Priorat,' ancient stone-built houses, and a primitive Romanesque chapel down by the river gorge. The castle was the Moors last stand in Catalunya, holding out until 1153.

A third important monastery in the province is nearby: **Santes Creus**, anciently walled and of elegant proportions, like Poblet founded by Ramón Berenguer IV in 1158, wasted in 1835, and since carefully restored. Particularly lovely is the **church**, completed in 1221 and containing the tombs of all the notables not buried in Poblet, including Pedro III (died 1285), Roger of Llauria, conqueror of Sicily, Jaume II and his wife Blanche d'Anjou; Ramón Berenguer IV is buried in the choir. As usual, the Cloister and Chapter house (both Gothic) are especially fine; the former resembles Poblet's with its mossy, hexagonal fountain. Concerts are performed in the monastery in July and August. The village of Santes Creus also has another of Martinell's bodegas.

Valls

Valls is famous through Catalunya for the daring and skill of its *castellers* (human towers), and its club, the Xiquets de Valls, is so good that the town erected a monument, depicting them in the act. A good time to see the real thing is at the city's midsummer festival in June or at the Firagost (the first part of August, when local farmers offer their best produce and flowers to Mother Earth). The most interesting streets in Valls belong to its **Call**, the Jewish quarter, still reached via its medieval arch and still well preserved; also worth a look are the Gothic **Sant Joan Baptista** and the **Chapel des Roser**, with a 17th-century portrayal of the Battle of Lepanto in *azulejos*.

In **Seguita** (between Valls and Tarragona) Gaudí's colleague Jujols designed a fine little Modernista church called **Vistabella**, its skyline spiked with rough stone.

Miravet

Across the Ebro from Mora la Nova stands Miravet, one of Spain's most remarkable Templar castles, given to the Order by Ramón Berenguer IV. One of their tasks was to safeguard the region's Moriscos, who enjoyed nearly total religious and economic freedom in return for their rent. The castle is located on a 308 m (1000 ft) precipice over the river, and may be reached from the village below on a narrow path from the Carrer Blanc; within its deathly silence you can explore the Templar's Romanesque chapel, with a spiral stair to the tower, the dormitory and refectory, and large vaulted rooms believed to have served as bodegas and granaries – though no one has ever found a trace of a chimney or kitchen. The upper patio is called the Patio de la Sang ('of the blood') – here the last Templars of Miravet were beheaded after resisting the order to disband and subsequent siege in 1308. There are wonderful views over the Ebro and the village below.

TOURIST INFORMATION

L'Espluga de Francolí: Torres Jordi 16, Tel: 87 04 56.
Montblanc: Placa Ajuntament 1, Tel: 86 00 09.
Villafranca del Penedés, Cort 14, Tel: 892 03 58.
Valls: Plaça del Blat 1, Tel: 60 10 43.

WHERE TO STAY AND EAT

Most visitors to this area base themselves in Tarragona, but if you'd like a tranquil night or two away from the coast one of the more pleasant places to stay is Montblanc. If you're driving, there's the scenic **Hotel Coll de Lilla****, Ctra. Nacional 240, Tel: 86 0907, on the road to L'Illa; its twelve pretty rooms are air-conditioned, with TV and bath; open all year, doubles are 5000 pts. It also has a good restaurant, specializing in game dishes and from December–March, *Calçatada* (grilled shalots and lamb, 1600 pts). Also in Montblanc centre, there's the amiable **Hostal dels Angels*** on the Pl. Angels, Tel: 86 01 73, with doubles for 1000 pts, without bath, and the grander **Hostal Ducal***, Disputacion 11, Tel: 86 00 25, with cosy doubles with bath for 2350 pts.

There's also a handful of *hostales* in Espluga, with **Del Senglar**, Pl. Montserrat Canals, Tel: 87 01 21, the pick, in the centre of the village, open all year, with a garden and decent restaurant. Doubles with bath are from 3700–3200 pts. Another pretty place to stay, near the monastery of Santes Creus, is the **Hostal Grau***, San Pedro III 3, Tel: 60 24 58; doubles are 2400 pts with bath, 1400 pts without.

EATING OUT

A good place to eat in Montblanc is the **Fonda Colom**, Crta. de Civadeira 5, with Catalan cuisine for 1200–1600 pts.

The Costa Dorada

Spain's 'Golden Coast' stretches from Barcelona to the southern tip of Tarragona province, and while its beaches are often long and even gold-coloured, they lack that most elusive quality in people and resorts – charm. The surrounding scenery tends to be featureless, the *urbanizaciones* are ugly or sleepy, or both, and unless you have young children who require nothing more than good castle-building sand, shallow sea, and their peers for a perfect holiday (most of the visitors are Spanish and French families) you may want to limit yourself to a nod from the train window.

GETTING AROUND

Cunit, Calafell, Torredembarra, Tamarit, Salou, Cambrils, L'Ametlla de Mar and Tortosa are all served by three Semidirecto trains a day between Valencia and Barcelona; the larger stations see considerably more action. Sant Carles de la Ràpita is linked by bus with Tortosa almost every hour.

WHAT TO SEE

For the record, from north to south – **Sitges** (see 'Around Barcelona', p. 101) is by far the most interesting and exciting resort on the coast; nearby **Cumit** is staider and boasts an exceptionally long, never crowded beach. A few miles inland, **El Vendrell**, like Valls famed for its *castellers*, was the birthplace of the great cellist and composer Pau Casals, a Catalan nationalist (he refused to speak anything but Catalán in public) whose opposition to Franco forbade him from ever seeing his beloved home after the Civil War. A plaque marks the house he was born in on Carrer Santa Anna in 1876, in 1979 his remains were brought from Puerto Rico and interred in El Vendrell's cemetery. The maestro bequeathed a considerable sum towards the creation of the Pau Casals Foundation (headed by the abbot of Montserrat), which has converted the family home in **Sant Salvador** on the sea into the **Casals Museum** devoted to his life, works, and memorabilia – including his first cello – and has constructed an auditorium next door.

Near Sant Salvador there's the vast beach, **Coma-ruga**, lined with holiday villas, and **Calafell**, a modest resort with a blank-walled castle as landmark. A ruined castle gave **Torredembarra** its name, and it has one of the coast's best beaches. Another castle from the 11th century stands right next to the beach at **Tamarit**; lovingly restored, the castle contains a fine museum of antiques.

South of Tarragona sprawls the Costa Dorada's Miami Beach-style resort, **Salou**, with nearby **Cambrils** yearning to achieve a similar status. The next resortlet south took a shortcut by simply dubbing itself **Miami Beach** (so tourists can tell their friends at home that they stopped there for a swim). Beyond Platja Miami it's desolate, literally, until the little fishing village-cum-resort, **L'Ametlla de Mar**.

Beyond stretches the **Ebro Delta** (Ebre in Catalán) as one writer described it, 'a strange amphibious landscape in the sea itself'. Malarial and abandoned until the beginning of this century, the delta is divided into rice paddies, criss-crossed by canals and dotted with Valencian *barracas*, farmhouses with thatched roofs, recalling the native province of many of the rice farmers. The delta is a fitting anticlimax to the 746 km (466 miles) of the Ebro, which, as great rivers go is a bit of a bore, though it has given its name to the entire peninsula, from the days when the Greeks knew it as the Iberus and the people on its banks as Iberes.

Tortosa is the most important city here, and with much of the surrounding farmland in its municipal boundaries, it claims to be Spain's second-largest city. No one seems to like it much. The Catalans regard it as somehow peculiar, and the natives prefer to call themselves Tortosans and not Catalans. The Battle of the Ebro, the last Republican offensive in the Civil War, took place here, and Tortosa, on the front line for a year, suffered considerable damage. A monument commemorating the battle, which cost 35,000 lives, was erected by the river.

If fate brings you to Tortosa, there are two sights worth your time. The **Cathedral**, though even more hemmed in than most by its neighbouring streets, has a charming Gothic interior and several fine chapels, especially that of the city's patroness, Nuestra Señora de Santa Cinta (Our Lady of the Ribbon). The citadel, **La Zuda**, was a Templar stronghold in the 12th century, when Tortosa's Moors, Jews and Christians lived in exemplary harmony. It's worth the ascent for the view, which extends across the great plain of the Ebro to 923 m (3000 ft) Sierra de Cardó and the rugged Ports de Bescuite, through which the river descends to the coast.

On the southern tip of the delta, **Sant Carles de la Ràpita** is the last resort on the Costa Dorada, splendidly located on Europe's largest natural harbour, **Los Alfaques**. The good Bourbon Carlos III (for whom the town is named) wanted to take advantage of nature's gift and make this a great seaport, but like so many of his fine plans it was buried with him. Yet in its semi-circular plaça and in some of its 17th-century buildings, the Bourbon colonial air lingers. The evidence of La Ràpita or *Ribbath*, the Sufi monastery that once stood here, is even more elusive.

TOURIST INFORMATION

Calafell: Vilamar 1, Tel: 69 17 59.
Cambrils: Pl. Creu de la Missió, Tel: 36 11 59.
Salou: Espigó del Moll, Tel: 38 02 33.
Torredembarra: Av. de Pompeu Fabra 3, Tel: 64 03 31.
El Vendrell: Dr. Robert 18, Tel: 66 02 92.
Tortosa: Pl. d'Espanya, Tel: 44 00 00.
Sant Carles de la Ràpita: Pl. Carles III, Tel: 74 07 17.

WHERE TO STAY AND EAT

Nearly all the hotels on the Costa Dorada close down from October to May. In Calafell, a pleasant family-resort hotel, the **Canadá****, Mossen Jaime Soler 44, Tel: 69 15 00, has a pool, a children's pool and playground, tennis courts and a reasonable restaurant (doubles 3400–4200 pts). More economical, but minus the restaurant and pools, the **Salomé***, Monturiol 19, Tel: 69 01 00, has a little garden and modern doubles with bath for 2400–2760 pts.

In Torredembarra the place to stay is **Hotel Morros****, Pérez Galdós 8, Tel:

64 02 25, a beach hotel in the traditional style, open March to September, its doubles with bath, 2650 pts in the spring, 3300 pts in the summer.

In Salou it's hard to tell one hotel from the next; in Cambrils you'd do well to stay at **Hostal Rovira*****, Avda. Disputación 6, Tel: 36 09 00, open all year, with doubles from 2950–3950 pts according to season. It's as modern and comfortable as the others by the beach, but has no restaurant, leaving you free to dine out at least once (see below).

Perhaps the only reason to spend a night in Tortosa is to sleep in its fine parador **Castillo de la Zuda******, Tel: 44 44 50, located in the great Templar citadel, with sterling views and a swimming pool, air-conditioning and a restaurant specializing in Catalan dishes. Open all year, its doubles range from 5000–6500 pts.

In Sant Carles de la Ràpita the **Hotel Blau***, Gov. Labadie 1, Tel: 74 01 51, is centrally located, open all year, and offers clean, comfortable doubles with bath for 1975 pts.

EATING OUT

Good Italian food and pizzas may be had in Calafell at **Da Giorgio**, Angel Guimerá 4; the works run around 1400 pts.

Beautifully located in a garden right on the sea at Torredembarra, the **Morros** restaurant on C. del Mar serves delicious seafood specialities (1500 pts).

In Cambrils there are three great seafood restaurants run by the Gatell dynasty of chefs: **Casa Gatell**, Psg. Miramar 26, **Ca'n Gatell**, Psg. Miramar 27, and **Eugenia**, Consolat de Mar 80, all in the 2500 pts range for a full-course meal, and worth it.

Part V

VALENCIA AND THE LEVANTE

Lady sorting figs in the sun

The modern autonomous region called *País Valenciano* (Valencian country) covers what was once the third kingdom of the Crown of Aragón, reconquered by Jaime I in the 13th century. It was a valuable asset, for the seemingly interminable Huerta de Valencia is Spain's most fertile region, irrigated since Roman times with the waters of the Turia. The Levante, or 'East' as this region is commonly known, has the highest rural density in Europe, with over 800 inhabitants per square kilometre, and their capital, Valencia, is Spain's third city and one of its most prosperous. This is the land of oranges and rice; the national dish, paella, was invented here and tastes better here than anywhere else. It is also the home of Costa del Azahar, with its string of modern resorts, and the Costa Blanca, which has entered the big leagues with the Costas Brava and Sol.

Most of the Christians who settled the new kingdom of Valencia were Catalan, but over the centuries their language has evolved into a new creature, Valencian, which in the fierce parochialism of post-Franco Spain is flaunted as an entirely different tongue. Yet like their cousin Catalans, the Valencians have their Generalitat and a long Republican tradition and pride themselves on their civility in public life. But for many it is Valencia's light that best defines the region, a clear, diaphanous light called *La Clara*, the light artists love, that illuminates the characteristic blue tiled steeples and cupolas, and casts a spell over the Albufera, the great lagoon south of the city, where changing patterns of light and colour are worthy of a Monet.

VALENCIA

The city of Valencia is an acquired taste. Those who arrive with visions of orange blossoms dancing in their heads will be disappointed once they leave the RENFE station (one of Spain's loveliest, a confection of ceramic oranges, tiles, and glittering mosaics of orange goddesses), for the first impression is of a big, bustling city, where grand bridges span a nonexistent river, where two magnificent gates recall the stupendous walls that the city knocked down to expand drably in all directions. A trip through the fine, old quarter is usually enough to dispel any initial misgivings, and if you linger a little longer, you'll begin to feel the charged atmosphere. There is an intensity in Valencia, a feeling that suggests if a revolution in Spain were to erupt, it would begin here. This smouldering feeling actually ignites every March in what must be the world's greatest pyromaniac's ball, Las Fallas, where hundreds of grotesque and satirical floats, painstakingly built in the streets and quarters of the city, are burnt in a saturnalia of gunpowder and fireworks.

History

As Mediterranean citys go, Valencia is a newcomer, founded in 138 BC specifically to settle a band of defeated legionaries from Lusitania, who called it Valentia Edetanorum. It especially prospered under the Moors, who irrigated the fertile Huerta with an elaborate system of canals. When the Almoravides took the city from the Moorish king of Valencia in 1092, the latter allied himself with the Cid, who captured Valencia in 1094 and ruled the city as a personal fief until his death five years later. Its permanent Reconquest waited until 1238 and a joint Aragonese–Catalan army under Jaime I. Most of the Moors stayed on and were valued agricultural workers and until the 17th-century, they constituted perhaps a third of the kingdom's total population. When the Turks threatened the coast, the archbishop of Valencia, Juan de Ribera, conjured up fears of a Morisco–Turkish conspiracy. Madrid readily believed the archbishop, and in 1609 the Moors had to go. Valencia which until then had been one of Spain's most prosperous cities, thriving on its silks and agriculture, suffered a near-total economic collapse. Worse came when Valencia, like Catalunya, picked the wrong side in the War of the Spanish Succession.

In the 1860s and 1870s, Valencia took a leading role in the Republican movement; at the same time, in a progressive mood, it tore down its great 14th-century walls as a public works project to give jobs to the needy. During the Civil War it served as the Republicans' capital after the government had fled from Madrid, a period remembered by plaques throughout the city.

GETTING AROUND

By air

There are regular flights between Valencia and Madrid, Ibiza, Mallorca and the Canary Islands. The airport is 12 km (7.5 miles) west of town in Manises (Tel: 370 95 00). Iberia's office is at C. de la Paz 14, Tel: 352 05 00.

By sea

Valencia's port is 4.8 km (3 miles) from town and has frequent connections with Mallorca and Ibiza, and the Canaries Transmediterránea's office is at Avda. Manuel Soto Ingeniero 15, Tel: 367 07 04. Bus 3 or 4 goes directly to the port from Plaza País Valenciano.

By train

The RENFE station is only a couple of blocks from the Pl. País Valenciano, Tel: 351 36 12. Ticket office is on the Pl. Alfonso el Magnámino, Tel: 351 26 15. There are eight trains a day from Madrid, vía Cuenca or Albacete; three connections with Zaragoza, five to Alicante, and eight to Barcelona and Castellón. There are also trains nearly every hour to Játiva.

The villages of the Huerta are served by the FEVE station near the Museo de Bellas Artes. There are connections to Lliria, Buñol, Paterna and Villanueva de Castellón. Valencians like to say their FEVE station is busier than Victoria Station.

By bus

Valencia's bus station is across the Turia at Avda. de Ménendez Pidal 3, Tel: 349 72 22; catch bus 28 from across the street for the Pl. País Valenciano. There are connections from here to most of the major cities of Spain, to the resorts along the coasts to the north and south, and a Eurolines bus direct to London. Autocares V. Edo go from Valencia to Castellón, Tarragona and Andorra once a day. In the summer there are buses to El Salér from the Plaza Porta del Mar every half hour.

The Cathedral

Looking at a map, it's easy to trace the line of the walls that once embraced old Valencia, the very heart of which is defined by the **Plaza Zaragoza** and the **Cathedral**, built over the Great Mosque and partnered by a sturdy, octagonal, minaret-like tower called the **Micalet**, completed by Pere Balanguer in 1429. If the thought of climbing 200 steps in a narrow spiral stair doesn't dismay you, the views from the top of the Micalet over Valencia and the Huerta are worth the trouble (open daily 10.30 am–12.30 pm and 5–7.30 pm). There are 13 bells in the Micalet, the largest weighing over 5 tons and dedicated on Michaelmas – hence the tower's name. The Cathedral, begun in 1262, has suffered a number of changes over the years. The main Baroque portal on the Plaza Zaragoza isn't much; walk around to see the Romanesque **Portal de Palau** and the Gothic **Puerta de los Apostales** (1354), facing the Plaza de la Virgen and adorned with sculpture and a star of David (locally called the Salomó) in the rose window.

If you happen to pass by the Puerta de los Apostoles on a Thursday at noon, you'll find a crowd gathered around eight seated men in black shirts. They are Valencia's famous **Tribunal de las Aguas** (Water Jury), where all disputes related to the irrigation water on the Huerta are settled. The eight-member court is elected every two years, and has been since the Tribunal was founded in 960, in the reign of the Caliph Abderraman III of Córdoba. Conducted in the Valencian language, nothing of the proceedings is ever written down, nor is there any appeal if a user is fined – not in pesetas,

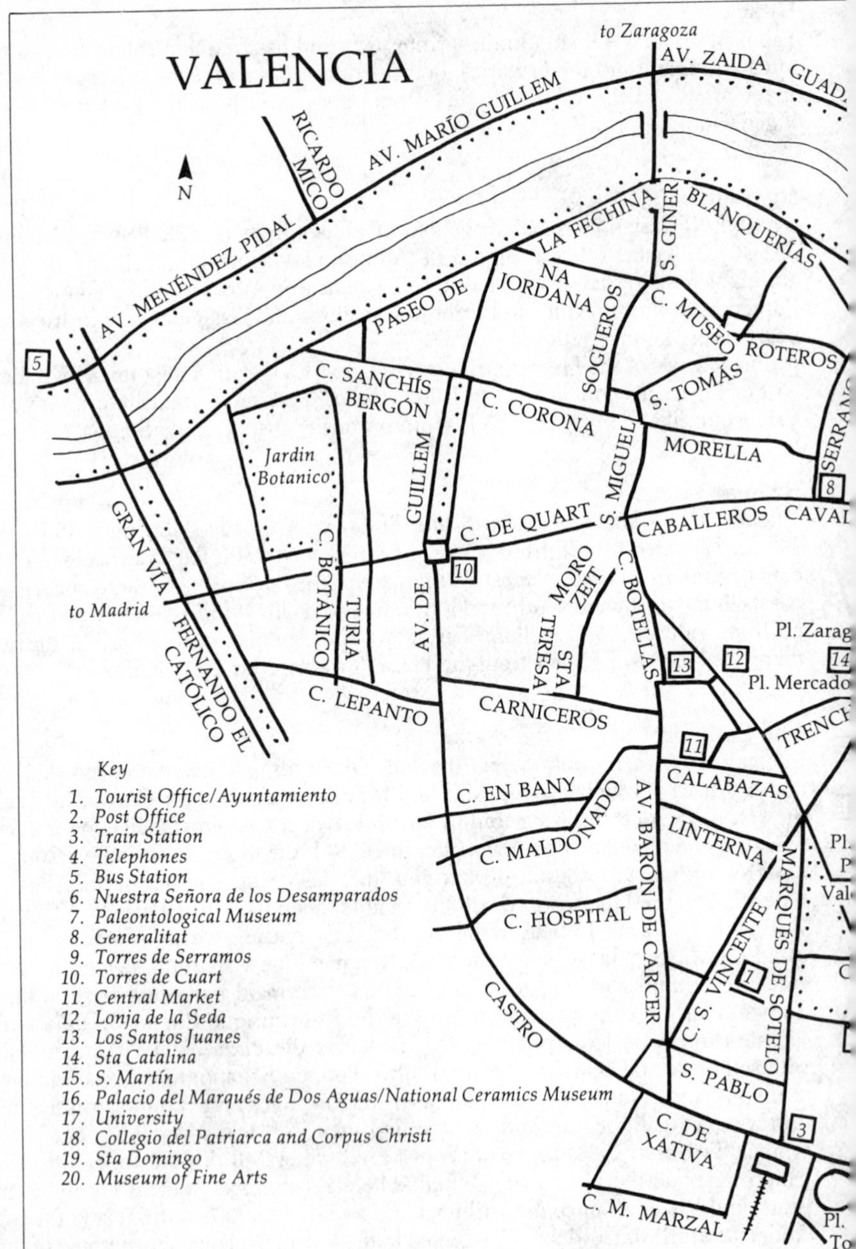

Key

1. Tourist Office/Ayuntamiento
2. Post Office
3. Train Station
4. Telephones
5. Bus Station
6. Nuestra Señora de los Desamparados
7. Paleontological Museum
8. Generalitat
9. Torres de Serramos
10. Torres de Cuart
11. Central Market
12. Lonja de la Seda
13. Los Santos Juanes
14. Sta Catalina
15. S. Martín
16. Palacio del Marqués de Dos Aguas/National Ceramics Museum
17. University
18. Collegio del Patriarca and Corpus Christi
19. Sta Domingo
20. Museum of Fine Arts

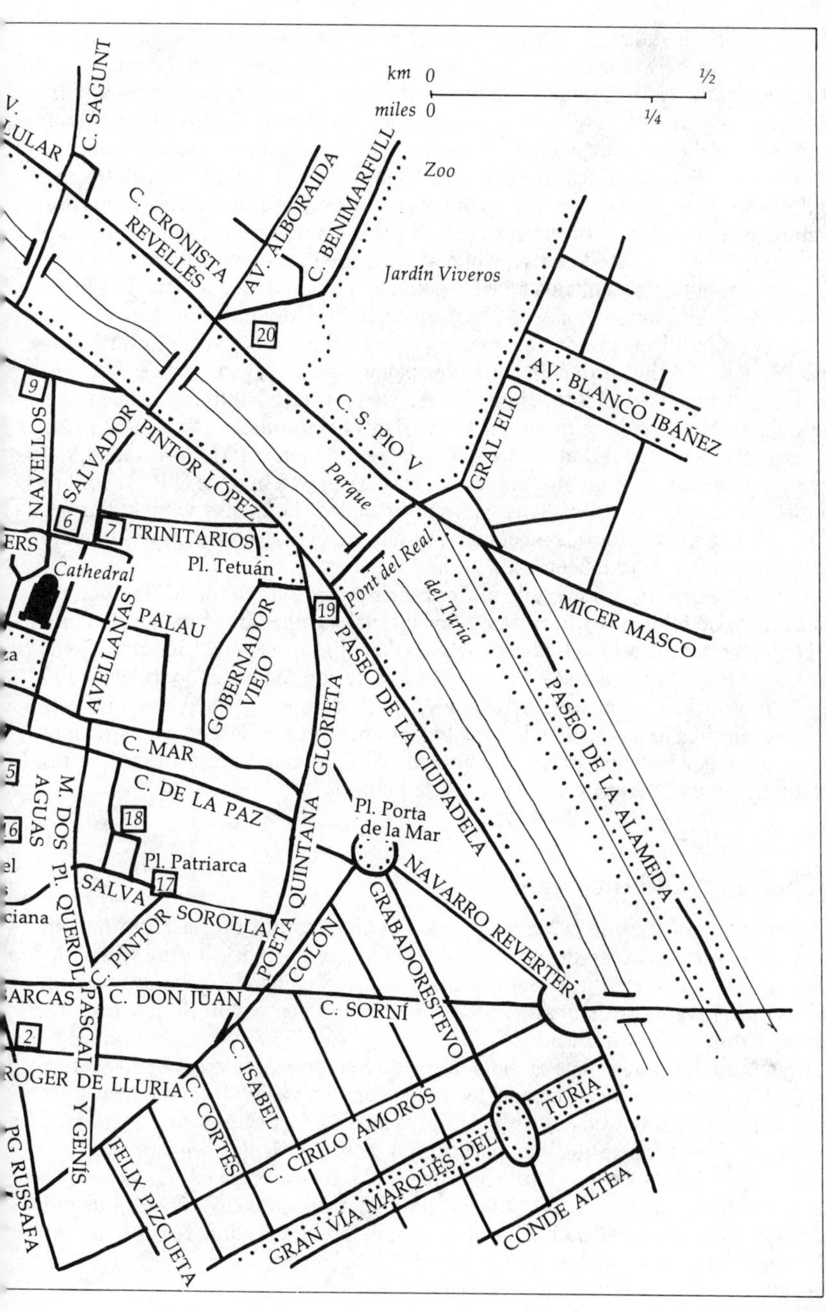
km 0 1/2
miles 0 1/4
Zoo
Jardín Viveros
C. SAGUNT
C. CRONISTA REVELLÉS
AV. ALBORAIDA
C. BENIMARFULL
20
9
NAVELLOS
SALVADOR
PINTOR LÓPEZ
C. S. PIO V
GRAL ELIO
AV. BLANCO IBÁÑEZ
Parque
6
7
TRINITARIOS
Cathedral
Pl. Tetuán
Pont del Real
del Turia
MICER MASCO
AVELLANAS
PALAU
GOBERNADOR VIEJO
19
PASEO DE LA CIUDADELA
PASEO DE LA ALAMEDA
GLORIETA
C. MAR
C. DE LA PAZ
M. DOS AGUAS
18
Pl. Porta de la Mar
Pl. Patriarca
17
SALVA
PINTOR SOROLLA
POETA QUINTANA
COLÓN
GRABADORESTEVO
NAVARRO REVERTER
PL. QUEROL
C. DON JUAN
C. SORNÍ
2
ROGER DE LLURIA
PASCAL Y GENÍS
C. ISABEL
C. CORTÉS
C. CIRILO AMORÓS
TURIA
GRAN VÍA MARQUÉS DEL
CONDE ALTEA
FELIX PIZCUETA
PG RUSSAFA

but in the medieval currency, *lliures valencianes*. The water laws of Valencia are so fair they were copied by the whole country and Spanish America in the 19th century.

The **interior** of the cathedral has been restored (since 1939) to reveal as much of its Gothic structure as possible. What impresses most, however, is the 14th-century *cimborio*, or lantern, over the crossing, with its translucent alabaster windows. The **museum**, in the 14th-century Sala Capitular, is worth a look, however (Monday–Saturday 10 am–1 pm and 4–6 pm), especially for a macabre painting by Goya that foreshadows his 'Black Paintings' in the Prado (the scene shows three grinning demons whispering into the ear of a graphically depicted corpse, while a priest attempts to ward them off with a crucifix). The museum also contains a lovely gold and coloured enamel Pax Tablet by Benvenuto Cellini, and for a climax, nothing less than the **Holy Grail**.

Spain has two Grail legends, one a primarily poetic tradition connected with Monserrat and Parsifal, and the second attached this bejewelled and agate chalice. According to the story, it was taken to Rome by St Peter, where it stayed until the 3rd century, when Pope Sixtus II, about to be martyred in Valerian's persecutions, entrusted it to his disciple Lawrence, who had it sent to Huesca in Aragón. When the Moors invaded, the chalice was hidden in the mountains, and the monastery of San Juan de la Peña built to house the precious relic. In 1399 King Martin persuaded the monks to give him the Grail, and it ended up here for safe-keeping. The chalice (Roman, 1st century) if nothing else, is old enough to have been used at the Last Supper.

The faithful of Valencia, however, do most of their praying at the round **Basilica de Nuestra Señora de los Desamparados**, adjacent to the cathedral on the lovely Plaza de la Virgen. The statue of 'Our Lady of the Forsaken' has its own legend: in the 14th century a group of pilgrims came to a charitable society and requested four days' food and lodging in a locked room without windows. Four days later, when the door was unlocked, the pilgrims had vanished, leaving behind the statue. Adorned with a radiant diamond crown and bejewelled gown, surrounded by a thousand flickering candles, this Virgin made by angels is the city's most venerated object.

The Generalitat and the gates

On the far side of the Plaza de la Virgen stands the **Generalitat of the Kingdom of Valencia** (1510), now again serving its original function, more-or-less, as the seat of the provincial council. The exterior is plain, but within are two chambers with wonderful *artesonado* ceilings, the **Salón Dorado** and the especially lovely **Salón de Cortes** with its gallery and 16th century murals.

From here Calle Serranos leads to the **Torres de Serranos**, the great 14th-century gate into the city. From the river the gate looks solid and imposing; from the rear it has the air of a stage prop, hollowed out with platforms and stairs. The gate that once stood to the east along the river near the Templar church (now a Guardia Civil barracks) was the famous Gate of the Cid, through which the Cid's corpse, decked out in warlike array and propped up on his faithful Babieca, led the attack on the Moorish besiegers who had taken courage from rumours of his death; in the film version, it was Charlton Heston's best scene. A second mighty souvenir of Valencia's walls, the **Torres de Quart** (1460), is just west of the Generalitat.

Plaza del Mercado

This square, where old Valencia held its *corridas* and *autos-de-fe*, is an exceptionally fine ensemble, though during market hours with triple-parked market vehicles it goes unnoticed. Befitting an argicultural queen, Valencia's **Municipal Market** is the city's true palace, Spain's largest and most beautiful market, a symphony of iron and glass, topped with a parrot-and-swordfish weathervane. Inside, the astounding cornucopia of the *huerta* is on display; sometimes you find oranges weighing up to 3 kg (6 or 7 lbs) apiece.

Opposite the market stands another cathedral of commerce, the 15th-century **Lonja de la Seda** (silk exchange), open Tuesday–Friday 11 am–2 pm (and 4–6 pm, weekends 10 am–2 pm). Notable here are the twisting, rope-like columns of the main hall, with its Latin inscription along the walls 'I am a famous building that took fifteen years to build' and an exhortation on the merits of honest trade. A spiral stair ascends to the **Salón del Consulado del Mar** with a great *artesonado* ceiling. Across from the Lonja, the plaza's third monument **Los Santos Juanes** is a medieval church with a Plateresque façade.

Behind the Lonja rises the second of Valencia's monumental towers, the hexagonal **Tower of Santa Catalina** (17th century). In the Plaza de Santa Catalina are two famous **Horchaterias** – cafes specializing in another Valencian creation, *Horchata de chufa*, made from the almonds of the Huerta. A flea market, liveliest on Sundays, extends from here into the curious, enclosed **Plaza Redonda** – a kind of residential bullring.

National Ceramics Museum

From here, Calle de La Paz passes the Baroque **S. Martin**, its gutted interior another victim of the Civil War. An alley in front of it leads to the 18th-century **Palacio del Marqués de Dos Aguas**, an outlandish Baroque wedding-cake with an amazing alabaster portal by Hipolito Ravira, who died a lunatic shortly after its completion.

Since 1954 it has housed the **National Ceramics Museum** (open Tuesday–Saturday 10 am–2 pm and 4–6 pm, Sunday 10 am–2 pm) with an excellent collection of *azulejos* (one portrays a giant mosquito chasing a dog); other ceramics are beautifully functional, like the all-tiled Valencian kitchen. There are whimsical 'popular' ceramics from nearby Manises – the ones on the third floor, from the 18th- and 19th-centuries, are strangely reminiscent of Picasso – beautiful green and blue medieval plates from Paterna, Spain's first great ceramics centre, as well as a fine collection of ex-libris designs from the 1920s, and on the top floor, the Gallery of Humourists, which is fascinating even if you don't get the jokes.

Plaza del Patriarca

Two blocks east lies the Plaza del Patriarca, named for the **Collegio del Patriarca**, founded by Bishop Juan de Ribera, the arch enemy of the Moriscos. Above its serene Renaissance patio is a small collection of painting, including three El Grecos and Ribaltas, and a Book of Miniatures once belonging to Philip the Handsome, with a scene of golfing in the Middle Ages (open daily 11 am–1 pm). Next to it is the 19th-century building of the 15th-century **University**, whose library contains the first book printed in Spain, *Les Trobes*.

Adjacent to the Patriarca, the **Church of Corpus Christi** offers some genuine Spanish Catholic hocus-pocus during its Friday morning *Miserere* service. During the chant the painting over the altar – *The Last Supper*, by Ribalta – sinks away, to be replaced by a series of four curtains that are parted at the climactic moment to reveal a starkly illuminated crucifix.

From here it's a short walk down the Calle de La Paz to the Glorieta; turn left for what is generally acclaimed as Valencia's finest church, **Santo Domingo**. Some tough customers have called its cloister home, beginning with St Vincente Ferrer, perhaps Spain's most ferocious religious bigot, and recently, General Milans del Bosch, mastermind of the abortive coup in February 1981, who called out the tanks in Valencia in support of his stooge Tejero, while the latter shot up the Cortes in Madrid. Although the cloister remains a barracks, you can see the porch designed by Philip II (who was no great shakes as an architect) and the Gothic **Chapel de los Reyes**, with the impressive 16th-century tombs of Rodrigo Mendoza and his wife.

Across the Turia

From Santo Domingo stretches Valencia's most attractive bridge, the **Puente del Real**. The once unpredictable Turia, which was either a squirt or a flood once it reached Valencia (after being 'bled' by the canals of the *huerta*) so often inundated the city that in 1957 Valencia lost its patience and dug a new channel. The city has turned part of the old river bed into a pretty park; there are trails for jogging (or 'footing' as the Spaniards call it) and even a baseball diamond.

Across the Puente del Real it's a short stroll to the **Museo de Bellas Artes** (open daily 10 am–2 pm, closed Monday), with a smattering of good works among the forgettable – there's a self-portrait by Velázquez, work by Ribalta and El Greco (*St John the Baptist*), a triptych by Bosch, medieval Valencian art, and, on the upper floors, some astoundingly lurid Spanish Impressionism. Next to the Museum you can recover from it all in the **Jardin Viveros**, and perhaps visit its cramped bit of zoo.

The Fallas and their Museum

The heart of modern Valencia is the large, triangular **Plaza del País Valenciano**, its bustling life tempered by the sweet scent of flowers from numerous stalls. From here you can catch bus 13 to the **Fallas Museum** (Plaza Monteolivete 4, open Tuesday–Sunday 10 am–2 pm and 4–7 pm) which can give you a hint of what you're missing if you're not in Valencia for Las Fallas itself (13–19 March). 20 March is the spring equinox, throughout the world a popular time for bonfires to welcome in spring, but no one does it with more enthusiasm than the Valencians.

The holiday began to take its present form in the 18th century, when as a rite of spring local carpenters and artisans would ceremoniously burn the wooden poles that had supported the lamps they had worked by in the winter. Because 18 March is also the feast of St Joseph, patron of carpenters, the rite took on a festive air, and the Valencians began to dress up the old poles as satrical effigies. Competitions between the neighbourhoods soon arose, and residents joined in, contributing towards the figure, or *ninot*, hoping theirs would be bigger and more humorous than the ninot from the next block.

In their present form, Las Fallas are a week-long carnival of parades, fireworks, bullfights – the first on the calendar – music and paella, all presided over by the *falleras*, the costumed neighbourhood beauties. You could spend the whole of Fallas week like the Valencians do, strolling through the city to see the over 300 papier-mâché tableaux of ninots, some several storeys high and based on the most outrageous themes that spare no one and need no translations – fat women, naked girls and tourists are peppered throughout, slick TV announcers pop out of cardboard screens with trays of sausages and coffins. *Barracas* (typical white Valencian houses with thatched roofs) are set up, dispensing *churros* and chocolate to the passing throngs. On the 18th, the huge offering of flowers takes place in the Plaza de la Virgen. The 19th is acrid with gunpowder as everyone hurries about to see their favourite ninots one last time before the *Nit de Foc*, 'the night of fire', when, at the stroke of midnight, with firemen poised with their hoses, the great holocaust, or *cremá*, takes place as the ninots burst into flames throughout the city. The largest pyre is in the centre of the Plaza del País Valenciano, and as it goes up hundreds of tons of fireworks explode overhead. Of all the weeks or work and millions of pesetas that went into Las Fallas, only the best ninot, the *Ninot Indulat*, is spared at the last minute from the flames of the cremá and installed in the 'Pantheon-hospice' of the museum.

Around Valencia

Valencia has two municipal beaches, **Levante** and **Malvarrosa** (bus 1 or 2 from the Plaza del País Valenciano) but they are as polluted as they are convenient. Levante, however, is the place to go for fresh seafood when in Valencia; the Avenida de Neptuno has some 27 restaurants alone.

Further south and far more pleasant and cleaner are the beaches at **Pinedo** and **El Saler**, which as yet are hardly developed. El Saler is also the best base for visiting the **Albufera**, Spain's largest fresh-water lagoon, separated from the sea by **La Dehesa**, a narrow sandbar shaded with pine groves. The Albufera is rimmed with rice paddies that turn gold in September; wildfowl (and duck hunters) flock here from September to March, and the waters are plied by scores of eel fishermen, some in their old-fashioned stately sailing boats. The Albufera is most dramatic at dusk, when the soft colours change by the second. You can hire boats from the little dock behind El Saler beach (a local bus passes by). Prices vary, so if you think one boatman's price too high, try another.

Sagunto

Some of Spain's best Roman remains are at **Sagunto** (ancient Saguntum) 25 km (15.6 miles) north of Valencia. Hannibal initiated the Second Punic War (219 BC) by taking Sagunto, which proved no easy task – after an eight-month siege, the defenders, unable to hold out any longer, burnt their belongings, their families and themselves. Historical

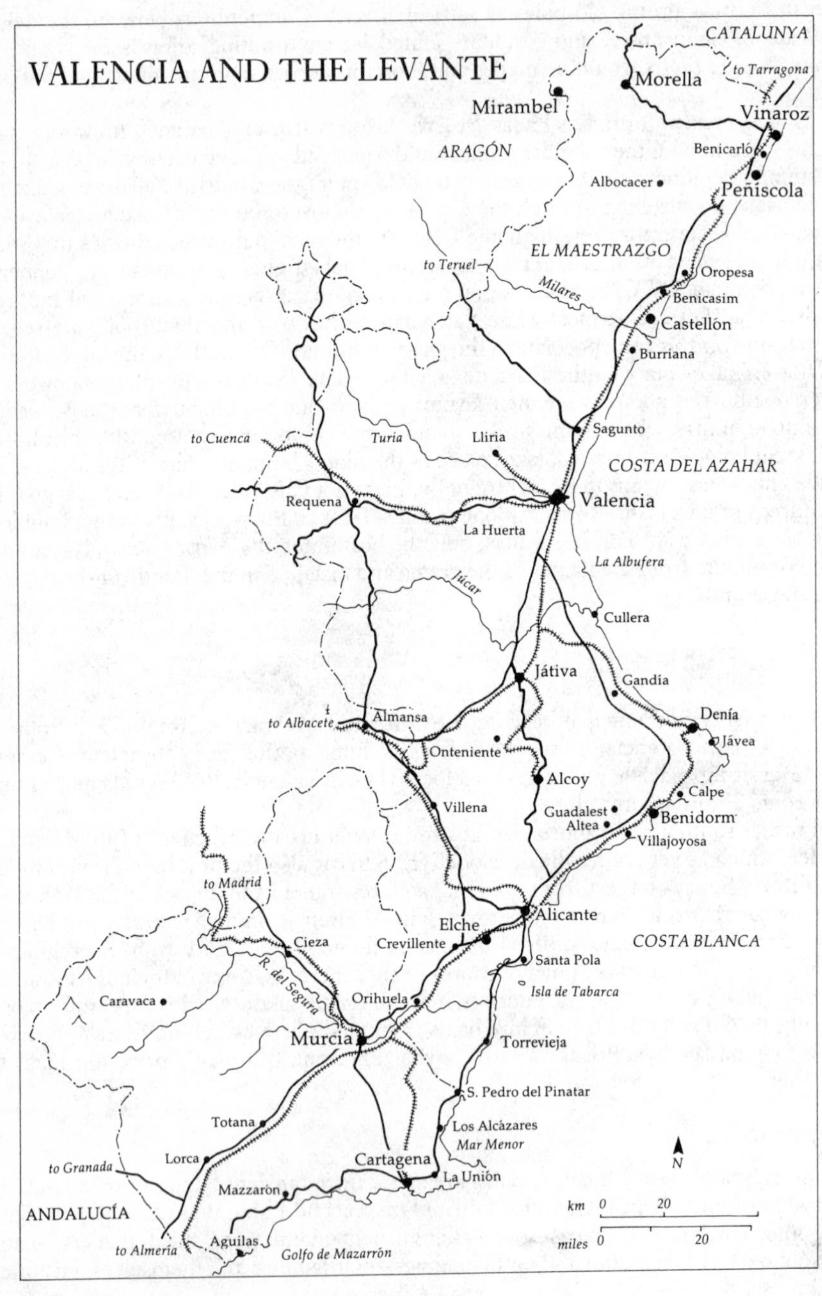
VALENCIA AND THE LEVANTE
CATALUNYA
to Tarragona
Morella
Mirambel
Vinaroz
ARAGÓN
Benicarló
Albocacer
Peñíscola
EL MAESTRAZGO
to Teruel
Oropesa
Milares
Benicasim
Castellón
Burriana
Sagunto
to Cuenca
Turia
Liria
COSTA DEL AZAHAR
Valencia
Requena
La Huerta
La Albufera
Júcar
Cullera
Játiva
Gandía
Denía
to Albacete
Almansa
Jávea
Onteniente
Alcoy
Calpe
Villena
Guadalest
Altea
Benidorm
Villajoyosa
to Madrid
Alicante
Elche
Crevillente
Cieza
COSTA BLANCA
Santa Pola
R. del Segura
Isla de Tabarca
Caravaca
Orihuela
Murcia
Torrevieja
S. Pedro del Pinatar
Totana
Los Alcázares
Mar Menor
Lorca
Cartagena
to Granada
La Unión
N
Mazzarón
km
0
20
ANDALUCÍA
miles
0
20
to Almería
Aguilas
Golfo de Mazarrón

hindsight suggests Hannibal ought to have taken the hint and parked his elephants there; indeed five years later, Rome easily took Sangunto back. The town never recovered, though the Moors added the great walls of the citadel over the Roman foundations, and the Spaniards added a giant steel mill. In 1902 the composer Joaquín Rodrigo, was born in Sagunto.

Traces of Roman Sagunto may be seen in the town itself – some of the arcades in the **Plaza Mayor** are supported by Roman columns. Calle del Castillo leads up to the **Roman Theatre**, a 2nd-century creation and one of the best-preserved in Spain, with fine views over the sea. Next to it the **Archaeology Museum** contains a modest collection of Roman bric-à-bac. From the theatre the road continues up to the drawbridge of the huge, rambling **citadel**, its 1 km (0.6 mile) of walls draped over the ancient acropolis. You can pick out the foundations of Roman temples and French buildings and ruins left by every king of the mountain in between. The views over the deep green *huerta* are excellent (all open Tuesday–Saturday 10 am–2 pm and 4–6 pm, Sundays 10 am–2 pm). A bus from Sagunto heads down to its beach, which isn't bad if you don't mind looking at the steel mill.

Játiva

Játiva (or Xátiva) is an hour's trip from Valencia, taking you across the *huerta* and past many a dilapidated but stylish orange warehouse. Located on a hill in the midst of the flat *huerta*, Játiva is one of the most scenic villages in the País Valenciano and is best known for three of its Italian exports, Ribera: born here in 1589 and known as 'El Españoleto' in Italy, and the two Borgia Popes, Calixtus III and the infamous Alexander VI, both born here when the family relocated from Borja and Aragón. Játiva (its Moorish name) was such a headache to Philip V that when he finally captured it in 1707, he burnt much of it and renamed it San Felipe for himself, so the inhabitants would never forget who was boss.

From the railway station it's a short walk up to the picturesque old town, divided from the new by Avenida de la Alameda. Numbers are posted in town, marking both a car and a pedestrian tour; a **tourist office** has just opened in the Plaza del Seo to offer assistance. The **Plaza del Seo** is itself one of the most scenic corners in town, with a Renaissance **Collegiate Church** even bigger than Valencia's cathedral, with several fine marbles and donations from the Borgias. Across the square from the church is Játiva's prettiest building, the **Municipal Hospital**, its Plateresque façade depicting an angelic chamber orchestra over the door.

On Carrer de la Corretgeria, the old Almudín (granary) now houses the **Municipal Museum** (Tuesday–Saturday 10 am–2 pm); inside are a few paintings by Ribera and an interesting archaeological collection. The road up to the castles passes **San Felix**, the town's Visigothic cathedral, remodelled in the 13th century with Roman columns. The two picturesque **castles** that crown Játiva date from the 15th century; from their ramparts you can see Valencia and the sea on the horizon (open Tuesday–Sunday 10 am–2 pm and 4.30–8 pm).

TOURIST INFORMATION

Valencia: Provincial office: Cataluña 1, Tel: 369 79 32. Municipal: Pl. del País

Valenciano 1, Tel: 351 04 17. Train station: Tel: 352 28 82. Airport: Tel: 153 03 25. Post Office: Pl. del País Valenciano 24. Telephones: Pl. del País Valenciano 27.

WHERE TO STAY

It usually isn't too hard to find a room in Valencia, except during Las Fallas, when a reservation certainly comes in handy. Most of the better hotels are clustered around the Plaza del País Valenciano; otherwise you take your chances in narrow, dimly lit streets in the older part of town.

Reina Victoria****, Barcas 4, Tel: 352 04 87, lies just off the Plaza del País Valenciano. This is the elegant grande dame of the city's hostelries, in an attractive Victorian monument; air-conditioned rooms can be a godsend in the summer. Doubles 7950 pts. **Excelsior***** Barcelonina 5, Tel: 351 46 12, is also just off the big square, its clean modern rooms also blessed with air-conditioning; 4900 pts a double. **Hotel Inglés*****, Marqués de Dos Aguas 6, Tel: 351 64 26, is in the same price range, and while lacking the air-conditioning offers much more in the way of style and old-fashioned atmosphere; at night the street is very quiet. **Hostal Mediterráneo*****, Avda Barón de Cárcer 45, Tel: 351 01 42, also conveniently located, is small and friendly and cool in the summer, with doubles for 3975 pts, no restaurant.

Hostal Bisbal**, Pie de la Cruz 9, Tel: 331 70 84, is right at the market's front door; noisy during the day but quiet at night. The owners speak English. Doubles, with bath, 2500 pts. **Hospederia del Pilar***, Mercado 19, Tel: 331 66 00, is clean and pleasant in the middle of the old town, with a lobby resembling an elementary school classroom. The price is right, though: doubles with bath 1800 pts, without bath 1300 pts. **Universal**, Barcas 5, Tel: 351 53 84, is your basic, faded but well-scrubbed *hostal*, just off the Pl. del País Valenciano, doubles without bath are 1500 pts.

Outside town

Parador Nacional Luis Vives****, Ctra Saler, Tel: 323 68 50, is located among the sand dunes and pine forests of the Dehesa near Saler. Very contemporary, air-conditioned and next to a fine 18-hole golf course and pool, the very plush doubles are 8500 pts in season, 6500 pts in the winter. **Patilla II****, Pinares 10, Tel: 367 94 11, also prettily located on Saler beach; small, with TVs in each room, and open all year, doubles are from 3500–4500 pts; breakfast, but no restaurant.

EATING OUT

Valencians are rightfully proud of their rice dishes, from the famous paella to other lesser-known dishes like *arros a la banda* and *arros en fesols i naps*. Another Valencian favourite, baby eels (elvers) from the Albufera, figures on many menus.

Two moderately priced restaurants in the new part of town specialize in Valencian cuisine. **El Romeral**, Gran Vía Marqués del Turia 62, on the big boulevard south of the Plaza Puerta de la Mar. Closed Monday and in August; 1200 pts for a home-cooked meal. On the next block, **El Plat**, Conde Altea 41, prides itself on its rice dishes, featuring a different *arros* each day of the week (closed Mondays; 1500 pts). For class and innovative cuisine, the place to go in Valencia is **Ma Cuina**, just south of the train station and bullring on Gran Vía Germanias 49; the menu always changes but Valencian rice and Basque dishes are permanent features (2200 pts).

If you're hungry but don't know what you'd like, the **Barrachina**, Pl. del País Valenciano is the place for you, with everything from three-course meals to chocolate pastries, cheap combination plates, sangria and *perros calientes (hot dogs!). Platos combinados* are around 800 pts. Another inexpensive place, **Flip**, just off the plaza at Marques de Sotelo 1, has dining upstairs, pizzas, and interesting set menus for 700 pts (try the grilled artichokes). Even cheaper is **La Nave**, on C. de la Nave in the old town, which has paella for 140 pts. If you prefer your rice with soy sauce, the **Restaurante Pekin** is just around the corner from the market of C. de los Ramilletes; the most expensive item on the extensive menu is sweet-and-sour shrimp for 340 pts.

NIGHT LIFE

Culture (two little theatres) and bars are slowly reclaiming the alleys of the old town; the city could help them along a bit by adding a few watts to the street lights. By reading the tantalizing personal ads in the local paper *Levante*, it's easy to think prostitution is the only game in town, especially in the maze of streets south and west of the Plaza de Mercado. Things are merrier south of the C. de Xátiva, west of the train station.

Costa de Azahar

The 'Orange Blossom Coast', as the shore of Castellón and Valencia provinces has been dubbed, is indeed lined with orange groves; Castellón has a huerta as rich as Valencia. While there are long stretches of sand, few of the beaches here are anything to write home about. There are plenty of villas and flats along the better stretches but few hotels.

GETTING AROUND

RENFE has frequent service up the coast from Valencia and down from Tarragona; there are stations at Burriana, Villareal, Castellón, Benicasim, Oropresa, Alcalá de Chivert, Benicarlo and Vinaroz. There are two buses a day from Valencia's bus station and from Castellón to Montanejos. Peñiscola, Benicarlo, and Vinaroz are linked by a municipal bus every hour; there are also three direct buses between Castellón, Benicarló and Peñiscola on weekdays (more in the summer), departing from C. Trinidad 166. Five other buses link Castellón and Valencia in an hour-and-a-half express service. Municipal buses leave Castellón's Plaza Hernan Cortes for the beaches from Grao de Castellón to Benicasim.

Two buses a day from Castellón and Vinaroz go to Morella, which is itself a terminus for buses that go once or twice a day to the villages of the Maestrazgo. Buses from Castellón pass through them all as well; get timetables from the tourist office.

WHAT TO SEE

From Sagunto to Castellón there's not much. **Burriana** is one of Spain's major orange ports; if you're passing through, stop to see the portal of the 16th-century parish church, flanked by two curious bears. Inland, **Villareal de los Infantes** is a busy citrus centre, founded in 1272 by Jaime I, who laid out its streets in a neat grid.

There are a handful of acceptable beaches here (**Playa de Nules** and **Playa de Chilches** near Almenara) but it's far more delightful to head inland up the River Mijares that irrigates the Huerta of Castellón. Before it reaches the plain, the Mijares passes through a deep, forested ravine, especially lovely around **Montanejos**, where you can paddle about in the clear, shallow water under the cliffs.

Castellón de la Plana

Castellón is not one of Spain's prettier provincial capitals, and the only real reason anyone stays here is for the fine stretch of beaches from the **Playa del Serrallo** with its golf course, north to **Benicasim**, served by frequent buses from Castellón. In town itself, the **Provincial Museum of Fine Arts**, on Calle Caballeros, has works by Ribera, Ribalta, and Sorolla, and good modern ceramics from the region (open Tuesday–Friday 3–8 pm, Saturday 10 am–1 pm). In one aspect, however, Castellón stands apart from other Spanish towns: it contains in its municipal boundaries a collection of tiny volcanic islets, the **Islas Columbretes**, 27 miles out to sea. Although not much more than rocks themselves, they are very popular with underwater fishermen, who can hire out excursions from **Oropresa**, the next town and beach north of Benicasim, crowned by a ruined castle like many in the region.

North of Oropresa the road is forced away from the coast by rugged Sierra de Irta, dotted with castles and towers. The finest of these **Alcalá de Chivert**, is an enormous ruined castle formerly belonging to the Templars, its ruins accessible by a dirt road.

Peñiscola

The belle of the Costa del Azahar, Peñiscola has been called Spain's Mont St Michel for its location on a rugged promontory linked to the mainland by a sandy isthmus. Some modest tourist development along the isthmus keeps Peñiscola from seeming as strikingly isolated as it once did; still, the heavily fortified medieval town, with its cobbled streets and castle, is one of the prettiest scenes ever to grace a Spanish postcard.

The Phoenicians, its first settlers, called it Tyriche, because it reminded them of Tyre; the Romans regarded it, in the 3rd century BC, as the boundary between their colonies and Carthage's. Hamilcar Barca used the town as his headquarters, and here his son Hannibal, chafing under Roman constraints, resolved to make war on the upstart young empire. Jaime I won Peñiscola from the Moors and handed it over to the Templars, who built the castle. When the Order of the Templars was dissolved, it passed to the Knights of Montesa, an Order that inherited all the Templars' possessions in the Kingdom of Valencia. They never spread outside Valencia, and according to most historians, quietly went about practising the same heresies and rituals that had condemned their predecessors. And it was these, the Knights of Montesa, who sheltered Peñiscola's best-loved historical personage, Papa Luna, the last of the Anti-Popes of Avignon, who reigned under the name Benedict XIII. Born in Aragón, Pedro de Luna (1338–1423) seems to have been a formidable character; he never once renounced his title of Benedict XIII, giving rise to the modern Spanish idiom, *mantenerse uno en sus trece*, 'to maintain one's thirteen', or as we would say, 'he stuck to his guns'.

The **Templar Castle**, where Papa Luna resided, has been vigorously restored and contains the few relics left by his stay in its fine Gothic halls (open 10 am–8 pm in the summer, 10 am–1 pm and 4.15–6.30 pm in winter); one of the gates into Peñiscola still bears his coat-of-arms. The façade of the 18th-century church near the castle is adorned with curious military symbols. If you're claustrophobic, you may want to avoid Peñiscola in July and August, when elbow room in its narrow streets is at a premium, the throngs further hemmed in by wall-to-wall souvenir stands. Yet from a distance it is always enchanting, especially at night when the walls and castle are are bathed in golden light.

Benicarló, Peñiscola's mainland connection, has a 'Valencian-style' Baroque church, with a dome frosted with blue *azulejos* and tower: **Vinaroz** nearby is a small but important fishing-port, famed for its sturgeon and lobsters; its Baroque church has an equally gaudy portal.

The Maestrazgo

Inland from here is a region called the Maestrazgo, which translates as 'the jurisdiction of a grand master of a military order'; and of Grand Masters you can take your pick between the Templars, the Knights of Montesa, and the Knights of St John, all of whom were here. It is a rugged, picturesque region, especially the Upper Maestrazgo (see 'Aragón'). The Lower Maestrazgo, while not as wild or remote, has a number of fascinating medieval villages.

Easiest to reach, on the Vinaroz–Zaragoza road, **Morella** is also one of the most picturesque, surrounded by medieval walls that look as if they were raised yesterday and surmounted by a steel, isolated rock and its mighty castle. Of the four gates into the city, the 14th-century **Puerta de San Miguel** is the most impressive. Of the churches, the **Basilica de Santa María la Mayor** (finished 1330) with its finely carved portals is not only the finest in town, but perhaps of the whole País Valenciano. Inside (open from 11 am–2 pm and 3.3)–6 pm) a pretty marble spiral stair ascends to the raised *coro*; the stained glass is also beautiful.

The streets of Morella are steep and lined with tall whitewashed houses embellished with wooden balconies. Near the top of them, just below the castle, is an old **Franscican monastery** with a local museum in its fine 13th-century **cloister**. From here you can take a path up to the castle itself, with magnificent views of the entire region; to the north look for the **Gothic Aqueduct**, built in the 14th century when the Roman style of building was a dim memory

From San Mateo a minor road heads 14 km (8.8 miles) south to **Albocácer**, a Templar town with a ruined castle; near this, just off the road from San Mateo is a **Calvario**. A Calvario is similar to the Stations of the Cross, a symbolic journey along the Via Dolorosa a typical one has a chapel atop a hill, reached by a winding path marked by intermittent shrines. There are quite a few in the Maestrazgo, but Albocácer's is exceptional – virtual maze of low, whitewashed, stone walls.

Another one in maze form may be seen in the **Covas de Vinroma** just to the south east. While the rest of Europe underwent the pangs of World War II, Spaniards were reading about the chapel atop the Covas de Vinroma's calvario, where the Francoists manufactured a miracle – several appearances of the Virgin, no less, who mouthed the philosophy of José Antonio Primo de Rivera and declared that Heaven, in league with Hitler, would soon clear the earth of the Marxist–Jewish menace that threatened it with extinction. In the euphoria of post-Civil victory, there were plans to make the village the Lourdes of Spain, but when the Vatican remained silent on the matter, and the war took its course, the miracles quickly declined. Nowadays the only 'sight' in the old village is its prehistoric cave paintings.

Two other scenic medieval towns, formerly Templar possessions, are **Culla** and **Ares de Maestre**, the latter impressively built around a soufflé of a rock and near some excellent paleolithic art in the **Cova Remigia**. The cave lies just along the road to another pretty village, **Villafranca del Cid**, which like several other places in the Maestrazgo, recalls in its name the Cid's frequent raids in the region.

TOURIST INFORMATION

Castellón: Plaza de María Agustina 5, Tel: 22 77 03.

Peñiscola: Paseo Maritimo, Tel: 48 02 08.

WHERE TO STAY

Burriana has a small and pleasant beach hotel in the **Aloha****, Conde Vallellano, Tel: 51 01 04, with a small pool and garden, and doubles with bath for 2800 pts. Montanejos has four modest *hostales*; the pick of the lot, and open all year round, **Rosaleda de Mijares***, Fuentes de Baños 30, Tel: 13 10 79, is prettily located near the small spa, offering doubles with bath for 1550 pts, without bath 1100 pts. Another *hostal*, **Xauen**, has the best food in the village.

In Castellón, the place to stay if you've brought along the clubs is the **Hotel del Golf*****, located on the Grao's Playa del Pinar, Tel: 22 19 50; besides golf, it offers tennis, a pool, and air-conditioned rooms in contemporary surroundings; 5000 pts in the summer, 4400 pts out of season for a double. **Hostal Brisamar** near the centre of Castellón at Avda. Buenavista 26, Tel: 22 29 22, is small and clean and located in one of the nicer corners of town, with doubles for 1550 pts with bath, open year round.

In Benicasim things are more expensive. A good bet is the **Hotel Azor*****, right on the beach (Paseo Maritimo, Tel: 30 03 50) open from March-mid November, and offering its guests tennis, golf, and pool facilities for 3800–4100 pts. For more reasonable prices, stay instead at Oropesa, where a small but good beach hotel like **El Cid***** (Las Playetas, Tel: 30 07 00) offers rooms in a pretty location, pool, tennis and a garden for 2900 pts with bath in season, without bath as low as 1800 pts (open April–September).

There are only two hotels on Peñiscola's promontory, the finest, **Hostal del Duc*** is located in an old mansion in the centre of town (C. Fuladosa 10, Tel: 48 07 68); open April-September, its elegant doubles go for 1600 pts. More typical beach fare, with fine views of the promontory, is **La Cabaña****, Primo de Rivera 29, Tel: 48 00 17, open all year, with doubles for 1400–1825 pts. It has many neighbours, all more-or-less the same.

In Benicarlo the best place to stay and eat is the parador **Costa de Azahar*****, Avda. Papa Luna 3, Tel: 47 01 00, a modern establishment with pool, garden and air-conditioned rooms for 5500–7000 pts; the restaurant features the freshest of seafood and Valencian specialities. Less expensive and also open all year, the **Almadraba***, Santo Tomás 137, Tel: 30 01 80, has clean double rooms with bath for 1485 pts; its annex, Almadraba II has more of the same.

Morella is the only town in the Maestrazgo prepared for visitors. Best here is the **Cardenal Ram****, Cuesta Suñer 1, Tel: 16 00 00, located in a restored palace, like a budget parador, with fine rooms near the centre for 2200 pts, open all year. It also has a good restaurant.

EATING OUT

For a good seafood meal in Burriana, the **Club Náutico**, right on the port, is the local favourite (1500 pts).

The classic place to dine in Castellón is the air conditioned **Casino Antiguo**, Puerta del Sol 2, a private club with a public dining room, classic Valencian rice dishes and good seafood (1200–1800 pts). More excellent seafood can be consumed at the charming **Restaurante Rafael**, Churruca 26, right off the fisherman's docks in El Grao, where you can watch the fleet come in. Closed Sundays; complete dinners around 1400 pts.

Benicasim has a number of French restaurants, reflecting the tastes of the majority of tourists – a good one is **Chez Renée** on C. Sevilla, offering traditional north-of-the-border favourites for 1400–1900 pts.

On the promontory of Peñiscola, **Casa Severino** at Principe 1, offers the provincial speciality, *paella marinara*, for 700 pts, with dining on the terrace overlooking the sea.

An even better restaurant than the Cardenal Ram's in Morella is **Mesón del Pastor**, Cuesta Jovani 5, which features the local cuisine of the mountains – lots of pork and lamb with curds and honey (*cuajada y miel*) for dessert (1400 pts).

Costa Blanca

The 'White Coast' of Spain started out as a refuge from the intensity of the Costa Brava, where pioneering Germans, followed by the British and French, could have an inexpensive if unexciting holiday. While not as dramatically beautiful as the Costa Brava, it's a rose compared to the toadstool monotony of the Costa del Sol. Yet the Costa Blanca is no longer inexpensive, and every year more sports activities and nightclubs accompany a growing number of hotels and apartment blocks – especially in the Babylon of Benidorm.

GETTING AROUND

There are at least 15 local trains daily between Valencia and Gandía, the terminus of the coast line. The Valencia–Alicante train, however, goes inland, through Játiva; another branch from Valencia terminates in Alcoy via Játiva (three a day). There are frequent RENFE buses between Valencia and Alicante as well, some direct on the Autopista, others stopping at the resorts along the Costa Blanca.

The Costa Blanca is also well served by its own FEVE narrow-gauge line out of Alicante (15 a day, once an hour), with stations at Denía, Teulada, Calpe, Altea, Benidorm and the beaches north of Alicante. Several buses a day link Denía with Javea, connecting with the train. FEVE information: Denía, Tel: 78 04 45; Benidorm, Tel: 86 18 95; Alicante, Tel: 26 27 31.

Denía is also a port with ferry links on the Flebasa/Isnasa line to Ibiza; for information, C. Marqués de Campas 62, Tel: 78 11 15, in Denía.

South of Valencia

The Costa Blanca officially begins at Denía; en route there are great rice plantations and minor beaches until **Gandía**, set back a couple of miles from the sea. It is best known for its dukes of the Borgia family; in the 15th century the branch of the family that remained in Spain settled down in the fine Renaissance **Palace of the Dukes**. The fourth duke of Gandía, Francisco Borgia, renounced the worldly vanities his family was famous for and became a Jesuit and saint. The palace now belongs to the Jesuits; the tourist office can tell you how to get in for a tour. There are frequent connections to the very developed beach. **Oliva**, 4 km (2.5 miles) away, is much quieter.

Just within Alicante province, **Denía** is located between Mount Montgó and the sea. The Greeks built a temple of Artemis here, the goddess the Romans knew as Diana, who in turn gave her name to the town. Only the ruined **castle** over the town evokes Denía's pre-tourist history, but the town with all its villas is one of the quieter on the Costa Blanca, and there are fine views from atop Mount Montgó. **Javea**, nestled beneath the villa-covered capes of San Antonio and San Martin, has preserved more of its character, and though it has only two small beaches, it is well endowed with scenic marine grottos and dramatic coves.

Next are the fairly quiet beaches of **Teulada**, and then the not-so-quiet but excellent beaches of **Calpe**. The Greeks called Gibraltar 'Calpe,' and this Calpe has it own mighty Rock, the **Peñon de Ifach**, bored with a tunnel to let you mount to the summit – 327 m (1063 ft) over the sea below. Beaches sweep around either side of it. **Altea** is quieter, located on a natural balcony over the sea; its beach isn't as good but its church has a fine blue-tiled Valencian dome.

Benidorm

The undisputed giant on the Costa Blanca, Benidorm has become synonomous with high rises and package tourism. The 6.4 km (4 miles) long wide, sandy beach has something to do with it, and the ensemble of skyscrapers huddled together in a dense forest is awesome in a Manhattanish way; certainly it has a verve most other costa resorts lack – as well as more discotheques and Las Vegas-type shows.

Behind Benidorm (easily visible from the autopista) there is a peculiar mountain with a neat, square notch taken out of it – a notch shaped exactly like the islet off the coast. There is an old Spanish legend that says a giant once lived near Benidorm. After many years of loneliness, he found a lady love, who eventually fell ill and told the giant that she would die when the sun went down that day. In despair the giant watched the sun sink behind the mountain, then at the last minute he wrenched out a piece of the summit and hurled it into the sea to give his lady another minute of life. Curiously enough, geologists who have studied islet and mount have found them indeed to be of the same composition.

Inland from Benidorm, it's 27 km (16.9 miles) to the medieval village of **Guadalest** with its much-ruined castle perched high atop a pinnacle. To capture it, Jaime I wrote that he had to attach wings to his soldiers' armour; the modern visitor can climb up through a tunnel. **Alcoy**, further west, celebrates St George's day with a Battle of Christian and Moors commemorating a personal appearance of the saint in a 1276 battle. It's been going on so long there's a museum of the holiday, as well as local costumes, armour, etc. at the **Casal de Sant Jordi**

Villajoyosa is the last big resort before Alicante but despite the pretty white nucleus of its old town it manages to have the least character.

TOURIST INFORMATION

Gandía: Rinconada del Padre Leandro Calvo, Tel: 287 35 36.
Denía: Patricio Ferrándiz, Tel: 78 09 57.
Jávea: Pl. Almirante Bastarreche, Tel: 79 07 36.
Calpe: Avda. Ejércitos Españoles 40, Tel: 83 12 50.
Altea: Paseo Maritimo, Tel: 88 88 23.
Benidorm: Martínez Alejos 16, Tel: 85 32 24.
Alcoy: Gral. Sanjurjo 3, Tel: 34 32 84.
Villajoyosa: Pl. de la Iglesia, Tel: 89 30 43.

WHERE TO STAY

In Gandía, the swanky hotels are on the beach, and the modest, inexpensive ones in the town. In the first category the **Bayren I******, (Paseo de Neptuno, Tel: 284 03 00) stands out, with a pleasant pool, garden and terraces, air-conditioned rooms and dancing in the evening; open all year round, doubles are 4835–6910 pts. It has an annex, the **Bayren II** on C. Mallorca with rates two-thirds that; both have good tennis courts.

In the town, the **Hostal Mangual****, Pl. del Mediterráneo 4, Tel: 284 21 02, is the most pleasant choice and open all year; doubles 2100–2300 pts; no restaurant but breakfast served.

In Denía, the **Hostal Rosa****, Partida Marines 197, Tel: 78 15 73, is a pleasant, seaside, family-oriented resort, with pools for the adults and children, a playground, tennis and breakfast, but no restaurant. Doubles are 2000–3000 pts, open March–October.

Javea boasts the new, finely situated **Parador Costa Blanca*****, Playa del Arenal, Tel: 79 02 00, air-conditioned, with a pool and garden and good restaurant focusing on the dishes of the Levante (6500–8500 pts). If you can't swing that, the **Hostal Javea***, in the middle of town on Pio X 5, Tel: 79 05 08, is small and friendly and open all year: doubles with bath 1500–2500 pts.

In Altea, a good bet on the beach is the **Hotel Altaya****, Generalísimo 113, Tel: 84 08 00, with pleasant rooms with sea views for 2600 pts, doubles with bath.

There are so many hotels in Benidorm, and so many of them so similar and so booked up with packagers in the summer that it's hard to tell them apart. Off-season you can get excellent rates – as little as half the high season's. Good value for money, **Los Alamos*****, located near the beach and the heart of Benidorm on Av. Gerona, Tel: 85 02 12, has a pool and garden but no restaurant – a blessing in Benidorm, where full-board requirements often force you to pay more and eat more than you care to.

Doubles at 2350–2700 pts, open all year. In the same category, but a bit further back from the sea, is the attractive **Hotel Don José****, Ctra, del Alt, Tel: 85 50 50; open March–October, doubles with bath are 2800 pts. A third choice without a restaurant isn't stylish, but it's centrally located and has a pool: **Hostal Nacional***, Verano 9, Tel: 85 04 32, open April–October with doubles and bath for 1800–2500 pts.

In Calpe the big favourite is the **Paradero Ifach****, Explanade del Puerto 50, Tel: 83 03 00, a small hotel located within spitting distance of the great rock. Tennis and gardens and the great seaviews complement the comfortable furnishings; doubles are 4000 pts; nice restaurant. A good bargain in Calpe is the **Hostal El Parque**, in the centre at C. Portalet, Tel: 83 07 70, its simple but clean rooms go for 900–1200 pts. doubles with bath – open all year.

EATING OUT

Most of the restaurants in Gandía are also on the beach: **La Gamba**, on the Ctra. Nazaret-Oliva, has a garden-terrace as a pretty setting for its delicious seafood (2000 pts). At the **As de Oros**, Paseo de Neptuno, shellfish are the speciality (2200 pts).

The place to eat in Denía is **El Trampoli**, Playa Les Rotes (where most of Denía's restaurants may be found), with a delicious menu of Valencian rice and seafood for 2400 pts.

Near the Javea parador on Avda. del Arenal, a little restaurant called **La Estrella** makes the best bouillabaise in Spain – order it in advance. Its other dishes are also very good, including the desserts (2400 pts).

La Costera, Costera Maestre de Musica 8 in Altea, is a good, moderate-priced eatery, with a delicious set menu for 1200 pts.

The posh place to dine in Benidorm is **Tiffany's**, Avda. Mediterráneo 3, Tel: 85 44 68, with high-class international cuisine, with full meals for 3500 pts. Also international, with a pretty atmosphere and terrace-dining in the summer is **La Caserola**, Avda. Bruseles 7 (1800 pts). In Benidorm's old town – the tiny, pre-holiday fishing village – **El Calpi**, Pl. de la Constitución, is a good bet for tapas dining.

The food in Calpe's restaurants, like Benidorm's tends to be international: good French dishes are featured at **L'Escale**, Puerto de Ifach (1500 pts).

ENTERTAINMENT

When you've had enough of the beach, the Costa Blanca seeks to entertain you in other ways. Nearly every town has its tennis courts; Altea, Benisa (near Calpe), Javea and Torrevieja (south of Alicante) have golf courses as well. Watersports of all kinds may be practised along the coast, especially at Benidorm, which has waterskiing facilities, boat rentals, sailing and diving on offer; windsurfing is popular all along the coast. Near Pego (by Denía), the Safari Park Vergel is for those with cars only – the lions and tigers run about freely; there's also a dolphin show and many children's activities; open all year. Tel: 75 02 85 for information. Benidorm has a permanent fun-fair just off the access route to the Autopista. The modern Casino Costa Blanca is between Benidorm and Villajoyosa; all along the old coastal road from Alicante are shopping centres with big parking lots (open and abandoned), putting courses and bowling alleys. Yachtsmen should obtain from the tourist offices the detailed folder on *Instalaciones Nauticas* on the

Costa; another big folder, *Deporte y Cultura* details every possible activity on the coast, from deep-sea diving to choral societies.

Benidorm counts its pubs, night clubs, and discotheques by the score, mostly international in flavour. Perhaps to compensate for this, Benidorm sponsors a Festival of Spanish Song to remind its visitors they're in Spain.

Alicante

Alicante is the air gateway to the Costa Blanca, and many of the 2 million people who fly in here decide to go no further. Unlike the other resorts on the coast, Alicante is a real Spanish city, with an air of its own along its seaside promenades and narrow back streets, it never tires of letting you know that, year after year, it has the warmest and sunniest winters in all Europe. And charter flights from London in January or February can be cheaper than staying at home.

GETTING AROUND

Alicante's *El Altet Airport*, is 20 km from the city (Tel: 28 50 11). Besides charters from Northern Europe, it handles a large number of regular flights, domestically from Madrid, Barcelona, Palma, Ibiza, Sevilla, Las Palmas, Tenerife and Vitoria. Iberia's office is at Avda. Federico Soto 9, Tel: 26 60 00; British Airways is at Explanada de España 3, Tel: 20 05 94. Airport buses leave from C. Portugal, by the bus station.

RENFE's station in Alicante is on the Avda. Salamanca (Tel: 22 01 27); ticket office is at Explanada de España 1, Tel: 21 13 03. There are connections with Murcia, Orihuela, Elche, Sax, Villena, Albacete, Madrid, Valencia, Barcelona, and Port Bou. In Elche, the RENFE station is called Elche Parque and is located on the edge of town on Avda. de la Llibertat, a block from the main bus terminal.

The FEVE station in Alicante (with connections to San Juan beach and the Costa Blanca north) is at the end of Playa del Postiguet (Tel: 26 27 31); bus C-1 goes there from downtown's Pl. de España.

Alicante's bus station is at the corner of C. Portugal and C. Italia, Tel: 22 07 00. There are frequent connections all along the Costa Blanca; also to Granada, Almería, Barcelona, Jaen, Málaga, and Valencia.

Bus C-1's route continues past the FEVE station to the Playa de San Juan and Playa de Muchavista, and takes in most of Alicante's discotheques as well. It runs approximately every half-hour.

There are buses down the coast from Alicante; connections between Torrevieja and points south are also very frequent from Murcia (see below).

WHAT TO SEE

Alicante was the mightiest citadel of the Kingdom of Valencia, and judging by the powerful **Castle of Santa Barbara** that crowns the city, it still is. The English garrisoned the castle during most of Spain's wars; Philip V blew both castle and troops up in 1707, but it was later restored, and is fun to explore for itself and the stunning views it commands (open 9 am till sundown; access by lift from the Paseo de Gomis, just above the Playa del Postiguet).

Below the castle is Alicante's lively and jovial old neighbourhood, **Santa Cruz**. Here you'll find the **Cathedral San Nicolás de Bari** (1662), a strong, well-proportioned church covered with red graffiti. The interior has been restored since its destruction in the Civil War. Republican passions burned white hot in Alicante – the founder and patron saint of the Falange, José Antonio Primo de Rivera was imprisoned in a local convent and hurriedly executed when the locals feared the Republican government might order him freed; at the end of the war, some 15,000 Republicans waited on the docks in vain for the Republican Navy to rescue them from Nationalist reprisals. Several hundred, it is said, committed suicide.

The other building worthy of mention, the **Ayuntamiento** on Calle R. Altamíra, has an elegant Baroque façade. The **Museum of 20th-Century Art** is near here, off the pedestrian Calle Mayor, with works by Picasso, Braque, Gris, Miró and more (open 10.30 am–1.30 pm and 6–9 pm summer, 10 am–1 pm and 5–8 pm winter, closed Mondays).

Most visitors, when they're not lounging on Alicante's fine beaches, are strolling down the shady **Explanada de España** with its flamboyant mosaics. The **Playa del Postiguet**, at the end of the Explanada, can get very, very crowded in the summer, and sometimes it seems just as many people take the bus or train 6 km (3.8 miles) north to bigger and cleaner **Playa de San Juan**.

Around Alicante

Between Alicante and San Juan beach, you can visit the **Monasterio de La Santa Faz**, built to enshrine the supposed handkerchief of Santa Veronica (open 10 am–1 pm and 4–8 pm). A secondary road off the coast here leads to Busot and the **Cave of Canalobre** (24 km (15 miles) from Alicante). The cave contains stalactites and strange formations, and in the summer is the scene of occasional concerts (open summer 10.30 am–8.30 pm, winter 11 am–6.30 pm).

All over Alicante the shops have stacks of *turrón*, a sweet made of local almonds and honey, and nearly all of it comes from **Jijona**, on the main road to Alcoy (try the 1880 *Crema de Jijona*) and there's even a Turrón Museum in town to show you how it's made. This is a busy region: nearby **Ibi** makes most of Spain's toys. One company claims to be the world's largest producer of dolls' eyeballs.

West of Ibi there are picturesque **castles** crowning the villages of **Biar, Sax** and, strikingly, **Villena**. Where the huge, square-towered castle dates from the 15th century, as do many of the old noble houses. The Gothic **church of Santiago** is the finest in Villena, especially interesting for its fluted columns and strange motifs. The Ayuntamiento (1707) has a gracious courtyard and in one of its wings, an **Archaeology Museum**, which has as its centrepiece 'the Treasure of Villena' – a hoard of solid gold bracelets, tiaras, bowls and rings discovered near the town in 1963. The pieces have been dated back to the Bronze Age (1000 BC) and were made by the ancestors of the Iberians.

Elche

Elche, 20 km (12.5 miles) from Alicante, makes two claims on the world's attention. First, Spain's most famous piece of ancient art was unearthed here, *La Dama de Elche* now in Madrid. Secondly, it has the only date-palm grove in Europe.

The Dama de Elche

The Moors planted the first palms, and now the approximately 200,000 trees nearly surround Elche. Although they produce a crop of dates (no other palms in Europe do), they are economically more valuable for their fronds, which are tied up to bleach a pale yellow in time for Palm Sunday, when they're shipped throughout Spain. Often you'll see one tied to a balcony, not because the owner has forgotten to take it down after Easter, but because the fronds are widely believed to ward off lightning. The palms are best seen in the garden setting of the **Huerto del Cura** just east of town on Calle Frederico Garcia Sanchis, the star of the garden is the unusual, eight-branched Imperial Palm, thought to be around 150 years old (open 8 am–9 pm). The Lady of Elche bust was discovered in 1897 in **La Alcudia** south of town. Since then further excavations have revealed nine successive civilizations, documented by a small **museum** on the site (Crta. a Dolores, 2 km (1.3 miles) from town; open 10 am–2 pm, closed Monday). The blue-domed **Basilica de Santa María** has an elaborate 17th-century Baroque façade; ask to climb the tower for the view across the palm plantations.

Orihuela, also on the road to Murcia, is an oasis – a prosperous town in its own very fertile *huerta*. It's worth a stop for its idiosyncratic **cathedral** (open mornings till 1 pm and from 4–6 pm). Finished in 1355, its interior is a fantasy of spiralling pillars and corkscrew-rib vaulting; the **cathedral museum** has a Velazquez and other masters in its fine collection.

South of Alicante

The scenery south and west of Alicante is mostly flat and not especially attractive, though in February the blossoming almonds give it a pretty lace edging. The resorts to the south are also less interesting. **Santa Pola**, the largest, has good beaches and a landmark, fortified **Isla de Tabarca**, which you can visit on an excursion boat. **Guardamat de Segura** is rather more scenic with its palms and pines; **Torrevieja** has modern hotels going up everywhere. To the south there are some tranquil beaches, as yet hardly developed, belonging to Orihuela.

Further south, into the Murcia region, the unusual **Mar Menor** is a warm, shallow and salty lagoon, covering 170 sq. km (66 sq. miles) and dotted with islets. It's separated from the sea by a narrow, beach-lined strip of land called **La Manga** ('the sleeve') where most of Murcia's holiday development has taken place. Along La Manga you can choose between the calm and warm beaches on the Mar Menor, or the cooler, beaches along the Mediterranean. In Moorish times the kings would come to the Mar Menor for their ritual 'nine baths'; today some of the ancient pools are still used in **San Pedro del Pinatar** for rheumatism therapy. Because of its warmth the Mar Menor is also used as a great prawn nursery, where Spain's favourite snacks may be harvested right up to the beginning of winter.

TOURIST INFORMATION

Alicante: Pl. de Ayuntamiento 1, Tel: 20 51 00, provincial office: Explanada de España 2, Tel: 21 22 85. Also in the bus station: C. Portugal 17, Tel: 22 38 02.

Elche: Parque Municipal, Tel: 45 27 47.

Orihuela: Pl. Condessa, Tel: 30 02 96.

Santa Pola: Pl. de la Diputación.

Torrevieja: Avda. de la Libertad, Tel: 71 07 22.

Los Alcázares (Mar Menor): C. de Julio Melero, Tel: 57 71 16.

La Manga del Mar Menor: Pl. Bohemia, Tel: 56 30 96.

WHERE TO STAY

In Alicante, hotels of all categories are spread throughout town, but the most popular are near the Explanada. The most beautiful is the elegant, if elderly, **Hotel Palas*****, Pl. del Mar 5, Tel: 20 93 10, with sea views and the Playa del Postiguet a stone's throw away. Rooms are quite spacious; doubles are 3920–4920 pts, open all year. Also on the beach, in a huge, totally self-contained complex, the **Meliá Alicante******, Playa Postiguet, Tel: 20 50 00, with three restaurants, two pools, and shops, open all year, doubles 7850–8800 pts. A few blocks from the Explanada, the **Hotel Crystal*****, López Torregrosa 9, Tel: 20 96 00, was named for its crystal façade. All rooms are attractive, have bath and air-conditioning, doubles 3400–3700 pts. **El Alamo***, San Fernando 56, Tel: 21 83 55, doesn't look like much from the outside, but has pleasant rooms within, from 2300–2700 pts with bath, 1900–2100 pts without, also open all year. The **Hostal Galicia**, Arquitecto Morell 1, Tel: 22 50 93, is two blocks from the bus station in a nice modern building; its doubles with bath are 2050 pts, 1600 pts without. The nicest budget *hostal*, the **Montecarlo****, San Francisco, 20, Tel: 20 67 22, is near the heart of town and near the beach; rooms are 1645–1800 pts with bath, 1350–1500 pts without.

In Elche, there's an associate Párador, the **Huerto del Cura******, F. Garcia Sanchiz 14, Tel: 45 80 40, with cabins in the palm grove. There's a pool and tennis courts; all rooms are air-conditioned and have private bars (doubles 7150–7650 pts). Near the train station, and in easy walking distance of the Parque Municipal and palm groves, the simple but clean **Hostal Maria***, Avda. Ferrocarril 4, Tel: 46 02 83, is a right for an overnight stay; bathless doubles 1410 pts.

The one hotel worthy of note in the interior is **Hostal El Molino*****, Jaime I 34, Tel: 47 48 42, in Sax, located in a 200-year-old mill; there's a pool, garden, and good restaurant featuring rabbit and partridge (1500 pts); the eight doubles, with bath, go for 1900–2600 pts (open all year). There are also a couple of *fondas* and pleasant restaurants in Villena (especially good, **Warynessy**, features kid for 800 pts on Isabel la Católica).

On the coast, **La Cibeles****, C. de Cartagena 10, Tel: 71 00 12, in Torrevieja is a pleasant, moderate, beach *hostal* open all year, and very near the centre. Doubles all with bath are 2200–2475 pts.

On Orihuela's beach Dehesa de Campoamor, the **Montepiedra*****, Tel: 32 03 00, overlooks the beach and has a pretty pool and garden; open all year, its modern doubles are 3000–4500 pts.

Around the Mar Menor, the most luxurious and pricey accommodation is on the Manga, like the huge **Cavanna******, Gran Vía de la Manga, Tel: 56 36 00, with a pool, tennis and children's activities between the two seas for 4000–5000 pts, open May–September. It's air-conditioned, as is the little **Hostal Mar Menor**** in Los Alcazares (Sta. Teresa 31, Tel: 57 51 25), which is on the beach and open all year round; doubles 2500–3400 pts with bath, 2100–2650 pts without. Also small and pleasant, open all year (except at Christmas) is the **Hostal Mariana**, Avda. Dr. Atero Guirao 54, Tel: 18 10 13, its doubles with bath 1500–2050 pts.

EATING OUT

The best restaurant in Alicante, **Delfin**, Explanada de España 12, not only serves delicious Alicantino versions of Valencian rice dishes, innovative international dishes and excellent seafood, but also has fine views of the sea (3000 pts). **Dársena**, boasts an even more scenic location on the Muelle de Costa just off the Explanada; it has a bright shiny interior and delicious rice dishes (2500 pts). **Quo Venit**, Pl. Santissima Faz, also near the Explanada, has outdoor dining on its terrace, and prides itself on its tapas, rice and grilled fish (2000 pts). Locals favour **La Parra**, Avda. de Maisonnave, with a good, filling set menu for 530 pts. There are lots of inexpensive restaurants right around the cathedral – **Bruno's** has pizza and couscous daily for about 875 pts, on C. Mayor.

The restaurant of Elche's parador, **Els Capellans**, is considered the town's finest, and has fine views over the palms and often live music (1700–2200 pts – some desserts have local dates in them).

The restaurant in the **Parque Municipal** specializes in rice dishes under the palms for around 1500 pts.

On the coast, **Miramar**, on the Paseo Vistalegre 6, overlooking the sea, is the best place to eat seafood (1600 pts).

In Orihuela, **La Barraca**, on the Avda. de las Adelfas has typical Spanish cuisine served on a seaside terrace for 1500 pts.

Murcia

In the division into autonomous regions of post-Franco Spain, no one wanted Murcia, so it became its own little region. In opinion polls, with questions like 'who would you like your daughter to marry?' the Murcians always come out at the very bottom. They don't really deserve it; they just happened to have been the first emigrants looking for work in Barcelona at the turn of the century. The snooty Catalans were appalled at their country ways, and 'Murcian' became an insult. Ironically, most of the Murcians are descendants from Catalan settlers who emigrated south in the 13th century after the Reconquista. The Moors, who gave it its name, *Musiyah*, loved it well and farmed its *huerta*; most Muslim scholars would say that Ibn Al-Arabi of Murcia (1165–1240), mystic and poet of love, was the greatest Spaniard that ever lived.

GETTING AROUND

Murcia's airport is located near the Mar Menor in San Javier (Tel: 57 00 73) and has daily connections with Madrid and Barcelona. Iberia's office is at Avda. Alfonso el Sabio, Edif, Velazquez, Tel: 24 00 50. The RENFE station (Estación de Carmen) is south of town, on C. Industria (bus 9 will take you to the centre); Tel: 25 21 54. There are connections with Aguilas, Cartagena, Lorca, Alicante, Valencia, Albacete, Madrid and Barcelona.

A narrow-gauge train links Cartagena with Los Nietos (near Cabo de Palos and its beaches) once every hour-and-a-half, a service complemented by hourly buses between Cartagena and Cabo de Palos run by FEVE.

Murcia's central bus station is on the west edge of town on Pl. de Casanova, Tel: 29 22 11 (good tapas in the station bar). There are buses every hour to Orihuela, seven to Caravaca, eight to Lorca, 13 to Cartagena, one to Aguilas, three to Mazzarrón. Towards the Mar Menor: six buses to San Pedro, three to Los Alcázares, and at 1.30 pm a bus through Cabo de Palos to La Manga del Mar Menor. Also connections with Granada, Sevilla, Almería, Mojácar, Barcelona, Málaga and Torrevieja.

WHAT TO SEE

Whatever other Spaniards may think, Murcia is a congenial, and atmospheric place. The **Cathedral**, not far from the river, is easy to find by its lofty, unusual **tower**, built by four different architects between 1521 and 1792; ask the museum custodian to open the door if you'd like to climb up. The cathedral itself has a fine Baroque façade and Gothic portals on either side. The interior is a mixture of styles, and is especially notable for its 15th-century **Vélez Chapel**, an exuberant Plateresque National Monument. An urn on the main altar contains an odd relic – the innards of Alfonso the Wise. In the **museum** (open daily 10 am–1 pm and 5–8 pm) a Roman sarcophagus relief of the muses shares space with good collection of religious artefacts.

From the cathedral head up the pedestrian Calle de Traperia, where, at the first block, stands the **Casino** (club), a charming 20th-century glass-topped arcade in the Alhambra style, site of frequent art exhibits. On the far side of the Gran Vía Escultor Salzillo, Murcia's main street, and near the bus station you'll find the **Salzillo Museum** (San Andrés 1, weekdays 9.30 am–1 pm and 4–7 pm, Sundays 10 am–1 pm), dedicated to the works of Murcian sculptor Francisco Salzillo (1707–83) who made many of the *pasos*, or floats, used in Murcia's Semana Santa processions, which make it one of Spain's best – compared to the great, overwrought *pasos* in Andalucía, Salzillo's have a vivacious if sentimental charm.

Lorca and Caravaca

There are two villages worth a visit in the Murcia region – **Lorca** on the main road to Granada and Almería, was an outpost against the Moors of Granada and a small artistic centre; its castle and some of its public buildings have been restored, many dating from the 16th-18th centuries. It is Murcia's prettiest village and easily accessible. **Caravaca**, further north, is a bit out of the way. On the hill overlooking the village is the large **Real Alcázar-Santuario de la Vera Cruz**, with a curious story – in 1231 (13 years before Caravaca was reconquered by the Christians), the Moorish lord asked a priest he had imprisoned to perform a mass so that he could see what it was like. The priest reluctantly agreed, and gathered together all the necessary items when he realized he had no cross. He was about to call it all off when two angels brought one in through the window. The Sanctuary, with its pink Baroque façade, was built in the 17th century to house this relic, but it was stolen during the Civil War and never found, (though the Vatican sent a copy containing a slivver of the True Cross). After the Reconquest, Caravaca was donated to the Templars who are vividly remembered in the villages' unique fiestas.

Cartagena

Cartagena was the major city of the Carthaginians in Spain, who honoured it by naming it after their own capital. It prospered by dint of its gold and silver mines, and it was a major blow to Hannibal when Scipio Africanus the elder besieged and captured it. In 1585 Francis Drake raided the port and snatched its guns. When the message of the First Internationale reached Spain, it was eagerly received here; revolts in Cartagena and Alcoy in 1873 by radicals led to the downfall of Spain's first Republican Government. The Civil War inflicted more damage; nor does the presence of a major naval base improve things.

Cartagena's port is dominated by its **Arsenal** (1782) and adorned with an early (1888) submarine, Isaac Peral's *Cartagena*, resembling a big white torpedo. The old town, with its narrow streets, Roman ruins, and dilapidated houses, is built around the ruined 13th-century cathedral. The best thing to do is head right up to the **Castillo de la Concepción** above the old cathedral for the view, or west to the beaches – there's a nudist one at **El Portus** and a fine one east at **Cabo de Palos**. **Mazarrón**, further west, is near more beaches and the **Enchanted City of Bolnuevo**, an area of strange, wind-eroded rocks and pinnacles. Ruined watchtowers from the 16th century guard the coast to **Aguilas**, the last resort before Andalucía. The Tartessians were the first to found a city here, on a promontory overlooking two bays, but Barbary pirates caused its abandonment until 1765, when Carlos III and the Count of Aranda laid out a new, modern town. English mining interests in Aguilas shipped away iron ore but left behind the game of football, which the locals claimed they played before anyone else in Spain.

TOURIST INFORMATION

Murcia: Municipal office, C. Tomás Mestre (near the cathedral), Tel: 21 61 15; provincial office, C. Alejandro Séiquer 3, Tel: 21 37 16.

Cartagena: Ayuntamiento, Tel: 50 64 83; also C. de Castellini 5, Tel: 50 75 49.
Aquilas: Av. de José Antonio 20, Tel: 41 29 63.
Mazarrón: C. Generalisimo 2, Tel: 59 45 08.

WHERE TO STAY

In Murcia, there are two elegant choices in the heart of the city. **Hotel Condé de Floridablanca**, Corbalán 7, Tel: 21 46 24, is in Baroque palace in the old town, but offering such modern conveniences as air-conditioning for 4995–5780 pts a double. More modern, and also air-conditioned (a definite plus when the torrid *leveche* wind blows in the summer) is the **Rincón de Pepe*****, Apóstoles 34, Tel: 21 22 39, with the most comfortable rooms in town for 6325–7273 pts. **Hispano I**** on the pedestrian Traperia 8, Tel: 21 61 52, also offers comfortable air-conditioned rooms, 3000–3600 pts. Even cheaper and just as cool, **Hostal Pacoche***, González Cebrián 9, Tel: 21 76 05, is large and a bit aging, but the price is right: doubles 1700–1900 pts, with bath; without bath 1350–1500 pts.

In Cartegena one of the best places to stay and eat is **Los Habaneros****, San Diego 60, Tel: 50 52 50, centrally located, air-conditioned and economical: doubles with bath are 2200 pts, without bath 1700 pts. The restaurant specializes in fish (1700 pts).

In Aguilas you can't do better than the **Hostal Carlos III*****, Rey Carlos III, 22, Tel: 41 16 50, small, prettily located near the sea, and open all year; doubles with bath 3025–3850 pts. For something cheaper, the **Hostal Vilar***, C. Málaga, Tel: 41 00 21, is also open all year and has good, clean rooms for 990–1100 pts. In the Puerto de Mazarrón, the **Residencia Durán****, Playa de la Isla, Tel: 59 40 50, is a fine, moderately priced holiday choice (open March–September, doubles 2000–3000 pts, all with bath). Of the innumerable cheap hostels in Lorca, the **Ciudad del Sol***, in the centre at Galicia 9, Tel: 46 78 72, beats the competition in August with its air-conditioned, clean if modest rooms: doubles 1500 pts with bath, 1200 pts without.

EATING OUT

An added attraction of the Rincón de Pepe in Murcia is that the same management runs the restaurant downstairs, by all votes the finest in Murcia; try the seafood or Murcian roast lamb (2500 pts.) Traditional Murcian cuisine, with a menu changed daily and pretty brick decor can be found at **Los Apóstoles**, Pl. de los Apóstoles 1 (1800 pts, closed August). **Paco's**, on Alfaro 7, has good, solid Spanish fare for 800 pts; **Feliz China**, C. de Conde de Valle de San Juan, just off Gran Vía Salzillo, has a good menu for 550 pts.

In Cartagena, try **Mare Nostrum**, near the submarine, for tapas.

Part VI

ARAGÓN

Detail of Mudejár Tower, Teruel

Not many people say to their travelling companion, 'Come on Cuddles, let's spend our holiday in Aragón.' It lacks a coast and first-rate monuments, though there are those who would argue that the Loarre castle is Spain's finest, and Teruel indisputedly has the best Mudejár ensemble anywhere. Yet most people going between Madrid and Barcelona see only the bleak plain of the Ebro out of the window and have little desire to see any more.

The best of Aragón lies off the beaten highway, in the seldom explored mountains in the south, and in the Pyrenees, here at their highest and most majestic, offering almost endless hiking and skiing possibilities. Another attraction is the villages, some of Spain's most medieval and remote, often set among unforgettable scenery.

Although an Aragonese nationalist was elected to the Cortes for the first time in 1986, the region as a whole is a kind of buffer-state between the independently minded Catalans and Basques. In the old days, the Aragonese, the most stubborn of Spaniards and boasting the oldest and some of the most liberal *fueros* or privileges, were not so tractable – Philip II had to put down a major revolt. Union with the Catalans in 1137 brought the crown of Aragón a Mediterranean empire and international renown.

At Aragonese fiestas, you're likely to see some brisk hoofing in the national dance, the *jota*, not one of Spain's more elegant ballets, but certainly one of the most energetic. In the Pyrenean valleys, sword dances are still performed. The region produces considerable quantities of wine – *Carineña* is perhaps the best, and served in many restaurants, along with hearty mountain cuisine and game dishes in season.

FRANCE
Anso
Hecho
Canfranc
Sallent de Gallego
Mt Aneto
*Cardanchu Astun
Bielsa
*Panticosa
Torla
*Benasque
to Pamplona
Berdún
Jaca
Parque Nacional de Ordesa
Castejón de Sos
S. Juan de la Peña
Ainsa
Sos de Rey Católico
NAVARRA
Uncastillo
Sta María
Jabarrella
Loarre
Sadaba
Ayerbe
Graus
Huesca
Alquezar
Benabarre
Ejea de los Caballeros
Barbastro
Monzón
to Logroño
Tauste
Tarazona
Sariñena
Lleida
Zaragoza
Castilla y León
Fraga
CATALUNYA
R. Ebro
Mequinenza
Belchite
Ateca
Calatayud
Caspe
to Guadalajara
Hijar
Daroca
Alcañiz
Valderrobles
Calamocha
Montalbán
CASTILLA LA MANCHA
Mirambel
Cantavieja
La Iglesuela del Cid
ARAGÓN
Albarracín
Teruel
Mora de Rubielos
R. Turia
Sarrión
to Cuenca
VALENCIA
Ademuz
N
km 0 50
miles 0 25
* Ski Resorts

Zaragoza and the South

Zaragoza, the capital of Aragón, is centrally located, and if not the most charming of cities, it has seduced the Aragonese, who have emptied much of countryside to move here. It can get very bitter in the winter and too warm in the middle of summer; still, it's the best base for visiting Aragón.

GETTING AROUND

Zaragoza's airport receives a number of ski-oriented charters from London in the winter, and domestic flights from most points in Spain all year round. The airport is some 20 km (12.5 miles) west of town, Tel: 34 90 50. Iberia's office is at Canfranc 22–24, Tel: 21 82 56. The airport bus leaves from Trovador 1, Tel: 43 28 29.

The train station is the modern Estación Portillo on Avda. Clavé, Tel: 21 42 66. There's a ticket office at San Clemente 23, Tel: 22 65 89. Trains go frequently to Madrid and Barcelona, also four times a day to Huesca, Jaca, and to France (Canfranc), to Teruel and Valencia, to Pamplona and San Sebastián, and to Logroño and Bilbao.

Buses can leave from anywhere. Points east and Catalunya are the domain of Agreda Automóvil, Paseo M. Augustin 7, Tel: 22 93 43 (not far from the train station); for Huesca and Jaca, La Oscense (Pso Echegaray y Caballero 94, Tel: 29 47 61) or Irigoyen (Allué Salvador 4, Tel: 22 32 21); for Soria, Borja and Tarazona: Hernández (Gral. Sueiro 22, Tel: 22 57 23). Basque country: Conda, Avda. de Navarra 77, Tel: 33 33 72. For others, check at the tourist office.

Zaragoza (Saragossa)

Don Quixote made it within sight of Zaragoza but refused to enter (because another author's false Don Quixote had been there already!). Even so, he enjoyed one of the best sights the city can offer: the view of its great towers and domes from the distance. Close up, Zaragoza reveals itself to be a busy city of half a million people over 70 per cent of all Aragonese call it home. Located on the Ebro, in the midst of a fertile *huerta*, it has been prominent ever since the Romans, who gave it its name – *Caesar Augusta*.

One peculiarity of Zaragoza is that it has two cathedrals, forcing the bishop to shuttle back and forth every six months. Newer and decidedly larger, the 19th century **Basilica de Nuestra Señora del Pilar** rises from the banks of the Ebro on the spot where, according to legend, the Virgin appeared on a pillar to Santiago and required a church to be built; from a distance it looks as if she got an Imperial Ottoman mosque instead, complete with four 'minarets' and a hierarchy of 11 domes. There's nothing like it elsewhere in Spain. The interior manages to be both vast and overdone. Goya had a hand in painting the domes – **Santa María, Queen of Martyrs** the most notable. A 14th-century, darkened image, adorned with countless diamonds and other gems, stands on the jasper pillar, on which the Virgin was transported to Spain by angels; she is the patroness of the Guardia Civil (during the Civil War she was Captain General of Zaragoza, and reputedly defused two Republican bombs dropped on the basilica – you can see them hanging in the chapel). The artistic highlight is the 16th-century *reredos* of alabaster by Damián Forment, who adorned many of Aragón's churches, Goya's sketches for the domes are in the **Museo Pilarista** next to the basilica (open 9 am–2 pm and 4–7 pm).

The old **cathedral, La Seo**, at the far end of the Plaza del Pilar, is a crazy quilt of styles – of its exterior, the Mudejár wall of brick and tile makes the most lasting impression. Within, it also has a lovely alabaster 15th-century *retablo* and capitals adorned with carved children. The **museum** in the Sacristy (works by Ribera and Zurbarán) and the **Tapestry Museum** next to La Seo (15th–18th-century French and Flemish) may be visited with the same ticket as the Museo Pilarista. A third monument, the Renaissance **Lonja** stands on the Plaza del Pilar in between the cathedrals; if it's open, step in to see its hall of tall Ionic columns, under which Aragón's grain dealers once met. Spain's plumpest pigeons reside in the Plaza del Pilar, nourished by the little plates of seeds pilgrims buy outside the basilica.

On the far side of the plaza, across from La Seo, the tourist office is shoe honed into **Zuda tower**, a vestige of the medieval walls, adjacent to some bits of Roman wall; when it was Caesar Augusta, the city had 200 towers. From here, walk up C. Augusto to Calle San Pablo and **San Pablo Church**, with the most beautiful of Zaragoza's many towers, a 13th-century Mudejár work, and a wooden *retablo* by Damián Forment. C. Augusto continues up to Coso, and near the corner, is the **Audiencia**, its door guarded by two fierce giants with clubs and topped with a tympanum portraying the Triumph of Caesar. This was the ancestral home of the Luna family, which produced not only Viceroys, but an anti-Pope (see 'Peñiscola') and an operatic villain (see below).

Continue down Coso, past the **Plaza España** and **Paseo Independencia**, the heart and main artery of city life, to Calle Rufas, that leads to the **Plaza de Los Sitios** (of the Sieges) commemorating Zaragoza's heroic resistance to Napoleon's troops in 1808. In 1908 the city held a Hispano–French centenary fair, for which the monument and exhibition palace, now the **Museum of Zaragoza** were erected. The ground floor is given over to archaeological exhibits, including bronze tablets in Iberian and Latin, while upstairs the best of the paintings are by Goya, who was a native of Fuendetodos, 48 km (30 miles) south of Zaragoza (open Tuesday–Sunday 10 am–2 pm).

Back towards the Paseo de Independencia via Calle Costa, you'll see the **Church of Santa Engracia**, founded by Ferdinand and Isabel, whose images kneel over the door; in the crypt, two 4th-century Palaeo–Christian sarcophagi supposedly contain the remains of countless local martyrs. From here, cross the large Plaza Aragón and Plaza Paraiso for Zaragoza's version of Barcelona's Passeig de Gràcia, the **Paseo Sagasta** where you'll find out what local Modernistas were up to – no. 11, The **Juncosa House** by Ricardo Magdalena (1906) is the best art nouveau work in the city. Near the Plaza Paraiso, reconstructed in the bank Caja de Ahorros de Zaragoza, is the 14th-century **Patio de la Infanta**, an elegant Renaissance work with medallions portraying the kings of Spain, that originally belonged to the palace of one of Charles V's biggest financiers, Gabriel Zaporta.

Zaragoza's prime attraction, the **Alijafería** is a short walk from the train station (alternatively, take bus 23 from the Basilica del Pilar or Plaza Aragón). This place, begun as a defensive work in the 9th century, later served as a residence of the local Berber–Moorish dynasty (its name is derived from the emir Abu Ya' far Ahmad) and after the reconquest, of the Aragonese kings. It was the seat of the Aragonese Inquisition until 1706, an institution regarded locally as an underhand attempt by the Castilians to sidestep the *fueros* of Aragón; the first Inquisitor sent by Ferdinand the Catholic was murdered in La Seo. Destroyed and misused for centuries since, restoration work on the Alijafería has been going on since the 1940s.

Walk around the huge walls to the entrance by the tiny jewel-like **Mosque**, in itself the best piece of Moorish architecture outside Andalucía. Also Moorish, and the oldest part of the Alijafería, the **Torre del Trovador** provided the set for García Gutirrez's play and Verdi's opera, *Il Trovatore*, where Manrico was imprisoned by the nasty Count de Luna. The Gothic additions – notably the stair and throne room with their fine *artesonado* ceilings – were added by Ferdinand and Isabel (open 11 am–1.30 pm and 4.30–6.30 pm, am only on Sunday, closed Tuesday).

TOURIST INFORMATION

Torréon de la Zuda, Glorieta de Pio XII (off Pl. del Pilar), Tel: 23 00 27. Provincial office; Alfonso I, 6, Tel: 22 26 73. Municipal office in Roman temple by the Lonja, Plaza del Pilar. Post office: Pso. Independéncia 31, telephones are next door.

WHERE TO STAY

For years Zaragoza's **Gran Hotel*******, Costa 5, Tel: 22 19 10 was the city's finest, and after extensive renovations, this elegant grande dame can reclaim her laurels; its air-conditioned, beautifully furnished doubles go for 6600–9600 pts. If it's hot and you're not a Rockefeller, try the **Conde Blanco****, Predicadores 84, Tel: 44 14 11, with pleasant, air-conditioned rooms a block from the Ebro for 2860 pts a double. The **Hostal Las Torres****, Pl. del Pilar 11, Tel: 21 58 20, has a number of rooms with views of the basilica (doubles 2600 pts with bath, 1950 pts without). So does **La Lonja***, Pl. del Pilar 16, Tel: 29 46 92, its modest rooms with bath 1830 pts, without bath 1545 pts. Even cheaper *fondas* may be found in the pedestrian-only alleys between Alfonso I and Don Jaime.

EATING OUT

Aragonese cuisine is substantial and simple, with lots of beans, potatoes, eggs, lamb, and codfish. One favourite, *bacalao al ajoarriero*, is one of many Aragonese dishes served at the **Mesón del Carmen**, Hernán Cortés 4, where Spaniards go on their nostalgia trips; it's also a good place to try Aragón's wine (order a *Cariñena*) – meals, 1500 pts. Hernán Cortés is the continuation of C. Augusto; from there C. Pamplona leads to Dr. Cerrada, a good street for restaurants and bars – here **Agustina de Aragón** is famed for its roast suckling-lamb (1800 pts). For good Chinese food near the Pl. Aragones, the **China-Sun**, C. Bilboa 2, has a tasty set menu for 450 pts. Other cheap offerings are around C. Don Jaime, like **Casa Pascualillo**, on Libertad (550 pts set menu).

West of Zaragoza: Tarazona

Not a few towns in Spain (we could mention Barcelona) give the impression of having just been dropped down from outer space. Tarazona, with its startling Mudejár towers hanging over the cliffs, is certainly one of them. Most of these are in the older quarter of town, across the Rio Queiles; the churches of **La Magdalena, La Concepción** and **San Miguel**. Tarazona is famous for its 16th-century **Ayuntamiento**, with reliefs of the capture of Granada across the façade; another landmark is the old, arcaded bull-ring, with its arches bricked up and turned into apartments (like the one in Tangier). Tarazona's **Cathedral** is odd too, with a dome like La Seo's in Zaragoza, a tower like La Giralda's in Seville, and several other styles mixed in.

On the way to Zaragoza, the road and railway line pass **Borja**, in the middle of a big wine-growing region, The peculiar crag with chimneys sticking out of it is explained as the ruins of Borja castle, the ancestral home of that celebrated family of schemers and connoisseurs of poison, the Borgias, petty-noble hoodlums in Aragón before they hit the big time in Renaissance Italy.

South of Zaragoza

Southern Aragón is a case of the blind man and the elephant – your opinion of it will depend entirely on which corners of it you see. The landscape is a jumble of awful, barren plateaux, scrublands and green, fertile valleys. Unfortunately there are more of the former, and this region, now as always, is one of the poorest in Spain.

More serious battles of the Civil War were fought here than anywhere else in the country, and that certainly did not help. **Belchite**, once an important town and now a ghostly ruin, was a victim of bitter house-to-house fighting in the 1938 Ebro offensive. The ruins include a Romanesque church and some fine old buildings, and the government has left them standing as a reminder.

GETTING AROUND

If you're relying on public transport, expect frustrations. This is a sparsely populated region, and both buses and trains are infrequent and slow. By train (about four daily) you can get to either Zaragoza or Valencia from Teruel, with no really interesting stops in between (in Teruel, Tel: 60 26 49). The bus station is on Ronda 18 Julio in Teruel; most frequent destination is Zaragoza, but there will be a daily bus to Cuenca and Madrid, to Valencia and to most of the provincial towns. In the Maestrazgo, the bus service is informal; it's no place to be in a hurry.

WHAT TO SEE

The Zaragoza–Valencia road, following the turgid Ebro, passes through mostly nondescript towns. **Caspe** can show a new **Roman mausoleum** in its town square, relocated from lands flooded by the big Maquinenza reservoir, which turns the Ebro into a lake for some 48 km (30 miles). Most of **Mequinenza** was drowned, too, but the remainder has a finer lakeside location than ever before. The well-preserved medieval **castle** above the town now belongs to the local electric company. **Alcañiz**, to the south, is a big town, with little to show the folks who stay in the Parador, installed in the 12th-century **castle** that once belonged to the Order of Calatrava. The 14th-century Ayuntamiento and Lonja buildings on the Plaza Mayor are the only sights. If you're heading towards the coast, tiny **Valderrobres** is worth a detour, for its improbably grand **Santa María la Mayor** (12th century) with a beautiful rose window; a castle of the Kings of

Aragón, a Renaissance Ayuntamiento, and a pretty main street along the Río Matarraña.

From Calatayud to Teruel

Sooner or later you'll pass through **Calatayud**, an important road and railway junction, but it's a dour and shabby place and there's little reason to stay. Calatayud (from the Arabic 'castle of Job') specializes in octagonal Mudejár church steeples; **Santa María La Mayor** has the best of them, along with an ornate Plateresque-Mudejár façade. Nearby, on the Sigüenza road, **Ateca** has a converted mosque for its main church, **Santa María**, with a later Mudejár tower much like those you'll see in Teruel. This one leans a little. There's a detour to the south to the **Piedra Monastery**, a 13th-century Cistercian house. Most of it is a hotel now, but the surroundings, with plenty of trees and a 46 m (150 ft) **waterfall** along the Río Piedra, has to be the garden spot of all southern Aragón.

South from Calatayud, **Daroca**'s pride is its **walls**, with 114 towers in varying states of decay. The gates are well-preserved and impressive. Charles V built them; Daroca was a thriving town in his time, as evidenced by several fine Mudejár churches, a lovely fountain called the **Fuente de Veinte Caños** ('20 spouts') outside the walls, and a half mile **tunnel** dug under a mountain to carry off flood waters – a very unusual fit of public works for 16th-century Spain.

About 20 km (12.5 miles) before Teruel, a side road follows the valley of the Río Turia up into the Montes Universales. The town of **Albarracín** is the centre of this bare and rocky district. There are no churches to attract visitors here, but the town itself is a national monument, one of the least-changed old towns of Spain. Its oldest streets are fairy-tale medieval, with narrow, cobbled lanes and half-timbered houses with projecting balconies leaning at precarious angles over them. Albarracín has an unusually long circuit of walls – not because the town was ever bigger than now, but to protect it from attacks from the dominating hillsides.

Teruel

As a provincial capital, Teruel looms large on the Spanish map. From up close, however, it is small and a little woebegone. Already a poor backwater, Teruel suffered as much as any Spanish city in the Civil War. In the freezing winter of 1937 (Teruel is famous for these), the Republicans fought their way up the steep slopes of this natural fortress above the Turia and took the town. Just two weeks later the Nationalists did the same and got it back. Since then the town has been repaired; a little prosperity has seeped in, and Teruel is probably in better shape than it's been for centuries. The reason for visiting is to see the best Mudejár churches in Spain – four of them, with tall glorious towers of delicately patterned brick and tiles. Teruel kept a large Moorish population after the 12th-century Reconquest, and it was Moorish craftsmen who gave the city its pride and its symbol.

If you come by train, you'll get an immediate introduction to Teruel Mudejár in the **terrace steps**, built in the 1920s, a long, elegant (though poorly maintained) stairway leading up from the station to the town. At the top, the most elaborate of the Mudejár towers is just a block to the left, that of **El Salvador**, built right over the street with a narrow arch to let pedestrians pass. Like minarets, the towers of Teruel are always separate from their churches. **San Martín**, the next tower, also has an arch underneath; it's a few blocks north down Calle Santiago. The **Cathedral**'s tower pales by comparison, but it compensates with a unique, Mudejár-style brick dome. There's a **provincial museum** around the back that may finally open some day.

San Pedro is the fourth Mudejár tower; a little chapel has been built to house the remains of **Los Amantes de Teruel**. Diego de Marcilla and Isabel de Segura were the star-crossed lovers of the old story. He had five years to go out and win his fortune; on the appointed day Isabel's impatient father married her off when Diego failed to appear. Diego had miscalculated, and when he turned up the next day there was nothing left to do but expire in each other's arms. The same tale is told in Boccaccio's *Decameron*, only the lovers are named Girolamo and Salvastra; scholars never get tired of speculating whether Teruel's lovers were the source for Boccaccio, or if some local light simply invented the story. There can't be fewer than 100 other versions of this folk-tale motif floating around Europe: you can take your pick. You may also join the young honeymooners in visiting this shrine of sorrow. Their effigies are beautifully sculpted, holding hands between the sarcophagi, and you can peek at the mummified remains if you care to. Meanwhile Spanish children have their nursery rhyme:

Los Amantes de Teruel,
Tonta ella y tonto el.

('The lovers of Teruel – she was crazy and him too.')

Teruel really is an unlikely honeymoon destination, but besides its Mudejár towers it has a few other things to see. The **Fountain of the Torico**, a bull with a star between its horns, is the symbol of the city, in the quiet Plaza Mayor; from there it's a short walk to the northern end of town and **Los Arcos**, a 16th-century aqueduct you can walk across, the work of the same French engineer who dug the tunnel at Daroca. There are no stories about the peculiar, eight-sided tower called the **Castillo de Amberes** nearby; nobody seems to know who built it, or why. Behind it, near the bus station, the streets around Plaza Juderia provide the most incongruous sight in Teruel on Saturday nights, when all southern Aragón's fast crowd congregates at the scores of hole-in-the-wall bars. Where does one little old-fashioned province get so many bikers?

Ademuz and the Maestrazgo

Quite a few of them speed in from these two pockets of quiet villages, where by day you're more likely to see shepherds with their flocks. If you're headed for Madrid or Cuenca, you'll pass through the **Rincón de Ademuz**, a spot of land that was independent through much of the Middle Ages, and now survives as an island of Valencia province within Aragón. The villages, such as Ademuz and Castelfabib, are among the least modern in Spain, and the countryside in the valley of the Río Turia is lovely.

In the **Maestrazgo**, between Teruel and Valencia, the scenery is wilder and the villages a little more colourful, with pointed arches overhanging the streets and Moorish *ajimez* windows. **La Iglesuela del Cid** is perhaps most characteristic, but tiny **Mirambel** is prettier; the town has recently won a national prize for the restoration of its modest monuments, including the old half-timbered gatehouses. Mirambel is reached through **Cantavieja**, a Templar foundation that was a stronghold of the Carlists in both their rebellions. Contavieja preserves an imposing 16th-century church, and Ayuntamiento, and if you have a car you may enjoy the view from a famous **mirador** outside the town called 'Muela Monchen'.

TOURIST INFORMATION

Teruel: C. Tomás Nogues (just off C. Ramón y Cajal, the **main** street; Tel: 60 22 79).

WHERE TO STAY

Southern Aragón sees few tourists, but you'll be able to find modest accommodation in all the towns and villages mentioned in this section. In Teruel, the **Parador de Teruel***** is nothing special, and inconveniently located outside the city (Tel: 60 22 53, doubles 5500–7000 pts); in town, the most comfortable spot is the **Reina Cristina***** (Paseo Generalísimo 1, near San Salvador tower, Tel: 60 68 60, doubles 5600 pts). For more modest lodgings in a quiet, central location, there's the **Goya***, near the tourist office on C. Tomás Nogues (Tel: 60 14 50, 2200 pts double with bath) and the **Casa de Huespedes Alcodoin**, on C. Temprado near San Mateo church (1000 pts a double, no bath).

Its worth going out of your way to spend a night at the **Monasterio de Piedra*****, mentioned above, near Ateca; the old monastery among the gardens and waterfalls has been converted into a first-rate hotel, with a pool, tennis courts, and a good restaurant (near the hamlet of Nuevalos, Tel: 84 90 11, doubles 4000 pts). Daroca is another nice place to stay; there are some good hotels including the Pension **El Ruejo**** (C. Mayor 112, Tel: 80 03 35, air-conditioned rooms in an old, restored house for 3400 pts a double with bath, 1600 pts without, meals a bargain at about 650 pts).

Alcañiz has its **Parador de la Concordia***** in the castle, one of the nicer paradors in this part of the country (Tel: 83 04 00, doubles with air-conditioning 5500–7500 pts). Otherwise, the **Guadalupe*** (2000 pts with bath) is the best bet in town. Tiny Valderrobres, surprisingly, has a hotel, the **Querol*** (C. Franco 6, Tel: 85 01 92, double with bath 2200 pts). Albarracín is becoming a small resort, as its charming streets and mountain views begin to attract visitors; its quality hotel is the **Albarracín***** (also in a restored building, in C. Azagra, Tel: 71 00 11, doubles 5400 pts). Anywhere else, especially in the Maestrazgo, you'll likely find only the sparest of *fondas* or rooms over a bar. In any season but summer remember to ask if there's heat, for this province has the worst climate in Spain.

EATING OUT

Teruel has only a few restaurants; you can get a better than average 700 pts *menú del día* at the **Tres Escudos**, on C. Santiago near the San Salvador tower.

Northern Aragón

Seldom visited except by skiers, Northern Aragón's prime attractions are its unspoilt medieval villages and mountain scenery. Public transport to nearly all points is possible but often time-consuming; the service is good but infrequent. Don't come with a tight schedule or a plane to catch in a couple of days – unless you have wheels.

GETTING AROUND

Monzón is on the train line between Lleida and Zaragozo (three a day); Barbastro and Monzón are also on the bus route between Huesca and Lleida (three times a day). Las Cinco Villas are served from Zaragoza by bus (Autocares Cinco Villas, Avda. de Navarra 80, Tel: 33 33 72 in Zaragoza). Sos del Rey Católico is easiest to reach, via any Pamplona–Zaragoza bus; RENFE buses from Zaragoza station will take you right there four times a day. Huesca and Jaca are easiest reached by train from Zaragoza (for bus connections, see 'Zaragoza').

In Huesca the train station is on C. Zaragoza; the bus station on the Avda. del Parque 3. To get to the Castillo de Loarre, catch the bus to Ayerbe and get off at Loarre – then walk 6.4 km (4 miles). Connections are limited so plan in advance.

In Jaca the train station is at the northern end of C. Juan XXIII. A local bus makes connections to the centre of town. The bus station is more convenient, on Avda. Jacetania behind the cathedral. From Jaca there is a daily bus to Anso and Hecho and more frequently to Biesca – 30 km (18.8 miles) to Torla and Ordessa Park – but ask at Jaca's tourist office before you take it and hitch the rest of the way; plans are afoot for some kind of shuttle. You may just want to rent a car and save yourself the hassle.

Benasque may be reached from Monzón (with its train station); buses are more frequent during the ski season. Jaca runs a fairly good shuttle service to the resorts in the winter.

East: Barbastro, Monzón and Torreciudad

One of the region's least-visited corners, and a good place to see the difference irrigation has made to the land – just to the south of Monzón, **Los Monegros** is as dry and barren a wasteland as anyone could wish. **Barbastro** is the largest town, with an interesting 16th-century **Cathedral** with a polychrome alabaster *retablo* by Damián Forment; buses from here go the 13 km (8.1 miles) to **Alquezar**, one of the Aragón's most picturesque villages, crowned by a well-preserved 12th-century **castle** and large **Colegiata** (16th century).

Monzón, the other large town of the region, was a very important Templar enclave. It came their way as part of a deal: when the King of Aragón, Alfonso el Batallador died without an heir in 1131, the Aragonese nobles upon reading his will were shocked to discover that he had bequeathed the kingdom to the Sepulchre of the Lord in Jerusalem and its guardians, the Knights Templar. The nobles quickly talked Alfonso's brother, Ramiro the Monk (Ramiro II) into taking the Crown. He dutifully married, sired a daughter, married her off aged two to Count Ramón Berenguer IV of Barcelona and went back to his monastery, letting the Catalans add 'King of Aragón' to their titles. The new king generously compensated the slighted Templars, giving them Monzón among many other properties. Jaime I, the Conqueror, received his education here, in the ruined **castle** that still dominates the town.

Near Graus, on the banks of a lake, **Torreciudad** has had a shrine of the Virgin since the 12th century. One of the shrine's fervent devotees was Escrivá de Balaguer, the Aragonese priest who in 1928 founded the Opus Dei – a shadowy organization of ultra conservative Catholic technocrats that ran most of Spain in the later Franco years and has since spread to some 80 countries around the world, with the blessing of John Paul II. Some of their rites, like flagellation, are downright medieval; and yet their main concerns are education (they run a university in Pamplona) and getting their members or sympathizers into the upper echelons of business and government. Opus Dei missed its chance to take over Spain and Mexico (in the 1950s), but in Spain a magazine issue is guaranteed success if it offers the latest dope on Opus Dei. In 1975, it built a new sanctuary next to the old church at Torreciudad, in memory of Escrivá and as a pilgrimage destination.

Las Cinco Villas

West of Zaragoza the region of Las Cinco Villas was named for five villages promoted to the status of towns by Philip V in gratitude for their help during the War of the Succession. The five (Tauste, Ejea de Los Caballeros, Sádaba, Uncastello and Sos del Rey Católico) have as their main allure their picturesque ensembles of old buildings and quiet atmosphere. **Tauste**, closest to Zaragoza, boasts a fine Mudejár church of the 13th century. **Ejea de los Caballeros** has a fortified Romanesque church, **San Salvador** (1222) with a stork-topped tower, more fitting to a castle than a church. In **Sádaba**, there's a large, square 13th-century castle just outside the village.

The last two, nearer the Pyrenees, are the most rewarding. **Uncastello**, seems entirely medieval, its houses adorned with proud escutcheons on steep streets beneath the great ruined castle. Of its numerous churches, the most interesting, **Santa María la Mayor** is Romanesque with a fine carved façade, and a battlemented Gothic tower. Nearby is the simple, arcaded **Plaza del Campo**. There are Roman remains by the hot springs at **Los Bañoles**.

Sos added 'del Rey Católico' to its name in 1924, honouring crafty old Ferdinand, who was a baby here. It is the most visited town of the five and the most beautiful; like Uncastello it has a number of noble mansions, most importantly, the **Palacio de Sada**, birthplace of Ferdinand and now a museum, housing artworks and historical odds and ends related to the king. The Romanesque church of **San Esteban** has fine murals in its crypt from the 14th century.

Huesca and Loarre Castle

Huesca, the provincial capital of northern Aragón, is unlovely but prosperous – it sits in the middle of its own fertile *hoya* (irrigated farmland). Spaniards associate Huesca with the *Legend de la Campana* ('of the bell'), illustrated by a painting in the **Ayuntamiento**: faced with rebellious nobles Ramiro II ('the Monk' – see above) summoned them to his palace to ask their advice on a bell he meant to cast, so big that it would be heard throughout all Aragón. As the nobles filed in, one by one, the king had their heads cut off. Ramiro II's admirers claim it's a lot of hooey, but you can visit the actual **Sala de la Campana** underneath the **Museum** in the Plaza de la Universidad, in a building that began its life as a Moorish alcazar, and served for many years as the palace of the kings of Aragón, then in 1354 as a university. Exhibits range from the prehistoric to medieval Aragonese painting (open 9 am–2 pm and 4–6 pm, closed Monday).

Ramiro II and his brother Alfonso el Batallador are buried in Huesca's oldest church, the 12th-century **San Pedro el Viejo** on Calle Cuatro Reyes; the cloister's capitals have some fine carvings of monsters (open 9 am–1.30 pm and 4–6 pm, closed Sunday). The lovely late Gothic **Cathedral** has a landmark octagonal tower, and a west portal topped by an unusual Mudejár gallery; within is another of Damián Forment's great alabaster *retablos*. The **cathedral museum** holds mainly primitive art from the region (open 11 am–1 pm and 4–6 pm).

The Castle of Loarre

Huesca is the base for visiting Aragón's showpiece **Castillo de Loarre**, an 11th century military masterpiece on a rocky eminence overlooking the great plain of Aragón. The castle, built by Sancho Ramirez, the great king of Navarre, so perfectly fits into its surroundings that we moderns would call it environmental art. It has been lovingly restored and is exciting to explore; outstanding are its three great towers – La Vigía, el Homenaje, and la Reina – and a gem of a Romanesque **chapel** (open 9 am–2 pm and 4–8 pm). If you pass through nearby **Ayerbe**, stop to see the **Gothic palace** of the local Marqués.

Jaca

Jaca, only 30 km (18.8 miles) from France, is the only real town in Aragón's Pyrenees and is nearly everyone's point of departure for the mountains to the north and east (far more rugged and less exploited than Catalunya's Pyrenees) and to the secluded valleys and villages to the west. In the Middle Ages, Jaca was also a point of departure – for Santiago de Compostela. Pilgrims taking the Aragonese road would cross the mountains near Canfranc, then the next day make for Jaca before turning west. Even earlier, Jaca served as the first capital of Aragón, regained from the Moors in 760 – in 795, when they tried to take it back, the women defended it so fiercely they never tried again.

French influence crossed the border with the pilgrims, and in Jaca Spain's first Romanesque church, the **Cathedral**, was constructed at the beginning of the 11th century and although meddled with over the years is still impressive; note the finely carved capitals. The **Diocesan Museum** in the cloister is especially worthwhile, featuring many Romanesque frescoes garnered from abandoned chapels in the Pyrenees (open 11.30 am–1.30 pm and 4.30–6.30 pm).

Jaca's other principal monument, the pentagonal **Ciudadela** was begun by Philip II after the Aragón revolt – one of the numerable headaches faced by His Majesty the Bureaucrat. The army still uses it, so you can't get in – but take a stroll along the ramparts of the Camino Monte Pago for fine views of the River Aragón, or walk down to the handsome medieval **Puente de San Miguel** on the pilgrims' road, 1 km (0.6 mile) from town. Before setting out on excursions, check at Jaca's tourist office, a goldmine of information on the Pyrenees; it can also sell you a good hiking map.

East of Jaca: Ordesa National Park

In the misty dawn of Aragón this was the county of Sobrarbe. Much of its heart is now part of the **Parque Nacional de Ordesa**, one of Spain's most beautiful, created in 1918, and crowned by the **Tres Sorores**, 'the three sisters' – three mountains over 3080 m (10,000 ft) high. In the late spring the park is filled with waterfalls cascading towards the Río Arazus in the valley; in summer edelweiss adorns the slopes. There are trails through the poplar groves for strollers and 300 m (1000 ft) cliffs for alpinists; the most beautiful is the 6–7 hour **Soasso Circle** route along the Río Arazus then up the valley for some spectacular scenery over the gorge, climaxing in the **Mirador Calcitarruego**. Anyone in reasonable shape can make it, but you should wear hiking boots and take lunch. This is obtainable in **Torla**, a small stone village at the entrance of the park, with plenty of accommodation as well.

Ainsa, south of the park, the capital of Sobrarbe, is the loveliest town in the region, its walled old town with an elegant **Plaza Mayor** overlooking the new quarters. **Bielsa** near the French border, is the departure point for the 15 km (9.4 miles) hike along the **Valle de Pineta**, Ordesa's 'twin' valley, on the banks of the Río Cinca. A pre-Romanesque hermitage, a lake and glacier and magnificent views are some of the highlights (and fewer fellow hikers).

Further east, the mountains become so formidable that the Spaniards call them **Les Montes Malditos** (the 'cursed mountains'). The tallest of the Pyrenees are here:

Aneto (3404 m: 11,063 ft) and its sister peak, **Maladeta** (3308 m: 10,751 ft). **Benasque** is the base for visiting them, for summer climbs and hikes, or winter skiing. The village itself, of stone houses with slate roofs, is hemmed in by the mountains and wonderfully picturesque and tranquil.

West of Jaca

The Monastery of San Juan de la Peña became the cradle of the Aragonese Reconquista; in 724, the nobles of Sobrarbe gathered here and swore to rid Aragón of the Moors. According to legend, the Holy Grail now in Valencia cathedral was hidden here for centuries; the old monastery itself is nearly hidden under an overhanging cliff. In the 18th century Carlos III had many of the kings of Aragón and Navarre interred with regal fittings. Now the monastery is being restored (a new one was built nearby); you can visit the crypt, the lovely Romanesque church and cloister, as usual, with fancy (and fanciful) capitals. The hamlet of **Santa Cruz de la Serós**, a short walk away, had an auxiliary convent, its surviving 11th-century church modelled on Jaca's cathedral.

Berdun was a day's journey for the pilgrim from Jaca. The beauty of the area, and its abundant and unusual plant and bird life, inspired an English artist, John Boucher, to found a field studies centre for painters, bird watchers, botanists, and architects, amateurs and professionals alike. It's one of the more interesting alternative holiday possibilities in Spain (see below).

This is the region of **Old Aragón**, and there are two secluded valleys here which have changed little since the Middle Ages. The eastern one, the **Valle de Hecho** was the birthplace of Alfonso el Batallador and still preserves its ancient Aragonese dialect; its principal village, **Hecho**, couldn't be more charming or better sited. In July and August Hecho and the surrounding hills turn into a contemporary sculpture garden as part of the 'Symposia de Escultura y Pintura Moderna'. The nearby hamlet of **Siresa** is an easy walk away; Alfonso el Batallador was educated here in the monastery of the ancient **church of San Pedro de Siresa**, currently under restoration. A number of lovely hikes begin here.

In the **Valle de Ansó** the old villagers speak yet another old dialect, and it's one of the few places in Spain where you may catch sight of a woman in her traditional costume any day of the week. Some of Ansó's houses are adorned with inexplicable symbols – thought to be a memory of the valley's once sizeable *agote* population (see 'Navarre'). Ansó is a bit more conscious of its own whitewashed charms than Hecho; an **Ethnographic museum** of odds and ends may be visited in the old church on the Plaza de San Pedro. Ansó is a good base for hikes in the beautiful **Valle de Zuriza**, 12.8 km (8 miles) north.

TOURIST INFORMATION

Ejea de los Caballeros: Costa 2 (Ayuntamiento).

Huesca: Coso Alto 23, Tel: 22 57 78.

Jaca: Pl. de Calvo Sotelo, Tel: 36 00 98.

There's a summer information office at the entrance of Ordessa Park.

WHERE TO STAY

In Monzón, the **Vianetto****, Avda. de Lérida 25, Tel: 40 19 00 has both air-conditioning and one of the town's best restaurants; doubles with bath 2750–3025; meals around 800 pts. Barbastro has a collection of cheap *hostales* – the **Roxi***, Corona de Aragón 21, Tel: 31 10 64 is well-run and in the middle of town; doubles with bath 1600 pts, without 1300 pts.

In Las Cinco Villas, there's an Aragonese-style *parador*, the **Fernando de Aragón*****, Sáinz de Vicuña (in town), Tel: 88 80 11. The kitchen serves Aragónese specialities and regional wines: try the rabbit with snails if you feel adventurous (air-conditioned doubles 5500 pts; meals around 2000 pts).

In Huesca, one of the prettier places to stay is the **Hostal Aragonesa****, Pl. de Lizana 15, Tel: 22 06 50, small and near the old centre; doubles are 3000 pts, all with bath. Of the cheap places, **Pondevila***, Ramón y Cajal 43, Tel: 22 00 24 is in an even nicer setting; it's small and friendly; doubles 1700 pts without bath.

In Jaca, the **Conde de Aznar****, Ps. Gral. Franco 3, Tel: 36 10 50, is comfortable and sports a garden in the middle of town. Its restaurant is also good, fresh vegetables and game in season are specialities (doubles 2990–3900, meals around 1400 pts). On lovely Calle Mayor, 41, the modern **Hostal La Paz**** offers very nice doubles with bath for 2600–3000 pts. A couple of doors down, **Galindo***, C Mayor 45, Tel: 36 13 67 has them for 2200 pts with bath, 1850 pts without. The tourist office in Jaca has a list of *casas particulares* (rooms in private houses) which many prefer.

In Torla, by Ordesa Park, you are guaranteed a mountain view. **Viñamala***, Nueva Plaza 1, Tel: 48 61 56, open all year, has a pool (doubles with bath 2200–2500 pts). Nothing is much cheaper, except for the two campsites.

Benasque has several relatively posh places along Ctra. Anciles; in town, try **Hostal El Puente****, San Pedro, Tel: 55 12 79, with mountain views and doubles for 2650–2800 pts with bath, 2200–2350 pts without.

In Hecho, **De la Val***, Cruz Alta 1, Tel: 37 50 28, with 20 bathless doubles for 1400 pts. In Ansó, there are all of three places to stay: a bed and complete board at the charming old **Fonda Estanés**, Tel: 37 01 46, for 4000 pts a double. The **Aísa**, Tel: 37 00 09, will give you a pleasant double without bath for 1060 pts. The new, upmarket **Posada Magoria**, Tel: 37 00 49 has doubles for 2000 pts and a vegetarian restaurant, with a set menu for 800 pts.

EATING OUT

A less expensive choice in Las Cinco Villas than the Parador, serving Aragonese dishes, is **Vinacua** on Pl. del Meson (1000–1500 kpts). For a good Aragonese meal in Huesca, topped off with a Havana cigar, **Navas**, San Lorenzo 15 is the place to go (1700 pts.) Good cheaper choices along C. San Orencio.

Good, solid and cheap food is served up in Jaca at the **Vivas**, C. Gil Berges 3; menu 750 pts.

SPECIAL HOLIDAYS

The John Boucher Centre for Field Studies in Berdun, C. Mayor 30, Berdun 22004, Huesca, Tel: 37 70 44 (open April to August), offers two-week holidays of botany and ornithology for £300, which includes room (in an Aragonese village house) and board. Painting holidays, etc. for one or two weeks also available; write for more information, or in the UK, contact Cox and Kings Special Interest Holidays, 46 Marshall St, London W1V 2PA, Tel: 01-439 3380.

WHERE TO SKI

Northern Aragón offers Spain's most varied and challenging skiing, and facilities are mostly up-to-date and quite reasonable compared to other installations in Europe; a bit out-of-the-way, they are also likely to be less crowded. Package deals are available in Madrid, Barcelona, Zaragoza and from travel agents anywhere in Aragón. All rent equipment.

Cerler, near Benasque, has very modern facilities and 22 pistes on the highest slopes the Pyrenees can offer. There are two hotels at the resort (and nine others in Benasque), an ice palace and a wide range of other activities (Tel: 55 10 12). Benasque also has a municipal ski facility in **La Maladeta**. **Astun**, near Jaca (near the Canfranc rail station) is new and has 20 pistes (nine difficult, three very difficult), two slalom courses (one giant), and easy transport from Jaca; Tel: 37 30 34. **Candanchu**, Astun's older sister on the other side of Canfranc, offers 31 pistes, cross-country skiing, 21 lifts and five hotels at the station; easy transport from Jaca (Tel: 37 31 92). **Formigal**, near Sallent de Gallego, has very open pistes without obstacles (one of its 23 is 7 km (4.4 miles) long), served by one telecabina and 15 other lifts. Most of the courses are rated difficult. There's a slalom course, lots of recreational facilities and seven hotels at the station (Tel: 48 81 25). **Panticosa**, also near Sallent de Gallego (Sabiñánigo, between Jaca and Huesca, is the closest train station – 40 km (25 miles) distant), has 11 pistes, a slalom course and seven hotels at the station (Tel: 48 71 12).

Part VII

THE BASQUE LANDS (EUSKADI), NAVARRE AND LA RIOJA

Mount Untzillatx Farm

Euskadi

The Basque lands, known in the Basque language as Euskadi ('collection of Basques') contain, according to Madrid, the three provinces of Viscaya, Guipúzcoa and Alava, but to the Basques themselves Euskadi includes all lands inhabited by Basques – the three provinces in France and the northern part of Navarre. Although subject to frequent rains (especially in the winter) Euskadi is one of the most charming corners of Spain – rural for the most part, lush and green, criss-crossed by a network of mountain streams that meander every which way through steep, narrow valleys in their search for the sea. Great stone country houses resembling Swiss chalets dot the hillsides and riverbanks – though the next valley over may have a grotty little town gathered about a mill. Spain's industrial revolution began in Euskadi, and even today the three Basque provinces are among the most industrialized and wealthiest (Basques run the country's leading banks). But in most of Euskadi, industry and finance seem remote. Basque nationalism on the other hand, is ever present; every bridge, underpass, and pelota court has been painted with the Basque flag and slogans of the *Euskadi Ta Askatasuna*,

'Freedom for Basques' – the notorious ETA – the small but violent minority that has given this ancient people a bad press – as they've had for most of their history.

The Basques and their Language

> Nomandsland, the territory of the Basques, in a region called Cornucopia, where the vines are tied up with sausages ... And in those parts there was a mountain made entirely of grated Parmesan cheese on whose slopes there were people who spent their whole time making macaroni and ravioli.
>
> *The Decameron*, VIII, 3

Wild stories like Boccaccio's have often been told about the Basques and their inscrutable language, but the conclusions of many scholars from different fields are almost as hard to believe. It seems likely that the Basques are no less than the original European aborigines, having survived in their secluded valleys after the great migrations of peoples from the east thousands of years ago; recent discoveries in Euskadi's caves suggest that they may even be descendants of Cro-Magnon man. The Basque language is unique – the only language ever found to have any kind of similarity to it is Berber – and it, too, seems to date back to the Stone Age (one clue is that the Basque words for many kinds of tools incorporate the word 'stone' or *aitz* – even scissors are *aitz-tturr*). Another clue to its antiquity is that Basque grammar is extraordinarily complex, with eight cases and an odd urge towards passivity. The sentence 'I am spinning' (*Iruten ari nuzu*) literally translates as 'in the act of spinning doing you have me' though the 'you' and 'me' might change, depending on our gender. Basque also has some fun onomatopoetics: looking at a menu in a Basque restaurant (they have the best cuisine in Spain, so you'll want to do this often) you may well be *keko-meko* (undecided); if you choose *birristi-barrasta* (carelessly), you might get *ttattu* (little cat), a supposed speciality in Bilbao in the 19th century. Basques do love to eat and drink; other Spaniards accuse them of *mauka-mauka* (gluttony). Curiously the language has no word for 'tree' (just as the Eskimos have no word for 'ice' but an infinite number of words for the infinite variations of ice), or 'king' except in Navarre, the Basques never had one; feudalism was unknown to them though both men and animals had a code of rights and responsibilities.

History

The Basques have no written records, and in other people's histories they always seem to be causing trouble. The Romans conquered but did not tame them, and the Visigoths, Moors and early Christian kingdoms did even less. Medieval clerics railed against them for fleecing and harassing pilgrims. Both organization into towns and Christianity came late to the Basques and when they did agree to recognize the suzerainty of Castile it was on their own terms, retaining intact their *fueros* (privileges) and ancient laws, the Viscayans insisted that every king upon being crowned should come to Guernica and swear under the sacred oak tree to uphold their laws. The Basques (except for Navarre) lost their *fueros* in retaliation for their support of Fernando VII's reactionary brother Don Carlos in the Carlist wars (1876). Around the

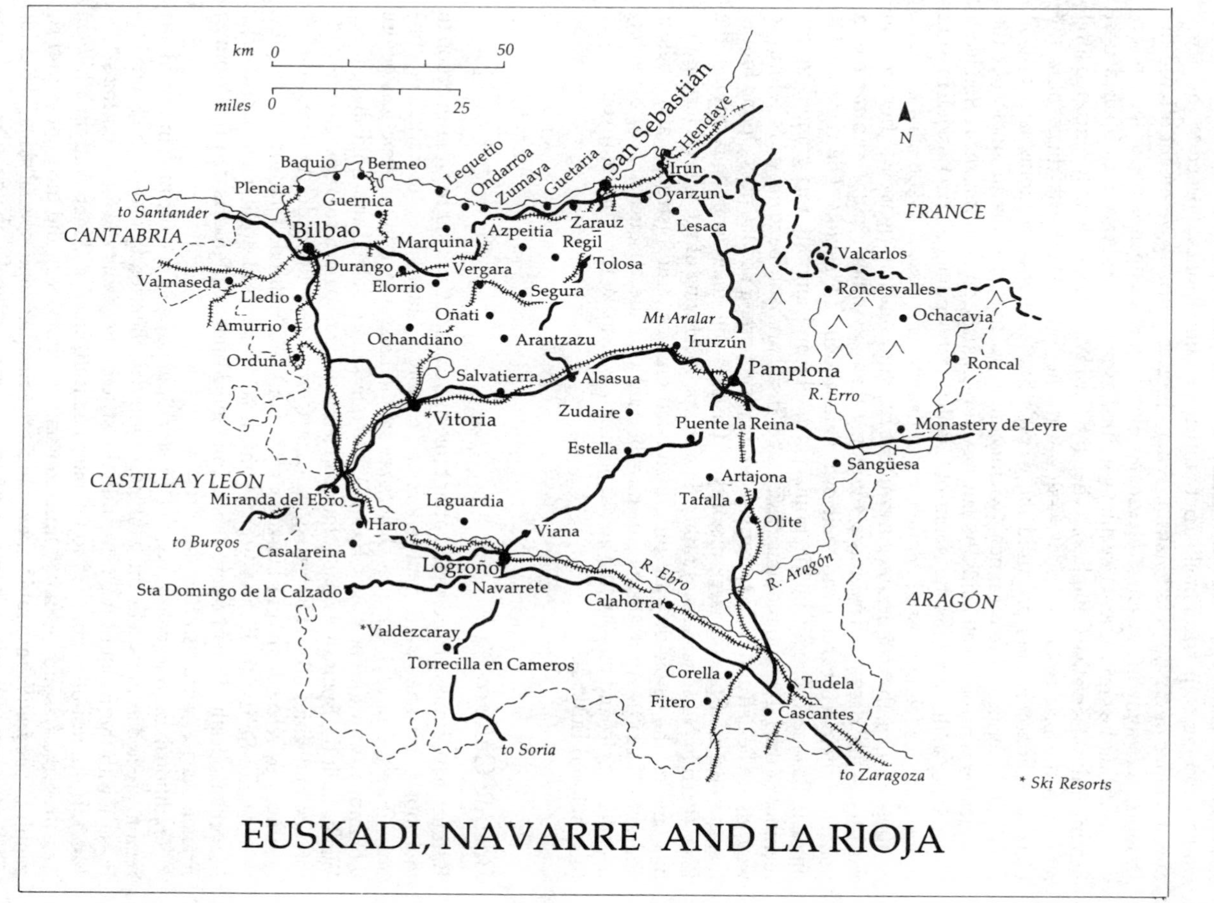

EUSKADI, NAVARRE AND LA RIOJA

same time Euskadi began to industrialize, and while many prospered, the majority of workers, seeing their traditional society threatened on all sides, flocked to the newly raised banner of Basque Nationalism. When the Republican government offered the Basques autonomy in exchange for their support, they snapped it up, despite reservations about the government's secularism (the Basques have always been Spain's most fervent and conservative Catholics). When the Civil War broke out, they remained loyal and even the priests fought side-by-side with the 'reds'. To break their spirit, the German Condor Legion practised the world's first saturation bombing of a civilian target at Guernica. After Franco's victory he took special pains to single out the Basques for reprisals of all kinds, outlawing their language and running the region like a police state, so that even the thousands of Castilians who immigrated to Euskadi to work in the factories felt oppressed enough to sympathize with Basque Nationalist goals.

Since Franco, the democratic government has done much to right past grievances in Euskadi – the Basques have more autonomy than any other region, with their own police (in their red berets) and their own independent TV station. The region is bilingual: Basque is taught in the primary schools, and amnesty was granted to any member of the ETA who renounced violence. It will probably be many years before the wounds are healed and ETA terrorists lose their support, or as Mao put it, 'pond for the fish to swim in'. Still, the large majority of Basques vote their aspirations through the PNV (Partido Nacional Vasco) rather than the political wing of the ETA, Herri Batisuna, and on the whole they are progressive-left on most issues (strongly anti-nuclear and anti-NATO). After all that, it must be said that the Basques are an extremely friendly people, and they'll often go out of their way to make sure you enjoy your stay in their beloved Euskadi.

Basque Culture

Basques have always played an important role in Spanish affairs, far out of proportion to their numbers. They were great sailors and explorers, shipbuilders and whalers, conquistadors and pirates. Basque whalers are said to have landed in the Americas before Columbus (whose pilot was a Basque); Basque sailors helped the English conquer Wales, built the Spanish Armada, founded a number of Spanish colonies like the Philippines and cities like Buenos Aires. The Conquistors Lope de Aguirre (so well portrayed by Klaus Kinski in Herzog's great film) and Pedro de Ursua were Basques; the Basque Sebastián Elcano became the first man to sail around the world after Magellan's death. Two of Spain's most influential saints, St Ignatius de Loyola and St Francis Xavier, were also Basque.

Traditional Basque culture is full of stories about the countless dolmens in the region, erected as houses by the gentiles, or *jentillak*, the friendly giants who lived side-by-side with the Basques (very much in the style of the giants in Doris Lessing's *Shikasta*). If the rest of Spain used to tell tales about the magical Moors and their hidden treasures, the Basques, who had little contact with the Moors, did the same with their gentiles. The *jentillak* are said to have taught the Basques some special skills, like cultivation, but one day, when strange omens appeared in the sky, the gentiles all disappeared under a dolmen, saying 'Kixmi (Jesus Christ) is born, our time is over' and they've never been seen again – although in some villages especially strong, tall people are believed to have descended from the *jentillak*.

Strength, endurance, agility and competitiveness are traditional Basques virtues in work, dancing and especially sports. The Basques invented *pelota* or *jai alai*, that combines two Basque loves, agility and gambling – though it originally seems to have been a sacred sport, played against the church wall. Less sacred and widespread are log-splitting, wrestling and heaving megakilo concrete weights over one's shoulders; sometimes oxen join in and drag stones across the town square. Traditional Basque instruments are the *txistu*, a three-holed flute played with one hand, while the other hand beats out the rhythm on the tambour, and to accompany their music the Basques dance some of the most furiously athletic dances in the world, especially the *Bolant Dantza* (the Flying Dance) or *La Espatadantza* (sword dance). They are also fond of improvising verses in competitions – to exercise the Basque language to keep it alive (not always an easy task: a new Basque gay organization could not imagine what the Basque equivalent of 'gay' might be).

Basque cuisine

Basques love to eat, and when they're not running banks or lifting weights, they're opening restaurants, not only in Euskadi but throughout Spain. Basque cuisine uses plenty of imaginative sauces; perhaps the most famous Basque dish is squid in its own ink (*chiperones*) – reputedly the only one in the world that's all black, and better than it sounds. Each Basque chef knows how to work wonders with elvers and cod, salmon and the famous 'txangurro' – spider crab; Basques like to wash it down with 'txakoli', a tangy wine produced on the coast with just a modicum of sunlight. Southern Alava produces an excellent Rioja (see 'La Rioja'), and you can top off your meal with the famous Basque hootch, Pacharán.

San Sebastián (Donostia)

GETTING AROUND

By Air

San Sebastián's airport to the east, by Fuenterrabía (Tel: 64 22 40), and has connections to Madrid and Barcelona. The bus to the airport and Fuenterrabía and Irún departs from C. Oquendo 16 (Tel: 42 30 50) every 12 minutes.

By Train

RENFE trains depart from the Paseo de Francia, in Gros, from Estación del Norte (Tel: 27 27 71): frequent connections with Irún and Hendaya, Paris, Burgos and Madrid; less frequent trains to Barcelona, Pamplona, Salamanca, Vitoria, Zaragoza and León; *talgos* whiz all the way to Málaga, Córdoba, Algeciras, Valencia, Alicante, Oviedo and Gijón.

The two narrow gauge lines have neighbouring stations on the C. de Easo: Topo trains (Tel: 45 51 60) depart from the Estación del Tranvia for Hendaya at 10 minutes past every hour, going by way of Oyarzun. Vascongados (Tel: 45 01 31) depart from the Estación de Amara less frequently for Bilbao, stopping everywhere on the way.

By Bus

Buses leave from the small station on Pl. de Pio XII near the southern end of town, a block from the river. The ticket office is nearby on C. Sancho el Sabio 33 (Tel: 42 30 50); there are buses to Pamplona, Madrid, Bilbao, Vitoria and coastal towns – except Fuenterrabía and Irún (see above).

There are 10 bus lines in San Sebastián itself; no. 6 goes to Igueldo and the funicular (daily 10 am–9 pm, every 15 minutes). Motor boats make excursions out to the Isla Santa Clara every half-hour from the port, where you can also rent a rowing boat to do the same yourself.

WHAT TO SEE

Long before there were any 'costas', wealthy Spaniards spent their summers bathing at San Sebastián following in the footsteps of the Queen Regent Maria Cristina, who made it all the rage in 1886. It's been a classy place to go ever since, a lovely, relaxed, seaside resort in a spectacular setting, built around one of the peninsula's most enchanting bays, the oyster-shaped **Bahia de La Concha**, protected from bad moods of the Atlantic by a wooded islet, the **Isla de Santa Clara** and **Mount Urgull**, the humpbacked sentinel on the easternmost tip of the bay. Sheltered within the bay is the magnificent golden crescent of the **Playa de La Concha**, San Sebastián's largest beach; on its western end stands a promontory topped by the mock-Tudor **Palace of Miramar** of Maria Cristina. The road passes through a tunnel underneath Miramar to the **Playa de Ondarreta**, a traditional Society retreat. Ondarreta ends where it meets **Mount Igueldo**, a seaside mountain topped by a **Parque de Atracciónes** (attainable by road or funicular), along with spectacular views over San Sebastián. Nearly all the city built around these beaches dates from the 19th century; San Sebastián is an ancient place, but has been burnt to the ground 12 times in its history, lastly by Wellington's drunken soldiery, who celebrated the conquest of the town with murder and mayhem.

A promenade-lined river, the **Urumea**, divides 19th-century Sanse (as it is affectionately known) from the newer quarter of **Gros**, the working-men's student-bohemian enclave, a lively place full of cheap bars and endowed with its own beach, the **Playa de Gros**, which is always less crowded but lies outside the sheltered bay, subject to the wind, waves and filthy debris. Of the three charming bridges that span the Urumea, the one named for Maria Cristina (near the station) most resembles a cream pastry.

Most of the action in town takes place beneath Monte Urgull in the narrow streets of **La Parte Vieja** – or old town. From La Concha beach, its entrance is guarded by a beautiful square, the **Parque de Alderdi Eder**, and the enormous 19th-century **Ayuntamiento**, or town hall, formerly the Casino (the new one is in the Hotel de Londres). What remains of the city's fishing-fleet may be seen in the harbour behind the Ayuntamiento, and at the far end of the harbour lies the **Aquarium**, with a few fish and sleeping tortoises and whale skeletons, along with other exhibits testifying to the Basques' great sea-faring past (open 10 am–1 pm and 3.30–8 pm, closed Mondays). From here you can stroll along the outer edge of Monte Urgull on the **Paseo Nuevo**, a splendid little walk between turf and surf. A popular late afternoon stroll is up one of the numerous paths to the summit of Monte Urgull with the half-ruined **Castillo de Santa Cruz de la Mota** (16th century) and an ungainly but huge statue of Christ, who keeps an eye on the holiday-makers on La Concha beach below.

The centre of La Parte Vieja is the arcaded **Plaza de la Constitución**, and within a few blocks of this local centre of Basque nationalism stand San Sebastián's three best monuments – the hyper-elaborate façade of **Santa María del Coro** (18th century) on Vía Coro, the fine Gothic **Church of San Vincente** on San Vincente, and nearby the old Dominican Monastery of San Telmo, now the fascinating **Museum of San Telmo** (open 10 am–1.30 pm and 3.30–5.30 pm). The monastery's church is adorned with golden murals by the Catalan artist Josep María Sert (1930) on the history of the Basque people. Old Basque tombstones, with round heads adorned with geometric patterns, are lined up in the cloister; upstairs the museum contains three El Grecos, two bear skeletons, Basque lucky charms and amulets, a history of Basque sports, the interior of a Basque cottage and more.

The main attraction of La Parte Vieja is its countless bars, where the evening crowds hasten to devour delectable seafood tapas and Basque goodies. Eating is the city's greatest obsession, and there are societies (all male) devoted to the preparation and devouring of enormous Basque meals. A fun excursion is to gather some of this good food and row it out to Isla Santa Clara for a picnic.

East to France

It's only 20 minutes by bus from San Sebastían to Irún on the frontier; connections are frequent by bus and train and not a few people watching their pesetas stay in Irún rather than in the more pricey capital. If you're not in a hurry, take the narrow-gauge 'El Topo', for a leisurely ride through some fine scenery.

Just east of San Sebastián, the long ribbon town of **Pasajes de San Juan** lines the east bank of a fjord, with picturesque old houses. Victor Hugo lived in one for a while, and the Marquis de Lafayette lodged in another before sailing off to aid the American colonies in their revolution. Philip built part of Invincible Armada here, though now all such business affairs are handled by San Juan's ugly step-sister across the fjord **Pasajes de San Pedro**.

If you're driving you can take the coastal road along **Monte Jaizkibel** offering superb views over the Bay of Biscay, the French coast and the Pyrenees. It descends at the lovely village of **Fuentarrabía** (Hondarribia), built up around the sandy ford of the Río Bidasoa that has endowed it with a fine, wide, and protected sandy beach. Fuenterrabía is known for its colour – its brightly painted houses, especially along **Calle San Nicolas**, balconies loaded with flowers, and its fishing-fleet that has not been afraid to take on France in the EEC's battle of fishing rights. The town has seen its share of sieges – you can still see the ancient walls and a **castle of Charles V** now a *parador* – and every summer sees an invasion of French tourists (the local defensive measure of raising prices has had little effect in repelling them). In the evening, head out towards the *faro* (lighthouse) on Cabo Higuer – the north-easternmost corner of Spain – for views of the sunset over the bay. **Irún**, up the Bidasoa, is the uncharming frontier town, with only plenty of cheap accommodation to recommend it. Inland you can flee the bustling coast for the serene **Valley of Oyarzun**, one of Euskadi's rural beauty spots, with the pretty villages of **Oyarzun**, **Lesaca** and **Vera de Bidasoa**.

TOURIST INFORMATION

San Sebastián: municipal: on the river, in the Victoria Eugenia Theatre, Tel: 42 10 02. Basque government: C. Andia 13, near La Concha, Tel: 42 17 74.

Irún: Puente de Santiago, Puente de Behobia, and in the train station.

WHERE TO STAY

San Sebastián is not the place to look for bargains, and many of the cheaper *hostales* and *fondas* are packed full of university students most of the year. In general, the further back you are from the sea, the less expensive the accommodation will be. The city's most luxurious address, the **Hotel Londres y Inglatierra******, on La Concha beach at Zubieta 2 (Tel: 42 69 89) has splendid views, first-class service, and plenty of charm, as well as one of the city's best restaurants (doubles 74000–9000 pts; meals around 2500 pts). The old grande dame, the **Maria Cristina******, Paseo Republica Argentina, Tel: 42 67 70, looks onto the Rio Urumea's promenade, a short walk from La Concha (doubles 5200–6200 pts). Quiet, small, comfortable, and located halfway up Monte Igueldo, the **Hotel Gudamendi*****, has superb views (Barrio de Igueldo, Tel: 21 41 11, doubles 4000–5000 pts); also in the Barrio de Igueldo, the **Leku-Eder****, Tel: 21 01 07 is even smaller, its 11 doubles with bath going for a bargain 2500 pts. In the middle of town a good bet is the **Ozcariz****, Fuentarrabía 8, Tel: 42 53 06, its bathless though stylish doubles going for 2200–2500 pts.

In Fuenterrabía, the castle that housed so many Spanish monarchs on French business over the centuries has been converted into the **Parador El Emperador*****, Pl. Armas del Castillo, Tel: 64 21 40, prettily situated, with only 16 rooms, doubles are 5500–7500 pts. For something just as different, although practical only for motorists, the **Hotel Provincial de Jáizkibel**, Tel: 64 11 00, is an attractive stone inn located in an isolated but magnificently scenic spot on the cliffs of Mt Jáizkibel, with the Atlantic crashing down below; many rooms have balconies; doubles are good value, at 1920–2280 pts with bath, 1320–1680 pts without, and there are good meals served in the dining-rooms for around 1000 pts.

Cheaper lodgings may be found in Irún: near the train station, the **Lizaso****, Aduana 5–7, Tel: 61 16 00, with pleasant doubles for 2850 pts, and only 1850 pts without bath. **Hostal Irún**, Zubiaurre 5, Tel: 61 22 83, has even cheaper but decent rooms for 1100–1500 pts.

EATING OUT

As eating is the municipal obsession, it's not surprising that the city can claim three of Spain's most renowned, award-winning restaurants, the three cathedrals of Basque cuisine: **Arzak**, Alto de Miracruz 2, offers a constantly changing menu of delights, and a bargain first-timers' menu for around 3000 pts to introduce you to the kitchen (à la carte meals run at around 4000 pts). **Akelaric**, in the Barrio Igueldo, combines exquisite meals with a beautiful setting and views over the sea 3500–4000 pts). The third culinary shrine, **Nicolasa** on Aldamar 4, specializes in classic Basque cookery and offers a large menu. Other good, and slightly less expensive, restaurants are **Urepel**, Paseo de Salamanca 3, and **Salduba** at Pescadería 6, both again serving fine Basque food for 2000–2500 pts. Another superb choice, specializing in grilled fish and meat and with a huge wine cellar, the **Rekondo** offers elegant dining on the Subida a Igueldo for 1600–2000 pts. Good seafood at reasonable prices is served at the **Bar Igueldo** near the fishing harbour on C. Pasealekua for around 800 pts; for something cheaper, follow the crowds through the tapas bars of the old town.

In Fuenterrabía, **Ramón Roteta** at Villa Ainar offers gracious dining in a lovely villa with a garden, grand cuisine and superb desserts (2500 pts). Next to the sea, the **Arrauniari**, Paseo Butrón, is the best bet, offering scrumptious seafood (1800 pts). In Irún, the **Romantxo** on Pl. de Urbanibia, has good home cooking for 1200–1600 pts. A number of places nearby are cheaper.

San Sebastián to Bilbao: the Coast

GETTING AROUND

Trains between San Sebastián and Madrid pass through Vitoria and Tolosa, and Salvatierra is a stop along RENFE's Vitoria–Pamplona run. Otherwise you'll have to take the bus – or hitchhike. Generally the more remote the area, the more likely you are to get a ride – friendly locals will often stop and ask you if you want a lift. If you want to bicycle in Spain you won't find a more pleasant region – cool summers, good country roads with little traffic, and easy hills.

In Vitoria the RENFE station is at the head of C. Eduardo Dato, six blocks from the old town (Tel: 23 20 30). The bus station is at C. Francia 34 (Tel: 25 84 00), just east of the old town.

The coast is served by frequent buses from San Sebastián and Bilbao; the narrow gauge Vascongados line stops four or five times a day at Zarauz, Guetaria, Zumaya, Deva and Durango; another branch runs out of Bilbao to Bermeo via Guernica.

WHAT TO SEE

Most of the **Costa Vasca** is simply beautiful and it's worth your while taking the old coastal highway for the great views. The first major town to the west of San Sebastián, **Zarauz**, is a big resort town, having first been made fashionable by more summering royalty – King Baudouin and Queen Fabiola of Belgium. The first ship to make it all the way around the world, the *Vitoria*, was built here – and the man who sailed it, Sebastián de Elcano, came from the nearby fishing port of **Guetaria**; a huge monument in his honour is as much of a landmark here as the islet **El Ratón** that shelters the harbour, named for its resemblance to a rat. Guetaria has been compared to a Cornish fishing-village, and besides its old charm it has two little beaches and a fine early 15th-century **church of San Salvador** containing a ship model and unusual altar. It also produces Euskadi's finest txakoli wine.

Zumaya is reached by a scenic stretch of road nicknamed the **Balcony of Cantabria**, from which it descends to Zumaya's long, serene **Zuloaga Beach** with its pine trees; it was named for the Basque painter Ignacio de Zuloaga, whose stone house, just behind the beach, is now the **Zuloaga Museum** (open June–September; Tel: 86 10 15 for current hours) with a fine collection of El Grecos and Goyas and two santas by Zubarán, displayed in a charming setting. Next to the house, the 12th-century chapel and cloister of **Santiago Echea** was a shrine for pilgrims taking the coastal route to Compostela. Zumaya itself is a pleasant town with few tourists, and has another beach to the west – **San Telmo**, a dramatic swathe of sand under steep red cliffs, known for the strength of its pounding surf.

After Zumaya the main road dives inland, but you can continue along the old winding coastal road to **Deva** and **Motrico**. Motrico is set back on a narrow inlet 3.2 km (2 miles) from the quiet beach of **Saturrarán** en route to Vizcaya province and **Ondárroa**, where the locals used to operate a provincial customs house near the old stone footbridge. The village is another pretty fishing-port, but most people prefer to continue west to **Lequeito** (Lekeitio), with its two good beaches, **Isuntza** and **Carraspio** further out. Lequeito still catches more fish than tourists, despite its gorgeous situation under the Cantabrian hills.

Guernica

The ancient, sacred city of the Basques is mostly rebuilt now, and most of the inhabitants are too young to remember the horror that occurred on a market day in 1937. But beyond the beautiful setting in the Mundaca valley and the oak tree by the old Basque parliament building (**Las Casas Juntas**) there's not much to see. The **tree**, the seedling of the ancient oak under which Spanish kings would swear to uphold Basque liberties (remnants of its 600-year-old trunk can be seen under a nearby pavilion), miraculously survived the saturation bombing as a potent symbol of freedom and hope, not only for the Basques, but for everyone – Guernica shocked the world because it was the first time modern technology was used as a tool of terror, a prelude to our own greatest nightmares. About 5 km (3.1 miles) east of Guernica, the **caves of Santimamiñe** have Euskadi's best paleolithic art (usually open in the morning – ask in town before setting out).

Guernica lies at the head of a pretty, pine-forested estuary, the Ria de Guernica, with a number of small, sandy beaches – at **Laida** and **Laga** near the mouth of the Ría, and **Pedernales** and **Mundaca** on the west bank. **Bermeo**, near Mundaca, is Euskadi's largest fishing-port, a colourful, working town that makes few concessions to tourism, though it has a fine collection of seafood restaurants. Off the shore of **Basquia** just to the west, the scenic, hermitage-topped islet of **San Juan de Gaztelugatxa** is linked to the mainland by an artificial bridge. In the old days it supported a castle; the best one remaining in the vicinity is the 11th-century **Castillo de Butrón**, rebuilt in fairy-tale style in the 19th century and located in the wooded hills (take the C-6313 west of Gatika).

Inland

From San Sebastían the main road leads to **Tolosa**, a riverside town tainted with the aroma of paper mills; better to continue up to **Regil**, a pretty mountain town with beautiful views from the Col de Regil (C-6324). This picturesque road continues to the ancient village of **Azpeitia** and the nearby **Sanctuary of St Ignatius of Loyola** (Iñigo López de Loyola), where in 1491 the future founder of the Jesuits was born, the last of 13 children of a noble family. The actual house, built by the saint's grandfather after a four-year exile among the Moors, is a fortress-like Mudejár structure. Next to it stands a large ornate basilica, with relics, the death mask, and scenes from the life of the General of the church militant.

Southwest of Tolosa lies the pretty mountain village of **Segura**, and further on, **Oñati**, capital of the Pretender in the Carlist wars. This was one of the few towns in Euskadi to be ruled by a noble, retaining its independence until 1845. For many years the town had the only Basque university, founded in 1540; this has a beautiful Plateresque façade and a plain Renaissance courtyard. Oñati is also known for its number of well-preserved medieval palaces; in one was born the conquistador, Lope de Aguirre. The parish **church San Miguel** (15th century) contains a number of treasures, including the alabaster tomb of the university's founder, Bishop Zuázola de Avila, attributed to Diego de Siloé, and an attractive Plateresque cloister. There are other fine buildings as well, especially the **Ayuntamiento** and the Franciscan **Convento de Bidaurreta**, but perhaps the greatest charm is the town's setting in a rich, rolling valley, dominated in the distance by the bluish pointed peaks of Mount Amboto and Udalaitz.

9 km (5.6 miles) up from Oñati a scenic road climbs to the sanctuary of **Arantzazu**. Here, in 1469, a shepherd found an icon of the Virgin by a thorn bush and a cow bell, and the church that houses it has been rebuilt innumerable times since, lastly in 1950. It is a curious temple of Basque modernism in a lonely and rugged setting, its towers covered with a distinctive skin of pyramidical concrete nubs.

Vitoria (Gasteiz)

The capital of the inland province of Alava, the city has grown to be one of Spain's most industrial, though at the same time it has carefully preserved its old core of neat, concentric streets. Although it was the scene of Wellington's sound victory over the forces of Joseph Bonaparte, its name has nothing to do with victory but with the slight height the city was built on (*Beturia* in Basque).

The **Plaza de la Virgen Blanca** is the centre of the old town, named for the statue in the niche over the door of **San Miguel**, the 14th-century church at the top of the square. Behind it, Calle Fray Zacarias leads to the **Cathedral Santa Maria** or the old cathedral, also from the 14th century, boasting a fine western doorway. There are a number of old houses surviving in the old town; the eastern quarter was the **Juderia**. The **Archaeology Museum** is in a lovely half-timbered house at Correría 116 near the Cathedral (open 10 am–2 pm and 5–7 pm, closed Monday) with Roman finds and Basque 'star' tombstones. Near the old town in Florida park stands the huge neo-Gothic **New Cathedral**, its masons immortalized in its gargoyles. Beyond the park, and just east of the train station the **Provincial Museum** (Paseo de Fray Francisco, open 11 am–2 pm and 5–7 pm, closed Monday and Saturday and Sunday pm) is located in an early 20th-century mansion with gardens, featuring a well-displayed collection ranging from Flemish paintings to Picasso and Miró, with a handful of great Spanish masters in between. The façade of a 13th-century hermitage was reconstructed in the garden; up the street at no. 3, the **Museum of Arms** (open 11 am–2 pm and 5–7 pm, closed Mondays) houses suits of armour, medieval weapons, and dioramas and displays on the Battle of Vitoria. A third museum, the **Museum of Playing Cards**, located in the grounds of Vitoria's card-manufacturing company at Heraclio Fournier 19 (off the Plaza San Cristobal, behind the east end of the train station), open Monday–Friday 8 am–12 noon and 3–5 pm, contains an interesting collection of cards (some decks dating back to the 15th century), card-making machinery and paintings.

Vitoria's most interesting building is a 20-minute walk to the south-west (from the Paseo de Fray Francisco, head down the Paseo de Cervantes and Avenida de San Prudencia), to the **Basilica of Armentia**, built at the end of the 12th century, with a fine doorway and unusual reliefs and capitals carved inside. East of Vitoria, **Salvatierra** is a fine old village within striking distance of two of Euskadi's best dolmens – **Aizkomendi** at Eguilaz, and **Sorginetxe** in Arizala.

Between Vitoria and Bilbao

There are several interesting old towns between the two provincial capitals. **Ochandiano** was the original Basque iron town, a fact commemorated by a statue of the god Vulcan in the main square. **Elorrio** is an attractive village full of grand palaces and impressive little squares; from the centre it's a lovely walk out to the hermitage of **San Adrián de Argiñeta**, where you can see the 9th- and 10th-century **tombs of Argiñeta**, carved out of rock, some adorned with pinwheel-like stars. **Durango** is another pretty town, with an attractive Baroque centre behind its **Portal de Santa Ana**, an ornate gateway surviving from the walls. There are several old churches – **San Pedro de Tavira** one of the oldest to survive in all Euskadi, and the porticoed **Santa María de Uribarri** – but the most remarkable single monument is the unique 19th-century **Kurutziaga Cross**, just outside the centre in a neighbourhood of same name.

North of Durango is the tiny village and valley of **Bolivar**, from whence came the family of the great Liberator of South America, Simón de Bolivar, to whom a large monument stands in the village square. Near the old parish church of **Santo Tomás** you can see the 'Cattle Trial Yards' and the huge stone weights hauled by oxen at festivals. **Marquina**, further north, is nicknamed the 'University of Pelota', its historic *fronton* has produced *pelota* and *jai-alai* champions who have made their mark around the world. Near Marquina, on the right bank of the Río Artibay, is the very unusual hermitage of **San Miguel de Arretxinaga**, its altar built by the giant Gentiles (or, according to some, fallen from heaven as a meteorite) consists of three huge boulders sheltering a statue of St Michael. It is a mysterious place that has never been satisfactorily explained. There's another 'Cattle Trial Yard' next to the church.

TOURIST INFORMATION

Vitoria: C. E. Dato 16, Tel: 23 25 79.

Lequeitio: Arranegiko Zabala 10.

Tolosa: C. San Juan.

Zarauz: Alameda Madoz.

WHERE TO STAY

There are relatively few hotels in Euskadi, though even in the smaller villages it doesn't hurt to enquire in bars about the availability of *casas particulares*. In Guetaria you can lodge near the beach at the **San Prudencia****, Tel: 83 24 11, open all year, with doubles for 1800 pts without bath. In Zumaya there's one *hostal*, the **Zurmaya****, Erribera 2–4, Tel: 86 10 96 (open April–September) with doubles for 3000 pts with bath, 2500 without. Lequeitio has a fine little pension, the **Piáupe**, Av. P. Abarcalo, Tel: 68 29 84 (doubles with bath 2900 pts).

Inland in Azpeitia, you can choose between the upmarket **Izarra***, near the basilica on Av. de Loyola, Tel: 81 07 50, complete with a swimming-pool, for 3800 pts, or the more modest **Hostal Uranga***, B. de Loyola, Tel: 81 25 43 (bathless doubles 1500 pts, meals 900 pts). Oñati has a pleasant, 10-room *hostal*, the **Echeverria***, R.M. Zuazola 14, Tel: 78 04 60, in the middle of town with doubles for 2500–2750 pts with bath, 1650–1900 pts without. In Aránzazu itself there's the large **Hospederia de Aránzazu***, Tel: 78 13 13, with simple, clean doubles with bath for 1920 pts.

In Vitoria, there are several large hotels in the newest part of town; the best value among them, the **General Alava*****, Av. de Gastiez 53, Tel: 22 22 00, offers modern, comfortable rooms with TV for 5000 pts; if you're driving, though, you may prefer the **Parador Argomaniz*****, on the Madrid–Irún highway 12 km (7.5 miles) from Vitoria, Tel: 28 22 00. Located in the ancient Palacio de los Lasses, it has excellent views, and its kitchen prepares good local dishes for 1800 pts (doubles 5000 pts). A cheaper alternative, **Francia****, Dato 33, Tel: 23 11 00, a short walk from the train station (doubles with bath 1600 pts).

To the north, Durango's one *hostal*, **Juego de Bolos****, San Agustinalde 2, Tel: 68 10 99, will make you pay 3800 pts for a double with bath, but only 1600 pts without. In Marquina you can sleep and eat well at the central **Hostal Vega****, Abesua 2, Tel: 686 60 15, where doubles are 2750 pts with bath, 2300 pts without, and Basque meals for around 1300 pts.

EATING OUT

You can taste Guetaria's famous txakoli wine at the portside **Kaia**, upstairs at Gral. Arnao 19, along with good Basque food (1500 pts); downstairs you can eat roast meats at the **Asador Kalpe**. **Jususkoa** in Zumaya's Barrio de Oikina, has good grilled fish meals for 1000 pts. In Lequeitio, good, abundant, and cheap fish dinners are served at **Zapiraia**, Igualdegui 3, for 750 pts. Near Guernica's Santimamiñe caves there's the **Lezika**, a fine restaurant located in an 18th-century Basque chalet in a charming woody grove (1400 pts). A good restaurant in Oñati, the **Txopekua** on the road to Aránzazu, is located in a Basque homestead (1500 pts).

Most of the good bars and restaurants in Vitoria are in the old town – especially good, **El Portalón**, Correría 151, with tables on three floors of a 16th-century building and traditional Basque food (1500 pts); **Amboto Oleagarena** on Cuchilleria 29, is another good bet for around 1000 pts.

Bilbao

With a metropolitan population of a million, Bilbao is Spain's sixth largest city and the capital of the Basques; much of Spain's banking, shipping, ship-building, steel and other industries take place here. It obviously offers few of the demands of the typical holiday maker, but it's hardly uninteresting. The people are very friendly and easy to meet, and the city's location, on the banks of the estuary of the Nervion river (which is so polluted along its length it sometimes looks as if it were literally made of milk and honey) is quite dramatic, the steep hills on either side forcing the city to grow in sinuous curves, the green slopes always in sight above. Americans will be struck by its resemblance to Pittsburgh.

GETTING AROUND

By Air

Bilbao's international airport is a few miles to the north at Erandio (Tel: 453 13 50); there are regular flights to Barcelona, Madrid, Las Palmas, Tenerife, Valencia, Vigo and London – Iberia' main office in the city is at Ercilla 20 (Tel: 424 10 90), Aviaco is at Buenos Aires 1 (Tel: 423 13 94), British Airways: Gran Vía 38 (Tel: 416 78 66). Airport buses leave from Henao 29, Tel: 424 41 35.

By Train

Bilbao has a confusing array of train stations. The RENFE station (Tel: 423 86 36), the Estación de Abando is on the Hurtado de Amézaga, just off the Plaza de España; trains from here go to most points on the peninsula. From the pretty Estación de Santander on Bailén 2 (between the RENFE station and the river and facing the Casco Viejo), the narrow-gauge FEVE connects Bilbao with Santander, and once a day La Linea de La Robla links the city with León (Tel: 423 22 66). Both trains are slow and marvellously scenic – the Santander train follows the Nevrion valley and the León train takes in part of the Picos de Europa (see León). From the Estación de Achuri, at Achuri 8 (Tel: 433 00 88) the Ferrocarriles Vascongadas have trains to San Sebastián, Irún, Bermeo, Durango, Guernica, etc. For Getxo and Sopelanas and Plencia, you can catch the very frequent suburban trains from the Estación Las Arenas, Plaza de San Nicolás (Tel: 416 14 11).

By Bus

Most of the bus companies depart from the vicinity of the Puente del Arenal near the Casco Viejo: for Vitoria, Logroño, and Pamplona buses depart from Henao 29 (Tel: 424 41 35). From the Pl. de la Encarnación 7, buses go to Guernica, Lequeitio, Bermeo and Castro Urdiales (Cantabria). From Urazurrutia 7 there are buses for Oñati, San Sebastián, Tolosa and Vergara (Tel: 416 46 10). From Autonomía 17 there are buses for Santander, Logroño, Burgos and Madrid (Tel: 432 32 00).

WHAT TO SEE

The **Casco Viejo**, the centre of the city from the 15th to the 19th century, is a snug little region on the east bank of the Nervion (take the Puente del Arenal from Bilbao's main street, the Gran Vía). Miguel de Unamuno was born on the Calle La Ronda here, not far from the **Basque Archaeological, Ethnographical and Historical Museum** on Cruz 4 (open 10.30 am–1.30 pm and 4–7 pm), located in an old Jesuit cloister – exhibits include a scale-model of Viscaya, a reconstruction of the rooms of the Consulate, the old merchants' organization, tools, ship-models and other ethnographic items, and Basque gravestones. In the middle of the cloister, the *Idolo de Mikeldi* is the museum's treasure – it looks like a primitive depiction of the cow that jumped over the moon. The churches in the Casco Viejo aren't all that impressive; there's an arcaded, enclosed **Plaza Nueva**, now a bit down-at-the-heels, but in its day the symbol of Bilbao's growth and prosperity. Behind the large church of San Nicolas an elevator ascends to the upper town, from where it's a short walk to the Viscayans' holy shrine, the **Basilica de Begoña** with its unusual spire stuck on an early 16th century church, holding a venerated image of the Virgin and some huge paintings by Lucas Giordano. There are fine views of the old town below.

There's better art across the Nevrion in the **Museo de Bellas Artes**, on the edge of the large and beautiful **Parque de Doña Casilda de Iturriza**, between the Gran Vía and the tourist office. Open 10.30 am–1 pm and 3.30–7 pm, it contains a worthy collection ranging from Flemish paintings (Metsys' *The Money Changers* is one of the best) to Spanish masters like Velázquez, El Greco, Zurbarán and Goya, to modern art by Picasso, Gaugin, Leger and Mary Cassat, and 19th and 20th-century Basque artists. In the summer you can join the locals at their beaches near **Getxo** (the Playa de Arrgúnaga), the metropolis' residential beauty-spot near the mouth of the estuary, and at **Sopelanas** and **Plencia** further up the coast.

TOURIST INFORMATION

Alameda Mazarredo, Tel: 424 48 19 – take a right off the Gran Vía, two blocks from the Pl. de España (near the RENFE station and Puente del Arenal) and follow it around to the modern pavilion near the intersection with C. Ercilla. The post office is on the Alameda de Urquijo 15; telephones are at Buenos Aires 10.

WHERE TO STAY

Bilbao has quite a few luxury hotels, catering for the businessmen who pass through. The average visitor, however, would probably prefer to stay in the Casco Viejo – there are several choices on Bidebarrieta, like the **Hostal Arana**** at no. 2, Tel: 415 64 11, with comfortable modern doubles for 2200 pts with bath, 1750 pts without, or the **Gurea****, at no. 14, Tel: 416 32 99, where the simple rooms are 1650 pts with bath, 1250 pts without. Just off the Bidebarrieta at Loteria there's the friendly **Hostal Roquefor**, with high ceilings and nice showers down the hall for 1500 pts a double.

EATING OUT

Eating out is a pleasure in Bilbao – you can splurge at the city's finest, the traditional and sumptuous **Guria**, Gran Vía 66, or the creative **Golzeko-Kabi**, Particular de Estraunza 476, both costing around 3500 pts for a full meal, or eat well for less at the **Casa Vasca**, Av. del Ejército 13, or the **Café Iruña**, Berastegui 5, both classic, moderately priced restaurants with full meals for around 1500 pts.

Navarre

Spanish history is full of the phrase 'except Navarre'. Even in a country full of different nations of peoples it has stood out, beginning in 605, when the Franks tried to harness it as part of the Duchy of Vasconia, a huge untenable territory that extended from the Garonne to the Ebro. Charlemagne himself came down in the year 824, either to discipline the unruly duchy or to force it to join his fight against the Moors. Whatever the cause, Charlemagne razed the walls of Pamplona and went back to France – except of course for his rear guard, which the vengeance-seeking Basques of Pamplona anihilated at the pass of Roncevalles. Historically the event was trivial, but it inspired one of the greatest medieval narrative epics *La Chanson de Roland*, which transformed the Franks into the good guys and the Basques into evil Moors.

Soon afterwards the Basques of Pamplona became independent, and in its heyday their kingdom of Navarre, under Sancho the Great (1004–34), ruled much of French Basque country and a large section of non-Basque lands south of Pamplona. Sancho dominated the other small kingdoms of Spain, taking Castile after the death of its last count and setting up his son Ferdinand I as king – the first to take the title of 'King of the Spains', ruling León, Castile, Galicia and Navarre. Such unity couldn't last, and by the time of Sancho III Navarre was a fierce rival of Castile, but avoided entanglements – marital or martial – by turning its face north to France. Three different French dynasties ruled Navarre until 1512, when Ferdinand the Catholic, warring with France at the time, demanded free passage of the Navarrese, was refused, and used the excuse to add Navarre south of the Pyrenees to Spain (French, or Basse Navarre, is a thimble-sized realm that gave France its long line of 'Kings of Navarre').

Yet even though Navarre was nominally Spanish, its *fueros* (or privileges) in practice gave it an independence enjoyed by no other region in Spain; it was ruled by a Viceroy, minted its own coins and had its own government. Napoleonic and Liberal attempts to do away with its privileges in the cause of central unity turned the Navarrese into fierce reactionaries and the most ardent of Carlists. Despite its sizeable Basque population, Navarre refused the Republic's offer of autonomy; instead, the Navarrese Carlist *requetés* in their distinctive red berets were among Franco's best troops, fighting for their old privileges and Catholicism – just as the Basques were, only on the Republican side. Franco rewarded Navarre by leaving its *fueros* intact, making it the only autonomous region in Spain until his death.

Just as Navarre combines the magnificent scenery of the misty western Pyrenees with sunny, vineyard-planted hillsides and Ebro valley flatlands, so it uncomfortably combines a sizeable Basque minority with conservative, non-Basque Navarrese, though now that most of the population has left the countryside for industrial jobs, things have been loosening up. As everyone must know by now, much of this 'loosening up' is concentrated into an ecstatic week-long bacchanalia of inebriated recklessness', bull-running and partying known as 'Las San Fermines' of Pamplona.

Pamplona

If you come outside the week of July 6–14, Pamplona (also known by its Basque name Iruña) is a pleasant if unremarkable place. Founded by the sons of Pompey and named for their father, the city is located on a plain at the foot of the Pyrenees and has long been known as the 'Gateway of Spain'. Besides the sacking by Charlemagne the city endured another famous siege in 1521, when a captain named Iñigo Lopez de Recalde suffered a wound that led to a lengthy convalescence, study – and the founding of the Jesuits, the stormtroopers of Christ. Lately, though, the Opus Dei, Christianity's fifth column, has made deeper inroads, building their university just south of the city.

GETTING AROUND

Pamplona has an airport 6 km (3.8 miles) south of the city (Tel: 31 72 02) with connections to Madrid, Barcelona, Santander and Vigo; information and tickets at the Aviaco office on Paulino Caballero, Tel: 24 13 00. A bus from the bus station (see below) leaves an hour before every departure.

Pamplona's train station is away out of town at Rochapea. Bus no. 9 makes connections from the centre every 10 minutes (Tel: 11 15 31). You can also pick up tickets and information at the travel office in town at Estella 8, Tel: 22 24 29. There are connections with Madrid, Burgos, Avila, Irún, San Sebastián, Vitoria, Zaragoza, Valladolid and Soria, and *talgos* to Barcelona, Alicante, Burgos, San Sebastián, Teruel, León, Lérida (Lleida), Palencia, Oviedo, Zaragoza and Valencia. Supplementary services are added during Las San Fermines.

The bus station is in town, near the citadel, at Conde de Oliveto 2; information Tel: 21 36 19; besides provincial connections, there are three buses to Vitoria, four to Bilbao, and three to San Sebastián, four to Zaragoza, two to Huesca and Jaca.

WHAT TO SEE

The **Plaza del Castillo** is the elegant, arcaded heart of town shaded by the intertwining boughs of the carefully pruned plane trees. A huge, overdone monument to Navarre's *fueros* looms to the southwest, on the Paseo de Sarasate; the symbolic figure on top is surrounded by the chains of Las Navas de Tolosa, where in the year 1212 Sancho VII ('the Strong') led the Navarrese to their greatest victory over the Moors. The chains are said to be part of those that bound ten thousand slaves at the ankle and wrist, forming a human fortress around the emir's tent, though even that failed to prevent the Christians from leaping over and carrying off the tent as booty.

The **Cathedral** is a few blocks to the south of the Plaza Castillo. A misguided dogooder slapped on a dull, Classical façade in the 18th century, but within it has retained much of its Gothic elegance. In the nave are the beautifully carved, alabaster tombs of the big-nosed Carlos III and his big-nosed queen Leonor of Castile. The **Cloister**, begun in the 14th century, is the cathedral's loveliest feature, and the **Diocesan Museum**, located in the old refectory and kitchen where pilgrims en route to Santiago could dine, contains two unusual reliquaries – the 1258 Relicario del Santo Sepulero and the 1401 Relicario del Lignum Crucis, adorned with precious stones (museum open 10.30 am–1.30 pm and 4–7 pm). Walk around back of the cathedral for a look at the old walls, the attractive **Portal de Zumalacárregui** (16th century, but renamed for the Carlist hero), and a fine view over the surrounding country and the winding Río Arga.

The **Museum of Navarre** is near the walls, off the Plaza Santo Domingo (open 10 am–2 pm, Sundays 11 am–2 pm, closed Monday), with the region's archaeological, historical and art collections (including a good Goya), well-displayed in a former hospital. Just below the terrace of the museum the wooden barricades remind you that this is the route of the *encierro* (running of the bulls) who leave their corral near Plaza Santo Domingo and head up Calles Mercaderes and Estafeta towards the bullring. Following their route towards the Plaza del Castillo you'll pass the fun Baroque **Ayuntamiento**, topped with jaunty allegorical figures. In front of the **Plaza de Toros** itself, the square has been renamed the Plaza Hemingway in honour of the man who made Pamplona a household word.

Las San Fermines

Before Hemingway and *The Sun Also Rises* (known as *Fiesta* in the UK) there was San Fermin, the first bishop of Pamplona, martyred by being dragged about by a bull. Obviously he had no hard feelings, for he has taken bullfighters under his special protection, and before every *encierro* the reckless ones who are about to risk life and limb running with the six bulls and six steers sing a hymn to the saint. And although the running of the bulls is the best-known part of the fiesta it's only the beginning of a week of non-stop merry-making, when for a few days (noon on 6 July to midnight 17 July) the locals and thousands of foreigners (especially Americans) come to burn the candle at both ends with plenty of company, plenty of wine, fireworks, and dancing in the streets to the numerous street bands who stagger through Pamplona. Good fellowship abounds and a spirit of child-like abandon is so infectious that even if you come determined not to run, you may find yourself joining in on the spur of the moment. (If you're a woman, though, the chances are good that you'll be yanked out of the *encierro* by the police.)

The *encierro* begins daily at 8 am, but if you want to run, or especially if you want a good place to watch, get there at least an hour earlier. The locals, as you'll soon notice, all carry a rolled-up newspaper to distract the bull's attention, since they charge at the nearest moving object – ideally at a flung newspaper instead of a falling runner. A rocket goes up as the first bull leaves the corral near Plaza Santo Domingo and hits the streets; a second rocket is fired when all are released; and a third signals that all have made it to the bullring – on a good run the whole thing only lasts two minutes. The most dangerous moments are when the runners and bulls have to squeeze into the runway of the bullring, making for some unpleasant congestion – or when a bull gets loose from his fellows and in a panic is liable to do anything. It's no use denying that people get hurt every year; you can hedge your bets by running on weekdays, when it's less crowded, and avoiding the *toros* of the Salvador Guardiola ranch, which have the most blood-stained record.

During the *encierro* the lower seats of the bullring are free (again, arrive early); from here you can watch the bulls and runners pile in, and afterwards, more fun and games as heifers with padded horns are released on the crowd in the ring. The bullfights themselves take place at 6.30 in the afternoon – tickets are quite expensive and sell out fast, so get yours as soon as possible. As it gets dark, stroll over to the citadel for the great fireworks show.

The first few days of the fiesta, before everyone is burned out from too much wine and partying, is the best time to go. Unless you have somehow conjured up a reservation before hand, expect to sleep out with hundreds of others in Pamplona's parks. The locals put up plenty of rooms in their houses for rent during San Fermin; ask in the tourist office about these *casas particulares*, especially if you arrive in Pamplona a few days before the festival. If you end up sleeping outside, keep a very close eye on your belongings, and check in what you don't need at the bus station's *consigna* (everyone else does, too, so get there early).

TOURIST INFORMATION
Duque de Ahumada, 3, Tel: 21 12 87, just off Pl. Castillo. Post office is on the Paseo Saraste 9; telephones on C. Amaya.

WHERE TO STAY
Los Tres Reyes****, Jardines de la Traconera, Tel: 22 66 00 is where Pamplona pampers its well-heeled guests with every possible convenience and an indoor, heated pool. It is also conveniently located in a park, a short walk from the Pl. Castillo; doubles 20,00 pts (during San Fermin); 10,000 pts other times. **Nuevo Hotel Maisonnave*****, Nueva 20, Tel: 22 26 00 is another good, very comfortable prestige hotel, where doubles are 4700 pts (also doubled during San Fermin).

Hostal Europa*, just off Pl. Castillo on Espoz y Mina 11, Tel: 22 18 00, is Pamplona's prettiest moderate choice, with its flower-bedecked balconies. Doubles with bath are 3450 pts, soaring up to 9500 pts at San Fermin. It has a very good restaurant as well (1300 pts). Cheaper *hostales* and *fondas* are mostly on C. San Gregorio and C. San Nicolás; the most interesting and least inexpensive, the **Casa García**, S. Gregorio 12, Tel: 21 36 38, offers 10 doubles without bath for 1150 pts, and an adequate *menú del día* in its restaurant at 375 pts. If you're sleeping out any of the gardens along the walls or river are preferable to the noisy, filthy, vomit-filled citadel.

EATING OUT
The cuisine in Pamplona is mostly Basque and very good; again, prices take seven league bootsteps upwards during San Fermin, places are crowded and service gets frazzled. An alternative is to bring your own food, or patronize the numerous food booths that spring up to feed the hoards. Otherwise, if you do eat out, try local specialities like *chuletas de cordero a la navarra* (lamb chops), *truchas con jamón* (trout stuffed with ham) or, for something out of the ordinary, *liebres con chocolate* (hare with chocolate), washed down by the good strong wines from Tudela and Estella. For dessert, try the *queso de Roncal*, one of Spain's best cheeses.

The best food in a most elegant setting is served at **Josetxo**, Principe de Viana 1, where local gourmets converge for perfectly prepared grilled and roast dishes (2500 pts). A fine second choice, **Hartza**, Labrit 19, is near the bullring and features the freshest of ingredients in dishes served in a garden setting (1800 pts). Near the walls behind the cathedral on C. de Redin, you can dine in a Renaissance setting at the **Osteria Caballo Blanco** (2400 pts.); for something considerably cheaper, **Ibanez** on C. S. Nicolás 45 has good dinners for around 800 pts. No matter what your bank account, you can have a coffee or beer in the **Cafe Iruña** on the Plaza Castillo, and get a taste of olde worlde elegance for free.

The Navarrese Pyrenees

The beautiful western third of the Pyrenees are not the highest, but are the most legendary. Roncevalles was not only the site of Charlemagne's great disaster, but for centuries was the pass most favoured by French pilgrims entering Spain. In these mountains Heinrich Heine set his lyrical narrative poem of the dancing bear, *Atatroll*, a bitter sweet yearning for the Middle Ages. Most of Navarre's Basque population lives up in the three great valleys of Batzán, Roncal and Salazar, where seemingly every house in every hamlet is emblazoned with a coat-of-arms of the hidalgo – for the Basques have traditionally considered themselves all equal and therefore all noble.

Yet in these same valleys, and in similar valleys across the mountains of Basse Navarre, lived some of Europe's best-known outcasts, the *agotes* (called *cagotes* in France). Accounts of who the agotes were are varied in the extreme: some say they were albinos covered with a blond down, others that they were New Christians, Moors or more likely Goths who failed to give up their Arian heresies, but took refuge in the mountains when the Moors invaded. History indeed refers to an expedition by Clovis, king of the Franks, against the Goths in the Pyrenees, and the Inquisition was originally conceived against their unorthodox faith. The *agotes* were also called lepers, giving rise to the belief that they were descended from a colony sent up to live in the remote valleys. Certainly for centuries they were treated as lepers – they were forced to live apart from other people, allowed to enter the parish church only by a certain door and to hear mass in a special corner, they had to dress differently, with a goose foot sewn on to the backs of their coats, and they had to sound castanets at the crossroads and other public places to warn passers-by of their presence. Trades were forbidden them – except as architects, stone masons, carpenters or healers (their skills in the latter art so impressive that they were accused by the Inquisition of dealing with the devil). And yet other researchers believe the *agotes* were only symbolic lepers, kept at a distance for the stigma of their heresies – Arianism or the kind of universal mysticism practised by the Templars, or another order of 'Knights' founded in the East even earlier than the Templars, known as the Order of St Lazarus, devoted to the care of lepers, and using Lazarus as the symbol of death within life. By the 16th century, however, the *agotes* had petitioned the Pope to give them their rights as citizens, since they were now all good Christians. The Pope agreed, but it is only in this century that the *agotes* have been fully integrated into society.

GETTING AROUND

No trains here; and in most cases the buses from Pamplona go only once a day. La Veloz Sangüesina goes to Sangüesa four times a day (Tel: 22 69 95). La Tafallesa (Tel: 21 28 54) and La Roncalesa (Tel: 21 20 79) both serve the Valle de Roncal; all of the above three also stop at Yesa, near the lake and 4 km (2.5 miles) from the monastery of Leyre. For the Valle de Salazar, La Salacenca has one bus daily to Ochagavia (Tel: 22 47 57). For Roncevalles, you can go as far as Burguete and walk 3.2 km (2 miles) (La Montañesa, Tel: 21 15 84). La Baztanesa y Aurrera, Tel: 22 67 12 serves the Valle de Baztán.

Sangüesa and the Monastery of Leyre

Sangüesa, in the foothills of the Pyrenees only 14.4 km (9 miles) from the interesting Aragonese town of Sos del Rey Católico (see p. xxx), was a main stop on the great pilgrims' road from Canfranc and is famous for the portal of the **Church of Santa María**, said to have been built by the *agotes* in the 12th century. For those who think the early *agotes* were on to something deeper than orthodox Catholicism could offer, this is their trump card, for Santa María is adorned with a remarkable set of symbols, all beautifully carved; even in the more conventional Last Judgement on the tympanum the damned are smiling. The *agotes* were almost certainly influenced by the Templars; this church originally formed part of a palace of the Aragonese King Alfonso el Battalador (who willed his kingdom to the knights). Another church in Sangüesa, the 12th-century **Santiago** recalls the pilgrims and has an interesting battlemented tower and carved capitals.

Sangüesa is the base for visiting two of Navarre's holy sites. 12.8 km (8 miles) away is the village of **Javier**, topped by a picturesque battlemented castle, the birthplace in 1506 of St Francis de Javier (Xavier), apostle of the Indies and Japan. Though the castle is now a Jesuit college, you can take the tour (10.30 am–1 pm and 4–7 pm) and learn a lot, both about St Francis Xavier and castles – this one dates back to the 11th century. Perhaps most fascinating are the murals of the *Dance of Death*, a reminder that the Pyrenees were especially hard hit by the plague.

The **Monastery of San Salvador de Leyre** is located 8 km (5 miles) away, on the opposite bank of the large **Yesa Reservoir**. According to legend, its earliest foundation predates the Moors, and in the 8th century, its most famous abbot San Virila so constantly prayed to heaven for a peek into infinity that he was granted his wish, by the lovely warbling of a bird. To the abbot, the vision was a sublime moment, but when he went to tell the monks of it he found that all had changed – his eternal second had lasted 300 years.

The oldest part of the monastery and its church date from the 11th century and were restored by its current residents, the Benedictines, in 1950; the 9th-century **crypt**, a dark, cold and gloomy place of mystery, contains the bones of the 10 earliest kings of Navarre in a simple wooden casket. There is a finely carved portal, though otherwise Leyre is an austere place. One of the best things to do is take the path up to the **Fountain of San Virila** for the magnificent view of the lake and Navarrese countryside that the abbot contemplated during his prayers.

The Valle de Roncal

Like many Pyrenean valleys, the Valley of Roncal was for many years so remote that the central authorities were content to let it have more-or-less political autonomy. Although the timber logged on its thickly-forested mountain slopes now travels by truck instead of careening down the Esca River, and the renowned Roncal cheese is now made in a factory instead of on the farm, residents of the valley still like to dress up in their old Basque costumes and observe such ancient rites as the Tribute of the Three Cows, given annually by their French counterparts in Béarne as a goodwill gesture for a long-forgotten feud.

Roncal is the largest village in the valley, a pretty place surrounded by pine forests, the birthplace of the great Basque tenor Julian Gayarre, whom the locals have honoured with a wonderfully rococola tomb just outside town. Even better as a base for exploring the magnificent mountain scenery is **Isaba**, further north, a pretty Pyrenean village often enveloped in mist, dominated by its fortress church of **San Cipriano** (1540).

From here you can hike up Navarre's highest peaks, **Mount Anie** (2504 m: 8138 ft and **Mesa de los Tres Reyes** (2431 m: 7901 ft) or continue up to the remote **refugio de Belagua** in a beautiful amphitheatre, once home of a glacier.

The next valley over, the **Valle de Salazar** is much less visited and almost as lovely, filled with streams, forests, and fine old Basque chalets with their pompous coats-of-arms. The main settlement is **Ochagavia**, a pretty village and a good base for mountain hikes; an easy one is up to the 13th-century chapel of Musquilda. Ochagavia is famous for its dance troupe, who perform Navarre's most ancient war dances. To the north stretches the large and ancient beech **Forest of Irati** and to the south, along the main valley road, the impressive sheer-sided gorge, the **Foz de Arbayún**.

Roncevalles

Misty and silent, few places are as evocative of the past as Roncevalles ('the Valley of thorns'), the traditional gateway into France. Pilgrims favoured the pass; and the *Chanson de Roland* would be on their lips as they paid their respects to the traditional sites related to the hero Roland, and said their first prayer to Santiago. The poem, it seems, purposely turned the angry Basques who destroyed Charlemagne's rearguard into Moors to drum up support for the Crusades; in a later version of the legend the Emperor was returning from a pilgrimage to St James when he was ambushed. From Roncevalles the fittest of pilgrims could reach Santiago in 20 days; those who made it no further than here, usually done in by 'false pilgrims' (thieves and murderers) were laid in a 7th-century **ossuary** under the decrepit 12th-century **Church of Santi Spiritus** (Silo de Charlemagne), built on the site where Roland sounded his great ivory horn Oliphaunt, belatedly summoning the emperor to his aid.

The most interesting building in Roncevalles, the **Colegiata**, is a fine Gothic church built by Sancho the Strong in 1219, and it was here, in this timeless pass, that he chose to be buried, next to his queen Clemencia; he was a giant of a man, as his 2 m (7 ft) plus effigy testifies, his battle maces, also in the Colegiata, were believed by pilgrims to belong to Roland, popularly believed to have been a giant himself. Among the other treasures are the emerald which fell from the turban of the Moorish emir when Sancho the Strong leapt over his human wall at the Battle of Las Navas de Tolosa; there are many fine reliquaries, and a much revered 13th-century image of the Virgin under her lovely baldichin. 1 km (0.6 mile) up the road is the famous **Puerto Ibañeta** where the Basques are said to have killed Charlemagne's rearguard by dropping boulders on their heads. **Valcarlos**, near the French border, is a charming little village, where Charlemagne and the vanguard camped that fatal day.

The next valley, the **Valle de Baztán**, had Spain's largest *agote* population and produced one of Spain's busiest conquistadors, Pedro de Ursua, who died in the mad Aguirre's search for El Dorado. The valley, and the **Bidasoa Basin**, benefit from the frequent rains of the Atlantic coast. Both areas are dotted with tiny white villages, trout streams, and quietly beautiful scenery: **Elizondo** and **Lesaca** are the major settlements in the region, which has been nicknamed the 'Navarrese Switzerland'.

TOURIST INFORMATION

Valcarlos: next to the Ayuntamiento.

Sangüesa: Mercado 2, Tel: 87 03 29.
Yesa, on the road to Huesca N-240, Tel: 88 40 40.

WHERE TO STAY AND EAT

In Sangüesa there's not a lot of choice – there are a couple of *fondas* and the **Yamaguchi**** on the road to Javier, Tel: 87 01 27 with a pool and nice restaurant; doubles with bath are 3450 pts. In Javier you can stay next to the castle in the **Hostal Xavier****, Tel: 88 40 06, with antique doubles for 2500 pts with bath, 1900 pts without. The Monastery of Leyre also has a *hostal* in the grounds (Tel: 88 41 00); doubles with bath 3000 pts.

In the Valle de Roncal you stay at the **Hostal López-Sanz***, Castillo 23, Tel: 89 50 08, with eight simple rooms without bath for 1500 pts in Roncal itself, or in Isaba at the new, luxurious **Isaba*****, Tel: 89 30 30, with the most modern rooms in the valley for 3500–4800 pts with bath. Isaba's **La Lola**, at Mendigatxa 17, has rooms and a good restaurant, with a set menu for 850 pts. There are also several places to choose from in Ochagavia: the biggest, with 12 rooms, is the **Posada Ory-Alde***, Urrutia 6, Tel: 89 00 27, with doubles for 2400 pts with bath, 2000 pts without, and meals for around 800 pts, featuring Basque cuisine. In Roncevalle there are two fine places to chose from: **La Posada****, Tel: 76 02 25, located in the monastery next to the Colegiata, with doubles for 2000–2500 pts with bath, and a restaurant located in the medieval inn that formerly served the pilgrims; dinners around 800 pts. **Casa Sabina***, Tel: 76 00 12, next to the monastery gate, has six pleasant rooms for 1265 pts without bath, and good Navarrese cooking for around 1000 pts.

In Elizondo, the **Saskaitz****, M. Azphilikueta 10, Tel: 58 04 88 is a cosy place to stay in the centre of town, with doubles for 3500 pts; there are several *casa particulares* as well that are a lot less expensive. For dinner, try the **Galarza** on Santiago 1, serving the cuisine and cheese of Baztán (which many prefer to its rival Roncal).

West of Pamplona

GETTING AROUND

Most trains between Pamplona and the main junction of Alsasua stop at Huarte-Araquil; trains linking Pamplona and Zaragoza call at Tafalla, Olite and Tudela. Otherwise you'll have to rely on buses from Pamplona–La Estellesa (Tel: 21 32 25) stops at Puente le Reina and Estella en route to Logroño five times a day; Conda (Tel: 21 10 08) stops at Tafalla, Olite and Tudela on the way to Zaragoza.

North-west of Pamplona lies a region called **La Barranca**, full of small Basque towns and one of Navarre's holy of holies, **Mt Aralar**, with no fewer than 13 dolmens and the **church of San Miguel**. A story is told of how a knight named Teodosio de Goñi went off to the crusades and, after an absence of several years, was returning home when he met a hermit who warned him that his wife was unfaithful. Seething with rage, the knight came into his house, saw two forms in his bed and without hesitation slew them both. He ran out and met his wife, who told him, to his horror that his own parents had been sleeping in the bed. Teodosio went to Rome to ask the pope's pardon, and was given the penance of wearing heavy chains in solitude until God should show his forgiveness by breaking them. Teodosio went up to the top of Mt Aralar and lived for some years bound in his chains, when all of a sudden a dragon appeared. Teodosio implored the aid of St Michael, who appeared to kill the dragon, strike off the knight's chains and leave a statue of himself. There are a number of similar sacred mountains throughout Europe (Mont St Michel and St Michael's Mount, for example) dedicated to the saint associated with serpents, or the 'lays' in the earth. But what is so strange about Mt Aralar is the image of St Michael – an angelic figure with a large cross on its head and an empty glass case where the face ought to be.

WHAT TO SEE

The **Sanctuary of San Miguel in Excelsis** (open 9 am–2 pm and 4 to sunset) which contains the image was consecrated in 1098 and is a simple chapel, where you can see the chains worn by Teodosio de Goñi and the hole through which the dragon appeared; it's still customary to stick one's head into it, though no one remembers what the old *rite de passage* signified. The shrine also contains a beautiful enamelled *reredos* donated by Sancho the Great. The path to the sanctuary, crowded with pilgrims on Corpus Christi, begins at Huarte-Araquil, halfway between Irurzun and Alsasua; if you're driving, the approach is from Lecumberri, off the N-240.

Zudaire, further south, is the head town in a broken terrain called **Las Améscoas**, the refuge of the Carlists and delight of speleologists for its many caves; many are located above Zudaire around Baquedano with its craggy ravine and streams.

From Pamplona to Logroño

A short turn off the main N-111 (about 15 km (9.4 miles) from Pamplona) leads to the old village of **Obanos**, and a mile beyond the village to a lonely field and **Santa María of Eunate**, a very unusual 12th century church built by the Templars. The Templars often built their chapels as octagons, but this one was purposely made irregular, and is surrounded by a unique arcade – hence its name 'Eunate' (the Hundred Doors). Many knights were buried here, and it's believed its peculiar structure had deep significance in the Templars' initiatory rites. During its restoration a large number of scallop shells were discovered along with the tombs – the church is just off the pilgrimage route. The two major routes through Canfranc-Somport in Aragón and Roncevalles converged nearby at **Puente la Reina**, named for the bridge the pilgrims crossed, dating from the 11th century. The village's **Rua Mayor**, leading to the bridge, preserves many of its old houses with coats-of-arms. The pilgrims traditionally entered Puente la Reina through the arch of another Templar foundation, the **Church of El Crucifijo**, another unusual church (it has two naves instead of the usual one or three), the smaller one added to house a peculiar 14th-century crucifix, where the Christ is nailed to the trunk and branches of a Y-shaped tree. On the walls of the church you can see the crosses carved by the Knights of St John, who inherited the church and hospital in the 14th century. 12

km (7.5 miles) south of Puente la Reina is the well-preserved, medieval walled village of **Artajona**, clustered beneath the Gothic, fortified **Church of San Saturnino**.

The main attraction in the area, however, is **Estella**, another town on the pilgrimage route. For many years it was the residence of the kings of Navarre and in the 19th century was the main centre of Carlism. Located along (and in some cases, leaning over) the banks of the River Ega, the old city was divided into three quarters: for Navarrese, Franks, and Jews (before Ferdinand swallowed up Navarre, it welcomed Jews fleeing the persecutions and, later, expulsion from Spain). Many of the old houses and fine churches have been preserved. Most date from the 12th century as does the rare **Palacio de los Reyes de Navarra**, perhaps the best-preserved civil structure of the period; on one of its capitals is the first-known depiction of Roland, in this case fighting the giant Ferragut. Above the palace, steps lead up to **San Pedro de la Rúa**, with a beautifully carved portal and cloister. **San Miguel Arcángel** has another beautiful portal; **Santo Sepulcro**, down the street from the palace, has been converted into a not-often-open **Museum of the Road to Santiago**. Across the river are the pretty, narrow alleys of the **Juderia; Santa María Jus del Castillo**, with its 11th-century interior, was the main synagogue. In August Spanish and foreign feminists come to Estella for its *encierro* – the only one in Spain where women are allowed to run with the bulls and get butted about by heifers with padded horns.

South of Pamplona to Tudela

The green valleys of the Pyrenees are a verdant memory the closer you get to Castile. A Dutchman named E. Cock wrote in the 17th century that two of the major towns here, **Tafalla** and **Olite** were the 'flowers of Navarre' and both have determinedly been calling themselves that ever since. Both have a fine old feel to them, but of the two Olite is the more interesting, dwarfed by its huge battlemented, lofty-towered **Castle of Carlos III**, built in 1407. Each of its towers has its own character, and restorers have made the whole thing seem startling new. Inside the decor is Mudejár; hanging gardens were suspended from the great arches of the terraces, and there is a 'Leonera' or lion pit – a rudimentary zoo – and a seemingly very busy set of dungeons; the Navarrese royal families led messy, frustrated lives. Also worth visiting in Olite is the enchanting façade of the castle's former chapel, now the **Church of Santa María**, and the earlier **San Pedro** (13th century) with its octagonal tower and portal adorned with two large stone eagles, one devouring the hare it has captured (symbolizing force) and the other, more friendly, said to represent gentleness.

Tudela on the Ebro is the capital of La Ríbera region, famous for its asparagus, though by dint of its industry it's Navarre's second city. Founded by the Moors, it was the last town to submit to Ferdinand; before its capture it had always made a point of welcoming Jews and heretics persecuted by the Inquisition of the Catholic kings. From its picturesque little labyrinthine Moorish, and later Jewish, quarter came three of Spain's greatest medieval writers, Benjamin of Tudela, the great traveller and chronicler (1127–73), the poet Judah Ha-Levi of the same period, and the doctor Miguel Servet (1511–53), the first to note the circulation of blood.

In Tudela head straight for the old town around the **Plaza de los Fueros** and the fine Gothic **Cathedral de Santa Ana**, built over the Mosque in the 12th century. The entire façade is devoted to the Last Judgement – 114 different scenes depict the joy of the righteous and the more fascinating macabre punishments of the damned. The main altar is adorned with a beautiful *retablo* painted by Pedro Diaz de Oviedo and yet more chains from Las Navas de Tolosa; the cloisters have some well-carved capitals with very expressive faces. The **Ayuntamiento** contains a plush 18th-century carriage in the vestibule. Among the palaces note the **Casa del Almirante** near the cathedral, and in the Calle de Magallón, the lovely Renaissance **Palace of the Marques de San Adrián**. An irregular, 17-arched, 13th-century **bridge** spans the Ebro and is still heavily used.

Near Tudela **Cascante** is known for its wines and its unusual church of Our Lady of the Rosemary Bush (**Virgen del Romero**), built in the 17th century and reached via a unique, arcaded 'cloister walk' from the village below. In **Fitero** there's the fine Cistercian **abbey of Santa María**; the abbot, San Raymundo, founded the Order of the Knights of Calatrava in 1158.

TOURIST INFORMATION

Estella: Bajos del Ayuntamiento, Paseo de la Immaculada 1, Tel: 55 08 14.

Tudela: Pl. de los Fueros, 14, Tel: 82 15 39.

WHERE TO STAY AND EAT

The closest place to stay near Aralar is in Lecumberri, where you'll find a modest resort *hostal* **Ayestarán II****, near the centre of town at San Juan 64, Tel: 50 41 27; it has a pleasant old atmosphere, tennis, children's recreational facilities, a pool and a garden; doubles with bath are 2350 pts, without 1600 pts. The restaurant serves good meals for around 880 pts. In Puente La Reina, the **Mesón del Peregrino****, on the Pamplona–Logroño, road, Tel: 34 00 75, is housed in a building old enough to have lodged the pilgrims; it also has a pool for modern wayfarers. Open March–November, doubles are 3200 pts, all with bath. In Estella there are several cheap *fondas* and the more upmarket **Tatan***, Sancho el Fuerte 6, Tel: 55 02 50, where doubles with bath are 2300–2500 pts, without bath 1750–1950 pts.

Next to Olite's Castle of Carlos III is the older Castillo de los Teobaldos, now converted into the **Parador Principe de Viana**, Tel: 74 00 00; a garden and air-conditioning and beautiful furnishings make castle-dwelling comfortable; doubles are 5500–7000 pts; delicious Navarrese gourmet treats in the dining-room (1800 pts). A much cheaper alternative is the little **Castillo***, Gral. Mola 16, Tel: 74 00 02, where a simple double with bath is 2000 pts, without bath 1800 pts.

In Tudela unfortunately there aren't any places to stay in the old town, and elsewhere prices are high. The best bet is the **Remegio****, Gaztambida 4, Tel: 82 08 50, adequate and comfortable with doubles for 2600 pts with bath, 2000 pts without.

EATING OUT

The finest restaurant in Estella is the **Tatana**, on Garcia el Restaurador 3 in the old town, with Navarrese specialities for 1500 pts. For dinner in Tudelo, if it's in season, order asparagus; the prettiest place to do so is **El Choko**, Pl. de los Fueros 5; full meals around 1600 pts.

La Rioja

The small autonomous region and province of La Rioja, wedged between the Ebro and the Basque country, is synonymous with Spain's best wine. The name comes from the Rio Oja, which eventually spills into the Ebro; along the latter you'll find most of the vineyards, especially in La Rioja Alta (by Haro) and La Rioja Alavesa north of the river. Wine was produced here long before the Romans came but the Rioja we imbibe today owes its origins to the French, who brought their techniques south of the border when the dread phylloxera knocked out all their own vines. The production of the wine is strictly controlled; La Rioja's best Gran Reserva spends two years maturing in oak barrels, then five more in bottles in the bodega before it's sold – though any Rioja from '78, '81 or '82 is certainly worth a try. Of late the region has begun to produce good, young white wines that skip the oaken barrels altogether

GETTING AROUND

Several trains a day link Haro, Logroño, and Calahorra (the Bilbao–Zaragoza route). By bus there are several other connections to Zaragoza (four a day), Burgos (via the towns on the pilgrims' route), Vitoria, Pamplona and elsewhere in the province. In Logroño the bus and train station are close to each other near the centre on C. Vara del Rey.

Logroño

Logroño, La Rioja's capital, is a large, rather nondescript town on the Ebro. Its name derives from the Germanic *Gronno*, or ford, and for many centuries that was its main reason for being. Here the pilgrims crossed the Ebro – only a single arch survives of the bridge built for them by San Juan de Ortega of Burgos. Nowadays most people use the iron bridge, near the 16th-century **Santiago el Real**. The most interesting church in town, **Santa María la Redonda** dates from the same period but is designed in the Catalan style, with fine Baroque towers.

East of Logroño, in La Rioja Baja, the main town is **Calahorra**, an important Celtiberian fortress-town that held out against Pompey and was conquered by Africans in 71 BC only when the defenders were all killed, through fighting or starvation. Now it is best known for its **Cathedral** on the banks of the Ebro, containing a magnificent sacristy, adorned with Flemish art and a 15th-century Custodia known as **El Ciprés**, made of gold and silver. The Gothic nave is also lovely, topped by graceful star vaulting.

South of Logroño, towards Soria, the road ascends through the **Valley of Iregua** with its rugged buttes and forests. At **Clavijo**, a tiny hamlet crowned by a large castle, Santiago Matamoros made a famous early appearance to help the Christians defeat the Moors. **Torrecilla en Cameros**, the main town in this quiet, seldom visited region, has a nicely preserved old centre and fine parish church, **San Martín**.

West of Logroño: pilgrims and bodegas

After Logroño there was a pilgrims' hospital in the pretty if somewhat decrepit town of **Navarrete**, though all that survives is the Romanesque arch leading to the present cemetery. More importantly **Nájera**, the next town to the west, was the residence of the kings of Navarre in the early Middle Ages; in 1052, only 25 years before the Navarrese had to surrender La Rioja to Castile, King Garcia founded the **church of Santa María la Real**, and a pilgrims' *hostal*; the latter is long gone but the church, rebuilt in the 15th century, has a beautiful Renaissance cloister, carved *coro*, and several royal tombs, most notably that of Sancho III's wife Blanca (died 1158).

From Nájera (if you have a car – it's 17 km (10.7 miles) you can detour south into the pretty Sierra de la Demanda and the village of **San Millán de la Cogolla**, that has grown up around the two ancient monasteries of **Yuso** and **Suso**. The more interesting Suso dates from 923, and is dug into the mountainside 2 km (1.3 miles) above town, a curious Mozarabic building with horseshoe arches, arcades, a finely carved, 12th-century tomb of San Millán; another belongs to the first poet of the Castilian language, Gonzalo de Berceo, who was an abbot here (died mid-13th century). Yuso, down below, is a Benedictine abbey founded in the 11th century and rebuilt in the 16th; the prize treasure here is an 11th-century ivory chest.

20 km (12.5 miles) from here or from Nájera, **Santo Domingo de la Calzada** ('of the road') was one of the highlights on the Camino de Santiago. Santo Domingo is named for an 11th-century friend of the pilgrims, who built bridges and *hostales*, and in druidical fashion cleared paths through the oak forests with a magic sickle, which is still displayed next to his tomb in the **Cathedral**, the star attraction of the town, built in the 13th century. The *retablo* is by Damián Foment, and there are some other fine works, but what everyone remembers best are the rooster and hen, cackling and crowing in their own little shrine, recalling the miracle that took place in the *hostal* (now a *parador*) next to the Cathedral: according to the story, a young German pilgrim refused the advances of the *hostal's* maid, who avenged herself by planting a silver cup in his pack and accusing him of theft. The pilgrim was summarily hanged, while his parents sadly continued to Compostela. On the way back, they passed the gallows and were amazed to find their son still alive and glad to see them. They hurried to the village judge and told him of this miracle of Santo Domingo; the judge, about to dig into a pair of roast fowl, laughed and said their son was as alive as the birds on his table, upon which both came to life and flew away. Since then, two similar birds have been kept in the cathedral and are killed and replaced every 12 May; pilgrims would take one of their feathers and stick it in their hats for good luck. Besides the cathedral, however, there's little to see in Santo Domingo.

To the north along the Ebro lies the **Rioja Alta**; some have over enthusiastically compared the region to Tuscany, although as in Tuscany you can make a **wine tour**, especially around **Haro**, a fine, dignified old town with many 16th-century houses. Perhaps best known among the bodegas, and one you can visit without advance notice, is the **Bodegas Bilbaínas** (open mornings and late afternoons); others open for visits – though it's best to book ahead – are Federico Paternina, La Rioja Alta and CUNE. Across the Ebro in **La Rioja Alavesa** is the walled, medieval town of **Laguardia**, where you can learn all about local wines and their production at **La Casa del Vino**, besides visiting several other bodegas. Don't miss the beautifully sculpted façade of Laguardia's Gothic **Santa María de los Reyes**.

TOURIST INFORMATION
Logroño: Miguel Villanueva 10, Tel: 25 54 97.

WHERE TO STAY AND EAT
There are a couple of fancy, modern hotels in Logroño but it's more fun to stay at the **Gran Hotel*****, General Vara del Rey 5, Tel: 25 21 00 with its bit of olde worlde charm and a garden and doubles for 3800 pts. For less style and fewer pesetas, **Gonzalo de Berceo***, Gran Vía del Rey D. Juan Carlos 37, Tel: 22 96 12, offers doubles with bath for 2225–2600 pts, without bath 1900–2180 pts. The cheapest places are on C. San Juan, like the **Sebastián*** at no. 21, Tel: 22 17 79, offering its bathless doubles for 1300 pts.

Calahorra has the modern **Parador Marco Fabio Quintiliano***** (Era Alta, Tel: 13 03 58), with comfortable rooms and air-conditioning for 5000–5500 pts; as usual, it has a good restaurant with regional cuisine (1800 pts). On the cheap side, try the **Teresa***, Sto. Domingo 2, Tel: 13 03 32, with doubles for 1400 pts with bath, without 1050 pts. The **Parador Nacional*****, Pl. del Santo 3, Tel: 34 03 00 in Santo Domingo is located in the ancient pilgrim's *hostal* built by the saint himself, though he would be shaken by the 5500–7000 pts the wayfarer is now asked to pay. Prices are less worldly at **Santa Teresita****, Gral. Mola 2, Tel: 34 07 00, where doubles with bath are 2575 pts, 1820 pts without. In Haro, you can lodge very comfortably at the **Higinia****, Vega 31, Tel: 31 01 00, where doubles are 2610 pts with bath or 1600 pts without.

EATING OUT
Logroño's best-known restaurant, located in an 18th-century palace, with exquisite furnishings and a vast bodega of Rioja wine, is **La Merced** on Marqués de San Nicolás 109. Prices here are around 2700 pts; the same owner operates the **Mesón** across the street with more reasonable prices, that remains open in August when La Merced closes. For a good *menestra*, go where the locals go: **El Cachetero** on Laurel 3 (1200 pts).

For good fish in Calahorra, **Chef Nino**, at Basconia 1, fills the bill except on Thursdays (1400 pts). In Haro the owner of the restaurant **Beethovan 2**, Sto. Tomás 3, specializes in growing *setas* (Spanish mushrooms) and they play a big role on the menu, along with roast meats (1800 pts).

Part VIII

CANTABRIA, ASTURIAS AND GALICIA

El Capricho, Comillas

Cantabria

Spain's emerald-green dairy-land, Cantabria is wedged between the extraordinary Picos de Europa mountains and a coastline of scenic beaches. Santander, the capital and only large city, is a major summer resort, and while there are a handful of other touristed spots (Laredo, Comillas, and the medieval Santillana del Mar) the bulk of Cantabria is serenely rural, claiming to have the highest density of cows in Europe. The majority of the bovine population lives indoors, and in the evening the most common Cantabrian sight is the farmer or his wife, driving home an ox-cart laden with grass which they have cut from their several lilliputian plots of land scattered over the hills. On rainy winter evenings they gather to hear the strains of the *rabel*, a stringed instrument from the Moors, made only of wood cut by the light of a full moon.

GETTING AROUND

There are buses from Bilbao and Santander along the coast; from Santander they depart from the terminal at the Bar Machichaco, on C. Calderón de la Barca, a block from the station.

West to Santander – The Costa Esmeralda

One of Cantabria's most scenic fishing-port-resorts, **Castro Urdiales**, is only an hour west of Bilbao. Important in the Middle Ages, the town preserves a fine, old quarter, the **Mediavilla**, and a striking harbour dominated by a ruined Templar castle (now sheltering a lighthouse) and the fortress-like **Church of Santa Maria**, a magnificent Gothic temple with massive buttresses and pinnacles. Constructed almost entirely in the 12th century, its Templar influences are revealed in the unusual symbolism of the figures carved in the lovely frieze wrapped around the body of the church – rabbits kissing oxen, dragons devouring serpents devouring birds, and more. There's a beach on the other end of town; if it's too crowded, head up the coast to **Islares**, a small village with a magnificent beach under the cliffs.

There's more fine scenery to the west at **Laredo**, the Roman *Portus Luliobrigensium*, where the Romans finally subdued the fiery natives in a great sea battle. The **Puebla Vieja**, or medieval town, over the harbour was walled in by Alfonso VIII of Castile to safeguard the region from pirates. Today Laredo is the nicest resort on the Atlantic coast, patronized especially by the French, who cover its splendid beach and fill the scores of cafes, bars, and discotheques in the Puebla Vieja. The outstanding building here is the 13th-century **Church of La Asunción**, unusual for its five naves and curiously carved capitals. In the sacristy there are two lecterns shaped like eagles, donated by the Emperor Charles, who landed here on his way to his retirement at Yuste. On either side of Laredo you'll find more attractive beaches, the **Playa de Oriñón** to the east and the **Playa de la Salvé** to the west, en route to **Santoña**, another fishing-port resort. A large monument commemorates its most famous native, Juan de La Cosa, the cartographer and companion of Columbus, who accompanied the admiral on his first voyage to America. Another lovely area, **Noja** has another stretch of fine, sandy beaches and a considerable villa and apartment development along the shore.

TOURIST INFORMATION

Laredo: Pl. de Generalisimo, Tel: 60 54 92.

Santoña: C. Santander, Tel: 66 00 66.

WHERE TO STAY

In Castro Urdiales you can be right on the beach in the stylish **Miramar****, Av. de La Playa, Tel: 86 02 00, open from March–October, (doubles with bath 3300–4000 pts) or stay in town in the antique **El Cordobés****, Ardigales 15, Tel: 86 00 89, prettily located in the Mediavilla (doubles without bath 2000 pts).

In Laredo the hotels are small and fairly dear, and reservations are essential in the summer. The **Montecristo***, Calvo Sotelo 2, Tel: 60 57 00, open mid-April to mid-September, offers one of the best beach deals in town (doubles with bath 3100 pts). The **Risco*****, Alto de Laredo, Tel: 60 50 30, is the classiest lodging in Laredo, its rooms enjoying great views of the protected bay and beach (open all year, doubles 4550–5775 pts). In Islares, there's one, pleasant little *hostal*, the **Arenillas****, Tel: 86 07 66, peaceful and near the beach, open all year (doubles with bath 2500–2800 pts).

EATING OUT

Castro Urdiales' well-known **Mesón Marinero**, next to the fishing port at Correria 23

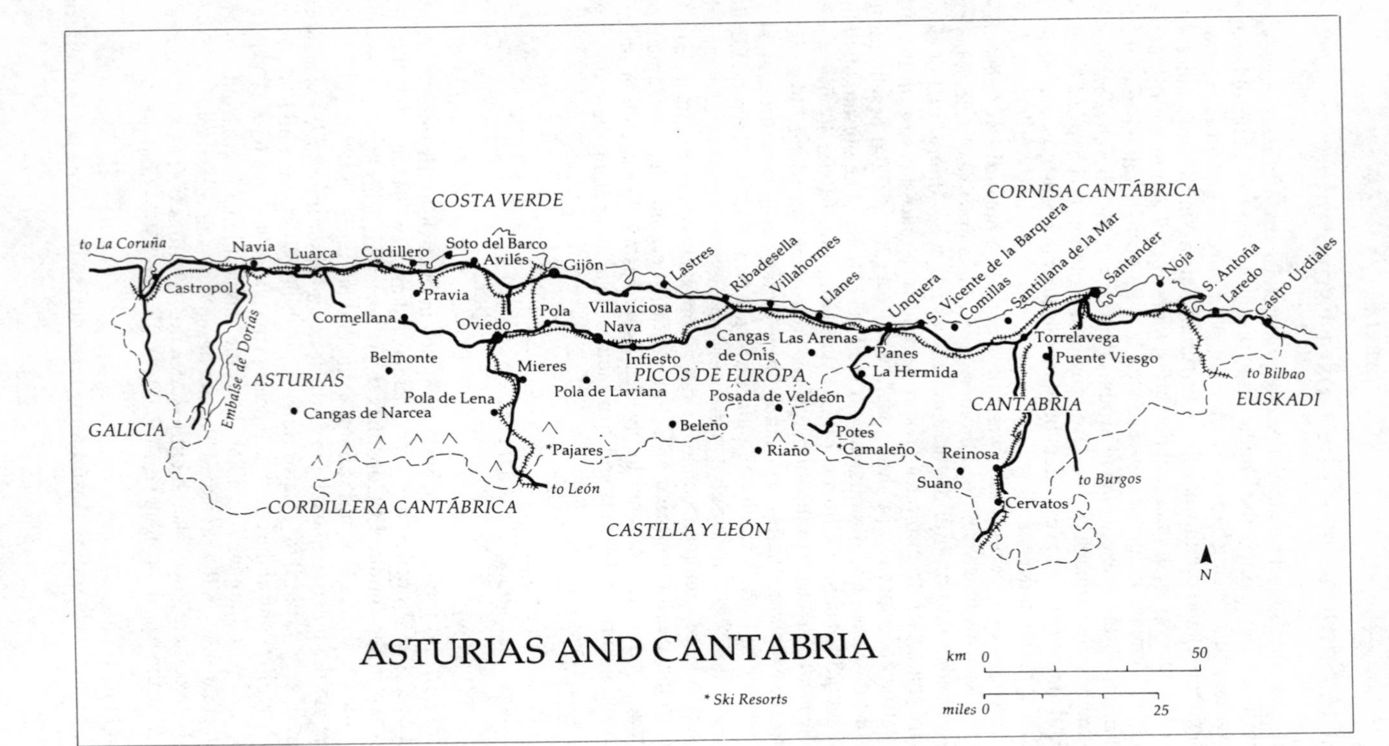

ASTURIAS AND CANTABRIA

is the place to go for delicious, fresh seafood at low prices – for even less than the typical 1000 pts meal, you can feast on a wide selection of tapas at the bar. The **Risco** has Laredo's finest restaurant, naturally featuring the fruits of the sea (meals around 2400 pts).

Santander

GETTING AROUND

From Santander, Brittany Ferries sails to Plymouth twice-weekly all year. For information in Santander, call 21 45 00 or visit the ticket office at the Estación Maritimo. Santander also has an airport 7 km (4.4 miles) away at Maliaño (no buses) with daily connections to Barcelona and Madrid. Iberia's office is at Paseo de Perda 18, Tel: 22 97 04; Aviaco: Calvo Sotelo 15, Tel: 22 32 00. The train stations are on C. Rodriguez, near the city centre. RENFE (Tel: 21 02 88) has connections with Madrid, Palencia, Reinosa, Segovia and Valladolid; tickets are available as well at the travel office at Paseo Pareda 25, Tel: 21 23 86. The narrow gauge FEVE (Tel: 21 16 87) has trains to Bilbao and Oviedo; unfortunately they miss the coast east of Santander, which is instead served by buses from the Bar Machichaco, a block from the station. Buses to other destinations depart from C. Federico Vial, also near the train station.

Within Santander itself, there are frequent buses and trolleys (nos. 1, 2 and 7) that run from the centre to El Sardinero 20 minutes away. Los Reginas runs the boat service to the beaches across the bay, with departures every 15 minutes from 10.30 am to 8.30 pm from the Muelle de Ferrys, two blocks from the cathedral.

WHAT TO SEE

The capital of Cantabria, Santander has a lot in common with San Sebastián – a large city beautifully situated on a protected bay, popularized by royalty as a summer resort. After World War I, it was *the* fashionable place to go, especially with the founding of an international summer university (named for Menéndez Pelayo, Santander's favourite son and Spain's greatest antiquarian), offering holiday-makers high-brow culture to complement its lovely beaches. In 1941 a tragic fire destroyed most of the city and most of its character, except in the suburb of **El Sardinero**, with its fine twin beaches, imaginatively named **Primera** (First) and **Segunda** (Second), backed by the enormous Belle Epoque **casino**, recently refurbished in an effort to revive some of the city's lost panache. Still, despite this and its widely acclaimed International Music Festival in July and August, Santander lacks the excitement and joie de vivre of San Sebastián.

El Sardinero is separated from the working end of the city by the beautiful **Peninsula de la Magdalena**, fringed by two more splendid beaches, the **Playa de la Magdalena** and the **Playa del Promontorio**. The Tudor palace at the end of the peninsula was a gift from the city to Alfonso XIII; when the king accepted it, Santander's success as a summer resort was guaranteed. In the middle of the city there's a much-altered and rebuilt **Cathedral**, most interesting for its early Gothic crypt, which now forms the separate church of **Santísimo Cristo**, where a glass floor has been installed over the remains of a Roman building. Of the museums, the best is the **Museo de Prehistoria**, next to the Provincial Council on C. Juan de la Cosa, with exhibits devoted to Cantabria's prehistoric cave-dwellers, including tools, reproductions of their art and large Celtic disc-shaped tombstones discovered in the valley of the Buelna (open Monday–Saturday 10 am–1 pm and 5–7 pm).

Besides the beaches in the city, there are several miles of golden dunes across the bay at **Somo, El Puntal**, and **Pedrena**, linked every 15 minutes by boat from the centre of town.

TOURIST INFORMATION

Jardines de Pereda, Tel: 21 61 20; also the Plaza de Velarde (where the music festival takes place), Tel: 21 14 17. The post office is at Alfonso XIII 2, Tel: 21 26 02; telephones are at Hernán Cortés 37.

WHERE TO STAY

July, August and September are the busy months here, especially the first two, when the music festival and international university are in full swing. Prices are as high as San Sebastián, though again there are plenty of *casas particulares* to preserve your budget.

At the other end of the scale, Santander's most elegant option is the **Hotel Real*******, Paseo de Perés Galdós 28, Tel: 27 25 50, located near the Playa de la Magdalena and offering marvellous views over the bay, lovely rooms and a fine garden, but open only from 1 July to 15 September (doubles 10,330 pts). Open all year round, the popular **Hotel Sardinero*****, Pl. de Italia 1, Tel: 27 11 00, is conveniently located near the beaches of Sardinero and the casino, with very pleasant doubles for 5720 pts in July–September, but only 3900 pts other times. Nearby, the **Hotel Paris****, Avda. de los Hoteles 8, Tel: 27 23 50 (open July–September), is an old-fashioned beach hotel with old-fashioned fittings and a garden, its doubles with bath 3600 pts, without bath an economical 2000 pts. The cheaper hotels, mostly located in the centre of town, have gained a certain amount of notoriety for being either dreary or rip-offs. Two safe ones are the **Hostal La Gran Antilla***, Isabel II 8, Tel: 27 31 00, especially nice with doubles from 2200–2500 pts, some with bath, and the **Rocamar****, Avda de los Castros (where there are several other choices), Tel: 27 72 68, open June–September, doubles with bath 2200 pts.

EATING OUT

Unlike San Sebastián, Santander is hardly known for its cuisine. The seafood, however, is always good, and the traditional place to get it is at the rather piquant **Barrio Pescadero**, in the fishing-port (take bus 4 from the centre). One of the best places here is the **Casa José**, C. Mocejon 2, with a good *menú del día* for 500 pts. More elaborate in every way, the fashionable **La Sardina** (Dr Fleming 3) in El Sardinero, offers imaginative renderings of the day's catch (especially *bonito*, or tunny fish), in a very pretty setting (2500 pts). More seafood in sumptuous displays is on offer in numerous eateries in the Puerto Chico, between the centre and the Playa Magdalena. Especially good are the **Bar del Puerto** on Hernán Cortés 63 (2000 pts) and **Iris**, at Castelar 5 (1600 pts). Nightlife is concentrated in El Sardinero, with its numerous bars and discotheques and the lavish **Gran Casino** where you can risk your pesetas from 7 pm to 4 am (dress up and bring your passport).

Around Santander

GETTING AROUND

For Puente Viesgo there are a couple of buses from Santander's main bus station to Burgos that stop in the town, in walking distance of the caves (Continental, Tel: 22 53 18). For Reinosa RENFE runs four trains a day here between Santander, Palencia and Madrid and nine others that run only between Reinosa and Santander. Other destinations in the south are linked by at least one bus daily out of Reinosa.

Santillana, Comillas and San Vincente are linked around six times daily to each other and Santander by La Cantabrica buses (Santander terminus: Pl. de las Estaciones); alternatively, you can take a FEVE train out of Santander as far as Torrelavega, with more frequent bus connections to Santillana. There's also a FEVE station about 3.2 km (2 miles) from San Vincente – a lovely walk if you're not carrying too much luggage.

Inland: south of Santander

South of the capital the land gradually rises to the Montañas de Santander, a pretty, hilly region dotted with small villages. Near one of them, **Puente Viesgo**, you can tour some of Cantabria's finely decorated prehistoric caves (the best after Altamira, which are inaccessible to the average visitor); there are five of them altogether in Monte Castillo – in **Pasiega**, **Monedas**, and **Castillo caves** you can see graceful line drawings of stags, horses and other animals, believed to predate the more eloquent art at Altamira (open Tuesday–Sunday 10 am–1 pm and 3–7 pm, closed Sunday pm).

Reinosa, on the rail line, is the main hub in Las Montañas, with most of the area's hotels and restaurants. It's an attractive old town on the banks of the new-born Ebro (its official source is just to the north-west in Fontibre); just below Reinosa the large **Embalse del Ebro** is a reservoir that follows the outline of a prehistoric lake. The most beautiful part of the region lies beyond Fontibre, in the virgin valleys of the **Saja National Reserve**, where beech oak and birch forests follow the courses of clear streams. Of the tiny vilages in the area, **Bárcena Mayor** has best preserved its medieval ambiance, with arcaded streets and wooded balconies; its woodworkers' shops are another attraction.

South of Reinosa there are several fine Romanesque churches – in **Bolmir** and more significantly in **Retortillo**. Retortillo is near the scanty remains of the Roman city of **Julióbriga**, once the most important city of Cantabria. Further south in **Cervatos**, you can visit perhaps the most singular Romanesque church in Spain, the 12th-century **Colegiata**, adorned with a tympanum with an oriental design, a frieze of lions – and unabashed by erotic figures carved onto the corbels and capitals in the apse. This unique, medieval tantric temple probably survived clerical prudishness over the centuries because of its remote location and the explanation that such sexual exhibitionism was meant to frighten the parishioners with the horrors of sin. To the south-east, in an even more remote region, there's another fine Romanesque church in **San Martin de Elines**, with a lofty cylindrical tower and ancient cloister and nothing to censor from the kids. Real explorers can make for **Suano** and the **Población de Suso**, villages that figure on few maps, but can claim a large number of dolmens, a huge cromlech and the ruins of a Templar castle. The region's most important ski installation, **Alto Campoo** lies to the west in the village of Hermandad Campoo de Suso.

The coast west of Santander: Santillana del Mar

The tour buses disgorge their hundreds daily upon the tiny village of Santillana del Mar, but it has yet to lose its special enchantment – though it may seem a bit more seductive if you can visit it out of season, or spend the night after the day-trippers have all gone. Popularly acclaimed as the most beautiful village in Spain, it is at once an evocative medieval town of grand palaces and a country village of dairy farmers, whose pastures lie on the hills just beyond the marvellous stone and half-timbered houses that line Santillana's one street. Santillana is famous as the birthplace of Spain's favourite fictional rogue, Gil Blas, and home of the real Marquis de Santillana, Iñigo López de Mendoza, the Spanish Sir Philip Sidney, a warrior and poet and courtly lover whose house still stands on the Calle del Cantón. Other houses have equally noble pedigrees; the one across from the **Colegiata** once belonged to the Archduchess of Austria. The church itself is a 12th-century Romanesque masterpiece, dedicated to St Juliana, whose remains have lain here since the 6th century and who gave her name to the town, albeit in a corrupt form. The church has an interesting façade and a beautiful cloister, with capitals carved with Bibical and hunting scenes (open 10 am–1 pm and 4–7.30 pm). The same ticket to the cloister will get you into the **Museo Diocesano**, on the other end of town near the parking lot, installed in the 17th-century **Convento de Regina Cocli**, a lovely building and cloister in itself, displaying an exceptional collection of ecclesiastical artefacts from all over Cantabria, some of definite Templar origin, and all perfectly restored by the nuns. Another museum has been installed in the tower house of Don Borja in the charming main **Plaza Ramón Pelayo**, entitled **Cantabria y la Mar en la Historia**, devoted to the region's seafaring past, and making up in a way for the town's anomalous name 'de Mar' when it's actually 3.2 km (2 miles) from the sea. On the same plaza stands the lovely **Ayuntamiento** and the palace of Barreda-Bracho, now a parador.

Many residents of Santillana still keep cattle on the ground floors of their beautiful homes and sell their delicious rich milk by the glass and tasty *bizcocho* (cake) by the piece all over town.

Altamira Caves

'Mira, papa, bueys!' ('Look, papa, cows!')
– Maria, aged 9, discoverer of the paintings at Altamira

From Santillana you can walk up to **Altamira caves** in 20 minutes, though don't expect to get in unless you've written months in advance (Centro de Investigación de Altamira, Santillana del Mar, Santander) and are one of the 10 lucky people permitted the 15-minute glimpse at what has been called 'the Sistine Chapel of Primitive Art'.

Still, an extraordinary number of people show up at the site almost with the fervour of pilgrims to pay homage to the masterpiece of our remote ancestors, who lived around 12,000 BC and covered the undulating ceiling of these caves with stunning, vividly coloured paintings of bison, horses, boars and stags. An ancient landslide sealed the caves' entrance until they were rediscovered in 1868; the fabulous ceiling, however, remained unnoticed until a speliologist took his little daughter to see the caves in 1879. Unfortunately, since then the ceiling has suffered deterioration and fading due to moisture – hence the severe limitations on visitors.

Nevertheless, you can do the next best thing at Altamira – see the video. This is part of the **museum** (open 9 am–1 pm and 4–6 pm, closed Sunday pm) installed on the site. Near here you can also explore the small **stalactite cave** which is prettily lit to emphasize nature's wonders as compensation for the inaccessibility of the more fragile works of man.

Comillas

To the west, the seaside town of Comillas is a bit of Catalan quirkiness in a gorgeous setting, framed by two endearing beaches – the **Playa Comillas** just below town and the longer **Playa de Oyambre**, a 20-minute walk away. Comillas' old town, with its rough cobbled streets and arcaded mansions with overhanging second storeys, has been a quiet watering-hole for the Madrid and Barcelona aristocracy for a long time; the latter brought along their favourite architects in the 19th century to add a little Modernista flair. Gaudí designed a curious arabesque of a palace with a minaret-like tower known as **El Capricho**, especially interesting for the patterns of brick and ceramics worked into the facade, though unfortunately there's no admittance; it's been empty for years awaiting a buyer. Next to it is the equally empty **summer palace** and Chapel of the Marquis de Comillas, by Gaudí's friend Joan Martorell, while over all looms the huge Jesuit **Seminario Pontificia** by Domenech i Montaner, who in this case chose to operate in neo-Gothic. All of them together form an exceedingly strange ensemble, and you may find yourself scurrying back to the safety of the beaches and their jovial crowds.

San Vincente de la Barquera, the next resort to the west, is still as much a fishing-port as a holiday retreat. Marvellously sited on a hill in the last elbow-bend of the wide and marshy Rio Escudo, it is linked by a long causeway to the eastern coast (near the town beach). Head up to the older, upper town, dominated by the rose-coloured parish church **Nuestra Señora de los Angeles**, a 13th-century transitional work containing the finely sculpted Renaissance tomb of the Inquisitor Antonio Corro. Nearby are several other Renaissance mansions, and the main plaza below is attractively shaded by interwoven branches of plane trees. Every quarter hour the bell tower of the church San Vincente booms out a recording of the first phrase of Schubert's **Ave Maria**, guaranteed to drive you nuts. The locals claim an enemy of their town had it installed – with any luck it will be a bad memory by the time you get there.

TOURIST INFORMATION

Reinosa: Pl. de España, Tel: 75 02 62.

Santillana del Mar: Pl. Ramón Pelayo, Tel: 81 82 51.

Comillas: C. La Aldea 2, Tel: 72 07 68.
San Vincente de la Barquera: Avda. Antonio Garelly, Tel: 71 07 97.

WHERE TO STAY AND EAT

In Puente Viesgo you can top off a morning in the caves with an afternoon in the spa at the old **Hotel Puente Viesgo****, Barrio de la Iglesia, Tel: 59 80 11, in the centre of town, open only from July–September (doubles 2190 pts). There are more choices in Reinosa: the most comfortable place in town, the **Vejo*****, Av. Cantabria 15, Tel: 75 17 00 is in the newer part, with a garden, bar and good restaurant (doubles 3740–4600 pts); the more economical **San Cristóbal**** at 14 de Agosto 1, Tel: 75 14 86 has simple, bathless doubles for 1750–2000 pts. If you're driving, a scenic place to stay is **La Casona***, on the Reinosa-Cabezón de la Sal highway, in Nestares, Tel: 75 17 88, an old inn with double rooms (without bath) for 1800 pts; open all year.

In Santillana there's the wonderfully atmospheric **Parador Gil Blas***** on the Pl. Ramon Pelay 11, Tel: 81 80 00 with medieval doubles for 6500–8500 pts; reserve well in advance in season, and request a room on the first or second floor. A good second choice, the **Hotel Altamira**** is installed in another palace nearby on Cantón 1, Tel: 81 80 25 with a patio and garden (doubles with bath 3200–4000 pts. Both of the above have elegant dining-rooms, especially the parador, where a full meal runs around 1800 pts. If you're lucky you can get one of the four rooms at the **Hostal Castillo***, that shares the plaza with the parador but at cut rates: doubles are 2000 pts in season, 1500 pts otherwise (Tel: 81 80 33). The tourist office also has a list of *casas particulares* in town, though most of them are in the newer suburbs en route to Altamira.

In Comillas the **Casal del Castro*****, San Jeronimo, Tel: 72 00 36, is in the centre of town in a fine old building with a pretty garden and rooms; open mid-June to mid-September, doubles are 3250 pts. The **Hostal Esmeralda*** is a good second choice close to the beach (Fernandez de Castro 6, Tel: 72 00 97; nice doubles for 1900 pts). The tourist office has a list of *casas particulares* for something even cheaper. In San Vincente, the **Luzón****, smack in the centre of town facing the tidal basin, Tel: 71 00 50, is a solid, square stone inn with doubles for 3000 pts with bath, 2700 pts without; **La Paz*** nearby (C. del Mercado 2, Tel: 71 01 80) has recently been remodelled and offers stylish, if bathless doubles for 1800–2400 pts. For something cheaper, try the **Fonda Liebana** just above Pl. el Cantón (Tel: 71 02 11) with doubles for 1000 pts.

EATING OUT

Barcena Mayor is famed for its mountain cuisine – try it at the **Rio Argoza** (750 pts). If you happen to be in Santillana at the weekend, you can feast on local and mountain specialities at **Los Blasones**, Pl. de la Gándara, for 1400 pts; otherwise there are good tapas and reasonably priced meals in the bar nearest the Colegiata. The food in Comillas is good – the long-established, friendly **Colasa**, on A. López 11 has especially good seafood (1400 pts); another old favourite, the ancient **Mesón el Torreán** (1000 pts) also has cheap rooms upstairs. There is a sizeable collection of seafood restaurants in San Vincente – **Augusto**, in the Pl. de Abastos, has more variety than most (1300 pts).

Asturias

The Principality of Asturias is the Spanish Wales, a rugged country of miners, stupendous mountains, and a romantically beautiful coast line. The inhabitants have traditionally been a hardy lot, beginning with the Iberian tribe of Astures who gave their name to the province and defied both the Romans and Visigoths. Yet the proudest date in Asturian history is 718, when a band of Visigoths, led by the legendary Pelayo, defeated the Moors in the misty mountain glen of Covadonga, officially beginning the 774 Reconquista and founding the first tiny Christian kingdom in Muslim Iberia. Their beautiful churches are Asturias' chief artistic patrimony; the language they spoke, Babel, has only barely survived the modern dominance of Castilian, its direct descendant.

Since the 14th century, the Spanish heir-apparent has had the title of 'Prince of Asturias', a practice initiated by John of Gaunt when his daughter married the son of Juan I. Except for that title, the region fell into an obscurity that lasted centuries. The discovery of iron ore and coal in the 19th century rapidly changed its traditional agricultural economy into one of mining. Asturias became one of the most radical provinces in Spain; the second great date in its history was October 1934, when the miners staged a well-prepared revolt against the conservative government of Gil Robles, that was intent on dismantling all the reforms of its Republican predecessor. Barcelona and Madrid rose up at the same time as Asturias but failed to follow through, yet on their own the Asturians formed a Revolutionary committee to govern the province, and a 30,000-strong Red Army. In a prelude to the first battle of the Civil War, Franco sent in the Foreign Legion and Moroccan troops to suppress the rebellion, which they did with the utmost ferocity – nearly 2000 Asturians were killed in reprisals after the surrender on October 19. Even after the Civil War, resistance to Franco continued in the wild mountains of the province.

The modern autonomous region of Asturias is in its quiet way one of the most progressive in Spain. One of the last areas to be touched by tourism, it is fighting to maintain its integrity against big developers who would exploit the Picos and the coast, prefering to develop a 'rural tourism' based in the villages, respecting local cultures and architecture, and preserving the environment. In 1985, the Asturian wildlife protection fund received the European Preservation of Nature (FAPAS) prize for its efforts to preserve the rare Cantabrian bear and the capercaillie from extinction.

At least once while in Asturias visit an old *'chigre'* or *'sidrería'* to taste the local poison *sidra* (cider) – natural but dangerous stuff always poured at arm's length to give it the proper bounce. If you drink enough of it, it even begins to taste good.

The Picos de Europa

We may thank Asturian ecologists for their efforts in keeping Spain's most beautiful mountains enchanting and unspoiled: what development there is (ski resorts, hotels) is in western Cantabria and northern León. The Picos are divided by rivers into three tremendous Massifs – **Andara**, mostly in Cantabria, **Urrieles** in the middle, and **Cornión** to the west. The highest peak, Torre Cerrado, stand 2648 m (8606 ft) – not all that much as mountains go. Yet for sheer beauty and rugged grandeur, for the contrast of tiny rural villages in fertile green valleys against a backdrop of sheer, twisted stone peaks crested with snow the year round, the Picos de Europa are hard to beat.

The range seems to have been dropped from heaven especially for hikers; there are trails for Sunday walkers and sheer cliffs for serious alpinists. Hiking boots, however, are universally recommended because of frequent patches of loose shale on the trails and slopes. If you're going for an extended holiday in the Picos, you'll want to get the detailed maps published by the Federación Española de Montañismo, generally available at Potes, the main base for visiting the mountains. The guide *Picos de Europa* by Robin Collomb (West Col, Reading) is a great help, and up-to-date detailed information on guides, itineraries and mountain *refugios* (free, overnight shelters) is available from the Federación Asturiana de Monatañismo, Calle Melquiades Alvarez 16, Oviedo, Tel: 21 10 99.

Hiking in the Picos is practical only from the end of May to October, but even then you may get a soaking – the Picos are only 32 km (20 miles) from the rainy Atlantic seaboard. Bring warm clothes and a lightweight plastic poncho, a sleeping bag and food for nights in the refuges, and consider a pair of binoculars to take in the wonderful array of wildlife and birds.

GETTING AROUND

There are two buses (one in the winter) daily between Santander and León that stop at Potes and Lebeña; departures are more frequent from Unquera (five buses daily to Potes). From Potes there are three buses from the central square to Fuente De and the teleferico; jeeps make the link between the upper station of the teleferico to the refugio de Aliva if you're not up to the walk. Also, a stable in Turieno next to Potes offers several guided **riding excursions** in the Picos.

There are daily buses between Arenas and Cangas along the northern rim of the Picos, and a Land Rover connection betwen Arenas and Poncebos. Cangas itself may be reached once daily by bus from Riaño; there are also a couple of buses daily from Oviedo to Cangas and Covadonga.

Posada de Valdeón is easiest reached from León, via Riaño or Portilla de La Reina (once a day).

Potes and the Valley of Liébana: the Massif de Andara

The eastern mountains of the Picos are the most visited and the most accessible. From **Unquera** (a FEVE stop to the west of San Vincente de la Barquera see p. 219) the N-621 climbs up through the **Desfiladero de La Hermida**, a dramatic, high, narrow gorge walling in the River Deva and the tiny hamlet of **La Hermida**, famous in sunny Spain for not seeing *el sol* at all from 26 October–28 March. The road climbs up from here into the idyllic little valley of apple orchards and vineyards around the town of **Lebeña**, with its jewel of a parish church – the 10th-century Mozarabic **Santa María**, with its gentle rhythm of horseshoe arches – a Christian microcosm of the great Mezquita of Córdoba.

Potes, the capital of the Valley of Liébana, is the metropolis of the Picos, where you can garner information, catch buses, change travellers' cheques and stock up on supplies. There are also a number of jeep excursions on offer. The main monument in

Potes itself is the 15th-century **Torre del Infantado**, a massive, square defensive-residential work. The most popular excursions from Potes include the walk up to the **Monasterio de Santo Toribio de Liébana**, some 3 km (1.9 miles) from town; it was founded early in the 8th century, though what you see today is mainly Romanesque and Gothic. It claims to have the world's largest sliver of the True Cross, and in its earliest days was ruled by the Abbot Beato de Liébana, whose *Commentaries on the Apocalypse* were popular in Spain in the Middle Ages (in Girona and El Burgo de Osma there are beautiful 10th-century copies of the manuscript). From the **mirador de Santo Toribio** there are splendid views over the Andara massif. Another, longer walk south will take you through **Cabezon de Biébana**, where some of the houses have coats-of-arms and there are two medieval bridges to the lovely church of **Santa María de Piasca**, built in 1172 with some fine Romanesque carvings on the capitals within. Typical for the mountains, but unusual elsewhere, the monastery was shared by monks and nuns.

Fuente De

The classic excursion from Potes is to catch the bus west up to the stunning old village of **Espinama** and a mile beyond, to **Fuente De**. Here you can catch the teleferico for an awesome, vertigo-inducing ride some 800 m (860 ft) up the sheer cliff to the **mirador del Cable** (in the peak season, arrive early or late or be resigned to wait in line). Once at the top, most people continue 4 more km (2.5 miles) to the **Refugio de Alvia**, a popular modern version of the old mountain refuge; a path from her leads down to Espinama – a pleasant day's circuit. From Espinama, you can make a longer, more serious hike through the eastern and central massifs north to **Sotres**, a good day's walk (jeep excursions also available from Espinama). The landmark near here, in the Central Massif of the Urrieles, is **Naranjo de Bulnes** (Pico Urriello on some maps) a distinct sheer-sided, tower-like pinnacle, loved and hated by daredevil alpinists. From Sotres, another day's hiking will bring you to **Arenas de Cabrales**, renowned for its powerful mountain cheese, and the most important village in the region, with buses to Cangas and Land Rovers to **Ponchebos** (see below).

The Divine Gorge

The **Cares Gorge** between Poncebos and Cain extends north to South across the Picos. It is a spectacular 25.6 km (16 miles) walk often over sheer drops down to the Río Cares, made relatively easy by a footpath sculpted into the mountainside much of the way. The classic approach is from **Cain** in the south, itself linked to civilization (the fine mountain village of **Posada de Valdeón**) by a regular four-wheel-drive service. Walking south from Poncebos isn't much more strenuous – only you risk either spending the night in Cain, which has no lodgings, or walking the 9 km (5.6 miles) further south to Posada. Other possible walks from Poncebos are to **Camarmeña** and **Bulnes**, two of the most remote villages in the Picos; in Bulnes there's a *refugio*; both villages have knockout views over the Naranjo de Bulnes.

Posada de Valdeón is the chief village of the Picos' highest valley, the **Valley of Valdeón**, a serenely magnificent place to rest up in before or after the Cares Gorge, with its tiny farming villages and their rustic granaries, or *hórreos*, built on stilts to protect their contents from moisture, all dwarfed by loftiest mountains in the Picos. One of the best views of the mountains is attainable from the **Mirador de El Tombo**, 1.6 km (1 mile) from Posada, framed by a statue to the chamois goat, occasionally seen in the flesh frisking over the steep slopes. The **Chorco de los Lobos** nearby was once used to trap the mountains' most fearsome predator, the wolf (now rare).

Cangas de Onís and Covadonga

The Río Sella defines the west edge of the western Massif de Cornión, which in its northernmost reaches forms part of **Covadonga National Park**. Easiest reached from Ribadsella on the Asturian coast, or through the stunning narrow gorge, **Desfiladero de los Beyos** (C-637) from León and Riaño, the region lacks the high drama of the mountains further east, but is nonetheless green and tranquil, and for Spaniards constitutes a pilgrimage. **Cangas de Onís** claims to be the first capital of Christian Spain, where the Asturian kings first set up shop after their victory at nearby Covadonga. The most beautiful things in Cangas de Onís are the high **medieval bridge**, with its great arch spanning the Río Sella, and the **Capilla de Santa Cruz**, where the kings worshipped. It was built over a dolmen, perhaps as early as the 5th century, and rebuilt in the 15th.

From Cangas you can walk north to **Villanueva**, where Alfonso I founded the **Monastero de San Pedro** in 746. Now deserted, it is known for its 12th-century doorway, with capitals carved with scenes of a bear hunt. East of Cangas, in Cardes, the **cave of Buxu** contains paleolithic drawings; from here it's 10 km (6.3 miles) to **Covadonga**, dominated by an enormous 19th-century basilica. Here Pelayo, a Visigothic noble and 300 followers managed to ambush a small Moorish expedition and defeat them, and the Moors, who didn't care for the climate much to begin with, made the mistake of letting them stay and consolidate their power, turning instead to the richer spoils in France. Next to the basilica is the **cave** where, according to legend, Pelayo fought with his back to the wall; now a chapel, it contains his and his wife's sarcophagi.

A beautiful excursion 20 km (12.5 miles) from Covadanga is through the national park to the mountain lakes of **La Ercina** and **Enol**, with the huge Peña Santa mountains as a backdrop.

TOURIST INFORMATION

Potes: Pl. Jesus del Monasterio (though more detailed information and maps may be purchased nearby at Bustamente's).

Arenas de Cabrales: Ctra. General, Tel: 84 41 88.

Cangas de Onis: Emilio Lara 2, Tel: 84 80 43.

WHERE TO STAY AND EAT

Nearly every village in the Picos has at least one *casa particular* or *fonda* of a place to camp, and you can purchase supplies (at least a hunk of cheese) or dine out in a traditional restaurant. Potes has the most in the way of accommodation in all price ranges – at the top of the line, there's the **Picos de Valdecoro****, at C. Roscabado, Tel: 73 00 25, open all year round, with doubles for 3500 pts; and the **Hostal Rubio****, San Roque 17, Tel: 73 00 15, where a double with bath runs from 1750–2450 pts, without bath 1200–1700 pts. The **Casa Gomez**, Tel: 73 02 18, near the Unquera and Santander bus stop, has doubles for 1400 pts and good inexpensive meals for around 600 pts.

In Fuente De, there's the magnificently sited **Parador Río Deva*****, Tel: 73 00 01, with doubles from 5000–6500 pts; the restaurant specializes in mountain and Castilian dishes for around 1800 pts. In Espinama, the **Remona***, Tel: 73 04 95 has a handful of simple rooms for 1800 pts with bath, 1600 pts without. The **Refuge of Aliva** (open 15 June to 30 September) has a restaurant and a number of comfortable rooms available on a first-come, first-served basis.

In Posada de Valdeón there are several *casas particulares*, some fine *fondas*, and the **Hostal Abascal**** (no tel.), open all year round, doubles with bath 1900–2200 pts, without bath, 1600–1900 pts, and a hearty breakfast for a bit more.

Cangas de Onís has a number of pricey *hostales*, though if you're lucky you can get one of the four rooms at **El Sella**, Av. Castilla, Tel: 84 80 11, where a double room (without bath) is 2000 pts, and dinner in the restaurant 750 pts; otherwise, head for the **Piloña****, De San Pelayo 19, Tel: 84 80 88, where rooms with bath are 2325–2970 pts. In Covadonga there's a cheap *fonda* and the **Hotel Pelayo*****, Tel: 84 60 00, with overpriced doubles (4300–5600 pts).

The Asturian Coast: East to West

Although the Picos attract mountaineers and hikers from all over the world, the coast of Asturias sees relatively few foreigners. Yet what it lacks in calm, sandy beaches it more than makes up for in breathtaking scenery and unspoiled villages. If you're driving, be sure to take the old scenic coastal road.

GETTING AROUND

FEVE trains along the coast take in some truly marvellous scenery. There are five trains a day between Santander and Oviedo, with stops at Unquera, Colombres, the beaches at Nueva and Villaharmes and Ribadesella. To continue up the coast from here you'll have to take a Gijón bound bus. FEVE has frequent connections between Gijón and Avilés, and west to Cudillero, Luarco, Soto de Luiña and Ortigueira. ALSA buses link all these towns as well with Oviedo, while RENE links Gijón with Oviedo, Madrid, Barcelona and the rest of the peninsula.

WHAT TO SEE

There's not much to detain you in **Llanes**, the first sizeable town, though to the east, near Vidiago and the **Playa La France**, there's a very strange Bronze Age monument called **Peña Tú** or the 'Cabeza de Gentil' (the gentile's head); even older cave drawings may be seen in the **Cueva del Pinal** near Colombres. This part of the coast is especially well endowed with beaches and quiet coves.

Ribadasella, at the meandering mouth of the Río Sella, is an excellent base from which to make forays along the coast or into the western Picos. It has a handful of old houses, a long protected beach, and the **Tito Bustillo Caves**, with some rather faint paintings in the Altamira style and stalactites.

Further west, into what is officially known as the Costa Verde, there are quiet beaches in the tiny hamlets of **Caravia** (Baja and Alta), and even lovelier ones around **Colunga**, renowned for its clams and **sidra** (cider) – the best beaches are **La Isla** to the east, **La Griega**, and **Lastres**, near a very picturesque fishing harbour, beneath a stack of red-tile-roofed houses. Some rare Asturian horses survive in the **Reserva Nacional de Sueve**, 3.2 km (2 miles) south of Colunga; the Romans used them for mountain duty. It's worth continuing to the **Mirador de Fito**, another 0.8 km (0.5 mile) to the south, for the views of the Picos de Europa and the coast.

Apple orchards line the coast around **Villaviciosa**, a fine old historic town and the first one in Spain to see the odd face of the future Emperor Charles V, who landed here from the Low Countries to claim his kingdom in 1517. Parts of town have changed little since that day. Some of Asturias' best pre-Romanesque churches lie in the outskirts of Villaviciosa; 9 km (5–6 miles) southwest in **Valdedíos**, there's the unusual San Salvador, better known as **El Conventín** (893) in the pretty Puelles valley. Next to it is the ruined **Santa Maria** (1218). Others are **San Salvador de Priesca** (921) with fine sculpture, **Santiasa de Gabiendes** (900), and the Romanesque **San Juan de Amandi**, noted for its beautiful sculpture. 3.2 km (2 miles) from Villaviciosa there's a good beach at **Rodiles**.

Gijón

Gijón is the largest city in Asturias, with long beaches, a pretty park and busy port. It is also a major industrial centre and was nearly totally rebuilt after the Nationalists devastated it in the Civil War. One small corner of town occupies the isthmus below the hill of Santa Catalina; the newly established Puebla de Asturias on the far side of the Rio del Piles there's an interesting **Museo de La Gaita**, with a collection of bagpipes from Celtic north-western Spain and around the world, as well as a workshop (open Monday–Friday 10 am–7 pm).

Up the headland from Gijón is the pretty fishing village **Luanco**; **Avilés** to the west is another large industrial town with a big steel mill, located at the head of a long, narrow inlet. Its main attraction is its 17th-century old town and the interesting Romanesque **Santo Tomás de Cantobery** (as in Salamanca, one of the earliest dedicated to the saint). There's a long beach at Salinas, and to the west, one of the coast's prettiest fishing villages, **Cudillero**. The same could be said of **Luarca**, an old whaling port with a sheltered harbour, near the mouth of the Rio Negro. It was one of the chief towns of the Vaqueros, one of Iberia's marginal peoples, who lived half of the year up in the mountain pastures with their herds of cattle, carrying all of their worldly goods with them in ox carts and building huts (*pallozas*) with conical thatched roofs, still visible in some of the rural regions further inland. Although ostracized from society (in most parishes they weren't even allowed to hear mass inside a church or be buried in holy ground), they themselves claimed to be far older than God, and returned disdain for disdain. Recent research based on their singular dialect, places them as First century AD immigrants from Italy. Those still in the area have traded in their ox carts for pick ups, though curiously enough, Franco, abolisher of so many ancient Spanish festivals, inaugurated a new one, ostensibly to preserve their customs, in the form of a 'Vaquero wedding' in **La Braña de Aristébano** 6 km (3.8 miles) to the south. On the last Sunday in July, prominent citizens are chosen to play the parts of the Vaqueros, who are duly married and escorted home with a procession that includes the neatly made matrimonial bed pulled by oxen.

There are good beaches along this stretch of coast: near Cudillero, **El Aguilan** and **Soto de Luiña** and, to the west of Luarca, **Tapia de Casariego**. A couple of miles inland from the fishing hamlet, **Ortigueira**, you can visit the extensive remains of a Celtic '*castro*' – walls, paved streets and the circular foundations of houses – the similarity between these and the Vaquero huts have led some to believe that the Vaqueros were a lost Celtic tribe. Near the main road, there's a monolith carved with the star symbol so widespread in Northern Spain.

TOURIST INFORMATION

Gijón: Marques de San Esteban 1, Tel: 34 60 46.
Avilés: Ruíz Gómez, Tel: 54 43 25.
Cudillero: El Pitom, Tel: 59 01 18.
Iuarca: Pl. Alfonso el Sabio, Tel: 64 00 83.
Llanes: Nemesio Sobrino, Tel: 40 01 64.
Ribadesella: Crta. Piconera, Tel: 86 00 38.
Tapia de Casariego: Pl. Constitución, Tel: 62 82 05.

WHERE TO STAY AND EAT

Ribadesella has more accommodation than most villages around the coast, and you can choose the posh, air-conditioned, beach-side splendour of the **Gran Hotel del Sella******, La Playa, Tel: 86 01 50, with a pool, tennis courts, a garden – a bit of Costa del Sol luxury on the Atlantic. Open April–September, doubles are 5700–7300 pts. Two less expensive hostels offer rooms and delicious food: the **Hostal Apolo****, by the beach on Gral. Franco, Tel: 86 04 42, with bathless doubles from 1800–2100 pts (open all year round) and good seafood for around 1200 pts; and the **Hostal El Pilar***, near the bridge, Tel: 86 04 46, with tennis, garden and spiffier rooms for 2500 pts; the restaurant features Asturian home cooking.

In Llanes, near the beach, the **Montemar*****, Jenaro Riestra, tel: 40 01 00 offers modern, comfortable doubles for 3975–4700 pts, but the **Venezuela***, in the nearby village of Villahormes, tel: 40 72 90, offers tranquillity and a better beach for 1500 pts a double, no bath (open all year).

Villaviciosa has some *casas particulares* and pricey hostels; it's better to stay in Lastres, where you can get a nice room on the port at **Miramar****, Tel: 85 01 20 for 2100–2400 pts with bath, or 2000–2200 pts without.

In Cudillero the best place to sleep and eat is **La Lupa****, on San Juan de la Piñera, (2 km (1.3 miles) east of the village), Tel: 59 00 63, an old inn with doubles for 2000–2500 pts, or 1700–2000 pts without bath, and local specialities like *merluza a la sidra* (hake in cider) for around 1200 pts. There are a handful of less expensive fish restaurants near the harbour in Cudillero (and a few rooms to rent).

Luarca is more ready for visitors, though prices are a bit high, one of the best places is 6 km (3.8 miles) outside town, the **Casa Consuelo**** at Otur, Tel: 64 08 44, where doubles with bath are 3500–4000 pts, and the food served in the large dining-rooms attract people for miles around with classic Asturian dishes like *fabada* (pork and bean stew) and good *sidra* (1300 pts). Look in town for cheaper *fondas* near the port.

You probably won't care to stay in Gijón, though you can eat at some of the best restaurants in Asturias here – **La Pondala** (1300 pts) on Avda. Dionisio Cifuentes 27 in the suburb of Somió, where you'll also find **Las Delicias** (Pl. de Villamanin), the city's oldest, famed for its desserts as well as its curious fish pudding (2000 pts). In Avilés, try the **Casa Lin**, Avda de los Telares 3, for seafood and *sidra* (800 pts).

Oviedo

The ancient and modern capital of Asturias, Oviedo is a working town but has a fine gritty charm, a university almost 400 years old, and two of Europe's most exquisite pre-Romanesque churches, built when the rest of the continent bumped about in the long night of the Dark Ages. The city was founded in 757 and served as the capital of what was in effect Christian Spain until the Asturian kings conquered León in 1002. The city suffered terribly in the insurrection of 1934 and during the Civil War; its modern prosperity is mainly due to the surrounding coal and iron mines. It continues to take up a variety of causes – walls are covered with graffiti encouraging the revival of Babel; pro-abortion, '*Viva la Virgen*,' and 'Free Rudolf Hess' rally posters are pasted side-by-side on the walls of the numerous *chigres* (Cider bars).

GETTING AROUND

Oviedo has three train stations, all near the centre of town. The RENFE station, with frequent connections to Gijón and less frequent links to León, Barcelona, Burgos, Zaragoza, Pamplona (*talgos*), and to Madrid, Valladolid and Palencia is at the head of the mainstreet C. Uria (Tel: 24 33 64); there's also a RENFE travel office on C. Cabo Noval 10, Tel: 21 25 82. FEVE trains to Santander depart from the neighbouring station on C. Economicas (Tel: 28 01 50); for Pravia and the western coast to El Ferrol, from C. Jovallanus 19 (Tel: 21 43 97) near the cathedral.

Buses depart from a variety of places; ALSA, the biggest company, with services throughout Asturias and to Madrid, Sevilla, Barcelona, Valladolid and Valencia as well as Paris, Geneva, Zurich and Brussels, depart from Pl. Primo de Rivera, Tel: 28 12 00.

The Cathedral

In the middle of Oviedo (take Calle Uria from the station) lies in a tranquil shady park where you can feed the ducks; from here Calle San Francisco leads to the oldest part of the city and the asymmetrical **Cathedral**, an attractive Gothic temple from the 14th century, its lovely tower Oviedo's landmark. It is built on the same site as the church of Alfonso el Casto (the Chaste), the builder of the city, of which all that survives it the **Camara Santa** (open daily 10 am–1 pm and 4–7 pm), strange and semi-barbaric, with fine carvings of the Apostles on the capitals of the outer chamber and disembodied heads on the wall. The inner chamber is thought to be unaltered since Alfonso el Casto built it in 802 to house the relics of Visigothic Toledo rescued after its capture by the Moors. Today it contains the Cruz de la Victoria, said to have been borne by Pelayo at Covadonga, the Cruz de los Angeles (808), a golden Maltese cross embedded with jewels, reputedly made by the angels themselves, and a beautiful, silver-plated reliquary chest (1073). The main cathedral and cloister are also worth a look; the former has an enormous florid 16th-century *retablo*.

Behind the cathedral the old convent of San Vincente now houses the **Museo Provincial** (open 10 am–1.30 pm and 4–6 pm, closed Monday and Sunday pm), featuring archaeological exhibits from the Paleolithic era to the days of the Asturian kingdom. There are a few attractive old streets to the south of the cathedral around the Plaza Mayor.

The Asturian churches

Oviedo has the finest of Asturias' post-Visigothic pre-Romanesque churches. Some scholars have noted a Carolingian influence in their structures, though much in them is original and beautiful. It's intriguing to speculate on what kind of architecture might have evolved in Spain if it had remained isolated from the French and their Romanesque fashions of the 10th and 11th centuries and developed a new style of Asturian and Mozarabic designs – as it is, these ancient churches remain as provocative prototypes that never made it to the assembly line. In 1985, UNESCO declared the churches, the best architecture of 9th century Christian Europe, as part of the 'Patrimony of Humanity'.

Alfonso el Casto built the oldest of these, **San Julian de Los Prados** (or Santullano), a short walk north-east of town on the Gijón road. This is a simple, solid building with three square apses, a secret compartment in the wall, and interesting murals by an artist who learn his craft from studying the monuments left by the Romans.

Santa Maria de Naranco, Oviedo

However, if you're pressed for time, head in the opposite direction up the Cuesta de Naranco, a hill overlooking the town (facing the RENFE station, turn left to the sign at the bridge over the tracks and walk up 3 km (1.9 mile) – it's not steep; city bus no. 6 makes cameo appearances as well). The two churches here, **Santa María del Naranco** and **San Miguel de Lillo** are open in the summer from 9.30 am–1 pm and 3–7 pm, winter from 10 am–1 pm and 3–5 pm, closed Sunday pm, and if one is closed when you arrive, the caretaker is probably at the other church and will soon return. Both of these were built by Alfonso's successor, Ramiro I (842–50); incredibly, the perfectly proportioned Santa María is believed to have been part of the king's hunting-lodge. Built of a fair golden stone and set in a small clearing, it is an enchanting building, supported by unusual flat buttresses and flanked by two porches. The lower level is believed to have served as a waiting chamber and bath; the upper, with a rough sort of altar on the porch, was the main hall, its interior designed with blind arches of subtly decreasing height, topped by round medallions.

46 m (50 yards) up the road, San Miguel is a more traditional cruciform church, although its stunted size causes many to believe that only a third of the original church still stands. Its round windows are adorned with beautiful stone tracery, and a circus scene is carved on the door jamb, along with some Visigothic arabesques.

TOURIST INFORMATION

Pl. de la Catedral 6, Tel: 21 33 85. Post office is on C. Alonso Quintanilla; telephones at Pl. de Porlier.

WHERE TO STAY

A couple of blocks from the Parque de San Francisco, a lovely 17th-century palace has been converted into the **Hotel de la Reconquista*******, Gil de Jaz 16, Tel: 24 11 00, a plush luxury hotel of the highest order (doubles 8800–10,400 pts). More modestly historic, a block from the Plaza Mayor, the **Fruela**** on Fruela 2, Tel: 21 82 78 offers doubles with bath for 2254–2789 pts, without bath 1855–2308 pts. The **Porlier***, Pl. de Porlier 3, Tel: 22 47 20 has five rooms in a good central location for 2000 pts (no bath); near the RENFE station, at C. Campoarmour 18, the **Pension Montreal** (Tel: 22 05 56) has pleasant doubles for 1200 pts.

EATING OUT

There are plenty of restaurants and *tapas* bars in Oviedo, but the oldest and best is **Casa Fermin** near the park on San Francisco 8, offering classic Asturian cuisine; if it's full the more recent **Trascorrales**, Pl. Trascorrales 18, in a charming building in the old town, offers the same with a flair to delight gourmets (both around 2500 pts). More good *fabada* at more moderate prices may be had at the popular **Meson del Labrador** on C. de Arguelles, which has a garden and *sidra* bar in a garden downstairs (700 pts). There's even cheaper dining at the **Casa Muñiz**, C. de la Lila, a jovial, local hole in the wall with dishes around 300 pts; university students and other cheapskates favour **La Pizzeria**, Pl. de Riego (a block from the Plaza Mayor and across the street from a good bookshop with English books), where a three-course pizza meal is 450 pts.

The Asturian Hinterland and Cantabrian mountains

The principality, beyond the coast and the Picos, is terra incognita for most foreigners – a hilly, wooded land of small mining-towns and agricultural villages. Much of it is protected, especially in the national hunting preserves that cover the northern slopes of the Cordillera Cantabrica, and criss-crossed by a network of hiking paths. Most of the villages have only limited public transport, and you'd do well to rent a car – and pack a big lunch – before setting out. Be sure to pick up one of the large new and detailed maps of the province available at the tourist office in Oviedo.

GETTING AROUND

If you're driving when the snow is flying, it's essential to call ahead for road conditions (Tel: 25 46 11). If you want to rent a car, the main companies in Oviedo are along C. Ventura Rodriguez, where you can shop around for the best deal.

Some points, however, can be reached by bus. ALSA buses from Oviedo (Pl. Primode Riveu) go to Salas, Puerto de Somiedo, Cangas del Narcea, Tineo and Pola de Allande. Empresa Fernández (Llamaquique, Oviedo, Tel: 23 83 90) has buses to Pola de Lena and Turón; Alcotán (Padre Suárez 27, Oviedo, Tel: 21 91 49) has buses to Pola de Laviana. The RENFE train between Oviedo and León stops at Pájares, and Pola de Lena.

Southeast of Oviedo

Southeast of Oviedo, the C-635 passes **Pola de Laviana**, famous as the typical Asturian mining-town (mostly copper), on its way to Reres National Reserve and the beautiful mountain pass, **Puerto de Tarna**; from a point just south, a seldom trod mountain path leads up to **Beleño**, on the edge of the Picos de Europa and offering a fine panorama over the mountains. The next mountain pass to the west **Puerto San Isidro** (both are linked with the Pueblo de Lillo in León province), is the site of a major ski installation. **Collanzo**, some 12 km (7.5 miles) below the pass, is a pretty area near the idyllic **Hoces de Río Aller**, a fine little gorge.

Directly south of Oviedo, along the train route and recently built highway to León (an engineering marvel Spain is not a little proud of) the views are uniformly magnificent. The second ski station is at the **Puerto de Pájares**, another dramatic pass. Just before you get there, 1.6 km (2 miles) south of **Pola de Lena**, is another of King Ramiro I's lovely churches, the hilltop **Santa Cristina de Lena**, a cruciform temple built around 845, with blind arches similar to Santa Maria de Naranco, Visigothic decorations and a lovely iconostasis inspired by the Mozarabs (the key is available in the house below by the bridge). The landmark in this part of the Cantabrian mountains is the **Peña Ubiña** (2417 m: 7855 ft), a jagged peak which you can ascend in some four-and-a-half hours from **Tuiza de Arriba** for incomparable views over the Picos de Europa and Somiedo. (To reach Tuizo, take the side road from the main highway at Campomanes.) From Pájares, you can make the much shorter climb up the **Pico de los Celleros** (1861 m: 6048 ft).

Somiedo

Southwest of Oviedo lies the Reserva Nacional de Somiedo, which may be approached via Trubia. 10 km (6.2 miles) south of Trubia, is **San Adrián de Tuñón**, built by Ramiro I's successor, Alfonso III (866–910), one of the last of the 'Asturian' churches, sombre in design and Mozarabic in decoration, especially in the murals. In **Proaza** there are a number of medieval buildings, and between it and the next village, **Caranga**, you can pass through the pretty gorge, the **Desfiladero de Peñas Xuntas**. The road continues through **La Plaza** with two fine Romanesque churches, **San Pedro** and the later, 12th-century, **Santa María de Villanueva**. From here the road continues south through a magnificent forest to the **Puerto de Ventana**, perhaps the least-used Cantabrian mountain pass. Just on the other side of the pass, from the Leonese village of **Torrestío** you can hike in three hours into the lovely heart of Somiedo and its mysterious lakes, home of the *xanas*, or mermaids who guard sunken treasures with which to please their lovers on the night of St John. The first lake, **Lago de la Cueva** is the source of the Rio Salencia; the third and largest, is the eerie **Lago Negro** – the Black Lake.

The second approach to Somiedo is via **Belmonte de Miranda** (C-633), an iron-mining area; a curiosity in the region is the **Machuco de Alvariza** (near Belmonte village), an ancient oak hydraulic hammer used in the 18th-century iron works. Many Vaqueros still live in the area – you'll see even more of their conical-roofed *pallozas* further south towards **Pola de Somiedo**, the chief town in the district. The region is also rich in Celtic castros. Somiedo is in the highest part of the Cantabrian mountains, and at the head of the path to the region's fourth lake, the **Lago del Valle** (four hours), passing several conical huts on the way. South of Pola are the ancient thatch-roofed hamlets of **Santa María de Puerto** and especially the remote **La Pornacal** (trail from Villar de Vildas).

West of Oviedo

Salas, on the main road west of Oviedo, a fairly large town, has an attractive old centre and a fine Renaissance church, the **Colegiata de Santa María** containing the beautiful alabaster tomb of the Inquisitor and church founder Valdes-Salas and a good *retablo*. This is a good area for picturesque *hórreos* (granaries), and to the north west are the lovely pasturelands and gentle hills around **Navelgas** and **Bárcena del Monasterio**, where the Vaqueros winter their herds.

Just west of Salas, the C-630 heads south to **Tineo**, a great trout-fishing area through which a branch of the Santiago pilgrimage route once passed. A number of medieval churches survive from that era – Tineo's 13th-century parish church and the ruined monastery and church in nearby **Obona**. Further south a dirt road leads up to the tiny borough of **Llamas del Mouro**, where potters, isolated from the rest of the world, still create the shiny black ceramic jugs and bowls made by their Celtic ancestors, 4000 years ago. The pieces are baked in the ancient style, in circular ovens buried in the earth – three are still in use in Llamas.

Cangas de Narcea, the largest town in south-west Asturias, is modern and has little to detain the traveller; head instead further south to **Pico de la Masa** (near Puerto del Connio) for the view over the magnificent 3302 hectare (8156 acres) **Bosque de Muniellos**, one of Europe's most extensive forests of primeval oaks and a strictly protected wildlife preserve, the last refuge in the world of the extremely rare *urogallo* (capercaillie), a funny-looking bird with red eyebrows. The trail through the forest begins at **Tablizas**, a short hike from Moal; the hike takes about five-and-a-half hours and is guaranteed to leave you mourning for the ancient times, when it is said that a squirrel could cross the whole of Iberia through forests without ever touching the ground. East of Muniellos lies the **Reserva Nacional de Degaña**, another lovely, wooded area, with pretty meadows and small lakes formed by glaciers. In the Roman era, Degaña was heavily mined for its gold.

Gold was also mined in the most westerly zone of the province, around **Pola de Allanda** and **Graundas**, both enchanting, seldom visited villages. In **Celón**, 5 km (3.1 miles) from Pola, there's a fine 12th-century church, **Santa María**, with murals and carvings; one of Asturias' best-preserved Celtic castros is up on **Pico San Chuis** to the west near Berducedo, whose ancient inhabitants, like the modern, exploited the region's minerals.

TOURIST INFORMATION
Salas: Pl. Generalisimo, Tel: 83 08 67

WHERE TO STAY AND EAT
In the smaller villages, you can always ask about rooms in *casas particulares*, though it's not something you should count on. On the whole it's best to base yourself in the towns and make forays from there. There are inexpensive rooms to be had in Mieres north of Pola de Lena, with the **Villa de Mieres***, Teodoro Cuesta 33, Tel: 46 70 04, a pleasant inn with doubles for 1700 pts with bath, or 1500 pts without. In Tineo, you'll find three *hostales*, each with only a handful of rooms: **Don Miguel****, El Viso, Tel: 80 03 25 offers doubles with baths for 2500 pts: **Casa Belarmino***, Campomanes 2, Tel: 80 02 35 has them without for 1000 pts; the third one, **Pertierra**, outside the village at Casares, has a little restaurant (Tel: 80 02 79).

Cangas de Narcea has the widest range of choices. The best place to stay and eat is the **Conde Piñolo****, Uria 21, Tel: 81 02 50, with nice rooms (showers down the hall) for 1700 pts; mountain cuisine in the dining-room for 750 pts. The **Acebo***, Hermanos Florez 1, Tel: 81 06 66, offers doubles for 3000 pts with bath, 2500 pts without; ask in the bars about cheaper rooms and *fondas*.

WHERE TO SKI
Valgrande Pájares, 3 km (1.9 miles) from the Busdongo train station, offers 10 slopes from the very difficult to the very easy, 10 lifts and two chairlifts (Tel: 49 61 23). The closest hotels are in León province, at La Pola de Gordon and Villamanin. **San Isidro** (León province) is near Puebla de Lillo, and offers three very difficult runs in the Cebolledo circuit, as well as five of average difficulty and four easy ones; there's a chair lift and seven ski lifts, Tel: 73 50 66. There are a couple of hotels at Puebla de Lillo, but no public transport. Other ski installations in the area are at San Emiliano, on the slopes of **Peña Ubiña**, at **Lietariegos Pass**, and **Maraña**, near Riaño in León.

Galicia

If Asturias is the Spanish Wales, then Galicia is in many ways its Ireland, for many years so far removed from the mainstream of Spanish life and history it might just as well have been an island. Here the Celtic invaders of 1000 BC found their cosiest niche, in the same kind of rain-swept, green land facing the setting sun that their race had settled further north. The Moors left no mark in Galicia, having been expelled in the 8th century by the kings of Asturias – who promptly turned their attention to the south and richer spoils. While the rest of the north had the newly won lands of the Reconquista to expand into, the Galicians, or Gallegos, were hemmed in by Portugal and forced to turn inwards, dividing their land into even smaller and smaller holdings. Famines were common, and as soon as the New World was opened up to them, they immigrated in droves – there are more Gallegos in Buenos Aires alone than all of Galicia. Even today Galicia is one of the poorest regions in Spain.

Yet few places in Spain have such a lasting charm. The coastline is pierced by a dozen estuaries, or *rías*, wild and scenic in the north, and sheltering serene beaches and coves in the south. Rivers in deep, narrow valleys with odd names – the Eo, the Ulla, the Lor, the Eume and Jallas – drift through the hills on their way to the sea. Bright green gardens cover every inch of cultivatible land, though a third of it is said to be covered by the granite fences each Gallego has carefully erected around his own little plot. It's hard to find a corner of Europe with more primitive agricultural techniques – the small size of the plots forbids machinery, and you'll often see ox carts rumbling down the narrow lanes between the granite houses. Each farm, however, has a sturdy, self-sufficient air to it, with its cow and conical hayrick, its trellis of vines (producing excellent white wines similar to Portugal's 'green' wines, like Ribero, Albariño and Condado) and tiny plots of turnips, peppers, maize, cabbage, peas and Spain's finest potatoes. Turnip greens (*grelos*) are an almost unavoidable item on local menus, but the tiny peppers (*pimientas de Padrón*) are worth asking for by name. Many cottages have granaries (*horréos*), monumental pieces of granite folk architecture, usually rectangular, set up on pillars, and topped by a gabled roof with crosses. Some are grand enough to have been mistaken for hermitages by early travellers. Chestnut, oak and furze forests cover the hills, while the Gallegos grow kiwi fruit, oranges, palm trees and camellias, which have been the rage since their introduction from Japan.

Galicia lacks the urban flair evident in the smallest Spanish town (exceptions are Pontevedra, Compostela and Lugo), and most of its population is spread in some 31,000 'villages' (population 100–200 people) sprinkled here and there with the showy new bungalows of the *americanos*, returned after making their fortunes in Argentina. Many of the older houses, especially along the coasts, have balconies closed in by glass 'crystal galleries', adorned with elaborate white mullions. La Coruña is famous for them. Another distinctive feature of the landscape is the granite crosses, often adorned with fine, Romanesque carving. Their purpose has long been forgotten, though some apparently guided pilgrims, marked out the high roads, or fulfilled vows, or perhaps even served the same mysterious purposes as the dolmens the Celts erected all over Galicia, but carved into acceptable Christian forms. Near the Rías Bajas, and especially along the rivers leading into them, you'll see the stately manor houses the Gallegos call *pazos*.

Galicia's languge, Gallego, is spoken by a greater percentage of the population than Basque or Catalan are in their respective regions. It's chock-full of x's, and more closely related to Portuguese than to Castilian. Two of Spain's greatest poets wrote in Gallego: Alfonso the Wise in his beautiful *Cantigas de Santa Maria* and Rosalia de Castro (1847–85), whose simple, evocative poetry (especially the *Cantares Galegos*) has an Emily Dick-

Ría de Sta María
Ría de Vivero
N
Ortigueira
Vivero
Cervo
RÍAS ALTAS
Sargadelos
Foz
Ría de Ribadeo
El Ferrol
Ria de Betanzos
Pontedeume
Lourenza
Ribadeo
Malpica
Mondoñedo
La Coruña
Miño
to Oviedo
Corme
Betanzos
Carballo
Villalba
ASTURIAS
Bayo
Fonsagrado
Corcubión
Ordenes
Finisterre
Sobrado
Lugo
Cabo Finisterre
Arzua
Muros
Santiago de Compostela
Noya
Ría de Muros y Noya
Portomarín
Padrón
Sarriá
Lalin
Embalse de Belesar
Villagarcía
Chantada
Ría de Arosa
Cambados
El Grove
to León
Bobras
Monforte de Lemos
Pontevedra
Isla de Ons
Marín
Carballino
Ría de Pontevedra
R. Sil
El Barco del Valdeorras
Cangas
Ribadavia
Orense
Islas Cies
Puebla de Trives
RÍAS BAJAS
Ría de Vigo
Vigo
*Manzaneda
Bayona
Allariz
R. Miño
Tuy
Celanova
Viana del Bollo
Oya
Forcadela
Valença
Bande
La Guardia
to Porto
to Zamora
Campobancos
PORTUGAL
km 0 50
GALICIA
miles 0 25
* Ski Resorts

inson feel. Rosalia was a key figure in Galicia's *Rexurdimento* (literary renaissance), inspired by the Catalans, and like theirs, the forerunner of the local nationalist movement, an increasingly important factor in local politics.

Culturally, Galicia has always looked to its ancient roots. The national instrument, the *gaita*, is very similar to Breton or Irish bagpipes, and Gallegos like nothing better than to blow them at festivals with their Celtic brethren (the best group playing traditional Galician music has long been *Milladoiro*). Celtic influences are also strong in Galicia's thousands of folk festivals (many associated with death, witches and evil spirits) and those with a special interest can buy a 400-page book that lists every one of them. Irish immigrants in the 16th century introduced lace-making, still done by women all along the coast.

Cuisine

One of the great pleasures in visiting Galicia is eating; in Spain the Gallego restaurants command almost as much respect as the Basque. The estuaries are rich in shellfish of all kinds, from the famous cockles of Santiago to lobster, mussels, shrimp, oysters, clams, squid, crab and some ugly creatures that English hasn't seen fit to name, but are fun to try. Some people consider Galician seafood the best in Europe – try hake or turbot*Allada* or in *empanadas* (turnovers), which can also include eels, sardines or scallops. *Caldo Gallego*, a broth of turnip greens, turnips and white beans, a typical first course, had been adopted throughout Spain; in the winter you may want to try *lacón con grelos* (pork shoulder with greens, sausages and potatoes). A meal to make a Gallego weep (and available as *tapas* in bars) is roast sardines, *pulpo a la Gallega* (octopus), *pimentas de Padrón*, with chewy hunks of bread and delicious breast-shaped *tertulla* cheese, washed down with glasses of Ribeira wine. For dessert try *tarta de almendras* (almond tart), and to top it all off, a glass of Galician fire water, *orujo*, properly burned (*queimada*), with lemon peel and sugar.

West from Asturias: Galicia's beaches

This is one of the least visited coasts in Spain, though parts of it are quite rugged and beautiful and endowed with fine beaches.

GETTING AROUND

The FEVE train from Gijón or Oviedo makes several trips a day along the scenic coast to El Ferrol, with stops at Ribadeo, Foz, Burella, Vivero, Covas, Barqueiro and Ortigueira. RENFE has frequent links between El Ferrol, Pontedeume and the main junction at Betanzos, where there are connections to La Coruña and beyond. El Rapido buses serve Betanzos and Monfero out of La Coruña. There are also bus connections from Betanzos, El Ferrol, Vivero, Foz, and Ribadeo to Lugo.

WHAT TO SEE

The first town beyond Asturias, **Ribadeo**, is one of the more popular – be sure to walk up to the **Church Santa Cruz**, for a great view of the *ría*. There are some nice stretches of sand between here and **Foz**. Inland from Foz, **Mondoñedo** is a curious old town in a green valley, with an interesting **cathedral**, begun in 1233. When it came time to slap on a Baroque façade, it was done with charm, preserving the Romanesque portal and Gothic rose window in harmonious blind arches. The good Romanesque murals inside are of the Massacre of the Innocents; a Gothic statue of the Virgin in one of the chapels was brought over from St Paul's in London during the Reformation. There's a small **museum** off the cloister. The pretty square in front of the cathedral is Mondoñedo's best, and there's a pretty walk (*alameda*) in front of the church Os Remedios. Nearer to Foz, about 1.6 km (1 mile) from the coast, is the region's best Romanesque church, **San Martín de Mondoñedo**.

Back on the coast, **Burela** is an important fishing-port; **Sargadelos**, near the coast, had one of Spain's earliest ironworks and a famous **Royal Ceramics Factory** that closed in 1860 but has recently been reopened. **Vivero**, at the head of a lovely *ría*, is a sardine port and has some lovely beaches – **Covas** under the pines, **Faro** up the *ría*. Within its old walls (note the escutcheon of Emperor Charles over the gate near the bridge) are picturesque streets paved with slabs, the pretty **Plaza de Pastor Diaz** and two ancient churches: **Santa María del Campo**, founded in the 9th century, and **San Pedro** (12th century). From the Mirador de San Roque there are splendid views along the *ría* and coast. On the tiny **island of Coelleira**, the Templars once had a castle but were all reportedly massacred in 1307.

To the west a road leads out to **Bares**, the northernmost point of Spain and retaining traces of walls from the days when it served as a Phoenician port. **Barqueiro**, at the foot of Bares peninsula, is a tiny village built in a scenic amphitheatre over the harbour. **Ortigueira**, at the head of another *ría*, has some more beaches. On 8 September pilgrims from all over Galicia head to the seaside **San Andrés de Teixido**, because, as the saying goes 'if you'd don't go while alive, you must go after death' – in the form of lizards or toads, which must never be harmed. Pilgrims build little mountains of stones en route to the church and collect a certain herb.

El Ferrol was formerly tagged 'Del Caudillo' ('of the Chief') in honour of its most famous native son, Francisco Franco, son of a naval supply officer who grew up to be the youngest General in Spanish history; his Gallego 'qualities' were most obvious in his maddening stubbornness and in keeping his own counsel – earning himself the nickname 'the sphinx without a secret'. El Ferrol can boast a handful of pretty houses with 'crystal galleries' and a couple of pretty walks, as well as Spain's biggest naval base, modern districts and industry.

There are a couple of interesting villages around El Ferrol; to the south lies the medieval town of **Pontedeume**, once the preserve of the Counts of Andrade, who built the great bridge over the Río Eume, originally containing 58 arches, and a 14th-century palace nearby, its tower emblazoned with a huge escutcheon. There are a couple of beaches along its *ría* and an unusual chapel on a hill 308 m (1000 ft) above town and sea, **San Miguel de Breamo** (1137), its façade pierced by a strange window with an 11-point star.

South of Pontedeume, **Monfero** is the site of an ancient Cistercian monastery, now derelict. It was rebuilt in the 17th and 18th centuries, unabashedly grandiose in its rustic setting, its church most memorable for a singular checker-board façade of granite and slate blocks. Further south, at the head of a small estuary, is a far more ancient place, **Betanzos**, the Roman *Brigantium Flavium*, itself built over a Celtic village. It is a fine old town, with picturesque, narrow streets. Within the gates of its medieval walls are three fine churches: 14th-century **Santa María del Azoygue** with a finely carved façade, **San Francisco**, of the same period, containing Galicia's most beautiful tomb, that of Férnan Pérez de Andrade 'O Boo' (the Good) supported on the backs of a boar and a bear and carved with a hunting scene, and the 15th-century **Santiago**, with an equestrian St James on the tympanum. Take time to walk around the town along the Río Mandeo, one of the prettiest in Galicia.

TOURIST INFORMATION
Foz: Hermanos López Real.
Ribadeo: Plaza de España.
Vivero: Plaza Mayor 1.

WHERE TO STAY
In a scenic spot overlooking its ria, Ribadeo has the **Parador de Ribadeo*****, Amador Fernandez, Tel: 11 08 25, its doubles ranging from 5000–7000 pts; the restaurant (1800 pts) features fresh seafood. Unless you're hooked on paradors, however, it's best to continue west. If you're driving, **Los Paredones*****, on the main road near Mondoñedo, Tel: 52 17 00, is a nice place to rest up near the coast, with a garden, pool, fine views and an average restaurant; doubles a bargain at 2800 pts, 1800 pts out of season. Less expensive, Mondoñedo's **Hostal Montero****, Av. San Lázaro 7, Tel: 52 17 51 has pleasant doubles in town for 1800–2300 pts, without bath for 1200–1600 pts; it also has the town's best cheap restaurant (700 pts). Vivero has many more choices, from the smart **Las Sirenas*****, near Covas beach, Tel: 56 02 00 (doubles 2200–3850 pts; open year round) to the more central **Hostal Vila****, N. Montenegros 57, Tel: 56 13 31, with doubles and bath for 1600–2500 pts. **Nito**, on Playa de Area, Tel: 56 09 87, has a handful of rooms above its fish restaurant.

Ortigueira's most comfortable lodgings is **La Perla****, Av. de la Penela in town, Tel: 40 01 50, open all year, with doubles for 1900–2450 pts with bath, 1600-2000 pts without, and there is a fair supply of cheaper *hostales* and *fondas*. Franco saw to it that El Ferrol got a **Parador Nacional*****, its rooms decorated with nautical themes (Almirante Vierna, Tel: 35 67 20, where doubles are 6000–6500 pts. Cheap rooms and eateries in El Ferrol are concentrated on **Pardo Bajo**, but it's more fun to stay in Betanzos at the modern **Los Angeles***, Los Angeles 11, Tel: 77 15 11 (doubles 2100–2750 pts) or the cheaper **Barreiros***, Argentina 6, Tel: 77 22 59, its nine rooms costing 1400–1700 pts with bath, 1200–1400 without. Both *hostales* have cheap restaurants.

EATING OUT
There's a good restaurant in El Ferrol, **Pataquiña** on Dolores 35, offering heaps of good, well-prepared Gallego specialities (1500 pts). The classic eatery in Betanzos is **La Casilla**, Av. de Madrid 90, renowned for its potato omelettes and *empanadas* and homemade wine (1000 pts).

The Galician Interior: the Road to Santiago

Pilgrims who made it as far as Villafranca del Bierzo (see León) had to gird their loins for one last big trial: the **Puerto Piedrafita** in the Sierra de Ancares. This is the wildest and bleakest part of Galicia, deceptively covered with blooms in the spring, but the haunt of werewolves and witches in the evening. Here, in 1809 Sir John Moore's troops, flying from Soult on their way to the ships at La Coruña, nearly rebelled. Discipline had already vanished in Villafranca, where the soldiers had sacked, raped and looted the homes of their Spanish allies; up in the pass and at **O Cebreiro**, famous for its tempests and blizzards, hundreds froze to death. Such was their haste that the army's pay, thousands of pounds in gold, had to be tossed over the cliff, along with hundreds of horses, while the women that accompanied the army were left to starve. It was one of the blackest pages in the history of the British army, and almost miraculous that Moore was able to restore order and make it to the coast.

Celtic Village

GETTING AROUND

Lugo is the transportation hub for Galicia, on the rail line to La Coruña, Orense and Vigo, as well as Madrid and León. There are also *talgos* to Zaragoza and Barcelona, Bilbao and Irún. Monforte de Lemas is a big interchange, but the only other town mentioned below on the line is Sarriá. In Lugo the station is in the new part of town on Pl. C. de Fontao (Tel: 22 21 41); take the steps down and walk along Rua de Castelao to the walls. There's a travel office at the Pl. de España 27, Tel: 22 55 03. The bus station (Tel: 22 39 85) is near the Puerta del Carmen on Plaza Angel López-Pérez, you'll find connections to most of the towns; buses to León pass through Becerreá and Pedrafita.

WHAT TO SEE

At O Cebreiro, a small colony of shepherds still makes use of the ancient Celtic style *pallozas* (circular, conical-roofed huts). The scene would have been familiar to a medieval pilgrim, who would also have been sure to pay his respects at the old squat church of **Santa María del Cebreiro**, where one of the greatest miracles of the Road took place. A grumbling priest in the 13th century, tired of celebrating Mass for just one shepherd, was amazed to see the Host transformed into flesh and the wine into a chalice of blood, a miracle inspired by the legend of the Holy Grail. Archaeologists have found the sturdy old chapel to be contemporary with the Asturian churches of the 9th century. Four of the *pallozas* have been fixed up to house the **Museo de Artes y Costumbres Populares** (usually open mornings 10 am–1 pm.)

O Cebreiro and the mountains to the north form part of the **Reserva Nacional de los Ancares**, which encompasses in its rugged mountains several other villages of *pallozas* – **Villarello, Cervantes, Donís** and especially **Piornedo**, which can only be reached by foot from Donís. **Becerreá**, on the Lugo road, is the main point of departure for excursions into Los Ancares.

From the pass, the pilgrims descended to **Samos**, where the ancient abbey of **San Julian** was burned down in 1951, preserving only a Baroque cloister with the grand Fountain of the Nereidas in its centre; it was long the home of Padre Feijóo the 'Spanish Voltaire'. **Sarriá**, the next town on the route, retains more of its medieval air with its church and tower of granite. It is an interesting detour from the **Camino de Santiago** south to **Monteforte de Lemos**, a picturesque old town dominated by the castle of the counts of Lemos. Once it had two important monasteries: **San Vincente del Pino**, Benedictine, of which the church in the late Romanesque ojival style survives, along with a 15th century image of St Anne, and, near the river and its medieval bridge, the colossal **Colegio del Cardenal**, Jesuit, its chapel containing a famous walnut *retablo* carved with the life of the Virgin, two El Grecos painted before he found his own style, and a lovely triptych attributed to Van der Goes. More of the same may be seen at the **Museum of Religious Art** installed in the Monasterio de Santa Clara, also near the bridge.

Back on the French road, **Portomarín** was a stop protected by the Templars; now the old village lies under the waters of the Embalse de Belesar. The new village is partially made of medieval buildings saved from the dam, most notably the Romanesque fortress-like **San Juan**, with an immense rose window. There are more Romanesque churches around the next stops, at **Mellid** (**Sancti Spiritus** and **Santa María** with murals, and an impressive dolmen, the 'Pedra de Raposo') and **Arzua** (**La Magdalena**). From here, it was an easy walk to **Labacolla**, where 'for the love of the Apostle' the pilgrims would bathe. Sentries were posted to make sure they performed the ritual, as much against lice as for St James. 5 km (3.1 miles) more would take them to Montjoy (**Monte del Gozo**) and the tremendous, long-awaited sight of Santiago. The first member of each band to sight the cathedral towers was called the 'King', a proud title that was passed down as a surname; if yours is King, Leroy or Rey, the chances are you had a sharp-eyed ancestor (for *Santiago*, see below).

Lugo

Many pilgrims made the detour, coming or going, to **Lugo**, a fine old town and one of Galicia's four provincial capitals. Its curious name is a direct survival from the great Celtic sun god Lug; the marvellous slate **walls** enclosing the old town are a magnificently preserved survival from the Roman Empire, the best ancient walls in Spain. 2.4 km (1.5 miles) in extent, 9.2 m (30 ft) high, containing 85 rounded towers and four ancient gates (Santiago, Carmen, La Falsa and Miña). A road circles the walls so you can get a good look at them.

Lugo's other five-star attraction is its **Cathedral**, with a Baroque skin built over the 1177 original modelled on the great church of Santiago. Its three great towers are Lugo's landmark, inside are fittings from a wide variety of periods – carved Romanesque tombs, a circular 18th-century chapel of 'Our Lady of the Big Eyes', and a beautifully carved *coro* by Francisco de Moure (1624). The Cathedral has the rare privilege of *manifestado* (having the Host always on display), an honour depicted on Galicia's coat-of-arms. Be sure to note the carving of the Almighty over the Gothic portal.

There are a number of picturesque squares and streets behind the cathedral. Past the 17th-century **Bishop's Palace** the Plaza Santa María gives on to Calle Cantones, leading to the Plaza España and a Rococo **Ayuntamiento**; Calle de la Reina from here heads north to the busy Plaza Santo Domingo with a 14th-century church of the same name and that of **San Francisco**, reputedly founded by St Francis himself on his return from his pilgrimage to Santiago; the cloister is now the interesting **Provincial Museum**, containing Celtic and Roman finds (note the golden, winged ram from the 2nd century BC, jet figures from Compostela, sun dials, ceramics from Sargadelos and more. Open Tuesday–Sunday 10 am–2 pm). The city's beauty-spots are along the Rio Miño, the most important of Galicia's numerous rivers; a mirador in the **Parque Rosalia de Castro**, just outside the Santiago gate, has fine views of the valley.

Some 16 km (10 miles) from Lugo is the extraordinary **Santa Eulalia de Bóveda**, built over a Celtic temple and later Roman Nymphaeum. The ancient church, discovered in 1962 next to the parish church, dates from the 4th century; it is entered through a brick horseshoe arch with mysterious reliefs of dancers on the side. Within, it has three naves, a shallow pool, and murals of birds and trees. According to tradition Santa Eulalia was the burial place of Galicia's first saint, Prisciliano, whose doctrines, a syncretism of old Celtic and Christian beliefs, attracted many followers in Galicia and León but upset the established clerics – Prisciliano believed works of the spirit obliterated sexual differences, and that monks and nuns should live together. His followers walked barefoot to stay in contact with the forces in the earth, were vegetarians, did a bit of sun-worshipping and retreated to hermitages (alone or with their families and servants) in the holy mountains of the Celts. The counsel of Zaragoza (380) condemned him, and a bishop had him beheaded five years later in Tréveris – one of the first saints to be martyred by the Church instead of by Romans. His death increased the popularity of his doctrines until the early 9th century, when, by an extraordinary coincidence, the *headless* body of St James was discovered in nearby Santiago. Some scholars and Galician nationalists openly suspect it was Prisciliano's body they found, that now lies in the cathedral crypt, in Santiago.

Another rewarding excursion from Lugo is northwest to **Sobrado** 'de los Monjes', the site of Galicia's greatest monastery (now ruined), founded in the 10th century and another popular detour for pilgrims from the Road. The chances were they could get a meal cooked in the monumental, ojival **kitchen** that has survived, along with the 13th-century **chapel de la Magdalena**, a sacristy (1571) by Juan de Herrera, Philip II's favourite architect, a 12th-century **Sala Capitular**, a Baroque church with a fine façade, and three 17th- and 18th-century **cloisters**. **Villalba**, further north, has 15th-century walls and a powerful castle, now a *parador*.

TOURIST INFORMATION

Lugo: Plaza de España 27, Tel: 23 13 61: the post office is on C. San Pedro 5; Telephones: Quiroga Ballesteros 4. In Cervantes, there's information on Los Ancares park at Monforte 12.

WHERE TO STAY AND EAT

Way up at Piedrafita del Cebreiro, **San Giraldo de Aurilac**** (no phone) offers doubles in an old-fashioned inn near the *pallozas* for 1900 pts a double with bath, 1500 pts without. Other lodgings in Los Ancares are in Bacerreá, where there are two basic hostels: **Herbón***, G. Jiménez 8, Tel: 36 01 34 (doubles 2000 pts with bath, 1300 pts without) and the **Rivera****, Ctra. General 468, Tel: 36 01 85, outside town; doubles with bath 2500–3000 pts, 1500–2000 pts). Both are open all year; a couple of bars in town serve meals as well. In Sarriá there's a *fonda* and the hostal-restaurant **Londres****, Tel: 53 06 89, where doubles with bath range from 1850–2325 pts, and meals are around 750 pts.

There's more choice in Lugo. At the top of the scale, with a pool, air-conditioning, and good restaurant **(Os Marisqueiros)** and other luxuries is the **Gran Hotel Lugo******, with doubles from 5950-7525 pts; a seafood dinner at the restaurant will run around 1700 pts. Within the walls, the **Méndez Núñez*****, Reina 1, Tel: 23 07 11, has modern rooms for 3500–4500 pts. If you're driving, the **Portón do Recanto****, on the road to Vegadeo in La Campiña, Tel: 22 34 55 is a pleasant option, in a memorable old building with a good restaurant and fine scenery (doubles 3000–3600 pts with bath). In town you can have a view of the walls at the **Mar de Plata****, Ronda Muralla 5, Tel: 22 89 10, where doubles range from 2000–3000 pts, all with bath. Cheaper choices within the Roman walls include **La Perla***, Catedral 20, Tel: 21 11 00, where doubles are 1000 pts.

At Monforte de Lemos, there are nice and nicely priced rooms at the **Río**** near the centre at R. Belmonde 30, Tel: 40 18 50, where doubles with bath are 1400; good cheap Gallego meals are cooked at **El Castillo**, which has slightly more pricey rooms at Huertas 36. The **Parador Condes de Vilalba*****, Valeriano Valdesuso, Tel: 51 00 11, bestows on its visitors feudal fancies – the windows in the 3 m (10 ft) thick walls were made to shoot arrows at attackers far below. Its six doubles go for 6500–7500 pts; since it's so small, it's best to call ahead. The restaurant features natural, hand-fed country capons (1800 pts).

Santiago de Compostela

The original European tourist destination, Santiago de Compostela, is still one of the best. Not only does it boast one of Spain's greatest cathedrals, but the moss-stained granite town with its red-tile roofs is pure magic, one of Europe's most harmonious and 'unspoiled' though that's not quite the word to use for a town that grew up primarily to receive visitors, or pilgrims, as they're still called today. Expect rain – the city is famous for it and never fails gently to remind you that rain is good for granite, fostering the elegant patina of Santiago's great monuments and the plants that sprout out of everywhere. A university, with an important medical school keeps the ancient city full of life and youth.

History

Tradition relates that a bright star led a monk of Iria Flavia (Padrón) to the long forgotten tomb of St James in 813, hence the name 'Compostela' ('Field of the star'). Alfonso II of Asturias ordered the first chapel built to house the relics in 829; a larger sanctuary was already needed in 896, built by Alfonso III. When the fierce Al-Mansur swept through in 997, he destroyed the church, took the bells, but left the tomb alone 'out of respect'. The present Cathedral was begun in 1075 on a grand scale, to accommodate the already considerable flow of pilgrims from all corners of Europe; Chaucer's Wife of Bath, like the other English, sailed to Bordeaux and walked from there. In 1236 Ferdinand III el Santo conquered Córdoba and brought back the bells from the Great Mosque. In the 16th century the saint's body was hidden to protect it from Francis Drake, who was ravaging the coast. Rather amazingly, it was lost and forgotten until 1879, when a workman repairing the church found it. How to make sure it was the genuine article? They brought in a sliver of the skull of St James back from Italy, which like a puzzle piece fitted in the skeleton perfectly.

There's a good deal about the legends of Santiago that beggar belief (see p. 41) but it's a great story. Many have remarked on the ulterior motives of the cult and the pilgrimage. The French monks of Cluny who did the most to develop the pilgrimage probably had their own hidden agenda. Early Spain needed Santiago on its side, both for Reconquista propaganda and the strong voodoo of his relics (the Moors, after all, attributed their prowess to an arm of the Prophet himself, kept in the mosque of Córdoba). The Church itself in the early 9th century needed a focal point to assert its control over the newborn kingdoms (and it seems, especially over the Galicians – see above for Lugo and San Prisciliano).

Yet we would probably be wrong to chuckle at the 'simplicity' of the devout medieval pilgrim. In the Middle Ages it took real courage to leave one's village and make such an arduous journey into the unknown literally to the End of the World (Finisterra), and it's hard not to think there was more behind it than just picking up a slip of paper, the *Compostela*, to deposit in one's personal account in the Bank of Grace. The pilgrimage was one of the few available opportunities for Everyman to attain a greater consciousness (as we'd call it today) than permitted in the dogma of the Official Church. The whole tradition is rife with symbolism and nuances far older than St James himself. The *Universal Way* to Compostela, the star way, the Milky Way, the Via Lactea to heaven, seems to have been a path of initiation into the mysteries of life and death and unity of all things. Certainly the magnificent laughing figures Master Mateo carved on the Portico de la Gloria seem to be in on the secret.

The Cockleshell

The symbol most closely associated with Santiago is the scallop, or cockleshell, a common bivalve of the Galician rias. Curiously, its Spanish name, *venera*, calls up associations with Venus, the goddess of love, born of the sea, but what she has to do with St James is anyone's guess. One of the first things a pilgrim would do upon arriving in the city is head to the Barrio de los Conchieros (shell-sellers' quarter), buy a scallop, eat it, and attach the shell to the bent-up brim of his hat; the symbol is emblazoned on half the churches in Spain and many coats-of-arms.

In Compostela the shell symbol is attributed to a miracle of St James. A young Gallego, on the eve of his wedding, was spirited into the sea by his untamed horse and believed drowned, though in truth the horse was running along the waves on its way to meet a stone boat bringing the body of St James to Galicia. When the bridegroom returned, escorting the boat, his body covered with an armour of milk-white shells, it was enough to convert the locals to the new faith. (The story is illustrated by a carving on the cloister in the Plaza de Las Platerias.) The shell also symbolized the end of the journey and unity in the world – the sea from which it came, the earth in its stony hardness, and the sun in its radiant lines. Of course, those who hunger more in the belly than the spirit will see it as the key ingredient of *coquilles de St Jacques*, a dish the French learned how to prepare in Compostela.

GETTING AROUND

Santiago's train station is a 10-minute walk from the centre down in the newer part of town at the end of C. Gral. Franco (Tel: 59 60 50), with daily connections to Madrid, Orense, Le Coruña, Vigo, Zamora and other points. The bus station is on San Cayetano, Tel: 58 77 00, at the opposite end of town from the train station, and further out – bus 10 will take you, in the Plaza de Galicia. Buses go to nearly all points in Galicia, especially the Rías Altas.

Santiago's airport (Tel: 59 74 00) is at Labacolla, 11 km (6.9 miles) to the east. It has regular flights to Barcelona, Madrid, Sevilla, Santa Cruz de Tenerife, Bilbao, Santander and San Sebastián, as well as direct flights to London, Paris and Amsterdam. Iberia's office is at Gral. Pardinas 24, Tel: 59 41 00; there are buses to the airport from the station run by the Empresa Freire, Tel: 58 81 11.

The Cathedral

All roads lead up to the cathedral, the culmination of the pilgrim's journey and magnificent enough to fulfil all their expectations. It is built over the site where the hermit Pelayo followed the star to Santiago's body, and excavations in the cathedral's foundations have revealed quite a few other graves from the Roman era, as well as a Celtic fortified settlement, or *castro*. The proper way to approach it is from the **Plaza del Obradoiro**, facing the main façade, the **Fachada del Obradoiro**. The effect is breathtaking; the square is one of the finest ensembles in Christendom and the moulded, grey granite façade of Fernando Casas y Novoa tacked on in the 18th century almost redeems the entire Baroque period, the typical mass of Churrigueresque detail enhancing the soaring forms – the two great towers have been compared to huge flames rising to heaven.

If you follow the cathedral around to the right you'll come to the **Façade of the Platerías** which many prefer to the Obradoiro, though it has been hemmed in by the bell tower. It faces the smallest of the jewel-like squares that encircle the church; this one in the Middle Ages was filled with silversmith's shops. The carvings are from the 11th century, the tympanum on the right adorned with scenes from the Passion, the one on the left featuring winged monkeys and the figure of a woman giving birth to a skull (one of the stranger mystic symbols). Further down is an excellent carving of King David playing the fiddle. Continuing to the right is the lovely enclosed **Plaza de la Quintana**, its upper section surnamed 'de los Vivos' (of the living), the lower patio 'de los Muertos' (of the dead), recalling the Roman cemetery that once occupied the site. From here you can get a good look at the Cathedral's highest tower, **La Berenguela**. Around the corner is the **Puerta Santa** (Holy Door), opened only during Jubilee years (every year when St James' day – 25 July – falls on a Sunday; the next ones will be 1993 and 1999); on 31 December it is opened by the Archbishop with a special silver hammer. The doorway is covered with carved figures removed from the ancient *coro*. The fourth (northern) façade faces the **Plaza de la Azacheria** (of the jet-makers), given a Baroque facelift in the 18th century that unfortunately obliterated the medieval 'Door of Paradise'. It was here that the pilgrims, descending into town from Montjoy and passing through the Barrio de los Concheiros, would first enter the cathedral. Those in rags would receive new clothes from the monks of **St Martin's** (facing the cathedral; note the upper carving of St Martin sharing his cloak with a poor man) and hang their rags on the iron cross still standing nearby, and they would buy souvenirs of their pilgrimage from the jet-makers; you couldn't get your picture taken next to St James then, but you could get little black figures of the Apostle with yourself praying at his feet. The jet itself is said to be in memory of a local coal-worker, Contolay, who helped St Francis of Assissi on his pilgrimage; in ancient traditions black stones in themselves are often held sacred.

THE INTERIOR

You can enter the cathedral from here or the Plaza de la Platerías (indeed most locals use those doors as a short cut across town, as their ancestors surely did in the Middle Ages, when cathedrals were as much covered public squares as religious shrines), but nothing beats climbing up the stairs and entering through the main doors of the Obradoiro façade, where you are met by the inner, 12th-century façade, the **Portico de la Gloria**, the greatest piece of 12th-century sculpture in Spain, and perhaps all Europe. It was begun in 1168 by the mysterious Master Mateo, of whom next to nothing is known except that he finished it 20 years later. The most remarkable thing about the 200 odd figures that adorn its three great arches is their animation and joy, from the smiling figures of St James, welcoming you into the cathedral, to the famous laughing Daniel (who is said to owe his good humour to the loveliness of Queen Esther, whom he appears to be eyeing across the way). The other prophets and Apostles on the pillars are smiling or chatting together, while the line of musicians over the central figure of the Almighty appear to be discussing their hopes for another gig during an intermission. St James himself stands on the Tree of Jesse, portraying Jesus Christ's family tree from Adam to the Virgin Mary; for centuries so many pilgrims have placed their fingers in its five niches that they have worn the stone smooth. The crouching figure below is the humble, curly-haired Master Mateo himself, who has been nicknamed '*O Santo dos Croques*' 'Saint Bump-on-the-Head' from the millions of people who have bowed their heads to touch Mateo's in the hope that some of his talent would rub off. The portico has other unusual features, on the left arch is an especially benign Christian portrayal of

Jews waiting for the Messiah; on the right arch is believed to be the first depiction of children suffering the torments of the damned with their parents – a powerful psychological trick to make parents behave.

The body of the cathedral is almost entirely Romanesque, in the form of the Latin cross. After the Portico de la Gloria it is almost austere in its architecture, though not in the treasures and artwork it houses. The huge, silver shrine on the high altar glimmers in the dim light, sheltering a 12th-century image of Santiago, and you do as millions have done before: climb the narrow stair behind the altar, kiss the image's robe and receive the modern equivalent of the *Compostela*. Below the altar you can pay your respects to the saint's bones in the crypt; one of its walls is from Alfonso III's 9th-century church. The alms boxes you see here and everywhere else were installed in the 16th century, replacing the ancient custom the pilgrims had of literally helping to build the cathedral by bringing in a stone from the quarry along the road.

Most of the chapels along the nave were added in the 16th and 17th centuries – in one you can see an 18th-century polychrome statue of Santiago 'Matamoros', cutting down the Moors at the legendary battle of Clavijo, the same scene is portrayed in a 10th-century scene on the tympanum near the entrance to the cloister. To the side of the high altar, notice the ropes and pulleys suspended from the *cimborio*, from which, on high feast days, Santiago's renowned *Botafumeiro*, the world's largest censer, is suspended and swung dramatically over the heads of the congregation in a comet-like arc of smoke and sparks. The current Botafumeiro dates from 1602 and weighs 53.6 kg (118 lb): it takes eight men, the *tiraboleiros*, to swing it properly. Don't miss it if you're in Santiago on a holy day, and try not to think about the time when Katherine of Aragón attended mass and the Botafumeiro broke loose and flew out of the window. Some think the Botafumeiro was used in the Middle Ages to sweeten the air inside the cathedral, where many pilgrims slept at night; others say it was invented to upstage the pilgrimage to Rome.

A ticket can get you into the cathedral's various museums, the cloister, and the crypt of Master Mateo (open 10.30 am–1.30 pm and 4–7 pm). It's odd that such a choice cathedral has such trifling museums – the **archaeological collections** still sit in boxes; the **tapestry museum** a few Goyas, mostly insipid (though head up here for a walk among the towers and the balcony of the Obradoiro façade). You can see the Botafumeiro in the library of the **Sala Capitular**, and the two best tapestries, Flemish representations of Hannibal crossing the Alps and Scipio with his Romans. The **cloister** is 16th century and offers good views of the towers as well as being attractive in itself. Most interesting of all is the **Crypt of Master Mateo** below the steps of the Obradoiro façade, built by Mateo, to distribute evenly the weight of the Portico de la Gloria, with ancient columns, elaborate capitals and sculptural odds and ends under the vaults.

Plaza del Obradoiro

Facing the main façade of the Cathedral, this square is one of the loveliest in Spain, filled with Gallegos holding demonstrations, vendors of postcards and plastic birds with flapping wings. On one side is the ornate Plateresque façade of the **Hospital Real**, constructed for poor pilgrims by Ferdinand and Isabel with booty from Granada. The founders face each other in medallions over the doorway, while Adam and Eve stand near the bottom of the columns of figures. Within there are four fine patios and a beautiful late Gothic chapel – and a five-star hotel with an exclusive air (you can make an appointment at the desk to tour it from 10–11 am or 4–7 pm). Next to the Hospital stands the magnificent 18th-century **Ayuntamiento**, and next to it the **Palacio de Gelmirez**, built in the 12th and 13th centuries by the two Archbishops whose worldly aplomb helped make Santiago great: Gelmirez, who received a licence to mint money, and Arias, 'one of the great ecclesiastical pirates of 13th-century Spain'. A new skin was added to the palace in the 18th century to keep it from collapsing, but it's still worth visiting (summers only, 10 am–10.30 pm and 3.30–7.30 pm) for the dining-hall, where the corbels beneath the ribs of the dome are carved with scenes of a medieval feast, one man dining on a Galician *empanada*. If you like the Obradoira façade, visit St Martin's in the Plaza de la Platerias, with a tremendous, elaborate *retablo* by the same artist.

Elsewhere in the city

Despite its fame, Santiago is a small town, and even from the Plaza del Obradoiro you can see beyond the houses below to the rolling green countryside. Nearly any walk you take through the narrow, arcaded streets paved with granite flagstones, opening up into small plazas, is bound to be delightful. Old palaces, churches, and monasteries that would stand out elsewhere are too numerous to mention.

In the immediate area around the cathedral there are a couple of places worth getting into: **San Martín Pinario** in the Plaza de la Azabacheria (see above) has one of Spain's grandest *retablos*, by the same artist of the Obradoiro façade, Casas Novoa (open 10 am–1 pm and 4–7 pm). On the Plaza Quintana (which also has a great Galician record shop) the **Monasterio de San Pelayo** has a good museum of sacred art (open summer only 10 am–1 pm and 4–7 pm) famous for the image of the Virgin, who holds the Child in one hand and thumps a devil with the other. Between these two, off Azabacheria street, is the **Casa de la Troya**, where much of the action of a well-known Spanish novel of Bohemian student life took place; it now houses a group of student merry-makers called a *tuna*, who carry on most nights in the Plaza Immaculada. The **Colegio de Fonseca** (16th century) across from the Palacio de Gelmirez on Calle Fonseca, has a lovely, peaceful **cloister**. Behind the cathedral there's a typical street called **Pregun-toiro** ('questioning' street) from all the pilgrims who asked for directions here.

The special place to aim for is the **Convento de Santo Domingo**, on the Puerto del Camino at the end of Calle de las Casas Reals. This, according to tradition, was founded by St Dominic himself on his pilgrimage to Santiago and is a large Romanesque-Gothic structure. Its cloister now serves as the **Museo do Pobo Galego** (open 10 am–1 pm and 4–7 pm, Sunday am only) with ethnographic collections on Galician rural life. Next to the collections is the stunning **triple spiral stair** built in 1700 by Domingo de Andrade: three different unsupported granite stairways interlace in a single tower, each leading to different doors – a Baroque architectural model of the Fibonacci sequence. One chapel of the church is called the Patheon of Illustrious Gallegos, last resting-place of poet Rosalia de Castro and the writer and caricaturist Castelao (died 1950), the Goya of the Civil War. A museum on the pilgrimage is planned to reopen soon in the Plaza San Miguel.

The best church after the Cathedral itself, **Santa María del Sar**, is 1.6 km (1 mile) from the centre (from Calvo Sotelo, take the Calle del Sar). This 12th-century church is a fine piece of Romanesque architecture, with a different slant – literally. Its piers have leaned at precarious angles as long as anyone can remember; one school of thought believes the tilt was caused by the subsidence of the soil, though the chances are it was done intentionally by the architects just to show it could be done – like the Tower of Pisa, also built in the 12th century. Supports were added after the Lisbon earthquake, but the church remains one of the jewels of Spanish Romanesque, its cloister is decorated with remarkable carvings (open Monday–Saturday 10 am–1 pm and 4–6 pm 10 pm in the summer).

For the classic view of Santiago's towers and roofs, walk along the **Paseo de Herradura** east of the cathedral, around the edge of a park where old men will take your photo with cameras as old as themselves.

TOURIST INFORMATION

Rua de Vilar 43, Tel: 58 40 81. Rua de Vilar is one of the city's loveliest streets and Turismo distributes a fine map of the city. If you're coming from the station, head up Franco Street and turn a block left at Pl. Canton. The post office is on the Travesia de Fonseca; Telephones are at Alfredo Brañas 2.

WHERE TO STAY

Finding a place to stay at any price is easy in the city that has received visitors for 1100 years; you'll probably be met at the bus or train station by landladies tempting you to their *hostales* or *casas particulares* for prices around 600 pts a head.

At the other end of the scale, you can play pilgrim in the **Hostal Los Reyes Católicos** *****, Plaza del Obradoira, Tel: 58 22 00, the antique fittings much more comfortable than anything the 16th-century devotee ever saw. Most rooms look onto one of the four shady patios; some are simple, while the bridal suites have been slept in by the famous from Franco up. Open since 1954, it is rated as one of Europe's best hotels – doubles are 11,950 to 13,805 pts. Far more sensible for most is the older **Hotel Compostela*****, Calvo Sotelo 1, Tel: 58 57 00, a grand old granite hotel still offering considerable elegance for 4300–5700 pts a double.

Moderate choices can also be fun. The **Suso****, Rúa del Villar 65, Tel: 58 66 11 is located on Santiago's prettiest street and run by a jovial fellow who knows everything. Doubles with bath are 1700–2300 pts, with tasty tapas in the bar downstairs. Another *hostal* with a patina of age is **La Estela***, near the cathedral on Rajoy 1, Tel: 58 27 96, charming and friendly, with doubles for 1375–2000 pts with bath, 1375–1775 pts without.

In Santiago the cheapest places have retained the antique name *hospedajes*. Real low-rollers should check out the pleasant if basic **Hospedaje Villa de Cruces**, on Patio de Madres 16 off Calvo Sotelo, Tel: 58 08 04, where you can expect to pay 400 pts a person. If it's full, try the **Hospedaje Rodriguez** nearby on C. Pison 4, Tel: 58 84 08, with doubles for 1400 pts.

EATING OUT

This is a pleasure – with all the students and visitors passing through, competition is keen and the food has to be good to succeed. Calle del Franco has the biggest concentration of restaurants and bars – one window of tempting seafood after another. It's one of the city's greatest charms that one of its best restaurants, **El Asesino**, is one of its cheapest, and has been for more than a 100 years – it's so well known it doesn't bother putting out a sign but can be found in the Plaza Universidad at no. 16. Great Gallego cooking for less than 500 pts.

The classy place to go is **Vilas** on the edge of town at Rosalia de Castro 88, featuring the freshest seafood and other Galician dishes (2500 pts). On C. Franco the queen is **Tacita de Oro** at no. 31, offering traditional dishes excellently prepared for around 1500 pts. The locals pack the **Victoria** nearby at Bautizados 5, with more tasty seafood and a *menú del día* for 1200 pts. More simple but delicious food can be found at **Mesón Candilejas** in the Pl. Mazarelos (350 pts).

Las Rías Altas

Las Rías Altas, or the upper estuaries of the Galician coast, have some of the best coastal scenery in Iberia, wild, windy, and beautiful. If you're a very good swimmer, or just a sun-bather seeking a cove of your own, Spain can't do better than the coast between La Coruña and the Ría de Muros y Noya.

GETTING AROUND

La Coruña and Santiago are the main bases for transport to this section of the *rías*, but buses are not all that frequent, and if you intend to visit more than one destination in a day, study bus schedules before setting out.

La Coruña can be reached by train from Santiago, El Ferrol, Lugo, Vigo, Madrid, Irún and Barcelona. The station San Cristobál is in the new city on the Av. de San Riego (Tel: 23 03 09) – bus no. 1 to la Ciudad Vieja. There's also a travel office on Fontán 3, Tel: 22 19 48. Padrón and Villagarcia de Arosa are linked by train to La Coruña, Santiago and Pontevedra.

La Coruña's bus station is on C. Caballeros near the RENFE station (Tel: 23 96 44) with buses to all the villages below at least once a day, though the destinations on the Ría Arosa are more frequently linked with Pontevedra. There are buses from Santiago to Noya, Finsterra, El Grove and points in between.

La Coruña

La Coruña, one of Spain's great ports, is the big, industrial provincial capital of the region. Emperor Charles V sailed from here to his coronation. Philip II left to wed Mary Tudor, and later his Invincible Armada made its last call here before its disaster at the hands of Sir Francis Drake. Drake rubbed salt in Philip's wounds by burning La Coruña a few months later, though in 1809 it was the British who suffered the most in the battle of Elviña; here Sir John Moore was mortally wounded by a cannonball before the British army, despite grievous losses, was able to embark intact under Soult's very nose – and soon return under the new commander, the Duke of Wellington. In 1851, it was the birthplace of Galicia's best-known novelist, the Countess Emilia Pardo Bazán.

For most visitors La Coruña has little to offer, despite its sandy beaches (too much industry nearby) and its superb location on an isthmus. Most of what you'd want to see is in the **Ciudad Vieja**, squeezed into a labyrinth of winding streets beyond the **Plaza María Pita**, named for Galicia's national heroine who stood up to Drake. Along the sea here you can see the lovely row of 'crystal galleries' (Avenida de la Marina) facing the busy fish harbour. At the upper end of the street you're only a block away from the Ciudad's prettiest square, the **Plaza de Azcarraga** and the city's best Romanesque church, the 12th-century **Santiago**; for pilgrims who sailed to La Coruña, it was their first stop; over one door Santiago Matamoros cuts down the Moors at Clavijo. Another Romanesque church stands nearby at the top of the plaza, just up Calle Damas: the 12th-century basilica of **Santa María de Campo**. Sir John Moore was buried in the shady little **Parque de San Carlos** off the Paseo del Parrote; some of the famous verses on his burial by Rev. Charles Wolfe, as well as stanzas in Gallego by Rosalia de Castro are engraved on the gate by the mirador overlooking the old harbour, its ancient walls, and the **Castillo de San Anton** (16th century), now home to the **Provincial Museum**, with a good archaeological collection with artefacts from the Celts, Romans, and other early folk (open 10–2 pm and in the summer also from 6–8 pm, closed Mondays). The Ciudad Vieja also has most of La Coruña's busy nightlife, a demi-monde of sailors and summer beachcombers; no wonder old British seadogs nicknamed it 'the Groyne'.

La Coruña is most proud of its **Torre de Hercules**, claimed to be the only extant Roman lighthouse in the world. It's located on the northernmost tip of the peninsula (bus no. 9 passes close by), but actually looks more like its 1791 restoration than the Roman original. Though it's still used as a lighthouse, you can climb to the top for the view (10 am–1 pm and 4 pm till twilight, closed Sundays). La Coruña's beaches are across the isthmus from the Ciudad Vieja: the **Playa de Riazor** is the most popular; quieter and cleaner and prettier strands are outside the city at **Mera** and **Lorbe** (14 km (8.8 miles) and 16 km (10 miles), respectively).

West of La Coruña

Both the scenery and the waves are dramatic. The Spaniards, who have recently given us the Costa del Sol and the Costa Blanca, long ago dubbed this region down to Finisterra **La Costa de la Muerte**: 'Death Coast'. Not surprisingly the region is full of Celtic memories; from the end of the western land Celtic warriors would sail out to their reward in the seven-towered castle of Arianhrod. Some of Galicia's best dolmens are to be seen around **Malpica, Corme** and **Laxe**, all tiny fishing villages. Malpica was an old whaling-port and has a nice, secluded beach and a dolmen called the **Pedra de Arca**; the islets of Sisargas nearby are a major nursery for seagulls. Corme and Laxe share a small *ría*, and both have fine town beaches. Laxe can also boast a Romanesque church of Santiago and two intriguing dolmens on the road to Bayo, 5 km (3.1 miles) inland towards the main road: signs point the way to the **Dolmen of Dombate** and the scant but ancient remains of **Borneiro**, a Celtic city founded in the 6th century BC. The best dolmen is the **Pedra Cuberta** another kilometre to the south, with a 6.2 m (20 ft) chamber.

After some very rugged coast, the rocks relent to admit another *ría* shared by the remote fishing hamlets of **Camariñas** and **Muxia**; from little, white Camariñas you can walk up to Cape Villano, wild piece of country, which makes you feel small and that civilization is far away. Muxia is a bit more important, attested by the escutcheons on some of the houses, it is also the holy city of the Costa de la Muerte, with the pilgrimage church of **Nuestra Señora de la Barca**, built in the 17th century, though the magic powers of healing attributed to the two huge boulders on the way are far older. Both Camarinãs and Muxia are renowned for their extraordinary lace.

Corcubión is a fine little town on one of the prettiest, narrowest *rías* and near one of Galicia's best beaches, the **Playa de Ezardo**; behind it the Río Xallas tumbles down a cliff in a charming waterfall feeding two pools that many people prefer to the colder waters of the Atlantic. There's another beach on the other side of Corcubión, **Langosteira** on the way to the tiny villages of **Finsterra** and beyond it, Cape Finisterra, the world's end, where pilgrims from Santiago frequently came to gaze at the sea and contemplate the legends of an ancient city sunk beneath the waves. The cape is also the official boundary between the Rías altas and bajas.

The Ría de Muros y Noya

The Rías Bajas almost at once have tamer, greener scenery than their wild cousins to the north. These less exposed *rías* can, however, get a bit dirty if you swim at the innermost coves; if that's the case, try a beach closer to the sea. Both **Muros** and **Noya** are fine, old fashioned Gallego towns with good beaches and a small number of tourist facilities, mostly at Noya. Muros is the prettier of the two, with its narrow lanes and arcaded buildings stacked under its Gothic parish church. This contains a startling Crucifix found in the sea, with long, flowing hair that is said to grow. There are good beaches at **Louro**, 1.6 km (1 mile) from Muros on the tip of the estuary, and at **Carnota**, which also claims Galicia's largest **horréo**, over 30 m (100 ft) long, and made entirely of granite.

Noya was named for Noah, whose dove is said to have found the olive branch here – a scene depicted on the city's coat-of-arms – while his ark found a solid base to anchor on the holy Celtic mountain **Barbanza** just to the south. This local Mt Ararat is adorned with numerous dolmens (see below) and in Noya itself you can visit the mysterious cemetery next to the 14th-century **Santa María de Noya** where local guildsmen in the Middle Ages had their headstones carved with symbols far more Celtic and pagan than Christian. Some of the 200 stones have symbols and designs relating to the trades of the deceased, and others are a total enigma to those who have studied them. Noya also has a medieval **bridge** and another church worth a visit, **San Martín**, an early 15th-century temple with a good rose window carved into its fortresslike façade, and fine carving on the portal. There are many fine beaches within striking distance of Noya – **Boa Grande, Avilleira** and **Area do Coido** among the best.

From **Oleiros** (or **La Puebla**, if you approach from the south) you can walk or drive up to the Mirador on Monte Barbanza, for great views from Cape Finisterra to Vigo on a clear day, and to an extraordinary dolmen, **Anxeitos** – an enormous rock supported on top of eight smaller ones. **Padrón**, capital of midget green peppers, is the ancient *Iria Flavia*, the legendary port where the followers of Santiago disembarked with their precious cargo. Its modern name means 'memorial pillar' and the stone pillar to which the stone boat was moored is displayed in the 17th century **Church of Santiago**. The legend tells that the boat was met by a pagan queen, who mockingly gave the disciples two wild bulls to transport the coffin. Miraculously, the bulls when yoked turned into peaceful oxen. Padrón was the town where the poet Rosalia de Castro was born, the illegitimate daughter of a priest, and here she unhappily married, had six children, wrote beautiful poetry and died young of cancer; her house, the **Pazo de Retén**, is now a museum. The bridge over the Río Ulla to Puentecesures was built by Master Mateo.

The **Ría de Arosa** is the most developed resort of the Rías. The main town here is **Villagarcia**, though on the whole **Cambados** is a better base for beach-hopping, facing the **Isla de la Toja**, a beach-rimmed, pine-clad islet united to land by bridge from **El Grove**. La Toja and El Grove are major resorts, La Toja, with its casino and fancy sports complex, for people with bags of money and El Grove for those who don't, but know how to have a good time. Many people consider the **Playa de la Lanzada**, 4 km (2.5 miles) from El Grove, to be Galicia's finest beach; the Celtic cure for sterility was for a woman to take nine dips into its sea. There are two smaller sheltered beaches on the **island of Arosa** in the middle of the *ría*.

TOURIST INFORMATION

La Coruña: Darsena de la Marina, Tel. 22 18 22, Post office: Alcalde Manuel Casas, a few blocks from the tourist office: telephones: San Andres 101.

Villagarcia: Plaza de la Revolla.

WHERE TO STAY

La Coruña fills up in the summer despite its many hotels, so you'll want to arrive early or call ahead. The best-located and most luxurious hotel in the city, **Finisterre******, Paseo del Parrote, Tel: 20 54 00, overlooks the sea in the Ciudad Vieja and has a pool, tennis courts, a nursery and children's pool and playground; its air-conditioned doubles are 7000 pts in season, 5300 pts otherwise. The **Riazor*****, Av. Barrio de la Maza, Tel: 25 34 00 has a fine beachside location and modern rooms for 3200–4200 pts. Also near the beach, the **Mar del Plata****, Paseo de Ronda 58, Tel: 25 79 62 has pleasant doubles with bath for 1815–2700 pts, without 1375–2200 pts. There are quite a few cheaper places in the Ciudad Vieja, especially along C. Riego Agua, a block behind the tourist office.

From La Coruña to Camariñas the only rooms are over bars or in private houses; you'll have to ask around. In Camariñas there are three small *hostales*: **La Marina***, M. Freijó 4, Tel: 73 60 30 is nearest the sea (doubles without bath 1400–1700 pts; there's a good restaurant downstairs (800 pts). Corcubión's **El Horreo*****, Santa Isabel, Tel: 74 55 00 is the largest and most pretentious hotel in the Rías Altas outside the cities; it has a pool and garden and is beautifully located near the sea (doubles 3200–4100 pts, open all year round). The more typical **Casa Pachin***, Av. Marina 4, Tel: 74 50 18 is on the fishing port (doubles without bath 1200–1500 pts). Finsterra has a few tiny places to stay. Muros has three cheap *hostales* and several *fondas* – the nicest is **La Muradana***, Av. de la Marina, Tel: 82 68 85 near the sea (doubles 2360 pts; meals in its restaurant, 850 pts). In Noya there are more choices, but again they're all about the same. The **Ceboleiro****, Gral Franco 15, Tel: 82 95 31, stands out by having the best restaurant (1000 pts); its doubles are 2000–2500 pts with bath, 1400–1700 pts without.

Padrón, again, has a wide selection of places to stay, all about the same, though the **Casa Cuco****, Av. de Compostela, Tel: 81 05 11, has the most memorable name and doubles with bath 1800–2300 pts, without 1450–1700 pts. If you feel homesick for London, stay or eat at the **Rivera**, Enlace Parque 7, Tel: 81 04 13, whose owner and chef paid their dues in a big London hotel (doubles 2000–2400 pts with bath, 1700–2000 without; dinners around 1500 pts).

Villagarcía has a handful of places (**Cortegada***, V. Viquiera, Tel: 50 03 83; doubles 2000–2500 pts with bath). In Cambados you can lodge in an old country *pazo* (manor house) at the **Parador del Albariño*****, Paseo de Cervantes, Tel: 54 22 50 with a beautiful garden and a restaurant featuring seafood (doubles 5500–7000 pts, meals around 1800 pts). Most people, however, continue down to El Grove, where you can put on the ritz at the **Gran Hotel de La Toja*******, Isla la Toja, Tel: 73 00 25, with golf, tennis, a spa, heated pool and everything else in a very exclusive, park setting for 14,200 pts in the summer, and half as much in the winter. A solid, moderate beach hotel in El Grove, **El Besugo***, Gonzalez Besada 102, Tel: 73 07 87, on the road to Toja, offers simple, clean rooms with bath for 2500–3000 pts, also open all year round. **Casa Pepe** nearby at Gonzalez Besada 149, has good *mariscos* for 1400 pts.

EATING OUT

La Coruña can boast some fine seafood restaurants – one of the fun things to do is watch the auctioning of the catch, the *Muro*, a strange ritual featuring fast-talking Gallegos and fish you've never seen before. It takes place around 6 or 7 am by the marina. You can eat the fish later at the **Coral**, Estrella 5, in the Ciudad Vieja near the port, with exceptional shellfish (*mariscos*) for around 2500 pts, or the equally good *marisqueiria* **El Rápido** on Estrella 7, which also does Gallego specialities (2200 pts). **La Marina**, Av. de la Marina, offers solid fish and regional dishes for 800 pts, and you can eat for even less in **La Granja**, a popular spot in the Plaza Maria Pita (around 600 pts).

The main allure at Villagarcía is Galicia's most famous restaurant, **Chocolate**, located in nearby Villajuán, with divine grilled fish prepared by the flamboyant owner, and delicious everything else; the decor features many tributes to the restaurant from celebrities, and yet the prices are surprisingly modest – around 2200 pts.

Las Rías Bajas: Pontevedra to Tuy

Nothing to the south is as developed as the Ría Arosa, though the hotels fill up in the summer with vacationing Spaniards and Portuguese. The scenery is domesticated, green and pretty and the beaches usually safe for the kids.

GETTING AROUND

This section of the coast is well served by buses, and there are several trains daily between Pontevedra and Vigo and beyond. In Pontevedra the RENFE station (Tel: 85 13 13) and bus station (Tel: 85 19 61) are next to each other, but a long walk from the centre on C. Conde Gondomar; a municipal bus can take you into town. In Vigo the train station is at the top of Calle Alfonso XIII, a 15-minute walk uphill from the port (Tel: 43 11 14). Most of the buses (to Tuy, La Guardia, Bayona, Pontevedra, El Grove, Villagarcía and Santiago) depart from the C. Uruguay, a couple of blocks down from the train station, just off Alfonso XIII. If you have a long wait, you can get in a few frames at the bowling bar at the end of the street.

You can also go to Tuy by train, though the station's a mile away; buses go to the centre of town. If you want to make a few hours' trip to Valença in Portugal, you'll save time by walking; traffic jams and long waits at customs in trains often last over an hour.

Boats to Cangas (every half hour), Moaña (every hour) and the Islas Cies (six daily) depart from Vigo's Estación Maritimo near El Berbes (Tapores de Pasaje, Tel: 43 77 77). If you're coming in the summer, buy your ticket to the islands as soon as you arrive; by law only 2200 people a day can make the crossing and boats fill up fast. The same company offers night excursions. The other one offers a once-a-day trip to Isla Ons.

Pontevedra

Pontevedra, a provincial capital, is a traditional, granite Gallego town par excellence located on the beautiful Ría de Pontevedra, adorned with arcaded streets, pretty squares with stone crosses, and more Pekinese dogs than Beijing. According to ancient tradition, it was once known as *Helenes*, founded by Teucer (Teucro), a Greek warrior who fought at Troy (interestingly, *Teucro* means 'Trojan' in Spanish, and it seems more likely that the Teucro who founded the city was the son of Scamander and a nephew of Priam, who is said to have led a band of Cretans to western Spain and founded a colony. It's also curious that the city was named after Helen, the sister of the twins Castor and Pollux, the favourite gods of Roman warriors. The cult of the warrior twins continued to inspire the soldiers of the Reconquista in a half-buried tradition that asserts that James (Santiago) was the twin brother of Jesus.

Pontevedra's **Old Town** is compact, its monuments all within a stone's throw of the Plaza Orense in the middle of town, where old meets the new. Here is the 18th-century **Virgen Peregrina** church (the 'Virgin Pilgrim') built in the shape of a cockleshell to house an image of the city's patron. It was one of the few instances where the Virgin had any role at all to play in the pilgrimages (Pontevedra lies on the route from Portugal). On the other side of the plaza there's a lovely 16th-century fountain in a small garden and the 14th-century **San Francisco** with some good tombs. From here, Calle Pasanteria descends to Pontevedra's most perfect little granite square, the **Plaza de Leña**, with an ancient cross as its centrepiece. On one side you'll find the **Museo Provincial**, one of the best in Galicia, with the best collection of jet figures from Santiago, prehistoric gold work, ancient headstones, paintings and sculpture (open 11 am–1 pm and 5–8 pm, closed Sunday pm). The museum's lapidary collection is in the 14th-century **Convento de Santo Domingo** in the Alameda; here too stands the **Basilica Menor de Santa María**, constructed in the 16th century by the local Seafarers' Guild, with a Plateresque façade by Cornelis of Holland. There are some pretty 'crystal galleries' on the **Plaza Teucro**; just below, where Calle Isabel II intersects with four other streets, there's a fine stone cross portraying Adam, Eve and the serpent – the numerous *tapas* bars in the vicinity are also tempting.

Around Pontevedra

A short way to the north, **Combarro** is worth the trip for the unique view of its *horréos* lined up along the shores of the *ría*. Made of granite, they stand on pillars to protect the grain from rodents, and vents like tiny windows permit air to circulate within. In the middle of the *ría* is the tiny **islet of Tambo**, where the body of Santa Trahamunda floated to in a stone boat from Córdoba. Further along, **Sangenjo** and its neighbour **Portonovo** are jumping little beach resorts, said to get more sun than the rest of Galicia. The southern shore of the *ría* is spoiled by a paper mill, often brewing an intolerable stink that reaches Pontevedra itself when the wind is up. Some 15 km (9.4 miles) further down is **Bueu**, a sleepy fishing-village and a great base from which to explore the surrounding undeveloped beaches. **Hio**, overlooking the **ría de Vigo**, boasts Galicia's most beautiful and elaborate stone crucifix, portraying the Descent from the Cross. From **Cangas** or **Moaña** (with an excellent beach) you can take the ferry across the ría de Vigo to Vigo city, an enchanting approach that takes all of 10 minutes.

Vigo

Spain's premier fishing port, Vigo occupies a privileged hillside spot on its own *ría*, protected from the winds by the Cies islets. It attracted ancient Phoenician and Greek seamen and the Romans called it *Vicus Spacorum*. The city likes to refer to an early 12th-century troubador, Martin Codex, as its founder; in his poems he speaks of waiting for his love among the other lovers bathing in Vigo. The city's history is full of unwanted English visits; two by Sir Francis Drake (1585 and 1589) and in 1702, when the English surprised a joint Spanish and French treasure fleet just returned from the New World, in the Battle of Bande. The English captured some of the ships but 11 were sunk (sources suggest the silver had already been unloaded, but it hasn't stopped treasure-seekers from looking). Today one of the greatest treasures of the ría de Vigo are mussels, which are grown on long ropes hung from wooden platforms stationed in the inner reaches of the estuary.

There's not much to see in Vigo. The old part of town, with rough, cobbled streets and granite arcades, called the **Barrio del Berbés** hugs the fishing port and is an atmospheric place for a stroll. As in La Coruña, there's a lively fish auction by the waterside here early in the morning; if you've had a rough night you can pick up a dozen oysters for a song in the **Rua da Pescaderia** morning market. The **Calle Real** has some noblemen's palaces. Head up to the **Parque del Castro** at the top of the city for a great view of the *ría* from the modern monument to the Galeones de Rande: the Celts had their settlement in this commanding position. The municipal museum is in the 17th century **Pazo de Castralos** on the south western edge of town, in the pretty **Parque Quiñones de Leon** with geometric gardens. The museum contains antique furniture, folklore paintings, local history, all beautifully displayed (Tuesday–Saturday 10 am–7 pm Sundays 10 am–1 pm).

The best thing to do is go for a swim, either at the city's beach **Playa Samil**, across the *ría* to Moaña or better yet, take a picnic out to the **Islas Cies** with their fine beaches and crystal waters, or sail beyond them to the **Islas Ons** near the ría de Pontevedra.

Bayona, down the coast, is a fine, small resort, topped by the walls of the 18th-century **Castillo de Monterreal**, with a pretty village in between and lovely beaches down below with soft sand, like **Ladeira, Santa Maria** and **America**. Just to the south of town you can be awed by a huge granite sculpture of 1910, the **Virgen de la Roca** (ancient rock worship dies hard). Wild horses have a free rein in the hills here, rounded up once a year in a *rapa das Bestas*, when Gallego cowboys tame them, run a race or two, and let them go again. In **Oya** there's a ruined 13th-century monastery.

La Guardia, at the mouth of the Río Miño, is worth a visit for the well-excavated Celtic castro up on **Monte Tecla**, a 40-minute walk up from the village. This is one of the most important *citanias* in Spain, inhabited from the 7th century BC up to the Roman period. Some of the huts have been reconstructed on the site, others are mere foundations, linked by cobbled lanes and encircled by walls. Further up there's a cromlech and a small **archaeological museum**, where you can learn about the strange carving discovered on the site, believed to be a map; if true, it would be one of the oldest ever found in the West. From the top of Monte Tecla there are fine views over the Valley of the Miño into Portugal. The nearest beach is at **Camposancos**, 3.2 km (2 miles) from La Guardia.

Tuy

For once it must be said that a frontier town is worth visiting in its own right. Tuy is a pleasant little place upon its 'acropolis' – like Pontevedra it has a tradition of ancient Greek foundation. Known as Tude in the Middle Ages, it was the capital of the Visigoth Witiza in 700, and has seen many battles since then. The wide and wooded Río Miño, that flows between Spain and Portugal, is Galicia's prettiest river.

The **Cathedral of San Télmo** with its powerful walls and keep, looks like a castle from the distance, and it was one, until the 13th century. Construction began in 1120 and though it wasn't completed until much later, the stone has mellowed into a kind of grey, vertical garden of wild flowers. It has a finely carved Romanesque porch and Gothic doorway; be sure to note the lovely but strange coat-of-arms carved on the side wall, with five stars and a crescent moon, rather feebly said to symbolize the burning of the town by Al-Mansur. The interior is also heavily fortified (against earthquakes); it contains the remains of San Telmo (died 1240), the patron saint of Spanish sailors; their British counterparts called him St Elmo and hoped for his mysterious fire to light on their masts, igniting even their finger-tips without burning them – an excellent omen. For a great panorama over the Río Miño, climb the tower of Alfonso VII.

The town itself is the main attraction, though **Santo Domingo** (1415) is worth a visit, especially for its finely carved effigies on the tombs. In half an hour you can walk from the centre of Tuy to the lovely Portuguese walled town of **Valença do Minho**, crossing an iron bridge built by Eiffel. The views from Valença to Tuy are lovely, as is the town – even though it's blanketed in bright towels, which Spaniards flock over to purchase. The Portuguese, on the other hand, come to Tuy for salt cod and plastic toys.

TOURIST INFORMATION

Pontevedra: General Mola 1, Tel: 85 08 14.

Vigo: in the undulating concrete pavilion at the Estación Maritimo (Tel: 21 30 57).

Tuy: on the road to Valença (Tel: 60 07 57)

WHERE TO STAY AND EAT

In Pontevedra, the **Parador Casa del Barón*****, Maceda, Tel: 85 58 00 offers a chance to live in a Gallego *pazo*, this one with a magnificent stone stair and a garden; doubles are 5500–6500 pts; meals in its good restaurant are around 1800 pts. Other than that, Pontevedra has relatively few hotels, and even *fondas* are on the scarce side – Calle Charino and other streets in the old town are good places to seek them out. The **Madrid***, Andres Mellado 11, Tel: 85 10 06 is near the centre, but the rooms are on the dingy side (1400–1550 pts with bath, 1300 without).

There's lots more choice in Sangenjo, though nearly all of these are open only from June to September. One exception to this is the **Panadeira***, on the Playo de Panadeira, Tel: 72 37 28, a friendly little establishment in a pretty spot (doubles with bath 2000–4000 pts). If you're driving, you can conveniently stay in a *pazo* in the vicinity, the **Pazo El Revel**** in Vilalonga, Tel: 74 30 00, which offers tennis and a pool as well as a dose of old Gallego life (doubles with bath 5200 pts, open mid-June to mid-September). Open during the same period, **La Playa**, Avda. Generalismo 36, Tel: 72 00 15, is a nice bargain on the beach for 2300 pts a double with bath, 2000 pts without.

Vigo is Galicia's cheap hotel capital, though you can luxuriate on the beach in the **Samil Playa******, Tel: 23 25 30, with a pool, tennis and cosy rooms for 4500–7500 pts. Otherwise, you may as well stay in the port at the pleasant **Estoril***, Lepanto 12, Tel: 21 56 28, where a double with bath is 2500 pts, without 2000 pts, or the **Argentina***, Lepanto 8, Tel: 22 20 25, adequate doubles with bath for 1400–1700 pts, or near the train station at the grandmotherly **Colonial***, Alfonso XIII 65, Tel: 43 55 79, where a double is 2500 pts with bath, 2000 pts without.

There is a cafe but no hotel on the Cies islands and a campsite with limited spaces.

Bayona has the **Parador Conde de Gondomar******, Galicia's finest, housed in a *pazo* within the walls of Monterreal, in a lovely park (Tel: 35 50 00); it offers a pool, tennis, children's recreation, and a short walk to the beach (doubles 6500–9000 pts). **Tres Carabelas***, Ventura Misa 72, Tel: 35 54 41, is a fine old inn in the middle of town (open all year; doubles with bath 2400–3500 pts).

In La Guardia you can stay near the top of Monte Tecla in the **Pazo Santa Tecla***, Tel: 61 00 02, open June–September; doubles 2200–2500 pts.

In Tuy you can enjoy views over the Miño in the **Parador San Telmo***, 1 km (0.6 mile) below the town centre, Tel: 60 03 09, located in a small castle (doubles 5000–7000 pts. Near the Cathedral, there are rooms above the restaurant **O Cabalo Furado**, the most popular in Tuy, where you can dine on eels and other good things for around 800 pts. The **Hostal Generosa***, Calvo Sotelo 37, Tel: 60 00 55, has fine rooms upstairs for 1200–1600 pts without bath, near the bus stop.

EATING OUT

Besides the bars along C. Isabel II, a good place to dine in Pontevedra is the long-established **Calixto**, Benito Corbal 14 (just outside the old town), with Gallego specialities for 1500 pts. In Sangenjo restaurants line the Playa de la Lanzada.

For seafood or roast leg of lamb, the people's choice in Vigo is **El Mosquito**, Pl. de Villavicencio 4 (near the port), with prices around 1500 pts. **Sibaris**, another good seafood place is on Garcia Barnón 168. At **El Castillo**, Monte del Casto, you can dine with a superb view; grilled seafood and meat are the specialities (1700 pts). At **Pepe**, near the port on Av. Montero Rios, the seafood is around 600–900 pts. Shellfish and *pimientos de Padrón* are the specialities served at **El Moscón** in Bayona on A. Barreiro 2. If you have a car, there's a very good restaurant, **Casa Delmiro** on the La Guardia road from Tuy, featuring creative Gallego cuisine (1600 pts).

Orense

Another provincial capital further down the Río Miño, **Orense** was named by the Romans for its unusual steaming hot springs, *Aquae Urentes*, now known as Las Burgas. If it's a cool day you can see the water rising in a cloud of steam in the *fountain* near the Ayuntamiento in the Plaza Mayor and elsewhere in the city. The locals have invented a hundred uses for the hot water – if you stick a chicken in it, they say, you can pluck it in only two minutes.

GETTING AROUND

Orense is the main hub here, with trains to Santiago, Lugo, La Coruña, Vigo, Ribadavia, Zamora, León and the rest of Spain. The RENFE station in Orense is on C. Peña Trevinca (Tel: 21 10 64), a 10-minute walk from the Pl. Mayor; tickets also on sale at Juan XXIII, Tel: 24 12 01. There's no central bus station: the tourist office has a list of all the various companies and their termini for destinations mentioned above; buses for Celanova and Santa Comba de Bande depart from Ervedelo 80 (Tel: 22 52 88); for Allariz and Verin, from Reza 21 (Tel: 22 42 38). For Ribadavia: Avda. Saénz Diaz, Tel: 24 26 26.

WHAT TO SEE

The oddest page in Orense's history was when it served for several months as John of Gaunt's capital in 1386–7, during his attempt to claim the throne of Castile. Its oddest attraction is the Santisimo Cristo in the **Cathedral**, also in the Plaza Mayor. Similar to the crucifix in Burgos, it has real hair and beard and a wood and fabric body; according to legend it was made by Nicodemus and found in the sea near Finisterra. The cathedral itself is another imitation of Compostela cathedral, with a 13th-century painted reproduction of Santiago's great Portico de la Gloria, here the **Portical del Paraiso**, which impresses more if you haven't yet seen the original, other Romanesque carving in and around the chapels is more original. There's a **museum** in the 13th-century remains of the cloister, with one of the first books printed in Galicia and the 'Treasure of San Rosendo' – chess pieces carved of rock crystal in the 10th century (open daily 11 am–1 pm and 4.30–6.30 pm, Sunday pm only). The prettiest thing in Orense is its graceful **old bridge**, with seven ojival arches high above the Miño, emerging from Roman bases.

East of Orense the mountains are high enough for a ski resort, **Manzaneda** near **Puebla de Trives**. Along the Portuguese frontier, if you're entering Galicia from Zamora, you may want to stop in **Verín**, the chief village of the Monterrey Valley; high up on one side of the valley looms the **Castle of Monterrey**, built in the 16th century, part of it converted into a parador. **Allariz** is closer to Orense with a Romanesque church of **Santiago** and **Convento de Santa Clara**, founded by the wife of Alfonso X.

Another excursion from Orense is into the south to **Celanova** a town especially noted for its **Plaza Mayor**, with the vast **Bendictine monastery of San Salvador** on one side and its **church**, also on the plaza, with an ornate façade of 1681, two elegant cloisters, and in the garden at the back, a simple Mozarabic jewel, the **chapel of San Miguel** (940). Inside the church there's a particularly good *retablo* and fine carvings on the choirs. 16 km (10 miles) further south, **Bande** is known for its Visigothic church (actually 10 km (6.3 miles) further south) of **Santa Comba**, overlooking a reservoir. The church was built around the year 700, with a Byzantine plan, and is remarkably well-preserved, with its Corinthian marble columns supporting a horseshoe arch. West of Orense, along the banks of the Miño is the famous wine-growing region of **Ribeiro**, where the chief town is the charming **Ribadavia**, typically Galician with its granite houses, arcaded streets, a beautiful **Plaza Mayor** and three interesting churches, the ruins of its walls and towers, and bars where you can taste the local brew. Be sure to walk up the hill to the **Calvario**, with its three granite crosses, overlooking a cluster of *horréos*.

TOURIST INFORMATION

Orense: Curros Enriquez 1, Tel: 23 47 17.

WHERE TO STAY AND EAT

The local ritz is a new hotel near the old part of Orense, **San Martín****** (Curros Enriquez 1, Tel: 23 56 11), its air-conditioned doubles for 4715–5555 pts. A quiet choice near the centre, the **Parque*** (Parque de San Lazaro 24, Tel: 23 36 11) looks onto greenery and offers doubles, all with bath, for 3000 pts. Less expensive choices lurk around the station, or there's the **Orensano*** on the main Gen. Franco 89, Tel: 22 00 07, where you can get a double and a bath for 1100–1400 pts, or stay dirty for 900–1000 pts.

Up at the ski resort of Manzaneda above Puebla de Trives, the **Queiza**** is open all year, Tel: 31 08 75, offering a heated pool, tennis, children's activities and more (doubles 2700–3850 pts). In Verin, the **Parador de Monterrey*****, Tel: 41 00 75, is located next to the 13th-century castle, with lovely views of the valley below (doubles 5000–6500 pts); its restaurant (1800 pts) has seafood and other Gallego treats. Down in Verín, you can look up the same hill from the **Dos Hermanas***, Avda de Sousas 106, Tel: 41 02 80 (doubles with bath 1500 pts, without 1100 pts); good food is served at the **Gallego**, L. Espada 24 (800 pts). There are many other choices in the valley, and a couple at remote little Viana del Bollo (**Somoza***, Gral. Franco 82, Tel: 34 01 22, with a pool and doubles for 1200–1500 pts with bath, 1000–1200 pts without, just outside town).

In Celanova there are simple rooms with bath at **Betanzos***, in C. E. Ferreiro 7, Tel: 45 00 11, open all year (2300 pts). The pleasant **Evencio*** in Ribadavia (Av. R. Valcarcel 30, Tel: 47 10 45) has a swimming-pool and garden to delight its guests, and the village's best restaurant (1675–1900 pts, meals around 750 pts).

EATING OUT

Orense makes up for its nondescript hotels with one of Galicia's best restaurants, **San Miguel** on San Miguel 12–14, specializing in seafood fresh from the coast and masterfully prepared, and Galicia's finest wines (2400 pts). There are two other good choices on the same street: **Carroleiro** with more seafood (1600 pts) and **Pingallo**, with solid Gallego homecooking (700 pts).

WHERE TO SKI

Manzaneda offers 10 different courses of all degrees of difficulty, served by a chair lift and four other ski lifts. Besides the Queixa hotel, there are three others nearby. For information, Tel: 31 08 75.

Part IX

CASTILLA Y LEÓN

San Lorenzo, Sahagún

The modern autonomous region of Castile and León encompasses the ancient kingdoms of Spain and the *meseta* – the great plateau ringed by the mountains of various sierras – a flat land of wheatfields that tends to get too hot in the summer and bitterly cold in the winter. Yet here was born a culture, language, and people who would dominate in their day not only the nations of Iberia, but a good part of two continents. Even today Burgos, seat of the first counts of Castile (so named for the forest of castles erected during the Reconquista) is the headquarters of all that is pure Castilian or *castizo*, down to proper pronunciation of the name of Castile's greatest hero, 'El Theed' (the Cid), who helped win much of the meseta from the Moors.

The region has three magnificent attractions in its cities of León, Burgos and Salamanca; Valladolid and Zamora have fine, unusual churches. And yet the most beautiful corners of Castile are rarely visited, especially by foreign tourists – the whole province of Soria is perhaps Spain's best-kept secret. The Southern part of Salamanca has its own little sierra and hamlets straight out of the Middle Ages, while western León is endowed with lovely, seldom visited valleys and bizarre landscapes. In between are picturesque little towns that have been collecting dust since Charles V sucked them dry in the 16th century, and others that have changed little since the last pilgrims wended their way west to Compostela. Note that we've included Segovia and Avila (part of Old Castile) in the chapter 'Around Madrid' since they are easiest reached, and possible day-trips, from the capital.

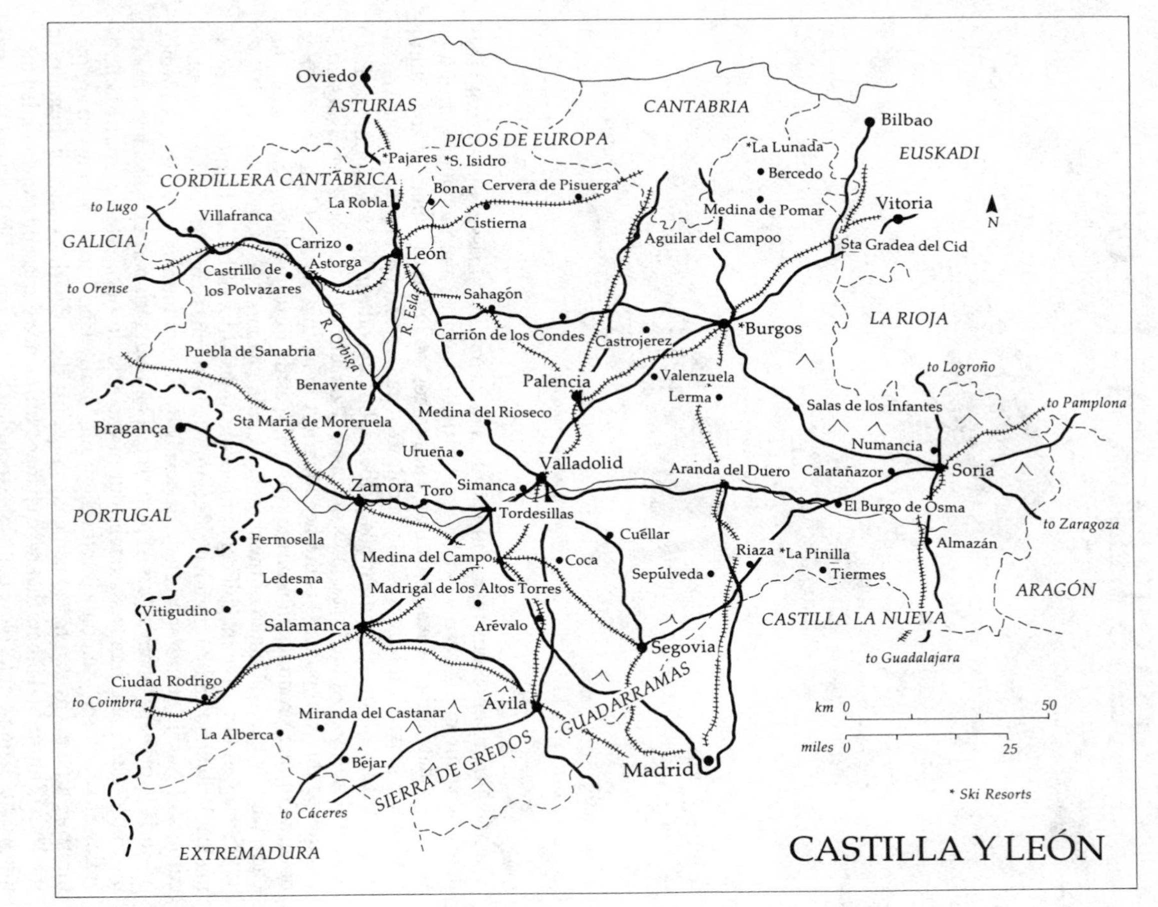
CASTILLA Y LEÓN
Oviedo
ASTURIAS
CANTABRIA
Bilbao
EUSKADI
PICOS DE EUROPA
*Pajares
*S. Isidro
*La Lunada
Bercedo
CORDILLERA CANTÁBRICA
Bonar
Cervera de Pisuerga
Medina de Pomar
Vitoria
to Lugo
La Robla
Villafranca
Cistierna
Aguilar del Campoo
Sta Gradea del Cid
GALICIA
Carrizo
León
Castrillo de los Polvazares
Astorga
to Orense
Sahagón
R. Esla
R. Orbiga
*Burgos
LA RIOJA
Carrión de los Condes
Castrojerez
Puebla de Sanabria
Palencia
Valenzuela
to Logroño
Benavente
Lerma
Medina del Rioseco
Salas de los Infantes
to Pamplona
Bragança
Sta Maria de Moreruela
Numancia
Urueña
Valladolid
Aranda del Duero
Calatañazor
Soria
Zamora
Toro
Simanca
Tordesillas
El Burgo de Osma
PORTUGAL
to Zaragoza
Cuéllar
Fermosella
Almazán
Medina del Campo
Coca
Riaza
*La Pinilla
Ledesma
Sepúlveda
Tiermes
Madrigal de los Altos Torres
ARAGÓN
Vitigudino
CASTILLA LA NUEVA
Salamanca
Arévalo
Segovia
to Guadalajara
Ciudad Rodrigo
GUADARRAMAS
to Coimbra
Ávila
km 0 50
Miranda del Castanar
La Alberca
miles 0 25
Béjar
Madrid
SIERRA DE GREDOS
* Ski Resorts
to Cáceres
EXTREMADURA

LEÓN

Radiant under the famous spires of its cathedral, León is a singularly happy city of clean boulevards shaded by horse-chestnut trees, one of the few places in Spain to achieve *urbanización* with grace and elegance. Part of the credit for this must go to its hyperactive Ayuntamiento (City Hall), which blankets the city with posters depicting itself as a friendly lion, advising the Leonese to ride the bus, recycle their glass, and not to use swear words in front of the children.

Although the lion has long been the city's symbol, its name actually comes from the Roman *Legio Septima*, from the days when the Seventh Legion guarded the plain. After reconquering it from the Moors, the kings of Asturias moved their capital here (913), and it became the main base for the reconquest of Castile. But as León eclipsed Asturias, Castile – first a county, then a separate kingdom as the Reconquest progressed – eclipsed León, and by the 13th century the kings of León y Castilla were spending a lot of their time elsewhere. Medieval pilgrims looked forward eagerly to León, with its Hilton of a *hostal*, where they could shake the dust off their wide-brimmed hats and catch their breath for the last leg of their journey. León has had little influence since then, though it has its share of modern autonomy atavists whose political slogan is '*León sin Castilla*' (León without Castile). As yet their movement has little support – it's too much like a mother rejecting her own child.

GETTING AROUND

León's main thoroughfare crosses the Río Bernesga to meet the RENFE station on Calle Astorga, Tel: 22 37 04; the central ticket office is on the Travesía Roa de la Vega 1, Tel: 22 26 25. There are frequent connections with Burgos, Palencia, Medina del Campo, Avila, El Escorial and Madrid; another train goes to Oviedo and Gijón nine times day through some magnificent mountain scenery and at least 500 tunnels. A third line to Galicia passes through Astorga and Ponferrada on its way to El Ferrol and La Coruña.

Buses depart from the terminal on C. de Cardenal Lorenzana to Astorga, Ponferrada, Oviedo, Valladolid, Burgos, Santander, Salamanca, and Madrid.

For something different and marvellously scenic, take the FEVE train to Bilbao from León's station on Avda. del Padre Isla; the one daily train leaves León at 8.50 am, stops for a half-hour lunch at Mataporquera near the Picos de Europa and arrives at Bilbao at 7.12 pm, stopping everywhere in between. For information in León, Tel: 22 59 19.

The Cathedral

The Spaniards call this, the most splendid articulation of Gothic in Spain, '*La Pulchra Leonina*' ('Belle of León'). Even if it were in France, where the style was born, León Cathedral would be remarkable for its superb walls of stained glass – a like amount caused its closest rival in glass-acreage, Beauvais, to collapse, a disaster León has avoided by adding greater support to the walls. Begun in 1205, the cathedral was built over the site of three earlier cathedrals as the exquisite symbol and culmination of the kingdom's golden age.

The magnificent **West Portal**, flanked by two lofty towers and crowned by a beauti-

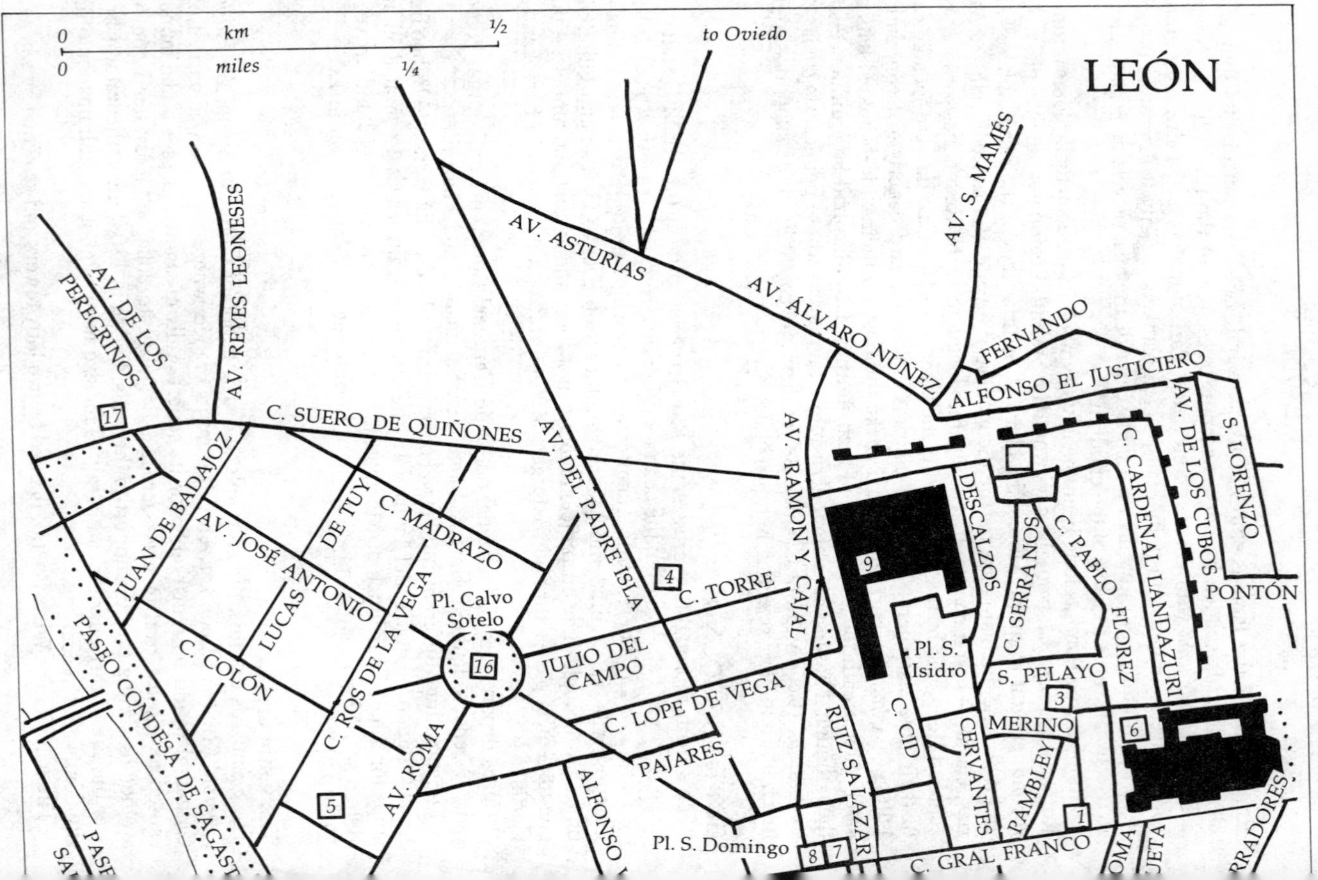
LEÓN
0 km ½
0 miles ¼
to Oviedo
AV. ASTURIAS
AV. S. MAMÉS
AV. ÁLVARO NÚÑEZ
FERNANDO
ALFONSO EL JUSTICIERO
AV. DE LOS CUBOS
S. LORENZO
PONTÓN
C. CARDENAL LANDAZURI
C. PABLO FLOREZ
C. SERRANOS
DESCALZOS
S. PELAYO
MERINO
PAMBLEY
CERVANTES
C. CID
Pl. S. Isidro
RUIZ SALAZAR
AV. RAMON Y CAJAL
C. GRAL FRANCO
Pl. S. Domingo
PAJARES
C. LOPE DE VEGA
JULIO DEL CAMPO
C. TORRE
AV. DEL PADRE ISLA
C. SUERO DE QUIÑONES
AV. REYES LEONESES
AV. DE LOS PEREGRINOS
JUAN DE BADAJOZ
AV. JOSÉ ANTONIO
DE TUY
C. MADRAZO
LUCAS
C. ROS DE LA VEGA
Pl. Calvo Sotelo
C. COLÓN
AV. ROMA
PASEO CONDESA DE SAGAST
1
3
4
5
6
7
8
9
16
17

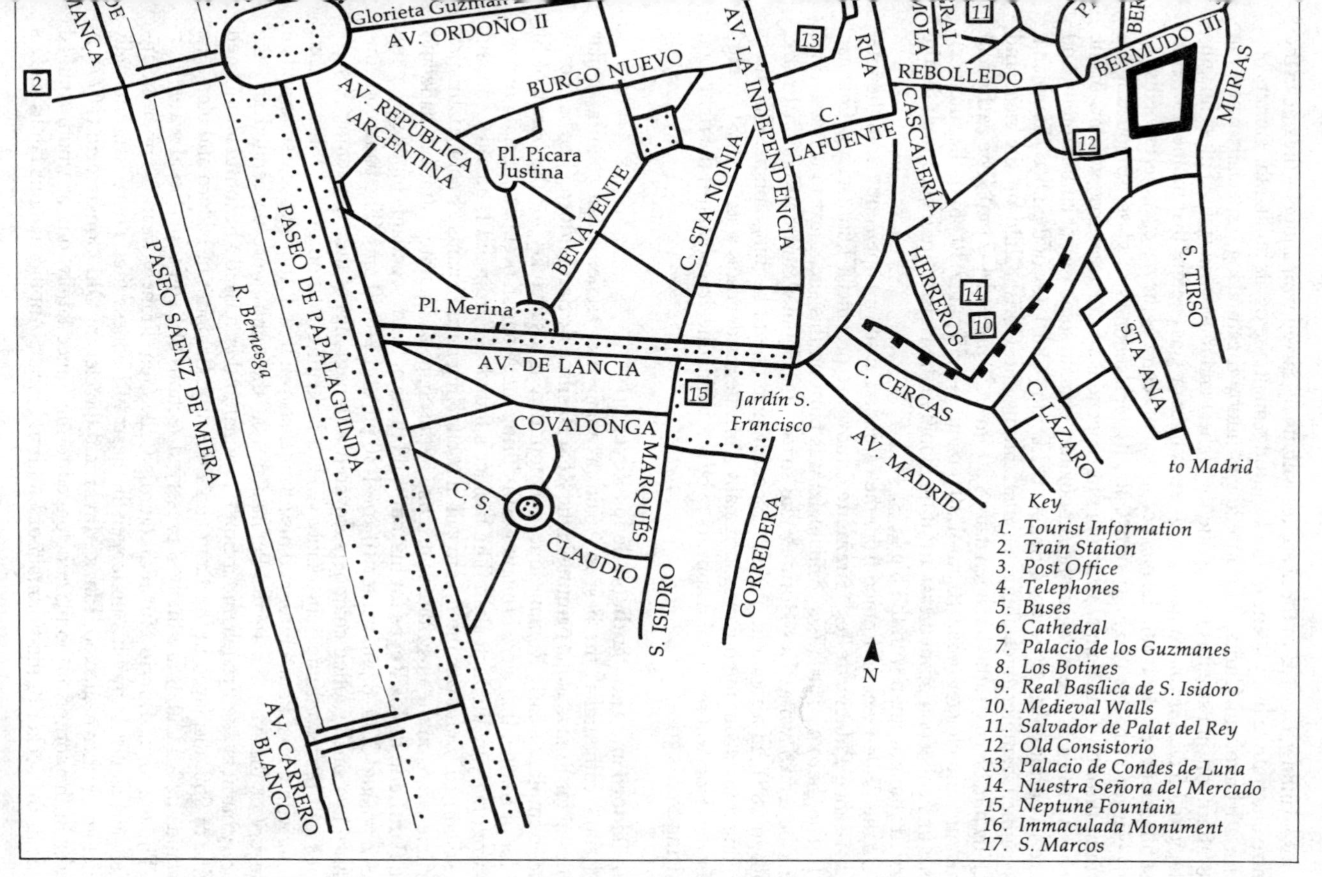

AV. ORDOÑO II
BURGO NUEVO
AV. REPÚBLICA ARGENTINA
Pl. Pícara Justina
BENAVENTE
C. STA NONIA
AV. LA INDEPENDENCIA
RUA
C. LAFUENTE
REBOLLEDO
CASCALERÍA
BERMUDO III
MURIAS
S. TIRSO
HERREROS
STA ANA
Pl. Merina
AV. DE LANCIA
PASEO DE PAPALAGUINDA
R. Bernesga
PASEO SÁENZ DE MIERA
AV. CARRERO BLANCO
COVADONGA
MARQUÉS
C. S.
CLAUDIO
S. ISIDRO
Jardín S. Francisco
CORREDERA
C. CERCAS
AV. MADRID
C. LÁZARO
to Madrid
N
Key
1. Tourist Information
2. Train Station
3. Post Office
4. Telephones
5. Buses
6. Cathedral
7. Palacio de los Guzmanes
8. Los Botines
9. Real Basílica de S. Isidoro
10. Medieval Walls
11. Salvador de Palat del Rey
12. Old Consistorio
13. Palacio de Condes de Luna
14. Nuestra Señora del Mercado
15. Neptune Fountain
16. Immaculada Monument
17. S. Marcos

ful rose window, consists of three arches with finely carved tympanums – the one in the centre illustrates a lively scene of the Last Judgement, the devils boiling the sinners beneath a triumphant Christ. The **interior** is utterly breathtaking, especially when the late-afternoon sun streams in to ignite the richest and most vivid stained glass imaginable; you'll feel as if you've never really seen light or glass before that moment when it first fills your eyes. As usual, the *coro* occupies the centre of the nave, and is embellished with elegant alabaster carvings; unusually, its midsection is of glass, so you can see straight through to the altar, swimming in reflections of the great rose window of the twelve Apostles. The chapels in the Ambulatory contain some very beautiful tombs, and there's a curious altar to Nuestra Señora del Dado ('Our Lady of the Dice') at which a disgruntled gambler once flung his dice, hitting the Christ Child on the nose and making him bleed (Cathedral open daily 8.30 am–1.30 pm and 4–7 pm). The **cathedral museum** and cloister (open 10 am–1.30 pm and 4–6.30 pm (7.30 pm in the summer)) has a fine collection of medieval art; if the doors in the cloister are locked, wait for the harried young woman with the big keys.

Up the Calle General Franco from the cathedral, a square opens out, with the fine, Renaissance **Palacio de les Guzmánes**, (now the provincial Diputación); Guzmán el Bueno, hero of Tarifa (see Andalucía) was born on this site. Next to it is a savings bank better known as **Les Botines** 'the spats'. It's Gaudí's most conventional work, built in 1891 'in a moment of doubt' according to one of his biographers. The most striking thing about the building, originally a private residence, is a statue of St George over the door, where the saint appears to be scratching the dragon in just the right spot, judging by his grin.

San Isidoro and the Pantheon de los Reyes

If León's cathedral is the best in Spain, as many may argue, it can claim a similar pedestal for Romanesque painting in the **Real Basilica de San Isidoro**. The basilica, a fine example, of early Romanesque, was founded as a sanctuary for the bones of St Isidor of Seville, that were brought north during the Moorish occupation, and are now in a reliquary by the high altar. The basilica's founder, Ferdinand I, united León and Castile in 1037 and was the first to call himself 'King of the Spains'. Feeling Christian fortunes were on the upswing, he had one of the chapels (separate entrance) made into the **Pantheon de los Reyes** for his tomb and those of his descendants (open summer 9 am–2 pm and 3.30–8 pm, winter 10 am–1.30 pm and 4–6.30 pm). The pantheon consists of two small vaulted chambers, covered with paintings of the 12th century, amazingly well preserved and remarkably vivid, a brilliant evocation of the Middle Ages. Along with Christ Pantocrator and his Evangelists you'll find Apocalyptic visions and an allegory of the Months. In the Peninsular War the tombs were desecrated and the library burnt by the French under Soult; fortunately they missed a beautiful illuminated Bible of 960, displayed in the Pantheon's treasury. Behind San Isidoro and along the Avenida de los Cubos are the best preserved sections of León's **medieval walls**.

The old town, **Barrio Húmedo** (across Calle Gen. Franco) wears a rather melancholy air, as if it knows it's no longer the heart of Leonese life. There's an unusually quiet and rather neglected, **Plaza Mayor** and the elegant **Old Consistorio** (1677). A tower in the corner of the plaza belonged to the Ponce family, one of whom attained fame as the seeker of the Fountain of Youth in Florida. Another famous family had its *solar* just south of the Plaza Santo Domingo, the 14th-century **Palace of the Condes de Luna**, of which only the tower and fine façade remain. The Romanesque and recently restored, **Nuestra Señora del Mercado** (open 11 am–12 noon and 7–8 pm) is on the pretty Plaza del Mercado.

San Marcos

León's third great monument lies at the end of the shady, riverside garden along the Paseo Condesa de Sagasta. **San Marcos** is one of Spain's most beautiful luxury hotels but in the 12th century admittance was free to pilgrims on the French road; this was a Monastery of the Order of the Knights of Santiago, founded originally for the pilgrims' protection. In the 16th century, when pilgrims were few and the Knights devoted to their own pleasure and status, the monastery was rebuilt with a lovely Plateresque façade, lined with a frieze of busts and the door topped by Santiago the Moor-slayer. Next to it, the **Church of San Marcos** with its cockleshell façade is Gothic and still in use, but its fine Chapterhouse and sacristry contain the **Provincial Archaeology Museum** (open 10 am–12 noon and 4–6 pm, closed Monday and Sunday pm). Its most prized exhibition is an 11th-century ivory Christ; there are also mementoes of the Roman Seventh Legion, and in one hall artefacts discovered in a **Punic** necropolis near the Maragato village of Santa Colomba de Somozo – a key discovery in unravelling the origins of the mysterious Maragatos (see below).

TOURIST INFORMATION

Plaza de Regla 4, across from the Cathedral, Tel: 23 70 82. Post office is on the same plaza; telephones, C. de la Torre 13.

WHERE TO STAY

The **Hotel de San Marcos*******, Pl. San Marcos 7, Tel: 23 73 00, is not only one of Spain's best hotels, it is a veritable antiques museum in its public rooms – even the bedrooms are furnished with unique pieces. Double rooms are 10,000 pts; its lordly restaurant specializes in meat dishes (2000 pts). A solid second choice is the very modern **Quindos****, Av. José Antonio 24, Tel: 23 62 00, where instead of antiques, the rooms are adorned with contemporary art (doubles 3550–3850 pts). Another moderate choice, the **Hotel Paris***, Generalísimo Franco 20, Tel: 23 86 00, is very near the cathedral, built into an old palace, though the rooms are modern. Doubles with bath are 2675–2805 pts, without bath 1935–2045 pts. Cheap *hostales* abound – one of the most pleasant is the **Hostal Oviedo***, Avda. Roma 26, Tel: 22 22 36, just off the Glorieta Guzmán el Bueno, easy walking distance from the train station. Its doubles are 1500–1700 pts; there are only nine rooms, so you may want to book ahead.

WHERE TO EAT

León is equally endowed with good restaurants, many serving garlic soup and trout, the queen of the local cuisine. Both trout and salmon, cooked in a variety of styles, are the speciality at **Casa Pozo**, Arco de Animas 15 (near the Ayuntamiento, a block south of Pl. Santo Domingo), closed Sunday, 1600 pts. Plaza San Martín is the inexpensive restaurant headquarters; of the six to choose from, the 12th-century **Bodega Regia** is the most atmospheric; good Léonese cuisine as well (1400 pts). **Fornos**, C. del Cid 8, also serves trout and other good food in sizeable quantities – you feel as if you really get your 1100 pts worth for a full meal. In the Bario Húmedo, not far from the Pl. San Martin, **La Gitana** (C. de Azabacheria and Trav. de Sarniceria) has a lively local atmosphere and lots of fish; set menu for 775 pts.

Around León

GETTING AROUND

RENFE links Astorga and Ponferrada with León and Lugo and beyond, four times a day; the same train goes to Sahagún on its way to Palencia. Otherwise you'll have to rely on provincial buses; Astorga is the point of departure for La Maragatería; Ponferrada for El Bierzo; and León for the villages in the south. The Cueva de Valporquero is accessible only by private transport, although there are often excursions organized from León.

West of León

West of León lies two unusual regions: **La Maragatería**, the homeland of the Maragatos and **El Bierzo**, where the tabletop lands of the meseta give way to a unique mountainous region, with some of the province's prettiest wooded valleys and landscapes, distorted and eroded by Roman strip-mining for gold. The *Universal Route* to Santiago (nowadays more prosaically known as N-120 and the VI until Lugo) passed through both areas.

One of the bridges the pilgrims crossed, the 13th-century **Puente de Orbigo** still stands parallel to the N-120, 23 km (14.4 miles) from León; it is well preserved in a tranquil green setting. Things weren't so tranquil during July 1434, when one of the models for Cervantes' Don Quixote, Don Suero de Quiñones, and his nine companions challenged every passing knight (and there were many, for it was the jubilee of Santiago) to declare his lady the fairest. It is said 727 knights took up his challenge and of the 12 who were wounded, one died. This incident, the last hurrah of Spanish chivalric romance, has gone down in history as the 'Paso de Honor.'

Astorga and the Maragatos

Astorga is an ancient town and the 'capital' of the Maragatos where many still live, occasionally donning their unusual ancient costumes for fiesta dancing and baking their justly famous *mantecadas*, available in every Astorga pastry shop. Otherwise they keep very much to themselves, marrying only other Maragatos, and if they've emigrated to Mexico, returning in the summer to be with their relatives. Until the advent of the railway, they were famous as muleteers and carriers, transporting nearly all the goods between Castile and Galicia, a line of work forced on them by their stubborn, almost uncultivatable land; indeed, their name has been traced back to the Latin 'mercator', or merchant.

For decades scholars from many branches of study have been trying to discover who the Maragatos are and where they came from. A common belief held that they were Berbers who came over in the 8th century and managed to hold on to this enclave after converting to Christianity. This belief, however, has been called into question by Dr Julio Carro, who in the late 1950s discovered a Punic necropolis near the village of Santa Colomba de Somoza west of Astorga – an unusual find, because the Phoenicians were sailors and León isn't exactly on the coast. Even more unusual was his discovery of figurines nearly identical to those found at Punic sites in Ibiza and dressed in a style very similar to the Maragato's traditional costumes. Carro's conclusion, based on his discoveries and on elements in Maragato culture was that the Maragato are the descendants of Phoenicians and Asturians enslaved by the Romans to work the great gold mines of El Bierzo. The Maragatos themselves agree, and to thank Carro for discovering their true origins, they put up a stone plaque to him in the village Quintanilla de Somoza.

Unless you're lucky, you won't see the Maragatos of Astorga in their old costumes, apart from the two figures that bang the hour atop the attractive 17th-century **Ayuntamiento**. Another Maragato ornament, a weathercock named Pedro Mato, crowns the **Cathedral**, on the north-east edge of town. Begun in the 14th century, the cathedral is a melange of styles and is best known for its *retablo*, in marble high relief, by Gaspar Becerra, a pupil of Michaelangelo. The **Museo Diocesano** (open daily 10 am–2 pm and 4–8 pm) is worth a visit, with its fine collection of early Romanesque artwork – including a casket of gold and silver (10th century) that belonged to Alfonso III.

Next to the cathedral stands the **Palacio Episcopal**, a work begun by Gaudí in 1887 but completed by other hands; Gaudí refused to finish it after his friend, the bishop who had commissioned the work, died. It isn't vintage Gaudí, but it's more representative of his work than the Casa Botines in León built like a pale castle, complete with a moat and pointed towers, with an interesting sloping front. These days it serves as the **Museo de los Caminos** (Museum of the Pilgrimage Routes, same hours and ticket as the Museo Diocesano) containing an interesting collection of pilgrimage paraphernalia, maps of the routes, Roman remains, and more.

From Astorga you can take a bus to **Castrillo de los Polvares** (just off the Pilgrimage Route) considered the finest of Maragato villages, with its street built wide for the passing of mule trains. It is a bit of a tourist destination, especially for Spaniards, for whom the Maragatos have a legendary quality; sometimes the very unusual wedding ceremony of the residents is performed for visitors. Less popularized Maragato villages are **Santa Colomba de Somoza** and **Rabanal del Camino**, both further west.

El Bierzo

In the old days the Romans dug for gold here; the modern Leonese extract the iron and cobalt. El Bierzo has bleak little mining towns, scenic vineyards, charming old villages ancient hermitages – its isolation attracted anchorites early on. **Ponferrada** is the largest town of El Bierzo, and sums up the regions split personality, part of it mine-blackened and shabby, the other half medievally pretty. The town's name, 'iron bridge', comes from an 11th-century bridge with iron balustrades, erected over the Río Sil for the pilgrims. On the east bank of the Sil stands Ponferrada's proudest monument, the

Castle of the Templars, though its fairy-tale gate and towers were added after the Templars in the 14th century.

Ponferrada is the base for exploring the best of El Bierzo. South of town, the Oza river winds through the beautiful **Valle del Silencio**, once home of many hermits and the 10th-century saint Genadio, who founded the Mozarabic **Church of Santiago** in the tiny medieval hamlet of **Santiago de Peñalba** at the head of the valley. To the south-west, **Carucedo** is the point of departure for an unusual hike through an ancient ecological ruin, **Las Médulas**. To extract the gold here, the Romans dug canals – one over 40 km (25 miles) long – to wash and erode the earth away; the left-over tailings were piled up by thousands of slaves over a couple of centuries, creating a bizarre landscape resembling a jagged spinal cord. You can clamber through the ancient canals and surreal caves – an eerie, haunted place.

After Ponferrada the pilgrimage route entered the Valley of Bierzo, a shallow depression that once held a lake, now crisscrossed by trout streams. The largest town here, **Villafranca del Bierzo**, was a French foundation. Here Pilgrims too weary or ill to continue down the last leg to Compostela could achieve the same indulgences at the Puerta del Perdón of the 12th-century **Church of Santiago**, which has recently been restored. Villafranca itself is a charming town, with many other old churches and palaces – **Calle del Agua** is an especially lovely street; the church of **San Francisco** has a pretty *artesonado* ceiling. **Corullón** near by has two more lovely Romanesque churches, **San Miguel** and **San Esteban**, the former adorned with many typically Romanesque funny faces. Walk up to Corullón's ivy-smothered **castle** for an excellent view of the valley. North of here is another lovely region, the **Ancares Leoneses**, with a wild-life and hunting reserve.

North of León

One of Spain's best caves, the **Cueva de Valporquero** lies 46 km (28.8 miles) north of León (open 10 am–2 pm and 4–8 pm tours). No paintings here, but a 3 km (1.9 miles) gallery with little lakes, esplanades, a stalactite 'cemetery', chamber of wonders, etc. (bring your non-skid shoes). The cave is up in the mountains – northern León encompasses the southern slopes of the Cordillera Cantabrica and the Picos de Europa (covered in 'Asturias'). The Leonese gateway to the Picos is **Riañe**, from where you can visit the **Valle de Valdeón** and **Valle de Sajambre**. Another beauty spot is the **Puerto de Pajares** (1379 m: 4524 ft), the lofty pass in the Cordillera Cantabrica between León and Oviedo.

Southeast of León

Before reaching León, the *French Route* passed through **Mansilla de las Mulas** (which has preserved much of its 12th-century walls and towers). Just before Mansilla, a road bears north-east 5 km (8 miles) for **San Miguel de Escalada**, one of Spain's most unusual monasteries, founded in 913 by a certain Abad Adefonso and his companions, refugees from Córdoba, who were inspired by the horseshoe arches they saw back home – the chapels are horseshoes, as are the naves, the exterior gallery and the iconostasis. Fine carving adorns the capitals; the tower is from the 11th century.

The gracefully decaying town of **Sahagún**, another rest stop for pilgrims, was built around one of Spain's most important Benedictine monasteries, now a ruin, but a National Historical ruin; its beautiful portal now serves as a decorative city gate. Sahagún is famous for its two churches with towers rising from their crossings like amputated skyscrapers, **San Tirso**, a fine 12th-century brick church, recently restored, and the 13th-century **San Lorenzo**. Near the medieval bridge that crosses the Río Cea stands a grove of poplars which, according to the medieval pilgrims guide, the *Codex Calixtinus*, are the flowering lances of Charlemagne's paladins!

Off to the west, **Valencia de Don Juan** was named for its first duke, the son of Alfonso the Wise, and is worth a detour only for its picturesque Gothic **castle**, which rises from the banks from the banks of the Río Esla and is featured on all León's tourist brochures, with its dramatic Homage Tower outlined by four slender turrets. Also in the area is **Valderas**, a wine-producing region with curious bunker-like bodegas.

TOURIST INFORMATION

Astorga: Ayuntamiento, Plaza de España, Tel: 61 68 38.

Ponferrada: Avda. de la Puebla 1, Tel: 41 22 50.

Valencia de Don Juan: Ayuntamiento, Pl. del Generalísimo, Tel: 75 04 64.

WHERE TO STAY AND EAT

In Astorga, the **Hotel Gaudí*****, Eduardo de Castro 6, Tel: 61 56 54, is the finest place to stay, not far from the Cathedral; all rooms have TVs (doubles 3800–4100 pts). Its restaurant features several Maragato dishes and fish (1600 pts). **La Peseta****, Pl. San Bartolomé 3, Tel: 61 53 00, is pleasant and centrally located; its doubles with bath go for 2550–2800 pts; it also has a good restaurant, where you can sample wines of El Bierzo. A fine, inexpensive pension, **La Concha**, Gen. Mola 2, Tel: 61 61 59 has doubles with basin only for 1200 pts.

In Ponferrada, the largest and best-endowed hotel is **El Temple******, Avda. Portugal, Tel: 41 00 58, located in a former palace, with a swimming pool; its luxurious doubles are 4430–5075 pts. In the old town, the **Hostal Lisboa****, Jardines 3, Tel: 41 13 50 is small and well-run; doubles 1940 pts with bath, 1390 pts without. The best restaurant in Ponferrada, **Ballesteros** (Fueros de León 12) has trout and Bierzo wines for 1500 pts.

Villafranca del Bierzo is blessed with the **Parador de Villafranca del Bierzo*****, Avda. Calvo Sotelo, Tel: 54 01 75, not one of the chain's showcases, but more like a comfortable motel in a scenic locale; doubles 5000 pts; dinners 1800 pts. A fine little alternative (there really isn't much in between) is the **Ponterrey***, Dr. Arén 17, Tel: 54 00 75, with bathless doubles for 1200 pts; it has the village's fanciest restaurant next door (1200 pts).

There's an overpriced *hostal* in Mansilla de las Mulas; you'll get a getter deal down the road in Sahagún at the **Hostal Hospital Benedictina***, Bermejo Calderón, Tel: 78 00 78, located, as the name implies, in the former hospital; doubles 1350 pts with bath, 1100 pts without.

Palencia

Sooner or later the wanderer in Castile ends up in Palencia, a leading candidate in the non-descript provincial capital sweepstakes. Part of the blame (as usual) rests squarely on the shoulders of Charles V, who rubbed out the city's prospects in revenge for its role in the Comunero revolt. In 1185 Alfonso VIII founded Spain's first university in Palencia, but in 1239 it was removed to Salamanca. The one thing they couldn't take away is its Gothic **cathedral**, nicknamed 'La Bella Desconocida' ('the Unknown Beauty'), south of the central Plaza Mayor. Its main entrance has some fine carvings; within its prize artwork is an early 16th-century *retablo*. Its intriguing crypt (673) belonged to the original Visigothic church on this site. Be sure to note the clock in the transept, where a Lion and Knight strike the hours with gusto.

GETTING AROUND

Palencia is easy to leave: there are frequent trains to Burgos, Valladolid, Avila, Madrid and Santander (via Frómista and Aguilar de Campo); trains to León call at Paredes de Nava. Carrión de los Condes and Villalcázar de Sirga are connected by bus with Frómista and Palencia three times a day.

North of Palencia

On the rail line to Sahagún, **Paredes de Nava** was the birthplace of two early and very influencial Castilian artists, Pedro Berruguete, court painter to Ferdinand and Isabel, and his son Alonso, a pupil of Michelangelo (though not with brilliant results), who served as court painter to Charles V. A few of their paintings remain in Santa Eulalia, the town's main church; the rest were stolen in 1979. **Carrión de los Condes** is named for the river Carrión and not for putrefying nobility, though it can't be denied the Infantes de Carrión, who married the Cid's daughters, were genuinely rotten villains. You can see their tombs in the pretty Renaissance cloisters of **San Zoilo**, a Benedictine monastery by the river just outside town. There are two good Romanesque churches in town: **Santiago**, with its frieze of the Almighty and four evangelists and **Santa María del Camino**, its finely carved portal depicting the cruel Tribute of 100 Maidens that the Castilians had to send yearly to the Moors (probably because they had nothing else the Moors could possibly want). Carrión was a halt on the *Universal Route*, and during the great days of the pilgrimage, the town produced two men of genius: Rabbi Shem Tov Ardutiel (Sem Tob) who died in 1370, and the Marqués de Santillana (died 1458), the poet.

Another town on the route, **Villalcázar de Sirga** is 7 km (4.4 miles) away; in the Middle Ages it was a key Templar possession. The Knights, at the start of the 13th century, built its **Santa María la Blanca** to house the image of the Virgin to whom Alfonso the Wise dedicated his famous *Cantigas*. You can still see her, a little worse for wear, with her peasant features and headless child. The church contains the beautifully carved tombs of the Infante Don Felipe (son of Fernando III) and his wife, curiously gagged. Another rarity is the tomb of a Knight Templar, with his hawk and sleeping lion.

A third town on the Santiago road, **Frómista**, is famous for its finely restored Romanesque church, **San Martín**, founded in 1035 and a model example of the architectural style, with its eight-sided lantern.

In the northern part of Palencia province the scenery improves as you near the Cantabrian mountains. The chief settlement, **Aguilar de Campoo** has a number of picturesque, if decidedly leaning, medieval houses. More good Romanesque churches may be seen here: **St Cecilia**, at the foot of the ruined castle, and the **Colegiata de San Miguel**. According to legend, Bernardo del Carpio, the doughty warrior in *La Chanson de Roland* is buried in a cave near the Romanesque monastery of **Santa María la Real** (1213), 2.4 km (1.5 miles) west of Aguilar.

Another scenic town, **Cervera de Pisuerga** has a Gothic church, **Santa María del Castillo**, built on the medieval citadel; the town is the base for exploring the surrounding mountains, rivers, and reservoirs.

TOURIST INFORMATION

Palencia: Mayor 105, Tel: 74 00 68.

Frómista: Paseo Central.

Aguilar de Campoo: Pl. Mayor 32.

WHERE TO STAY

In Palencia **Rey Sancho de Castilla*****, Avda. Ponce de León, Tel: 72 53 00, offers the guest a number of diversions – swimming, tennis, TV, bingo – and as many activities for the children as well; pleasant doubles for 4500–5000 pts. **Hostal Emilio***, Mayor 53, Tel: 74 07 00, offers none of the above, though it's good enough for a night and is centrally located; doubles without bath are 1450–1700 pts.

The rest of the province isn't exactly overbrimming with hotels. There's one in Frómista, however, that's unique, the **Hosteria de Los Palmeros**, Pl. Mayor, Tel: 81 00 67, formerly served as a *hostal* for pilgrims, although the medieval has been seasoned with several styles since; furnished with a number of antiques, the ten rooms are complemented by a fine restaurant, with an *artesonado* ceiling. Doubles are 2200 pts; dinners around 1300 pts.

In Aguilar de Campoo, there's a scenic mountain hotel, **Valentin*****, Avda. Generalisimo 21, Tel: 12 21 25, in an elegant old building, with a garden and a good restaurant: doubles 3850–4700 pts. On the Pl. España you'll find a couple of inexpensive choices: the **Siglo XX***, no. 11, Tel: 12 29 00, offers bathless doubles for 1500 pts and average food for around 800 pts. In Cervera de Pisguera, up in the mountains near the manmade lakes and newborn rivers, is the **Parador Fuentes Carrionas*****, Tel: 87 00 75, a plush headquarters for nature-lovers; doubles are 5000–6500 pts; a good restaurant, as usual.

EATING OUT

Neither of the hotels in Palencia mentioned above has a restaurant, but there are two on Casado del Alisal: the elegant, **Lorenzo** at no. 10 features haute cuisine; among its specialities is *pisto* – creamed tomatoes, peppers, onions, etc (1600 pts). At no. 26, **Castilla Vieja** offers Castilian dishes for around 1000 pts.

In Villálcazar de Sirga, there's nowhere to spend the night but a charming old posada to have lunch in called the **Mesón Villasirga** on the main square, featuring baked suckling-pig with almonds for 1400 pts.

BURGOS

First it must be said that Burgos is a genteel and quite pleasant town, its river, the Arlanzón, so filled with frogs in the spring and early summer that they drown out the traffic with their croaking, and that the favourite promenade, the Paseo del Espolón, is one of Spain's prettiest, adorned with amazing topiary hedges. It also contains one of the greatest collections of Gothic art and monuments in Spain. Yet throughout much of its history, Burgos' role has been that of a stern, military camp, from the day of El Cid Campeador to Franco el Caudillo, who during the Civil War made Burgos his temporary capital, the city where, it was said, 'the very stones are Nationalist'. Here in 1970, Franco held the infamous Burgos trials in which 16 Basque Nationalists (two of them priests) were tried and after a hearing bordering on the scandalous, six were sentenced to death. Outraged world opinion convinced Franco to commute the sentences.

The Kingdom of Castile was born in Burgos, and it is fitting that the city itself began as a castle erected on the Moorish frontier in 884. By 926 the city took its first step away from Leonese rule, electing its own two judges; in 950, one of their successors, Fernán González, declared his independence as Count of Castile. His descendant, Fernando I, elevated the title to king and married the heiress of León. Burgos remained sole capital of Castile until 1087, when Alfonso VI moved to Toledo (one reason must have been to put some distance between himself and the overbearing Cid). After that the capital was sometimes one city, sometimes the other.

GETTING AROUND

This is easy in Burgos. Both trains and buses have their stations in easy walking distance of the centre: RENFE at Avda. Conde Guadalhorce, Tel: 20 35 60; tickets also dispensed from the office at Moneda 21, Tel: 20 91 31. Burgos is on the main rail line from Irún to Madrid (connections to Pamplone, Vitoria, Bilbao, Valladolid etc); less frequent links with Zaragoza, Palencia, León, and La Coruña; also to Salamanca, Barcelona, Málaga, Madrid, Córdoba and Vigo on various *talgos*. The bus terminal is on C. Miranda, across the river from the Arco de Sta María, Tel: 20 55 75; there are daily buses to León, Santander, Madrid, Soria, San Sebastián and the province.

WHAT TO SEE

Burgos' glistening white, fairy-tale front door, the **Arco de Santa María** was originally part of the medieval walls, but after the Comunero revolt it was embellished to appease Charles V; the Emperor himself is portrayed in the Burgos Pantheon, which includes the first judges, Fernán González, and the Cid. Directly behind it loom the great spires of the Cathedral, to some viewers, transparent conduits of light, to others, ungainly oil derricks.

The Cathedral

Along with León and Toledo, Burgos is one of Spain's greatest Gothic cathedrals. Yet while León has an instant, sublime appeal, Burgos' power lies in its awesome number of masterworks and details from the tiniest carving in the choir stalls to its beautiful star-vaulted domes.

In 1221, in honour of his marriage with Beatrice of Swabia, Fernando III (the saint) and the English bishop Maurice laid the first cornerstone. The first portal to be finished, the upper-level **Puerta Alta de la Coronería** (1257) is the most interesting, with its Apostles, Almighty, and a peculiar row of mere mortals in between. The door is never opened; Burgos is prey to a biting wind in the late afternoon, and the cross-current would blow the congregation away. From up here, though, you can get a good view of the forest of spires, especially on the lantern, adorned with scores of figures. Three generations of the Colonia family devoted itself to moulding the soft grey stone of Burgos into the cathedral's intricate towers and pinnacles. At night they are illuminated, along with the Arco de Santa María for a dazzling tour de force.

The main, **West Façade** incorporates two Stars of David, a reminder that more than one of Burgos' bishops hailed from a Jewish family, as did the city's greatest sculptors, Diego and Gil de Siloé, the undisputed masters of Isabelline Gothic. One of Diego's masterpieces, the diamond-shaped **Golden Stair** (1523), is the most strikingly original feature of the interior, the perfectly proportioned solution to the Puerta Alta, 7.7 m (25 ft) above the floor of the cathedral.

Of all Spanish cathedrals, the *coro* of Burgos is the most self-contained, almost entirely shut off from the rest of the church. You can peer through the grill work to see the magnificent gold-trimmed star vault of the **lantern** which Philip II declared couldn't have been built by men, but by angels. Underneath its celestial beauty a simple slab marks the **tomb of the Cid and his wife Jimena**, their bones relocated here with great pomp in 1921. The other tomb in the *coro* belongs to Bishop Maurice, topped by his enamelled copper effigy; try to get in to see the magnificent carving on the wood and inlaid stalls – unabashed pagan figures on the seats, New Testament scenes above. They were done by Philip Vigarni, who also sculpted the dramatic scene on the ambulatory behind the main altar.

The side chapels are as magnificent as the main church. First, to the right as you enter, is the plainest but most venerated, the glass-doored **Capilla del Santo Cristo**, where ladies in mantillas gather to worship one of the strangest cult idols any religion has ever conjured up – the 13th-century Cristo de Burgos, a figure made of old buffalo hide (long-reputed to be human skin), real hair and fingernails (according to an old tale, both trimmed every few days) dressed in a red skirt and warm to the touch. Nearly as famous is the 15th-century mechanical clock across the nave near the roof, the **Papamoscas** ('fly-catcher') a grinning devil who pops out of a hole in the wall to strike the hour. The second chapel from the Papamoscas, **Santa Ana**, has a retablo of Jesus' family tree by Gil de Siloé and a fine Bishop's tomb by his son Diego. The most magnificent chapel, the great octagonal **Chapel of the High Constable of Castile**, was built by Simon de Colonia for Pedro Hernández de Velasco in 1486, whose tomb, accompanied by that of his wife, Doña Mencía de Mendoza, faces the elaborate altar by Vigarni and Diego de Siloé. The Constable, the head of the Castilian army, clutches his sword even after death; his lady's little dog sleeps at her feet. Velasco was Constable during the war in Granada, whose Moorish craftsmen inspired the great, geometric star-vaulting that crowns the chapel. The sacristy of the chapel is a chest full of trinkets

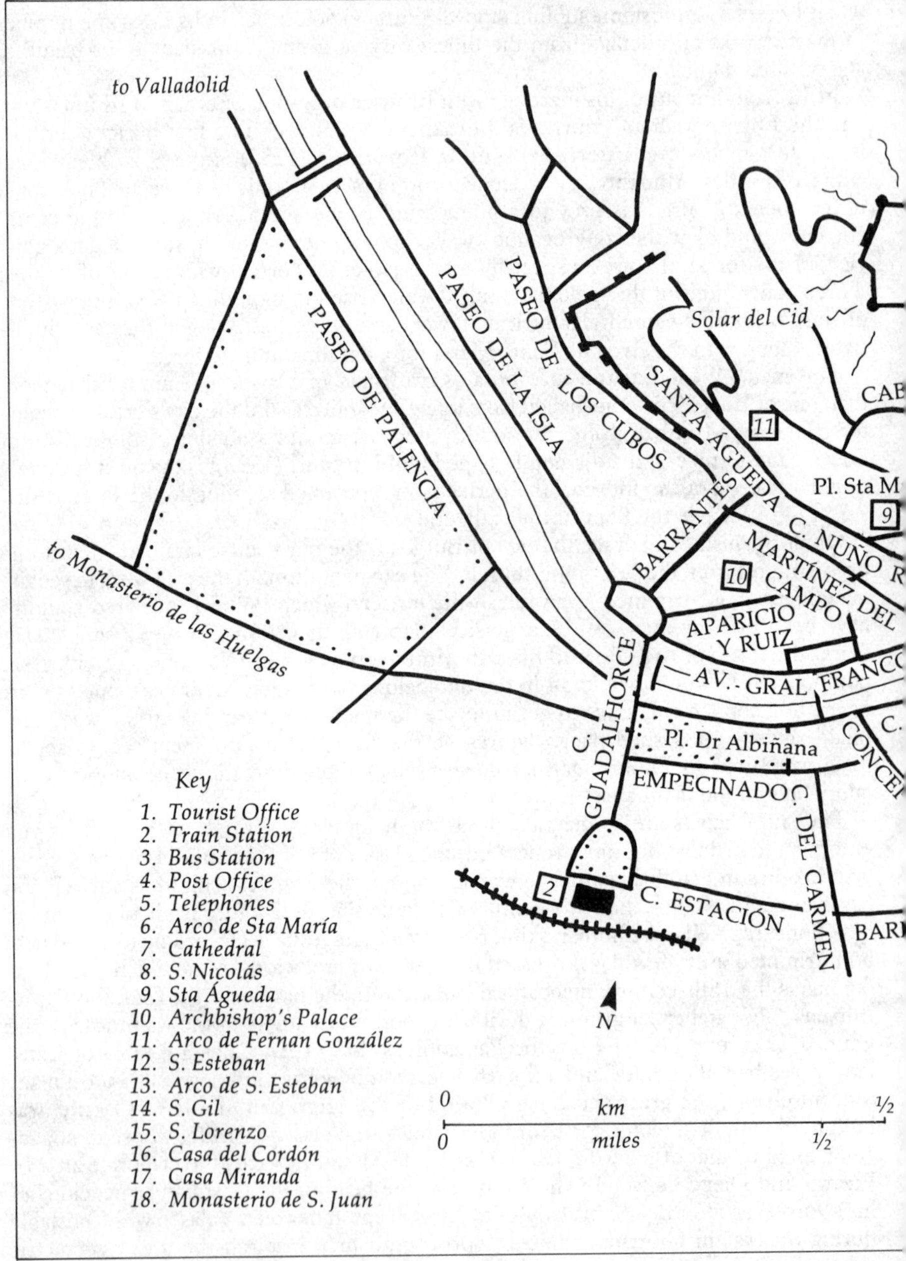

to Valladolid
to Monasterio de las Huelgas
PASEO DE PALENCIA
PASEO DE LA ISLA
PASEO DE LOS CUBOS
Solar del Cid
SANTA ÁGUEDA
BARRANTES
C. NUÑO R
MARTÍNEZ DEL CAMPO
Pl. Sta M
APARICIO Y RUIZ
AV.- GRAL FRANCO
C. GUADALHORCE
Pl. Dr Albiñana
EMPECINADO
C. DEL CARMEN
C. ESTACIÓN
CONCE
BAR
CAB
11
9
10
2
N
0
km
½
0
miles
½
Key
1. Tourist Office
2. Train Station
3. Bus Station
4. Post Office
5. Telephones
6. Arco de Sta María
7. Cathedral
8. S. Nicolás
9. Sta Águeda
10. Archbishop's Palace
11. Arco de Fernan González
12. S. Esteban
13. Arco de S. Esteban
14. S. Gil
15. S. Lorenzo
16. Casa del Cordón
17. Casa Miranda
18. Monasterio de S. Juan

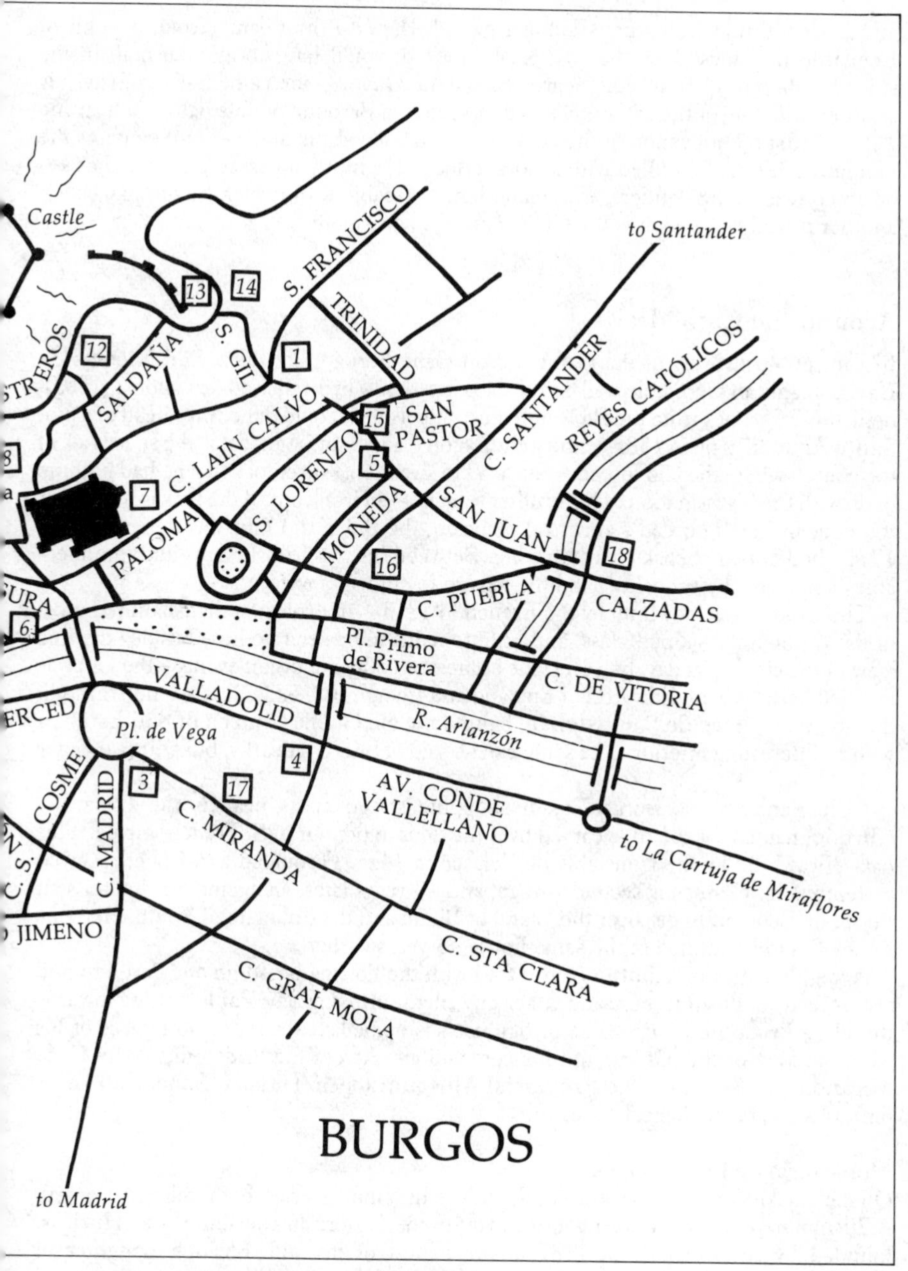
Castle
to Santander
S. FRANCISCO
TRINIDAD
SALDAÑA
S. GIL
C. LAIN CALVO
SAN PASTOR
C. SANTANDER
REYES CATÓLICOS
S. LORENZO
MONEDA
SAN JUAN
PALOMA
C. PUEBLA
CALZADAS
Pl. Primo de Rivera
C. DE VITORIA
VALLADOLID
R. Arlanzón
Pl. de Vega
AV. CONDE VALLELLANO
to La Cartuja de Miraflores
COSME
C. MADRID
C. MIRANDA
C. STA CLARA
C. GRAL MOLA
BURGOS
to Madrid
1
3
4
5
6
7
8
12
13
14
15
16
17
18

and a wonderfully voluptuous auburn-haired *Magdalen* by Giampetrino, a pupil of Leonardo da Vinci. The chest is usually locked; you'll have to ask the man in the souvenir shop to open it. The nearby **Sacristia Mayor** – the cathedral's sacristy – is adorned with one of the cathedral's lighter scenes, a Baroque bubble bath of a heaven.

The **Museo Diocesano** in the cloisters (open 9 am–1 pm and 3–7 pm) contains the famous coffer the Cid filled with sand and locked tight, then passed off as gold as security to two money-lenders, who made him a sizeable loan (which he did pay back); another prized possession is the Cid's marriage agreement.

Around the Cathedral

Just to the north-west of the Cathedral on Calle Fernán González, **San Nicolas de Bari** contains an incredible wall-sized alabaster *retablo* by Francisco de Colonia (1505), depicting 36 scenes from the Bible and more angels than could dance on a head of a pin. **Santa Agueda**, a plain 15th-century church on Calle Santa Aguada, is the successor of the church where the Cid forced Alfonso VI to swear on a silver lock that he had nothing to do with the assassination of his brother Sancho – an iron copy of the lock is hung over the door inside. The Cid's ancestral mansion, the **Solar del Cid** was demolished in 1771, though two obelisks mark the site. Between his two banishments and innumerable campaigns, he probably had little leisure to enjoy it anyway.

The **Castle** was blown up by the French in 1813 – an explosion that shattered most of the Cathedral's stained glass, and little remains to be seen up here besides the fine view of the city. In its day, however, the castle saw many important events – the Cid was married here, as were Edward I of England and Leonor of Castile. It is reached through the horseshoe **Arco de San Esteban**, behind the old Gothic **Church of San Esteban** with an interesting interior. The same can be said of **San Gil** nearby, built 40 years later in 1399.

Calle Santander is Burgos' main shopping street; at its head is the **Casa del Cordón**, named for the rope carved over the door in honour of St Francis' girdle. This palace was built by the Constable de Velasco in 1485. Ferdinand and Isabel received Columbus here after his second voyage, and 18 years later, an ageing Ferdinand sent Ponce de León off to discover the Island of Binini and the Fountain of Youth. His son-in-law Philip I had died in the same house six years earlier.

A mighty equestrian **statue of the Cid** with the flowing beard no one dared to pull seems ready to fly off its base and attack any enemy crossing **San Pablo bridge** towards the Plaza Primo de Rivera. The bridge itself is embellished with stone figures of his wife, the king of the Moors, and his companions. Across the bridge the lovely **Casa Miranda** (1545) houses the **Provincial Museum** (open Tuesday–Sunday 10 am–1 pm) with an archaeological collection.

Monasterio de Las Huelgas

On the outskirts of Burgos lie two of Spain's richest monasteries, both well worth a visit. A 20-minute walk to the west will take you to the Cistercian convent of Las Huelgas, founded by Alfonso VIII in 1187 at the behest of his wife Eleanor, daughter of England's Henry II. The abbess of Las Huelgas enjoyed more power and influence than any woman in Spain except the Queen herself, until her powers were revoked in the 19th century. In 1219 Saint Fernando III started the custom of Castilian kings of going to Las Huelgas to be knighted into the Order of Santiago – not by any inferior, mind you, but by Santiago himself; a statue was made of the saint holding out a sword especially for the purpose. Guided tours (in Spanish) are run Tuesday–Saturday 11 am–2 pm and 4–6 pm, Sundays 11 am–2 pm, and take you through the English Gothic church: statues of Alfonso VIII and Eleanor kneel before the altar, and there's a curious painted iron pulpit that gyrated to allow the priest to address the choir or congregation. The church also serves as a royal Pantheon of Castilian kings and royal ladies. The French, as usual, desecrated the tombs, though the one they missed, that of Alfonso X's son Fernando de la Cerda, produced such a fine collection of goods as to form the nucleus of Las Huelgas' **Museo de Ricas Telas**, a fascinating collection of fabrics and medieval dress, showing considerable Eastern influences. These are not the only Moorish touches in Las Huelgas: note the Geometric tomb of the Infanta Doña Blanca, the peacock and stars in the **Mudejár cloister**, and the **Capilla de Santiago**. The grandest chamber, the **Sala Capitular**, contains a trophy from Alfonso VIII's great Battle of Las Navas – the beautiful silk flap of the Moorish commander's tent – as well as Don Juan's banner from Lepanto, which he later gave to his daughter Ana, abbess of Las Huelgas. If the guide's in a good mood, he'll play a scale on the well-tuned columns in the halls.

Noble and wealthy pilgrims would receive a fair welcome at Las Huelgas, but Alfonso VIII also built the **Hospital del Rey** for the needs of poor pilgrims. Most impressive here are the 16th-century Plateresque gateway and the court.

La Cartuja de Miraflores

Burgos' second great monastery is a half hour's walk to the east, through a lovely park of shady trees. **Miraflores** (open 10 am–3 pm and 4–6 pm, Sunday 11.15 am–12.30 pm, 1–3 pm and 4–6 pm) was founded by Juan II in 1441 and is still used as such, so you can see only the church, built by the Colonia family; yet this alone contains more great art than many a cathedral. Here Isabel la Católica commissioned the great Gil de Siloé to sculpt the **Tomb of Juan II and Isabel of Portugal** as a memorial to her parents, and after four years of steady work he created the most elaborately detailed tomb of all time, 'imprisoning Death inside an alabaster star' as a local guidebook poetically put it. Instead of a chisel, it looks as if Siloé used an alabaster needle to sew the gorgeous alabaster robes of the effigies – Juan pensive, his wife reading a book. Isabel owed her succession primarily to death of her brother, and as a posthumous thank-you had Siloé carve his memorial as well. The **Tomb of the Infante Don Alfonso** portrays the young prince (1453–68) kneeling at prayer surrounded by a wonderfully playful menagerie of animals, putti and birds entwined in the vines. Master Siloé also did most of the gilt *retablo* of the high altar, said to be gilded with the gold Columbus presented to the Catholic kings at the Casa de Cordón.

There are other works of art: a lovely painting of the Annunciation by Pedro Berruguete, the carvings on the stalls of the laybrothers' choir (the middle section of the Carthusian church's traditional three divisions – the monks' choir is in the front, the general public in the back, by the painting of the Virgin sending the infernal spirits packing). In the side chapel there's a wooden polychrome **statue of St Bruno** carved by the Portuguese Manuel Pereira, so lifelike 'it would speak if it weren't a Carthusian monk' as the Burgoese like to say.

Below Miraflores and 10 km (6.3 miles) further down the road is the **Abbey of San Pedro de Cardeña**, founded in 899. Here the Cid left his family when banished by Alfonso VI, and here he requested to be buried by his wife Jimena. The French stole the bones from their tombs and when the Spanish government finally got them back it was to inter them in the more secure precincts of the Cathedral. Now a Trappist monastery, you can visit the original tombs with their effigies in a chapel off the **Cloister of Martyrs**, where 200 Benedictines were beheaded during a 10th-century Moorish raid. The Cid's faithful charger Babieca is buried just outside the gate.

TOURIST INFORMATION

Pl. de Alonso Martinez 7, Tel: 20 18 46.

WHERE TO STAY

Just outside Burgos on the Madrid road, the **Landa Palace*******, Tel: 20 63 43 is a memorable stay in a medieval tower, furnished with antiques, an indoor atrium and swimming-pool and beautiful rooms: doubles at 9900 pts. A meal in the Landa's equally palatial restaurant, the region's finest, will set you back some 3600 pts. In the centre of Burgos, the **Hotel Condestable******, Vitoria 8, Tel: 26 71 25, is the city's long-running traditional favourite in an elegant setting (doubles 4900–5600 pts). With even more reasonable charm and elegance in the middle of town is the **Hotel Norte y Londres**** on Pl. Alonso Martinez 10, Tel: 26 41 25, doubles with bath 2500–3200 pts. For fun you can stay near the river in the **Hilton**** Vitoria 165, Tel: 22 51 16, with doubles for 1850–2100 pts with bath, 1450–1700 pts without; it's situated near the park. The **Vitoria***, San Juan 3, Tel: 20 15 42 is nothing special but clean and priced right: 1200 pts a double.

EATING OUT

Burgos has quite a few restaurants. For medieval atmosphere in a 15th-century building, facing the Cathedral, and delicious, roast suckling-lamb, the **Mesón del Cid**, Pl. Santa Maria 8, is the place to go. The dining-rooms are on various levels throughout the building, which held one of Spain's first printing presses (around 1800 pts). Just inside the Arco de Santa Maria, the **Corral de los Infantes** offers Castilian specialities like *olla podrida* and 'medieval lentils' for 1100 pts; outdoor dining in the summer. The Chinese restaurant next door has *platos combinados* for 480 pts. **Gaona**, Virgen de la Paloma 41, near the cathedral, has Basque cooking; peppers stuffed with cod is a treat for 1400 pts. Near the statue of the Cid, the **Casa Alonso** offers good roast lamb for 900 pts. The most popular place in town, **Casa Ojeda** on Vitoria 5, has the best tapas in the bar and good local cuisine in its dining-room (around 1800 pts).

Burgos Province

GETTING AROUND

Miranda del Ebro is a major railway junction; all other destinations are linked with no great frequency by bus. Santo Domingo de Silos, off the main routes, is attainable only by car.

WHAT TO SEE

In the north, on the route to Bilbao, **Miranda de Ebro** is the major town, with little to see besides the glass balconies of its decrepit houses hanging over the river; to the west, however, **Frias** is an exceedingly picturesque village, with its unique **castle** spiralling up a rocky outcrop high above the medieval whitewashed 'hanging houses', similar to those of Cuenca. Far fewer tourists visit Frias, however, and if it's hot you can join the locals for a dip in the Ebro in the shadow of a medieval **bridge**, complete with a mighty gate. Another pretty town near Frias, **Medina del Pomar**, also boasts a powerful castle (both Frias and Medina belonged to the Velasco family, the hereditary Constables of Castile); Medina also has a fine early Gothic church with star-vaulting in the **Convent of Santa Clara**.

Frias

If you're following the *Pilgrimage Road*, there's little to see but quiet forests between Logroño and Burgos. There is a Romanesque church in **San Juan de Ortega**, where the titular saint is buried; like Santo Domingo, he was canonized for his assistance to pilgrims. An old hospital can be seen in **Villafranco**. Towards Palencia, there are interesting churches in **Castrojerez** and Santa María with a fine door in **Sasamón**.

Southeast towards Soria

This is the prettiest part of Burgos province. Off the main road (N-234) near **Quintanilla** there's a Visigothic church, **Nuestra Señora de las Viñas**, an unusual 7th-century basilica adorned with strips of beautiful relief. Within, carved on the capitals, the Visigoths attempted a bit of syncretism, identifying God with the sun and the Virgin with the moon. The church is a 4 km (2.5 mile) walk up from Quintanilla; inquire in the village about the key. **Covarrubias**, in the Arlanza valley, is a showcase medieval village linked with exploits of Count Fernán González, who is buried in a Roman sarcophagus in the 14th-century **Colegiata**; here too is a *Triptych of the Magi*, attributed to Gil de Siloé and a beautiful 17th-century organ. The tower guarding Covarrubia is named for Doña Urraca, the irrepressible daughter of Fernán González – who locked her in there.

Further south, **Santo Domingo de Silos** was founded by Fernán González in 919 and rebuilt after al-Mansur burned it to the ground. The glory of the monastery is the ground floor of its two-storey **cloister** was its magnificently carved capitals of the mid-12th century. The cloister's **Mudejár ceiling** has recently been restored (tours, Tuesday–Sunday 10 am–7 pm).

TOURIST INFORMATION

Miranda del Ebro: on the Madrid–Irún road.

WHERE TO STAY AND EAT

Unfortunately there are no places to stay in Frias, apart from a few rooms in private houses, but in Medina de Pomar you can chose from **Las Merindades*****, Pl. Somovilla, Tel: 11 08 22, located in a pretty, historical building with the village's best restaurant downstairs; doubles are 3600–3800 pts. **Hostal Madrugada***, Buen Conde de Haro 16, Tel: 11 03 30, offers simple doubles for 1100–1500 pts with baths, 1110–1300 pts without, and a set menu in its restaurant for 600 pts.

In the south, Covarrubias has a lovely associate-Parador in the **Arlanza*****, Pl. Mayor 11, Tel: 40 30 25 in a refurbished mansion (closed mid-November to mid-March; doubles 4250–3850 pts). The Arlanza's restaurant serves local dishes for 1200 pts. There are also a couple of places to stay in Sto Domingo de Silos: the **Tres Coronas*****, Pl. Mayor 6, Tel: 38 07 27, another inn located in a centuries-old building, its intimate 16 rooms 4000–4350 pts for double with bath; its restaurant, **Casa Emeterio**, features Castilian cuisine (1800 pts). **Hostal Amaya***, Pradera de San Juan, Tel: 38 07 94, also in Sto Domingo offers a roof, a bed, and heating in the winter for 930 pts a double.

VALLADOLID

Valladolid, sovereign of infirmity
The priest's early death, the maggot's Compostela

Such was the opinion of Guillem de la Gonagal, the 16th-century 'François Villon of Extremadura', said to have died in a brothel here in 1546. The judgement seems harsh for a city that has experienced so much of Spain's history and culture. Philip II was born in Valladolid, and Columbus died here in 1506, impoverished and almost forgotten. Valladolid was twice capital of Spain, and Cervantes wrote the first part of *Don Quixote* in a little house on Calle del Rastro.

Valladolid has attractions that almost make it worth a short stay, but to see them you'll have a pay a price. For all its history, Valladolid is a stupefyingly ugly city, and probably always has been. Lately it has enjoyed considerable industrial growth, becoming by far the largest city of Old Castile. Many writers have blamed it for destroying much of its older quarters in the process, but this is one city where you may want to cheer on the wrecking crews. The new developments are neither better nor worse than elsewhere in Spain, but the old, an amorphous blot of shabby alleys, ghastly misbegotten churches and abandoned palaces, will not be the memory of Spain you would wish to take home with you. Nobody in Valladolid seems unhappy to see it go.

But if you want to see San Pablo Church and the Colegio San Gregorio, two of the most unusual architectural fantasies in all Spain, steel yourself and plunge in.

GETTING AROUND

Lots of trains pass through Valladolid, with regular connections daily to all the cities of Old Castile and León (except Soria) as well as Galicia and the northern coast. There are always at least eight daily trains to Madrid, some passing through Segovia, some through Avila. In this region, there may be quicker connections than you see up on the boards at the station. Always ask at the information desk or the ticket counter; all trains pass through the big junction at Medina del Campo, and by changing there you may reach your destination faster. In Valladolid the station is on the southern edge of town, on the Paseo de Campo Grande (information Tel: 22 33 57, or in the centre at the RENFE office at Atreo de Santiago 3, Tel: 22 28 73).

The bus station is a 10-minute walk west of the train station, at Puente Lodgante 2, under a highway overpass (Tel: 23 63 08) with connections to all the same places, also Soria, Barcelona and provincial towns like Toro, Tordesillas and Arevelo.

The city

Most people's introduction to Valladolid will seem innocuous enough; both the bus and train stations are near the **Campo Grande**, a large park on the eastern edge of town. From here, follow the pedestrian Calle de Santiago to the city centre and the **Plaza Mayor**, grimy but not unpleasant, with most of the restaurants and cheap hotels on or around it. In the 16th century the plaza earned renown for spectacular *autos-de-fé*, a practice inaugurated by Philip II in 1559 after a secret community of religious free-thinkers was discovered in the town. Heading west down San Francisco Ferrari, you'll come to the **Cathedral**. It was begun in 1580 as one of the first works of Juan de Herrera, and in the 1720s Alberto Churriguera was given a chance to try and complete it. This combination of Spain's apostle of austerity and its most exuberant Baroque master explains the mess you see; plenty of hacks have monkeyed with it since, but quite understandably the city has given up; the cathedral will never be finished and fair-sized shrubs are already growing out of the cornice. Just behind it is a small 14th-century Gothic jewel, **Santa María la Antigua**; its Italian Romanesque tower survives from an earlier church.

San Pablo and San Gregorio

It is hard to explain the presence of these two buildings in Valladolid (they are next to each other on the Plaza de San Pablo, just down Calle de las Angustias from the cathedral) – their façades are as eccentric as Toledo Cathedral's Transparente, and completely unlike anything else in Spain. Both façades are huge curtains of sculpture, woven with fantastical forms and ornate decoration, completely disregarding the norms of religious architecture. **San Pablo**, where Philip II was baptized, had its façade added in 1601. The big coat-of-arms also displayed on it is that of the Duke of Lerma, who picked up the bill. Its great lions and dozens of saints and angels seem like figures of some mechanical clock, ready to come alive at the stroke of the hour. The Castilian Cortes often met here, and the interior is full of tombs of Spanish notables, but there hasn't been much to see inside since the thorough looting done by the French in 1809. Napoleon could have overseen the job himself; he made the **Capitania General** across the square, a former royal palace, his headquarters on his visit to Spain.

San Pablo's anonymous sculptors were undoubtedly inspired by the earlier (1496) **Colegio de San Gregorio**, very similar in conception. Its architect, Mattias Carpontera, is said to have committed suicide just before the façade was completed. At its centre a pomegranite tree, commemorating the recent conquest of Granada, springs from a fountain full of cherubs. Ragged wild men with clubs called *maceros* guard the doors, a curious fashion copied in other Spanish churches, such as Avila cathedral.

National Museum of Sculpture

Inside, the Colegio San Gregorio has been restored to house this large collection (open 10 am–1.30 pm and 4–7 pm, Sunday 10 am–1.30 pm, closed Monday). The name is a little misleading; it's all polychrome wood sculpture of religious subjects, taken from churches in Valladolid and elsewhere in Castile. Very little is of any merit – the anonymous 1463 **Retablo de San Jeronimo** and some well-carved choir stalls up on the 2nd floor. The rest, room after room of gaping Virgins and blood-splattered Christs, will either make you queasy or make you laugh. With so much of it in one place, the Spanish obsession with pain and death dissolves into pure kitsch. Juan de Juni (c. 1540) is the master of this, and his tableau *El Entierro de Cristo* is rivalled only by Gregorio Fernandez's *Cristo Yacente* in the expression of anguish and the correct depiction of wounds.

The school's restored chapel may also be visited, where there's a lovely statue of *Death* himself, and in the cloister, restorers of the 1880s tried to clear the air with some fanciful silly **gargoyles**, which bear a closer inspection than anything in the museum.

Other sights in town

Both Cervantes' and Columbus' houses have been turned into museums. The **Casa de Cervantes** (Calle del Rastro, open daily except Monday, 10 am–6 pm, Sunday 10 am–2 pm) and **Casa de Colón** (Calle Colón, open daily except Monday, 10 am–1 pm and 4–7 pm, Sunday 11 am–1 pm). Better than these, the old **Philippines Convent** behind the Campo Grande has an **Oriental Museum** of works acquired in centuries of missionary work in the Far East – nine rooms filled with fine paintings and porcelain from China, and three more with folk art of the Philippines and elsewhere.

Around Valladolid

In the heartland of Castile you would expect castles, and these are the major attraction of the flat, monotonous country around Valladolid. Few ever served any military purpose, apart from intimidating the populace and defending the nobility during the civil wars. That they survived while so much else has been lost is a key to Castile's history. In the 15th century this was indeed the heartland, a region of rich and growing new towns whose prosperity was based on the *Mesta*, that peculiar half-corporation, half-cooperative that kept all Europe supplied with prized merino wool. The Habsburgs destroyed the region's economy for ever, and towns like Toro and Tordesillas, that figured so prominently in the chronicles of Ferdinand and Isabel, never fulfilled their early promise.

Medina del Campo, like Valladolid, stands as a symbol of so much that went wrong in 16th-century Spain. Once this was one of the greatest trade fair towns of the continent, and merchants from as far as Germany and England made the annual trip here over the Pyrenees to expedite the trade in wool (the most important commodity of the age), Vizcaya iron and Toledo silk. Medina's fairs inaugurated the use of letters of exchange among merchants – the beginning of modern banking – and the city's financiers arranged the exchequers of all Castile's kings up to Charles V. The Habsburg bankruptcies put an end to all this, and Medina dwindled to an insignificant village in little more than a century. Spain's biggest sheep-market is still held here, but there's almost nothing to see of the old Medina – Charles V's army razed it to the ground during the Comunero revolt. **La Mota Castle** survives, east of town; Queen Isabel often used it as a residence, and in the town itself is a little palace where she died in 1504.

Madrigal and Toro

Some 30 km (18.8 miles) south, **Madrigal de las Altas Torres** makes a fine sight, with its crumbling 14th-century walls rising above the plain. There's little left inside them, but you can visit Isabel's birthplace here at the **Convento de las Angustias** – she wasn't born in a nunnery; the building incorporates an old palace of Isabel's family. **Toro**, north of Medina on the Zamora–Valladolid road, has a site almost as picturesque, on red cliffs above the Duero; it has grown old more gracefully than Madrigal, though it's only a shadow of the important town it was in the 15th century. Toro's landmark is a remarkable 12th-century Romanesque church, the **Colegiata**, with a broad 16-sided *cimborio*, or tower over the crossing, that looks like a castle keep. The same peculiar design can be seen in Zamora and Salamanca – and nowhere else. The Colegiata's west front, the **Portico de la Gloria**, is one of the best works of Spanish Romanesque sculpture.

The Battle of Toro, fought during the civil war that followed the death of Enrique IV, inaugurated Spain's golden age, by making Ferdinand and Isabel undisputed masters of the country. Ferdinand's army did not really defeat the partisans of Juana la Beltraneja; the battle was a draw, but Juana's Portuguese supporters gave up and went home, ensuring Isabel's hold on the throne of Castile.

Tordesillas

Here, too, an important battle was fought. Just a few miles outside the town, Charles V's army of veterans scattered the rabble militia of the Comuneros at the Battle of Villalar in

1521. Coming just 45 years after Isabel's triumph at Toro, Villalar meant the defeat of Castile's last chance to control its own destiny. Juan Bravo and the other Comunero leaders were captured and executed the next day, and Toledo fell to the royalists soon afterwards. Tordesillas is better known as the last abode of Queen Juana the Mad. Her son, Charles V, kept her locked up here for 46 years under guard. The rumours that Juana was sane never ceased, and Charles allowed her no visitors to confirm or deny it. When the Comuneros took Tordesillas, they reported she was sane enough, but she refused to sign the papers that would legitimize their revolt, and perhaps have assured its success.

Tordesillas, like Toro, was once a thriving town, its lovely arcaded **Plaza Mayor** survives, but from its better days the only monument left is the **Convent of Santa Clara**, parts of which were begun as a palace by Alfonso XI in 1340. The older parts, notably the **Patio de San Pedro** and the **Capilla Mayor**, are done in the Mudejár style with lovely arches and lattice-work façades (open daily except Monday and Tuesday, 9 am–1 pm and 3–7 pm).

As for castles, there are fine ones at **Fuentesaldaña, Simancas** (this one has housed the state archives of Spain since the time of Charles V) and **Cuellar**, a village famous for its annual *encierro*, or 'running of the bulls' as in Pamplona. **Coca Castle** may be the strangest in Spain, a 14th-century stronghold of notorious local tyrants, the Fonseca family. This one looks as if it was built much more for decoration than defence, with unique fluted turrets that seem to be cogs and gears in some mysterious piece of machinery.

TOURIST INFORMATION

Valladolid: on the other side of the Campo Grande from the train station, Pl. de Zorilla 3, Tel: 22 16 29.

WHERE TO STAY AND EAT

Rooms in Valladolid are priced quite high. If you must stay, you can indulge at the **Olid Melia******, an unremarkable chain hotel but probably the best in town (Pl. San Miguel 10, two blocks from San Pedro, Tel: 35 72 00, 6830 pts a double). The **Imperial****, a slightly worn, middle-range establishment (C. Paso 4, Tel: 33 03 00, 3500–3850 pts a double). Nobody has ever said a kind word about any budget *hostal* in Valladolid, but you'll find a wide choice on the back streets around the Pl. Mayor.

Few hotels in the province are in any way remarkable. Tordesillas has a **Parador Nacional***** in a modern building (highway 620, Tel: 22 00 51, doubles 5000–6500 pts) but it gets stiff competition from **El Montico*****, in a restored farmhouse, with a pool and tennis, but an overpriced restaurant (also on highway 620, towards Salamanca, Tel: 77 07 51, 3500–4700 pts doubles). Madrigal has a more inexpensive *hostal*, the **Madrigal***, on the road to Peñaranda (1200 doubles, no bath) and there are a few modest hotels each in Medina del Campo, Toro and Simancas.

EATING OUT

In Valladolid, the back streets around the Pl. Mayor is the area to look for restaurants. The **Restaurante El Nogal** on C. del Conde Ansurez has imaginative *menus del día* for 600 pts. The **Hosteria de la Cueva**, C. Correos, is just slightly more expensive and has good, modest seafood dinners in a traditional setting. For a more elegant dinner, try **El Lugar** on C. Manlilla 1, where Castilian cuisine seems more refined than most places (1600 pts).

Around the province, Fuensaldaña north of Valladolid is a wine-making area, and has some inexpensive *bodegas* offering Castilian cooking with their wines; the **Bodega Sorbona** (800–1200 pts) is an agreeable one.

From Valladolid to Soria

Coca Castle has a worthy competitor at **Peñafiel**, on a narrow ridge overlooking the Duero and the quaint old village. This castle, built to follow the crest of its difficult site, is 214 m (695 ft) long and only 24 m (77 ft) wide, giving it the appearance of a stage property. Like Coca, it is in a near perfect state of preservation.

The road to Soria generally follows the Duero, and the countryside becomes considerably greener and prettier in the neighbourhood of **El Burgo de Osma**. This town, important until the 1700s, has shrunk into one of the truly beautiful villages of Castile, with bits of its old walls crumbling beneath the trees, and fields and gardens encroaching on its very centre. The town is worth a stay for itself, but Burgo de Osma also has an exceptional little **Cathedral**, with a beautiful 13th-century Gothic façade leading into a hotch potch of different ages and styles within. The Cathedral's tower, Burgo de Osma's landmark, is a Baroque addition and there are some arches of the original Romanesque church within. Its founder, San Pedro de Osma, is entombed inside in a sarcophagus covered with lively and colourful medieval scenes. The cathedral's small **musuem** should be seen; you may be fortunate enough to get them to show you their important collection of illuminated medieval manuscripts, especially the *Beato*, a 1065 codex of commentaries on the Apocalypse.

Burgo de Osma is not the original town here; its predecessor, Osma, was a Roman city called *Uxema*, but has now declined to a tiny hamlet just a short distance away. Both are overlooked by a ruined **castle** on Roman foundations. About 14.4 km (9 miles) north of town, there is some wild and rugged scenery around the **Canyon of the Rio Lobos**; here, just outside the village of Varo, the church of **San Juan de Otero** (now called San Bartolemé) was built in the 12th century by the Templars. In this isolated spot the Templars could afford to express some of their heretical doctrines in the design. One of the windows is in the form of an inverted pentangle, and there are other unusual geometric forms and patterns inside.

From Burgo de Osma, it's a short jump to Soria, the only city of this region, but you may consider a detour through the fascinating and little visited country to the south-east, in the valley of the Duero.

The Upper Duero

The landscape, if you're not alert for it, may pass without notice, but you'll find it sticks in your memory after you go. Most of Soria province is like this – unusual, intense shades of green and gold, wrinkled hills ploughed into subtle patterns of furrows, bare mountains topped with crumbling castles. The towns and villages, little changed since the Middle Ages, come in the same gold and brown as the hills. Most are genteel and decaying, seemingly ready at any moment to seep back into the land that gave them birth.

Heading north from Burgo de Osma, you meet the Duero under the walls of **Gormaz Castle**, a huge, half-ruined, barbaric-looking pile built by the Moors in the 10th century. The walls are almost half a mile around. It's worth the climb, for the fine Moorish gateway and the view. From Gormaz, a long detour to the south will take you to **Termancia** in a small patch of mountains called the Sierra de Pela, near the village of Tiermes. This was an important Celtiberian town, and though unexcavated it's an exceedingly strange site, with tunnels and stairs and caves dug out of the bare rock; scanty ruins of the Roman Termancia that succeeded it can be seen below.

The next town up the river from Gormaz, **Berlanga de Duero**, has a squat, round-towered castle, arcaded streets and medieval gates, and the fine, plain early Gothic **Colegiata Church**. Friar Romas de Berlanga, the town's favourite son, is buried here. He was a 16th-century Bishop of Panama, who changed the course of history by introducing bananas into the New World from Africa, so making possible banana splits and banana republics. At nearby Casillas de Berlanga, you can get the key for an entirely unique and curious church, the 10th-century Mozarabic **San Baudelio Hermitage**. Behind its blank walls is a chapel with horseshoe arches radiating from a central column – like a palm tree in stone – covered with remnants of frescoes. The best, unfortunately, have been spirited away to the Prado in Madrid.

Almazán, a growing town of some 6000 people, second-largest in the province, has some of its old walls and gates, and the 12th-century **San Miguel Church**, with a Moorish dome of interlaced arches, much like the famous one over the mihrab of the mosque in Córdoba. A nearby village, **Morón de Almazán**, has a lovely plaza surrounded by a Renaissance church and palaces. Heading south from Almazán, you meet the main Madrid–Barcelona road at **Medinaceli**, an ancient, half-deserted town on a hill where stands a Roman **triumphal arch**, its inscriptions so ground away by wind and rain that nobody has any idea what triumph it commemorates. Some 30 km (18.8 miles) to the east, at **Santa María de Huerta**, is a Cistercian monastery of the same name. Shut down with the rest in 1853, this one was restored to the order in 1927. It is like a small museum of Gothic architecture and sculpture, with an especially fine chapel and refectory (open 9 am–1 pm, and 3.30–7 pm daily except Monday).

SORIA

It may be one of Spain's smallest provincial capitals, but Soria will seem like a metropolis after the bitsy villages of the rest of the province. It is a town of distinction, full of early medieval monuments in a beautiful setting among forested hills overlooking the Duero; out of the way, but a tranquil place to stop over on your way to or from Madrid and the south.

GETTING AROUND

Soria's only train service is five a day to Madrid, and two to Logroño and Pamplona; it's easy to reach Zaragoza or Bilbao, though, with a change at Castejon del Ebro. You'll have to take a cab to the station, outside Soria; there's no bus. RENFE information is Tel: 21 10 95.

The city has a new bus station, on the western edge of town with a few daily runs to Logroño, Pamplona, Zaragoza, Burgos, Valladolid, and Madrid – and also to Burgo de Osma, Almazán and, less regularly, to the smaller villages of the province. There are also two daily direct buses from Burgo de Osma to Madrid.

WHAT TO SEE

Soria's centre, connecting the old town with the new, is the **Plaza Ramón y Cajal**. The plaza faces a big park, the **Alameda de Cervantes**, with perhaps Spain's only public tree-house, and the **Museo Numantino**, with finds from the ancient city of Numantia (see below). The museum has been 'under restoration' for years; no one knows when the province will reopen it.

Soria's two finest medieval churches stand at the northern and southern edges of the old town. **San Juan de Rabarera**, on Calle Caballeros (c. 1200) with an unusual apse, in transition from Romanesque to Gothic, and **Santo Domingo** (c. 1160), on Calle La Aduana Vieja, with a spectacular carved tympanum over the west portal, displaying hundreds of figures of saints and angels, even musicians.

Behind the Plaza Mayor, Calle Real traverses the middle of the old town, passing two more churches, the ruined **San Nicolas** and **San Pedro**, both 13th century, on its way to the banks of the Duero.

San Juan de Duero

Soria's stretch of riverfront, strung between two hills (one has a monastery, the other a parador and a ruined castle) is an attraction in itself, a lovely, peaceful spot with groves of poplars, an island, and a weir on the lazy Duero. You can rent canoes from the bar next to the old stone bridge, or cross to the other side and see **San Juan de Duero**, a house of the Knights of St John, founded around 1200. The arcade of its ruined **cloister**, standing strangely alone in a field, is unlike any other in Spain – half of it Gothic, the remainder intertwined, pointed arches that look from a distance like spiral loops. Whoever built it for the Knights knew what they were doing; even where one of the pillars has fallen, the arches above it hang suspended in space. The church next to the cloister is still in good shape, with vivid scenes of the Massacre of the Innocents on its capitals. A small museum has been installed. Medieval Soria was an important Jewish city, and many of the artefacts – headstones and sarcophagi, mostly – are reminders of this.

Take a walk down the avenue of poplars on the eastern bank of the river, and you'll pass two other old monuments: the 13th-century **San Polo Church**, a Templar foundation built right over the road, with an arch to let traffic through (now a private home) and, further on, the octagonal Hermitage of **San Saturio**, romantically set into a cliff over the river. It isn't surprising that these sites should be out of the ordinary. As the Templars and Hospitallers would have known, this corner of the Duero must have been a holy site since remotest antiquity. Forget the made-up story of a San Saturio, hermit and patron of Soria – and don't even bother guessing who San Polo might have been. It

Ruined Cloister of Saint Juan de Duero, Soria

was the common early Christian practice to appropriate ancient deities and turn them into saints. For Saturio and Polo, read *Saturn* and *Apollo*.

Numantia

In this ancient city, 19 years of the Iberian Arevaco tribe's struggle against the Romans culminated in one of the famous events of antiquity. A year-long Roman siege in 132 BC seemed on the verge of success when the people of Numantia chose not to accept the inevitable. Instead they set fire to their town with themselves in it, a grand gesture of heroic defiance that Spanish poets and politicians haven't yet tired of talking about. There's little to see on the site (6 km (3.8 miles) north of Soria); a few straight streets and foundations from the later, Roman town on a hillside overlooking the modern village of Garraz, and traces of the 6.4 km (4 miles) of walls.

In the northern reaches of Soria province, you can trace the source of the Duero into a landscape of grey mountains and pine forests. **Vinuesa**, off the road to Burgos, is a beautiful, untouched village on the way to the sequestered **Laguna Negra** ('black lagoon') and other sights of the Sierra de la Hormaza.

TOURIST INFORMATION
Soria: Pl. Ramón y Cajal, Tel: 21 20 52.

WHERE TO STAY AND EAT
Don't expect anything fashionable in this province, perhaps the least visited in northern Spain – just simple accommodation and honest, heavy Castilian cooking. In Soria, the **Parador Antonio Machado***** heads the list of the city's hotels, a plain and modern, but comfortable place on a hill among the ruins of the old castle, perhaps a bit overpriced for the area (Tel: 21 34 45, 6000–7000 pts for a double). In town, the **Viena**** is a good night's sleep (Tel: 22 21 09, 1900–2300 pts with bath, 1500–1900 pts without)

and most of the cheaper *fondas* off Pl. Ramón y Cajal will not disappoint. **Huespedes Sol** is a grandmotherly place on C. Sta. Maria (1100 pts a double, no bath).

You'll be able to find comfortable lodging in most of the towns mentioned in this section: the **Hoz La**** in Berlanga de Duero (C. Postigo, Tel: 34 31 69, doubles 1500–2000 pts with bath); the **Casa Agapito**** in Burgo de Osma (C. Universidad, Tel: 34 02 12, 1800 pts double with bath, 1200 pts without) and a wider choice in Medinaceli, along the Madrid–Zaragoza highway. Also in this area, the **Parador Nacional Santa María de Huerta***** has recently been built, near that monastery, between Medinaceli and Calatayud (Tel: 32 70 11, 5000 pts a double).

EATING OUT

Among Soria's restaurants, **Maroto** stands out, with unusual dishes like mushroom and truffle soup (1400–1800 pts) on the Paseo del Espolon. In the town centre, most restaurants are off Pl. Ramón y Cajal. The **Palafox** on C. Vincente Tutor and the **Capri** on C. San Benito have better-than-average *menús del día* for 500–600 pts.

ZAMORA

Zamora is a fine old city on the banks of the River Duero, boasting a golden necklace of small Romanesque churches and a jewel of a cathedral. Despite these treasures, it's off the main tourist route – even in June it's very likely that you'll have it to yourself. Needless to say, this wasn't always the case. Zamora 'the well-walled' under the great shepherd-chieftain and escaped Roman slave Viriato, was a nightmare for the Romans. In 1072, the siege of Zamora was a nightmare for the Cid, who at the time served as a standard-bearer to Sancho II of Castile. Sancho was besieging his sister Urraca, whom the Cid refused to fight as she was his foster sister; in the end Sancho was treacherously murdered and succeeded by his brother Alonso VI. The city was a leader in the Comunero revolt under Antonio de Acuña, the last of the great battling bishops, who had to seize and defend his bishopric in Zamora by force against the mayor. When finally thrown out of town for leading the Comuneros, he built up a private army, captured Toledo and had himself proclaimed archbishop. When Franco, like Charles V, faced dissenting priests, he built a notorious prison in Zamora to contain them all – more were imprisoned here, it is said, than in the whole of the Warsaw pact countries.

GETTING AROUND

Zamora's Plateresque train station lies at the bottom of the hill at C. Tres Cruces; from the top of the hill (Pl. Alemania) the bus terminal is a couple of blocks north near the bullring. Zamora is on the main line between Madrid, Avila and Galicia, with several regular trains and *talgos* daily. Buses go every hour or so to Salamanca; less frequently to Toro, Valladolid, Madrid and Barcelona.

The Churches

The dusty **Plaza Canovas**, with a dramatic statue of Viriato and a battering ram '*The*

Terror Romanorum' is the core of old Zamora, with its churches, which on the map circle the plaza like the numbers on a clock. All are lovely, if not spectacular, and specific ones to aim for are **Santa María la Nueva** behind the old hospital, with its unusual 8th-century capitals in the Byzantine style and a **Museum of Pasos** (Semana Santa floats). If the hospital is at 'noon' on the Plaza, at six o'clock, **Santa María del Orta**, built by the Templars, is perhaps the most visually striking with its tower; at three o'clock **San Andres** has a fine interior and *artesonado* ceiling. Calle Ramos Carrion (nine o'clock) leads towards the cathedral, passing by way of the 1160 **La Magdalena** with its pretty rose window and to **San Ildefonso**, with its photogenic arches, buttresses and a Flemish tryptich, said to have been brought over by Charles V.

The Cathedral

At the far west end of Zamora stands the Cathedral crowned by its peculiar dome and with its ring turrets – a style unique to this western corner of Castile that lends the Cathedral its Byzantine air. A huge tower on the west was built for defence; it overlooks the remains of Zamora's **castle** and walls. Within are a couple of works by Fernando Gallego, the 15th-century master, but what everyone remembers best are the fine carvings on the choir stalls – Decameronesque vignettes of nuns and monks that were censored for many a year.

However, the **Museum** off the cloister (open 11 am–2 pm and 4–8 pm) contains a treasure that even the most respectable cathedral would envy – the **Black Tapestries**, magnificent masterpieces of the weaver's art, made in Belgium in the 15th century. The nickname seems to derive from the sheer density of stitches and details put into scenes of the Trojan War, the battles of Hannibal, and the Parable of the Vine.

Behind the Cathedral, near the bishop's palace, is an 11th-century residence known as the **Casa del Cid**. From here the Peñas de Santa Marta follows the Duero up to a fine **medieval bridge**. If you have a car, head up N-122 and turn at the sign for **San Pedro de la Nave**, a fine 7th-century Visigothic–Asturian church, relocated after the construction of the Ricobayo dam nearby. It has a lovely carved frieze and capitals inside; ask at Zamora's tourist office for opening hours.

TOURIST INFORMATION

Santa Clara 20, Tel: 51 18 45.

WHERE TO STAY

Zamora's **Parador Condes de Alba de Aliste******, Pl. Cánovas, Tel: 51 44 97, is one of the most atmospheric and elegant in all Spain, even if it has only 19 rooms. It is located in the 15th-century ducal palace – with an added swimming-pool – and is furnished with antiques and coats of armour; its restaurant features the finest of local cuisine; doubles, 5500–7500 pts. Spanking new, the **Hotel Dos Infantes*****, Cortinas de San Miguel 3, Tel: 51 28 75, is conveniently located and offers its modern and comfortable doubles for 4100–4600 pts. Three of Zamora's cheaper *hostales* are all in one modern building at Benavente 2, all rated at one star: **Toary**, Tel: 51 37 02, **Luz**, Tel: 51 31 52, and **Chiqui**, Tel: 51 14 80, all offering doubles with bath for 1800–1950 pts.

EATING OUT
For good tapas or a fish dinner, the **Serafin**, Pl. Maestro Haedo 2, is the local favourite; for the latter expect to pay around 2000 pts. Just off the Pl. Mayor, the elegant olde worlde **España** has a Castilian menu for 600 pts; **Pozo** on the same street has roast kid for 725 pts.

Around Zamora

Zamora divides itself as a province between the **Tierra del Vino** (wine land) south of the Duero, and the **Tierra del Pan** (bread land) north of the river, which sums it up quite well.

GETTING AROUND
Puebla de Sanabria and Toro (see Valladolid) are both on the rail line from Zamora; there are buses four times a day to Benavente from Zamora, and two to Fermosella.

WHAT TO SEE
In the **Tierra del Pan** the most scenic excursion is to the north-west near Galicia, where the pretty glacial lake, **Lago de Sanabria**, is the centre of Spain's newest national park. The **Puebla de Sanabria** is the main town scenically located on a cliff over the river Tera, dominated by a well-preserved 15th-century castle; in the parish church, note the four curious slate figures in 11th-century dress. In **Benavente** one of Spain's most elaborate alcazars was built in the 15th century; only the **Torre de Caracol** ('snail tower') survived the 19th-century demolition and now houses a parador. There are a couple of interesting churches – **San Juan de Mercador** houses an unusual image of the Virgin, holding a Templar cross in a wheel.

In the **Tierra del Vino** the most important town is **Fermosella** on the Portuguese border, the last refuge of Bishop Acuña's Comuneros. The Gothic parish church is quite imposing and contains a collection of Romanesque and Gothic icons.

WHERE TO STAY AND EAT
There are quite a few places to stay in Puebla de Sanabria, where holiday-makers come to swim in the lake and fish in the streams of the park. The modern **Parador Puebla de Sanabria*****, Crta de Zamora, Tel: 62 00 01 is actually near to the town, with fine views and a good restaurant; doubles 5000–6500 pts, meals around 2000 pts. In the village itself a good bet is **Victoria***, Arrabal 29, Tel: 62 00 12, its 10 comfortable doubles with bath are 3200–3500 pts. If you seek a clean bed without the frills, the **Galicia**, Animas 22, Tel: 62 01 06 has doubles for under 1000 pts and a cheap restaurant (700 pts set menu) as well.

In Benavente, the **Parador Rey Fernando II de León******, Paseo Ramón y Cajal, Tel: 63 03 00, has been elegantly furnished in the Torre del Caracol, complete with an *artesonado* ceiling brought in from another demolished monument. Its restaurant serves local Castilian specialities (1800 pts); doubles here are 5500–7000 pts. A less expensive and centrally located alternative, the **Hostal Mercantil****, Avda. de José Antonio 9, Tel: 63 13 00 has bathless doubles for 945–1115 pts.

SALAMANCA

Spain's great medieval university town, Salamanca, is also one of the country's charmers, a dream city of deep golden stone embroidered by the prolific Churriguera family. Although the university was ranked in the Middle Ages as one of Europe's finest it began to decline in the strict clericalism and intolerance initiated by Philip II; Francoism, virulently anti-intellectual, was almost a death blow to Salamanca. Although the glamour of its name continues to lend it status, its slowly awakening scholarship still has a long way to catch up with that of Barcelona's and Madrid's universities. But there's nothing like thousands of students to keep a town awake, and their lively presence compliments the serene magnificence of Salamanca's monuments.

GETTING AROUND

Salamanca's train station is a 20-minute walk north of the centre via Plaza de España, in the Plaza de la Libertad, Tel: 22 02 95; there are trains to Avila and Madrid, Ciudad Rodrigo and into Portugal; others go up through Valladolid to Burgos, Irún, Zaragoza, etc.

The bus station is a 15-minute walk from the Plaza Mayor in the Avda de Filiberto Villalobos 73–85, Tel: 23 67 17; there are 13 buses daily to Zamora (fewer at the weekends), 1 to León, Valladolid, Cáceres and six *rapidos* to Madrid. Frequent buses to Ciudad Rodrigo.

Plaza Mayor

Despite its prominent place in Spanish history, Salamanca is not a big town, and you can walk nearly everywhere from the central **Plaza Mayor**. This endearing urban heart of gold was built at the beginning of the 18th century and is rivalled in beauty only by the Plaza Mayor in Madrid itself. A happy collaboration by Alberto Churriguera and Andrés Garcia de Quiñones, members of the two greatest dynasties of the Plateresque, the plaza is made of the stone of Villamayor – the fine grained sandstone that is pale, moist, and easy to handle when freshly quarried, but when left in the sun slowly hardens and darkens to a deep, golden-brown patina. The Plaza Mayor is Salamanca's public stage, its crossroads, focal point, and general meeting-place, and in the evening the whole city relaxes in the numerous bars and cafes spilling out of its shady arcades, on occasion entertained by the *Tuna de Salamanca*, the jolly groups of minstrels in black Renaissance costume. The plaza doubles as a Spanish hall of fame, with busts of the national greats – and Franco – carved on medallions around the arcades.

South of the plaza, the Rua Mayor passes another Salamantine landmark, the **Casa de las Conchas** ('house of the shells'), the *solar* of Dr Talavera Maldonada, a member of Ferdinand and Isabel's royal council and a Knight of Santiago, who had his palace adorned with the scallop-shell symbol of St James. They give the house a wonderful nubby texture, and even adorn the iron grills over the windows, masterpieces of Gothic metalwork. The great, domed **La Clericia** (1750) nearby belonged to a Jesuit seminary, and nowadays to the University's college of religion.

The Cathedrals

Rua Mayor continues down to the **Plaza de Anaya** and Salamanca's two cathedrals.

These are built side-by-side although from the outside the much larger **New Cathedral** (completed in 1560 as a symbol of Salamanca's aspirations and prestige just as Philip prepared to undermine both) dominates. This, one of Gothic's last hurrahs, is adorned with pinnacles, cosmic Plateresque details (even an elephant makes an appearance) and a tower modelled after the one in Toledo. Dwarfed in comparison the Romanesque cathedral makes itself known from the outside through its **Torre del Gallo** – an unusual silvery 'fish-scale' dome with turrets and topped by a rooster; believed to be Byzantine in inspiration, its only cousins in Spain are in Toro and Zamora.

Inside, the New Cathedral is lofty and elegant. Among its chapels near the main altar is the talisman *Christ of the Battles* – a simple Romanesque image carried by the Cid and invoked before his battles, surrounded by some of the frothiest Baroque imaginable. Underneath lies the tomb of Bishop Jerónimo, the Cid's chaplain and founder of the old cathedral. Another chapel, next to the door of the old cathedral, is crowded with wooden sculptures of every conceivable saint and the Memento Mori – Death – in its window.

The **Old Cathedral**, built in 1160, is a magnificent Romanesque temple that the New Cathedral failed to surpass. Brightly lit by the ring of windows at the base of the dome, the main *retablo*'s rich colours are wonderfully vivid – its 53 paintings crowned by an awesome vision of the Last Judgement. Paintings on the side walls depict various miracles – including one that occurred during the building of this very cathedral, when a stone block fell on the head of a mason, inflicting only a headache (judging by his expression). The block itself hangs from one of the columns, which have beautiful capitals. In the back of the church a door leads to the **Capilla de Saint Martin** with the late 13th-century frescoes portraying saints and another view of the Apocalypse.

The chapels off the former cloister (modernized out of existence in the 18th-century) are especially interesting. The first, the **Capilla de Talavera**, has unique star-vaulting, the tattered standard of the Comuneros – a rare memento of the great revolt – and the privilege, bestowed when the chapel was built in the 12th century, of celebrating mass according the Mozarabic rite. The **Capilla de Santa Barbara** (1340) has in its centre the tomb of Bishop Lucero of the well-worn feet, polished by countless anxious candidates for Doctorate degrees – it was customary to pass the night before the examination in the chair before the altar, feet propped up on the bishop's in a vigil of study. The examiners would come to the chapel in the morning and grill the student, who, if successful, would leave in a triumphal procession, attend a bullfight and, mixing the bull's blood with olive oil, inscribe his name on the cathedral or university building for all posterity to see.

Another chapel, the **Capilla de Los Anayas**, contains another bishop's tomb, enclosed in an awesome *verja* (ornate fence); against the wall is a beautifully crafted organ with Mudejár designs, believed to be the oldest in Europe. The **chapter house** contains a triptych by Fernando Gallego (a native of Salamanca); it was here, in 1316, that the Knights Templar were tried for heresy (both Old and New Cathedrals are open daily 10 am–2 pm and 4–8 pm; ticket required for the old cathedral).

The University

A block from the cathedral is the **Patio de las Escuelas**, with a statue of the mystic and poet Fray Luis de León, Salamanca's most famous professor. This is the main

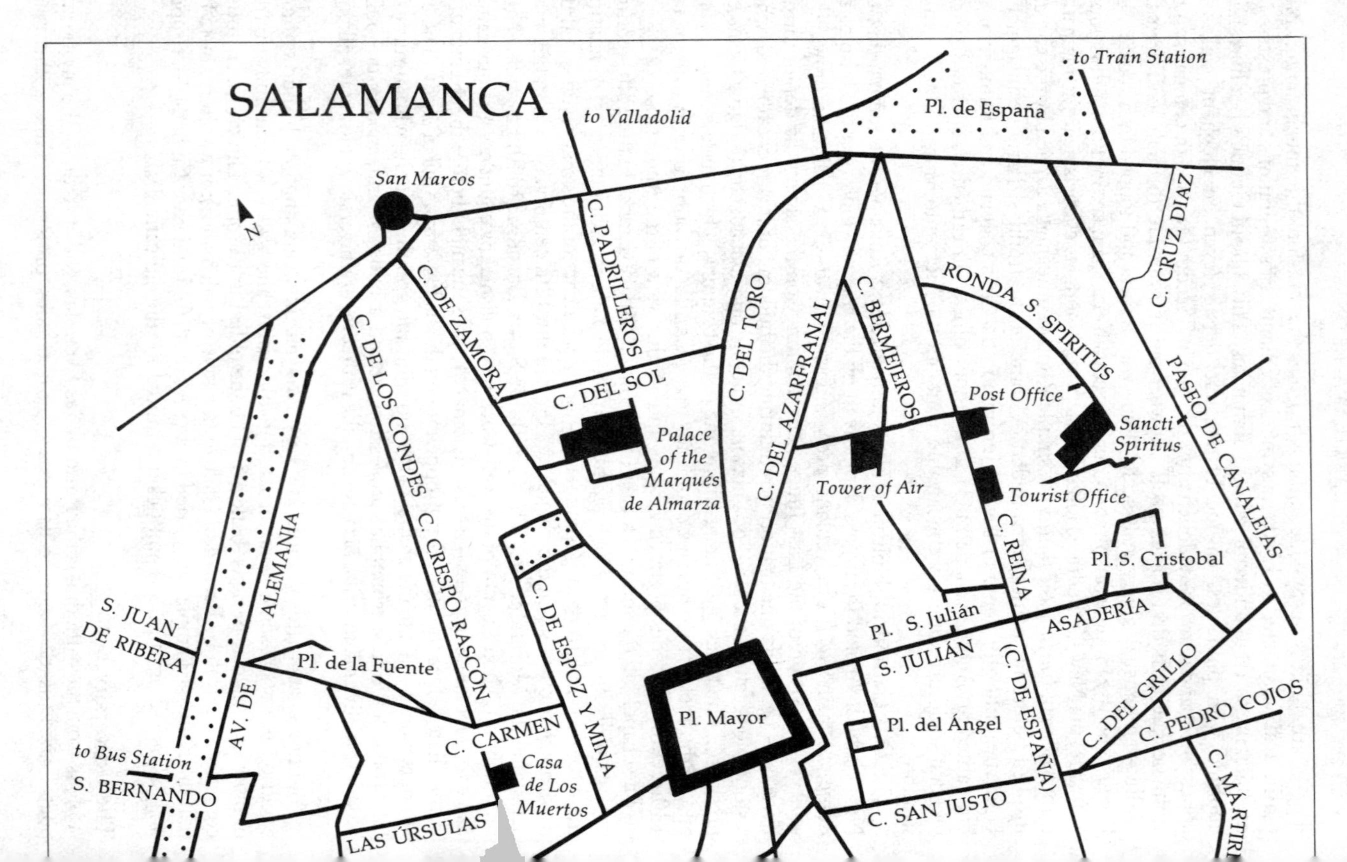
SALAMANCA
to Valladolid
to Train Station
Pl. de España
San Marcos
N
C. PADRILLEROS
C. DEL TORO
C. DEL AZARFRANAL
C. BERMEJEROS
RONDA S. SPIRITUS
C. CRUZ DIAZ
PASEO DE CANALEJAS
C. DE ZAMORA
C. DE LOS CONDES
C. CRESPO RASCÓN
C. DEL SOL
Palace of the Marqués de Almarza
Post Office
Sancti Spiritus
Tower of Air
Tourist Office
C. REINA
Pl. S. Cristobal
Pl. S. Julián
ASADERÍA
S. JULIÁN
(C. DE ESPAÑA)
C. DEL GRILLO
C. PEDRO COJOS
C. MÁRTIRI
ALEMANIA
AV. DE
S. JUAN DE RIBERA
Pl. de la Fuente
C. DE ESPOZ Y MINA
Pl. Mayor
Pl. del Ángel
C. CARMEN
Casa de Los Muertos
to Bus Station
S. BERNANDO
LAS ÚRSULAS
C. SAN JUSTO

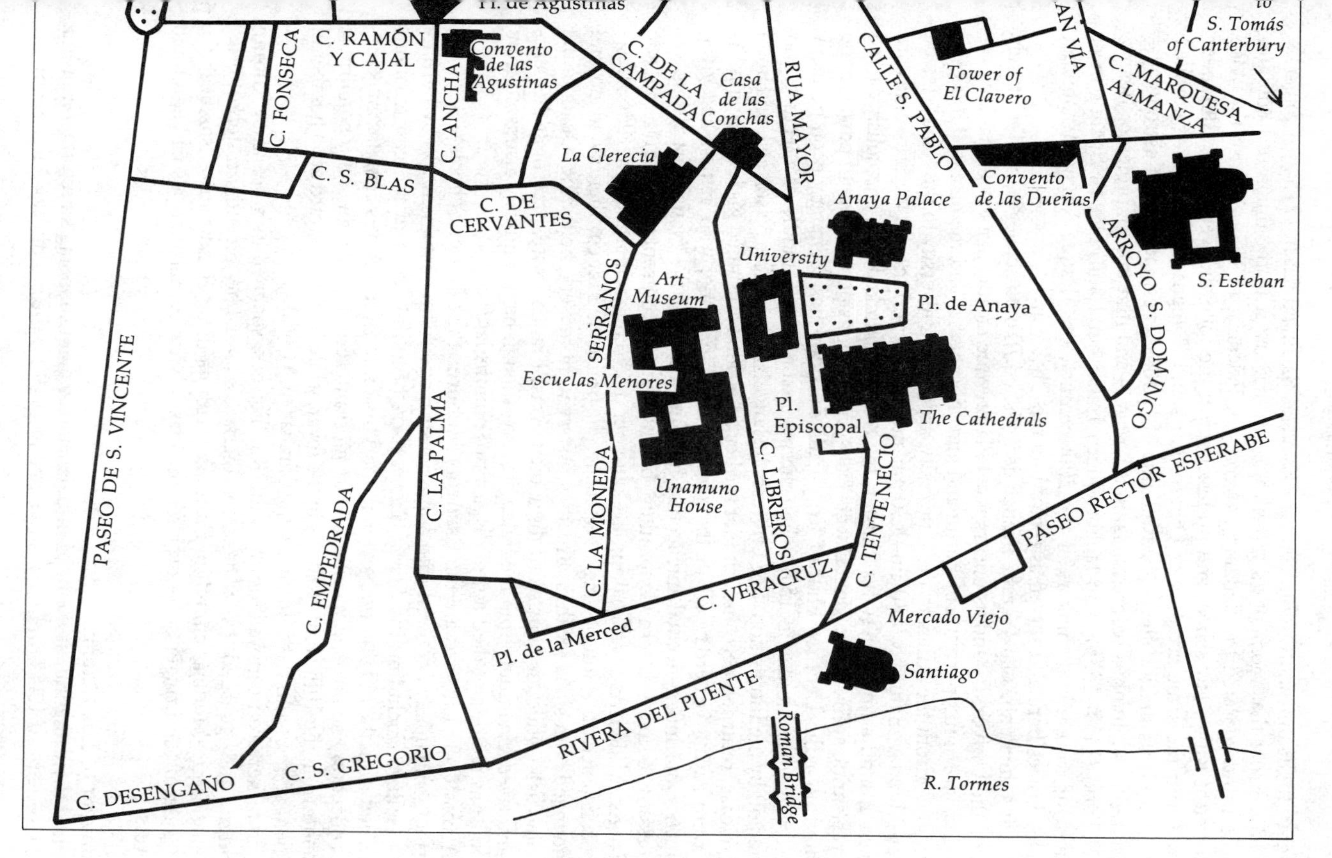

Pl. de Agustinas
to S. Tomás of Canterbury
C. RAMÓN Y CAJAL
Convento de las Agustinas
C. DE LA CAMPADA
Casa de las Conchas
RUA MAYOR
CALLE S. PABLO
Tower of El Clavero
GRAN VÍA
C. MARQUESA ALMANZA
C. FONSECA
C. ANCHA
La Clerecia
C. S. BLAS
C. DE CERVANTES
Convento de las Dueñas
Anaya Palace
ARROYO S. DOMINGO
S. Esteban
University
Art Museum
Pl. de Anaya
SERRANOS
Escuelas Menores
Pl. Episcopal
The Cathedrals
PASEO DE S. VINCENTE
C. LA PALMA
C. LA MONEDA
Unamuno House
C. LIBREROS
C. TENTENECIO
PASEO RECTOR ESPERABE
C. EMPEDRADA
C. VERACRUZ
Mercado Viejo
Pl. de la Merced
Santiago
RIVERA DEL PUENTE
Roman Bridge
C. S. GREGORIO
C. DESENGAÑO
R. Tormes

entrance to the university, founded as the Escuelas Salamantinas in 1218 by Alfonso IX of León. From that moment its growth was prodigious; with the union of León and Castile it incorporated the fledging university of Palencia; in 1254 Alfonso the Wise endowed it with a law school and professorships; the following year Pope Alexander ranked it in the same category as Oxford, Paris and Bologna. At its peak it enrolled 10,000 students in 25 colleges, boasted one of Europe's best faculties of astronomy – consulted by Columbus before his famous voyage – and first woman professor Beatriz de Galindo (1457–1535), who taught Queen Isabel her Latin. One of Spain's most prominent writers and thinkers of the 20th century, the Basque Miguel Unamuno, taught classics here and served as rector into the Civil War.

During the Peninsular War the French demolished 20 of the colleges, but fortunately spared the **University** and its unsurpassed Plateresque façade; in a low medallion over the door are smug portraits of Ferdinand and 'Elisabetha' and the elegant Greek inscription: 'From the Kings to the University; from the University to the Kings. Inside (open Monday–Saturday 9.30 am–1.30 pm and 4.30–7 pm) the old lecture-rooms are placed around a fine two-storey cloister, the two floors linked by a gorgeously carved **Renaissance stair**, where giant insects frolic with bishops popping out of pots. On the ground floor the **Lecture Hall of Fray Luis de León** has seemingly been perfectly preserved since the day in 1573 when the professor, in the middle of a lecture, was carted off by the Inquisition. For five years he languished in a dire prison cell, and upon his release, returned here and without further ado, calmly resumed his lecture with 'As we were saying yesterday...' In the same room, Unamuno, who at first had given Franco some much-needed intellectual backing, claiming the Nationalist rising was 'necessary to save Western Civilization', had his famous confrontation with the lunatic Falangist Millán Astray. Chairing a Columbus Day commemoration in 1936, Unamuno listened to a long string of speeches in praise of Franco, then stood up and denounced both sides for their atrocities. Astray went berserk, bellowing 'Death to the intellectuals' while his bodyguard drew their arms. Franco's wife, present at the ceremony, saved Unamuno from the Falangist fury, though he was quickly dismissed from his post as rector and died out of disgust two months later.

Across Calle Libreros are the **Escuelas Menores** ('the Lesser Schools' – for non-aristocrats), equally endowed with a fine cloister; one room contains works by Ferdinand Gallego, including his *Sky of Salamanca* a beautiful scene of the constellations salvaged from the old library. Next to it, the **Museo de Bellas Artes** contains an eclectic collection and *artesonado* ceilings. The most interesting piece, an anthropomorphic menhir from the 10th century BC, is in the foyer, while in the courtyard are a number of ancient *verracos* and *cerdos* (male swine) (similar to Avila's).

From here you can walk down to the Río Tormes, spanned by a beautiful **Roman bridge**, and guarded by a headless Iberian *cerdo*. The recently restored brick Romanesque-Mudejár church of **Santiago**, with its three elegant apses, sits near the city side of the bridge; cross over for the classic view of Salamanca's cathedral and towers.

Convent of Las Dueñas

Behind the cathedral, at the head of Salamanca's main shopping street, the Gran Vía, the **Convent of Las Dueñas** was founded in 1419 for the Dominican Mothers. In the

16th century, an unusual five-sided **cloister** was added, its upper gallery adorned with capitals carved by some Plateresque Edvard Munch – nightmarish, twisted torsos, skulls, hundreds of screaming faces, generally lumped under the heading of 'grotesques'. These scenes from Dante's **Inferno**, however, are the most disturbing grotesques you'll ever see (open daily 10 am–1 pm and 4–7 pm).

Across from Las Dueñas stands another Plateresque masterpiece, **San Esteban**, with a façade that is as filigreed and delicate as the University; inside it has a lovely (and tranquil) cloister, and a huge wedding-cake of a *retablo* by José Churriguera. The frescoes near the upper choir are unintentionally funny, depicting rows of martyred saints, all holding their heads like a queue of bewildered waiters (open 9 am–1 pm and 4–7 pm). Behind this is another Romanesque church, **Santo Tomás de Canterbury**, erected just three years after his martyrdom; reputedly it was the first in the world dedicated to St Thomas, built by English residents of Salamanca.

Elsewhere in Salamanca

West of the Plaza Mayor, the triangular **Plaza de Agustinas** is one of the city's scenic corners, framed by the **Convent of Las Agustinas** (containing the well-known *Immaculada* by Ribera) and the ornate **Palace of Monterrey** (16th century). A block down is the **Casa de los Muertos** ('the house of the dead'), its name of unknown origin although the Plateresque façade incorporates skulls in the design. Unamuno died in the house next door, at no. 4, and his neo-Rodinesque statue, anguished and bound in matter, broods across the square. Further north, **San Marcos** is an unusual round Romanesque church (1202). Two towers from great aristocratic *solars* survive as landmarks east of the Plaza Mayor: the **Tower of Air** with its elaborate windows, and the **Tower of El Clavero** with its picturesque crown of turrets. As you stroll through the city, look for the brass door-knockers shaped like a hand – the 'Hand of Salamanca', a memory of the Islamic lucky charm, the 'Hand of Fatima'.

TOURIST INFORMATION

Gran Vía 39, Tel: 24 37 30. Municipal information booth: Plaza Mayor, Tel: 21 83 42.

WHERE TO STAY

Salamanca's **Parador de Salamanca******, Tesode Feria 2, Tel: 22 97 00, is located just across the Roman bridge with a fine view of the city's enchanting skyline. The *parador*, one of Spain's newest, is hardly the loveliest, but it offers a pool, garden and air-conditioning for 6500–7000 pts a double. A more moderate choice in the middle of town, the **Hotel Emperatriz****, Compañia 44, Tel: 21 92 00, located in a pretty monumental building, with TV in every room; 2300–2650 pts a double. Even better is **Las Torres****, Plaza Mayor 26, Tel: 21 21 00, some rooms with balconies overlooking Salamanca's front parlour (doubles with bath 2300 pts). There are at least a score of inexpensive *fondas* and pensions: the **Hostal Tormes**, Rua Mayor 20, Tel: 21 96 83, stands out by dint of its great location, between the Plaza Mayor and University; the rooms are also clean and pleasant, and doubles with bath are 1500–1800 pts, 1350–1550 pts without.

EATING OUT

You can eat well in Salamanca for little, thanks to the student population – in spots like the **Roma** on C. Aguilera near the Plaza Mayor, there are 'Quick meals' at 295 pts a throw, and there are many other places like it. For something more elegant, eat at **El Caudil** on Ruiz Aguilera 10, where a stuffed, bespectacled pig in the window toots a horn proclaiming the good *cochinillo* inside; good tapas at the bar (1500 pts). **La Posada** on Aire 1, near the Tower of Air, has a wide selection but is best known for its dishes with *alubias* – French beans (1200 pts). Good Chinese food may be had at **King Long**, Pl. de la Libertad – Peking prawns are good, at 690 pts; other dishes are less costly.

Around Salamanca

The province of Salamanca for the most part resembles a northern extension of Extremadura. A good part of the land is devoted to raising fighting bulls, who roam vast fields dotted with holm oaks. Some of Spain's most remote villages are located in Salamanca's sierra – reputedly some of them hadn't even heard of God until the 20th century.

GETTING AROUND

There are six trains a day from Salamanca to Ciudad Rodrigo; otherwise you'll have to rely on buses from Salamanca to Alba de Tormes, Ledesma, and to Béjar and the villages of the Sierra. Connections exist, if not particularly often. Remember, life is a journey . . . not a destination.

WHAT TO SEE

One of the more scenic parts of the province is to the north-west of the city near the River Duero, which forms for many miles the border with Portugal. **Ledesma** is a pretty, walled town at the tip of the **Embalse de Almendra**, a huge lake formed by a dam on the Tormes, close to its confluence with the Duero. The town itself has a pretty Plaza Mayor, a couple of medieval churches and a bridge from the same period. Up the river towards Salamanca there are beaches along the Tormes; the whole area is pretty, green and wooded and very un-Castilian.

The **Arribes del Duero** is a region of steep, 310 m (1000 ft) walled canyons, lakes and rugged hills. **Saucelle** is one of its most scenic villages, in the centre of a large almond-growing area.

Ciudad Rodrigo

On the Portuguese frontier, **Cuidad Rodrigo**, was captured from the Moors in the early 12th century and named for the Count Rodrigo González Girón, who led its resettlement. A magnificent set of walls added in 1190 is still almost intact; Spaniards are fond of aerial views of the city, enclosed in its multi-pointed star. During the Peninsular War, Wellington took it after a bitter, 11-day siege, earning himself the Spanish title of

Duque de Ciudad Rodrigo. Since then much of the damage inflicted by British guns has been restored – namely the much-battered **Cathedral**, an elegant Gothic temple built soon after the founding by Count Rodrigo. It has three lovely carved portals; note especially the twelve figures from the Old Testament over the south door, and the beautiful Portico del Perdón of the main façade. The **choir stalls** are the work of the fertile imagination and delicate chisel of Rodrigo Alemán (who is also credited with the naughty choir in Zamora), and there is more fine carving to be seen on the capitals in the cathedral and its **cloister**, added in 1325.

Ciudad Rodrigo has a charming, 17th-century **Plaza Mayor** with an unusual **Ayuntamiento**, more Latin American than Spanish. Indeed, many of the fine 16th-century palaces that ennoble the city's quiet streets were built by men who had made their fortunes with the Conquistadores. One of the highlights of the city is the 2.4 km (1.5 mile) walk around the **medieval walls**. The **castle of Enrique II** that dominates them has been converted into a parador.

South of Salamanca: Alba de Tormes and the Sierra

Between Salamanca and Avila, **Alba de Tormes** has a history bound up with the proud Dukes of Alba and Santa Teresa, who in 1571 founded the **Convento de La Anunciación** with the Duke's support. She returned to the convent to die, and her remains (or at least her heart and arm) are venerated in the church; a beautiful relief over its door depicts the Annunciation, with the Angel Gabriel carrying a caduces like the god Mercury. Of the castle of the Dukes of Alba, only the **Homage Tower** remains. Here, when the Grand Duke was in residence, Lope de Vega's plays were often premiered before being performed in Madrid; some of its 16th-century frescoes have been restored. Alba is famous for its several Romanesque–Mudejár churches and the unusual filigree work of its potters.

In the rugged **Sierra de Béjar** and the **Sierra de Francia** in the southern extreme of the province, tiny villages were secluded for centuries. They are wonderfully atmospheric places, their narrow medieval streets lined with leaning, half-timbered houses, piled before scenic mountain backdrops, refreshingly cool in the summer when parboiled Spaniards ascend, seeking relief from the plains of Extremadura and Castile. Most beautiful and most visited is **La Alberca**, a gem of a village in a magnificent setting, surrounded by oak and chestnut forests. The parish church has a unique pulpit of coloured granite, and if you're lucky, you'll run into one of the village's semi-pagan celebrations, when the women don the most ornate costumes in Spain; when they're not dressing up, they're stitching gorgeous, primitively exuberant embroideries. Nearby there are fantastic views over the valley of **Las Batuecas** and its mirador **El Portillo**, and in the summer you can hike up the conical **Peña de Francia** (1730 m; 5623 ft) where a Gothic church houses an image of a Virgin discovered by a French pilgrim (hence its name). Other beautiful old villages of the Sierra are **Candelario** only two miles from the major town of **Béjar**, which itself boasts some fine streets, and the **Mirador de Extremadura**. If the above are too cosmopolitan, try **Miranda del Castañar**, or the even smaller **San Martín del Castañar**, or head south into **Las Hurdes** (see Extremadura, p. 373).

TOURIST INFORMATION

Ciudad Rodrigo: Arco de las Amayuelas 6, Tel: 46 05 61 (across from the Cathedral).
Béjar: Plaza Mayor.

WHERE TO STAY AND EAT

Ledesma's only hotel belongs to a spa, the **Balneario de Ledesna*****, Tel: 57 02 50, a large and fairly modern establishment open mid-May to mid-October; doubles are 3200 pts. The **Parador Enrique II*****, Pl. Castillo, Tel: 46 01 50 in Ciudad Rodrigo has its entrance just under the Homage Tower; with only 27 rooms, it is intimate and charmingly furnished; doubles are from 5500–7500 pts. The **Conde Rodrigo**** (Pl. de Salvador 9, Tel: 46 14 04) next to the Cathedral in an old palace, is a close second to the parador – or better, if you like to wake up to Spanish cartoons on your room's TV (3000–4200 pts double). Most of Ciudad Rodrigo's other accommodation, and restaurants as well, are on the Salamanca–Lisbon road, though there are a couple of adequate *fondas* near the tourist office.

The villages of the Sierra are mostly unspoiled, but hardly undiscovered, and if you'd like to stay over in the summer, you'll need a reservation. In Alberca the two main hotels are open all year: **Las Batuecas**** on the road to Las Batuecas, Tel: 5, doubles with bath, 3000 pts, and **Hostal Paris***, La Chanca, Tel: 12, doubles 2000 pts with bath, 1800 pts without; both are very pleasant in wonderful settings and have average restaurants. In Candelario the **Hostal Cristi****, Pl. Béjar 1, Tel: 40 29 76 is the village 'Ritz', open from June until the end of September; doubles with bath range from 1950–2425 pts, without 1200–1600 pts. If you come out of season, the best bet is the **Travieso****, El Rincón, Tel: 40 24 77, with nine comfortable rooms for 2200 pts a double, 2000 pts without bath.

Béjar has the Sierra's best hotel (**Colón*****, Colón 42, Tel: 40 06 50, with a bar, garden and restaurant; doubles with bath 3600 pts down to 2900 pts from November to March). Also open all year, the **Hotel Commercio***, Puerta de Avila 5, Tel: 40 02 19 has cosy rooms in the centre for 2200–2600 pts a double with bath, 1800–2200 pts without.

There's a pension in Miranda de Castañar – the **Condado de Miranda**, Parajela Perdiza, Tel: 16, open all year with rooms with bath for 1400–1700 pts, without 1000–1200 pts, which also has the town's sole restaurant (700 pts).

In Alba de Tormes you can get a fine, air-conditioned double in a quiet corner of town at the **Alameda****, Avda. Juan Pablo II, Tel: 30 00 31, with bath for only 1850 pts; it also has a very reasonable restaurant, though the food is only par.

EATING OUT

In Ledesma, the **Parador's** restaurant (1800 pts) is the town's best; for good, inexpensive tapas try **El Rodeo** at Gigantes 6, or one of the bars in the Plaza Mayor.

A good place to eat in Béjar, **Tres Coronas**, Ctra. de Salamanca, features Castilian roast meats for around 1500 pts.

Part X

MADRID

Coat of Arms of Madrid – the Bear and the Berry Tree

Through all the books that have ever been written about Spain, opinion on this unlikely capital seems about evenly divided. Some writers are sure it's the heart and soul of the nation, but the dissent has been coming in ever since the city has been on the map; many follow Richard Ford in counselling that the less time you spend in Madrid, the better you'll like it. Like Bonn or Washington, it is an entirely artificial capital, created on the whim of the early Habsburg kings. The city has great museums, wide boulevards and a cosmopolitan air. It doesn't have a beautiful setting, or a tolerable climate, or many noteworthy churches or monuments – it's difficult to imagine a capital more impoverished architecturally.

So why stay long, when fascinating places like Toledo and Segovia are just a short train-ride away? Art is one reason; not surprisingly, the city of Velázquez and Goya and connoisseur Habsburg and Bourbon kings has one of this planet's greatest hoards of fine paintings stored in its museums. Old Madrid, the area around the Plaza Mayor that has changed little since the 17th century, would be another. The biggest reason for many, though, will be that Madrid is better equipped than any city in Spain to give you a good time. The Madrileños proudly claim their city stays up later than any in Europe; there's good cause to stay up, with an infinite variety of *tapas* bars, night life and attractions that may make you forget all about Velázquez and Goya.

And that's a clue to the real story of Madrid. Now that the democrats are in and the Francoist bogeys a dim memory, this very alive and self-conscious capital has its destiny in its hands, and the freedom to do whatever it likes. It will be worth at least a short stay just to see what they do with it.

History

Settlements have come and gone here since the Paleolithic era, but the first permanent town seems to have been built by the Arabs, who constructed a fortress Alcazar on the site of today's Royal Palace, and a small circuit of walls that extended only as far as the Plaza Mayor and the Plaza Isabel II. Their name for it, *Majrit*, came from the Matriz, a little stream that ran in the valley where Calle de Segovia is now. Majrit met the Reconquista in 1083, two years before Toledo; the Cid may have been around to assist Alfonso VI in its capture. The walls were extended to the 11th and 12th centuries. The new southern gate, the Puerta del Sol, gave its name to the square that later replaced it, standing at the centre of Madrid today.

One strange interlude in the city's history came in the 1380s, when King Juan I gave the city in fief to the exiled last king of Little Armenia, Leon VI. In the centuries that followed, the town's growth was steady and slow. Royal patronage came first with Enrique IV, who tacked a Renaissance façade onto the old Moorish Alcazar to make it one of his palaces, but it was Charles V who first began to spend much time here, both he and his son Philip II found the climate eased their bad cases of gout. Up to that time Spain had had no real capital. The Cortes traditionally alternated its meetings in all the Castilian cities, so that none would be offended, and the necessity of an occasional royal presence in all of Spain's diverse regions made vagabonds of all the earlier kings. Philip declared Madrid the permanent capital in 1561, giving the Habsburg monarchy a strong, central, specifically Castilian capital from which to combat the separatist tendencies of the outlying regions, and at the same time creating a counterweight to the contentious older cities of Castile, most of which had supported the Comunero revolt just 40 years earlier.

Unfortunately, neither the Habsburgs nor the Bourbons went out of their way to replan or embellish their capital. Besides palaces, their only important contributions are the two great parks, the Retiro and the Casa del Campo, that define the eastern and western boundaries of the old town and help so much to make Madrid liveable. Most travellers of that era, from the 16th to 18th centuries, write of Madrid as crowded, unpleasant, even unhealthy; sanitation and other urban amenities did lag far behind other European capitals of the day. The city must have seemed a curious juxtaposition of a sophisticated royal court, with its palaces and gardens on top of an overgrown Castilian provincial town. Nevertheless, in this era Madrid was home to Velázquez and Goya, to Calderón and Lope de Vega, as well as many other important figures of the 'Golden Age of Spain'.

Politically the city learned to speak for itself in 1808, in the famous revolt of the 'Dos de Mayo'. When Napoleon's men attempted to kidnap the Spanish royal family, a spontaneous patriotic uprising occurred; though soon suppressed by the French, it has been a golden memory for the Spanish ever since. Madrid's next chance for heroism came with the Civil War. In the early days of that conflict, four Nationalist columns, including most of Franco's Army of Africa, advanced to positions within sight of the Royal palace (General Mola mentioned a 'fifth column' of sympathizers supposedly hidden within the city: it was just propaganda, but a new phrase was born). Bitter street fighting in the western suburbs continued until March 1937. At first, the defence of the city was almost entirely in the hands of the newly formed Socialist, Communist and Anarchist militias. Their untrained fighters, many women among them, wore street clothes, held meetings to discuss tactics with the officers, and some actually commuted daily to the front on the Metro, or in cars commandeered from the wealthy.

The Republican government soon fled to Valencia, but as the world watched in suspense, Madrid held. *'No pasarán'* – 'they shall not pass' – was the famous slogan, coined by La Pasionaria, and the city became a symbol that caught the imagination of Europe, the first community in that dark time to make a successful stand against fascism. In November 1936 the International Brigades and the first squadrons of Soviet airplanes began to arrive, and they helped defeat the last Nationalist attempts to encircle the city. Madrid held out until the last days of the war, remaining calm and disciplined, with little of the frenetic revolutionary craziness of Barcelona.

Before the Civil War, Madrid had grown into a bright and cosmopolitan cultural capital; its cafes and clubs frequented by the artists and writers of the 'Generation of '98' as well as the politicians and the Spanish elite. Though most of the glitter, as well as the substance, disappeared under 40 years of Franco, the city grew tremendously. The Franco government, determined to see their capital outstrip Barcelona, encouraged new industry and migration from other corners of Spain. Though the city flourished, the environmental cost was high; once lovely boulevards were flattened into urban motorways, and the outskirts of the city were disfigured by the wasteland of factories, junkyards, and shantytowns you see today.

After 1976, however, Madrid's civic pride was allowed to resurface. A remarkable mayor, Enrique Tierno, dedicated himself to improving the city's quality of life; he planted thousands of trees, created new parks in the outlying districts, repaired some of the damage done by the traffic planners, and even found some water to direct through the dusty stream bed of the Manzanares. Madrileños called Tierno 'the old Professor' for his habit of lecturing them on the importance of trees and greenery, and all of them, regardless of politics, mourned his death in 1986.

GETTING IN AND OUT

First of all, Madrid is smaller than most great European capitals, and transportation is surprisingly easy and convenient.

By Air

Yellow buses regularly connect Barajas Airport with the Plaza de Colón (terminal in the underground car park), a few blocks north of Retiro Park. The service is fast and cheap (150 pts) and infinitely preferable to a very expensive taxi ride (no service from 1.15–4.15 am). **Iberia** information's number is 411 25 45; call 411 20 11 for tickets and reservations. For **Aviaco** call 254 51 13; **Spantax** 205 44 69.

By Train

There are two main stations: **Atocha**, quite close to the city centre at end of the Paseo del Prado, handles trains to Andalucía and all points south, also Portugal and Valencia. Quite a few trains to the north also stop here. **Chamartin**, way out in the northern suburbs (the Metro is the best way to get there) is new and has the air of a shopping mall. It takes most of the trains going north. Note that these two stations are connected by an underground rail line, with stops at **Recoletos** (just north of Retiro Park) and

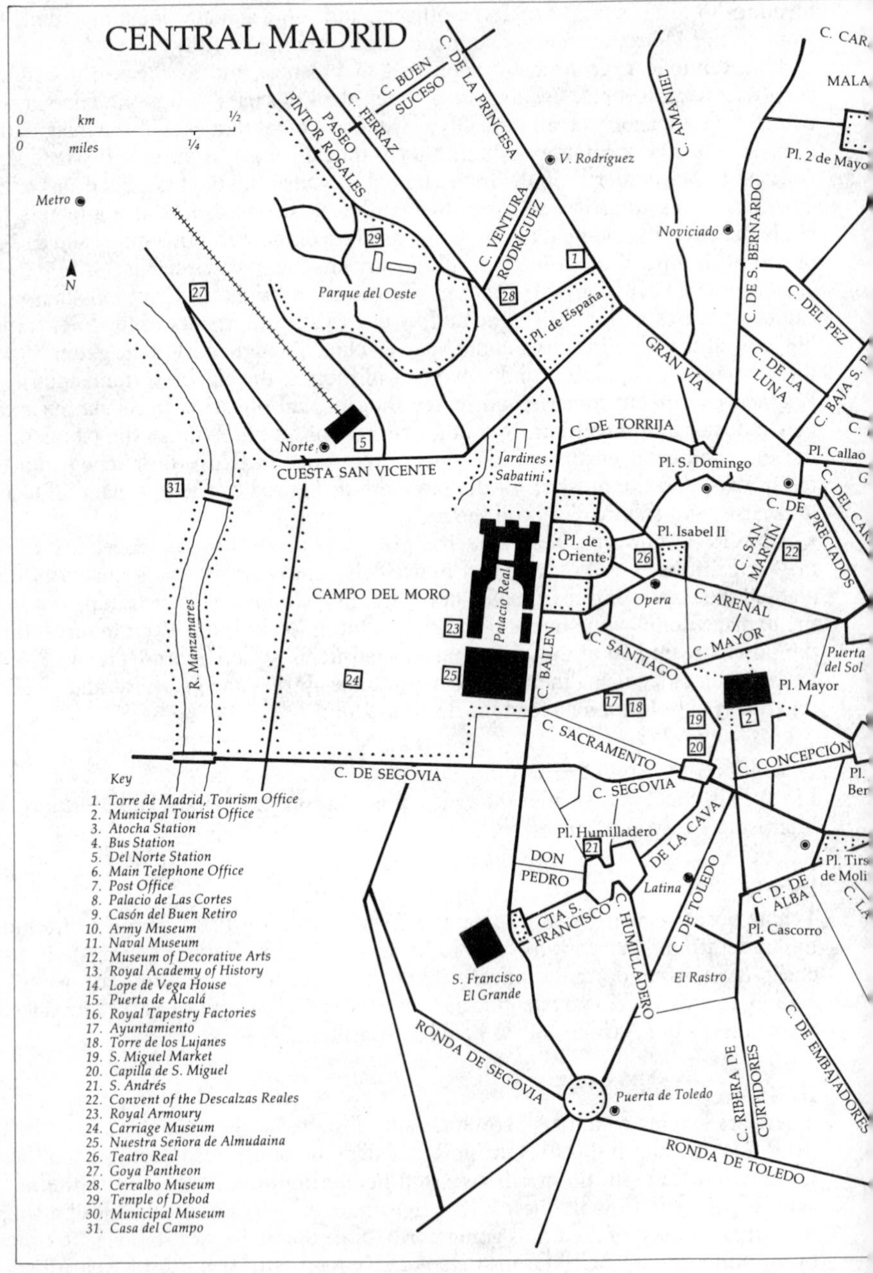
CENTRAL MADRID
0 km ½
0 miles ¼
Metro
N
C. BUEN SUCESO
C. DE LA PRINCESA
C. FERRAZ
PASEO PINTOR ROSALES
C. AMANIEL
C. CAR
MALA
Pl. 2 de Mayo
V. Rodríguez
C. VENTURA RODRÍGUEZ
Noviciado
C. DE S. BERNARDO
Parque del Oeste
Pl. de España
C. DEL PEZ
GRAN VÍA
C. DE LA LUNA
C. BAJA S.
C. DE TORRIJA
Norte
CUESTA SAN VICENTE
Jardines Sabatini
Pl. S. Domingo
Pl. Callao
C. DEL CA
C. DE PRECIADOS
Pl. Isabel II
Pl. de Oriente
C. SAN MARTÍN
CAMPO DEL MORO
Palacio Real
Opera
C. ARENAL
R. Manzanares
C. BAILEN
C. SANTIAGO
C. MAYOR
Puerta del Sol
Pl. Mayor
C. SACRAMENTO
C. CONCEPCIÓN
C. DE SEGOVIA
C. SEGOVIA
Pl. Humilladero
DON PEDRO
DE LA CAVA
C. DE TOLEDO
Latina
Pl. Tirs de Moli
C. D. DE ALBA
Pl. Cascorro
CTA S. FRANCISCO
C. HUMILLADERO
S. Francisco El Grande
El Rastro
C. DE EMBAJADORES
RONDA DE SEGOVIA
Puerta de Toledo
C. RIBERA DE CURTIDORES
RONDA DE TOLEDO
Key
1. Torre de Madrid, Tourism Office
2. Municipal Tourist Office
3. Atocha Station
4. Bus Station
5. Del Norte Station
6. Main Telephone Office
7. Post Office
8. Palacio de Las Cortes
9. Casón del Buen Retiro
10. Army Museum
11. Naval Museum
12. Museum of Decorative Arts
13. Royal Academy of History
14. Lope de Vega House
15. Puerta de Alcalá
16. Royal Tapestry Factories
17. Ayuntamiento
18. Torre de los Lujanes
19. S. Miguel Market
20. Capilla de S. Miguel
21. S. Andrés
22. Convent of the Descalzas Reales
23. Royal Armoury
24. Carriage Museum
25. Nuestra Señora de Almudaina
26. Teatro Real
27. Goya Pantheon
28. Cerralbo Museum
29. Temple of Debod
30. Municipal Museum
31. Casa del Campo

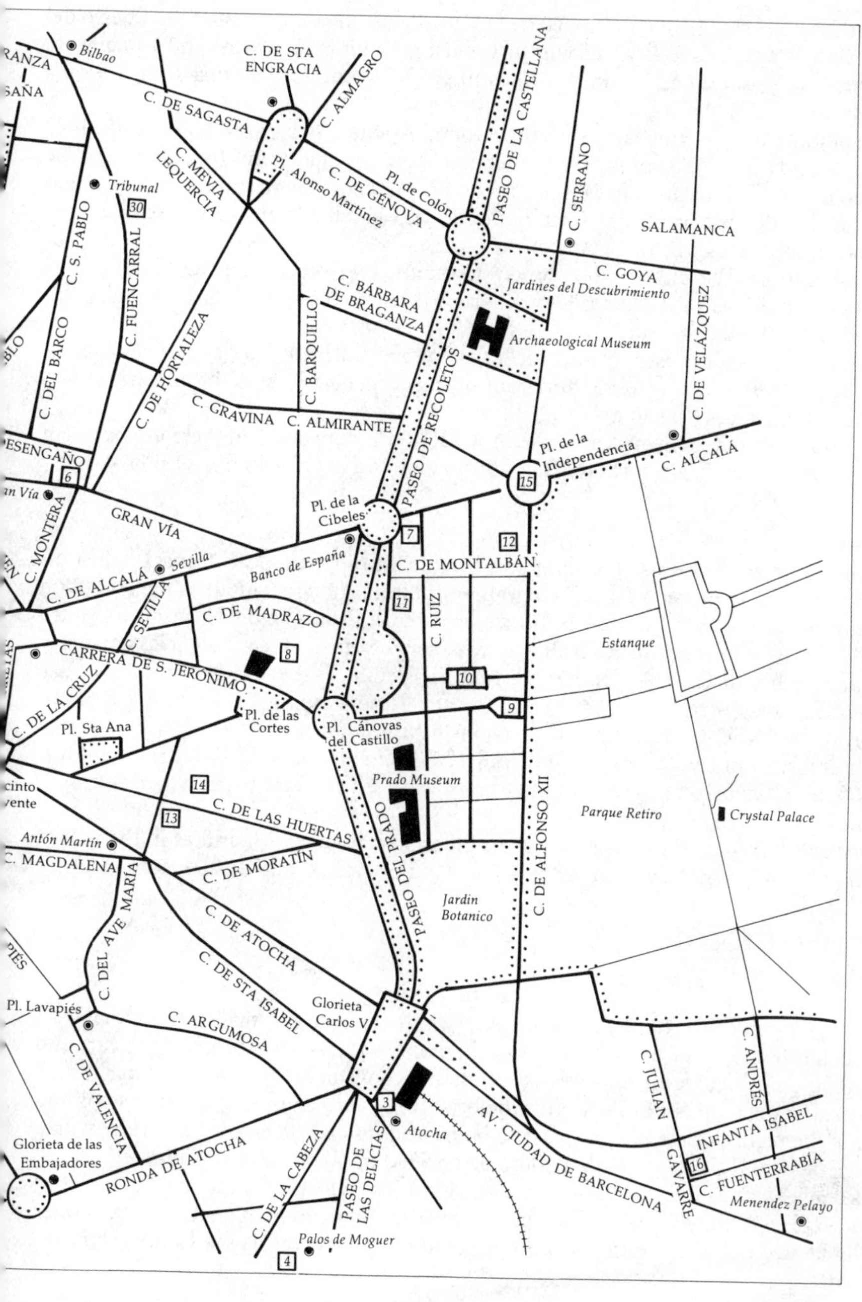

Bilbao
C. DE STA ENGRACIA
C. ALMAGRO
C. DE SAGASTA
C. MEVIA LEQUERCIA
Pl. Alonso Martínez
C. DE GÉNOVA
Pl. de Colón
PASEO DE LA CASTELLANA
C. SERRANO
SALAMANCA
Tribunal
30
C. S. PABLO
C. FUENCARRAL
C. DEL BARCO
C. DE HORTALEZA
C. BARQUILLO
C. BÁRBARA DE BRAGANZA
C. GOYA
Jardines del Descubrimiento
Archaeological Museum
C. DE VELÁZQUEZ
C. GRAVINA
C. ALMIRANTE
PASEO DE RECOLETOS
Pl. de la Independencia
15
C. ALCALÁ
6
GRAN VÍA
C. MONTERA
Pl. de la Cibeles
7
12
Banco de España
Sevilla
C. DE ALCALÁ
C. SEVILLA
C. DE MONTALBÁN
C. DE MADRAZO
11
C. RUIZ
Estanque
8
CARRERA DE S. JERÓNIMO
10
9
C. DE LA CRUZ
Pl. de las Cortes
Pl. Cánovas del Castillo
Pl. Sta Ana
Prado Museum
14
C. DE ALFONSO XII
Parque Retiro
Crystal Palace
13
C. DE LAS HUERTAS
Antón Martín
C. MAGDALENA
C. DE MORATÍN
PASEO DEL PRADO
C. DEL AVE MARÍA
C. DE ATOCHA
Jardin Botanico
C. DE STA ISABEL
Pl. Lavapiés
C. ARGUMOSA
Glorieta Carlos V
C. DE VALENCIA
C. JULIAN GAVARRE
C. ANDRÉS
3
Atocha
AV. CIUDAD DE BARCELONA
INFANTA ISABEL
16
C. FUENTERRABÍA
Glorieta de las Embajadores
RONDA DE ATOCHA
C. DE LA CABEZA
PASEO DE LAS DELICIAS
Menendez Pelayo
Palos de Moguer
4

Nuevo Ministerios (along the Paseo de la Castellana, one mile north of the Puerto del Sol). Many trains to and from distant places use it to hit both Atocha and Chamartin, and you may jump on any train that does to get from one to the other (buy a 35 pta ticket).

In addition, next to Atocha, there's the **Atocha Apeadero**, a grimy, nightmarish hole in the ground where most of the commuter and short-distance trains (*cercanias*) go. The connection to Chamartin is here – not in the big Atocha. Chamartin has its Apeadero also, but it's downstairs in the same building, and handles many of the same short-distance trains that go through Atocha Apeadero.

Besides these, there is the big, lonely **Estación Del Norte**, on the Cuesta de S Vicente near the Royal Palace (metro: Norte); it has trains only to Galicia and Salamanca, and sometimes Avila.

If that's confusing, just buy your ticket at the main RENFE office at C Alcalá 44 (Tel: 222 76 09) or at any of the hundreds of travel agencies that do it (long trips only) and they'll tell you where to go.

Madrid is of course the nerve-centre of the RENFE network, and there are frequent connections to nearly everywhere. Rail information is Tel: 733 30 00, 24 hours.

By Bus

Most, but not all, buses use the **Estación Sur de Autobuses**, on C Canarias (just off the Paseo de las Delicias, a 10-minute walk south from Atocha station). A big exception is the *Auto Res* company, which has its own terminal at Plaza Conde de Casals 6 (Metro Conde Casal, south-east of Retiro Park) with services to Cuenca, Valencia, Extremadura, and parts of Castile. *Continental Auto*, C Alenza 20 (head north from the Rias Rosas Metro stop) takes you up to Burgos and Basque country. For towns close to Madrid, check the 'Getting Around' sections for those towns.

For information: Estación de Sur: 468 42 00. Continental: 233 37 11. Auto Res: 251 66 44. Of course the Tourist Office can always tell you how to get where you want to go.

Note on left luggage. There's no office in the train stations in Madrid as in the rest of Spain. The only convenient public *consigna* is in the Estación de Sur de Autobuses.

GETTING AROUND

Metro

It is fast, clean, cheap (40 pts) and goes everywhere in town. Its only faults are that it's a little colourless (except the old lines, like the no. 1, with its ancient half-open cars and bare light bulbs) and that connections are often inconvenient. You can get a map of the system at any station; study it carefully before setting out. There are so many stops and lines in the centre of the city, it's easy to be tricked into taking a half-hour ride (with a change or two) for a distance that could be covered in 10 minutes on foot.

As convenient as it is, try to not use the Metro too much. Even though Madrid isn't the most pleasant city to walk in, the more time you spend up in the open air, the better you'll like it. Madrid's Metro is almost as conducive to anomie as the London Underground.

Trains run from 6 to 1.30 am. Stations are distinguished by a red diamond over the entrance, as in Barcelona. You can purchase 10-trip *tarjetas* for 380 pts.

Taxis
Any city taxi that has a meter (some don't; avoid them) is expected to use it, but don't be surprised if the fare comes out a little higher; there are surcharges for the airports, train stations, and double the rate shown if you leave the city limits. As elsewhere in Spain, taxis are cheap enough, the average ride in the city centre going for about 350 pts.

Buses
Only a few lines will be of use to the visitor – but buses can be preferable to the Metro if you want to see Madrid. Many buses go through the Plaza de la Cibeles, where there is an information booth.

Line 1: Pl. España – Gran Via – Cibeles – C. Velázquez and C. Serrano – Ortega y Gasset (Salamanca area).
Line 3: Pl. Alonso Martinez – C. Fuencarral and Hortaleza – Sol – C. Mayor – Pl. San Francisco
Line 14: Glorieta Carlos V (Atocha) – Cibeles – Paseo Castellana – Chamartin
Line 19: C. Velázquez and Serrano – C. Alfonso XII (Retiro Park) – Atocha – Paseo de Las Delicias (bus station Sur)
Line 33: Pl. Isabel II – Casa del Campo (Zoo and fun fair).

MICRO BUSES
Line M1: Opera (Teatro Real) – C. Arenal and C. Mayor - Sol - C Alcalá – Cibeles
Line M8: Pl. España – Pl. Callas – C. Alcalá – Bullring
Most buses stop at midnight; the all-nighters all converge at the Plaza de la Cibeles. Fares can be either 40 or 45 pts; the drivers do give change.

ORIENTATION

Madrid goes on and on – today it is home for 3 or 4 million people, depending on how much of the surrounding area is included. Don't trouble yourself about that; almost everything of conceivable interest to any traveller will be found within one mile of the **Puerta del Sol**. Here, in the centre of the city, Madrid is squeezed into a kind of isthmus by two huge parks. On the west, old Madrid is bounded by the wall of the **Royal Palace**, its gardens opening into the larger of these parks, the **Casa del Campo**. Nearby is the **Plaza de España**, where you'll find the tourist information office. The smaller, eastern park is the **Retiro**. Between it and the broad boulevard called the **Paseo del Prado**, most of Madrid's famous museums can be found. The Puerta del Sol sits squarely in the centre, and the oldest quarter of the city, around the **Plaza Mayor**, is just to the east of it. Keep these in mind, and learn a few of the main streets, and you'll not get too lost – Madrid isn't nearly as complicated as it looks on the map.

WHAT TO SEE

Puerta del Sol
Ten streets meet here, as well as three Metro lines and dozens of buses; however you're

travelling in Madrid, you're soon likely to cross the 'Gate of the Sun', the centre of Spain. All distances in the nation are measured from the marker in front of the police headquarters, in the south-west corner of the square. The gate (*puerta*) from Alfonso's walls is long gone, and the plaza is chaotic, dirty and crowded as it always has been, but it endears itself to the Madrileños in a way no formal plaza with fountains, traffic roundabouts and a postcard view ever could. Nothing that is *autentico* in Madrid ever strays far from the Sol, and the spider's web of narrow streets around it; curious old shops, the *tascas* south of the plaza with their windows piled high with shellfish and other delicacies, the oldest and best-known bars in town.

From here, you'll have the choice of heading either west to the old town and the Royal Palace, or east to the Retiro and the museums. It's almost a tradition for visitors to Madrid to begin with a morning in the Prado, one of the half-dozen great museums of the world, and the major attraction Madrid has to offer. If that's your destination, the Carrera de San Geronimo on the eastern end of the square will take you right to it.

The Cortes

Along the way, if you blink you may miss the **Palacio de las Cortes** (1850), the home of the Spanish parliament. Many cities one-tenth Madrid's size have larger and more elegant post offices. Certainly, few nations would be content to house their lawmakers in such a dowdy and insignificant structure; from it we can see how little Spaniards thought of their corrupt and manipulated governments of the 19th century. Today, important sessions of the Cortes are broadcast on the radio, and it was on one such occasion in February 1981 when the right-wing zealot, Civil Guard Colonel Tejero, and his men stormed in, shooting off their pistols while the nation listened. Tejero held the Cortes hostage for 24 hours, finally surrendering when it became clear that the majority of the army was supporting the King and democracy. The following day saw the biggest demonstration in the city's history, led by the leaders of all the political parties, marching arm-in-arm down the Calle de Alcalá.

The Prado

When, in the early 19th century, the Spanish royal house realized that the paintings adorning its various palaces added up to perhaps Europe's greatest artistic treasure, it was resolved to bring all of them together under one roof; credit for the creation of the Museo del Prado goes to Fernando VII, that most hated of kings, who took over this rambling neo-Classical structure, intended as a natural history museum when it was begun in 1785, and opened the collection to the public in 1819. Since then the building has been restored several times, but the collection has changed little. The Spanish noble families who collected paintings in centuries past are likely still to have them; the habit of donating to museums never took root as much here as in the rest of Europe. For the best of the Prado we can thank the practised eyes of Charles V, Philip II and Philip IV. Whatever else history can blame them for, they knew good painting when they saw it.

Expect crowds, especially on weekends. The earlier you go, the less you'll have to contend with – and don't be dismayed by huge mobs at the entrance; they're likely to be disorganized tour groups counting heads, and you should be able to pass right through (hours: Sunday 10 am–1.45 pm, Tuesday, Thursday, Friday and Saturday 10 am–4.45 pm; Wednesday 3–8.45 pm; admission includes the two museums in the Casón del Buen Retiro, discussed below).

THE COLLECTIONS: GROUND FLOOR

The first rooms are devoted to medieval religious art. Don't be in too much of a hurry to see Velázquez; some of the best art in the Prado is here, including two 15th-century retablos, the *Legend of St Michael* by the Maestro de Arguis, and *The Life of the Virgin and St Francis*, by Nicolas Frances. From here, the next galleries are arranged more-or-less chronologically, providing a running history of the development of Spanish art, along with contributions from the Flemings. Even before Philip II, who valued Flemish art above all others, the Low Countries' close commercial and dynastic ties ensured that some would turn up here. Among them is one of the greatest works of Brueghel, the untitled 'snowy landscape', very small and hidden away in a corner. A room nearby contains the famous collaboration of Brueghel and Rubens, the *Allegory of the Five Senses*, a complete universe of philosophy in its five enormous canvases. Rubens, another favourite of the Spanish monarchs, is well represented here, with his chubby *Three Graces* among a whole roomful of mythological subjects. His paintings of Biblical subjects fill the adjacent gallery.

The huge collection of early Spanish painting, from the beginning of the 16th century, clearly shows the influence of the Renaissance in such works as Fernando Gallego's eerie *Cristo Benificiendo*. Pedro Berruguete contributes a scene of an *Auto-de-Fé* that is almost satirical, with bored and sleepy church apparatchiks dozing under a baldachin while the woebegone heretics, in clothes emblazoned with flames and devils, are led off to the slaughter. By the 17th century, the religious pathology of the age becomes manifest in the Prado's Spanish collection, notably in a disturbing painting by Francisco Ribalta of the crucified Christ leaning down off the Cross to embrace St Bernard.

This should prepare you for one of the Prado's greatest treasures, the *'Black paintings'* of Goya, hidden away here behind a room of indifferent Flemings, as if it were feared they would contaminate Goya's sunnier works upstairs. All the well-known images are here: Saturn devouring his children, the duel with cudgels, the Panic. One, a nightmarish vision of the procession at Madrid's festival of San Isidro, can be compared with another, naturalistic painting he did of the festival that can be seen upstairs.

FIRST FLOOR

From the central rotunda, near the stairs and elevator, three doorways open to the galleries dedicated to the Italian, Spanish and Flemish sections. In the Italian, there are several paintings by Raphael, all religious subjects – and an unusual Botticelli pair, a scene from the *Decameron* (fifth day, VIII). Andrea del Sarto, Mantegna, Antonello da Messina and Corregio, among the other Italian masters, are all represented, and there are rooms full of Titians, including two portraits of the artist's patron, Charles V. Titian never painted anything small, and perhaps his biggest canvas of all is *La Gloria*, a colourful, preposterous cloud-bedecked imagining of the Holy Trinity that gently nudges the boundries of kitsch. Charles (who is also in the picture, sometimes called his 'Apotheosis'), is said to have gazed upon this picture constantly while on his deathbed.

In the Dutch rooms, pride of place is given to the work of Van Dyck, a number of portraits including one of Charles I of England. The biggest crowds, though, will be around the works of Hieronymous Bosch (1450–1516, known in Spain as El Bosco). His psychological fantasies, including the *Garden of Earthly Delights*, the *Hay Wain* (and several others you may not know e.g. the *Extraction of the Stone of Madness*) and the table in the centre of the room decorated with the *Seven Deadly Sins* are too familiar to need any comment. Philip II bought every one he could get his hands on, and it should not be surprising to find the most complex of all Spanish kings attracted to this dark surrealism as we moderns are. More works by Bosch can be seen in Philip's apartments at El Escorial.

Probably no other museum has such a large complement of terror to balance the beauty of it; between Goya, Bosch, the other northern painters and the religious hacks, a trip to the Prado can seem like a long ride in a carnival funhouse. If you approach it in this way, the climax will undoubtably be Brueghel's *The Triumph of Death*, with its phalanxes of leering skeletons turned loose upon a doomed, terrified world. To Philip II, who is said to have kept a crowned skull on his night table, it must have seemed a deeply religious work. The Dutch, though, in the middle of their war of independence, would probably have been reminded of the horrors of intolerance and militant religion that were searing contemporary Europe – much of it emanating from this very city.

If you like Bosch, you should also get to know his countryman Joachim Patinir, some of whose best work can also be found in this section. The Prado has few German paintings, but they are choice: Albrecht Dürer's *Self Portrait* and *Adam and Eve*, the angular Teutonic *Three Graces* of Hans Baldung Grien, and works by Cranach and Memling.

VELAZQUEZ

On a day when there are as many Spaniards as foreigners in the Prado, you may find the crowds in the rooms of Velázquez (1599–1660) even more daunting. Many Spanish consider their countryman to be the greatest artist of all, and you may find his several rooms here, the largest Velázquez collection by far, to be a convincing argument. Many of the works have recently been cleaned or restored, making the audacity of his use of light and colour stand out even more clearly. Almost all of his best-known paintings are here: *Los Borrachos* (the Drunkards), *Las Hilanderas* (the Spinning-women), and *The Surrender of Breda*, which the Spaniards call *Las Lanzas* (the Spears). Also present are the royal portraits; lumpy, bewildered Philip IV, a king aware enough of his own inadequacies to let Velázquez express them on canvas, appears in various poses – as a hunter, a warrior, or simply standing around wondering what's for dinner. Of his children, we see the 6-year-old *Don Baltazar Carlos*, in a charming, mock-heroic pose on horseback, and again at the age of 16. It was this prince's untimely death soon after the latter portrait that gave the throne to the idiot Charles II. His sister, the doll-like *Infanta Margarita Maria*, appears by herself and in the most celebrated of all Velázquez's works, *Las Meninas* (the Maids-of-Honour), a composition of such inexhaustible complexity and beauty that the Prado gives it a room to itself. Velázquez painted himself in it, but the red cross on his tunic, the badge of the Order of Santiago, was added by the King's own hand, as a graceful way of informing the artist of the honour he was conferring on him.

Uneven works by Velázquez' contemporaries fill a dozen nearby galleries: Jose Ribera, Francisco Zurbarán and Murillo among others. St Bernard comes in for more abuse, this time at the hand of Alonso Cano, who illustrates the old tale of the praying saint receiving a squirt of milk in his mouth from the breast of an image of the Virgin. Among the works of El Greco are some fine examples of what are sometimes called his 'vertical pictures', including the *Annunciation* and the *Baptism of Jesus*.

GOYA

Like Velázquez, Francisco de Goya (1746–1828) held the office of court painter, in this case at the service of an even more useless monarch, Charles IV. Also like Velázquez, he was hardly inclined to flattery. Critics ever since have wondered how he got away with making his royal patron look so foolish, and the job he did on Charles' wife, the hook-nosed, ignorant and ill-tempered Queen Maria Louisa, is legendary. In every portrait and family scene, she comes out looking half fairy-tale witch, half washerwoman. Her son, later to be the reactionary King Ferdinand VII, is pictured as a teenager, and Goya makes him merely disagreeable and menacing.

Among the other famous Goyas you may compare the *Maja Desnuda* and the *Maja Vestida* (the Naked and Clothed Majas), and the *Dos de Mayo* and *Los Fusilamentos de la Moncloa*, the pair commemorating the uprising of 1808 and its aftermath. The latter, much the better known, shows the impassioned patriots' faces caught in the glare of a lantern, facing the firing squad of grim, almost mechanical French soldiers. Nothing like it had ever been painted before, an unforgettable image and a prophetic prelude to the era of revolutions, mass politics and total war that was just beginning, inaugurated by the French Revolution and Napoleon. The setting is Madrid's Casa del Campo, and the spires of the old town can be made out clearly in the background.

Goya, however, will give you a chance to shake the terrors of the Prado from your mind before you go. His remarkable *cartoons* – designs for tapestries to be made by the Royal Factories for the king's palaces – provide a massive dose of joy and sweetness, with their vivid colours bathed in clear Castilian sunshine. Most, such as *El Quitasol* (the Parasol) and the *Fiesta de San Isidro* are idealized scenes of festivals or country life, and the creatures inhabiting them seem less Spaniards than angels.

Casón del Buen Retiro

Your ticket to the Prado will also get you into the museum's annex, an ungainly 17th-century building intended as a ballroom for Philip IV, three blocks behind the Prado on Calle Felipe II, near the entrance to the Retiro Park. One end of the building is entirely devoted to Picasso's *Guernica*, and the rest (separate entrance) to the 'Sección de Arte Español del Siglo XIX'.

These paintings, differing little from the tepid naturalistic art of the rest of 19th-century Europe, should not detain you long. Painters like Madrazo, Fortuny, Rusiñol and Sorolla were popular in their day, but here the only really memorable works are the marvellously blatant female nudes in the manner of Bouguereau, the kind they liked to hang in saloons 100 years ago.

GUERNICA

Picasso had made New York's Museum of Modern Art promise to return it to Spain when liberty was restored there. The promise was kept in 1981, and millions of Spaniards since have come to see a part of their history denied them under 40 years of dictatorship.

When the German Condor Legion practised its new theory of saturation bombing on the little Basque town of Guernica in April 1937, Franco most likley had not even been informed. Nevertheless, the Nationalists were forced to create an elaborate lie – they said the Communists had planted bombs in the sewers – and it became the official version up until Franco's death. As for the painting itself, there are as many interpretations as critics; *Guernica* is much more than a monument of terror caught in the glare of an electric bulb. As can be seen from Picasso's preliminary sketches displayed on either side of the painting, the fallen horse and rider in the centre were on the artist's mind from the beginning. In them perhaps we can see the origins of Guernica's destroyers: the man on horseback, the bully, the crusader, the caudillo, meeting a bad end from his own designs, while Picasso's primeval bull looks dispassionately on.

The huge black and grey painting is hung in what was Philip IV's grand ballroom, incongruously under a silly Baroque ceiling painted by Luca Giordano. The plate glass in front is ominously thick; Spain still has its share of right-wing cranks. Besides the preliminary sketches and paintings, the adjacent corridors include the wickedly humorous series *Dreams and Lies of Franco*.

The Retiro Park

In the days of Philip IV, this entire area was a royal preserve, including a fortress, a palace (of which only the Casón del Buen Retiro survives) and this park, begun by the Conde-Duque Olivares in 1636 for Philip. Apart from growing smaller – it once extended westwards to the Paseo del Prado – the Parque del Buen Retiro has changed essentially little since, an elegant, formal garden, perfect for the decorous pageants and dalliances of the Baroque era.

Visit the Retiro in spring, when the tulips and horse-chestnut trees are in bloom; failing that, come on any Sunday, when all Madrid comes to see the flowers, concerts, puppet-shows and other impromptu entertainments. If you would like a carriage ride, wait at the little cabin marked 'servicio de simones' near the entrance opposite Calle Antonio Maura.

The centre of the Retiro is a broad lagoon called **El Estanque**, where you may rent canoes or paddleboats. No king ever did less to earn such a grandiose memorial than Alfonso XII (1874–86), but that's him up on horseback decorating the eastern end of the Estanque. In the 17th century, this was a favourite spot for the royal diversions: water pageants and plays. One of the best remembered was a royal performance of Calderón's *Polifemo y Circe* and *Los Incantos de Circe* in 1663; artificial islands were built for the action, while the audience sat around the edge of the Estanque. The whole of it took nine hours, including battles, sea voyages in miniature galleys and Odysseus' trip to the Underworld.

Other attractions of the Retiro include the **Palacio de Exhibiciones** and the great, glass **Palacio de Cristal** (Crystal Palace), built in the 1890s; both have a regular schedule of cultural exhibits and shows. Among the 160-odd hectares (400 acres) of the Park are the **Jardines Botanicos** (Botanical Gardens: entrance near the Prado Museum), a Japanese garden, and towards the south, a seemingly endless expanse of quiet paths among old shady trees, hedges and gardens where you can easily forget you're in the centre of a metropolis of 3 million people.

Museums near the Prado and Retiro Park

This neighbourhood has been Madrid's centre of fashion for three centuries, and consequently has attracted quite a few museums, devoted to all manner of things. Museums are about all, for this is one of the duller corners of Madrid.

Closest to the Prado, the **Museo del Ejercito** (Army Museum) at Calle Mendez Nuñez 1 pokes its scores of old cannons menacingly out at the surrounding apartment blocks. Most of the exhibits are from better days: armour and arms from the conquistadores, and from the nearly invincible infantry that made Spain a European power in the days of the Catholic Kings. El Cid's sword is here, and Boabdil el Chico's, among rooms full of shiny military bric-à-brac. The Carlist and Napoleonic wars are covered, and the Civil War, too – you can get the Army's side of the story (open daily 10 am–5 pm, Sundays 10 am–1.30 pm, closed Mondays).

More interesting is the **Naval Museum** (open daily 10.30 am–1.30 pm, closed August), in a corner of the Ministry of Defence offices on the Paseo del Prado. Whatever relics of the age of explorations were not locked away in Seville's Archive of the Indies ended up here. Some of the most fascinating are the maps and charts, not simple sailors' tools, but lovely works in which art and scholarship are joined. The 1375 *Atlas Catalan* is one of these, and Juan de la Casa's *Mapa Mundi* of 1500 is the first Spanish map to show parts of the American coast. Another, made by Diego Rivera just 29 years later, has almost all of the Americas' Atlantic coasts, and some of the Pacific, a tribute to the work Spanish explorers had done in such a short time.

Much of the Naval Museum is given over to ships' models. Some wonderfully detailed and precise, giving real insight into the complexity and artfulness of the age of sail. Columbus' *Santa María* is one of these, and it is a reminder of the Admiral of Ocean Sea's achievement to see how small and frail his craft really were.

Just around the corner at Calle Montalban 12, the **Museo de Artes Decorativas** (National Museum of Decorative Arts) (open Tuesday–Friday 10 am–5 pm, weekends 10 am–2 pm), has a comprehensive collection of furniture, costume, ceramics, and work in wood, textiles, gold and silver from the 15th to the 20th century – six floors of it, in fact, covering every aspect of Spanish design. One favourite exhibit is the lovely, tiled 18th-century Valencian kitchen on the top floor.

A few blocks west of the Prado on Calle Heurtas, the **Academía Real de la Historía** (Royal Academy of History) (open irregularly, call 239 82 63), maintains a small museum with some paintings by Goya, Iberian and Roman antiquities and religious art of the Middle Ages. Two blocks north, at Calle Cervantes 11, the **House of Lope de Vega** has been restored by educated guesswork to how it might have looked when that great and very prolific dramatist lived there. This is also the old neighbourhood Cervantes (1547–1616). Though he and Lope de Vega were said to have been bitter enemies since the days they served together in the wars against the Turk, Cervantes lived on the same street, on the corner of Calle de Leon. *Don Quixote* was first printed nearby on Calle Atocha, and its author is buried in an unmarked grave in the Trinitarias Convent, on Calle Lope de Vega.

Museo Arqueológico (Archaeology Museum)

In the Madrid of the 19th century, architectural tastes favoured the grandiose and overdone. There is no better example, perhaps, than the florid monumental pile on the

Paseo de Recoletas that houses this museum as well as National Library (the Museum's entrance is the back door, at Calle Serrano 13, but you may first want to check the Library's **Salas de Picasso**, a gallery that often hosts important travelling exhibitions of modern painting from the world's museums).

By any measure, this is the only comprehensive archaeology museum in Spain (open daily 9.30 am–1.30 pm, closed Monday). If you can read a little Spanish, the explanations posted around the exhibits will provide a thorough education in the obscure comings and goings of Spain's shadowy prehistory. Not that the museum is limited to Spain – there is a surprisingly good collection of Greek vases, and an Egyptian room full of mummies and gaping school-children, along with some very fine jewellery and engraved seals. Many of the Greek and Egyptian relics were actually found in Spain, testimony to the close trade relations ancient Iberia enjoyed with the rest of the Mediterranean world.

A visit to this museum, however, is really a pilgrimage to the first and greatest of the great ladies of Spain, *La Dama de Elche*. Nothing we know of the history and culture of the Iberians can properly explain the presence of this beautiful 5th-century BC cult image. As a work of art she ranks among the very greatest productions of antiquity. Pre-Roman Spain was one of the backwaters of the Mediterranean, and while it would be sacrilege in Spain to suggest this lady was the work of a foreign hand, the conclusion seems inescapable. The dress and figure have much in them that is reminiscent of some eastern Mediterranean image of Cybele, and the Greeks could often capture the same expression of cold majesty on the face of an Artemis or Ariadne or Persephone. Elche, where the bust was discovered, was then in the Carthaginian zone, and that meant easy access to all the Mediterranean world; an artist from anywhere could conceivably have turned up to execute the high priests' commission.

Nevertheless, many experts disagree, and find in the lady's unapproachable hauteur something distinctly Spanish. She holds court these days from a large glass case on a pedestal in the museum's main hall; when the hordes of school-children run up, pressing their noses on the glass and shouting, as thousands of them do every day, you will see the lady's expression intensify into a look of chilly disdain that is a wonder to behold. She shares the room with her less formidable cousins, the very few other Iberian goddesses that have ever been found, including the 4th-century *Dama de Baza* and the *Dama de Cerra de Los Santos*.

The Iberians of the Bronze Age were at least up-to-date in metalworking, and the collection of small expressionistic *bronze figurines* shows a fine talent; these are similar in many ways to the famous bronzes from the same period found in Sardinia. Spain's entry into the literate world is chronicled in a host of inscriptions from all over the country. Scholars think the language was related to modern Basque, and not surprisingly they haven't completely deciphered any of them.

From the Romans, there are indifferent mosaics and copies of Greek sculpture, along with larger-than-life statues of emperors. The bronze tablets from AD 176, inscribed with the laws and orations of Septimus Severus, would have been set up in public places – a landmark in the development of political propaganda. The practice was begun by Augustus and used by several of the more energetic emperors that followed. There are also working models of the Roman catapult and ballista (a kind of gigantic crossbow) if you've ever wondered how they worked.

Spanish Early Christian art is one of the museum's surprises. The architectural sculpture and mosaics show a strong and original sense of design, and a tendency to contemplative geometry that seems almost Islamic. The Visigoths haven't much to offer outside the **Treasure of Gurrazar**, a collection of vigorously barbaric bejewelled crowns and crosses, all in solid glittering gold, that were found in the Visigothic capital, Toledo. **King Reccesvinth's crown** (c. 650) the richest of all, has his name dangling from it in enamelled golden letters; to the mainly illiterate Visigoths, these must have seemed like magic symbols. A small number of Moorish and medieval Christian works complete the collection.

Outside, near the gate, a small cave has been dug to house replicas of the famous **rock paintings of Altamira**, very artistic representations of bisons, bulls, and other animals in red and black. The museum has gone to great lengths to copy the atmosphere of the real cave (which is now closed to the general public) – the lighting is so realistically dim, you can barely make out the pictures.

Across the street from the museum, the **Jardines del Descubrimiento** is one of Madrid's new parks, and the great blocks of sandstone decorating it are all part of an interesting modern monument to Columbus, carved with reliefs and quotes from the explorer's journals. Behind is a more old-fashioned Columbus monument, in the broad intersection called the **Plaza del Colón**. Since the Bourbons, this area has been the most self-consciously monumental corner of Madrid, spread with impossibly wide boulevards and roundabouts, and not much fun for walking. One of the circles, the Plaza de la Independencia, has for a centrepiece the stately Baroque **Puerta de Alcalá**, a sort of triumphal arch with triumph to commemorate, built during the reign of Charles III. Before Madrid's last set of walls was demolished in the last century, this was the actual gate on the road to Alcalá de Henares. The next circle west, the Plaza de la Cibeles, shows off a fanciful 1780 fountain of the goddess Cybele in a car drawn by lions. The grand marble palace on the corner is nothing more than the **main post office**, but in a city as unimaginative in its architecture as Madrid, such a flagrant example of the movie-palace style popular under Dictator Primo de Rivera in the 1920s truly stands out. Madrileños have been making fun of it since it was built; one of the nicknames it has acquired is 'Nuestra Santa de Comunicaciones'.

South of the Prado

In this direction, the Paseo del Prado passes the Botanical Gardens towards the shadowy districts around Atocha Station. The broad square in front of the station, the **Glorieta de Carlos V**, may still seem a grim desolation for years to come, but it is in fact the most significant environmental victory of the civic-minded Madrid of the 1980s. Not long ago, the entire plaza was buried under a ghastly, multi-level highway interchange Madrileños called the 'scalextric' after a popular amusement park ride. Mayor Tierno saw it dismantled just before he died, but it will be a long time before the area is habitable again. Already they're making a start with the conversion of a rambling, 17th-century hospital into the **Reina Sofia Art Centre**, opened in 1986.

A few blocks to the west, at Calle Fuenterrabia 2, you may visit a handcrafts workshop fit for kings. In the Royal Palace, the Escorial, and in all the other royal residences around Madrid hang works of the **Real Fábrica de Tapices** (Royal Tapestry Factory).

Ever since Philip IV founded it in the 1640s, the weavers of the Real Fábrica have served the Spanish elite's love of fine, pictorial tapestries – not only decorative, but a positive asset to any drafty palace during the chill Castilian winters. Its best-known productions, of course, are those woven to the designs Goya created when he was court painter, the cartoons for which are now hanging in the Prado. They are still the favoured subjects today. You may watch the master weavers at work on any weekday morning (9.30 am–12 noon), and those with gargantuan bank accounts may even order a genuine tapestry as a souvenir.

Old Madrid

Shoehorned into a tight 0.5 km (0.3 mile) between the Puerta del Sol and the Royal Palace is a solid, enduring Castilian town, as evocative in its own way as Segovia or Toledo. Old Madrid has changed little since Goya painted its delicate skyline of cupolas and spires. Neither menaced by modern office blocks nor done up picture-pretty for the tourists, the quarter has enjoyed the best of possible fates – to remain as it was. Its residents are perhaps poorer than the city average but their presence keeps the place a living neighbourhood, loud, busy and unkempt, but still Madrid's best and cosiest refuge from the cosmopolitan greyness of the rest of the city.

Plaza Mayor

Few squares in Spain are lovelier, and none is better used. Between concerts, festivals, political rallies and the popular Sunday market for stamps, coins, and trinkets, something is likely to be on when you visit. If there isn't, at least someone will be strumming a guitar on the pedestal of Philip III's equestrian statue while all Madrid passes through and the tourists observe from the cafes. In the old days it was much the same. Kings of Spain were crowned here, and they would often return to preside over fiestas, bullfights, *autos-de-fé*, even archaic knightly tournaments. Although the Plaza is as old as Madrid, the present buildings were constructed in 1620 for Philip III. During events, the city council would rent the balconies from their owners to seat the distinguished visitors. Kings traditionally take their places in the elegant building with twin spires on the north side, the **Casa Panaderia**, so called after the bakery that preceded it on the site.

Take time to look in the shop windows. Besides some of Madrid's best restaurants and ancient, but still popular *tascas*, the streets around the Plaza Mayor are home to the queerest shops in all Spain. Just outside the Plaza there's a place that sells comic books from around the world; another, on the Calle Mayor, features Guardia Civil regalia and little ceramic statues of Franco. Off the Calle de Toledo is a shop claiming to sell the biggest sizes of ladies' lingerie in the world. Its lovingly designed window displays may well be the most unforgettable sight Madrid can offer.

Plaza de la Villa

Just a few blocks west of the Plaza Mayor, on Calle Mayor, some of Madrid's oldest buildings can be seen around the **Plaza de la Villa**. The **Ayuntamiento**, built in 1640 by Gomez de Mora, the same architect who created the Plaza Mayor, is one of Madrid's finest buildings. Across the square, the 15th-century **Torre de los Lujanes** once served as a prison for no less than King Francis I of France. This monarch, bitterest enemy of Charles V and Habsburg ambition, was captured by the Spanish at the Battle of Pavia in Italy in 1525. He spent a few months as Charles' unwilling guest here, and won his release by signing a treaty and agreeing to marry Charles' sister; once safely over the border, he said it was all a joke, and he and Charles were at war for most of the next 20 years. Near the square, at Calle Mayor 59, is a rare example of blooming Art Nouveau, a style that was never as popular in this serious city as elsewhere in Spain. The old house next door was once home to Calderón de la Barca. Just a block or two west, the streets around the charmingly rickety glass-and-steel **San Miguel Market** make up the busiest and most colourful corner of old Madrid.

To the south, the **Plaza del Humilladero**, the **Plaza de Cascórro**, and the **Plaza Tirso de Molina** are centres of the La Latina neighbourhood, the heart of old Madrid and a run-down but pleasant place for a stroll. Every morning, but especially on Sundays, the stretch of Calle Ribera de Curtadores south of Cascorro is home to Spain's best-known and longest running flea market, the **Rastro**, where items running the entire spectrum from rare antiques to unsaleable junk change hands at a brisk pace. Now that the Rastro has become as popular with tourists as with the Madrileños, the bargains are harder to come by, but if you've the time, and room in your suitcase, it's worth a look.

Just a few old churches

Despite its four centuries as capital of Catholic Spain, Madrid amazingly does not have a proper cathedral, or even a single church worth going out of your way to visit. The one that comes closest, the 18th-century **Capilla de San Miguel**, was designed by Italians; located on Plaza Puerta Cerrada, it has an elaborate Churrigueresque façade. A few blocks away, on the Plaza de la Paja, the **San Andres** church is more typical of the blank, severe style of Madrid's older parishes. San Andres was burnt during the Civil War, and both it and the Plaza are currently undergoing restoration. Many others of the neighbourhood's churches are, too – in fact, recently it has been hard to see anything of this area for the scaffolding. The city has an elaborate plan of rehabilitation here that it hopes will lead to a rebirth of interest in this quiet, pretty corner of town. Madrid's largest church, **San Francisco el Grande** (1785, restored 1890) is nearby at the foot of Calle San Francisco. With a dome almost 30 m (100 ft) in diameter, it does live up to its name, but there's little more to say for it, only that it too is under restoration.

North of the Calle Mayor, on Calle Arenal, is the **Convent of the Descalzas Reales** (5 pm Monday–Thursday, 10.30 am–1.30 pm, 4–5.45 pm, Friday–Sunday 10.30 am–12.45 pm). To visit it, you'll have to submit to a guided tour, but there are paintings by Brueghel and Zurbarán inside, and several centuries' accumulation of rich tapestries, furniture, art and holy relics. The convent, from the 17th century, is the branch office of the order founded by Santa Teresa, the shoeless (descalza) Carmelites, sworn to poverty and an excess of pious observance. When Charles V's daughter, Juana of Austria, entered, though, fashion was not far behind, and the Royal Barefoots soon became the richest prestige nunnery in Christendom, attracting even a German empress for a short stay. You may notice one of the dusty portraits is of Charles' sister, the one Francis I agreed to marry. You'll see what changed his mind.

Palacio Real (The Royal Palace)
Any self-respecting Bourbon had to have one. Philip V, who ordered it 1738, had to be talked out of an even grander version by his wife, who thought 2800 rooms would probably suffice to meet her needs.

The palace entrance is off the broad **Plaza Oriente**, filled with statues of Spanish kings originally intended to go on the building (they were too heavy). The guided tour (hours: summer 10 am–1.30 pm, 4–6.15 pm; winter, 10 am–12.45 pm and 3.30–5.15 pm; 10 am–1.30 pm Sundays and holidays) may well take you through all 2800 rooms; a mild delirium soon sets in, and one loses count. Each has a tapestry from the Real Fábrica, portraits of bewigged sycophants, a nice inlaid table, a half-ton chandelier, and indolent mythological deities painted on the ceiling. If you're serious about such things, persevere, and you will be rewarded with works by El Greco and Goya, as well as Rubens, Van der Weyden and Watteau, and many other favourites of the age. One room is full of gold clocks, and if your tour is lucky enough to hit it at noon, you can hear them all go off, a delicate symphony of bells and chimes.

Originally this was the site of the Moorish Alcazar, converted by Enrique IV into Madrid's first Royal Palace. It was here that Velazquez lived and painted for Philip IV, and many of his works are infused with the atmosphere of its old, dark chambers. A great fire occasioned the 18th-century replacement, very much in the style of Versailles and other contemporary palaces. The exterior is grand and elegant enough, the effect heightened by its setting on a bluff above the Manzanares. Alfonso XIII was the last king to use the Palace as a residence. Juan Carlos' tastes are much more modest; he lives quite comfortably at the suburban Zarzuela Palace, without any semblance of an old-style court. The Palace is used today only for important state occasions. During these it will be closed, but otherwise you may visit – tours given in English and other languages. Tickets are sold separately for the Palace, the **Royal Armoury**, and the **Museum of Carriages**, both situated in the palace grounds.

The Armoury is interesting. Charles V, living in an age when the medieval manner of warfare was rapidly becoming obsolete, had a truly Quixotic fascination for armour. His collection makes up most of what you see today. Some of the suits and weapons are functional, but most were never meant to be anything but decorative, something a king could cut a fine figure in on campaigns or in the old-fashioned jousts that were still popular with the nobility.

Two formal parks make up the grounds of the Royal Palace, the **Campo del Moro** towards the Manzanares, and the smaller **Jardines Sabatini**. The southern wings of the palace enclose a courtyard big enough to hold the entire Plaza Mayor, buildings and all; bordering it on the southern edge is the monstrous bulk of what is to be Madrid's cathedral, **Nuestra Señora de Almudaina**, ungainly, unvisited and unfinished, even more of a dubious undertaking now than when it was begun a century ago.

The Goya Pantheon (San Antonio de la Florida)
From the Campo del Moro, you can walk a few blocks up the bank of the Manzanares, flowing gamely with its borrowed water, to a plain, tiny chapel tucked between the river and the rail-yards of the Estación de Norte. Few tourists ever find their way up here, but inside is one of the milestones of Spanish art. In 1798, Goya was commissioned to do a series of frescoes on the walls, ceiling and dome, and he did them in a way no

church had ever been decorated before. St Anthony, in the dome, is clearly recognizable, but that is Goya's only concession to the usual conventions of religious art. The scores of figures with which he covered the ceilings seem almost to be the same faces from his celebrated cartoons, only instead of angelic Madrileños they have become angels in fact. Every one has the quality of a portrait; the peaceful rapture expressed in their faces has at its source nothing the Church could give, but a particular secret perhaps known only to Goya. The artist is buried here, and the church has become his monument (open: winter 11 am–1.30 pm, 3–6 pm, Sunday 11 am–1.30 pm; summer 10 am–1 pm, 4–7 pm, Sunday 10 am–1 pm).

Plaza de España and the Gran Vía

This is Madrid's shopping and business district replete with awkward skyscrapers, grand imperial cinemas, American hamburger joints, and unyielding traffic swarms. You're likely to pass through the broad Plaza de España, with its famous bronze figures of Don Quixote and Sancho Panza, at least once; the tourist office is located here, in the city's tallest building, the **Torre de Madrid**. Just off the Plaza at Calle Ventura Rodriguez 17 the **Museo Cerralbo** is one of Madrid's several private collections that have become museums in their original settings – in this case, the home of a Marques who died in the 1920s. There are paintings by Ribera and El Greco, and the ambient bric-à-brac is thickly spread (open daily except Tuesday, 9 am–2 pm; closed in August).

In recent years the modest hill that rises above this area has gradually been landscaped into the new **Parque del Oeste**. For a centrepiece, this park has just what you least expected, an Egyptian temple of the 4th century BC. The **Temple of Debod** is nothing very elaborate, but it is genuine. The Egyptian government sent it, block by block, as a gift of appreciation for Spanish help in the relocation of monuments during the building of the Aswan dam. However far it has strayed from the Nile, the little temple seems cheerfully at home, oriented to the same sunrise, looking over the peculiar city below. In July 1936, this spot was occupied by the Montaña Barracks, scene of one of the earliest and bloodiest actions of the Civil War. When the government decided to arm the popular militias, it was found that the bolts for most of the rifles available were locked away in the barracks, held at the time by a group of rebellious officers and Falangists. After a brief siege, some miners from Asturias managed to blow a hole in the walls, and the barracks was stormed by a mob, who killed most of those inside.

Casa del Campo

When the Habsburgs decided to make Madrid their capital, they didn't give much thought to amenities. One of their tricks was to chop down every tree of the forests that once surrounded Madrid; they sold them as firewood all over Castile, and used the money to embellish their palaces. Philip II, an avid hunter like most of the Habsburgs, soon regretted this, and he caused this tract of several square miles to be reforested.

There was no altruism in Philip's motives. He simply wanted a royal hunting preserve, but the Casa del Campo was the happy result, a stretch of quiet countryside, just a short walk (or Metro ride) from the centre of the city. Within its boundaries are a fairground, an amusement park, and the **Madrid Zoo**, the stars of which are two clowning panda bears, one the first born in captivity in the West.

Museo Municipal (The Municipal Museum)
North of the Gran Via, neighbourhoods like Malasaña and Fuencarral have very much the same atmosphere as the oldest parts of Madrid – modest, working-class areas acting out colourful street scenes under a backdrop of drab brick tenements. It's the real Madrid, and a perfect setting for the city's very good **Municipal Museum** on Calle Fuencarral. Housed in the 18th-century Hospicis de San Fernando, with an exuberant Churrigueresque portal, the museum has been renovated and greatly expanded in recent years (open Tuesday–Saturday 10 am–2 pm and 5–9 pm, Sundays 10 am–2.30 pm).

More Madrileños come here than tourists, and you can sense their growing civic pride as you watch them scrutinizing the old maps and prints, pointing out landmarks and discussing how their city has changed. The collection is large, and you can learn as much as you care to about Madrid and its history – except the period during the Civil War, which is discreetly omitted. Spaniards love to make room-sized models of their cities, and there is one here that accurately reproduces the Madrid of the 18th century.

Ciudad Universitaria (The University City)
Miguel Primo de Rivera always liked to think of himself as a great benefactor of education, and it exasperated him that Spain's university students spent most of the 1920s out in the streets calling him names. He began this sprawling, suburban campus in 1927, partly to appease them but mostly to get them out of town. This institution, the nation's largest, began as the Complutensian University, founded by Cardinal Cisneros in Alcalá de Henares. After it moved to Madrid, its buildings stood in the quarter north of the Gran Via, where many may still be seen. Primo de Rivera's new campus was unfinished when the Civil War broke out; in the battles for Madrid the University found itself in the front line, providing a potent symbol of the nature of the war as Franco's artillery pounded the halls of knowledge to rubble.

Franco rebuilt them after the war in a stolid, authoritarian style. Today the campus is green and well-kept but as dull to visit as it must be for the students who attend it. Two museums are near the southern end. The **Museo de America** (Calle Reyes Catolicos 6) has one of the largest collections in Europe of artefacts from the Aztecs, Incas and other native cultures of the New World. At the time of writing the museum is closed for a major renovation, and the reopening date uncertain. One long block down Avenida Arco de la Victoria is the **Museo Español de Arte Contemporanes** (Spanish Museum of Contemporary Art; Av. Juan de Herrera 2) hidden away like the Museo de America in a shady park where it's hard to see from the street (Tuesday–Saturday 10 am–6 pm; Sunday 10 am–3 pm).

The best reason to visit this museum is likely to be one of the block-buster special exhibitions from somewhere else regularly assembled here. The permanent collection contains some Picassos (the 'Pintor y Modela' series) and Mirós, but the remainder is a tired lot, production-line abstract expressionism and paintings that ostentatiously flaunt primeval elements and archetypes already done to death by artists elsewhere.

Salamanca Quarter and the Museo Lazaro Goldiano
Ever since Madrid's last city walls were knocked down in the 1860s, opening this

district to development, it has been Madrid's fashionable address. Today much of its cheerless grid of swank avenues bears an eerie resemblance to the neighbourhoods around New York's Park Avenue, with a scattering of old mansions, trendy show-offs peering in the windows of the Calle de Serrano boutiques, illegally parked cars with diplomatic licence plates, and concierges walking other people's Pekingeses. Many of the surviving mansions have a certain Victorian panache, but the only building in Salamanca that really stands out is the US Embassy on Calle de Serrano, done in that style only possible to American embassies, half-fortress and half-kitchen-appliance.

You'll pass by it on the way to one of Madrid's best museums, the **Museo Lázaro Galdiano** (Calle Serrano 122). The founder, who died in 1948, had a better eye and deeper pockets than the other Madrid collectors whose homes have been turned into museums. Among the 37 rooms of art, he assembled one work by nearly every important Spanish painter, two visionary paintings by Hieronymous Bosch, a Rembrandt portrait and, something you won't see much of in any other Spanish museum, English painting, including works by Gainsborough, Turner and Reynolds. The founder's tastes were remarkably eclectic, and on the ground floor articles from the Moors, Byzantines, Persians and Celts share space with medieval enamels, swords and armour, and early clocks and watches (open daily except Monday 10 am–2 pm, closed in August).

Peripheral Attractions

There's not much reason to leave the central area of Madrid, but a few museums in the outlying districts may catch your fancy. **El Pardo**, another overdone Bourbon palace, built by Charles III, stands in a planted forest some 13km (8 miles) north of the centre. Franco used it as his residence throughout the dictatorship, and now it is open to guided tours (daily 10 am–1 pm, 4–7 pm summer, 10 am–1 pm, 3–6 pm winter).

Madrid's main bullring, the **Plaza de Toros Monumental**, along the Calle Alcalá 0.8 km (0.5 mile) east of the Retiro, is the busiest and most prestigious in Spain. Around the back is the **Museo Taurino**, the largest and most complete museum of bullfighting, with special exhibitions on famous toreros like Manolete, who met the horn in this ring in 1947 (open daily except Monday, 9 am–3 pm). South of Atocha, on the Paseo de las Delicias, the century-old Delicias Station has been converted into the **National Railway Museum**, with RENFE's oldest and proudest warhorses (some from the 1840s) shined up as good as new. If you were interested in the works of the 19th-century painter Sorolla shown in the Casón del Buen Retiro, you can get a whole building full at the **Sorolla Museum**, Calle Martinez Campos 37 (open daily except Monday 10 am–2 pm).

Finally, there is a museum in Madrid – the **Real Academia de Bellas Artes de San Fernando**, on Alcalá 13 that to many in the know is the country's second-best, containing 1500 works, 15 Goyas, 15 Riberas and more. The catch is, it hasn't the money to stay open. At writing it is down to one morning and one afternoon a week; call 276 25 64 to find out what days.

TOURIST INFORMATION

The main office is in the Torre de Madrid (open 9 am–7 pm, weekdays, 9.30 am–1.30 pm Saturday), the big skyscraper on the Plaza de España (Tel: 241 23 25) and there are branch offices (don't count on their being open) at Barajas Airport and Chamartin Station (both supposedly 8 am–8 pm Monday–Saturday, and 8 am–2 pm Sunday), and an information booth at Atocha that specializes in helping you find lodgings. In addition, the city of Madrid has an office right in the Plaza Mayor (Tel: 266 54 77). While in Madrid, keep an eye out for the *Columnas Informativas* scattered about town, with maps and all sorts of information posted. They have a way of turning up miraculously when you're lost.

Maps

The one handed out by the tourist offices is good enough, but if you want total detail, the map published by *Almax Editores* is a wonder to behold.

Embassies

Great Britain: Fernando el Santo 16, Tel: 419 02 00; also for New Zealanders with embassy business
US: C. Serrano 75, Tel: 276 38 00
Canada: Nuñez de Balboa 35, Tel: 225 91 19
Australia: Paseo de la Castellana 143, Tel: 279 85 01
Ireland: Hermanos Becquer 10, Tel: 225 16 85

Bookstores

Turner's, C. Genova 3 (Metro: Colón) would be a good English book-shop in London, and it's certainly the best in Spain, with the best collection of books about Spain in English anywhere. For scholarly and obscure matters about Spain in any language, try **Meissner**, C. Ortega y Gasset (Metro: Nuñez de Balboa). Most Madrid bookshops have a small selection in English.

Foreign newspapers are available at any number of stands along Gran Vía, Plaza de Cibeles, and in the Salamanca area.

Post Office and Telephones

The main post office is on the Plaza de la Cibeles (Monday–Saturday 9 am–10 pm). You can also make international phone calls and send telegrams from there; otherwise the main telephone office is in the Telefonica skyscraper at Gran Vía 28 (open 9 am–10 pm; Sundays 10 am–2 pm and 5–9 pm).

Police: Puerta del Sol 7 (emergency phone 092).

American Express: Plaza de las Cortes 2, tel. 429 68 75.

WHERE TO STAY

With some 50,000 hotel rooms in Madrid, there are always enough to go around. Regrettably, few are at all interesting. At the top of the scale, Madrid has well over a third of all the luxury hotels in Spain, and if you're fixed you can pamper yourself at the **Ritz** (God knows what they have there that's worth 35,000 pts a night), choose from all the world's big chains (even a Holiday Inn, on a street named for Juan Perón), or stay at any of a hundred three- , four- or five-star hotels, all pleasant and well-staffed, and all pretty much the same. Many of Madrid's finest are along the Gran Vía or other major streets; convenient but likely to be intolerably noisy.

Some places just as close, in, where you can stay calm: **Reyes Católicos*****, C. Angel 18, Tel: 265 86 00, is in a very nice old neighbourhood around San Francisco El Grande Basilica (4500–4750 pts); and **Carlos V*****, C. Maestro Vitoria, Tel: 231 41 00, around the corner from the Descalzas Reales and close to the Puerta del Sol (doubles 4950 pts). Besides the quiet locations, both of these have air-conditioned rooms (not all, though, so specify), are small, personal and good bargains for the services offered.

Madrid has plenty of hotels more expensive – there's a large international expense-account crowd to keep them filled. If you want to make a big splurge, however, you'd be better off doing it somewhere else. If you insist, though, one place in a good location near the Prado is the **Hotel Palace*******, Plaza de los Cortes 7, Tel: 429 75 51, in a fine old building and second only to the Ritz in prestige (and much cheaper); many bullfighters and entertainers make it their base in Madrid; 16,500 pts a double (Metro: Sevilla).

In Old Madrid

A taxi ride or a fair trek from any of the stations, but still, the most atmospheric place to experience Madrid (all closest to Metro: Opera). **La Macarena****, Cava de San Miguel 8, Tel: 256 92 21, is just off the Plaza Mayor. Clean, cosy, and family-run, its doubles are 2500 pts with bath, 1800 pts without. **Almundéna****, Calle Mayor 71, Tel: 248 64 25, just around the corner from La Macarena, is more modest, with doubles for 1300 pts without bath.

On Calle Arenal, two acceptable and inexpensive hostels are just across the street from one another: **Capricorno***, no. 23, Tel: 242 16 45, doubles without bath 1400 pts, and the **Caritel***, no. 26, Tel: 247 31 29, offering slightly more upscale doubles with bath for 2400–2600 pts, without bath 1400–1500 pts. **Rober***, a *hostal* in the same building as Caritel (Tel: 241 91 75) may be the cheapest in the area, with doubles for 1800 pts with bath.

Around the Prado

Close to the museums, but a little walk to most of the central restaurants: **Cosme****, C. Principe, Tel: 429 03 01, is a find in the boisterous area of tapas bars and restaurants east of the Puerta del Sol – fine if you stay up as late as the Madrileños; rooms with bath 1700 pts (Metro: Sol). **Roso***, Plaza de los Cortes 3, Tel: 429 83 29 is simple, well-kept and tranquil, with doubles with bath for 2400 pts. **Mori****, in the same building, Tel: 429 72 08, offers similar rooms for the same prices (Metro: Sevilla). **Sud Americana***, Tel: 429 52 64 and **Coruña***, Tel: 429 25 43, also occupy the same fine old building on the Paseo del Prado 12, overlooking the museum. These are two of the most friendly and quiet lodgings in all Madrid; both offer doubles with bath for 2000 pts (Metro: Banco de España).

Far enough from Atocha Station

If you stay too close, you take your chances in Madrid's jumpiest transient neighbourhood. Both of these are in walking distance of Puerta del Sol (all Metro: Anton Martin).

Santa Ana*, Plaza S. Ana 1, Tel: 221 30 58, is in an area still rundown, but much more genteel than the immediate Atocha environs, a steal at 1200 pts with bath for a double, 1000 pts without. **Matute*****, Pl. de Matute 11, Tel: 228 69 04, is a block south of Santa Ana, classier, with a little garden (3500 pts double with bath), **Rozas Diaz***, C. Atocha 51, Tel: 228 69 12, is a good budget choice close to the station. Doubles here are 1100 pts without bath.

Around Calle Fuencarral

This district, close to the night spots of Malesaña and the Gran Vía, has much to offer: relatively quiet locations and convenience, as well as a look into one of Madrid's real neighbourhoods. Walk up C. Fuencarral or C. Hortaleza and you'll find an enormous choice of low-cost *hostales* (all Metro: Gran Vía). Three of the best here are: **Ribidavia***, Fuencarral 25, Tel: 231 10 58, well recommended, with doubles for 1800 pts with bath, 1500 pts without. **Lopez***, C. Barco 25, Tel: 221 04 32, doubles 1500 pts with bath. **Veguin**, Fuencarral 16, Tel: 231 47 91, doubles 1400 pts with bath.

If everything's full, continue up to the end of C. Hortaleza, where a few modest hotels have begun to appear in the pleasant and respectable environs of Plaza Alonzo Martinez. **Santa Bárbara****, Pl. Alonzo Martinez 4, Tel: 445 73 34 is very pleasant but often very full, and worth the 2900 pts for a double with bath, 2600 pts without (Metro: Alonso Martinez).

EATING OUT

No place in Spain, except perhaps the Costa del Sol, can offer such a wide choice of places. Besides the country's best gourmet restaurants, you can sample the cuisine of every region in Spain and a score of other lands without straying 0.8 km (0.5 mile) from the Puerta del Sol. Most of the old, well-known establishments are in Old Madrid.

Casa Botin, C. Cuchilleros 17 (Metro: Opera); one of Ernest Hemingway's favourites, but the management doesn't make as big a deal about it as other places in Madrid – they've been around since 1725 and have a little sense of perspective. Certainly this is Madrid's prettiest restaurant, with its old, varnished façade off the Calle Mayor copied by dozens of competitors. The Castilian cuisine includes roast suckling-pig and roast lamb, as good as any in Segovia, as well as seafood and lots more (2400 pts for the set menu, and up from there). **Casa Ciriaco**, C. Mayor 84 (Metro: Opera) offers simple but first-rate home-cooking that attracts Madrid celebrities as well as neighbourhood locals. Chicken *pepitoria* (like a fricassee) is a speciality (1200 pts and up). **Aroca**, Plaza de los Carros 3 (Metro: Latina) is just off the Plaza de Humilladeros. A little fancier than the Ciriaco and slightly more expensive, the Aroca is a fashionable spot, in a lovely old building; it has won prizes for its menu of seafood dishes and other local favourites (around 1800 pts). **Esteban**, Pl. Humilladeros 4 (Metro: Latina), is another popular spot in the vicinity. If you think of tripe (*callos*) as a gourmet dish, as the Madrileños certainly do, this is the place to go. Good roast lamb and seafood, too (1200 pts and up).

Restaurants offering Basque and Galician cuisine are becoming increasingly popular in Madrid; here are some of the best: **Principe de Viana**, C. Manuel de Falla 5 (Metro: Cuzco); it's way up north, off Paseo de Castellana behind the Bernabeú Stadium, but some consider this Madrid's best restaurant. Besides Basque specialities, partridge, duck and seafood prepared in imaginative ways are on the menu (2800–3500 pts). **Ordago**, C. Sancho Davila 15 (Metro: Ventas), near the bullring, at Plaza de Ventas.

Another first-rate Basque restaurant, but at more affordable prices (1400–2000 pts). **O'Pozo**, Reina Mercedes 20 (Metro: N. Ministerios), up north again, in the Nuevas Ministerios area. Galician and Cantabrian cuisine means mostly seafood; this place has the widest selection anywhere (2500 pts, average). **Arrumbamlaza**, C. Libertad 23, near the Plaza de Chueca (Metro: Chueca); *Caldo gallego* and fresh seafood right from the coast (1000–1800 pts). **Hogar de Gallegos**, Plaza del Comandante de Las Morenas, off C. Mayor (Metro: Opera); another very good Galician restaurant, with a nice outdoor garden (average 1900 pts).

Here are some places to try if you want something different: **Edelweiss**, C. Jovellanos 7, near the Cortes (Metro: Sevilla); German and Spanish dishes and Hungarian goulash. Knock down a few beers in the company of politicians and parliamentary clerks (500–1500 pts). **El Viejo Uno**, Ribera de Manzamores 123 (Metro: Norte), across the river from the Goya Pantheon; Madrid's only Polish restaurant is a good one. Duck and game dishes are the specialities (800–1600 pts). **Goffredo**, C. Silva 11, (Metro: Callao); Madrid has quite a few Italian restaurants; this one makes a good *saltimboca alla Romana*, among other things, and is relatively cheap (1600 pts).

Central Madrid is full of inexpensive Chinese restaurants – all mysteriously the same, as if a Chinese restaurant academy were operating in some hidden corner of the capital. Most are decent, and the chicken with almonds is good anywhere. **Victoria**, C. de la Estrella, north of Gran Via (Metro: Callao) is a cut above the average Chinese restaurant (700–1300 pts).

Inexpensive Restaurants

In parts of Madrid, around the Puerta del Sol, the San Miguel Market, the Plaza Hummilladeros and the C. Fuencarral, the streets are packed with them; many have good tapas bars in front and a small dining-room in the back. Anywhere south of the Sol, you can't go wrong; every shop front is bar or restaurant along C. Victoria, C. de la Cruz, and C. Espóz y Mina; just look in the windows and see what's on display. On the Pasaje Mathieu, just off C. Victoria, some of the places have outdoor tables.

Cerveceria Danubio offers one of the largest selections of good tapas on Espóz y Mina, and *platas del dia* as low as 300 pts (Metro: Sol). **Restaurant Platero**: about the same, but better platas average around 600 pts. Also on Espoz y Mina. **Da Queimada**, C. Echagary (Metro: Sol); a distinguished paella for 400 pts, full dinner average 1200 pts. **Casa Ramon**, C. Ventura de la Vega (Metro: Sol); there are literally no businesses that aren't restaurants on this street. This one has a 700 pts set menu, as well as specialities like *cocido Madrileño* and roast lamb (1100 pts average à la carte).

The streets around Pl. Humilladero and Pl. Tirso de Molina (Metro: Latina) are also good places to look. Some inexpensive choices are: **Tormes**, C. Humilladero, with distinctive specialities and a 500 pts *plata del día*. **La Latina**, C. Cava Alta, *conejo* (rabbit) and more Spanish favourites; full dinners as low as 800 pts. **Oliveros**, C. San Millan; authoritatively Madrileño both in ambiance and cuisine (*menú* 660 pts). **Asadero Fronton**, Pl. Tirso de Molina; Basque and run by a former frontón star; *menú* 800 pts, or an excellent Basque meal for up to 1600 pts.

Bars and attractions

Cafe society, in Madrid, includes everyone who cares to participate. With one bar for every 96 inhabitants, according to the last census, there's always some place to go when you just can't look at another museum, from beloved ancient holes in the wall where the walls haven't been painted since Alfonso XII to chic cafes on the boulevard where young sports with New York haircuts discuss modern art. You'll find one close to your hotel good for sending an entire afternoon down the drain, but here are some of the most famous.

Gíjon, Paseo de Recoletas 21, a decorative, turn-of-the-century cafe with good tapas, popular with nostalgic young intellectuals and always packed. **El Espejo**, Paseo de Recoletas 31, a competitor to the above and just as pretty, with a cafe terrace and a restaurant. **Nuevo Oliver**, C. Conde de Xiquena 3, a little too much perhaps, but very, very fashionable; drink with Madrid society in a clubby atmosphere. **Viva Madrid**, C. Manuel Gonzales, off the Pl. Santa Ana, is another trendy favourite and a good place to meet people. **El Anciano**, C. Bailen 19, across from the Royal Palace, a very old and picturesque wine shop. **Cerveceria Alemaná**, Plaza Santa Ana, a perfect German–Spanish beerhall and another old Hemingway watering-hole. **La Bobia**, C. San Millan, old and funky, the traditional place to go after a shopping trip to the Rastro.

ENTERTAINMENT

Nightlife

For current listings, the best sources are *El Pais* and the weekly *Guia del Ocio*. Fashions change quickly; the scene is especially volatile among discos and clubs featuring contemporary music; one thing that never changes is the habit of going very late – the rest of Spain calls the Madrileños, 'los gatos' (the cats) for their habit of prowling around in the small hours of the morning.

Jazz clubs and bars with good music and atmosphere are the **Bar Cafe Clamores**, C. Albuquerque 14; **Whisky Jazz Club**, Diego Leon 7, and **Cafe Central**, Plaza del Angel 10. For music and dancing, currently the most popular area is **Malasaña**, west of C. Fuencarral in the streets around the Plaza Dos de Mayo, and especially on C. San Vicente Ferrer. Flamenco shows in Madrid are largely for tourists, and there are quite a few. One with pretensions to seriousness is the **Corral de la Moreria**, C. Moreria 7.

Theatre

Madrid comes in second to Barcelona in importance in Spanish theatre these days, but there a number of houses, with classical Spanish theatre, the works of Garcia Lorca, and new plays in the repertory; much is expected from the newly created **Compañia Nacional de Teatro Clásico**. Check out the listing in *El Pais*, and look out for performances of *zarzuela*, the specifically, Madrileño, turn-of-the-century operetta – a genre that enjoys a popularity much greater than just occasional revivals. The **Teatro de la Zarzuela,** C. Jovellanos 4, where it all began, is the most likely place to find it, though this theatre now runs mostly classical opera.

Other attractions

Madrid's bullring, the **Plaza de Toros Monumental**, sometimes referred to simply as **Las Ventas**, at C. Alcalá 237, has the biggest schedule of any in Spain, and is the place you're most likely to catch up with a *corrida* on your trip. The best way to get tickets is to go to the ring early in the day of the event – places in central Madrid also sell them in advance, but at a higher price. Basque *jai-alai* is played at the **Fronton,** Dr. Cortazo 10 (south of C. Atocha). Madrid has a **racetrack**, the Zarzuela, out in the northern suburbs near El Pardo, and there are 10 **golf courses** in the metropolitan area; ask at the tourist office for details. **Real Madrid**, the 'government's' football club in the Franco years, now struggles manfully to keep up with Barcelona, its traditional rival; they play at Bernabeú Stadium, up north off the Paseo de la Castellana at Av. Concha Espina. Also, you can throw your money away at the **Casino de Madrid,** 28 km (17.5 miles) from town on the N-VI highway (free bus service from Plaza de España 6).

Part XI

AROUND MADRID

Alcazar, Segovia

If anything, beyond the caprice of Charles V and Philip II, made Madrid the logical site for Spain's capital, it was the location. Not only is Madrid roughly central to the country as a whole, but its growth filled a vacuum at the centre of a region containing many of the most important cities of 16th-century Spain. Philip's new capital thus had a sort of ready-made Île-de-France around it, a garland of historic and lovely towns, each with something different to offer the visitor.

Everyone goes to **Toledo**, of course, and romantically beautiful **Segovia** also comes in for its share of travellers. But beyond these, you may also conveniently use Madrid as a base for visiting **Avila**, resolutely medieval behind its famous walls, the distinguished old university town of **Alcalá de Henares**, quiet, seldom-visited **Sigüenza**, the steep citadel of **Cuenca** with its cliffside houses, the royal palaces at **Aranjuez**, or Philip II's **El Escorial**.

Whenever Madrid's traffic, cacophonous nightclubs, and endless museum corridors become too much, any of these towns can provide a day's diversion and a little peace and quiet. And if Madrid is just the kind of metropolis you're trying to get away from, you can always set yourself up in one of them – and make a day-trip to Madrid.

EL ESCORIAL

The Spaniards aren't shy; they matter-of-factly refer to Philip II's combination palace-secretariat-monastery-mausoleum as 'the eighth wonder of the world'. Any building

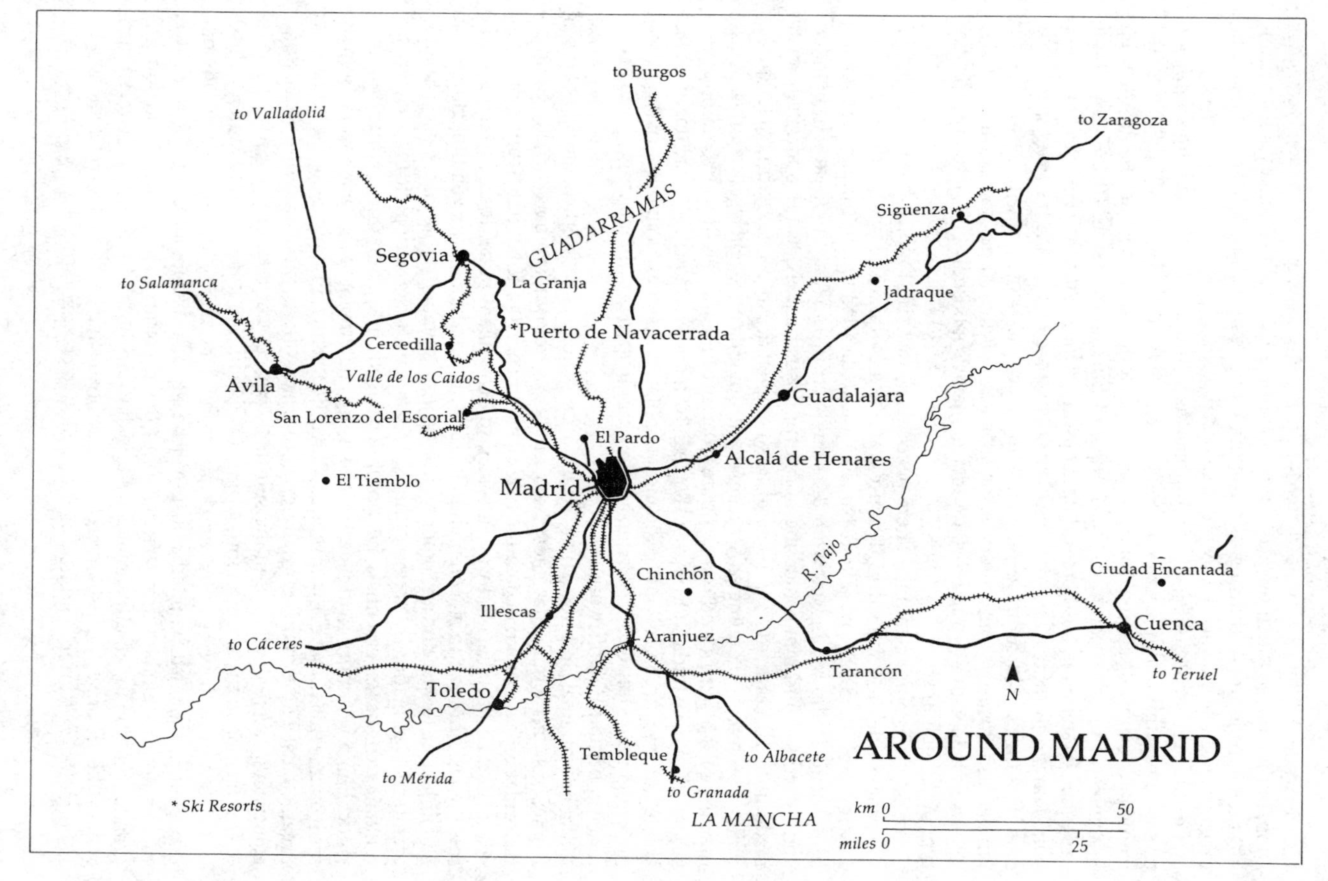
AROUND MADRID
to Burgos
to Valladolid
to Zaragoza
GUADARRAMAS
Sigüenza
Segovia
La Granja
to Salamanca
Jadraque
*Puerto de Navacerrada
Cercedilla
Avila
Valle de los Caidos
Guadalajara
San Lorenzo del Escorial
El Pardo
Alcalá de Henares
El Tiemblo
Madrid
R. Tajo
Chinchón
Ciudad Encantada
Illescas
Cuenca
Aranjuez
to Cáceres
Tarancón
to Teruel
N
Toledo
Tembleque
to Albacete
to Mérida
to Granada
* Ski Resorts
LA MANCHA
km 0
50
miles 0
25

with a façade 0.2 km (0.13 mile) wide and 2673 windows is entitled to some consideration, but it's not so much the glass and stone of the Escorial that makes it remarkable, but the neurotic will of the king who conjured it up. This is the vortex of Spain, full of magnificence and poison, a folly on an imperial scale.

To the Protestants of Northern Europe, hard-pressed to keep Philip's armies of priests at bay, this building was a diabolic horror, the seat of evil on earth. Philip himself would have calmly disagreed (for he was always calm), explaining that what he really had in mind was the re-creation of the Temple of Solomon. Despite all the effort Philip expended in stamping out heretical opinions in his long reign, he seems to have entertained on the sly quite a few of his own, possibly picked up during his years spent in the Low Countries. He found geomancers to select the proper site for the millennial temple, astrologers to pick the date for laying the corner stone, and hermetic philosophers to help with the numerical mysticism that is supposedly built into every proportion of the building.

An *escorial* is a mine-tailing. There once was some sort of mine on this site – and so the proper title of Philip's dream-house translates as the Royal Seat of the Royal Saint Lawrence of the Slagheap. The reasons for the dedication to San Lorenzo are unclear. Supposedly Philip won a victory on the saint's day in 1557, at St Quentin in Flanders, and vowed to build him something in return; this is unlikely, as the dedication wasn't made until 10 years after El Escorial was completed. An even less probable tale has Philip's architects planning this rectangle of buildings and enclosed courtyards as a memory of the saint's gridiron attribute (St Lawrence was roasted alive on one; he is supposed to have told the Romans: 'You can turn me over now; I'm done on this side.') While St Lawrence is not one of the most popular saints, there's an obscure legend that he brought the Holy Grail to Spain, and this may help to explain the tangled web of esotericism behind Philip's work.

Philip's original architect, Juan Bautista de Toledo, had worked on St Peter's in Rome; you may find that these two chilly, overblown symbols of the Counter-Reformation have much in common. Work commenced in 1563, but Bautista died four years later, and the Escorial was entrusted to his brilliant pupil, Juan de Herrera, who saw the task through to its completion in 1584. It kept him busy; even though Herrera had little time to spare on any other buildings, his reputation as one of the great Spanish architects was made. By creating the *estilo desornamentado*, stripping the Renaissance building to its barest essentials, he captured perfectly the nation's mood of austere militancy. Philip was more than pleased, and as he contemplated the rising work from the spot on the hills above the Escorial still called 'King Philip's Seat' he must have dreamed just a little of the dawn of new classic age, where Christianity and Renaissance achievement were combined in the spiritually perfect world empire of Spain.

If you come to the Escorial for a classic revelation, you'll have to settle for dry classicism; those who have read too much about the dark side of Philip's Spain and come expecting a monkish haunted house will be equally disappointed. As huge as it is, there's nothing gloomy or menacing about the Escorial. Its clean lines and soft grey granite combine for an effect that is tranquil and airy both inside and out. Everything is remarkably clean, as if dust and age had been banished by royal decree; somehow the Escorial looks as bright and new as the day it was completed.

GETTING AROUND

Keep in mind that the town's proper name is San Lorenzo del Escorial, and appears that way in bus and train schedules. The **bus** is faster, run by the Herranz line from Paseo Moret near the Moncloa Metro stop in Madrid, to the stop on C. Reina Victoria, very near the monastery (about 12 buses daily). Herranz also has a twice-daily service from the Escorial to the Valle de los Caídos, allowing enough time to see the place. Tickets are sold from a little office in a bar on C. Reina Victoria; the bar also has bowling lanes, so you can get in a few frames while reflecting on Habsburg eccentricity. **Trains** to El Escorial start from Atocha Apeadero, and also stop at Chamartin. They usually run every hour, or less, and it would be easy to combine Avila with El Escorial for a slightly hectic day-trip. The station is outside town, but a bus will always be there to meet trains.

El Escorial has fallen into the clutches of the Patrimonio Nacional. They sell their complicated tickets and dull guidebooks from the north entrance, but if you go right in and begin the tour, you may never get a good sense of the layout (James Michener was not ashamed to admit he came here twice without realizing it had a church, though a 13,000 sq. m (40,000 sq. ft) basilica with a 90 m (300 ft) high dome would elsewhere be hard to miss). The Temple, as the church is called, can be visited without a ticket; you may walk right in, through the monumental western entrance, under the statue of St Lawrence with his gridirons. From here, along the central axis of the complex, the symmetrical grandeur of Bautista's and Herrera's plan will begin to unfold. The complex is open daily [except Monday], 10 am–1 pm and 3.30–6 pm. Try not to go on Sunday – everyone else does.

WHAT TO SEE

The Temple

The western entrance leads into the Escorial's main courtyard, the **Patio of the Kings**, so called for the six mighty Kings of Israel adorning the façade of the Temple. The two statues in the centre represent David and Solomon. Once inside the huge, square church, you will quickly become aware of the heightened atmosphere of a holy-of-holies. With very few windows, the temple was purposely kept dark as a contrast to the airiness of the rest of the Escorial. No church in Spain is colder inside; even in the hottest days of July the thin air seems pure distilled essence of Castile. Just inside the entrance, in the narrow **lower choir**, note the unusual ceiling and its 'flat vaulting', an architectural trick of very shallow vaulting that creates the illusion of flatness.

From here, the eye is drawn to the bright retablo, framed in darkness. Its paintings are by several then-fashionable Italian artists, including Pellegrino Tebaldi, who like Juan Bautista was a pupil of Michelangelo. Above them all is a golden figure of Christ on the cross, and at its foot a tiny golden skull that stands out even across the great distance; its hollow eyes seem to follow you as you pass through the Temple. These are really only of gilded bronze; if they weren't, they wouldn't be here. Originally the Temple was full of real gold ornaments, and the precious stones of the Tabernacle were some of the most valuable that the Spanish royal house possessed. Napoleon's troops did a thorough job of looting the Escorial in 1808, making off with them all. Connoisseurs that they were, they left the artwork in peace. Notable are the gilded bronze ensembles to the sides of the altar, the families of Charles V and Philip II (with all three of his wives) at prayer. Beneath the high altar is the **primera piedra**, the cornerstone of the Escorial, and below it are the tombs of the Spanish kings, which you will see later on the tour.

The Royal Palace

The unavoidable escorted tour begins at the north entrance, through a quarter of the Escorial never used by Philip II, but converted by the Bourbons Charles III and Charles IV into a royal residence. These two do not seem to have had any interest in Philip's conception of the Escorial, but used it only as a sort of glorified hunting-lodge. Not surprisingly, they refurbished these rooms as a similar, though smaller version of the Bourbon Royal Palace in Madrid. They are almost habitable, all sweetness and colour and light, the walls hung with tapestries after works of Goya and others. One of the most interesting rooms is called the **Hall of the Battles**, with a fresco nearly 62 m (200 ft) long representing every detail of the 1431 Battle of Higuerela, an encounter between King John II and the Moors of Granada.

From here the tour leads down to the **Royal Mausoleums** beneath the Temple. All manner of stories have grown up around this pantheon of bad kings. Charles II, it is said, spent whole days down here, ordering the tombs opened so that he might gaze on his mummified ancestors. As in the Temple, the most expensive stone from around the Mediterranean was used in its construction; the red jasper of the pavement and pilasters is so hard it had to be cut with diamond-tipped saws. The adjacent room is called, charmingly, the **Pudredero**, where Habsburg and Bourbon potentates spent a few years mouldering until they became sufficiently dried out for their interments. Royal relations fill a maze of corridors beyond the Pantheon of the Kings, guarded by enormous white heralds with golden maces. Don Juan, victor of Lepanto, is the best known of them, though the tomb everyone notices is the tall, marble wedding-cake that holds 60 baby princes and princesses.

Palace of Philip II

Such a reputation Philip earned for himself – the evil genius of the Inquisition and all – that it comes as a genuine surprise to visit the little palace he tacked onto the back of the Escorial for himself. Few kings anywhere have ever chosen a more delightful abode: a few simple rooms reminiscent of the interiors from paintings of Vermeer, with white walls, Delft-blue tiles, and big windows opening to gardens and forests on all sides. These rooms suggest that Philip's famous self-isolation had less of monkishness about it than the desire of a cultured, bookish monarch to ensure the necessary serenity for the execution of the royal duty he took so seriously. Philip did not like courtiers, and he didn't care to go out. Alone with his trusted secretaries, he governed the affairs of his empire meticulously, reading, re-reading and annotating vast heaps of documents and reports. Aesthete and mystic, he approached politics with the soul of a clerk, and each of all the long list of mistakes he made was decided upon with the greatest of care.

It was here that Philip received nervous, respectful ambassadors on a throne 'hardly grander than a kitchen chair'. Here, in his perfect temple, where the wisdom of Solomon was to be reborn, they brought him the news of the Armada's disaster, the two national bankruptcies, the independence of the Netherlands, and all the little pinpricks in-between. Here he endured the wasting disease that killed him, stinking so badly that neither servants nor visitors could bear his presence, observing the endless masses and bad art of his Temple through the spy-hole he had cut in the wall. With only that crowned skull on his night table to keep him company, here he awaited the reward of the virtuous.

The art and furnishings of the apartments may not necessarily be an accurate representation of Philip's tastes, but there is a copy Philip had made of Bosch's *Hay Wain*, one of his favourites, the original of which hangs in the Prado. In the throne room, be sure to see the marvellous inlaid wood **doors**, decorated with trompe-l'oeil scenes and architectural fantasies, done by an anonymous German artist of the 16th century; they are quite the most beautiful things in the entire Escorial.

New Museums and Library

Between the palaces of Philip and the Bourbons, the **New Museums** occupy a long corridor along the eastern walls. More of Philip's collections are displayed here, including works by Bosch, Patinir and Dürer; later additions include a Velázquez. Much of the southern end of the Escorial is not open to visitors, being still in use as a monastery.

One other section that may be seen is the **Library**, entered by a stair near the Escorial's main gate. Philip's books meant as much to him as his paintings. His librarian, Benito Arias Montano, contributed much to the esoteric conception of the Escorial, and he built Philip one of the largest collections of Greek, Hebrew and Arabic philosophical and mystical works in Europe. His agents watched over all the book-burnings of the Inquisition, and saved from the flames anything that was especially interesting. That his hoard of 40,000 volumes survives almost unchanged since Philip's day is due only to the benign neglect of the generations that followed; 18th-century travellers reported that the monks watching over the collection were all illiterate. The frescoes that cover the vaulted ceiling, also by Pellegrino Tebaldi, are an allegory of the seven liberal arts, portraying most of the famous philosophers and scientists of antiquity. The large globe of nested spheres in the centre of the library is Philip's orrery, used in making astronomical calculations.

Two little country-houses within walking distance of the Escorial are included in the admission ticket. The **Casita del Principe** and the **Casita de Arriba**, both built in the 1770s for Charles IV, are tasteful, cosy and full of pretty pictures, but unless you just can't get enough of those Bourbons or have time to kill before the bus comes, you won't find them worth the trouble.

Since the building of the Escorial, a pleasant little town has grown up here; not only the palace, but the setting in the cool, forested foothills of the Guadarramas makes it a popular summertime resort for Madrileños escaping their city of baking concrete. Expect crowds on any summer Sunday.

Valle de Los Caídos

If you're one of those who came to the Escorial expecting freakishness and gloom, don't be disappointed yet. From the town, there's a regular bus service to Francisco Franco's own idea of building for the ages. The **Valley of the Fallen** is supposedly meant as a memorial to soldiers from both sides of the Civil War, but it was old Republicans and other political unfortunates languishing in Franco's jails who got to do the work in the 1950s, blasting a 245 m (800 ft) tunnel-like church out of the mountainside, and erecting a 150 m (490 ft) stone cross above. The crowds of Spaniards who come here in a holiday mood on any weekend seem to care little for history or politics; they linger at one of Spain's most outrageous souvenir stands, then take the children up the funicular railway to the base of the cross. For local colour, there'll be a few ancient widows in black who come very week, and perhaps a pair of maladjusted teenagers in Falangist blue shirts.

The **cross**, held up by faith and structural steel, is claimed to be the largest in the world. Around its base are a series of titanic sculptured figures in some lost, murky symbolism: lions, eagles and pensive giants lurching out above you. The view takes in the hills and valleys for miles, as well as the monastery Franco built for the monks who look after the **basilica** below.

This cave church is impressive, in the way the palace of a troll-king might be. The nave goes on and on, past giant, disconcerting Fascist angels with big swords, past dim chapels and holy images, finally ending in a plain, circular altar. José Antonio Primo de Rivera, founder of the Falangists, is buried here. His original interment in the royal crypt of the Escorial was too much even for many of Franco's supporters, and he eventually had to be moved here. Franco is here, too; the company he chose for his last resting-place is perhaps the last word on what kind of man he really was. **Franco's tomb** is a plain stone slab on the floor near the altar, opposite José Antonio's. The gentlemen behind you in sunglasses and Hawaiian sport shirts are, if you haven't guessed, plain-clothes policemen, waiting for someone to try and spit on the old Caudillo.

TOURIST INFORMATION

C. Floridablanca, Tel: 896 07 09, near the bus station.

WHERE TO STAY AND EATING OUT

As a summer resort, El Escorial has quite a few hotels around it. Visiting nabobs check in at the **Victoria Palace******, C. Juan de Toledo, Tel. 890 15 11, with a pool – and a bingo hall! Pretty doubles with balconies go for 4800–6000 pts. The budget choice is the **Hostal Vasco****, Plaza de Santiago, Tel: 890 16 19; doubles 1600 pts with bath, 1400 without. It also has a good, inexpensive restaurant – a consideration in this town where dining isn't cheap – with a set menu for 575 pts and Basque specialities for a bit more. Otherwise for restaurants, you may check out the outdoor places in the pretty square across from the Escorial (there are quite a few, and all about the same in quality and price).

SEGOVIA AND AVILA

For whatever cool breezes refresh Madrid in its torrid summers, thank the **Guadarramas**, the chain of low mountains north of the city that stretches from Avila in the west almost as far as Soria. Its highest peaks are near Madrid, and the snow on them lasts often until May or June. The Guadarramas have a near monopoly of pretty scenery in this part of Spain; though the heights are drab and grey, the lower regions contain green patches of forest and pastureland with a bit of the same Alpine ambiance found in the Pyrenees and Cantabrian chains.

Once over the crests of the Guadarramas, the traditional boundary between the two Castiles, you're back in the medieval atmosphere of Old Castile, with its Romanesque churches, flocks of sheep and lonely castles. Two of its cities, Avila and Segovia, are within easy reach of Madrid and make convenient day-trips. Segovia, though, one of the most beautiful cities of Spain, is a place where you may wish to spend some time.

Segovia

Three distinct cultures have endowed this once-prominent town with three famous monuments. The Romans left Segovia a great aqueduct, and the age of Charles V contributed an equally famous cathedral. The third, Segovia's Alcazar, should be as well known. Though begun by the Moors and rebuilt in the Middle Ages, its present incarnation is pure 19th-century fantasy, a lost stage set from a Wagnerian opera. Segovia has its other monuments – a unique style of Romanesque church, and the *esgrafiado* façades of its old mansions, but the memory the visitor takes away is likely to be mostly a fond impression. The delicate skyline silhouetted on a high narrow promontory between two green river valleys gives the city the appearance of a great ship among the rolling hills of Castile. To enter it is to climb into a lost medieval dream-Spain of unusually quiet streets, where the buildings are all of a single, lovely shade of warm, tan stone, making all old Segovia like one work of art.

When the Emperor Trajan built the aqueduct in the early 2nd century, this was *Segobriga*. It was already an old town when the Romans came. Under Rome, and later the Visigoths and Moors, it attained little distinction, but it survived. After it fell to the Christians in the 11th century, Segovia blossomed in the great cultural and economic expansion of medieval Castile. Its Romanesque churches and palaces were built on the profits of an important textile industry, and by the time of the Catholic kings it was one of the leading cities of Spain.

Like most of Europe's medieval cities that have survived intact, Segovia's present-day serenity hides a dark secret. The economic policies and foreign wars of Charles V and Philip II ruined Segovia as thoroughly as the rest of Old Castile, and it is only the four centuries of stagnation that followed that allow us to see old Segovia as it was.

GETTING AROUND

Some **trains** from Madrid (Chamartin), Santander and Valladolid stop at Segovia, as well as a regular Madrid–Segovia line – they run better than one per hour. The trip takes two hours (about halfway there you can see the Valle de los Caídos out of the left-hand windows). The **bus** is faster, 1½ hours from La Sepulveda office on Paeso de la Florida (near Norte Station) to Segovia's station, inconspicuously located under a big apartment block on C. Eusebio Gonzalez. On weekdays there are five buses a day to

SEGOVIA
El Parral
ALAMEDA DEL GRESMA
R. Gresma
PASEO DEL OBISPO
C. TRINIDAD
SERAFÍN
9
3
Pl. Mayor
1
C. VICTORIA
7
6
C. SANTIAGO
C. MARQUÉS ARCO
5
15
C. VELARDE
8
Pl. Merced
C. CÁDIZ
Vera Cruz
14
Jardines
del
Aleázar
R. Clamores
HOYAS
DE LAS
CUESTA
Alcázar
km 0
miles 0

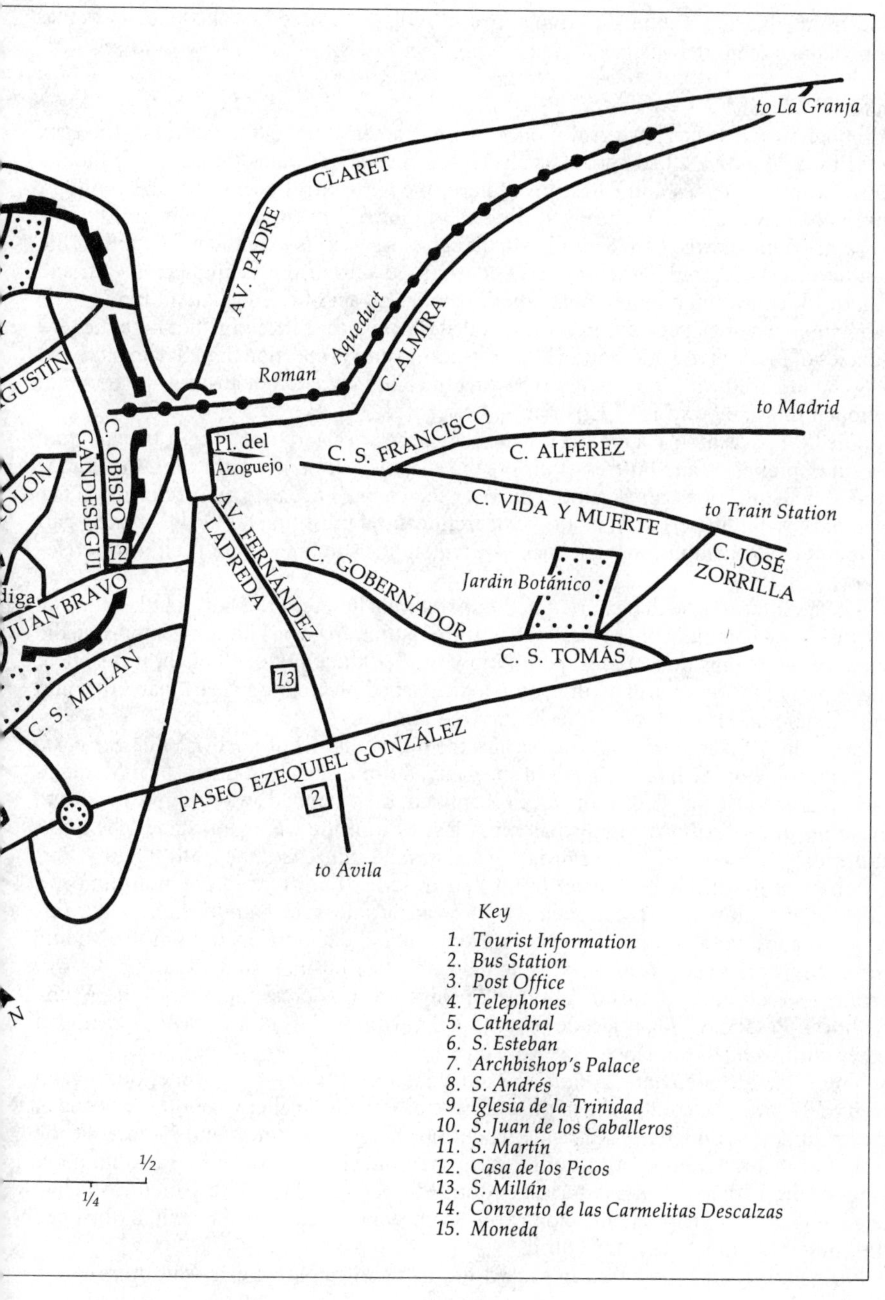
to La Granja
CLARET
AV. PADRE
Aqueduct
Roman
C. ALMIRA
GUSTÍN
C. OBISPO
GANDESEGUI
Pl. del
Azoguejo
C. S. FRANCISCO
to Madrid
C. ALFÉREZ
C. VIDA Y MUERTE
to Train Station
C. JOSÉ
ZORRILLA
OLÓN
AV. FERNÁNDEZ
LADREDA
C. GOBERNADOR
Jardin Botánico
12
diga
JUAN BRAVO
C. S. TOMÁS
13
C. S. MILLÁN
PASEO EZEQUIEL GONZÁLEZ
2
to Ávila
N
½
¼
Key
1. Tourist Information
2. Bus Station
3. Post Office
4. Telephones
5. Cathedral
6. S. Esteban
7. Archbishop's Palace
8. S. Andrés
9. Iglesia de la Trinidad
10. S. Juan de los Caballeros
11. S. Martín
12. Casa de los Picos
13. S. Millán
14. Convento de las Carmelitas Descalzas
15. Moneda

and from Madrid, nine to La Granja, two to Avila and three to Valladolid, as well as connections to all the villages in Segovia province.

WHAT TO SEE

Although new districts have grown out past the Roman aqueduct to the south and east, the **Plaza Mayor** (still sometimes called Plaza Franco), remains the centre of the old town, with its arcades and cafes. From here, the **Cathedral** peeks over the rooftops, just a block away. This has been called the 'last Gothic cathedral' of Spain; most of the work was done between 1525 and 1590, though parts were not completed until the 18th century. Segovia's old cathedral had been burned during the Comunero revolt, and Charles V contributed much to its replacement as an act of reconciliation. Juan Gil de Hontánon, who designed the new cathedral at Salamanca, carried further here the tendencies of his earlier work. Segovia is finer in form and proportion than Salamanca, and less encumbered with ornament, expressing the national mood of austerity in grandeur in much the same way as El Escorial.

The best parts of this cathedral are the semicircular eastern end, where an exuberant ascent of pinnacles and buttresses covers the chapels behind the main altar, the unique square bell-tower and an elegant dome over the choir. The latter two are Renaissance elements that fit in perfectly; in an age of architectural transition it was the greatest part of Juan Gil's accomplishment to make a harmonious combination of such diverse elements.

The architect chose to be buried in the spare, well-lit interior. There's little to see on the inside – a comment on the hard times 16th-century Segovia had come into – and the small **museum** inside is almost painful to visit. See the **cloister**, though, if it's open; this is part of the original cathedral, built in the Isabelline Gothic style by Juan Guas and moved here and reassembled after it survived the fire.

Between the Cathedral and Alcazar lies the oldest district of Segovia. The *esgrafiado* work on some of the houses is a local speciality, more common in the eastern Mediterranean than in Spain – a coat of stucco is applied, then scraped away around stencils to make decorative patterns. In a small plaza just west of the Cathedral stands the finest and most representative of Segovia's Romanesque churches, the 13th-century **San Esteban**, with a lively bell-tower in the Italian style. The arcaded porch around two sides of the church is the trademark of Segovia's Romanesque. Porches like this adorned all the old churches, and most likely the old cathedral as well; in the Middle Ages they were busy places, serving as the centres of business and social life the way arcaded streets and squares do in other Spanish towns. Across the plaza is the **Archbishop's Palace**, its plain façade relieved only by the reliefs of a serpent-woman and other curious medieval fancies over the entrance.

The **Alcazar** (open daily 10 am–7.30 pm in summer, 10 am–6 pm winter) jutting out on its cliffs over the confluence of the Rio Eresma and the smaller Clamores, was one of the great royal residences of Castile when San Esteban was new and Segovia at the height of its prominence. Alfonso the Wise spent much of his reign here, as did other kings of the 12th and 13th centuries. By the 19th, though, the old, forgotten castle had declined into a military school, and in 1862, some young cadets set fire to it, in the hope they might be transferred to Madrid.

No one, it seems, bothered to record the name of the architects who oversaw the

Alcazar's restoration in the 1880s. Even worse, some writers have sniffed that the job they did is 'not authentic'. Just because these forgotten heroes of the picturesque saw fit to turn the Alcazar into a flight of fancy worthy of the Mad King Ludwig, with pointed turrets and curving crenellated walks, some people find fault. The German tourists look puzzled, and a little disappointed to find a castle on the Rhine in Castile; still they admit it's a very good Rhine castle. The Alcazar is *better* than authentic.

As if the architects had ordered them for effect, sombre ravens perch on the turrets and walls. The people of Segovia who look after the castle have joined in the fun, fitting out the interior in a fashion that would make the characters of any Sir Walter Scott novel feel right at home. There are plenty of 14th-century cannons and armour, an arquebus or two, stained glass and dusty paintings of Visigothic kings. Some of the interiors survived the fire; there are fine *artesonado* ceilings in the Sala de Las Pinas and in the throne room, built by Enrique IV but furnished as it might have been in days of Ferdinand and Isabella. The **Plaza** at the Alcazar's entrance, with old mortars left over from the days of the military school, was the site of Segovia's original cathedral.

Old Quarters and Romanesque Churches

Within Segovia's walls, the streets meander languidly; to meander along with them is a treat, and fortunately the old town is small enough so that you will never get entirely lost. The medieval parish churches are everywhere: **San Andres**, a solid, simple work from the 12th century on the Plaza Merced; the **Iglesia de la Trinidad** on the Plaza Dr. Laguna, with an interior restored to something like its original appearance; **San Martin** on Calle Juan Bravo and **San Juan de los Caballeros** on the Plaza de Colmenares, both smaller versions of San Esteban (though both are older) with the characteristic arcades and towers. Calle Juan Bravo is named for the military leader of the Comunero revolt, who was executed after the defeat at Villalar in 1521. Segovia remembers enough of its ancient pride and liberty to keep him as a hero to this day, and his statue can be seen in the plaza. Nearby, the **Casa de los Picos** is another Segovia landmark, a 14th-century mansion with a façade like a waffle-iron, a style copied in many later buildings in Spain and even one famous palace in Naples.

One of Segovia's best churches is outside the walls, near the centre of the new town on Avenido Fernandez Ladreda. **San Millan** is also the oldest, but the capitals of its arcade, charmingly sculpted with scenes from the Bible and from everyday life, have survived much more clearly than at the other churches.

The Aqueduct

Nothing else remains from Roman Segobriga, but for the city to have merited such an elaborate water-supply it must have had nearly as many inhabitants as modern Segovia's 50,000. Trajan, one of the Spanish emperors, most likely ordered its construction. Its two-storey arcade rises 39 m (128 ft) over the busy Plaza Azoguejo below, making it the tallest surviving Roman aqueduct anywhere.

The Romans, antiquity's master plumbers, did not build it there just to show off. An aqueduct's purpose is to bring water from a distant source, in this case the Rio Frio, several miles to the east. Over the length of it a constant downward slope must be maintained to sustain the flow, and wherever it crosses a valley like this an arcade must be built to keep the flow level. The actual water-course, a channel cut into the stone and lined with lead, is at the very top. What you see is only a small part of the system; the

Romans built an underground water course from here to the Alcazar, and from the other end you can follow the arcade, ever shallower as the ground rises, up Calle Fernan Garcia from the Plaza Azoguejo and right out of the city.

Note the notches cut into the rough stone on the arcade; these allowed the stones to be picked up easily by a block and tackle. Once in place, they were used to help secure the scaffolding around the arcade. The Romans never cut corners; this was built for the centuries to come, and most likely would have survived unchanged had not several of the arches been destroyed in a siege by the Moors in the 11th century. 400 years later, Queen Isabel hired the monks of El Parral monastery to oversee the reconstruction, and when they had finished, they replaced the little statue of Hercules that stood in a niche over the centre with an image of the Virgin Mary.

A Templar Church and a Rogue's Retreat

By all means do not leave Segovia without a walk through the valley of the Eresma. Through either of the old Mudejar gates in the city's northern walls, the road leads down to the river through willow and poplar woods dotted with wild flowers. Following the road under the walls of the Alcazar, you cross the river and arrive at the church of **Vera Cruz**, one of the most interesting surviving Templar foundations, standing on a low hill in open countryside.

Iglesia de la Vera Cruz, Segovia

It is known that this church was built in 1208, and with the dissolution of the Templars in 1312 it became a regular parish church. The last few centuries have seen it abandoned, and its relic of the True Cross (*vera cruz*) moved to the little village of Zamarramala, 0.6 km (1 mile) away. Today the church is used by a Catholic brotherhood that grandiosely styles itself the 'Knights of St John'. Like many Templar churches, this one is round, with 12 sides; at its centre is the two-storeyed chamber, the 'inner temple' where the Templar secret rites took place, as opposed to the 'outer temple' which belonged to the common Church rituals (open daily except Monday, 10 am–1 pm and 3–7 pm).

None of the paintings or furnishings are as old as the Templars, but one 15th-century picture of the Last Supper, with the apostles seated at a round table, is worth a look. You may climb the belltower for one of the best views of Segovia and the Alcazar, taking in a number of churches and monasteries nearby in this holy valley, now largely unused. The closest, the 17th-century **Convento de las Carmelitas Descalzas**, has the tomb of the gentle St John of the Cross – or what's left of him, since like any Spanish saint his corpse was chopped up finely for holy relics.

To reach the most interesting of the monasteries, **El Parral**, retrace your steps to the river and continue up the opposite bank. On the way you'll pass the remains of the **Moneda**, or mint, where American gold and silver were turned into coins before 1730.

El Parral's founder, Juan Pachero, Marqués de Villena, is generally ranked among the slipperiest of all Castilian court intriguers. A protégé of the famous favourite Alvaro de Luna during the reign of John II, he played a role in the wars between the partisans of Isabella and Juana la Beltraneja by taking first one side, then the other, and occasionally both. He apparently chose this site because it had brought him luck – he had killed three men here in duels. In its day, El Parral was famous throughout Spain for its woods and gardens. The place is still lovely, and the long neglected church has been restored, with a number of interesting tombs of famous Segovians (and some of the Marqués' illegitimate children). Open daily 9 am–1 pm and 3.30–6 pm; Sunday 9 am–12 noon, 3–6 pm.

Another Bourbon Palace

La Granja de San Ildefonso is an easy excursion from Segovia, only 11 km (7 miles) east of town. This is one of the works of Charles IV, he of the insatiable appetite for palaces. La Granja ('the farm') has a certain rococo elegance of the sort American millionaires love to copy, but its fame has always been its **gardens**, laid out in the 1740s in immitation of Versailles. There are some 70 acres of them, with remarkable fountains everywhere, decorated with pretty pagan deities. One, the **Cascades Nievas**, descends the main axis of the gardens in a series of pools like a stairway; another throws water over 30 m (100 ft) in the air. The fountains are turned on only on Thursday, Saturday and Sunday afternoons at 5.30 (palace open 10 am–1 pm, 3–5.30 pm daily).

TOURIST INFORMATION

South side of the Plaza Mayor, Tel: 43 03 28; even if it's closed, everything you could want to know is posted up on the doors and windows outside.

WHERE TO STAY

Segovia's **Parador Nacional******, 2 km (1.3 miles) out of town on the Valladolid road, Tel: 43 04 62, is not convenient unless you have a car, and it's in a plain modern building. On the other hand, it has fine views of the town, a pool and one of the best restaurants of any Parador (6500–8500 pts doubles). Still, to experience Segovia the better choice would be **Los Linajes*****, Dr. Velasco 9, Tel: 43 12 01, in what certainly must be the most serenely pretty location of any hotel in Castile, on the northern walls overlooking the valley of the Eresma. It has a garden, and is only a few blocks from the cathedral (4700 pts for a double). Less expensively, there are the **Victoria*** on the Plaza

Mayor, Tel: 43 57 11, clean and simple; some rooms have views of the cathedral over Segovia's rooftops and clothes lines (2000 pts a double) and the **Plaza***, C. Cronista Lecca, just off the Plaza Mayor, Tel: 43 12 28; double with bath 2500 pts, without 1800 pts. There are *fondas* in the building next to the Victoria where the prices are even lower.

EATING OUT

More than anywhere else in Castile, Segovia takes dining seriously, and the streets around the Plaza Mayor and the Aqueduct are packed with dimly lit *típico* restaurants, where master *asadors* of reputation, bedecked in ribbons and medals, serve up Spain's best *cochinillo* (roast suckling-pig, traditionally only 21 days old), along with roast lamb and other formidable heavy Castilian specialities. Heading the list for 50 years or so now has been the **Mesón de Candido**, with its picturesque façade (shown on most of Segovia's tourist brochures) on the Plaza Azoquejo. Señor Candido is the expert – he writes cookbooks on Castilian cuisine – and he has played host to all the famous folk who have ever passed through Segovia (autographed photos on the walls, of course, to prove it). Dinners here will put you back 1700–2500 pts.

The young contender in Segovia is the **Restaurant Jose Maria**, off the Plaza Mayor on C. Cronista Lecca, where everything is first-rate (try the breaded frogs' legs, another local treat) and the prices kept relatively low – 1000–1600 pts for an à la carte dinner. Other renowned **asadors** hold court at the **Mesón Duque**, C. Cervantes 12 (1200–2100 pts), **La Oficina**, C. Cronista Lecca (1200–1800 pts) and **El Bernardino**, C. Cervantes (1000–1500 pts).

Less expensive restaurants abound, in the same areas, like the **Restaurant Lazaró** on C. de la Infanta Isabel (700 pts *menú del día*, but you can get *cochinello* here, too), the **Galicia**, C. Santa Columba (various set menus 700–900 pts). Sensitive souls should lay off the *sopa castellana* (and some other dishes), especially in the cheaper places, with enough grease to lubricate a locomotive. It's not bad, though.

WHERE TO SKI

There are three resorts in the Guadarramas between Madrid and Segovia, popular with Madrileños, as they're easy day-trips; if you'd like to join them, catch any train to Segovia, disembark at the small resort town of Cercedillas, and take the funicular up to Puerto Navacerrada or Puerto de Cotos. There are four three-star hotels in Navacerrada, the most fashionable place to stay.

Navacerrada has 12 pistes, a slalom and cross-country course served by 12 lifts; there are three hotels at the ski station. Navacerrada offers the most challenging skiing in the Guadarramas; Tel: 852 14 35. **Valcotos** has two very difficult courses among its 11 pistes; there are eight lifts and an emphasis on instruction; Tel: 852 08 57. **Valdesqui**, at Puerto de Cotos, has six pistes and 11 lifts, and like the other two, rents out skis if you didn't bring your own; Tel: 852 04 16.

Avila

For two cities so close together and with so much history in common, Segovia and Avila could hardly appear more unlike. Chance, with a little help from the geography, has made them into stone images of complementary sides of the Spanish character. Secure on its natural hilltop fortress, Segovia had the leisure to become a city of kings and merchants, aesthetic and relaxed and full of trees. Avila stands more exposed and it has always had the air of a frontier camp, coarse and ugly, a city first of soldiers, and later of mystics.

Avila's **walls** are its main attraction, the only complete circuit of fortifications around any Spanish city. Though medieval, they rest on Roman foundations, and their rectangular layout is the classic form of the Roman *castrum*. For Rome, this was a frontier-post against the Celtic tribes they had displaced from the area, and after the 8th century Avila found itself performing the same role in the constant wars between Moor and Christian. Through most of the 11th century it was the front line, often changing hands, until Alfonso VI decided in 1088 to construct these walls and make the town a secure base for further Christian advance. Except for Saint Teresa, who was a native and spent much of her career as a writer and monastic reformer behind Avila's walls, the town has been heard from but little since. The walls survive only because there was never the energy or incentive to knock them down.

GETTING AROUND

Avila is two hours from Madrid by train or bus. The same trains that go to El Escorial, running every hour or so from Madrid (Chamartin), arrive at the station in the new town on C. José Antonio. Most of the trains to and from Galicia, Asturias, Salamanca and even the Basque provinces and Burgos pass through here. The city has a brand-new bus station nearby on the Avenida de Madrid. (Buses from Madrid leave from the La Sepulveda terminal on Paseo de la Florida, near the Norte rail station.) Both stations are a five-minute walk from the city's old walls. There are regular bus connections to Segovia, Salamanca, and to all the provincial towns mentioned below from Avila, less regularly to points outside the province.

WHAT TO SEE

San Vincente

Modern Avila has almost completely forsaken the old walled town. The bus and train stations are out in the eastern extension, and however you arrive you are likely to approach this historic centre from this direction. Here, just where the Avenida de Portugal reaches the walls, is **San Vincente**, the most interesting of Avila's churches (open daily except Sunday, 10 am–2 pm and 4–6 pm). Parts of it are as old as the late 12th century, including the fine sculptural work on the west portal. St Vincent was another native of Avila, who was martyred along with his sisters, SS. Sabina and Cristeta, during the persecutions of Emperor Diocletian. There's more graphic, vigorous sculpture inside, where scenes of St Vincent on the rack and suffering other tortures decorate his sarcophagus. The church, probably succeeding an earlier Visigothic structure, was built over the site of the martyrdom, and if the attendant will agree to take you down to the crypt you can see the rock where the Romans did them in. Watch out for snakes; there's a legend of a serpent who guarded the saints' graves while Avila was occupied by the Moors. A custom grew up whereby the people of Avila would come down here to make bargains and swear oaths; if they lied, the serpent would come out and sting them (the only recorded victim was a bishop). Also down in the crypt is a much-venerated icon called **Nuestra Señora de la Soterana** (Our Lady of the Underground).

Los Verracos

This part of town, just east of the walls, is really as old as anything inside. A block from the walls, on the Plaza de Italia, an old ecclesiastical residence called the Palacio de los Deanes has been converted into Avila's very good **Provincial Museum**, with a folk-costume and crafts collection, Roman artefacts and some fine local medieval pictures – displayed where you can see them much more clearly than in Avila's dim churches. The museum provides a good introduction to an interesting aspect of Avila's ancient history. All of Avila province was a busy place when the Celts lived here, something as close to a capital or religious centre as this determinedly non-urban people cared to have. Remains of their castles and monuments can be seen all over the countryside, as well as hundreds of unique stone grave-markers called '*verracos*' (boars), carved in the shape of boars or bulls. These continued to be erected under Roman rule, as late as AD 300, and some carry Latin inscriptions, such as 'to the gods Manes and Titillo'.

Two blocks south, outside the **Puerta de Alcazar**, main gate of the old town, is the **Plaza de Santa Teresa**, the only really lovely corner of Avila, with most of the modest restaurants and hotels nearby. The church here with the lovely rose window is **San Pedro**, from the 13th century.

The Walls

Calle San Segundo runs along the eastern side of the fortification, towards the Puerta de Alcazar. In this section of the walls, you will see some stones with Roman inscriptions, and a good many others with a rectangular niche and a groove cut into them. These were the bases of the *verracos*, and the niches held the ashes of the departed chiefs and warriors. The Castilians under Raymond of Burgundy dragged in dozens of them to help build their walls. (A few *verracos* can be seen in the Plaza Calvo Sotelo, just inside the Puerta de Alcazar.) Though simple, the walls were up-to-date for the military needs of the 11th century; an engineer from Rome was called in to help with the design. The distinctive rounded towers are called *cubos*, but the biggest bulge, facing Calle San Segundo, comes as a surprise. It is the apse of Avila's cathedral, built right into the walls as if to symbolize the Church Militant of old Castile, helping man the battlements of the Reconquista.

It's a pleasant 2.4 km (1.5 mile) walk around the walls; on the southern and western sides they face open country, and the setting is sufficiently medieval to have been used for the shooting of several movies. On the narrow west end, they overlook old bridges spanning the River Adaja and the 12th-century Church of **San Segundo**, yet another local saint, who supposedly converted Avila back in the 1st century. If you wish to have a look at Avila from the top of the walls, the only entrance is in the garden of the Avila Parador, inside the northern face of the walls.

The Cathedral

It isn't much, though one of the earliest Gothic churches in Spain, and though a king of León (Alfonso IX) once lived here in sanctuary during a civil war. From the front it has no character at all, apart from the two bizarre stone wild men with clubs, added in the 18th century, who guard the portal. Avila's cathedral, literally half-church and half-fortress, does however have a little stage presence. The critics like to speak of Gothic architecture at its best as an eloquent argument for the Christian faith; this church was for a people who needed no convincing. Strong and plain, it has the air of an outsized chapel for warrior knights. The men of the Reconquista adorned it richly inside as if it were their treasure-house, and they lined its walls with niches for tombs where they expected to be buried.

Some of the sculpted tombs are among the best works in the cathedral, and there are some good reliefs in the north portal, and paintings and sculpture inside from quieter times when the wars of the Reconquista had passed on. One work very famous in Spain is the tomb of a learned 15th-century bishop named Alfonso de Madrigal (better known as 'El Tostado' for his swarthy complexion), with a statue of the bishop deep in his books, wearing robes carved with finely detailed scenes from the scriptures.

Little else within the walls is worth searching for. Old Avila, stagnant for centuries, has for the most part been reduced to a jumble of weedy lots, ruins and modern houses; in many places you can see faded coats of arms on the façades of once-proud noble mansions, now empty and crumbling or converted to other uses.

Santa Teresa de Avila

The Avilians celebrate her memory as ostentatiously as the Corsicans do Napoleon's. Even if it were possible to escape hearing about her for a while, there would still be the ubiquitous, nasty, candied egg-yolks called 'Yemas de Santa Teresa' to remind you. A traditional speciality of the local nuns, they are sold in every shop in town.

Teresa de Cepeda y Ahumada, of a wealthy family of Jewish converts, was born here in 1515. The faith was in her from an early age; when she was 7 she and her brother tried to run away and get themselves martyred by Moors. An old stone cross called **Las Cuatro Postes**, just across the Adaja from the town, is the spot where her uncle caught her and brought her back. Teresa took vows as a Carmelite at 18, and lived uneventfully for 22 years until her famous vision – an angel pierced her heart with a burning arrow during prayer.

At this point her career as a contemplative mystic began. Her works, notably the *Autobiography* her confessor ordered her to write, and the *Inner Castle* are read to this day; only 20 years ago Pope Paul VI declared her one of the Doctors of the Church, a position that has her keeping company with the likes of St Augustine and St Jerome. Just as her approach to mystical union with God was essentially practical, so was her very busy life in the world. Another vision, while praying at the chapel of Nuestra Señora de la Soterana in San Vicente, bade her reform her Carmelite order and return it to its original regimen of poverty and simplicity. The subterranean Virgin also had her take off her shoes, and wearing sandals became the symbol of the new *descalzada* (shoeless) order of Carmelites she founded. For the rest of her life she travelled throughout Spain founding new convents and reforming old ones. For all the good work she did, the end of the story is sad, and typical. Directly after her death the timeservers among the Carmelites staged a successful revolt; the convents and priories that remained faithful to her principles gradually backslid until they were as bad as the rest, and as for Teresa herself, while the Church disapproved of her books it saw fit to canonize her, repackaging the honest mystic into a miracle worker and an object of popular devotion whose chopped-off fingers soon became prized holy relics.

In her writings, Santa Teresa had little kind to say about Avila; apparently it was not a place where reforming ideas were very welcome. Nevertheless, Avila is happy to show off memories of her life in a number of convents about town. On the spot where she was born they built the **Convento de Santa Teresa**, just inside the southern gate. There is a squat church in the Herreran style, with a collection of relics and paintings of imagined scenes from the saint's life. More of these can be seen at the **Convento de la Encarnación** where she lived for 27 years, just north of the walled town on Calle de la Encarnación (open daily 9 am–1 pm, 5–7 pm) and at the **Convento de Las Madres** on Calle del Duque three blocks east of the Plaza de Santa Teresa.

Around Avila

The countryside is pretty and often quite unusual – green, rolling hills broken by rocky outcrops that often have the appearance of ancient ruins. South of the city, near the village of El Tiemblo, a great number of *verracos* can be seen in a field called **Los Toros de Guisando**. In 1468, at an assembly here, King Enrique IV was forced to accept Isabella's right to the throne of Castile. Only 6 km (3.8 miles) north of Avila, there are more *verracos* around the scanty remains of **Las Cagotas**, an ancient Celtic fortress whose inhabitants gave the advancing Romans fits for centuries.

Some of the more interesting villages of the province are **Arevalo**, little changed since the 1600s, with its walls, old churches and a bridge across the Adaja, and **Arenas de San Pedro**, a pretty town full of trees, with a little square castle right next to its town plaza. This is the base for visiting the **Sierra de Gredos**, a patch of dark, spare mountains with pleasant green valleys in-between and old villages like **Guisando** and **Mombeltran**, where there is a very well-preserved 14th-century castle.

TOURIST INFORMATION

In Avila, across the square from the cathedral, Tel: 21 13 87.

WHERE TO STAY

At the luxury end of the scale, Avila's **Parador Raimundo de Borgoña**, C. Marqués de Canales y Chozas (Tel: 21 13 40, doubles 5500–7000 pts) has a worthy competitor in the **Hotel Palacio de Valderrabanos****** across from the Cathedral, Tel: 21 10 23. Both are in old, historic buildings, but the Valderrabanos is a little less expensive – and it's air-conditioned (5400–6200 pts a double).

In the middle range, the preferred choice is **El Rastro****, in the shadow of Avila's walls on the Plaza del Rastro, Tel: 21 12 19. The rooms are plain (1700 pts for a double with bath, 1400 pts without) but there's a garden and a very popular restaurant, the **Meson del Rastro**, where local specialities such as veal and *judias del Barco* (famous beans from Barco de Avila with sausage) figure in the 800 pts menu. If the Rastro is booked up – as many of even Avila's hotels are likely to be in July and August – try the **Hotel Jardin***, also in an old building near the walls, San Segundo 38, Tel: 21 10 74, doubles: 1750–1975 pts with bath, 1425–1625 pts without. Most of the town's inexpensive hostels can be found around the train station on C. José Antonio, but you'll do better to take the time and find one closer in. The **Elena*** across from the Parador on C. Marques de Canals, Tel: 21 31 61, has doubles with bath for 1500 pts, 1100 pts without.

As for the Sierra de Gredos, there's the **Parador Nacional de Gredos*****, 3.2 km (2 miles) from Navarredonda, on the edge of the mountains, Tel: 34 80 48 with a good restaurant (5000–6500 pts a double); and if you have your own transport, you can enjoy these other simple, inexpensive retreats: the **Refugio de Gredos***, also near Navarredonda, Tel: 34 80 47, doubles with bath 2000 pts and the **Mirador de Gredos*** in La Adrada, Tel: 867 07 09, with a good, inexpensive restaurant (2200 double with bath). There are only very modest hostels and restaurants in Arevalo, Aremas and the other towns mentioned at the end of this section.

EATING OUT

Avila is full of good, solid, inexpensive restaurants, more than you would expect in a small town with lots of tourists. Most are near the eastern end of the wall, inside or out. At **El Rincón**, Pl. de Zurraquin 15, near the cathedral, there's a 700 pts set menu and you can get *cochinillo* and other Castilian specialities for slightly more. Others worthy of mention are **Casa Patus**, on C. San Millan just off the Plaza S. Teresa (various platters for 700 pts) and **Los Leales**, on the Plazuela de Italia near the museum (425 pts *menú del día*).

East of Madrid

Alcalá de Henares

Anyone from the Arab world would recognize the name's origin right off – *Al-kala*, a fortress – and it was the Moors who began this town, on the site of the abandoned Roman city of Complutum. In the 12th century, warrior bishops from Toledo captured it for Christianity and built it up; the long tradition of Church control may be one of the reasons Cardinal Jimenez de Cisneros founded his great Complutensian University here in 1508, an institution that almost immediately rivalled Salamanca as the foremost centre of learning in Spain.

In 16th-century Castile, it was no mean trick for a man like Cisneros to be on one hand an imperialist and a disturbingly fierce religious bigot, and on the other a champion of the new humanist scholarship that was sweeping Europe. For a brief, brilliant period the University became one of the intellectual lights of the continent; its great achievement, indeed its main reason for being, was the creation of the Complutensian Polyglot Bible, the first authoritative scholarly edition in modern Europe, with Latin, Greek, Hebrew and Aramaic originals in parallel columns. Even today it remains the standard work for Biblical scholars; in its day it was an academic revolution. Among the University's graduates in Spain's golden age, can be counted Calderón, Lope de Vega and Ignatius Loyola.

Through the 17th and 18th centuries the University's degeneration was gradual but complete, and half its buildings lay in ruins by 1837, when the sad remnants were moved to Madrid. Some of the old colleges were used as the Communist headquarters during the Civil War. Today, Alcalá without its university is one of the fastest growing cities of Spain, from industrial growth and the presence of a huge US air base nearby at Torrijón (a popular rendezvous for anti-NATO protesters from Madrid). Many of the old University's buildings are currently under restoration, and Alcalá is hoping it will be able to find some use for them.

GETTING AROUND

Lots of trains pass through, on their way from Madrid (Atocha and Atocha Apeadero) to Soria, Bilbao, Zaragoza and Barcelona, and it would be possible to see both Sigüenza and Alcalá de Henares in one day without really rushing. This is one case where the train is so convenient that you needn't worry about buses.

WHAT TO SEE

Alcalá's centre is the **Plaza Cervantes** with the arcaded **Calle Mayor**, the lively and pretty, old main street touching its edge. The University buildings are spread all over town, but the best of them, the **Collegio Mayor de San Ildefonso**, is just off the Plaza Cervantes and has a wonderful Plateresque façade, with the arms of Cisneros (note the swans – *cisnes*). Inside are a Plateresque chapel and a famous hall called the **Paraninfo** with an *artesando* ceiling. Other noteworthy buildings are the **Colegio de la Palma** on Calle Colegios and the **Casa de los Lizana**, with its brave stone lions, on Calle Postigo. Both are under restoration. Most of the University colleges are done in a very austere, Herreran style, as are Alcalá's churches.

On the Calle Mayor is a small museum devoted to Alcalá's most famous son, Miguel de Cervantes. The **Cervantes House** is one of two in Alcalá that claims to be the author's birthplace, but it has very much the air of a house a city might build or restore to pretend it were a famous author's birthplace. Modern Alcalá's only monument is on the street leading from the train station. The **Hotel Laredo** or *Quinta de la Gloria*, presently boarded up, is an incredible confection of brick Moorish arches and turrets piled up by some forgotten madman of the 19th century. Its style is not really 'neo-Mudejár' as the sign says, but more honestly 'hyper Mudejár'.

Guadalajara

The next stop up the rail line from Madrid, this once great town of new Castile was almost completely wrecked during the long battles for Madrid during the Civil War. Rebuilt as a modern, industrial city, the only reason to stop is the **Palace of the Dukes of Infantado**, built by Juan Guas in 1461 for the founder of what was to become one of Spain's most powerful noble houses, the Mendozas. Among its members it counted statesmen, authors, even a Viceroy of New Spain. The palace, in the Plateresque style, has a façade and courtyard florid enough to please any duke. Most of the palace has been restored or rebuilt, and it now houses a provincial art museum.

On the way to Sigüenza, both the highway and rail line pass the impressive, round-towered 15th-century **Castle of Jadraque**, built by the Dukes of Osuna. There are a number of pretty, old villages in this region, around the Río Henares and its tributaries: **Hita, Brihuega**, and **Atienza** have been little disturbed since the 14th century at least, and each has a castle and some ancient churches to add to the atmosphere. Sigüenza, on the rail line from Madrid, is much the same, though a little bigger.

Sigüenza

The cathedral is worth the trip, but what makes Sigüenza a pleasant excursion from Madrid is its setting in the hills around the Henares. From the quiet, arcaded **Plaza de España** you can walk through a little gate into the marketplace on the cliffs above the valley, and from there pass directly into the lovely forested hillsides that surround the town. Sigüenza is altogether much too cosy and charming to be in Castile.

The **Cathedral** has a good deal in common with the one in Avila; both were built at about the same time and show the influence of the French Gothic with a distinctive Castilian twist. Like Avila's it stands honest and foursquare – a castle with rose windows. They are very good rose windows, especially over the north portal, but the best things are inside. In the chapel of the Arce family is the tomb of Martin Vasquez de Arce, a young man who died in the wars with Moorish Granada. An unknown artist carved his figure in alabaster on the top of the sarcophagus, gently smiling and musing over a book. The image, as evocative of the medieval world as any passage from Tennyson, has become so well known it is referred to simply as *El Doncel de Sigüenza. Doncel*, in this case, means a king's page; Arce was an attendant of Ferdinand and Isabella. His crossed legs are not just an expression of nonchalance. It was a convention of Spanish medieval art, used to show that the deceased was a Crusader.

To stroll through the rest of Sigüenza will require a little climbing up narrow streets to the **castle** that dominates the town. Like Guadalajara, Sigüenza suffered greatly in the Civil War. The castle, now a Parador, and the Plaza de España have been almost completely restored, and plenty of bullet scars can still be seen on the cathedral tower. Several other Romanesque and Gothic churches, all quite plain, have also been restored, including the 12th-century **San Vicente** on Calle del Jesus. There is a **museum**, with works by El Greco and Zurbarán and some early religious art, across the plaza from the cathedral.

TOURIST INFORMATION

In Alcalá, Callejon de Santa María; none elsewhere.

WHERE TO STAY

Few tourists spend much time in this area, close as it is to Madrid. Alcalá has only one hotel with pretensions, the **El Bedel*****, C. San Diego, Tel: 88 93700 (very adequate rooms 3680 pts with bath), and several one-star establishments and *fondas* around the train station. Sigüenza's **Parador Castillo de Sigüenza******, in the old castle atop the old city, Tel: 39 01 00, is somewhat spartan by parador standards, a recent renovation from the ground up (doubles 5500–7000 pts). Everything else in town is quite modest: **El Doncel****, on C. General Mola, has rooms with bath for 2400 pts (Tel: 391 09 90) and the **Hotel Venancio***, around the corner at C. San Roque 1 (Tel: 390 347) offers comfortable old rooms without bath for 1600 pts.

If you get to Brihuega, there's a good inexpensive hotel there, **El Torréon****, on Paseo Maria Christina (doubles 1200–1500 pts; Tel: 28 03 00).

EATING OUT

Most of Sigüenza's few restaurants also cluster in the town. **El Laberinto**, always full of locals, has an unusually wide choice of dishes on its 500 pts set menu; it's on C. Grl Mola.

Alcalá de Henares has one restaurant so well-known it attracts a regular clientele from Madrid. The **Hostal del Estudiante**, on C. Colegio in an annex of Cardinal Cisneros famous University building (the Colegio Mayor), has been faithfully restored to a 16th-century atmosphere, right down to the oil lamps and uncomfortable chairs. The old fashioned Castilian cuisine is studiously maintained, and if you're up to spending 1700 pts for dinner in this corner of Castile, this is the place.

Aranjuez: yet another Bourbon Palace

There has been a royal residence in Aranjuez since the days of Philip II. His palace, built by Bautista and Herrera, the architects of El Escorial, was burned down in the 17th century, and we can only wonder what sort of pleasure-dome those two grinds could have created. Philip V began the replacement at the same time as he was building his palace at La Granja. It is hard to tell the two apart. Like La Granja, Aranjuez is an attempt to emulate some of the grandeur of Versailles; it isn't surprising, with Louis XIV meddling in Spain's affairs at every step, that the junior Bourbon wanted to show that he, too, was somebody.

Aranjuez is a natural location for a palace. The water of the Río Tajo makes it an oasis among the brown hills, on the threshold of La Mancha. Centuries of royal attention have given the area more trees than any other corner of Castile, and even today it is famous in Spain for its strawberries and asparagus. A small town has grown up around the palace since the 16th century.

GETTING AROUND

Most trains from Madrid (Atocha) to Cuenca, Alicante and Andalucía stop here, so there's no problem in getting there or back. A city bus will take you right from the station to the palace.

WHAT TO SEE

As at La Granja, the prime attraction here is the **gardens**, full of sculptural allegory and fountains in the most surprising places, shady avenues and walks along the Tajo, even an informal garden of the sort that were called 'English gardens' in the 18th century. They'll drag you through a guided tour of the **palace**, packed full of chandeliers and mirrors, with collections of porcelain, fancy clocks and court costume of the period. Among the gardens is another small palace, the **Casa del Labrador**, modelled after the Petit Trianon, and along the river a **museum of boats**; the conscientious Charles III built the structure as part of a forgotten project to make the Tajo navigable, but his successors turned it into a boathouse, and their pleasure craft are on display.

Aranjuez fills up with day-trippers from Madrid on weekends, and more than a few also find their way to **Chinchón**, a pretty, largely restored village some 19 km (12 miles) to the northwest. *Anis*, the anise-flavoured liqueur, is not quite as popular in Spain as in the south of France, but the Spaniards down their share of it; most of it made in Chinchón.

TOURIST INFORMATION
Plaza Santiago Rusiñol, Tel: 891 01 27.

EATING OUT
The local asparagus and strawberries figure prominently on most of the town's restaurant menus. Most of the restaurants are expensive, though, and you may settle for strawberries and cream from one of the little stands around town. Many restaurants have elegant settings along the riverfront, like **La Rana Verde**, where paying the extra for one of the fish or game specialities is preferable to the simple 1000 pts menu. **Casa Pablo**, on C. Altimbar, takes the cuisine and the wine a little more seriously, and is a little more expensive.

Cuenca

West of Aranjuez, the empty northern corner of La Mancha gradually rises into an attractive, rolling countryside, the foothills of the **Serrania de Cuenca**, a low, dishevelled chain that marks the traditional boundary between New Castile and Aragón. Cuenca, one of the most unusual and dramatic fortress-cities of Spain, stands at the base of this chain.

On the way, anyone interested in Roman Spain who can't make it to Tarragona or Mérida may want to take the detour south-east of Tarancón to **Segóbriga**, an important city for the Iberians and Visigoths as well as the Romans. The theatre, amphitheatre and some other buildings have been excavated, and there is a small museum on the site.

GETTING AROUND
Cuenca isn't really a comfortable day-trip from Madrid, unless the slow trains (three-hour trip) and quirky RENFE schedules hold no terrors for you. There are six trains a day (from Atocha) going in both directions; those going east continue to Valencia. Bus service (four a day) is handled by the Auto Res line (C. Fernandez Shaw in Madrid, C. Republica de Argentina in Cuenca). They also handle service to Teruel, the logical next step if you're going east towards Catalunya.

Depending on how you enter Cuenca, you may not see the old town at all when you arrive. A fair-sized modern city fills up all the space in the valley of the Río Jucar that once held medieval Cuenca's market gardens. Nearly all the hotels and restaurants are down here, but to see the real Cuenca, you'll have either to do a very stiff climb or to take the city bus up from the Plaza Trinidad, near the confluence of the Jucar and the little Huecar.

WHAT TO SEE
Old Cuenca waits upon a high rock between the two valleys, a position that helps to explain the city's history – or lack of one. Save only a few odd sackings, at the hands of

Alfonso VIII and during the Napoleonic Wars, Cuenca has been quiet for a long time, guarded by its nearly impregnable setting. The cliffs are steep, particularly on the Huecar side, and the **Casas Colgadas**, 'hanging houses', draped over them are the town's most prominent and picturesque feature.

Once you're up, you can rest while regarding the **Mangana Tower**, the last remnant of the town's Moorish alcazaba; no one is quite sure whether it was a minaret or part of the fortifications. It's hard to find, on a rise tucked behind the main street, Calle Alfonso XIII. That street leads to the **Plaza Mayor**, passing underneath the arches of the lovely 18th-century **Ayuntamiento** that closes off the square. The Plaza Mayor, with its cafes and plane trees, would be perfect but for the screamingly atrocious façade of the **Cathedral** (open 9 am–1.30 pm, 4.30–7.30 pm). Inside, the church reveals itself as an austerely graceful Gothic work of the 12th century, but the front was rebuilt in the 1660s in someone's bright idea of what Gothic really ought to have looked like. The original features of the interior are worth a trip inside, some noble tombs, stained glass and sculpture; note the very unusual subjects portrayed on the inside of the north transept. The **treasury** contains two paintings by El Greco.

Museum of Abstract Art

Just behind the cathedral, on Calle Canonigos, there is a small **Archaeology Museum**, with finds from Segóbriga and other Roman sites around Cuenca (open Tuesday–Saturday 11 am–2 pm, 4–6 pm, Sunday 10 am–2 pm). And just behind this, on the cliff's edge, some of the most decorative of the hanging houses have been converted into one of Spain's most unusual museums, the **Spanish Museum of Abstract Art** (open Tuesday–Friday 10 am–2 pm and 4–6 pm, Saturday 11 am–2 pm and 4–8 pm, Sunday 11 am–2 pm, closed Monday). Many visitors come to Cuenca expressly to see this audacious undertaking, showing off the avant-garde in a medieval setting, and the museum has acquired an international reputation. Only Spanish contemporary artists are represented, and while only fervent devotees of the abstract may spend much time on the paintings, anyone will enjoy the views from the old wooden balconies high above the Huecar. The houses – several of them have been connected for the museum – are interesting in themselves, though restored in a trendy manner with white walls and exposed beam ceilings.

The museum, now 20 years old, is one of the many projects of the Juan March Foundation, one of the most important forces in the Spanish art world. Its founder, the late Juan March, is worth a mention. Spain's greatest robber baron, a poor boy from Mallorca, made his fortune in contraband tobacco, eventually almost running the state tobacco monopoly out of business. After that he cornered the Spanish shipping business (with his Transmediterranea Line), put the entire Spanish Coast Guard on his payroll, stole the Barcelona street-car service from the foreign syndicate that built it, and still found time to assist British intelligence in two world wars. The Republic finally managed to land him in jail, but friends who visited him there reported finding March's private chef in attendance, tapestries on the cell walls, and three newly installed telephone lines. In return for the annoyance, March arranged all the financing for the Nationalist war effort in 1935. He died in 1962, from injuries received in the crash of his Cadilllac, and his billions are now building hospitals around Spain and buying up abstract art.

The Devil's Handprint

On the opposite side of Cuenca, facing the Jucar, a road called the Ronda del Jucar leads down into the valley past a number of old churches, monasteries and shrines, a corner of Cuenca that has been a holy place probably for millennia. Past the chapel of Nuestra Señora de las Angustias, patroness of the city, there is a small sunken garden with an unusual stone cross, decorated at the base with radiant suns. There's a legend in Cuenca of a young wastrel, long ago, who was seduced by a mysterious lady into arranging a midnight tryst outside the walls (at Halloween!). Lost in her charms, he did not realize that he was about to become the subject of old legend until he slid his hand up her dress and saw the cloven hoof – for she was the Devil himself, concealed in feminity. The wastrel escaped with his life only by reaching the refuge of this cross just as the fiend was about to snatch him, and you may see the mark of the Devil's hand on it today. More prosaically, you may consider the hand to be a symbol from some discreet and long-forgotten heresy, perhaps a version of the Islamic 'Hand of Fatima', a common symbol in the Middle East that survives in Salamanca and other cities of Spain in the form of door-knockers.

The Hoz del Huecar

Returning to the Huecar side of the town, just behind the apse of the Cathedral near the Abstract Museum, there is a long, narrow footbridge called **Puente de San Pedro** that begins one of the most beautiful walks you can take in this part of Spain, over the gorge (*hoz*) of the Huecar and then down into it, passing through pine-woods and fields along the riverbank with a view of the Casas Colgadas high above. Only from here does it become apparent just how unusual some of these are. What seemed like simple houses from on top turn out to be the lobbies of upside-down medieval skyscrapers ('*rascacielos*' as the Cuencans call them) hanging as much as 12 storeys down the side of the cliff. The road along the Huecar re-enters the city at the picturesque **Calle de los Tintes**, a boundary between the old Cuenca and the new.

Excursions from Cuenca

The rough mountains of the Serrania de Cuenca are full of natural curiosities, which can be seen only with a car and a little determination. By taking a loop of backroads north and east of the city can you visit the **Ciudad Encantado**, near Villalba, a region of curious wind-blown rock formations among pine woods. Some, like the 15.4 m (50 ft) 'big lump' are balanced precariously on narrow stems, like mushrooms; others have acquired names like the 'elephant' and the 'sea of stone' (open sunrise to sunset every day). To the southwest, **Las Torcas** are a group of strange, conical sinkholes, formed by the action of underground streams; some have filled up from below to become small lakes. The truly determined may find their way to the paleolithic **cave paintings** near the village of Villar del Humo, interesting though not as well preserved as the caves of Altamira. They are quite away off even the back roads; ask at the tourist office Cuenca if they may still be visited, and for explicit directions. The road east from Cuenca, heading for Teruel, is wonderfully scenic, especially after it passes through the Valley of Ademuz into Aragón. The Castilian section is called the **Vía Pecunaria**, the old 'cattle road'; there are more sheep than cattle grazing on its hillsides these days, but this is still one of the more traditional and out-of-the-way corners of Spain.

TOURIST INFORMATION

It's just moved, so all the maps on the brochures are wrong – C. Fermin Caballero, at the corner of Garcia Izcara, three blocks north of the train station, Tel: 22 22 31.

WHERE TO STAY

Accommodation of all sorts is easy to find, though nothing really special. Most are in the new, lower town, like the **Alfonso VIII******, across from a pretty garden, the Parque San Julian, Tel: 21 43 25 with doubles for 4180–5670 pts. Most of the cheaper hotels and *fondas* are on C. Ramon y Cajal, on the way from the train station to the old town, including the **Fonda Marin**, closest to the train station (1000 pts for a double without bath) and the **Del Pilar***, Ramon y Cajal 35, Tel: 21 16 84 (1100 pts a double, but with heat – essential in the winter). The only hotel up in the old town is the **Posada de San José***, C. Julian Romero 4, Tel: 21 13 00, two blocks north of the cathedral. It's very nice and some of the rooms have great views (2900 pts with bath, 1900 pts without).

EATING OUT

Cuenca's best restaurant, by consensus, is the **Figón de Pedro** on C. Cervantes, with such local specialities as *morteruelo*, made with grated pig's liver, traditionally finished off with a glass of *resolí*, a local potion of brandy, oranges, cinnamon and coffee (up to 2500 pts). The **Taverna de Petro**, in a lovely setting by the river on C. de los Tintes, specializes in seafood (1500 pts *menú del día*, and up from there). Some of the less expensive restaurants are good; the **Baviera** on C. Hurtado de Mendoza has a 600 pts menu that often includes river trout, and you can get by for even less (450 pts) at the **Fonda Tintes**, also on C. de los Tintes.

TOLEDO

No city in Spain has seen more, or learned more, or stayed true to itself for so long through the shifting fortunes of a discouraging history. Under the rule of Madrid the usurper, though, the last 400 years have been murder for Toledo; its pride humbled, its talents and achievements dried up, this city with little political or economic function is entirely at the mercy of the tourists. It would be a ghost town without them.

It isn't Toledo's fault that it has become a museum city, but it carries out the role with considerable grace. Its monuments are perfectly restored and well-scrubbed, its streets lively and pleasant, and the city can usually summon a smile and a welcome for even the most befuddled package tourist. No matter how you come to Toledo, you'll be glad when you finally arrive. The surrounding countryside, once all irrigated farmland or forest, is a desolation, a desert with a tinge of green. Toledo has a beautiful setting on a plateau above the Rio Tajo, and its little plazas and narrow streets are like an oasis in brick and stone.

Toledo was a capital of sorts when the Romans found it, a centre for the local Celtiberian tribes called the Carpetani. As a Roman town, Toletum did not gain much distinction, but scanty remains of temples and a circus, still visible just north of town off the Avenida de la Reconquista, indicate it must have been fairly large. The Visigoths made it their capital in the 6th century; their palace may have been on the site of the Alcazar. The Visigoths were not great builders, and relatively little is left from their two centuries of rule.

The Coming of the Moors

Toledo is full of stories. One of the oldest speaks of a tower, built by Hercules, that stood on the edge of the city. No one knew what was in it, and it became a tradition for every Spanish king to add a new padlock to the scores of them that already secured the tower's thick brass door. Roderick, that scoundrel who was to be the last of the Visigoths, neglected this, and was confronted one day by two magicians in mysterious dress to remind him of his duty. Roderick's curiosity was piqued, and instead of carrying on the old custom he resolved to find out what was inside the ancient tower. The bishops and counsellors did their best to dissuade him, but in the end Roderick had the centuries' accumulation of locks pried off, one by one, and threw open the brass door. An air as chill as death issued from inside, but the king entered, alone, and climbed a narrow stair to the top of the tower.

There he met the figure of a bronze warrior, larger than life, swinging a great mace back and forth and barring his entrance to the tower's inner chamber. Still undaunted, the king commanded it to stop and it obeyed. Behind it lay a chamber with walls covered in gold and precious stones, empty save for a small table bearing a small chest. This the king opened greedily, finding nothing inside but a large folded linen scroll. He saw that it was covered with scenes of battle; as he unrolled it the figures on it came to life, and Roderick saw his own army go down to defeat at the hands of unknown invaders in outlandish costume. While he blinked in astonishment at the moving pictures, a loud crash like thunder sounded from the depths of the tower; he dropped the linen scroll and hurriedly fled, escaping just in time to see an eagle with a burning brand in its claws soaring over Hercules' tower. With a scream it dropped the flame directly over it, and in scarcely more time than it took Roderick and his knights to heave a sigh, the tower burnt to the ground. Just as quickly a great flock of birds flew up from the ashes and sped off to the four winds.

Of course the invaders were the Moors; both Toledo and Roderick fell to them in the year 712. The beauty and strangeness of the old legend betray its Moorish origins, and Toledo, under its new masters, was about to embark on a career that itself would be the stuff of legends. Here, long before the Crusades, the Christian and Islamic worlds first met, in a city renowned throughout the Mediterranean world for learning. A school of translators grew up over the centuries in which Arab, Jewish and Christian scholars transmitted Greek and Arabic science, as well as Islamic and Jewish theology and mysticism, to the lands of the north. The first medieval troubadours most likely gained their inspiration from the Arab originals here. Toledo, conveniently close to the mercury mine at Almadén, became the great centre for the study of alchemy. Schools of occult philosophy and mathematics proliferated, attracting students from all over Christian Europe. One was Gerbert, the late 10th-century Pope, who was said to have stolen a

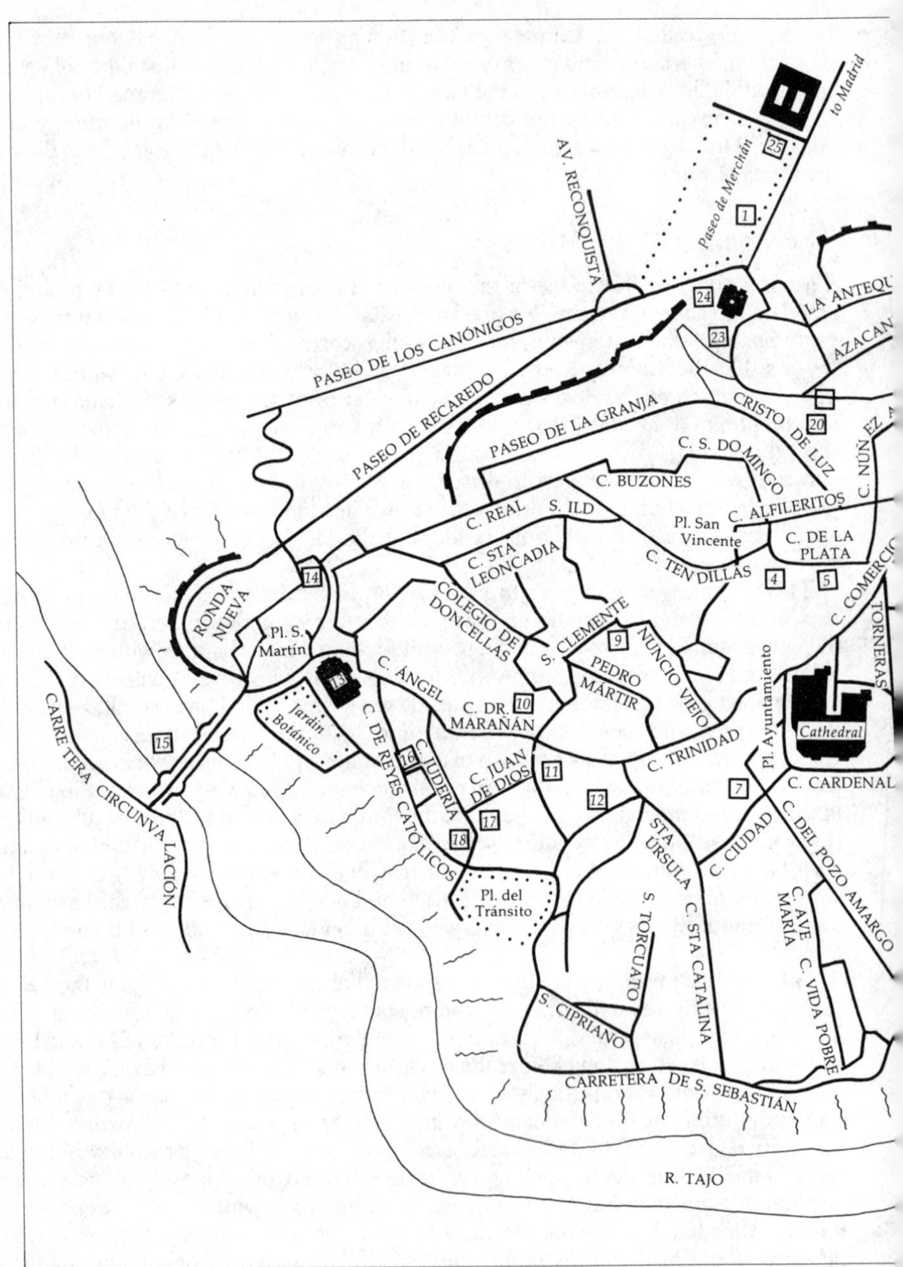

to Madrid
25
1
Paseo de Merchán
AV. RECONQUISTA
24
23
LA ANTEQU
AZACAN
PASEO DE LOS CANÓNIGOS
PASEO DE RECAREDO
PASEO DE LA GRANJA
CRISTO DE LUZ
20
C. S. DOMINGO
C. BUZONES
C. NÚÑEZ A
C. REAL
S. ILD
C. ALFILERITOS
Pl. San Vincente
C. DE LA PLATA
C. STA LEONCADIA
C. TENDILLAS
4
5
C. COMERCIO
14
RONDA NUEVA
COLEGIO DE DONCELLAS
S. CLEMENTE
9
NUNCIO VIEJO
TORNERAS
Pl. S. Martín
13
PEDRO MÁRTIR
Pl. Ayuntamiento
Cathedral
Jardín Botánico
C. ÁNGEL
C. DR. MARAÑÁN
10
CARRETERA CIRCUNVALACIÓN
15
C. DE REYES CATÓLICOS
16
C. JUDERÍA
C. JUAN DE DIOS
11
C. TRINIDAD
7
C. CARDENAL
12
17
18
STA ÚRSULA
C. CIUDAD
C. DEL POZO AMARGO
Pl. del Tránsito
S. TORCUATO
C. STA CATALINA
C. AVE MARÍA
C. VIDA POBRE
S. CIPRIANO
CARRETERA DE S. SEBASTIÁN
R. TAJO

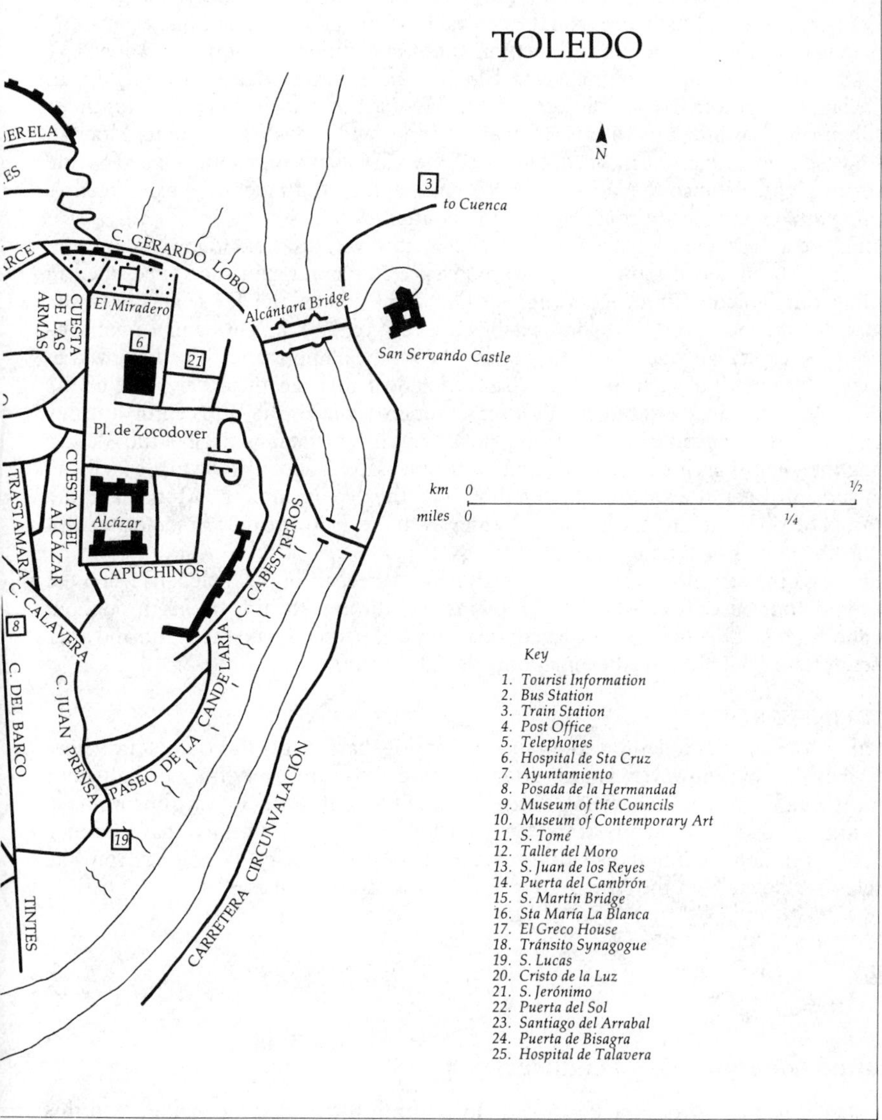
TOLEDO
N
3
to Cuenca
C. GERARDO LOBO
El Miradero
CUESTA DE LAS ARMAS
Alcántara Bridge
San Servando Castle
6
21
Pl. de Zocodover
CUESTA DEL ALCÁZAR
Alcázar
TRASTAMARA
CAPUCHINOS
C. CABESTREROS
C. CALAVERA
8
C. DEL BARCO
C. JUAN PRENSA
PASEO DE LA CANDELARIA
CARRETERA CIRCUNVALACIÓN
19
TINTES
km 0 ½
miles 0 ¼
Key
1. Tourist Information
2. Bus Station
3. Train Station
4. Post Office
5. Telephones
6. Hospital de Sta Cruz
7. Ayuntamiento
8. Posada de la Hermandad
9. Museum of the Councils
10. Museum of Contemporary Art
11. S. Tomé
12. Taller del Moro
13. S. Juan de los Reyes
14. Puerta del Cambrón
15. S. Martín Bridge
16. Sta María La Blanca
17. El Greco House
18. Tránsito Synagogue
19. S. Lucas
20. Cristo de la Luz
21. S. Jerónimo
22. Puerta del Sol
23. Santiago del Arrabal
24. Puerta de Bisagra
25. Hospital de Talavera

famous book of magic from Toledo, and was accused during his papacy of consulting with a prophetic magic 'head' of gold called a 'Baphomet' (the same charge that was later raised against the Templars).

Moorish Toledo was a city of some 200,000 people, over three times as large as it is today. Even so, it was never a centre of political power, and to the sultans and emirs of Al-Andalus it meant little more than the central bastion of their defence line against the rapacious Christians of the north. In a moment of inattention they lost it to Alfonso VI and the Cid. The conquest of the city in 1085 was never reversed, and probably tipped the balance of power irreparably against the Moors. For a long time, Toledo under Castilian rule continued its role as a city of tolerance and scholarship, and its Moorish and Jewish populations easily accommodated the Christian settlers introduced by the Castilian kings. Alfonso the Wise was born here, and he did much to make Toledo's learning and experience become Spain's in common.

After the accession of Ferdinand and Isabella, however, disasters followed thick and fast. The church and the Inquisition were given a free hand, and soon succeeded in snuffing out Toledo's intellectual lights. The expulsion of the Jews, and later the Moors, put an end to the city's long-established culture, and the permanent establishment of the capital at Madrid ended for ever the political importance it had enjoyed in medieval Castile. To make matters worse, Toledo had been the focal point of the Comunero revolt, and suffered greatly after its suppression. By the 18th century the city had become an impoverished backwater, and except for the famous siege of the Alcazar during the Civil War, little has happened there since. Long ago, Toledo made its living from silk and steel; the silk industry died off with the expulsion of the Moors, and the famous Toledo blades, tempered in cold water from the Tajo, are only a memory except for the cheap versions the tourists buy.

The visitors keep this town going, though it is the despair of the Toledans when the convoys of tour buses from Madrid stuff themselves through the tiny streets throughout July and August. Do not be discouraged; relatively few people spend the night, and after museum hours the old town becomes surprisingly tranquil.

GETTING AROUND

Toledo is off the main highway and rail lines, and its hard to get there from anywhere but Madrid. That, however, is easy enough; there are trains every hour or half-hour from Atocha to Toledo's charming Mudejár station east of town (any city bus will take you in), and buses frequently from the Estación de Sur. Toledo may have Spain's oddest bus station, built into the cliffs on the north edge of the city. To reach it, you take the elevator down from the Miradero off the Cuesta de las Armas.

WHAT TO SEE

Around the Plaza de Zocodover

The name, like the *socco* of a Moroccan city, is from the Arabic for market, and this square – triangle, really – has always been the centre of Toledo. The traditional market is still held here on Tuesdays. On the long, eastern edge of the triangle, the stately building with the clock is the seat of the provincial government, rebuilt after it burned down during the Civil War. From the archway under the clock, stairs lead down to the Calle Cervantes and the enormous, fascinating museum contained within the 1544 **Hospital de Santa Cruz**, a building by Enrique de Egas with a wildly decorated façade. A little bit of everything has been assembled here, archaeological finds from Toletum, paintings and tapestries, Toledo swords and daggers; the building itself is worth a visit, its long airy halls are typical of hospitals of the period, with beautiful ceilings and staircases. Spanish medicine was quite advanced in the 16th century (most of the physicians were Jewish and exempt from the persecutions) and the surroundings were held to be an important part of the cure.

Notable among the displays are Don Juan's huge standard from his flagship at the Battle of Lepanto, paintings by El Greco (*Santiago, Saint John*, an *Assumption*, and a *Crucifixion* with a view of Toledo in the background), some eccentric holy scenes by the 16th-century Maestro de Sigena, and a sculptural frieze from a pre-Roman Toledo house. A lovely 15th-century Flemish tapestry, the *Tapiz de los Astrolabios*, shows the northern constellations in a kind of celestial garden; other tapestries detail scenes from the life of Alexander the Great (open daily except Monday, 10 am–7 pm).

Just around the corner of Calle de la Concepción, the chapel of **San Jerónimo** is one of the best examples of Toledo's 16th-century Mudejar churches.

Gates of the town

North from the Zocodover, the Cuesta de las Armas is the old main road to Madrid. The street descends gradually, past the **Mirador**, and overlook with cafes, to the **Puerta del Sol**, a pretty gate-house from the 12th century. In the 14th century, the Knights of St John rebuilt it and added the curious relief medallion, much commented on as a late example of Toledan mysticism; it shows the sun, moon, and a large triangle around a scene of San Ildefonso, patron and 4th-century bishop of Toledo, receiving a chasuble woven by angels from the hands of the Virgin. According to local legend, it was a presented in return for a treatise the saint wrote on the meaning of the Immaculate Conception.

Further down, in the old quarter called the **Arrabal** outside the Moorish walls, is another fine Mudejar church, a joyous excess of pointed arches and towers done in brick, the 11th-century **Santiago del Arrabal**. In the 1480s, this was the church of San Vincente Ferrer, the anti-Semitic fire-eater whose sermons started regular riots and helped force the expulsion of the Jews. Here the modern road curves around the **New Bisagra Gate**, more like a palace than a gate with its pointed spires and courtyard. Charles V built it, strictly for decoration, and added his enormous coat-of-arms in stone after the Comunero wars, to remind the Toledans who was boss.

Just outside the gate, the city's tourist office is in a large park called the **Paseo de Marchan**, on the other side of which stands another 16th-century charitable institution converted into a museum, the **Hospital de Tavera**. Cardinal Tavera was a member of the house of Mendoza, a grandee of Spain, and an adviser to Charles V. His collection, including his portrait among several works by El Greco, and the memorable *Bearded Woman* by Ribera, share space with objects and furnishings from the Cardinal's time (open daily except Monday, 10.30 am–1.30 pm; 3.30–6 pm).

The Alcazar

Romans, Goths and Moors all had some sort of fortress on this spot, at the highest point of the city. The present plan of the big, square palace-fortress, the same that stands out so clearly in El Greco's famous *View of Toledo*, was constructed by Charles V, though rebuilt after destructions in the Napoleonic Wars and again in the Civil War. The second siege was a bitter one, and gave Toledo's Alcazar the curious fate of becoming the holy-of-holies for Spain's fascists and Francoists. Toledo declared for the Republic in July 1936, but a number of soldiers, civilians and Guardia Civil barred themselves inside with the idea that the coup would soon be over. Instead, what they got was a two-month ordeal, with Republican irregulars – there were no real troops on hand – keeping them under constant fire. When the Nationalists began to exploit the brave defence for propaganda, the Republicans got serious, and finally Asturian miners succeeded in collapsing most of the fortress with dynamite charges. Still the defenders held out, under the leadership of Colonel José Moscardó, in the ruins and underground tunnels, until a relief column finally arrived in September.

The courage shown by the men of the Alcazar was quite real, but Francoist Spain was never content to leave it at that. The climax of the visit here is Colonel Moscardó's office, where plaques in 19 languages record a telephone conversation in which the Republican commander threatened to kill Moscardó's son, whom he had captured, if the Alcazar did not surrender. With his son on the line, Moscardó intoned 'Shout *Viva España* and die like a hero!' The story is a blatant copy of that of Guzman el Bueno in Tarifa. In this case, unfortunately, it's all a fake, and Moscardó's son is reported to be still alive and well in Madrid.

The trip through the dungeons is interesting, with relics like the old motorcycle that was hooked up to a mill to grind flour for the defenders, and the spot where two babies were born during the siege. The corridors are covered with plaques sent from overseas to honour the memory of the besieged soldiers, contributed by such groups as the Chilean army and an association of Croatian Nazis in exile. Most of the plaques seem to be from various branches of the Argentine armed forces, but the biggest was sent by Paraguay's General Stroessner (open daily 9.30 am–7 pm, 6pm in winter).

Cristo de la Luz

From Zocodover, Calle Comercio leads off towards Toledo's great cathedral; on the way, you'll notice a big street sign proclaiming Calle de Toledo de Ohio, decorated with the Ohio state seal in azulejos (Toledans are proud of their little sister on Erie's shore, with its newspaper called the *Blade*; few of them have probably ever seen it). You may consider a detour here, up typically Toledan steep, narrow streets, to the church of **Cristo de la Luz**, in reality a mosque built around 980 and incorporating elements of an earlier Visigothic church. When Alfonso VI captured the city (the story goes) he and the Cid were making their triumphal entrance when the king's horse knelt down in front of the mosque and refused to move. Taking this as a portent, the king ordered the mosque searched, and a hidden niche was discovered, bricked up in the walls, with a crucifix and a lamp that had been miraculously burning since the days of the Goths. The tiny mosque, one of the oldest surviving Moorish buildings in Spain, is an exceptional example of their work, with horseshoe arches and beautiful vaulting.

The Cathedral

This isn't a building that may be approached directly; most of its bulk is hidden behind walls and rows of old buildings, with corners peeking out where you least expect them. The best of its portals, the **Puerta del Reloj** is tucked away in a small courtyard where few ever see it, at the end of Calle Chapineria. Circumnavigating the great building will take you all through the neighbourhood. On Calle Sixto Romano, behind the apse, you'll pass an old inn called the **Posada de la Hermandad**, seat of permanent militia-police force called the 'Holy Brotherhood' that kept the peace in medieval Castile. Coming around Calle Rombre de Palo, past the cathedral cloister, you pass the entrance used today, the **Puerta de las Molletes** (rolls) where bread was once distributed to the needy.

Finally, arriving at the Plaza Ayuntamiento (still often referred to as the Plaza del Generalisimo) you may enjoy the final revelation of the west front. It's a little disappointing. Too many cooks have been at work, and the great rose windows are hidden behind superfluous arches, over three big portals where the sculpture is indifferent but grandiose. Before too long, the interest fades; look across the square and you'll see one of Spain's most beautiful city halls, the 1618 **Ayuntamiento**, by El Greco's son, Jorge Theotocópulos.

Don't give up on the cathedral yet; few Gothic churches in Spain can match its interior, unusually light and airy and with memorable works of art in every corner. Some 800 fine stained-glass windows from the 15th and 16th centuries dispel the gloom. Unlike most other cathedrals of Spain, sculpture takes the place of honour before painting. Some of the best work is in the Old Testament scenes around the wall of the *coro*, at the centre of the Cathedral (note the interesting versions of the Creation and story of Adam and Eve). The coro's choir stalls are famous, decorated with highly detailed scenes from the conquest of Granada, done just three years after the event by Rodrigo Aleman.

Behind the coro is the freestanding **Chapel of the Descent**, dedicated to San Ildefonso; with its golden pinnacle it seems to be some giant monstrance left in the aisle. Another oddity is the 9.2 m (30 ft) painting of St Christopher on the south wall. The **Capilla Mayor**, around the main altar, contains some fine sculpture. A famous statue on the left-hand wall is that of Martin Alhagam, a mysterious shepherd who guided Alfonso VIII's army through the mountains before its victory at Navas de Tobosa, then disappeared; only the king saw his face, and he directed the sculptor at his work. On the right, another statue honours the memory of Alfaque Abu Walid. When Alfonso VI conquered Toledo, he promised this Moorish alcalde that the great mosque, on the site of the cathedral, would be left in peace. While he was on a campaign, however, the bishop and the king's French wife Constance conspired to tear it down; upon his return the enraged Alfonso was only dissuaded from punishing them by the entreaties of the generous Moor. Behind the altar, the beautiful *retablo* reaches almost to the vaulting, a saintly hierarchy of colourful carved wooden figures.

THE TRANSPARENTE

Even in a cathedral where so much is unusual, this takes the cake. Early in the 18th century, someone decided that mass here would seem even more transcendent if somehow a shaft of light could be directed over the altar. To do this a hole was chopped in the wall of the Capilla Mayor, and another in the vaulting of the ambulatory. The difficult question of how to reconcile this intrusion was given to the sculptor Nariso Tomé and his four sons, and in several years' work, they transformed the ungainly openings into a Baroque spectacular, combining painting, sculpture and architecture into a cloud of saints, angels and men that grow magically out of the cathedral's stones – many of the figures are partly painted, partly sculpture fixed to the walls. The upper window becomes a kind of vortex, through which the Virgin at the top and all the rest appear in the process of being vacuumed up to heaven. Even those who usually find Baroque extravagance a big bore will at least raise a smile for the Transparente. Antoni Gaudí would have approved, and it's hard to believe he did not gain just a little of his inspiration from this eccentric masterpiece.

Near the Transparente, the ratty old bit of cloth hanging from the vaulting is a Cardinal's hat – cardinals in Spain have the privilege of hanging them wherever they like before they die. It is one of several in the cathedral. Toledo's archbishop is still the Primate of Spain, and of cardinals it has known quite a few.

THE MOZARABIC CHAPEL

After the Christian conquest of Toledo, a dispute arose immediately between the city's old Christians and the officious Castilian prelates over which form of the liturgy would be used in masses, the ancient Mozarabic form descended from the time of the Visigoths, or the modern, Church-sanctioned style of the rest of Europe. Alfonso, as any good Crusader might have done, decided on a trial by combat to decide the issue. The Mozarabic champion won, but the Churchmen weren't satisfied, and demanded a trial by fire.

So they ignited some prayer-books. The Roman version was blown from the flames by a sudden wind, the Mozarabic wouldn't burn, and Alfonso decreed that the two versions of the faith would co-exist on equal footing. Though the numbers of those faithful to the Mozarabic liturgy have dwindled, their mass is still regularly celebrated in the large chapel in the south-west corner of the cathedral, built by Cardinal Cisneros, a friend and protector of the Mozarabs. You'll be lucky to see it; this chapel, the only home of the oldest surviving Christian ritual in Western Europe, is usually locked up tight.

Other sections of the cathedral are open by separate admission, from the enormous souvenir stand inside the Puerta de las Molletes. The **Treasury** has little of interest, though the 3m (10 ft) high silver reliquary does not fail to impress. In the **Sala Capitular**, a richly decorated room with a gilt *artesonado* ceiling, you can see some unusual frescoes and portraits of all Toledo's archbishops. El Greco painted the frescoes and altarpiece of the **Sacristy**, and there are other works of his, as well as a Holy Family by Van Dyck, and a gloomy representation of the arrest of Christ by Goya that makes an interesting contrast to his famous *Los Fusilamientos de Moncloa* in Madrid (cathedral hours: 10.30 am–1pm, 3.30–7 pm, 6 pm in the winter).

West of the Cathedral

Here the streets become even narrower and more winding; it's surprising just how long you can stay lost in a town only 1 sq. km (0.4 sq. mile) in size. Just three intractable blocks north-west of the cathedral, the 13th-century church of San Ramón has been converted into the **Museum of the Councils and Visigothic Art** (open daily except Monday 10 am–2 pm and 4–6 pm), the only one of its kind in Spain. 'Councils' refers to the several General Councils of the Western Church that were held in Toledo in the days of Visigothic rule, but the majority of the museum's exhibits are simple Visigothic relics, jewellery and religious artworks. Some of the buckles, brooches and carved stones show an idiosyncratic talent, but the lesson here is that the artistic inspiration of Spain did not really change in the transition from Roman to Visigothic rule – only there was much less of it. The building itself is much more interesting, half-Christian and half-Moorish, with nave, original frescoes of the Last Judgement and the 12 apostles in a garden. Painted angels and saints peer out from the ceilings and horshoe arches.

There is a small **Museum of Contemporary Art** just two blocks west of here on Calle de los Bulos.

The Juderia

As long as the streets continue to slope downwards, you'll know you're going in the right direction. The **Juderia**, Toledo's Jewish quarter before 1492, occupies a narrow strip of land overlooking the Tajo in the south-western corner of the city. El Greco too lived here, and the back streets of the Juderia are a concentration of some of old Toledo's most interesting monuments.

The church of **Santo Tomé**, on the street of the same name, is unremarkable in itself, but in a little chamber to the side, surrounded by souvenir stands, they'll show you El Greco's *Burial of the Count of Orgaz*. The tourists come here in greater numbers than to any sight in Toledo, and more nonsense has been written about this work, perhaps, than any other Spanish painting. A miracle was recorded at this obscure count's burial in 1323. SS. Stephen and Augustine themselves came down from heaven to assist with the obsequies, and this is the scene El Greco portrays. A group of the Count's friends and descendants had petitioned Rome for his beatification, and it is perhaps in support of this that El Greco received the commission, over 200 years later. The portrayal of the burial has for a background a row of gravely serious men, each one a notable portrait in itself (the artist is said to have included himself, sixth from the right, and his son, the small boy in the foreground, and some commentators have claimed to find even Lope de Vega and Cervantes among the group of mourners!). Above, the earthly scene is paralleled by the Count's reception into heaven.

This painting is perhaps the ultimate expression of the intense, and a little twisted, spirituality of 16th-century Castile. Its heaven, packed with grim, staring faces, seems more of an inferno. Nowhere in the work is there any sense of joy or release, or even wonder at the miraculous apparition of the saints. It is an exaltation of the mysteries of power and death, and the longer you look at it, the more disturbing it becomes.

The **House and Museum of El Greco**, not far away on Calle Samuel Levi, is the surviving wing of a palace where the painter lodged for most of the 33 years he lived in Toledo (open daily except Monday 10 am–2 pm and 4–7 pm). Domenico Theotokopopulos, a Cretan who had studied art in Venice, came to Spain hoping to find work at the building of El Escorial. Philip II didn't care much for him, but 'the Greek' found Spanish life and Spanish religion amenable, and spent the remainder of his life in Toledo. The city itself, as seen from across the Tajo, was one of his favourite subjects (though his most famous *View of Toledo* is now in the US). The best parts of the restored house are the courtyard and cosy tiled kitchen, and of the number of El Greco's paintings here only a few are of special merit – notably a portrait of *St. Peter*, another favourite subject. The museum guards are friendly and very talkative, and they'll tell you more than you ever wanted to know.

The **Taller del Moro** (Moor's Workshop), just around the corner from Santo Tomé church, gets its name from the days it spent as a shop for the cathedral workmen. The building itself is an interesting work of Mudejar architecture; inside is a collection of the sort of things the craftsmen made. Next door is the 15th-century **Palace of Fuensalida**, restored and also opened as a museum.

The Synagogues

Not surprisingly, in a city where Jews played such a prominent and constructive role for so long, two of Toledo's best buildings are synagogues, saved only by good luck after centuries of neglect. **Santa María la Blanca** (c. 1180) so called from its days as a church, is stunning and small, a glistening white confection of horsehoe arches, elaborately carved capitals and geometric medallions that is rightly considered one of the masterpieces of Mudejar architecture (open daily except Monday, 10 am–2 pm and 3.30–7 pm).

Just as good, though in an entirely different style, is the **Sinagoga del Tránsito** (open same hours) built by Samuel Halevy, treasurer to Pedro the Cruel before that whimsical monarch had him executed. The synagogue is much later than la Blanca, and shows the influence of the Granada Moors – the interior could be a room in the Alhambra, with its ornate ceiling and carved arabesques, except that the calligraphic inscriptions are in Hebrew instead of Arabic, and the Star of David is interspersed with the arms of Castile and León. The building now houses the **Sephardic Museum**, assembled out of a few surviving relics around the city. Elements of Jewish life and culture such as wedding costumes, a torah, and a shofar are displayed with explanatory notes, to reacquaint Spaniards with a part of their heritage they have quite forgotten.

San Juan de los Reyes

Before the conquest of Granada, Ferdinand and Isabella built this church with the intention of making it their last resting-place. The architect was Juan Guas, working the perpendicular elegance of Isabelline Gothic to perfection in every detail. Los Reyes Catolicos wanted no doubt as to whose monument this was; their F and Y monogram, coats-of-arms, and yoke-and-arrows symbols are everywhere, even on the stained glass. There's little of the elaborate furnishings of Toledo's cathedral here, but one of the side chapels contains one of the most grotesque, emaciated carved Jesuses in Spain. The exterior of the church is famous, with its western wall covered with the chains of prisoners released from the Moors during the Granada campaigns.

The **Cloister**, surrounding a peaceful courtyard where a lone orange tree keeps meditative company with a lone pine, is another of Toledo's architectural treasures, with elegant windows and vaultings, on the lower level. The same merry band of 1880s restorationists who did Vallodolid's San Gregorio were let loose here, and if you go up to the second floor and gaze up from the arches you will see the hilarious collection of **gargoyles** they added – all manner of monsters, a farting monk, a frog riding a fish, a lady playing bagpipes; see if you can find the cat (open 10 am–1.30 pm, 3.30–6 pm, closed Monday).

The **Plaza de San Martín**, in the front of the church, has a wide prospect over the valley of the Tajo; from here you can see another of Toledo's fancy 16th-century gateways, the **Puerta del Cambron**, and the fortified, medieval **San Martín Bridge**. If you would like to take the measure of this famous town from a little distance, on the other side of the Tajo there's a peripheral road called the **Carretera Circunvalación** that will give you more views of Toledo than El Greco ever did. On its way it passes a goodly number of country houses called 'cigarrales', the Parador, and finally, the 14th-century **Castle of San Servando**, rebuilt from an older Templar foundation. Beneath the castle, the **Alcantara Bridge**, even better than the San Martín, will take you back across the Tajo in the neighbourhood of the Zocodover.

Toledo's Countryside

It isn't pretty, and most of the attractions are castles – over 20 of them within a 48 km (30 mile) radius of the city. **Guadamur** and **Barcience**, both west of Toledo, are two of the most interesting. Among the towns and villages, **Talavera de la Reina** is a famous pottery centre, and **Illescas** has five El Grecos on display in its **Hospital de la Caridad. Orgaz** and **Tembleque**, on the threshold of La Mancha, are suitably ancient and evocative; each has an interesting Plaza Mayor. At Melque, on a back road south-west of Toledo, is one of the oldest churches in Spain, the 9th-century **Santa María de Melque**. Ask at the Toledo tourist office if it's open yet.

TOURIST INFORMATION

Just outside the Bisagra gate, on the road from Madrid (stop on your way if you can, so you won't have to make the steep trip down again), Tel: 22 08 43. Sometimes staffed by genial dilapidated gentlemen who'll talk your ear off once they get started.

WHERE TO STAY

Even though most visitors don't stay overnight (it's their loss!) you may need a reservation in July and August. At the top of the list, there's the showcase **National Parador Conde de Orgaz****** (Crta. Circunvalación, south of the city, Tel: 22 18 50. It's inconvenient for seeing the town, but there is a lovely view of it from the terrace, and a very good restaurant. A double room will set you back 7500–8500 pts. Less grandiosely, you can enjoy almost as good a view from the town (though not in every room) at the elegant and correct **Carlos V*****, tucked away on a quiet street near the Alcazar and Zocodover (C. Trastemaral, Tel: 22 21 00), doubles 2680–4900 pts.

In the middle range you have a choice between the modern and pleasant **Imperio*** (C. Cadenas, Tel: 22 76 50, double 2875 pts.), or a peculiar establishment in a peculiar old building, the **Lino*** (C. Santa Justa, Tel: 22 33 50, doubles 2024–2227 pts). Both are close to the Zocodover, off C. del Comercio. Among Toledo's cheapest are the **Labrador**** (C. Labrador 16, Tel: 22 26 20, 2200 pts for a double with bath, 1500 pts without; with 40 rooms there's usually a vacancy) and a few *fondas* scattered about town, like the **Fonda Segovia**, a block north of the Zocodover on C. Segovia (1000 pts for a double without bath).

EATING OUT

Dining in Toledo is largely a matter of avoiding overpriced tourist troughs. You'll get your money's worth (2500–3000 pts, though) at the fine restaurant of the **Hostal Cardenal**, outside the city walls at C. Recurado 24. As elsewhere in Toledo, stuffed partridge is a speciality, well-hung and gamey the way the Spaniards like it. You can eat kosher at the **Sinai**, on C. Reyes Catolicas in the Juderia, with a menu of Jewish and Moroccan specialities anywhere from 700 to 2000 pts.

Inexpensive restaurants are not as hard to find as you may think; there's a small colony of them along the C. Barrio Rey, just off the Zocodover, including **El Nido** (500 pts set menu). Also around the cathedral, on C. del Pozo Amargo, the **Restaurant Bar Paco**, and the **El Arrabal** on the road leading up from the Bisagra gate (both offer unremarkable 600 pts set menus). At least once, you should try Toledo's old speciality *mazapán*, made from almond paste; it's available everywhere.

Part XII

CASTILLA LA NUEVA: EXTREMADURA AND LA MANCHA

Temple of Mars, Santa Eulalia, Mérida

First-year students of Spanish often think Extremadura means 'extremely hard' – a translation that seems all the more true once they find out that this was the native land of those hard men – Pizarro, Cortés, Balboa and hundreds of others like them – who sailed to 'conquer' the New World for Spain at the expense of the Aztecs and Incas. Actually Extremadura means 'beyond the Douro River' – the territory conquered by the kings of León and held for centuries as a buffer zone between Christians and Moors. And hard as it may seem to its natives, who have left vast tracts of countryside empty for the bright lights of the city and jobs in Germany, Extremadura is not without a sweeping kind of beauty, one of endless rolling fields of wheat, dappled by the shadows of the evergreen holm oak, cork trees and olives. Blue mountains sunder the horizon; sleek black bulls share their pastures with storks, whose shaggy nests give a hairy crown to every church tower and castle turret in the region. Villages consist of low, whitewashed rows of houses, snaking over the contours of the hills, or towns filled with palaces embellished with the huge coats-of-arms of the nouveau riche Conquistadores.

The jewels of Extremadura are its cities Cáceres, Trujillo and Zafra, the extensive Roman ruins at Mérida, the famous shrine of Guadalupe and the Monastery of Yuste, where Charles V retired from his Empire. And lovers of scenic, out-of-the-way places can hardly do better than Las Hurdes.

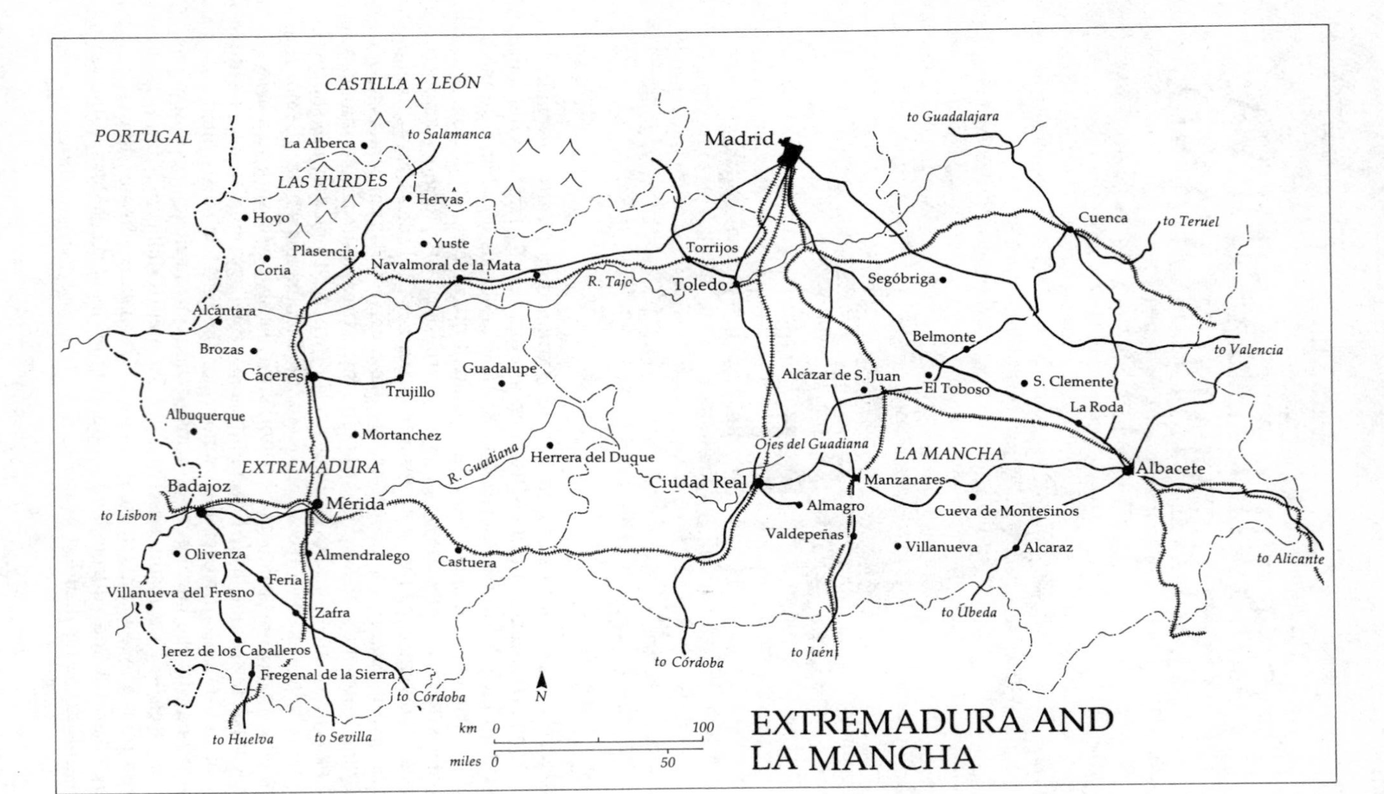

EXTREMADURA AND
LA MANCHA
CASTILLA Y LEÓN
PORTUGAL
LAS HURDES
EXTREMADURA
LA MANCHA
Madrid
La Alberca
to Salamanca
Hervás
Hoyo
Yuste
Plasencia
Coria
Navalmoral de la Mata
R. Tajo
Torrijos
Toledo
Alcántara
Brozas
Cáceres
Trujillo
Guadalupe
Albuquerque
Mortanchez
R. Guadiana
Herrera del Duque
Badajoz
Mérida
to Lisbon
Olivenza
Almendralego
Castuera
Feria
Villanueva del Fresno
Zafra
Jerez de los Caballeros
Fregenal de la Sierra
to Córdoba
to Huelva
to Sevilla
to Guadalajara
Cuenca
to Teruel
Segóbriga
Belmonte
to Valencia
Alcázar de S. Juan
El Toboso
S. Clemente
La Roda
Ojes del Guadiana
Ciudad Real
Manzanares
Albacete
Almagro
Cueva de Montesinos
Valdepeñas
Villanueva
Alcaraz
to Alicante
to Úbeda
to Jaén
to Córdoba
N
km 0 100
miles 0 50

Upper Extremadura

GETTING AROUND

Cáceres is the transport hub here, with rail links to Mérida, Badajoz, Lisbon, Madrid, Sevilla, Zafra – but not to Salamanca, though many maps still show the connection. Plasencia is connected by a short spur to Palazuelo on a couple of trains between Madrid and Extremadura. Palazuelo is the nearest station to Montfragüe national park – 20 km (12.5 miles) from its entrance at Puerta Serrana. The RENFE station in Cáceres (Tel: 22 50 71) at Ctra. Nacional 630, is 3.2 km (2 miles) from the Plaza Gral. Mola; a city bus connects the two every 20 minutes or so.

There are several connections daily between Salamanca, Plasencia and Cáceres by bus, and several to Trujillo (the bus station is just off the main Madrid–Cáceres road on C. Badajoz), and one daily from Cáceres and Trujillo to Guadalupe. There are also several express connections between Cáceres and Madrid (4 hours), and two RENFE buses that pass through the city daily on the way between Badajoz and Irun. Cáceres' bus station is out in the new town, about a mile from Pl. Gral. Mola on C. Gil Cordero, Tel: 22 06 00

Las Hurdes: if you're driving, C512 and C515 are the main roads through the region; if you're taking the bus from Plasencia (the bus station is near the river, not far from the Puente Nuevo), be prepared for some hiking; the few buses up that way tend to go no further than Pinofranquedo or Caminomorisco, the two largest villages in the Lower Hurdas. Plasencia is also the base for buses to Hervas (two a day), to Yuste (Cuacos) and the villages of La Vera (two a day). Coria, Alcántara and Garrovillas are easiest reached from Cáceres (two a day).

Las Hurdes

The northernmost zone of Extremadura is scenically the best and one of the least-known corners of rural Spain. The sierra of the southern Salamanca province (see p. 301) extends south into an untamed region with three valleys called **Las Hurdes**. For the Spanish the name is a dark shadow, a legendary place ruled by demons, where the inhabitants of the 40 tiny hamlets were brute savages, running about naked, devoid of religion, eating raw chestnuts, and practising everything from polygamy to cannibalism. A popular tale has a pair of noble lovers, somehow encountering the disapproval of the Duke of Alba, fleeing to Las Hurdes, only to be discovered a short time later in a state of of dire bestiality. The demons, it is said, were exorcised by a Carmelite monastery founded in 1599 in the valley of **Las Batuacas**, just south of La Alberca, but the misery lingered into this century; in 1932 Luis Buñuel finding the appalling poverty surreal, shot a film here, introducing the region to the rest of Spain. Over the last few decades Las Hurdes has received special attention to bring it into line with the rest of Spain: new schools, dams and roads were built and efforts made to prop up the local economy. Yet, from the outside the little villages of whitewash and slate have changed little, and wild boars trampling kitchen gardens are still a major nuisance.

Exploring Las Hurdes requires a car, or a willingness to tramp through some delightful scenery. The prettiest route is along the **Río Malvellido** in the **Altas** (High) **Hurdes**, taking in picturesque villages like **Fragosa, Nuñomoral, El Asegur** and, perhaps most unchanged of all, **La Huetre. El Gasco**, another of the more remote settlements, has a 55.4 m (180 ft) waterfall under the **Chorro de la Miacera**, one of the beauty spots of Las Hurdes.

On the other side of the **Reservoir Gabriel y Galán** – with an organized sailing Club, a good place to take a cool dip in the summer – you can explore the castle-crowned **Granadilla**, Spain's prettiest ghost town, though even if you're driving it's a bit of a walk from the local road C513. Going North, this road joins the N630 near **Hervás** in a pretty region of cherry orchards; the village has one of the best preserved *aljamas*, or Jewish quarters, in Spain, complete with a ruined synagogue and crooked half-timbered houses. Not surprisingly, the community owed much of its prosperity to the protection of the Templars, who aided in the conquest of Extremadura and were rewarded with large tracts of land.

Plasencia and Yuste

When Alfonso VIII of León founded this settlement, he declared '*placeat Deo et hominibus*' ('may it be pleasing to God and man'), from whence came its name Plasencia, a name Alfonso hoped would attract much-needed settlers to the frontier. It is known for its fine location, in a bend of the Río Jerte, and for its walls, now entirely integrated into the houses. The two **Cathedrals**' odd silhouettes dominate Plasencia, twice begun and twice unfinished. The pointy Gothic bulk of the 'new' one is more interesting inside, boasting a fine *reja* (1604) and more choir stalls by the ever-inventive, talented and profane Rodrigo Aleman. The older of the two cathedrals, begun in the 13th century, has a peculiar Salamanca–Zamora-style dome over its Sala Capitular. The **Plaza Mayor** a couple of blocks away is the home of the **Ayuntamiento**, with a funny man in green who strikes the hours on top and a main hall with an *artesonado* ceiling down below. Otherwise, Plasencia is a pleasant place to stroll through, as well as the base for visiting the **Monastery of Yuste**. The bus goes as far as the picturesque old village of **Cuacos**; from there it's a 2 km (1.3 mile) walk uphill to the monastery.

After ruling a hefty percentage of the Western World for 40 years, Charles V chose this isolated corner of Extremadura for his final retirement, accompanied by his cat and parrot, his friend the engineer and clockmaker Torriano de Cremona and 100 servants. Whatever excesses and seeds of disaster were sown by the old Habsburg during his reign, his retirement captured the popular imagination; here the somewhat world-weary emperor discomfited by gout (you can still see his gout chair, and the ramp especially constructed to give him easy access to his apartments) could fish, feed the ducks, look out over the Gredos mountains. Although Yuste was ruined after the depredations of the Peninsular War and suppression of the monasteries, Charles' apartments have been maintained as they were when he died in 1558, still draped in black (but minus the cartloads of Titians and Flemish tapestries); from his deathbed he could hear mass in the church below (guided tours, 10 am–1 pm and 4–7 pm.)

Cuacos and the pretty villages to the east in the **Valle de la Vera** are tobacco towns, and you can often see the local product hanging from the medieval overhanging second floors, many adorned with carved wooden balconies. **Jarandilla de la Vera**, the castle where Charles lived while waiting for his quarters at Yuste to be completed is now a parador; other pretty villages in the valley are **Villanueva de la Vera** with a fine plaza and **Losar de la Vera**, with many dilapidated 16th-century houses.

Coria and the Embalse de Alcántara

Located on the Río Alagón, a tributary of the Tajo, **Coria** is another old town, with a **bridge** remaining from Roman times, a lovely **castle** with a pentagonal tower, and a **Gothic cathedral** with a refined interior. At **Alcántara**, where the Alagón joins the Tajo, a dam was built creating the vast **Embalse de Alcántara**, one of several irrigation schemes of the Badajoz Plan, designed to bring the dry but fertile lands of Extremadura under cultivation. Alcántara takes its name from the Arabic word for 'bridge', given by the Moors for the remarkable example that now spans the often dry gorge below the dam. Built for Trajan in the year 105, its six lofty arches have often been destroyed and restored but still make a brave sight with their triumphal arch in the middle. Alcántara was the headquarters of the Order of Alcántara, founded to defend the frontier in the 12th century; Grand Masters' tombs may be seen in the 13th-century church, and ruins of the knights' castle remain above town. The prettiest church in town belongs to the 16th-century **Convento de San Benito**, with a fine, recently restored Plateresque façade.

East along the reservoir lies **Garrovillas**, site of a Templar convent. Its **Plaza Mayor** is an undulating, whitewashed work of art; its 15th-century **church of San Pedro** has a curious façade.

Further east, the government created **Monfragüe National Park** in 1979 to protect the unusual flora and fauna of this traditionally remote region. Another company of Knights, the Order of Montfrag, had its headquarters in the once mighty and now much-ruined **Castillo de Monfragüe**, located at the south end of the park near the scenic **Sierra de Peñafalcon**; a cult image of the Virgin brought from Palestine by the Knights is still the subject of local devotion. Much of the park is an inaccessible wildlife preserve for Iberian lynxes, boars, foxes, badgers, black storks, imperial eagles and several kinds of vultures but many of these animals can be seen in the accessible areas of the park's centre, around **Villareal de San Carlos**. This village was founded by Carlos III to police the once notorious bandits of Monfragüe. A booth here has information on trails, the best bird-watching spots and camping.

Cáceres

The provincial capital, Cáceres, is the most atmospheric of Extremaduran cities. Three sides of its large, central **Plaza General Mola** face the attractive, lively whitewashed new town, home of the region's university; the fourth side adjoins the nearly perfectly preserved **Roman-Moorish walls and towers** that enclose a beautiful 16th-century city inhabited mainly by storks. Much of it was built with gold from the Americas, and seemingly little has happened to it since the conquistadores returned to flount their wealth before their fellow citizens. If you come out of season, or in the dead of night, it's a wonderfully introspective experience to stroll its cobbled streets preserved unchanged by an enchantment like Sleeping Beauty's castle.

The **Torre Bujaco**, dominating the Plaza Mola is almost entirely Roman, and it's a startling experience to be in Cáceres during a fiesta, when the fireworks (and frightened storks) come careening off its roof just over the heads of the crowd below. The gate next to it, the **Arco de Estrella**, is an 18th-century addition by one of the prolific Churriguerras. Immediately to the right is the huge, decrepit **Casa de Toledo-Moctezuma**, home of the descendants of Cortés' follower Juan Cano and his wife, the daughter of Montezuma. All of the narrow streets near here converge in the elegant **Plaza de Santa María**, with a fine Gothic church of the same name and a beautiful 16th-century reredos. Among the many lovely palaces in the Old Town, the **Casa de los Golfines de Abajo**, just around the corner from Santa Maria at Cuesta de la Compañia, has the best façade, dating back to the 15th century. The lane in front of the palace descends through the last Roman gate that remains substantially intact, the **Arco Cristo**.

The other major architectural ensemble, the **Plaza de San Mateo** was the Moorish centre of town. Tall, Gothic **San Mateo** stands on the site of the old mosque; the **Casa de las Veletas** incorporates part of the Moorish Alcazar and its pretty cistern, or *algibe*, with its horseshoe arches. The building now contains part of the collection of the **Museo de Cáceres** (historical and ethnographic artefacts); the other section devoted to fine arts, is nearby in the **Casa del Mono** ('monkey house'), named for the very peculiar, bright-coloured gargoyles on the façade. Both are as interesting for their buildings as for their contents (open 9 am–1 pm and 4–7 pm, closed Mondays). On the same plaza, the 1477 **Casa de las Cigueñas** ('storks' house') is pointed out as the only one in town to retain the battlements on its tower; originally there were some 30 similar towers in Cáceres, but the nobles were so prone to fighting that Isabel la Católica ordered them knocked down. The tower still serves as a barracks and you can't enter. Nor can you get into the Gothic **Convento de San Pablo** which also shares the square, though in the doorway beneath the Arabic inscription you may purchase the best biscuits in town from the nuns, who use a lazy susan under a wooden hatch to preserve their anonymity.

Trujillo

An hour east, Cáceres' quieter twin-sister, Trujillo, is nicknamed the 'Cradle of Conquistadors' – the birthplace of the remorseless Pizarros, who almost singlehandedly wasted the Inca civilization, as well as of Francisco Orellana, first explorer of the Amazon; in the same epoch the town also produced another extreme character in Diego Garcia de Parades, a giant of a man who was the great companion-in-arms of the Gran Capitan, known for holding off entire armies by himself with a 1.8 m (6 ft) sword, earning the nickname 'the Samson of Extremadura'

Trujillo has an especially fine **Plaza Mayor**, dominated by an equestrian **statue of Francisco Pizarro**, man and horse wearing conquistador helmets; if it looks familiar, you've seen its double in Lima, Peru. Diagonally opposite across the plaza stands the **Palacio de la Conquista**, one of Trujillo's most grandiose, originally built by Hernando Pizarro. Of the five Pizarros who led the expedition to Peru, Hernando was the only legitimate son and also the cleverest, able not only to avoid the bloody intrigues that caused the untimely deaths of his brothers, but also to marry his brother Francisco's half-Inca daughter Francisca and settle here, where his descendants received the honorary title of Marqués de la Conquista. Behind this palace, the **Palacio Orellana-Pizarro** (now a school) contains an elegant Renaissance courtyard and doorway.

From here you can enter the old walled town via one of its seven gates, the **Puerta de San Andres**, and take the Calle de las Palomas up to the church **Santa María**, a fine Gothic temple with a retablos by the Flemish-inspired Fernando Gallego, and the tombs of numerous Pizarros and Diego Garcia de Paredes. Further up, the restored Roman-Moorish-Castilian **castle** nowadays defends kitchen gardens; from its commanding height there are fine views over Trujillo and its environs, so bleak and comfortless that you can understand how the Pizarros could leave it all behind and sail into the unknown to take the main chance, even if history will always condemn their cruelty and avarice, shocking even by the standards of the Age of Rapacity.

Guadalupe

One thing the Conquistadors took to, rather than from, the New World was the cult of their Extremaduran goddess, the Virgin of Guadalupe. The little dark image, said to have been carved by St Luke, was discovered by a shepherd in the 13th century in the pretty verdant oasis of the Sierra de Guadalupe, but the figure had to wait until 1340 for a proper shrine in a Hieronymite monastery founded expressly to house her. Soon Guadalupe became a pilgrimage destination, so popular that a Caribbean island was given the name.

Deserted in the 19th century, the monastery (now Franciscan) has been reopened; its fortress-like bulk, its pinnacles, towers and domes dominate the tiny, medieval town that over the centuries has grown up around the central plaza in front of the church. The setting is as superb as it is difficult to attain – Guadalupe is one of the most out of the way destinations in Spain.

The **Old Church** (which is always open) has attractive lacey stonework over its bronze doors, all dating from the 15th century. In the glittering gloom within you can barely make out the image on her throne high over the altar, though on all sides the rich gifts of her devotees, many locked behind elaborate *rejas* (grills) are testimonies of her mystique.

The **Monastery** (open daily 9.30 am–1.30 pm and 3.30–7 pm guided tours) adjoins the church in the plaza. Most intriguing here is the **Mudejár Cloister**, with two storeys of horseshoe arches enclosing Extremadura's most singular and provocative piece of architecture, the 1405 **Templete**, a Mudejár pavilion topped by an octagonal spire consisting of three tiers of blind, gabled arches, built over a Moorish fountain. The **Sacristia** is also unique, for its eight paintings by Zurbarán, still hanging in the room that was designed for them in the 17th century. Few paintings are as fortunate as these, to be seen as they were meant to be seen, in a sumptuous decor far removed from the sterile white walls of the museums. There's also a **museum** crammed full of more treasures – illuminated manuscripts and embroidered vestments, reliquaries and paintings – and for the climax, a trip up to the **Camarín** high above the altar, where the

Virgin of Guadalupe is turned around on her enamelled gyrating throne to receive the homage of the faithful and the scrutiny of the merely curious. She is certainly old, her mysterious, dark, Byzantine face peering out from her rich and gaudy attire. Then, if the good friar lets you linger, you notice that, among the enamels depicting the glory of the Virgin before Santa Teresa and San Juan de Dios, there are two scenes from the Civil War: one depicting a Guardia Civil killed on the monastery ramparts during 'the siege' and in the next panel, the triumphant entry of the Nationalists into Guadalupe, welcomed by a friar with a fascist salute. One can't help but wonder if this was a back-handed slap at Mexico, of whom Guadalupe is patroness, but was the one country in Latin America never to recognize the Franco government.

TOURIST INFORMATION

Cáceres: Pl. Gral. Mola, Tel: 21 21 17.

Plasencia: C. Truliio, a block from the Cathedral.

Trujillo: Plaza Mayor, near the steps.

In the summer there are also information booths in Pinofranqueado and Alcántara.

WHERE TO STAY

Up in Las Hurdes, there are *fondas* in Pinofranqueado and Nuñomoral (one here, **La Extremeña**, has rooms and natural food). Near Caminomorisco, the **Pensión Abuelo**, Ctra. de Salamanca, Tel: 43 61 14, has eight simple rooms; 1100 pts with bath, 800 pts without, meals for 600 pts. Up in Casares de Las Hurdes, the **Montesol***, Lindon 7, Tel: 43 30 25, has doubles for 1200 pts with bath, 1000 pts without.

In Plasencia a friendly and central choice, the **Rincón Extremeño**, Vidrieras 6, Tel: 41 11 50, has simple doubles with bath for 1500–1800 pts, without 1200–1300 pts. Visitors heading out to Yuste, however, can stay in the castle Charles V stayed in while waiting for his apartments at the monastery, at Jarandilla de la Vera's **Parador Carlos V**,*** Ctra. de Plasencia, Tel: 56 01 17, in a lovely location; doubles are air-conditioned and go for 6000–7000 pts. A cheaper option in Jarandilla, **Marbella***, Calvo Sotelo, Tel: 56 02 18 offers ten pleasant doubles, all with bath, for 2100 pts.

In Cáceres, the up-market hotels are in the dull, new part of town, but it's more fun to stay in the Pl. General Mola, either at the **Goya**, Tel: 24 99 50 (doubles with bath 2300–2600 pts) or the elderly **Fonda Carretero** or **Fonda Soraya** (both 1200 pts without bath for modest doubles), all of which have balconies on to the square and views of the old town.

The 17th-century convent of Santa Clara in Trujillo is now the **Parador de Trujillo**,**** Pl. Sta. Clara, Tel: 32 13 50, with attractive, air-conditioned rooms and a pretty garden (6500–7500 pts doubles); the restaurant serves local specialities for 1800 pts. There's also the little **Hostal Pizarro*** on the Plaza Mayor, Tel: 32 02 55, with simple rooms at the heart of things for 1500 pts without bath. It also has a good, cheap restaurant with homecooking (800 pts).

There are two special places to stay in Guadalupe: the **Parador Zurbarán*****, Marqués de la Romana 10, Tel: 36 70 75, located in a 16th-century palace with a lovely garden, pool and walls adorned with reproductions by Extremeño artists; it's only a short walk to the church (doubles 5500–7000 pts). The other, the **Hospedería Real Monasterio****, Tel: 36 70 00, is located in a spare wing of the monastery, its bar in the Gothic cloister (doubles with bath 3500 pts); it has a good restaurant as well (1500 pts), where you can top off a meal with a glass of the home-brewed *licor de Guadalupe*. Guadalupe also has a couple of *fondas* near the square and good, inexpensive meals (set menu 700 pts) at **Mesón el Cordero**, Convento 11.

EATING OUT
There's a memorable place to dine in Cáceres: the recently reopened **Hostería El Comendador**, at Ancha 6 in the old town, in a Renaissance palace, with a menu featuring Extremeño dishes (around 1700 pts). Equally good regional food is served at **El Figon de Eustaquio** nearby at 12–14 Pl. San Juan (try the *jamón iberico*, Extremadura's justly famous ham, reputedly made of swine fed on rattlesnakes! (1400–1750 pts). Cheaper choices are clustered about the Pl. Mola: try **El Gran Mesón**, Gral. Ezponda 7, with a 650 pts set menu and good artichokes, or **El Pato** in the plaza itself, where you can dine outside on fried trout or partridge (1000 pts) or try the set menu for 650 pts.

Lower Extremadura

GETTING AROUND
By rail: Badajoz and Mérida are linked by two *Talgos* daily with Barcelona and Valencia; Mérida has seven trains daily to Cáceres and eight to Badajoz; the Madrid train to Badajoz (four a day) passes through Mérida and Medellin. From Sevilla there's one train (at 5.30 pm) that connects Llerena and Zafra on its way to Mérida and Cáceres. From Huelva there's one train to Zafra, and two to Fregenal de la Sierra. For Portugal there are two trains from Mérida and Badajoz. In all of the above cities the train stations are within walking distance from the centre, except Badajoz, where the station is across the river, 1.6 km (1 mile) from the centre (Tel: 22 11 70); ticket office at A. de Celada 3, Tel: 22 45 62.

On the whole you may find it more convenient to take the bus, as RENFE is doing its best to close the local trains of Extremadura (going so far as to put its most uncomfortable carriages on the route). Again Badajoz and Mérida are the hubs; there's a daily RENFE bus connection to Córdoba and Málaga; another route twice a day to Salamanca and points north. The main bus station in Mérida is near the train station; in Badajoz buses leave from several locations. Most of the destinations described in the text are served from the station south of the walls on Av. Pardaleras. Buses between Badajoz and Sevilla (four a day) go by way of Jerez or Zafra.

Mérida

Not a few cities in Spain were founded by the Romans to settle their legions after the peninsula had been won. León and Zaragoza leap to mind, but in its day Mérida (founded in 23 BC as *Augusta Emerita*) outshone them all, growing to become the capital

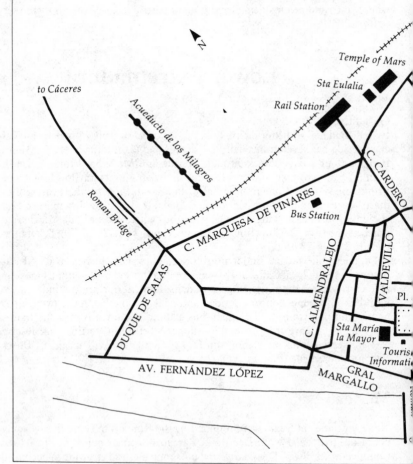

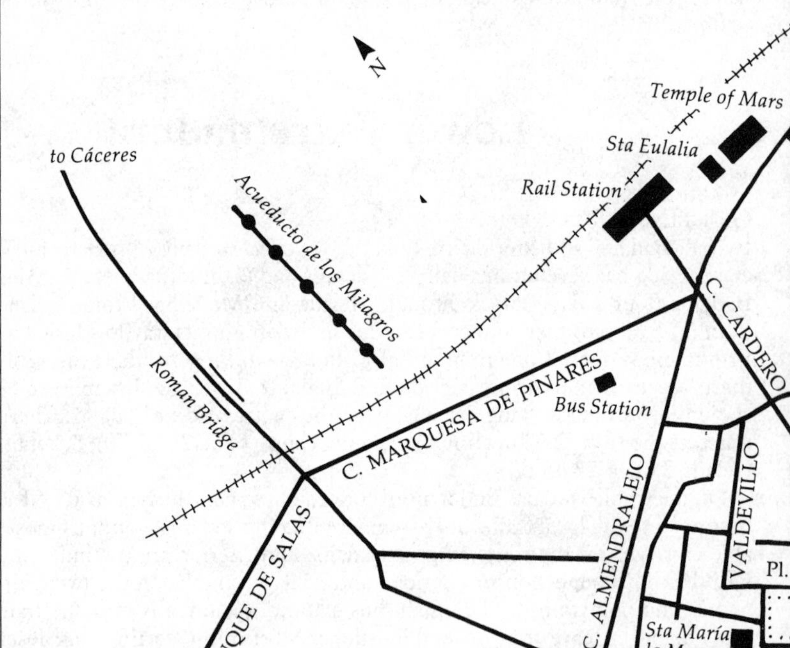
MÉRIDA
0
km
½
0
miles
¼
N
to Cáceres
Acueducto de los Milagros
Roman Bridge
Temple of Mars
Sta Eulalia
Rail Station
C. CARDERO
C. MARQUESA DE PINARES
Bus Station
DUQUE DE SALAS
C. ALMENDRALEJO
VALDEVILLO
Pl.
Sta María
la Mayor
AV. FERNÁNDEZ LÓPEZ
GRAL
MARGALLO

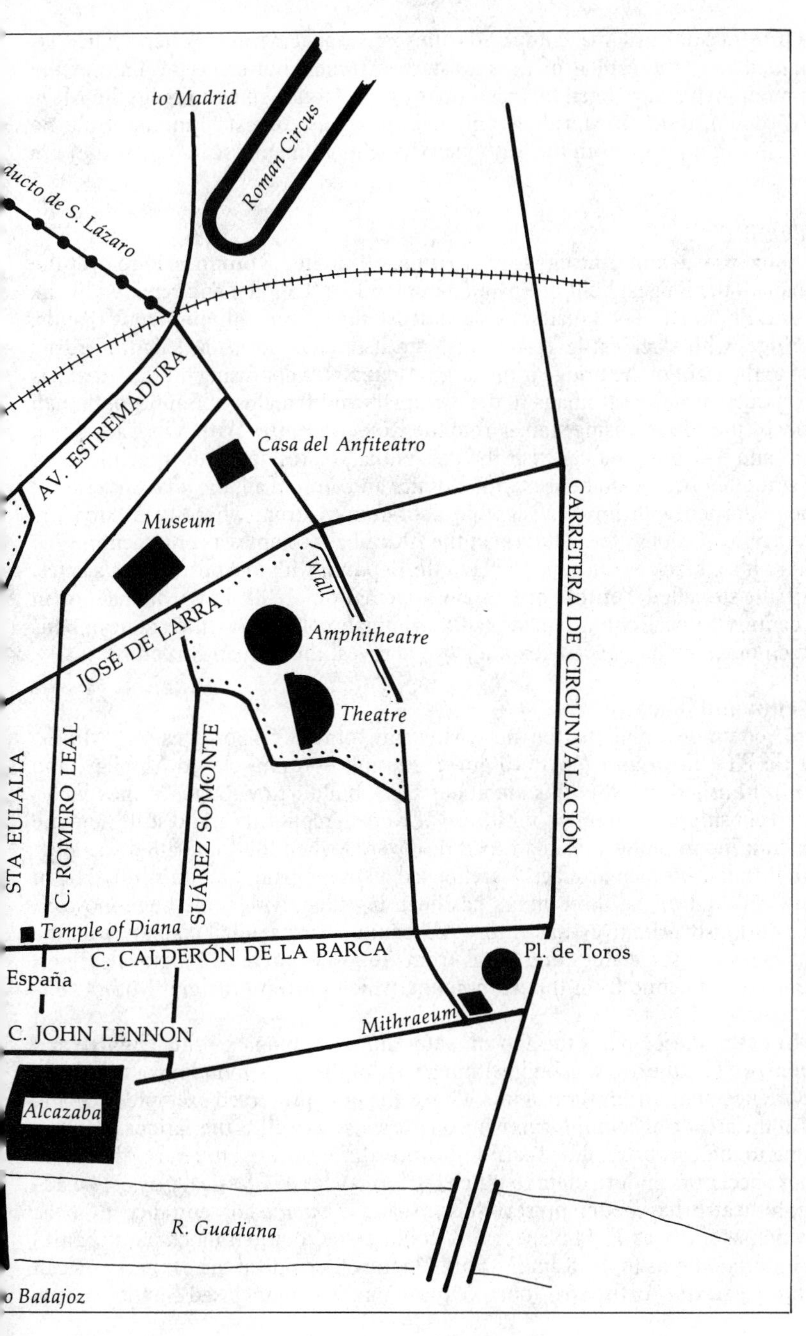

to Madrid
Roman Circus
ducto de S. Lázaro
AV. ESTREMADURA
Casa del Anfiteatro
Museum
Wall
JOSÉ DE LARRA
Amphitheatre
Theatre
CARRETERA DE CIRCUNVALACIÓN
STA EULALIA
C. ROMERO LEAL
SUÁREZ SOMONTE
Temple of Diana
C. CALDERÓN DE LA BARCA
Pl. de Toros
España
Mithraeum
C. JOHN LENNON
Alcazaba
R. Guadiana
o Badajoz

of the vast province of Lusitania, compared with some exaggeration to Athens. The Visigoths retained it as the capital of their western marches, but since the time of the Moors its monuments have been quarried (many of its stones going to build the Mezquita in Córdoba); modern Mérida is only half as big as Augusta Emerita. Still, no place in Spain can offer more in the way of surviving monuments, scattered as they are all over the city.

WHAT TO SEE

The traditional way to enter the city is to cross the 60-arched **Roman bridge** over the Río Guadiana – the longest built in Spain (about 0.8 km: 0.5 mile) and repaired by the Visigoths and Philip III. The Guadiana is a wide, shallow river with numerous islands, and the bridge, with sleek cattle grazing beneath its arches, forms a delightful rustic scene. Just to the right of the bridge is the large **Alcazaba**, a confusing bulwark that has served every ruler from the Romans to the Templars and Knights of Santiago, though built mainly by the Moors, using stones from the Roman theatre. Within its walls (open 8 am–1 pm and 4–7 pm) you can visit the conventual, or residence of the Knights of Santiago, a number of Roman houses with mosaics and, best of all, the *aljibe*, or cistern, its entrance adorned with lovely Visigothic door-frames, from where twin corridors descend to a pool of cool water. The rest of the Alcazaba resembles a construction site.

From here it's a block to the central **Plaza de España**, with most of Mérida's cafes. Further up, the so-called **Temple of Diana** was actually more likely a Nymphaeum; in the 16th century a local count had its tall Corinthian columns as the frame for his palace, much of which has since been cut away to reveal the Roman Structure.

The Museum and Theatre

From here, continue uphill to the new Museum, officially known as the **Museo Nacional de Arte Romano** (open 10 am–2 pm and 4–6 pm, closed Monday, and Sunday pm). Finished in 1986, this ambitious brick building by Rafael Mones Valles has attracted considerable attention for its use of Roman motifs, its grand scale, and the way in which it incorporates a Roman road discovered when the foundation was dug. Plans are to bring in Roman artefacts warehoused all over Spain, though at the time of writing only the first of the three floors has been installed, with some huge mosaics, including a curiously primitive 4th-century AD banquet scene, a tall column from the Temple of Diana, busts, statues and items from Augusta Emerita's religious shrines, most interestingly a statue from the Mithraeum, which portrays the god Mithras entwined in a snake.

Across from the museum lies the ancient entertainment complex – the **Theatre** and **Amphitheatre**. The theatre was built within a year of the city's founding, a testimony to the importance of drama in Roman life. This is the best-preserved example in Spain, with most of the arcade of columns surviving on the stage, as well as the various passageways leading to the orchestra. The seats of the *cavea* have suffered the most, though in the summer spectators endure them to watch performances of Classical plays. The adjacent amphitheatre has better-preserved seats and *vomitoria*, or entrance tunnels, through which as many as 15,000 spectators could come to watch mock naval-battles and other entertainments (open 8 am–10 pm). On the other side of the car park you can also visit the **Casa del Anfiteatro** (open 8 am–1 pm, 4–7 pm, closed Sunday pm), a large villa with a few mosaics, including a fine representation of winemaking. The first road left after the villa joins Avenida Extremadura near the scanty remains of the **Aquaduct San Lázaro** and the **Roman Circus**, where the Lusitanians watched their local hero Diocles chalk up some of his 1462 victories on the chariot-race circuits of the Roman Empire. You can make out the centre section, where the obelisks and turning-posts once stood, as well as parts of the stands that sat 30,000 people.

Heading back down Avenida Extremadura to the centre you'll pass Mérida's best-loved shrine, the **Church of Santa Eulalia**, dedicated to the child martyr who, according to legend, was baked in an oven on the site for spitting in the eye of a pagan priest. Whatever the real story, here is as tidy an example of syncretism as you'll find in Spain, for in front of the church is a well-preserved **Temple of Mars** (though the dedication is uncertain), better known as the 'Hornito de Santa Eulalia' (her 'little oven'), closed in by a grille, through which little girls traditionally dedicate locks of their hair to the saint! A bit further down towards the Guadiana stands the impressive triple-tiered **Aqueduct de Los Milagros**, a lovely work of engineering that greets visitors who arrive by train, another **Roman bridge** next to it spans a tributary of the Guadiana.

The most beautiful artwork in Mérida, however, is on the other side of town next to the Plaza de Toros, in the **Mithraeum** (open daily 8 am–1 pm, 4–7 pm). For the Romans, the cult of Mithras was like the Eleusian Mysteries for the ancient Greeks – the real religion, as opposed to official state rites performed in the Temples of Diana and Mars. Oddly enough (seeing the bullring next door) the sacrifice of bulls played an important part in Mithraic rites – rites to which the old legionaries of Augusta Meritus were especially devoted. Signs of frescoes remain on the walls of the underground *taurobolium* (where the bulls were killed) which you can peer down into, near a rectangular pool full of turtles. In the enclosed **Casa del Mitreo** there is a brilliant-coloured mosaic floor devoted to river gods that come vividly to life when the caretaker moistens them with the mop he keeps in the corner; be sure to ask.

Badajoz

Downstream from Mérida, on the Portuguese border, lies the provincial capital of Badajoz, its name deriving from its Roman appellation *Pax Augusta*. Few places have ever been so misnamed; instead of Augustian peace Badajoz' story is essentially one of sanguinary sieges and warfare – between Moor and Moor when *Bataljoz* was an independent kingdom, then Moor and Christian until Alfonso IX finally captured it for good in 1229, and then, as the 'key to Portugal' between Christians of several nationalities, most terribly in 1812, when Wellington lost a third of his 15,000 troops storming the French-held walls. Yet the nightmare that still haunts Badajoz is one that occurred after the siege in the Civil War, when the city was captured by Moors and foreign legionaries under Colonel Juan Yagüe, and the defenders, or any would-be refugees turned away from the Portuguese border (by order of the dictator Salazar), were coralled in the bullring and machine-gunned. Widely reported to a horrified world, this first major atrocity of the Civil War tragically set the stage for countless others on both sides.

Unless you're continuing on to Portugal, there's little reason to visit Badajoz; in an effort to forget its bloodstained past, Badajoz has bulldozed most of itself and covered it over with bland *urbanizaciónes*. The most elegant thing in the city is a bridge, the **Puente de Palmas**, built by Herrera in 1596, leading to a monumental gateway with round towers surviving from the old walls. From the plaza inside the gate, take Calle Yagüe to Meléndez Valdes 32 and the **Museo Provincial de Bellas Artes**, which among its contemporary works contains a handful of paintings by Badajoz native Luis ('El Divino') Morales and his fellow Extremeño Zurbarán (open 10 am–2 pm, closed Sunday). From here it's a couple of blocks to the **Plaza de España**, the unlovely heart of the city and home of its more-or-less Gothic **Cathedral**, begun by Alfonso the Wise and containing a pretty Renaissance choir, and paintings by Morales, Zurbarán and Ribera in the chapels and Sala Capitular – though none apparently did their best work when at home. In the same area you can find Badajoz's 'Giralda' – a dead ringer for the famous tower of Sevilla, stuck over a commercial block. The biggest sight in town is the rambling Moorish **Alcazaba** (1100) overlooking both the city and the Guadiana (open 9 am–1 pm and 3–6 pm); from its walls you can look out over the irrigated Vegas Bajas, a happy result of the 'Badajoz Plan' that has brought new growth to the city. Below the fortress stands its octagonal tower, the **Torre del Apendiz**, better known as the 'Torre Espantaperros', or 'dog-scarer'. An **Archaeology Museum** has been lodged in the former mosque of the Plaza Alta, the now-forlorn centre of Badajoz in the good old days.

Small towns where no one ever goes

From Badajoz you can take a side-trip north to the picturesque frontier town of **Albuquerque**, in the centre of a cork-producing region; it 14th-century **castle** saw plenty of action, and through its namesake in New Mexico it has gained immortal fame as the town where Bugs Bunny knew he 'shoulda made a left'. **Olivenza** to the south was Portuguese until 1801, when Godoy wrote a treaty that moved the border a bit to the west, gaining in Olievenza's church **Santa María Magdalena** Spain's finest example of Manueline Gothic architecture, with its graceful spiralling pillars and an altar crowned with the genealogical tree of the Virgin. Up the hill from the church stands the **castle**, built in 1488; an Extremeño **Ethnographic Museum** has been installed in the old Royal Bakery (open Saturday pm and Sunday am only). Exiting through the Puerta de los Angeles you'll find the **Santa Casá de Misericordia**, with one chapel done up sumptuously in Portuguese azulejos, installed in 1723.

From Mérida you can head out east along the Guadiana to tiny, whitewashed **Medellin**, birthplace of the ruthless Conquistador Cortés; the biggest thing in town (after the hilltop castle) is his monument. In Mexico, the land he won for Spain, such a memorial would be illegal. South-east of here is a forbidding land known as the 'Siberia of Extremadura'. South of Mérida on the route to Zafra, **Almendralejo** is the capital of the **Tierra de Barros** – the land of clay which produces, besides ceramics, a tasty wine.

Zafra

Zafra is the belle of Lower Extremadura. Known as Zafar under the Moors, it was the seat of the Dukes of Feria, the first of whom in 1437 built the **Alcazar** with its great round towers. Towering over the centre of town, this is Zafra's landmark and one of Spain's finest paradors – even if you're not a guest, you can duck inside to see the marble patio attributed to Herrera, the Sala Dorada and the Chapel. The nearby Plaza Mayor is better known as its two components, the **Plaza Grande** and **Plaza Chica**, separated an archway, both of them charming and whitewashed over their brick arcades, with Zafra's finest streets on either side. Of its churches, the **Colegiata**, built by the Dukes of Feria in 1546, is the most notable with its nine paintings by Zurbarán in the retablo; the first duke and his wife lie in their fine alabaster tombs in the **Convento de Santa Clara** near the Plaza de España; in here and around town see if you can find the duke's fig-leaf symbol, a play on his name, Figueroa.

Jerez de los Caballeros

Although named for the Knights ('Caballeros' – either Templar or Santiago – both were here in the 13th century), Jerez de los Caballeros likes to point out that it's far older, having in its environs a number of megalithic monuments, especially the **Dolmen del Toriñuelo**, with its unusual carvings of sun symbols, located 4.8 km (3 miles) north-west of town in the Dehesa (pasture) of La Granja. Jerez produced its share of conquistadors; Balboa, discoverer of the Pacific, was born here, and Hernando de Soto, first to explore the Mississippi River, was from Barcarrota just to the north.

Jerez went two better than Sevilla with its 'Giralda' towers; their silhouettes form the city's distinctive skyline. Nearest the heart of town (**Plaza de España**) towers the brick **Torre de San Miguel** (1756), carved and intricately decorated, a few blocks away, the even more lavish **Torre de San Bartolomé** (1759) is embellished with polychrome azulejos to match the blue and gold façade of the church below. On the opposite side of the Plaza España you can climb up to **Castle of the Templars**, which the knights held until their dissolution in 1307, when, according to legend, a number of them held out and were cut down in the **Torre Sangrienta** ('Bloody Tower'). The castle has recently been restored, and you can still see many traces of the Moorish alcazaba that preceded it. **Santa María**, next to the castle, was consecrated in 556, though the Visigothic has been swamped by the Baroque. Jerez' third 'Giralda' tower, **Santa Catalina** (1772), can be seen off to the left; its church has an impressive Baroque interior.

South of Jerez, **Fregenal de La Sierra** is a pretty village in the mountains near Andalucía, full of hermitages and traditional holy places; it was the birthplace of Philip II's great librarian and reviser of the Polyglot Bible, Arias Montano, who gathered the great collection of heterodox books in the library at El Escorial. Another town near Andalucía – and indeed, far more Andalucian and 'white' than an Extremeño town – is **Llerena**, with a beautiful **Plaza Mayor** and its idiosyncratic church of **Nuestra Señora de Granada**, with its huge 'Giralda' tower and a façade featuring a double-arcaded gallery.

TOURIST INFORMATION

Mérida, El Puente 9, just above the bridge Tel: 30 21 61.

Badajoz: Pasaje de San Juan 2, Tel: 22 27 63.

Zafra: Pl. España.

WHERE TO STAY

Mérida is endowed with the charming **Parador Vía de La Plata******, Pl. de la Constitución 3, Tel: 31 38 00, a former convent on a quiet square in the centre of town. The cloister is now a sitting-room and all rooms are air-conditioned (6000–7500 pts). A former palace on the main Pl. de España is now the **Hotel Emperatriz***** (Tel: 31 31 11), with a terrace in the front where you can take your morning coffee; all rooms have private bath (doubles 3700–4000 pts). The little **Hostal Nueva España***, Avda. Extremadura 6, Tel: 31 33 56, is near the bus and train stations, has simple, modern rooms and the best showers in Extremadura (all rooms with bath, 2000 pts). In the same area you can find a couple of cheaper *fondas.*

In Badajoz, the **Hotel Río*****, Avda. Adolfo Diaz Ambrona, Tel: 23 76 00, offers a fine view of the river and trees, as well as modern, air-conditioned rooms and a pool; doubles 3475 pts. If like most people you're just passing through, a good bargain choice is the **Hostal Menacho***, Abril 12, Tel: 22 14 46, which has clean, air-conditioned but bathless doubles for 1200 pts.

In Zafra, the Dukes' castle has been carefully converted into the **Parador Hernán Cortés*****, Pl. Corazón María, Tel: 55 02 00; Cortés indeed slept here as a guest of the Dukes of Feria. The decor may be Renaissance, but the comforts (pool, garden and good Extremeño cuisine served in a magnificent setting) are up-to-date and first-class (doubles 5500–6500 pts; dinner around 2000 pts). A lovely second choice, **Huerta Honda**** on Lopez Asme 32, Tel: 55 08 00, has fine doubles and views of the castle, a pretty patio and pool and an excellent restaurant, specializing in such regional delights as *ajo blanco* (white garlic) soup and golden cod (1200 pts). In Jerez, **Los Torres***, Ctra. Jerez a Oliva, Tel: 73 11 68, has 12 simple rooms near the centre for 1800–2000 pts with bath, 1400–1600 pts without.

EATING OUT

Mérida has a number of inexpensive restaurants (and an excellent one serving Extremeño dishes in the parador for around 2000 pts). The **Borroso** on the pedestrian C. St. Eulalia just off the Pl. España has a set menu featuring pork loins for 900 pts. Also just off Pl. España on Pl. St. Clarathe **Mesón el Emperador** offers local and Asturian dishes for around 800 pts. Near the bus station, the **Aragón** is funky but popular with a 600 pts set menu (José Antonio 20).

In Badajoz, the **Hostal Menacho** has a solid, inexpensive restaurant (600 pts); for something with a little more pizzaz, try the most popular restaurant in Badajoz, **El Tronco**, Muñoz Torrero 16, with a pleasant atmosphere and even better food (1600 pts); for something cheaper, dine off the tapas at El Tronco's amiable bar.

La Mancha

We've been unfair to this region, chopping off its most interesting sections (Toledo, Cuenca, and Sigüenza) and including them in the section around Madrid. What's left is the Spanish Nebraska, a moderately fertile but astoundingly empty corner of the

The Windmills of La Mancha

nation, covering about 160 by 320 km (100 by 200 miles) between the capital and Andalucía. Iberians, Romans and Moors trod these lonely plains, all no doubt wondering why they were doing it. Medieval Spain exerted itself mightily to wrest it from the Moors and make it the 'New Castile', but like their predecessors the Castilians were never able to make anything of it. The centuries have left this land utterly devoid of notable towns and monuments, and the lack of interest complements the monotonous scenery nicely.

It isn't so oppressive in the spring, when red carpets of poppies fill the gaps between endless fields of young wheat and budding vines, but even then, you're likely to find a quick trip through on your way to the south is more than enough.

GETTING AROUND

The region is well served by RENFE: all the southern routes from Madrid must pass through it. Madrid-Badajoz trains pass through Ciudad Real, and there are two a day that stop at Almagro. Trains to Andalucía pass through Valdepeñas and the big, dull towns of Manzanares and Alcazar de San Juan, and all lines from Madrid to Murcia and Alicante stop at Albacete. For the other towns, you'll have to depend on bus services from the two provincial capitals, Ciudad Real and Albacete.

WHAT TO SEE

If you pass down the main road from Madrid, there are a few diversions en route. After **Tembleque**, near Toledo (see p. 125) the first landmark is the decaying castle on the hill over **Consuegra**: one of the characteristic white conical-roofed windmill stands near it to remind us we are on the western borders of La Mancha. Near Daimiel, north of Ciudad Real, is one of the region's curiosities, the **Ojos de Guadiana**, a marshy area where the river Guadiana disappears underground, and pops back up a few miles to the west. Numerous species of migratory birds favour the area as a stop over, and it is included in the recently designated **Parque Nacional de las Tablas de Daimiel**.

Ciudad Real, capital of the province, is a small and somewhat dismal town, with only a lone Moorish gateway from its old fortifications to show visitors. A better stop would be **Almagro**, changed little since its period of prosperity in the 16th century. Among its monuments are a lovely, arcaded **Plaza Mayor**, a convent of the Knights of Calatrava, and the oldest theatre in Spain, the **Corral de Comedias**. This relic of the golden age of Spanish theatre makes an interesting comparison with its northern contemporaries – like Shakespeare's Globe, it has a row of balconies all around for the gentlemen and ladies, and a small floor in the centre for the 'pitlings' below the stage (only it's square instead of round). It's been restored and productions of classical Spanish plays are put on from time to time. Almost everything you see in Almagro was built by Jakob Fugger of Germany and his descendants, who started Europe's first great banking-house and at times controlled most of the continent's cloth trade. The Fuggers prospered greatly from Charles V's imperialist extravagance, and Almagro was their Spanish headquarters.

The back road south from Almagro passes through the **Campo de Calatrava**, scene of many battles of the Reconquista. The religious knightly Order of Calatrava, right arm of the Castilian kings in these wars, was founded here, and the ruins of their monastery headquarters at **Calatrava La Nueva**, including the rough, fortress-like church with its rose window, are evocative of that grim age of the Church Militant. An excursion from here into the bleak **Sierra de Alandia** to the south-west would be a novelty – this is undoubtedly the least visited part of Spain; and not without reason. Villages like Tirteafuera and Gargantiel, Cabeza del Buey ('ox-head') and Pueblonuevo del Terrible are more interesting on the map than in person. Much mining goes on here, coal and zinc, and the famous mercury mine at **Almaden** that supplied the alchemists of Toledo.

The main road is a better bet, passing through the country's biggest wine region, around **Valdepeñas**. Several bodegas in the town centre and off the highway would welcome your visit. Much of Spain's dependable 70-peseta-a-bottle brew comes from here, but also some of its finest vintages. The highway and railroad pass in to Andalucía through the **Desfiladero de Despeñaperros**, 'overthrow of the dogs', a wild rocky chute long the haunt of bandits.

Don Quixote's La Mancha

There's little evidence that Miguel de Cervantes ever cared to spend much time here. Certainly he would have had a big laugh at the expense of the Manchegans and literary critics who drone on about the 'poetic, essentially Spanish' landscape. Nothing could be less poetic than the bleak expanses of the region called 'the blot' (or 'the stain'), and Cervantes found its empty spaces the perfect setting for his hopeless knight errant and his parable of a burnt-out, disillusioned Spain.

You needn't come here to follow the tracks of Don Quixote; La Mancha is all too easy to imagine. Scholars have spent their careers tracing out the knight's imagined itinerary, and schools contend endlessly over which blank-faced, anonymous Manchegan village was the scene of the Encounter with the Windmills, the Adventures of the Inn, or

Camacho's Marriage. But unless you can tell one Manchegan village from another, such scholarship may seen extravagant.

El Toboso, home of the peerless Dulcinea, and one of the very few villages Cervantes ever actually names, might be a good stopover for determined Quixotic pilgrims. Of course they'll show you Dulcinea's house, now restored and turned into a humble Quixote **museum**. Two of the nicer villages are **San Clemente** and **Campo de Criptana**, around which several much-honoured windmills can be seen. There's a grandly exotic 15th-century castle outside **Belmonte**. An empty 80 km (50 miles) to the south-east, a series of small lakes and low waterfalls called the **Lagunas de Ruidera** are La Mancha's modest scenic wonder. **Alcaraz** nearby, is a town of some distinction; with its ensemble of interesting 16th-century buildings it seems a minor version of Ubeda. And not surprisingly Ubeda's architect, Andrés de Vendelvira, was a native and built many of them.

Albacete, the Manchegan metropolis, makes its living from artichokes and saffron from the country around it; it leads Spain in both these products, and has grown into a city of 100,000 people with dull, straight streets and little to see. Albacete was a ferociously Republican town during the Civil War, the training-ground of the International Brigades, and few of its old churches survived. From here you can choose between highways for Valencia, Murcia or Alicante, the last passing a 15th-century castle over the town of **Almansa**.

TOURIST INFORMATION

Ciudad Real: Avda Martires 31, Tel: 21 29 25.
Almagro: C. Corniceria 11.
Albacete: Avda. Rodriguez Acosta 3, Tel: 22 33 80.

WHERE TO STAY

One reason to stop in Almagro would be the **Parador Nacional de Almagro****** in the restored, 16th-century Convento de San Francisco, one of the finer paradores, in a most unexpected location (Ronda de San Francisco, Tel: 86 01 00, air-conditioned doubles 5500–7000 pts). Beyond that, Almagro has only a few *fondas*. Most of the hotels in Valdepeñas are on the Madrid highway outside town, but the **Cervantes**** is a reasonable spot in the centre (C. 6 Junio, Tel: 32 36 00, doubles 2850 pts with bath, 1700 pts without). Modest lodgings can be found in Ciudad Real, Almadén, Alcazar de San Juan, Campo de Criptana (the **Sancho***, on Pl. del Generalisimo, 1200 pts double with bath) and at Ruidera near the lagoons. A bargain in Daimiel is **Las Tablas***, modest, air-conditioned rooms with TV, for 2750 pts (C. Virgen de Los Cruces, Tel: 85 21 07). The **Parador de La Mancha***** in Albacete is a colourless place, but the most comfortable in town (C.N. 301, Tel: 22 95 40, air-conditioning and pool, doubles 5000 pts). A less expensive but satisfying place to stay if you're passing through is the **Albacete*****, C. Carcelen 8 (Tel: 22 71 50, 1900–2900 pts double with bath, 1350–1485 pts without).

EATING OUT

Game dishes are the speciality of most Manchegan restaurants; *perdiz con judias*, partridge with beans or other partridge dishes are those you are most likely to find, as at

Mesón Las Rejas in Albacete (C. Guerdiola 7, 1600–1800 pts) the **Miami Park** in Ciudad Real (C. Cirulo 48, 1400–1750 pts) and **Las Brujas** in Daimiel (highway 240, 800–1200 pts).

Part XIII

ANDALUCÍA

Detail of a window in the Great Mosque at Córdoba

A vision of the lost Islamic civilization of Al-Andalus may come upon you where you least expect it. In the cities – Sevilla, Córdoba and Granada most of all – it is obvious, a separate reality that shines through centuries of Spanish veneer. In the whitewashed villages, still so like their counterparts across the Straits of Gibraltar, it is present in spirit. But it is in the countryside where the Moorish heritage shows up most surprisingly. One of Andalucía's most beautiful views unfolds from the *mirador* at the eastern end of Ubeda; the rolling hills recede towards the distant mountains, covered with olive trees planted in neat, varying patterns, and down below near the stream a small farm has its rows of carrots and beans arranged in patterns even more intricate and maze-like. Moorish poets sang of their land as a terrestrial paradise, and Moorish farmers – their love and care for the soil still half-remembered today – shaped it into a great garden, landscaped as a work of art in the same play of geometry and arabesques that decorate the Alhambra and the great mosque of Córdoba.

Think of that picture when you visit. Al-Andalus was a culture totally unlike any Europe has known, and it requires an effort of the imagination to appreciate its subtlety and delicacy. Its destruction was a tragedy, not just for Spain, but the world. The ill-fortune that put Al-Andalus in the hands of Castile was like someone giving a complicated music-box to a small child; unable even to comprehend, let alone use it, the Castilians banged and pounded it until it broke. Many of the bits and pieces survive to this day, but it would take a greater talent than a magician's from the Arabian Nights to put them back together.

In just a few centuries, Andalucía went from being the richest and most cultured province in Europe to one of the poorest and most backward. It managed this feat

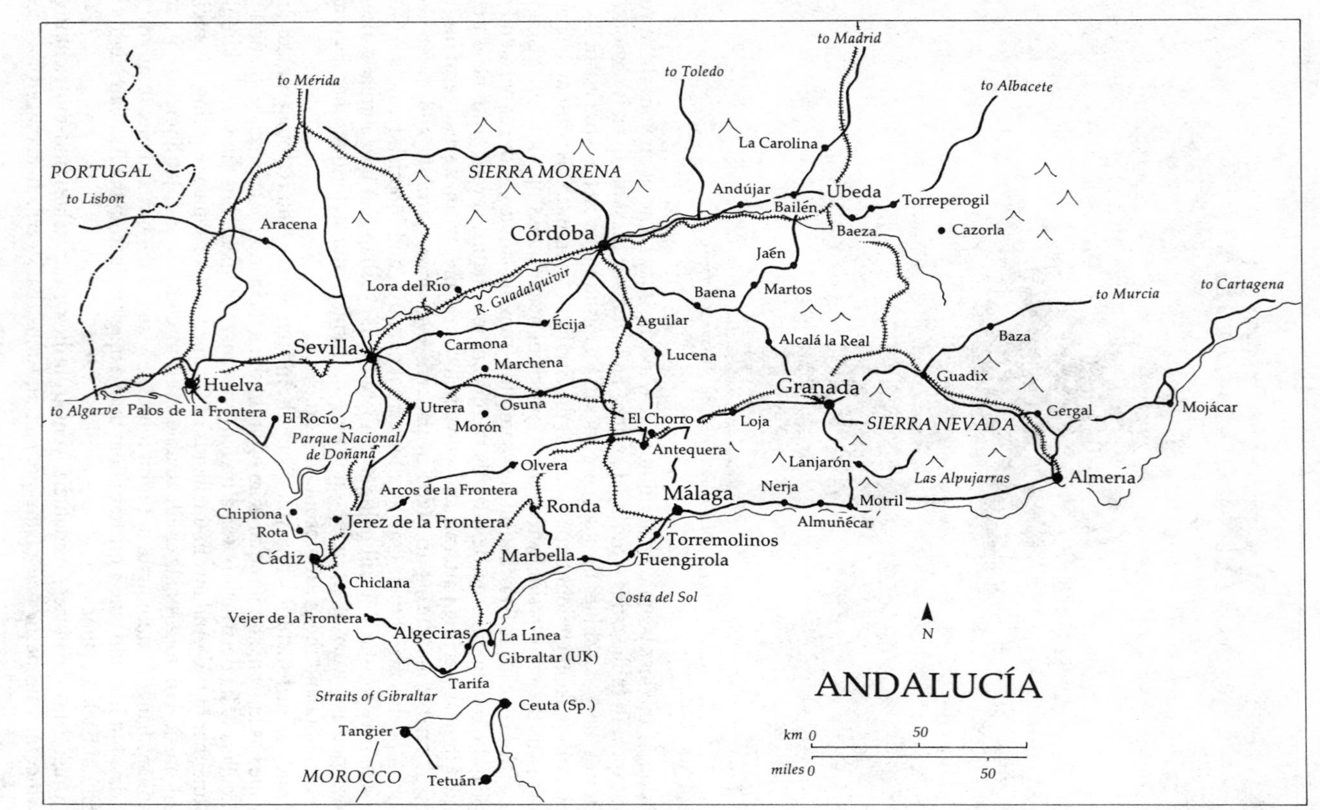
ANDALUCÍA
to Madrid
to Mérida
to Toledo
to Albacete
PORTUGAL
to Lisbon
SIERRA MORENA
La Carolina
Andújar
Ubeda
Torreperogil
Bailén
Baeza
Cazorla
Aracena
Córdoba
Jaén
Lora del Río
R. Guadalquivir
Baena
Martos
to Murcia
to Cartagena
Aguilar
Écija
Carmona
Alcalá la Real
Baza
Sevilla
Lucena
Marchena
Guadix
Huelva
Granada
Osuna
to Algarve
Palos de la Frontera
El Rocío
Utrera
El Chorro
Loja
SIERRA NEVADA
Gergal
Mojácar
Morón
Parque Nacional de Doñana
Antequera
Lanjarón
Las Alpujarras
Almería
Olvera
Arcos de la Frontera
Málaga
Nerja
Motril
Ronda
Chipiona
Jerez de la Frontera
Almuñécar
Rota
Torremolinos
Cádiz
Marbella
Fuengirola
Chiclana
Costa del Sol
Vejer de la Frontera
Algeciras
La Línea
N
Gibraltar (UK)
Tarifa
Straits of Gibraltar
Ceuta (Sp.)
Tangier
MOROCCO
Tetuán
km 0
50
miles 0
50

during the period of Spain's colonial empire, when the booty of an entire continent was being poured through its ports. Queen Isabel herself, so arrogantly proud of her conquest of the godless Moor, supplies us with a telling clue to this sad history. The Moors were the great architects of water, making dry plains into irrigated fields and gardens; Spanish folktales often speak of them almost as sorcerers, so superior were their works to anything the Castilians could create after the Reconquista. During the campaigns against Granada, Isabel found herself lodging at the Alcazar of Córdoba, where an old Moorish water wheel in the Guadalquivir churned up water for the pools and fountains of the Alcazar gardens. After a few nights Isabel ordered it dismantled – it disturbed her sleep.

In the long dark night of its conquerors, Andalucía fell under the hand of one of the most useless and predatory aristocracies Europe has ever known, heirs of the warriors of the Reconquista. As a result, its impoverished peasants became the most radicalized population in Spain, as manifested in frequent local revolts throughout the 19th and 20th centuries. Only now is Andalucía emerging from this situation – Felipe Gonzalez is an Andalucian, and so is his vice-President. A big land-reform programme is under way, and the growth of tourism along the southern coasts has pumped plenty of money into Andalucía's economy. A hundred years ago travellers in this region never failed to note the wretchedness of the villages and the glaring contrasts of wealth and poverty. You'll see little of that now.

Today, with its new green and white flag flying proudly on every public building, autonomous, Socialist-run Andalucía may have the chance to rediscover itself. With a fifth of Spain's population, its biggest tourist industry, and potentially its richest agriculture, it has great promise for the future. And as the part of Spain with the longest and most brilliant artistic heritage – not only from the Moors, but from the troubled, creative, post-Reconquista Andalucía that has given Spain flamenco and bullfighting, Velazquez, García Lorca and Manuel de Falla – the region may find it still has the resources to once more become the leader, and not a follower in Spain's cultural life.

For convenience, we've divided Andalucía's complicated geography into four parts: Sevilla, Córdoba, and the valley of the Guadalquivir; then the coasts, of which the famous Costa del Sol is only a small part; next come the inimitable white villages of the mountains, between the Guadalquivir and the sea; and finally, Granada and the Sierra Nevada.

For its size, Andalucía contains a remarkable diversity of landscapes – from Spain's highest mountains to endless rolling hills covered with olive trees, Europe's biggest marshland preserve and even some patches of desert. And no other part of Spain can offer so many interesting large cities. Andalucía, like Catalunya, is a world unto itself; it has as many delights to offer as you have time to spend on it.

Sevilla, Córdoba and the Guadalquivir

Sevilla

Apart from the Alhambra in Granada, the place where the lushness and sensuality of Al-Andalus survives best is Andalucía's capital. Sevilla may be Spain's fourth-largest city, but it is a city where you can pick oranges from the trees, and see open countryside from the centre of town. Come in spring if you can, when the gardens are drowned in birdsong and the air becomes intoxicated from jasmine and a hundred other blooms. If you can find a hotel room, and don't mind the crowds, Sevilla in spring can treat you to the April **Feria**, one of Spain's biggest parties, and also the most elaborate and grotesque Holy Week observances in Andalucía. If you come in summer, though, you might melt; the lower valley of the Guadalquivir is one of the hottest places in Europe.

The pageant of Sevilla unfolds in the shadow of **La Giralda**, the Moorish tower that means so much to Sevilla ('the mother of artists, the mould for bullfighters' according to a Sevillan poet). It is still the loftiest tower in Spain, and its size and the ostentatious play of its arches and arabesques make it the perfect landmark and symbol for this city, full of the romance of the south and the perfume of excess. At times Sevilla has been a capital, and it remains Spain's eternal city; neither past reverses nor modern industry have been able to shake it from its dreams.

From Hispalis to Isbiliya to Sevilla

One of Sevilla's distinctions is its long historical continuity. Few cities in Western Europe can claim to have never suffered a dark age, but Sevilla did well after the fall of Rome – and even after the coming of the Castilians. Roman Hispalis was founded over an Iberian settlement, and soon became one of the leading cities of the province of Baetica. So was Italica (see below) the now ruined city just to the north-west; it is difficult to say which was the more important. During the Roman twilight, Sevilla seems to have been a thriving town. Its first famous citizen, St Isidore, is one of the Doctors of the Church and the most learned man of the age, famous for his great *Encyclopedia* and his *Seven Books Against the Pagans*, an attempt to prove that the coming of Christianity was not the cause of Rome's fall. Sevilla was an important town under the Visigoths, and after the Moorish conquest it was second only to Córdoba as a political power and a centre of learning; for a while after the demise of the Western Caliphate, in 1023, it became an independent kingdom, paying tribute to the kings of Castile. Sevilla suffered under the Almoravids after 1091, but enjoyed a revival under their successors the Almohades.

The disaster came for Moslem Isbiliya in 1248, 18 years after the union of Castile and León. Ferdinand III's conquest of the city is not a well-documented event, but it seems that more than half the population found exile in Granada or Africa preferable to Castilian rule; their property was divided among settlers from the north. Despite the dislocation, the city survived, and found a new prosperity as Castile's window on the Mediterranean and South Atlantic trade routes (the Río Guadalquivir is navigable as far as Sevilla). Everywhere in the city you will see its emblem, the word NODO (knot) with a double knot between the O and D. It recalls the civil wars of the 1270s, when Sevilla was one of the few cities in Spain to remain loyal to Alfonso the Wise. *'No m'a dejado'* ('She has not forsaken me') Alfonso is recorded as saying; *madeja* is another word for knot, and placed between the syllables NO and DO it makes a clever rebus besides a tribute to Sevilla's loyalty to medieval Castile's greatest king.

From 1503 to 1680, Sevilla enjoyed a legal monopoly of trade with the Americas.

The giddy prosperity this brought, in the years when the silver fleet ran full, contributed much to the festive, caution-to-the-winds atmosphere that is often revealed in Sevilla's character. Sevilla never found a way to hold on to much of the American wealth, and what little it managed to grab was soon dissipated in showy excess.

It was in this period, of course, that Sevilla was perfecting its charm. Almost every other city in Spain secretly envies Sevilla for the way it lives, its gardens and festivals, the legendary dash of its *caballeros* and the beauty of its women. Poets and composers have always favoured it as a setting. Bizet's Carmen of course rolled her cigars in the Royal Tobacco Factory, and for her male counterpart Sevilla contributed Don Juan Tenorio, who evolved through Spanish theatre in plays by Tirso de Molino and Zoròlla to become Mozart's *Don Giovanni*, the same composer also used the city as a setting for *The Marriage of Figaro*. Modern Sevilla has been loth to leave all this behind, even though the city has shaken itself out of centuries of economic lethargy to become one of Spain's biggest ports and industrial centres. At present they're planning a World's Fair for 1992, the 500th anniversary of Columbus' voyage, where they hope to show off not only the Sevilla of orange blossoms and guitars, but the Sevilla of the future.

GETTING AROUND

By Air

Sevilla has regular flights from Madrid, Málaga, and Barcelona, less regularly from Lisbon, the Canary Islands and Valencia. The airport is 12 km (7.5 miles) east of the city, and the airport bus leaves from the Iberia office on C. Almirante Lobos, near the southern end of Av. de la Constitución (Tel: 51 06 77).

By Train

There are two stations, each of which has two names so it's easy to get confused. **Estación Plaza de Armas**, or Estación de Córdoba, is near the Guadalquivir and handles most of Sevilla's train connections – to Madrid, a daily *Talgo* to Barcelona, and to Córdoba, Granada and Málaga; for these last three, watch out for possible train changes at Bobadilla Junction, the black hole of Andalucian railways where all lines cross. The other station, **Estación de San Bernardo**, or Estación de Cádiz, has trains only for Jerez and Cádiz. The central RENFE office is at C. Zaragoza 29 (Tel: 22 25 77).

By Bus

Almost all lines for Madrid, the Levante, Andalucía and Portugal, leave from the Estación de Autobuses. Buses for Jerez and Cádiz run about every 1½ hours, and there are frequent connections to most other points in Andalucía (five daily to Granada, four to Málaga three to Córdoba and Ubeda, two to Costa del Sol, Ayamonte, Aracena, Almería, La Linea, Tarifa and Algeciras, also two each to Madrid, Valencia and Barcelona. Buses for Badajoz leave from the La Estellesa office at 3 C. Arenal; other buses to Extremadura depart from the main station, though the ticket office is on the outside and the buses aren't listed on the main schedule. Buses for Santiponce (Italica ruins) from in front of the Estación de Córdoba, every hour or so during the day.

AV. CRUZ ROJA
C. JOSÉ LAGUILLO
C. GONZALO BILBAO
C. JÚPITER
C. LUIS MONTOTO
AMADOR DE RÍOS
MARÍA AUXILIADORA
RONDA DE CAPUCHINOS
C. DEL SOL
C. NAVARROS
C. SANTIAGO
S. ESTEBAN
GARCÍA PÉREZ
CÉSPEDES
Pl. Ponce de Léon
Pl. Pilatos
CONDE IBARRA
S. LUIS
SOCORRO
S. JUAN RIBERA
DIEGO DE CÁDIZ
C. BUSTA TAVERA
Pl. San Leandro
C. S. LUIS
C. GERONA
ALHÓNDIGA
CABEZA DEL REY ARGOTE
MARMOLES
ABADES
DON FADRIQUE
C. RELATOR
C. JUAN PALMA
Pl. Cristo de Burgos
CUESTA ROSARIO
C. REGINA
Pl. Encarnación
C. DE LA FERIA
CONTEROS
Pl. El Salvador
C. COLÓN
C. PERAL
OROPESA
C. SIERPES
La Campana
TETUÁN
Pl. Nueva
AV. DE CONSTIT
CALATRAVA
C. JESÚS DEL GRAN PODER
VELÁZQUEZ
CARDINALE SPINOLA
Pl. de la Concordia
C. STA CLARA
C. MENDEZ NÚÑEZ
C. ZARAGOZA
C. ADRIANO
GARCÍA VINUESA
S. ELOY
ALFONSO XII
C. S. JUAN ÁVILA
C. LUMBERAS
C. JUAN RABADÁN
C. S. VICENTE
S. ROQUE
CANALEJAS
CÉSAR
REYES CATÓLICOS
C. TORNEO
C. BAÑOS
BAILÉN
MARQUÉS DE PARADAS
C. ARJONA
C. LA LEGIÓN
2
6
17
20
21
22
23
24
25
26
27
28
29
30
km 0 ½
miles 0 ¼
to Huelva

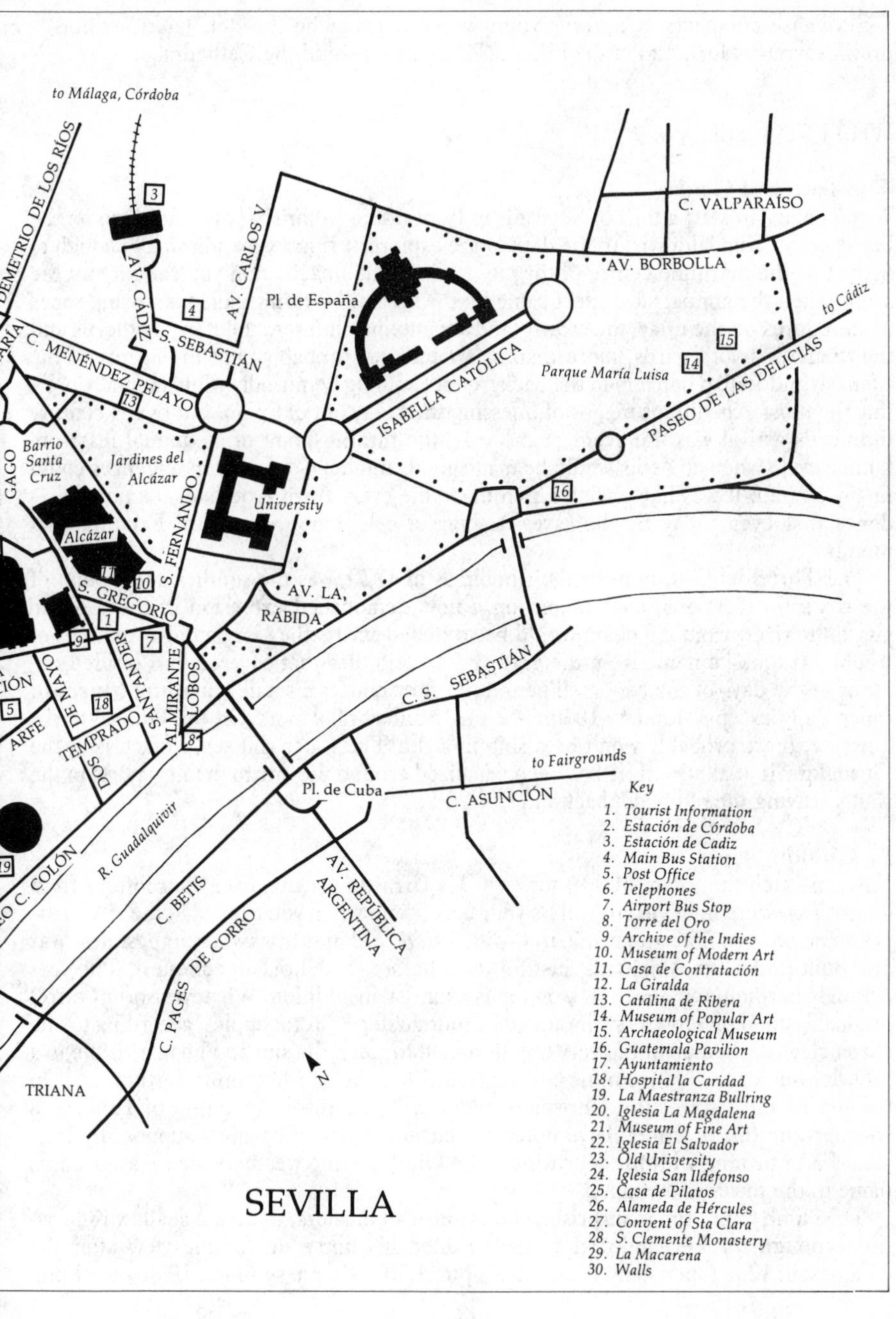
to Málaga, Córdoba
DEMETRIO DE LOS RÍOS
AV. CÁDIZ
AV. CARLOS V
C. VALPARAÍSO
AV. BORBOLLA
Pl. de España
to Cádiz
S. SEBASTIÁN
C. MENÉNDEZ PELAYO
ISABELLA CATÓLICA
Parque María Luisa
PASEO DE LAS DELICIAS
Barrio Santa Cruz
Jardines del Alcázar
S. FERNANDO
University
Alcázar
S. GREGORIO
AV. LA, RÁBIDA
C. S. SEBASTIÁN
DE MAYO
SANTANDER
ALMIRANTE LOBOS
ARFE
TEMPRADO
DOS
to Fairgrounds
Pl. de Cuba
C. ASUNCIÓN
R. Guadalquivir
C. BETIS
AV. REPÚBLICA ARGENTINA
C. PAGES DE CORRO
TRIANA
N
SEVILLA
Key
1. Tourist Information
2. Estación de Córdoba
3. Estación de Cadiz
4. Main Bus Station
5. Post Office
6. Telephones
7. Airport Bus Stop
8. Torre del Oro
9. Archive of the Indies
10. Museum of Modern Art
11. Casa de Contratación
12. La Giralda
13. Catalina de Ribera
14. Museum of Popular Art
15. Archaeological Museum
16. Guatemala Pavilion
17. Ayuntamiento
18. Hospital la Caridad
19. La Maestranza Bullring
20. Iglesia La Magdalena
21. Museum of Fine Art
22. Iglesia El Salvador
23. Old University
24. Iglesia San Ildefonso
25. Casa de Pilatos
26. Alameda de Hércules
27. Convent of Sta Clara
28. S. Clemente Monastery
29. La Macarena
30. Walls

Sevilla is a compact city, and everything in it can be reached by foot. There are horse-drawn carriages for tours in the Plaza del Triumfo, behind the Cathedral.

WHAT TO SEE

The Tower of Gold

A good place to start a tour of Sevilla is in front of the Moorish **Torre del Oro** on the banks of the Guadalquivir. In the days of the explorers, ships were still small enough to make this the maritime centre of the city; with a little imagination you can picture the scene when the annual silver fleet came in: the great, low-riding galleons tossing ropes to stevedores on the quay, the crowds and scrambling children, the King's officials and their battalions of guards, more than a few Indians, probably, and the agents of the Flemish and Italian bankers in the background, smiling bemusedly while mentally plotting the most expeditious means of finessing the booty out of Spain. For over a century the fleet's arrival was the event of the year, the turning-point of an annual feast-or-famine cycle when all debts would be made good, and long-deferred indulgences could finally be had. It was like having a rich uncle die every April – perhaps it's no coincidence that even today Sevilla saves its biggest celebration, the April Fair, for that month.

The Torre del Oro, built by the Almohads in 1220, was the southernmost point of the city's fortifications, constructed on a now demolished extension of the walls to guard the river; from it a chain would be stretched across the Guadalquivir in times of trouble. It took its name from the gold and azulejo tiles that covered its 12-sided exterior in the days of the Moors. The interior now houses a small **Maritime Museum** (open daily except Monday, 10 am – 2 pm, Sunday till 1 pm). On the Guadalquivir, however, there probably won't be a ship in sight. The water you see, in fact, isn't the Guadalquivir at all; the river has been canalized around the city to the new ports to the south, leaving the old bed a backwater.

La Giralda

You can catch the 92 m (300 ft) tower of **La Giralda** peeking over the rooftops from almost anywhere in Sevilla; it will be your best friend when you get lost in the city's labyrinthine streets. This great minaret, with its *ajimeces* and brickwork arabesques, was also built under the Almohads, just 50 years before the Christian conquest. The surprisingly harmonious spire stuck on top is a Christian addition. Whatever sort of turret originally stood on top was surmounted by four golden balls (or apples, according to one chronicler) stacked up at the very top, designed to catch the sun and be just visible to a traveller one day's ride from the city; all came down in a 13th-century earthquake. On the top of their spire, the Christians added a huge, revolving statue of Faith as a weathervane (many writers have noted the curious fancy of having a supposedly constant Faith turning with the four winds). La Giralda – the weathervane – has given its name to the tower as a whole.

The climb to the top is surprisingly easy; instead of stairs, there are shallow ramps – wide enough for Fernando III to have ridden his horse up for the view after the conquest in 1248 (open daily 10.30 am – 1 pm, 4.30–6.30 pm summer; 10.30am – 1 pm,

3.30–5.30 pm winter). If you're up to the climb, the view over the city of patios and gardens is priceless.

The Biggest Gothic Building in the Whole World

For a while after the conquest, the Castilians who repopulated Sevilla were content to use the great Almohad mosque, built at the same time as La Giralda. At the turn of the 1400s, in a fit of pious excess, it was decided to build a new Cathedral so grand that 'future ages shall call us mad for attempting it'. If they were mad, at least they were good organizers – they got it up in slightly over a century. The architects are unknown, though there has been speculation that the original master was either a Frenchman or a German.

The exterior, with its great rose window and double buttresses, is as fine as any of the Gothic cathedrals of northern Spain – if we could only see it. Especially on the west front, facing Sevilla's main street, the Avenida de la Constitución, the buildings close in; walking around its vast bulk past the fence of Roman columns joined by thick chains is like passing under a steep and ragged cliff. It's long overdue for a cleaning, and the grime contributes to the effect. The groundplan of this monster, roughly 120 by 185 m (400 by 600 ft), probably covers the same area as did the mosque. On the northern side, the **Patio de los Naranjas** preserves the outline of the mosque courtyard, now planted with orange trees. The Moslem fountain, and some of the walls and arches survive; in one corner, the 'Gate of the Lizard' has hanging from it a stuffed crocodile, said to have been a present from an Egyptian emir asking for the hand of a Spanish infanta. Another prize is an elephant's tusk, found in the Roman ruins of Italica.

The cavernous interior overpowers the faithful with its size more than its grace or beauty. The main altarpiece is the World's Biggest Retablo, almost 37 m (120 ft) high and entirely covered with carved figures and golden Gothic ornament; it took 82 years to make, and takes about a minute to look at. The cathedral is dark and cold inside, and without the usual nave and transept (like the mosque that preceded it, the cathedral is rectangular) the enormous space is ill-defined and disorienting, like some subterranean grotto with vaulting. Just behind the Capilla Mayor and the main altar, the **Capilla Real** contains the tombs of St Ferdinand (Fernando III) and Alfonso the Wise; Pedro the Cruel and his mistress Maria de Padilla are regulated to the crypt underneath. The art of the various chapels around the cathedral is lost in the gloom, but there are paintings by Murillo in the Capilla de San Antonio, and an altarpiece by Zurbarán in the Capilla de San Pedro. On the southern aisle, four stern pall-bearers on a high pedestal support the **Tomb of Christopher Columbus**. They represent the kingdoms of Castile, León, Navarre and Aragón. Columbus has been something of a refugee since his death. In the 16th century his remains were moved for unknown reasons from Valladolid to the island of Santo Domingo, and after Dominican independence from there to the Havana Cathedral. In 1899, after Cuba became independent, he was brought to Sevilla, and this idiosyncratic monument put up to honour him.

THE SACRISTY

Most of the Cathedral's collections are housed in a few chambers near the turn-stiles at the main entrance. In the **Sala Capitular**, Sevilla's bishop can sit on his throne and pontificate under the unusual acoustics of an elliptical Baroque ceiling, with paintings by Murillo. The adjacent **Sacristy** contains paintings by Zurbarán, Murillo, Van Dyck and others, most in dire need of restoration. Spare a moment for the reliquaries. Juan de Arfe, maker of the world's biggest silver monstrances, is represented here with one that seems almost a small palace, complete with marble columns. Most of the relics have become a little jumbled with age; there's a skull in a fancy box – nobody's sure whose – and some 'bones of St Felix'. Spain's most famous, and possibly most bizarre reliquary, is the **Alfonsine Tables**, said to have belonged to Alfonso the Wise. It is a set of folding cases, filled with tiny bits of bone and tooth – over 200 of them, all neatly labelled. But for the gold and jewels of the settings, the thing resembles nothing so much as a salesman's sample case. It was made in this fashion to provide extra-powerful juju for Alfonso to carry into battle.

The Archive of the Indies

As in most medieval cathedrals, Sevilla's porches, the Patio of the Orange Trees, and often even the naves and chapels were public ground, used to transact all sorts of business. A 16th-century bishop put an end to this practice, but prevailed upon Philip II to construct an exchange, or **Lonja**, for the merchants next to the Cathedral. Philip sent his favourite architect, Juan de Herrera, then still busy with El Escorial, to design it. The severe, elegant façades are typically Herreran, and the stone balls and pyramids on top are practically the architect's signature. By the 1780s, little commerce was still going on in Sevilla, and what was left of the American trade passed through Cádiz, so Charles III converted the lonely old building to hold the **Archive of the Indies**, the repository of all the reports, maps, drawings and documents the crown collected during the age of exploration. The collection, the richest in the world, has not even yet been entirely sifted through by scholars; some of it is always on display, and though the exhibits change constantly they are always worth a look (open daily except Sunday 10 am–1 pm).

The Alcazar

It's easy to be fooled into thinking this is a Moorish palace; some of its rooms and courtyards seem to come straight from the Alhambra. All of them, however, were built – by Moorish workmen, to be sure – for King Pedro the Cruel of Castile in the 1360s. The Alcazar and its king represent a fascinating dead end of Spanish history and culture, the possibility that Al-Andalus might have assimilated its conquerors instead of being destroyed by them.

Pedro was an interesting character. In Froissart's *Chronicle*, we have him described as 'full of marveylous opinyons ... rude and rebell agaynst the commandements of holy churche'. Certainly he didn't mind having his Moorish artists, lent by the Kings of Granada, adorn his palace with sayings from the Koran in Kufic calligraphy. Pedro preferred Sevilla, still half-Moorish and more than half-decadent, to Old Castile, and he filled his court here with Moorish poets and dancers, and Moorish bodyguards – the only ones he trusted. Unfortunately he was not the man for the job of cultural synthesis. The evidence, in as far as it is reliable, suggests he richly deserved his honorific 'the Cruel'; his brother Don Fadrique is only one of many he is said to have assassinated in this palace.

The Alcazar is entered through a little gate on the Plaza del Triumfo, on the south side of the Cathedral (open weekdays 9 am–12.45 pm, 3–5.30 pm, Saturday and Sunday 9 am–1.30 pm). The first courtyard, the **Patio de la Monteria**, has beautiful arabesques, with lions amid castles for Castile and León mixed in; much of the best Mudejar work can be seen in the adjacent halls and courts; their seemingly haphazard arrangement was in fact a principle of the art, to increase the surprise and delight in passing from one to the next. The **Patio de Yeso** (plaster) is largely a survival of the Almoravid palace of the 1170s, itself built on the site of a Roman *praetorium*. The **Patio de las Doncellas** is the largest of them, a little more ornate than the rooms of the Alhambra – built at the same time and possibly by some of the same craftsmen. It leads to the **Salon de los Embajadores**, a small, domed chamber that is the finest in the Alcazar despite jarring additions from the time of Charles V. Another small court, the **Patio de la Muñecas** ('of the dolls') where King Pedro's bodyguards cut down Don Fadrique, takes its name from two tiny faces on medallions at the base of one of the horseshoe arches – a little joke on the part of the Muslim stone-carvers.

Spanish kings after Pedro couldn't leave the Alcazar alone. Ferdinand and Isabel spoiled a large corner of it for their **Casa de Contratación**, a planning centre for the colonization of the Indies. There's little to see in it: a big conference table, Isabel's bedroom, a model of the *Santa María* in wood and a model of the royal family (Isabel's) in silver. Charles V added a **palace** of his own, as he did in the Alhambra. This one isn't much, either, but it contains a spectacular set of **Flemish tapestries** showing finely detailed scenes of Charles' campaigns in Tunisia.

Within its walls, the Alcazar has extensive and lovely **gardens**, with reflecting pools and palm trees, avenues of clipped hedges, and lemons and oranges everywhere. The park is deceptively large, but you can't get lost unless you find the little **labyrinth** near the pavilion built for Charles V in the lower gardens. Outside the walls, there are more gardens, a formal promenade called the **Plaza Catalina de Ribera**, with two monuments to Columbus, and the **Jardines de Murillo**, small though beautifully landscaped, bordering the northern wall of the Alcazar.

Barrio Santa Cruz

If Spain envies Sevilla, Sevilla envies this neighbourhood, a tiny, exceptionally lovely quarter of narrow streets and whitewashed houses. It is the true homeland of everything **Sevillana**, with flower-bedecked patios and iron-bound windows through which the occasional nostalgic young man still gets up the nerve to embarrass his sweetheart with a serenade. The presence of guitars, for that matter, seems mandatory, and there will usually be one playing at any given time in the Santa Cruz' little squares.

Before 1492, this was the Jewish quarter of Sevilla; today it's the most aristocratic corner of town. It's also full of cheap *hostales* and restaurants, and the two worlds co-exist peacefully. In the old days there was a wall around the barrio; today you may enter through the Jardines de Murillo, the Calle Mateos Gago behind the cathedral apse, or from the **Patio de las Banderas**, a pretty Plaza Mayor-style square next to the Alcazar.

The University

Sevilla has a building even larger than its cathedral – twice as large, in fact, and probably better known to the outside world. Since the 1950s it has housed parts of the city's **University** and it does have the presence of a college building, but it began its life in the 1750s as the state Tobacco Factory. Spaniards in the old days took smoking seriously –

this was the 'second largest building in Spain' (after El Escorial) in its time, placed in the centre of town and grandly embellished with an Allegory of Tobacco over its main entrance.

In the 19th century, it employed as many as 12,000 women to roll cigars – as historians note, the biggest female urban proletariat in the world. One of its members, of course, was Bizet's Carmen. These sturdy women, with 'carnations in their hair and daggers in their garters', hung their capes on the altars of the factory chapels each morning, rocked their babies in cradles while they rolled cigars, and took no nonsense from anybody.

María Luisa Park

For all its old-fashioned grace Sevilla has been one of the most forward-looking and progressive cities of Spain in this century. In the 1920s, while they were redirecting the Guadalquivir and building the new port and factories that are the foundation of the city's growth today, the Sevillanos decided to put on an exposition. In a tremendous burst of energy, they turned the entire southern end of the city into an expanse of gardens and grand boulevards. The centre of it is **María Luisa Park**, a paradisical half a kilometre of palms and orange trees, elms and Mediterranean pines, covered with flower beds and dotted with hidden bowers, ponds and pavilions. Now that the trees and shrubs have reached their maturity, the genius of the landscapers can be appreciated – this is one of the loveliest parks in Europe.

Some crumbling, audacious remnants of the 1929 *Exposición Iberoamericana* can be seen on the edges of the park – notably the **Guatemalan Pavilion**, covered with tiles in quirky Mayan Art Deco. Two of the largest, on the **Plaza de America**, have been turned into museums; the **Archaeological Museum** (open daily except Sunday and Monday, 10 am–2 pm) has one of the best collections of pre-Roman jewellery and icons, reproductions of the fine goldwork of the 'Treasure of Carambelo', and some tantalizing artefacts from mysterious Tartessos. The Romans are represented – as in every other Mediterranean archaeology museum – with copies of Greek sculpture and oversized statues of emperors. Across the plaza, the **Museum of Popular Art and Customs** (open daily except Monday, 10 am–2 pm) is Andalucía's attic, with everything from ploughs and saucepans to *azulejo* tiles, flamenco dresses (polka dots weren't always the style), musical instruments, religious bric-à-brac and exhibits for the city's two famous celebrations, Holy Week and the April Fair.

The Plaza de España

In the 1920s at least, excess was still a way of life in Sevilla, and to call attention to the Exposición Iberoamericana they put up a building even bigger than the Tobacco Factory.

Actually, that mighty edifice could almost fit inside the semi-circular courtyard of the **Plaza de España**, centrepiece of the fair on the eastern edge of María Luisa Park. With its grand Baroque towers (stolen gracefully from Santiago de Compostela), fancy bridges, staircases and immense colonnade, it is world fair architecture at its grandest and most outrageous. It would not be surprising if much of the fanciful neo-Spanish architecture of 1930's Florida and California were inspired by this building. Sevillanos gravitate naturally to it at weekends, to row canoes in the Plaza's canals and nibble curious pastries. One of the things Sevilla is famous for is its painted *azulejo* tiles; they adorn nearly every building in town, but here on the colonnade a few million of them are devoted to maps and historical scenes from every province in Spain.

West of the Cathedral

Avenida de la Constitución, before it fades off into an orgy of name-changing in the northern quarters, is Sevilla's main street. Between it and the Guadalquivir are mostly quiet neighbourhoods, without the distinction of the Barrio Santa Cruz but still with a charm of their own. On Calle Temprado, behind a colourful Baroque façade, is the **Hospital de la Caridad**. Though it still serves its original purpose as a charity-home for the aged, visitors come to see the art in the hospital chapel. The best is gone, unfortunately – in the lobby they'll show you photographs of the Murillos Napoleon stole. Among what remains are three works of art ghoulish even by Spanish standards. Juan de Valdes Leal (1622–90) was a competent enough painter, but warmed to the task only with such subjects as you see here: a bishop in full regalia decomposing in his coffin, and Death snuffing out your candle while bestriding paintings, church paraphernalia, and books. Even better than these is the anonymous, polychrome bloody Jesus, surrounded by smiling Baroque *putti*, who carry, instead of harps and bouquets, whips and scourges.

On the river is another citadel of Sevillan *duende,* **La Maestranza bullring** (1760). Not as big as Madrid's, it is still a lovely building, and perhaps the most prestigious of all *Plazas de toros*. It also carries the third busiest schedule, after Madrid and Barcelona, and you may be fortunate enough to see a *corrida* while in town.

Continuing north, as you near the San Eloy district, full of raucous bars and hotels, you'll pass the 1704 **La Magdalena**, on San Pablo, with an eccentrically Sevillan Baroque façade decorated with sundials.

Museo de Bellas Artes

This excellent collection is housed in the 1612 **Convento de la Merced**, on Calle San Roque (open daily except Monday 10 am–2 pm, 4–7 pm; Saturday and Sunday mornings only). There are some fine medieval works – sweetly naive-looking virgins, and an especially expressive triptych by the 'Master of Burgos' from the 13th century. The Italian sculptor Torregiano (who died in a Sevilla prison) has left an uncanny barbaric wooden **St Jerome**. This saint, Jeromino in Spanish, is a favourite in Sevilla, always pictured with a rock and a rugged cross instead of his usual lion; as the Doctor of the Church who helped most to define the concepts of heresy and self-mortification he has meant a lot to the Spanish church.

The museum has a roomful of Murillos (the painter was Sevillan and is buried in the Barrio Santa Cruz) including his *Immaculate Conception* and many other artful missal-pictures. Much more interesting are the works of Zurbarán, who could express spirituality without the simpering of Murillo or the hysteria of the others. His series of **female saints** is especially good, and the *Miracle of Saint Hugo* is perhaps his most acclaimed work. Occasionally even Zurbarán slips up; you may enjoy the '*Eternal Father*' with great fat toes and a triangle on his head, a *St Gregory* who looks like a scheming church executive, and the wonderful *Apotheosis of St Thomas Aquinas*, where the great Scholastic philosopher rises to his feet as if to say 'I've got it!' surrounded by a circle of his colleagues, all reading huge dusty books in the clouds. Don't miss El Greco's **portrait of his son Jorge**. There are also more Valdes Leal – heads on plates, and such – and works by Jan Brueghel and Ribera.

Calle Sierpes

Sevilla's business and shopping area has been, since Moorish times, the patch of narrow streets north of La Giralda. **Calle Sierpes** ('serpent street') is its heart, a sinuous pedestrian lane lined with every sort of old shop. Just to the north, **El Salvador** is a fine Baroque church, picturesquely mouldering; the base of its tower was the minaret of an important mosque that once stood here; the plaza in front is a popular hangout of Sevilla's youth, as well as their backpacking cousins from northern Europe.

On the **Plaza Nueva**, Sevilla's modern centre, you can see the grimy 1564 **Ayuntamiento**, with a fine, elaborate Plateresque façade. From here, Avenida de la Constitución changes its name to Calle Tetuan. Sevilla has found 100 ways to use its *azulejos*, but the best has to be in the **billboard** on this street for 1932 Studebaker cars; so pretty that no one's had the heart to take it down.

More Neighbourhoods

On the eastern fringes of the old town, the Barrio de Santa Cruz fades gently into other peaceful pretty areas – ironically less ritzy, though their old streets wear more palaces. One of these, built by the Dukes of Medinaceli (1480–1571) is the **Casa de Pilatos** on Plaza Pilatos. The dukes like to tell people that it is replica of 'Pontius Pilate's house' in Jerusalem (Pilate, without whom Holy Week would not be possible, is a popular figure; there's a common belief that he was a Spaniard); instead, it is a pleasant jumble of Mudéjar and Renaissance work, with a lovely patio and lots of *azulejos* everywhere (open daily except Sunday 9 am–1 pm, 3–6 pm, closed Saturday pm). Nearby the church of **San Ildefonso**, has a pretty yellow and white 18th-century façade.

The north end of Sevilla contains few monuments; most of it is solid, working-class neighbourhoods clustered around Baroque parish churches. The **Alameda de Hercules**, a once fashionable promenade adorned with copies of ancient statues, is in the middle of one of the shabbier parts. **Santa Clara** and **San Clemente** are two interesting monasteries in this area; Santa Clara includes a Gothic tower built by Don Fadrique, Pedro the Cruel's brother. North of Calle San Luis, a stretch of the city's **walls** survive, near the **Basilica of La Macarena**, home of the best-worshipped of Sevilla's idols, a delicate Virgin with glass tears on her cheeks who always steals the show in the Holy Week parades. **San Marcos**, down the street, has one of Sevilla's last surviving Mudejar towers. Finally, across the Guadalquivir from the bullring is the neighbourhood of **Triana**, an ancient suburb that takes its name from the Emperor Trajan. It has a reputation as the 'cradle of flamenco' and its workmen make all Sevilla's *azulejo* tiles. Queipo de Llaro's troops wrecked a lot of it at the start of the Civil War, but there are still picturesque, white streets overlooking the Guadalquivir, and quite a few bars and clubs.

Italica

8 km (5 miles) north of the city, the only significant Roman ruins in Andalucía are at **Italica**, a city founded in the 3rd century BC by Scipio Africanus as a home for his veterans. Italica thrived in the Imperial age. The Guadalquivir had a reputation for constantly changing its course in the old days, and this may explain the presence of two important cities so close together; the river may have temporarily deserted Sevilla, later returning to leave Italica without a port. Three great emperors, Trajan, Hadrian and Theodosius, were born here. The biggest ruins are an **amphitheatre**, with seating for 40,000, some remains of temples, and a street of foundations of villas, some with surviving mosaics.

The village of Santiponce, near the ruins, has a fine Gothic-Mudéjar monastery built for the Cistercians in 1301; **San Isidoro del Campo**, with another gruesome Saint Jerome, carved in the 1600s, on the altarpiece.

TOURIST INFORMATION

The permanent tourist office is an especially helpful one, at Avenida de la Constitución 21 near the Cathedral (Tel: 22 14 04). The municipal information centre is just outside the Alcazar, Puerta de Leon, Tel: 22 95 74.

WHERE TO STAY

Not many of Sevilla's hotels are distinctive in any way, but there are plenty of rooms all over the centre (except during Holy Week and the April Fair, when you should book well in advance even for inexpensive hostals).

Alfonso XIII***** (C. San Fernando 2, Tel: 22 28 50); built for the Exposición Iberoamericana in 1929, this luxury hotel is named for the unfortunate monarch then reigning. Probably *the* prestige hotel of southern Spain, in a huge building in landscaped grounds next to the University. It's been recently remodelled, and all the brass is polished up nicely; Sevilla society still meets around its lobby fountain and bars (12–18000 pts for a palatial double). **Doña María****** (Don Remondo 19, Tel: 22 49 90); Sevilla's number two hotel is just around the corner from the Giralda, a beautifully furnished place that's small and very popular. Unfortunately, it doesn't have its own parking (7000–11500 pts for doubles). **Hotel Simon*** (Garcia de Vinuesa 14, Tel: 22 66 60); just off the Av. de la Constitución by the Cathedral, this one is in a restored 18th-century town mansion, and is also quite popular (2900–4000 pts for a double with bath, 1900–2400 pts without; high season is March and April). **Hostal Residencia Goya**** (C. Mateos Gago 31, Tel: 21 11 70); nothing special, but a beautiful location in the heart of the Barrio Santa Cruz, doubles 2480–3000 pts. **Hostal Atenas**** (C. Caballerizas 1, Tel: 21 80 47), quiet and very nice, in a good location between the Pl. Pilatos and Cathedral. Take a cab, it's hard to find. Doubles 2500–3000 pts with bath, 2000–2500 pts without.

For inexpensive hostels, the Barrio Santa Cruz is surprisingly the best place to look. Even in July and August, you'll be able to find a place on the quiet side-streets off Mateos Gago. The **Monreal*** is closest to the Cathedral, a lively place with almost too much character and a good cheap restaurant when they feel like opening it (C. Rodrigo

Caro 8, Tel: 21 41 66, doubles 2500 pts with bath, 1500 pts without). **Pensión Vergara**, Ximenez de Enciso 11, is respectable and cheap, doubles 800 pts.

A larger selection – important when Sevilla is crowded – can be found in the area around C. San Esteban and the Plaza Curtidores, just south of C. Menendez Pelayo on the edge of Barrio Santa Cruz. C. Tintes and Vidrio are good streets to check. The **Venezuela*** is a good choice at Tintes 23 (1000 pts for a double). The biggest selection of all, however, is along **C. San Eloy** just east of the Córdoba station. **La Española*** has indifferent rooms, but a pretty patio (San Eloy 17, 1200–1350 pts a double) and there are many more from the respectable to the rock bottom. C. San Eloy may have little of the classical Sevillian grace about it, but it's theatrically urban any hour of the day, and there are plenty of bars to divert you (or keep you awake) at night.

EATING OUT

Andalucía is generally not the place to seek out grand culinary experiences, but Sevilla is a big enough city to have a wide variety of restaurants, and some quite good ones. They are a little more expensive than in most of Spain, but even around the Cathedral and the Barrio Santa Cruz, there are few places that can simply be dismissed as tourist traps.

A few places have attractions beyond the cuisine: **Mesón del Moro**, very popular with visitors, serves up specialities like *corvina* (a local fish) *a la marmera* and quail in a restored 12th-century Moorish bathhouse (C. Meson del Moro in Santa Cruz, around 2400 pts for a complete dinner). Along the Triana side of the Guadalquivir, you can dine with a view of the Torre de Oro and La Giralda at **El Puerto**, with seafood and a 700 pts *menu del dia* (C. Betis 57) or the **Río Grande** (C. Betis near the bridge) with a wide choice of dishes – average 2000 pts a complete meal – and homemade desserts. James Michener wrote about **El Mesón** at C. Dos de Mayo 26, and it has become popular since with visiting Americans (1600 pts).

If you don't mind going out of your way for some delicious Andalucían favourites (*cocida Andaluz* and *gazpacho con guarnación*) in an old taverna that few tourists ever find, try the **Casa Senra** on C. Becquer 4, near the walls at the northern tip of the old town (1800 pts).

Around the Cathedral: nothing really special here – but a wide choice. **Punta del Diamante** isn't as expensive as its well-appointed dining-room might suggest; there are *plato combinados* for as little as 450 pts (corner of Av. de la Constitucíon and C. Alemanes, across from the cathedral). **Las Duendes** on C. Quintero has *platos* for about the same price – only tastier.

Sevilla's cheapest restaurants lurk around C. San Eloy. Some almost give meals away, and they're worth the price. It's better to stick with the tapas and mariscos bars there and in the little streets of C. Tetuan and C. Sierpes. The **Bodega Gongora** on C. Albareda, is a seafood extravaganza, and there are a few others like it in the area.

OTHER DIVERSIONS

While we're waiting for the World's Fair Sevilla has planned for 1992 (the 500th anniversary of Columbus' voyage), the city has a few other ways to keep us busy. Take a **river cruise** along the Guadalquivir. Two companies do it daily (at 3.45 and 4.30 pm), both from around the Torre del Oro. See a **bullfight** in the famous Maestranza if you can (but don't just try to get tickets at the event! Do it as far ahead as you can; prices at the ring office will be cheaper than at the little stands on C. Sierpes).

If you must subject yourself to **flamenco**, Sevilla is probably the place to do it. The touristy flamenco factories will hit you for 1000 pts and up per drink. Bars in Triana and other areas do it better for less, but try to find an enthusiast (it shouldn't be hard) to steer you straight. They do play other kinds of music in Sevilla, and a little publication called *El Giraldilla*, available around town, has listings.

Handicrafts

All the paraphernalia associated with Spanish fantasy, like mantillas, castanets, wrought iron, gypsy dresses and Andalucian dandy suites, *azulejo* tiles and embroidery, is available here. Most of it's made here, and if you're interested in tours or just shopping, ask the Tourist Information office what's currently available.

Travelling from Sevilla

GETTING AROUND

There is no train service for the towns around Sevilla, but plenty of buses – especially for Carmona and Ecija, from where you can easily find a connecting bus for Córdoba.

South from Sevilla

If you're on your way to Jerez or Cádiz, stops at a few towns on the way will make an interesting alternative to the big four-lane highway. **Alcalá de Guadaira** is jocularly known in Sevilla as Alcalá de los Panadores ('of the bakers'), as it used to supply the city with its daily bread. Its **castle** is the best-preserved Almohad fortress in Andalucía. Just outside Utrera, the tiny village of **Palmar de Troya** received a visit from the Virgin Mary in 1968 (to little girls, as usual) that has led to the founding of a new church, the 'Orden de la Santa Faz'. They have their own Pope in Palmar and include among their saints Franco, José Antonio and Ramon Llull. In **Lebrija**, the church of **Santa María de la Oliva** is really a 12th-century Almohad mosque, with a typical Middle-Eastern roof of small domes and a tower that fits it perfectly, a miniature version of La Giralda, built by a Basque architect in the 19th century. Take care before you start any rambles in the countryside; this area south of Sevilla contains some of the best-known ranches where fighting bulls are bred, and the bulls are always allowed to run free.

Aracena and the Sierra Morena

If, on the other hand, you're heading for Extremadura and Old Castile, the route leads through the **Sierra Morena**, a chain of low mountains hardly worthy of the name, separating Andalucía from the empty lands to the north. Consider a detour to **Aracena**, the largest town of the region, with a Moorish castle, later occupied by the Templars, and the **Gruta de las Maravillas**, a stalactite cave with underground streams and lagoons. Not many people get to see it, but it's better than the more famous caves at Nerja (open daily except Monday, 10 am–7 pm).

From Sevilla to Córdoba

There are two ways to go, both of approximately equal length. The train, and most of the buses, unfortunately take the duller route through the flat lands along the Guadalquivir. The only landmark here is the Spanish–Moorish **castle of Almodovar del Río** perched romantically on a height planted with olive trees, overlooking the river.

The southern route also follows the Guadalquivir valley, though the scenery is a little more varied. The first town it passes, **Carmona**, seems a miniature Sevilla. Pedro the Cruel favoured it and built most of its extensive **Alcazar**. Under the Romans and Moors Carmona was an important city; some of its Moorish fortifications remain, including a grand gateway on the road from Sevilla. With its old quarters, and an ensemble of fine palaces and Mudejár and Renaissance churches – one, **San Pedro** (1466), has another imitation of La Giralda for a tower – Carmona is well worth a day's exploration. The prime attraction is just west of the town, the **Roman necropolis**, a series of rock-cut tombs; some are elaborate creations with subterranean chambers and vestibules, pillars, domed ceilings and carved reliefs (open daily except Monday, 10 am–2 pm).

Ecija makes much of one of its nicknames, the 'city of towers' and tries to play down the other – the 'frying-pan of Andalucía'. It isn't exactly fair. Any Andalucian town can brown you thoroughly on a typical summer day, and if Ecija is a degree hotter and a little less breezier, only a born Andaluz could tell the difference. Ask one, and you'll soon learn that the Andaluces are the only people yet discovered who talk about the weather more than the English – they do it even in summer, when it seems to the uninitiated to be just one hot, sunny day after another.

Most of the **towers** are sumptuously ornate Baroque, in churches like **San Juan Bautista, Santa María** and **San Gil**. Ecija has also a set of Renaissance and baroque palaces second only to Ubeda's in Andalucía; most of these showy façades can be seen on or near the **Calle de los Caballeros**.

WHERE TO STAY

Most of these towns are really more likely to be day-trips, but there is a *parador* in Carmona, the **Parador Alcazar del Rey Don Pedro******, Tel: 14 10 10, occupying a section of Cruel Pete's castle, with a garden and a pool and luxurious furnishings for 7500–8000 pts for a double. Ecija's hotels are mostly motels on the outskirts, serving traffic on the Madrid–Cádiz highway. **Ciudad del Sol**** (C. Cervantes 42, Tel: 83 03 00; 2200 pts for a double) is the best in town.

EATING OUT

Carmona has one very popular restaurant, **El Molino**, just outside town, on the road to Sevilla; *cazuela de gambas* (a kind of shrimp casserole) is a speciality, along with other seafood dishes, lamb stew and chicken curry.

Córdoba

There are a few distinct spots around the Mediterranean where the presence of past glories becomes almost tangible, a mixture of mythic antiquity, lost power and dissipated energy that broods over a place like a ghost. In Istanbul you can find it, in Rome, or among the monuments of Egypt, and also here on the banks of the Guadalquivir at Córdoba's southern gate. Looking around, you can see reminders of three defunct empires; a Roman bridge, a triumphal arch built for Philip II and Córdoba's great Mosque, over 1000 years old. The first reminds us of the city's beginnings, the second of its decline; the last one scarcely seems credible, as it speaks of an age when Córdoba was the brilliant metropolis of all Europe, city of half a million souls, a place faraway story-tellers would use to enthrall audiences in the rude halls of the Saxons and Franks.

The little plaza by the bridge concentrates melancholy like a magnet; there isn't much left for the rest of the town. Unlike Rome or Istanbul, Córdoba seems largely free of the burden of the past. Its recent growth has allowed it a chance to renovate its sparkling old quarters and monuments. With the new prosperity has come a contentment the city probably hasn't known since the Reconquista.

Everyone who visits Andalucía comes for the Great Mosque, but you should spare some time to explore the city itself. More than Sevilla, it retains its Moorish character, in a maze of whitewashed alleys opening into the loveliest patios in all Andalucía.

History

Roman *Corduba*, built on the site of an Iberian town, was almost from the start the leading city of interior Spain, capital of the province of Hispania Ulterior, and later of the reorganized province of Baetica. Córdoba had a reputation as the garden spot of Hispania; it gave Roman letters Lucan and both Senecas among others, testimony to its prominence as a city of learning. Córdoba became Christianized at an early date. Another favourite son, the fanatic Bishop Hosius, led the forces of orthodoxy in the great Church Council at Nicaea in 325 against the Arian heresy.

Ironically, the True Faith got its come-uppance in Córdoba in 572, when the Arian Visigoths under Leovigild captured the city from Byzantine rule. When the Arabs arrived, they found it an important town still, and it became the capital of Al-Andalus when Abd ar-Rahman established the independent Caliphate in 756. For 300 years, Córdoba enjoyed the position of unqualified leader of Al-Andalus. It is hard to take the chroniclers at face value – 3,000 mosques and 80,000 shops, a library of 400,000 volumes, in a city stretching for 16 km (10 miles) along the banks of the Guadalquivir. We can settle for half that, for accuracy's sake, and still be impressed. Beyond doubt, Córdoba was a city without equal in the West as a centre of learning; it would be enough to mention two 12th-century contemporaries, Averroës, the Muslim scientist and Aristotelian philosopher who contributed so much to the rebirth of classical learning in Europe, and Moses Maimonides, the Jewish philosopher (and later personal doctor to Saladin in Palestine) whose reconciliation of faith and reason were assumed into Christianity by Thomas Aquinas.

Medieval Córdoba was a great trading centre, and its luxury goods were coveted throughout Western Europe; the old word *cordwainer* is a memory of Córdoba's skill in leather goods. At its height, picture Córdoba as a city of bustling international markets,

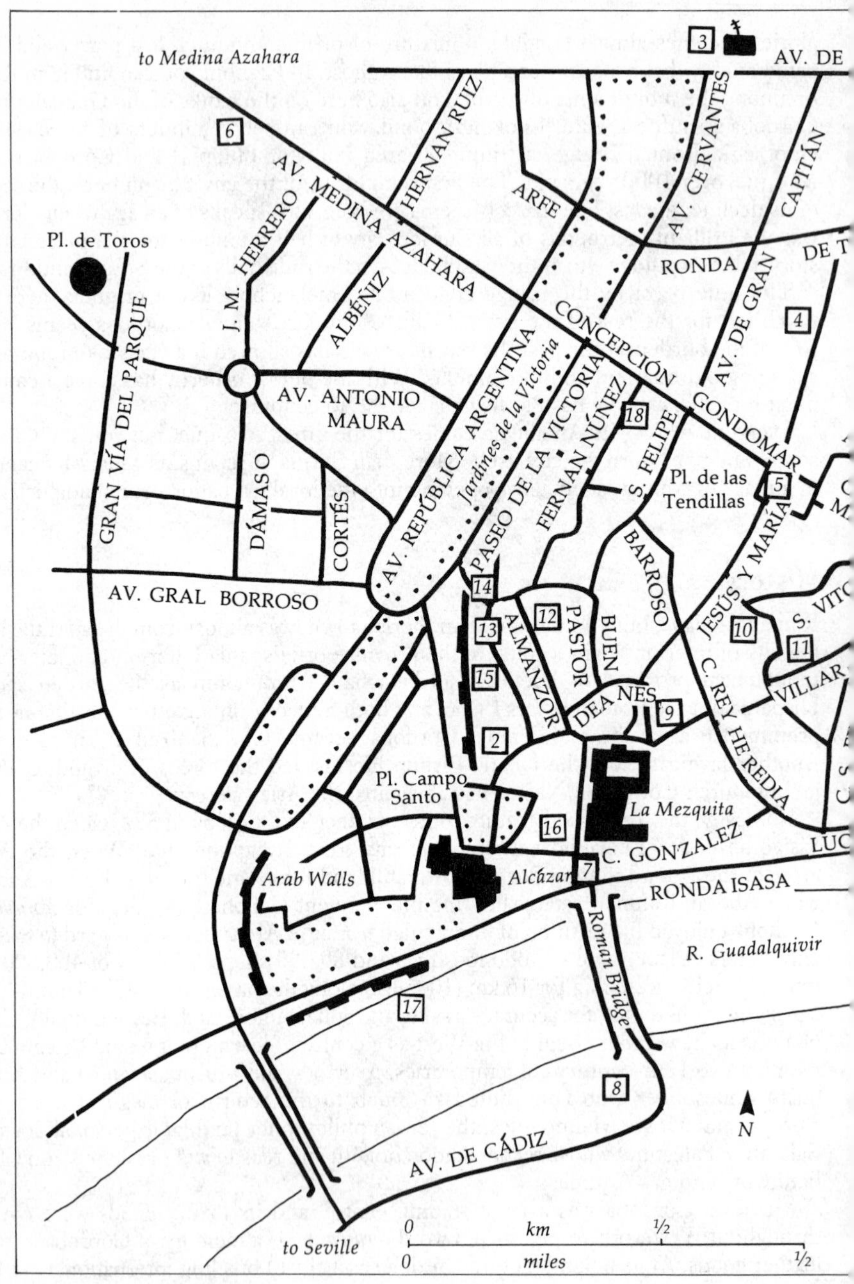
to Medina Azahara
3
AV. DE
6
HERNAN RUIZ
AV. CERVANTES
CAPITÁN
ARFE
AV. MEDINA AZAHARA
J. M. HERRERO
Pl. de Toros
RONDA
AV. DE GRAN
4
ALBÉNIZ
GRAN VÍA DEL PARQUE
CONCEPCIÓN
AV. REPÚBLICA ARGENTINA
Jardines de la Victoria
PASEO DE LA VICTORIA
FERNAN NÚÑEZ
18
GONDOMAR
S. FELIPE
Pl. de las Tendillas
5
AV. ANTONIO MAURA
DÁMASO
CORTÉS
AV. GRAL BORROSO
BARROSO
JESÚS Y MARÍA
14
13
12
ALMANZOR
PASTOR
BUEN
10
11
15
2
DEA NES
9
C. REY HEREDIA
VILLAR
Pl. Campo Santo
La Mezquita
16
C. GONZALEZ
7
Alcázar
Arab Walls
RONDA ISASA
Roman Bridge
R. Guadalquivir
17
8
N
AV. DE CÁDIZ
to Seville
0 km ½
0 miles ½

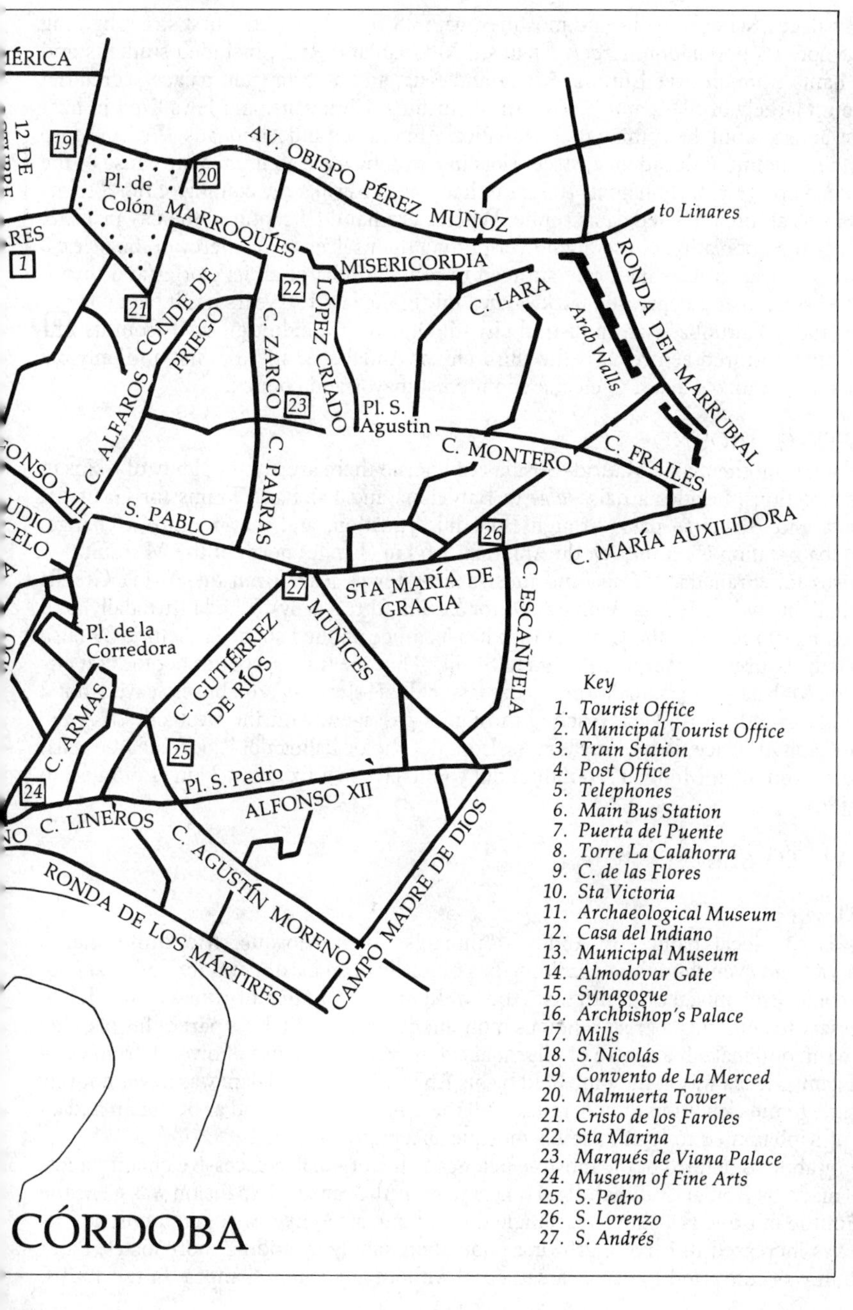
AV. OBISPO PÉREZ MUÑOZ
to Linares
Pl. de Colón
MARROQUÍES
MISERICORDIA
RONDA DEL MARRUBIAL
Arab Walls
C. LARA
CONDE DE PRIEGO
C. ZARCO
LÓPEZ CRIADO
C. ALFAROS
Pl. S. Agustin
C. MONTERO
C. FRAILES
C. PARRAS
S. PABLO
C. MARÍA AUXILIDORA
STA MARÍA DE GRACIA
C. ESCAÑUELA
MUÑICES
Pl. de la Corredora
C. GUTIÉRREZ DE RÍOS
C. ARMAS
Pl. S. Pedro
ALFONSO XII
C. LINEROS
C. AGUSTÍN MORENO
CAMPO MADRE DE DIOS
RONDA DE LOS MÁRTIRES
CÓRDOBA
Key
1. Tourist Office
2. Municipal Tourist Office
3. Train Station
4. Post Office
5. Telephones
6. Main Bus Station
7. Puerta del Puente
8. Torre La Calahorra
9. C. de las Flores
10. Sta Victoria
11. Archaeological Museum
12. Casa del Indiano
13. Municipal Museum
14. Almodovar Gate
15. Synagogue
16. Archbishop's Palace
17. Mills
18. S. Nicolás
19. Convento de La Merced
20. Malmuerta Tower
21. Cristo de los Faroles
22. Sta Marina
23. Marqués de Viana Palace
24. Museum of Fine Arts
25. S. Pedro
26. S. Lorenzo
27. S. Andrés

great palaces, schools, baths and mosques, with 28 suburbs and the first street lighting in Europe. Its population, largely Spanish, Moorish and Arab, included students and merchants from all over Europe, Africa and Asia, and an army and palace secretariat made up largely of Slavs and Blacks. In it Muslims, Christians, and Jews lived in harmony, at least until the coming of the fanatical Almoravids and Almohads. We can sense a certain amount of decadence; street riots in Córdoba were an immediate cause of the breaking-up of the Caliphate in 1031, but here, as in Sevilla, the coming of the Reconquista was an unparalleled catastrophe. When Ferdinand III captured the city in 1236, much of the population chose flight over putting themselves at the mercy of the priests. Three centuries of Castilian rule sufficed to rob Córdoba of all its glories and turn it into a shrunken and depressed backwater. Only in the last 100 years has it begun to recover; today Córdoba is an industrial city, though you wouldn't guess it from its immaculately restored centre. It is the third city of Andalucía, and the first and only big town since Franco's death to elect a communist mayor and council.

GETTING AROUND

Córdoba is on the major Madrid–Sevilla rail line, so there are always plenty of trains in both directions, besides a daily *talgo* to Barcelona and Valencia. Trains for Granada, Málaga and Algeciras pass through Bobadilla Junction, and may require a change. Córdoba's station is on the Av. de America, 1.6 km (1 mile) north of the Mezquita.

Buses for Granada, Málaga and most nearby towns leave from the Alsina Graells terminal on Avda. Medina Azahara 29; for Sevilla (three daily), Ubeda (five daily) and Barcelona (three daily) the UBESA firm has its office on the Pso. de la Victoria 29 (also for Madrid buses). Other firms do go to Sevilla – but the train's a better bet for that city and for Málaga. To Granada the bus is faster. Ecija–Jerez–Cádiz buses leave from a tiny alley called La Bodega, reached through a passageway off the west side of Avda. Gran Capitan (twice daily). Any bus for Lora del Rio or Palma del Rio (Alsina Graells) will drop you off at Medinat Az-Zahra, but you'll have to walk about 2 km (1.3 miles) to the site.

WHAT TO SEE

La Mezquita

This is the local name for Abd ar-Rahman's Great Mosque. **Mezquita** means 'mosque' and even though the building has officially been a cathedral for 750 years, no one could ever mistake its origins. Abd ar-Rahman, founder of a new state, felt it necessary to construct a great religious monument for his capital. As part of his plan, he also wished to make it a centre of pilgrimage to increase the sense of divorce from eastern Islam; Mecca was at the time held by his Abbasid enemies. Islam was never entirely immune to the exaltation of holy relics, and there is a story that Abd ar-Rahman had an arm of Mohammed to legitimize his mosque as a pilgrimage site.

Only about one third of the mosque belongs to the original. Successive enlargements were made by Abd ar-Rahman II, al-Hakam, and Al-Mansur. Expansion was easy; the plan of the mosque is a simple rectangle divided into aisles by rows of columns, and its size was increased to serve a growing population simply by adding more aisles. After 1236, it was converted to use as a cathedral without any major changes. In the 1520s, however, the city's clerics succeeded in convincing Charles V to allow the construction of a choir and high altar, enclosed structures as is typical in Spanish cathedrals. Charles is said to have strongly reproached them for the desecration when he saw the finished work – though he himself had done even worse to the Alhambra and Sevilla's Alcazar.

Most people come away from a visit to the Mezquita somewhat confused. The endless rows of columns and red-and-white striped arches make a picture familiar to most of us, but actually to see them in this gloomy old hall may not increase one's understanding of the work. They make a pretty pattern, but what does it mean? It's worth going into some detail, for learning to see the Mezquita the way its builders did is the best key we have to understanding the refined world of Al-Andalus.

The only entrance to the mosque today is the **Puerta del Perdón**, a fine Mudéjar gateway added in 1377, opening to the **Patio de los Naranjos**, the original mosque courtyard, planted with orange trees, where the old Moorish fountain can still be seen. Built into the wall of the courtyard, over the gate, the original minaret – a legendary fane said to be the model for all the others in Al-Andalus – has been replaced by an ill-proportioned 16th-century bell tower. From the courtyard, the mosque is entered through a little door, the **Puerta de las Palmas**, where they'll sell you a ticket and tell you to take off your hat. Inside, it's as chill and old as Sevilla Cathedral.

Now here is the first surprise. The building is gloomy only because the Spanish clerics wanted it that way. Originally there was no wall separating the mosque from the courtyard, and that side of the mosque was entirely open. In the courtyard, trees were planted to continue the rows of columns, translating inside to outside in a remarkable tour-de-force that has never been equalled in architecture. To add to the effect, the other three walls are lined with entrances, the beautifully decorated **gates**, now all sealed up, that you see when you walk around the building. It isn't just a trick of architecture, but a way of relating a holy building to the life of the city around it. In the Middle East, there are many medieval mosques built on the same plan as this one. In Turkey they call them 'forest' mosques, and the townspeople use them like indoor parks, places to sit and reflect or talk over everyday affairs. In medieval Christian cathedrals, whose doors were always open, it was much the same. The sacred and the secular become blurred, or rather the latter is elevated to a higher plane. In Córdoba, this principle is perfected.

In the aesthetics of this mosque, too, there is more than meets the eye. Many European writers have seen it as devoid of spirituality, a plain prayer-hall with pretty arches. To the Christian mind it is difficult to comprehend. Christian churches are modelled after the Roman basilica, a government hall, a seat of authority with a long central aisle designed to humble the suppliant as he approaches the Praetor's throne – or altar. Mosques are designed with great care to free the mind from such behaviour patterns. In this one, the guiding principle is a rarefied abstraction – the same kind of abstraction that governs Islamic geometric decoration. The repetition of columns is like a meditation in stone, a mirror of Creation where unity and harmony radiate from innumerable centres.

Another telling contrast with Christian churches can be found in an obscure matter – the distribution of weight. The Gothic masters of the Middle Ages learned to pile stone upwards from great piers and buttresses to amazing heights, to build an edifice that seems to aspire upwards to heaven. Córdoba's architects amplified the height of their mosque only modestly by a daring invention – adding a second tier of arches on top of the first. They had to, constrained as they were by the short columns they were recycling from Roman buildings, but the result was to make an 'upside-down' building, where weight increases the higher it goes, a play of balance and equilibrium that adds much to the mosque's effect.

There are about 400 of these columns, mostly from Roman ruins and Visigothic churches the Muslims pulled down. Others came from as far as Constantinople, a present from the emperors. The same variety can be seen in the capitals – Roman, Visigothic, Moorish and a few mysteries. The surviving jewel of the mosque is its **mihrab**, added in the 10th century, an octagonal chamber set into the wall and covered by a beautiful dome of interlocking arches. Another Byzantine emperor sent artists to help with its mosaic decoration – and a few tons of enamel chips for them to work with. That these two states should have had such warm relations isn't that surprising; any enemy of the Pope and the Western Christian states in those days was a friend of Constantinople. Near the mihrab is the **Capilla de Villaviciosa**, a Christian addition of 1377 with fancy convoluted Mudejár arches that almost succeed in upstaging the Moorish work.

Far more serious intrusions are the 16th-century **Coro** and **Capilla Mayor** (high altar). They are done in the Plateresque style, with a gaudy ceiling, but they would not offend anywhere else but here. Fortunately the Mezquita is so large that from many parts of it you won't even notice them. Dozens of locked, mouldering chapels line the outer walls of the mosque; never comfortable as a Christian building, today the Cathedral seems to be hardly used at all, and regular Sunday masses are regulated to a small corner of the building.

Around the Mezquita

The masses of souvenir stands, cafes and tourists that surround the Mezquita on its busiest days do their best to recreate the atmosphere of the Moorish *souks* that once thrived here, but walk a block in any direction and you'll enter the essential Córdoba – whitewashed lanes with glimpses into dreamily beautiful patios, each one a floral extravaganza. One of the best is a famous little alley called **Calle de los Flores** ('street of the flowers') just a block north of the Mezquita.

Below the Mezquita, along the Guadalquivir, the plaza called **Puerta del Puente** (mentioned above) marks the site of Córdoba's southern gate with a decorative **arch** put up in 1571. The very curious Churrigueresque monument next to it is called the **Triunfo** (1651) with a statue of San Rafael (the angel Raphael). The **Roman Bridge** over the Guadalquivir probably isn't Roman at all any more; it has been patched and repaired so often practically nothing remains of the Roman work. Another statue of Raphael can be seen in the middle – probably replacing an old Roman image of Jupiter or Mercury. The stern-looking **Calahorra Tower** (1369) once guarded the southern approaches of the bridge; now it contains a small **museum** of Córdoba's history, with old views and plans of the city, and the armour of Gonzalo Fernández de Córdoba, the 'Gran Capitan' who won much of Italy for Ferdinand and Isabel (museum closed at time of writing).

Just to the west, along the river, Córdoba's **Alcazar** was rebuilt in the 14th century and used for 300 years by the officers of the Inquisition. There's little to see, but a good view of the Mezquita and the town from the belvedere atop the walls. The **gardens** are peaceful and lovely, an Andalucían amenity much like those in Sevilla's Alcazar. On the river's edge you'll see an ancient **water wheel**. At least some of the Moors' talent for putting water to good use was retained for a while after the Reconquista. This is the mill that disturbed Isabel's dreams when she stayed at the Alcazar; it was rebuilt only in the early 1900s. If you continue walking along the Guadalquivir, in about a kilometre you'll come to Cruz Conde Park and the new **Córdoba Zoo**, where you can see a rare black lion who probably doesn't enjoy being called 'Chico' (open daily 10 am to sunset).

The Juderia

As in Sevilla, Córdoba's ancient Jewish quarter has recently become a fashionable area, a nest of tiny streets between the Mezquita and Avenida Dr Fleming. Part of the Moorish walls can be seen along this street, and the northern entrance of the Juderia is the old **Almodovar gate**. The streets are tricky, and it will take some effort to find Calle Maimonides and the 14th-century **Synagogue**, of which little remains but a wall of Alhambra-style arabesques and Hebrew inscriptions. On Calle Ruano Torres, the 15th-century **Casa del Indiano** is a palace with an eccentric façade.

The name of the **Municipal Museum** is somewhat misleading – it's mostly about bullfights. Manolete and El Cordobés are the city's two recent contributions to Spanish culture; here you can see a replica of Manolete's sarcophagus, his furniture (!) and the hide of the bull that did him in, along with more bullfight memorabilia than you ever thought existed. The turn-of-the-century art nouveau posters are beautiful, and among the old prints you can pay homage to the memory of the famous taurine malcontent Moñudo, who ignored the *toreros* and went up into the stands after the audience (on Plaza Maimonides, open daily 9 am–1.30 pm, 4–7 pm).

White neighbourhoods

The quarters around the Mezquita hardly exhaust the limits of old Córdoba. From the mosque you can walk eastwards through well over a mile of twisting white alleys, a place where the best map in the world wouldn't keep you from getting lost and staying lost. Though it all looks much the same, it's never monotonous: every little square, fountain or church stands out boldly, and forces you to look at it differently than you would in a modern city where your senses are assaulted from all sides. It is another lesson in the Moorish aesthetic – these streets have probably changed little since 1236 – but their best buildings are a series of **Gothic churches** built soon after the Reconquista. Though small and plain, most are exquisite in a quiet way. Few have any of the usual Gothic sculptural work on their façades; this was a matter of policy, to avoid offending a people accustomed to Islam's prohibition of images. The lack of decoration somehow adds to their charm. There are a score of these around Córdoba, and nothing like them elsewhere in the south of Spain. **San Lorenzo**, on Calle María Auxiliadora, is perhaps the best, with a rose window designed in a common Moorish motif of interlocking circles. **San Andres**, on Calle San Pablo, **San Pedro** off Calle Alfonso XII, **Santa Marina** on Calle Morales, and the **Cristo de los Faroles** on Calle Alfaros are some of the others. Have a look inside any you find open; most have some Moorish or Mudejár work in their interiors, and many of their towers (like San Lorenzo's) were originally minarets.

The neighbourhoods have other surprises, if you have the persistence to find them. **Santa Victoria** is a huge austere Baroque church on Calle Jesus y María, modelled after the Roman Pantheon. Nearby on Plaza Paez, a fine 16th-century palace houses the **National Archaeological Museum**, the largest in Andalucía (open daily 10 am–2 pm, 4–8 pm, Sunday 10 am–2 pm) with Roman mosaics, an unusual icon of Mithras, some Moorish-looking early Christian art, and early funeral steles with odd hieroglyphs. The large collection of Moorish art includes some of the best work from the age of the Caliphate. In the approximate centre of the city is the **Plaza de la Corredera**, an enclosed 'Plaza Mayor', picturesque though neglected. The **Museo de Belles Artes** is to the south on the lovely **Plaza del Petro** (mentioned by Cervantes, along with the little *posada* that still survives on it); its collections include works of Goya and Zurbarán. Beware the 'museum' across the plaza, dedicated entirely to the works of a local hack named Julio Romero de Torres.

Plaza de las Tendillas

The centre of Roman Córdoba, by chance, has become the centre of the modern city. Córdoba is probably the slickest and most up-to-date city in Andalucía (Sevilla would argue), and it shows in this busy district of crowded pavements, modern shops, cafes and wayward youth. The contrast with the old neighbourhoods is startling, but just a block off the plaza on Calle Gondomar, the beautiful 15th-century **San Nicolas Church** will remind you you're still in Córdoba. And in the other direction, well-preserved remains of a collapsed **Roman Temple** have been discovered on the Calle Nueva. The city has been at work re-assembling the walls and columns; already it is one of the most complete Roman monuments in Spain.

Next to the **Plaza de Colón**, a park a few blocks north of the Plaza de las Tendillas, the **Torre de Malmuerta** ('Bad Death') takes its name from a commander of this part of the old fortifications who murdered his wife in a fit of passion; it became the subject of a well-known play by Lope de Vega, *Los Comendadores de Córdoba*. Across the plaza is a real surprise, the Baroque **Convento de Merced**, an enormous building that has recently been restored to house the provincial government and often hosts cultural exhibitions on various subjects. Don't miss it: the façade has been redone in its original painted *esgrafido*, almost decadently colourful in red and green, and the courtyards and grand staircases inside are incredible – more a palace than a monastery.

Medinat az-Zahra

Five miles north-west of the centre of Córdoba, the Caliph Abd ar-Rahman III began to build a palace in the year 936. The undertaking soon got out of hand, and with the almost infinite resources of the Caliphate to play with, he and his successors turned Medinat az-Zahra ('city of the flowers', named for one of Abd ar-Rahman's wives) into a city in itself, with mosques, schools and gardens, a place where the last Caliphs could live in isolation from the world. Ḥisham II was kept a virtual prisoner here by his able vizir Al-Mansur.

The scale of it is pure Arabian Nights. One chronicler records an ambassador, being taken from Córdoba to the palace, finding his path carpeted the entire 8 km (5 mile) route and lined from end to end with maidens to hold parasols and refreshments for him. Stories were told of the palace's African menageries, its chamber with pillars and domes of crystal, and curtains of falling water for walls; another fountain was filled with flowing mercury. Such carrying-on must have aroused a good deal of resentment; in the disturbances that put an end to the Caliphate, Medinat az-Zahra was sacked and razed by Berber troops in 1013.

After serving as a quarry for 900 years it's surprising anything is left at all, but in 1944 the royal apartments were discovered, with enough fragments to permit a restoration of a few arches with floral decorations. One hall has a roof on, and more work is under way, but as yet the rest is only foundations.

TOURIST INFORMATION

The Provincial Office is on C. Gonzalez Murga, just off the Ronda de los Tejares (Tel: 47 12 35). The Municipal office (friendlier but less paper to hand out) is in the Juderia on Pl. Judah Levi (Tel: 29 07 40). It's definitely worth a stop at either to get a detailed map, for Córdoba has the biggest and most labyrinthine old quarter in Spain.

WHERE TO STAY

Near the Mezquita, of course. Even during big tourist assaults the advantages outweigh the liabilities.

Melia Córdoba****, a big modern hotel right in the middle of the Jardines de la Victoria on the edge of the Juderia. It has every conceivable luxury the chain is known for, including a pool and TV – but a double room will set you back 8650 pts. (Tel: 29 80 66). **Marisa****, C. Cardinal Herrero (Tel: 47 31 42) is a simple but well-run establishment opposite the Patio de los Naranjos. The location is the only real amenity, but it will do for the price (3350 pts for a double with the bath). **Hostal Seneca***, C. Conde y Ligue 7, just north of the Mezquita (Tel: 47 32 34), this is the real find among the inexpensive *hostales*, with a beautiful patio full of flowers, nice rooms and sympathetic management. Not surprisingly, it's hard to get a room (1400–1600 pts a double without bath). **El León***, C. Cespedes 6, just north of the Mezquita (Tel: 22 30 21), the rooms aren't as nice as at the Seneca, but the patio is just as lovely and the tribes of cats are good company (doubles 1400–1600 pts). Plenty of other inexpensive *fondas* can be found in the area east of the Mezquita, especially on and around C. Rey Heredia.

If all this area is full, or if you have a car and do not care to brave the old town's narrow streets and lack of parking, there are a few hotels in the new town and on the periphery worth mentioning. The **Parador Nacional La Arruzafa******, on the outskirts of town (Avda de la Arruzafa, Tel: 22 59 00) isn't in a historic building, but offers a pool, tennis courts and air-conditioned rooms and a view (doubles 7500–8000 pts). Off the Plaza de Tendillas, the **Boston**** (C. Malaga 2, Tel: 22 24 13, 2350 pts for a double with a bath) and the **Hostal Tendillas**** (C. Jesus y María 1, Tel: 22 30 29, 1350 pts a double, no bath) are simple and unpretentious – though at times a little noisy.

EATING OUT

There's no doubt that **El Caballo Rojo** is one of the premier restaurants of Andalucía. *Rabo de toro* (the bull's tail) is a Córdoba speciality, and they do things to it that have never been done before. Among other offerings of the prize-winning chef is roast lamb with eucalyptus honey; fancy dishes like this can raise the bill considerably (2600–3850 pts for full-course dinner, it's on C. Cardinal Herrero 28 by the Mezquita). Another famous establishment, **El Churrasco**, specializes in grilled meats (*churrasco* is a pork dish with pepper sauce) and seafood, with surprises like breaded aubergines (eggplant) for a change of pace (C. Romero 16, 1600–2600 pts; if you're not up to that the bar has an enormous variety of tapas). *Churrasco* is also a speciality at **Mesón Don Oscar**, C. Virgen del Perpetuo Socorro 16, 1200–2000 pts).

Among the more modest places, **El Aguila** on C. Conde y Luque has inexpensive dinners (800–1200 pts) and even cheaper combination plates with dining around a pretty Córdoba patio. Most of the inexpensive choices are around Pl. de las Tendillas. C. Victoriano Reyes, north of the plaza, is a whole street of them, including a good cheap Chinese restaurant **China Pekin** (850 pts). The **Restaurante Antonio** on nearby C. Eduardo Lucera is a very unpretentious spot with solid good cooking – local specialities and seafood figure prominently and there are set dinners from 625 pts up. Don't forget that Córdoba is the heart of a wine-growing region; there are a few bodegas in town that appreciate visitors: **Bodega Campos,** on C. Colonel Cascajo, and **Bodega Doña Antonia**, Avda. Virgen Milagrosa 5, really a small restaurant serving its own wines.

From Córdoba to Ubeda

In this section of the Guadalquivir valley the river rises into the heights of the Sierra Morena. The scenery isn't spectacular, but the endless rolling hills covered with neat rows of olive trees and small farms make a memorable Andalucian landscape. The three large towns along the way, **Andujar, Bailen**, and **Linares**, are much alike, amiable industrial towns still painted a gleaming white; Andujar is dominated by huge, blue, ultramodern sunflower-oil refineries that look like fallen space stations. Sunflowers, like olives, are a big crop in the region and much in evidence in late summer.

This area is a major crossroads for rails, roads and armies – Andalucía's front door, where the routes from Madrid branch off for Sevilla and Granada. Many important battles have been fought nearby, including Navas de Tolosa near La Carolina, in 1212, that opened the way for the conquest of Al-Andalus, and Bailen, in 1808, where a Spanish–English force gave Napoleon's boys a sound thrashing and built up Spanish morale for what they call their War of Independence. Not surprisingly, there are a few castles around; an elegant one over the road to Ubeda at **Canena**, and a well-preserved Moorish one in the village of **Baños de la Encina**, 10 km (6.3 miles) north of Bailen.

Baeza

The 16th century was good to Baeza, a distinguished little town of neatly clipped trees and tan stone buildings. It seems a happy town, serene and quiet as the olive groves that surround it. Among the 16th-century monuments are the **Cathedral** with some surviving portals from the Isabelline Gothic church that preceded it, and the early **Palacio de Jabalquinto**, with an eccentric façade covered with coats-of-arms and pyramidal stone studs. The fountain in front of the cathedral, the **Fuente de Santa María**, with a little triumphal arch at its centre, is Baeza's landmark and symbol. The prettiest corner of the town is a small square, the **Plaza de los Leones**, enclosed by decorative pointed arches, containing a fountain with four half-effaced lions.

GETTING AROUND

Come to Baeza by train at your own risk. The nearest station, officially named Linares-Baeza, is far off in the open countryside. A bus to Baeza usually meets the train, but if you turn up at night or on a Sunday you may be stranded. Baeza's bus station, in a residential area without many street signs is nearly unfindable – keep asking. Baeza is a stop on the Ubeda-Córdoba bus line. Ubeda has a new bus station on C. San José, at the western end of town, and various lines connect the city directly to Madrid, Valencia and Barcelona, at least once daily, and more frequently to Baeza, Córdoba, Sevilla, Jaen and Granada. Cazorla and other villages in the region can easily be reached from Ubeda.

Ubeda

Even with Baeza for an introduction, the presence of this nearly perfect little city comes as a surprise. If the 16th century did well by Baeza, it was a golden age for Ubeda, leaving a city a 'town built for gentlemen' as the Spanish used to say, endowed with one of the finest collections of Renaissance architecture in all of Spain. Two men can take much of the credit: Andrés de Vandelvira, an Andalucian architect who created most of Ubeda's best buildings, and Francisco de los Cobos, Imperial Secretary to Charles V, who paid for them. Cobos is a forgotten hero of Spanish history. While Charles was off campaigning in Germany, Cobos had the job of running Castile. By the most delicate management, he kept the kingdom afloat while meeting Charles' ever more exhorbitant demands for money and men. He could postpone the inevitable disaster, but not prevent it. Like most public officials in the Spanish Age of Rapacity, though, he also managed to salt away a few hundred thousand ducats for himself, and he spent most of them embellishing his hometown.

Like Baeza, Ubeda is a peaceful and happy town; it wears its Renaissance heritage gracefully, and is always glad to have visitors. Tourism is still something of a novelty here.

WHAT TO SEE

Ubeda today leaves no doubt how its local politics are going. In the **Plaza de Andalucía**, joining the old and new districts, there is an old metal statue of a fascist Civil War general named Sero, haughtily glaring down from his pedestal. The townspeople have put so many bullets into it, it looks like a Swiss cheese (including one shotgun blast right between the eyes). They've left it here as a joke, and have merrily renamed another square from Plaza de Generalsimo to Plaza 1 Mayo. The **Torre de Reloj**, in the Plaza de Andalucía, is a 14th-century defensive tower now adorned with a clock. The plaque near the base, under a painting of the Virgin, records a visit of Charles V and his pledge to defend the city's 'ancient rights and privileges'.

From here, Calle Real takes you into the heart of the old town. Nearly every corner has at least one lovely palace or church on it. Two of the best can be seen on this street: the **Palacio de Condé Guadiana**, with an ornate tower and distinctive windows cut out of the corners of the building, a common conceit in Ubeda's palaces. Two blocks down, the **Palacio Vela de los Cobos** is in the same style, with a loggia on the top storey.

The home of Francisco de los Cobos' nephew, another Royal Counsellor, was the **Palacio de las Cadenas**, now serving as Ubeda's Ayuntamiento, on a quiet plaza at the end of Calle Real. The side facing the plaza is simple and dignified (the tourist office is here) but the main faąde, facing the **Plaza Vazquez de Molina**, is a stately Italian Renaissance creation, the work of Vandelvira.

Plaza Vazquez de Molina

This is the only place in Andalucía where you can look around and not regret the passing of the Moors, for it is the only truly beautiful thing in all this great region that was not built either by the Moors or under their influence. The Renaissance buildings around the Palacio de las Cadenas make a wonderful ensemble, and the austere landscaping, old cobbles, and a plain six-sided fountain create the same effect of contemplative serendipity as any chamber of the Alhambra. Among the buildings are the **Santa María Church**, a renaissance façade on an older building with a fine Gothic cloister around the back, two sedate palaces, and Vandelvira's **Sacra Capilla del Salvador**, the finest of Ubeda's churches, where Cobos is buried.

All the sculpture on the façades of Ubeda is first-class work, and the west front of the Salvador is especially good. This is very much a monument of the time when Spain was in the mainstream of Renaissance ideas, and humanist classicism was still respectable. Note the mythological subjects on the west front and elsewhere in the church, and be sure to look under the arch of the main door. Instead of Biblical scenes, it has beautifully carved panels of the ancient gods representing the five planets; Phoebus and Diana with the sun and moon and Heracles, Aeolus, Vulcan and Neptune to represent the four elements. The interior, with its great dome, is worth a look despite a thorough sacking in 1936 (the sacristan lives on the first door on the left of Calle Francisco Cobos, on the north side of the church). Behind El Salvador, the **Hospital de los Honrados** has a delightful open patio – but only because the other half of the building was never completed. South of the plaza, the end of town is only a few blocks away, encompassed by a street called the **Redonda de Miradores**, a quiet spot favoured by small children and goats, with remnants of Ubeda's wall and exceptional views over the Sierra de Cazorla to the east.

Around town

Calle Montiel, north of El Salvador, has a few more fine palaces; at the foot of the street, Plaza 1 de Mayo has the 13th-century **San Pablo Church**, much renovated in the 16th. **San Nicolas de Bari**, further north, tells the same story, which has left it with one Gothic door and the other by Vandelvira.

On the outskirts of town, near the bus station on Calle Nueva is Vandelvira's most remarkable building, the **Hospital de Santiago**. This huge edifice, currently under thorough restoration after long years of neglect, has been called the 'Escorial of Andalucía'. Both have the same plan, a great quadrangle with a church inside. Oddly, both were begun at about the same time, though this one seems to have been started a year earlier in 1568. Both are also two supreme examples of the *estilo desornamentado*. The façade here is not as plain as Herrera's; its quirky decoration and clean, angular lines are unique, more like a product of the 20th century than the 16th.

East of Ubeda

If you go this way, you'll be entering a zone few visitors ever reach; the **Sierra de Cazorla**, a jumble of ragged peaks, pine forests, and olive-covered lowlands, offers some memorable mountain scenery, especially around **Cazorla**, a lovely, undiscovered white village of narrow alleys hung at alarming angles down the hillsides. Cazorla's landmarks are a ruined Renaissance church, half-open to the sky, and its castle, but there's an even better castle, possibly built by the Templars, just east of town. **La Iruela** is romantically ruined, with a Homage tower on a dizzying height behind.

TOURIST INFORMATION

Ubeda: Pl. de Ayuntamiento, Tel: 75 08 97.

Baeza: Pl. de los Leones, Tel: 74 04 44.

WHERE TO STAY

Of course they found one old palace in Ubeda to convert into a parador. The **Parador Condestable Dávalos******, with its glassed-in courtyard, is one of the loveliest and most popular of the chain. All the beamed ceilings and fireplaces have been preserved and the restaurant is the best in town, featuring local specialities from 1600–2100 pts a full dinner. Ask to see the ancient wine cellar (Pl. Vazquez de Molina, Tel: 75 03 45, 5500–7500 pts for a big double room). The rest of Ubeda's hotels are all good bargains; you'll find a large selection on C. Ramón y Cajal, just east of the bus station. At the **Sevilla****, Ramón y Cajal 9, Tel: 75 06 12, you can get a clean and pleasant double with bath for 1800–1900 pts, while at the **Consuelo****, Ramón y Cajal 12, Tel: 75 08 40, the rooms are a bit fancier for 2300 pts.

In Baeza there are no hotels with pretensions, but the **Comercio****, C. San Pablo 21 (Tel: 47 01 00), is a reasonably comfortable lodging.

Cazorla has a surprising number of hotels, both in town and up in the mountains on the road to the dam and reservoir at El Tranco, 20 km (12.5 miles) north in a beautiful mountain setting. One of these is the **Mirasierra** (no telephone, doubles with bath 1600–1800 pts). The **Parador El Adelantado*****, is a small mountain chalet – only 20 rooms – in another pretty setting in the mountains outside Cazorla, a base for hunting, fishing and walking in the Sierra (Tel: 72 10 75, doubles 5000–7000 pts).

EATING OUT

Apart from the *parador*, there aren't any really good restaurants in Ubeda – a smattering of unremarkable places around C. Ramón y Cajal.

In Baeza the restaurant of the **Hotel Juanito**, Pso. Arca del Agua, is a good one; try the *pastel de perdiz* (partridge in a pastry crust). Dinners average 1200–1600 pts.

Jaén

The largest city and provincial capital of all this area, Jaén is a decent, modern town, but without any of the attractions of Ubeda or Baeza. It does have a good archaeological collection in the **Museo Provincial** (open daily except Monday, 10 am–2 pm, 4–7 pm, on the Paseo de la Estación) and a big **Cathedral** by Andrés Vandelvira with a flattish, Renaissance façade full of statues looming over the humble buildings of the old town.

If you're on the way to Granada, a possible detour is **Alcalá de Real**, with an unusual town square and another picturesque castle, the **Castle of la Mota** on top of a hill. The **Castle of Solera**, in that tiny village just east of Huelina, is an even finer sight; the castle seems to grow out of its narrow crag. Like Cazorla, the views are breathtaking but it will be some trouble to get up to them.

GETTING AROUND
Jaén has direct rail links only with Córdoba (three trains daily) and Madrid (about six). Buses are the best bet for Ubeda or Granada. The bus station is on the Avda. de Madrid, two blocks west of the tourist office. The RENFE station is on the Pso. de la Estación, the main street, at the northern edge of town.

TOURIST INFORMATION
Pso. de la Estación 30, Tel: 22 92 00.

WHERE TO STAY AND EAT
The **Parador Castillo de Santa Catalina****** is in the castle overlooking Jaén (Tel: 26 44 11, 5500–7500 double) but here you might do better at the **Condestable Iranzo*****, near the tourist office on Paseo de la Estación. It doesn't have the view, but more luxuries at a better price (4200–4500 pts a double, for an air conditioned room with TV, Tel: 22 28 00). An acceptable budget hotel is **Los Cazadores**, Paseo de la Estación 51 (Tel: 25 21 42, doubles 1500 pts with bath, 1400 pts without). For dining, roast kid (*cabrito asado*) is a local favourite, and the best place for it is the **Restaurante Nelson**, Pso. de la Estación 33 (about 1600–2000 pts).

The Andalucian Coasts

Everyone has heard of the Costa del Sol (probably you get tired of hearing about it each winter, when the publicity machines start cranking up). But there is a good deal more to Andalucía's coasts than just that narrow strip of salty Babylon – about 640 km (400 miles) of it, from the empty spaces of Huelva to the empty spaces of Almería. A brief introduction will help to get things straight:

Andalucía's Atlantic coast, from Portugal to the Straits of Gibraltar, is not at all scenic, but it has plenty of long golden beaches that haven't yet become too crowded. The image-makers of the Spanish Tourism Ministry have bestowed upon it the name **Costa de la Luz**. The piquant, sea-washed town of **Cádiz** is its major attraction. After Cádiz the mountains close in, and there's little to see until **Algeciras**, a port town with the promise of a side-trip to Morocco, or to a tiny remnant of Spain's colonial empire in Africa, **Ceuta**. Next we stop for fish and chips in **Gibraltar**; there the endless *urbanizaciónes* of the **Costa del Sol** begin, reaching their greatest intensity around **Marbella** and **Torremolinos. Málaga** comes next, a big but not very pleasant city, and after it the only section of the coast with any pretensions to scenery, around **Nerja**. After **Motril**, and the road to Granada, there's more solitude on the **Costa de Almería**, that is in parts pretty, in others nearly a desert.

Altogether, these coasts have only one real purpose – planting yourself on a beach and dozing off. There are the inevitable peripheral attractions (mini-golf, seafood dinners, funfairs, English beer on tap, etc.) but little else. Pack a potent sunscreen and have a good time.

Costa de la Luz: around Huelva

GETTING AROUND

Ayamonte is the border crossing for anyone passing to or from the Portuguese resorts of the Algarve. It is a fishing village grown into a low-key resort, with some 8 km (5 miles) of beaches at **Isla Cristina**, more popular with vacationing Spaniards than foreigners. The same could be said about **Punta Umbria**, a small peninsula surrounded by beach that is also a growing resort.

The important thing to remember is that the two resort strips are not connected by road to each other. To get to the western section, Mazagon, Ayamonte, and Isla Cristina, you'll have to go through Sevilla to Huelva, the provincial capital. Huelva has regular bus service to all the resorts, mostly from the Empresa Damas office at Avenida de Portugal 9. There are also direct buses from Huelva to Sevilla and Granada, and trains to Madrid, Sevilla and Extremadura (RENFE on Avda. de Italia in Huelva, Tel: 24 66 66).

WHAT TO SEE

Huelva, the provincial capital, is full of factories and freshly laid cement. Its local tourist brochure, in a unique and disarmingly modest display of candour, states it 'has no particular historic interest' in the vicinity, though, you may visit the once-important town of **Niebla**, now forgotten behind its decayed Romano-Moorish walls. There's a Roman bridge and some interesting old churches and Moorish buildings. Christopher Columbus set out on his epic voyage from **Palos de la Frontera**; his two captains and most of the crews came from the town. Some 4 km (2.5 miles) to the west, the **Convento de la Rabida** was Columbus' home while he planned the trip, and the rooms he used are maintained as they were.

Mazagon, further down the coast, is another resort of last resort, and from here it's a straight shot to Torre de la Higuera, and the big hotel developments around the endless

Matalascañas Beach. This is a dead end of the coastal highway; the only place you can go is the tiny village of **El Rocio**, which would not even be on the map were it not for the annual *Romeria* at Pentecost, the biggest and perhaps the oldest in Spain. Every year hundreds of thousands of pilgrims, from as far away as Barcelona and the Canaries, bring their families for a few days of merry-making in the fields; it is traditional to arrive in a horse-drawn, covered wagon, decorated with flowers and streamers.

Las Marismas

Add the water of the broad Guadalquivir to this flat plain, and the result is southern Europe's greatest marshland wildlife preserve. Las Marismas is another world, a bit of the Everglades in a country better known for dry heated mountains. Hundreds of species of migratory birds pass through in the spring and autumn – storks and geese among them – but the Marismas have a fantastically varied population of their own: rare golden eagles, snowy egrets, flamingos, griffin vultures, tortoises, red deer, foxes and European lynx.

As in the Everglades, wildlife congregates around 'islands' among the wetlands; here they're called *corrales*, built of patches of dune anchored by surrounding shrubs and stands of low pines. Also like the Everglades, Las Marismas is threatened by development. Sevilla stands practically at the gateway of the wetlands, but it is the growing resorts like Matalascañas that are the real villains. It has become Spain's top environmental concern, and the government has limited coastal development and also set aside a large slice of the area as the **Parque Nacional de la Cota Doñana**.

For visitors, the park conducts tours by Land Rover from a station about half-way between El Rocio and Matalascañas; check with the tourist offices in Huelva or Sevilla for details before you go. Keep in mind that the wetlands are largely dried up in the summer, and whenever you come, bring a few gallons of mosquito repellent. If you go off by yourself, watch out for quicksand.

TOURIST INFORMATION
Huelva: C. Plus Ultra 10, Tel: 24 50 92.
Matalascañas, in the Urbanización Playa de Matalascañas.

WHERE TO STAY
In Ayamonte, the **Parador Costa de la Luz****, isn't on the beach, but has fine views over the sea (it occupies the site of a long-gone Moorish castle) and a big swimming-pool (Tel: 32 07 00; doubles 5000–7000 pts). Ayamonte has a number of inexpensive places to stay in the town if you're passing through on the way to Portugal, like the **Hostal La Ribera*** (Tel: 32 02 89, doubles 1500 pts) at Pso. de la Ribera 1. At Isla Cristina, you have a choice on the beach between the **Mary Nina**** (Tel: 33 18 00, doubles 3200–3600 pts) and the **El Paraiso**** (Tel: 33 18 73, doubles 2300–2900 pts). At Punta Umbria the choice is wider: **La Florida****(Avda. Oceanus 75, Tel: 31 11 07, doubles 2850 pts) is the cheapest hotel on the beach. All these little resorts have cheaper hotels within reasonable distances of the beaches, If you don't have a car, it might be best to get a list first at the Huelva Information Office and make some calls; it's surprisingly tight in the busy season.

EATING OUT
In Ayamonte the **Restaurante Barbieri**, Pso. de la Ribera at 11 is a good bet for seafood (1100–1500 pts).

Sanlucar and Rota

Like those to the east, the beaches around Cádiz are popular mostly with Spaniards – they're much more crowded, though, at least in July and August. Just the same, the beaches are lovely and huge, the towns behind them relatively unspoiled; there may be few better places in Spain to baste yourself. Most of these towns also make a living from wine – Jerez isn't very far away – and there will be plenty of opportunities for exploring *bodegas*.

GETTING AROUND
Cádiz is the base for visiting Jerez and the coasts. There is regular bus service (Amarillo company) from Cádiz to all the coastal towns, and at least five daily to Jerez. Infrequent buses connect Jerez with Rota, Sanlucar and Puerto. Almost all the Sevilla–Cádiz buses stop in Jerez and Puerto as do the trains. Jerez stations for buses and trains are together on the eastern edge of town (Tel: 33 66 82). You can also go by bus from Jerez to Arcos de la Frontera and Ronda.

There's a regular 20-minute ferry service from Puerto to Cádiz – more fun than the bus.

WHAT TO SEE
Sanlucar de Barrameda makes *manzanilla*, most ethereal of sherries, and it is known as the port that launched Magellan on his way around the world, and Columbus on his second voyage to the Indies. It stands at the mouth of the Guadalquivir, and the only beach is a quiet spot facing the river. **Chipiona** is a family resort, full of small pensions and *hostals*, with a good beach at **Playa de Regla** near the lighthouse. Next, on the edge of the bay of Cádiz, comes **Rota**, a bigger, flashier resort taking advantage of the best and longest beach on the coast; the town is pretty, though it's beginning to get a bit overbuilt. It's also full of unpicturesque Americans from the largest naval base in the region, just outside town. This was the key base Franco gave up in the 1953 deal with President Eisenhower; in the recent dealings over the future of Spain's role in NATO, the Americans made it unpleasantly clear this base is not a subject of negotiations. The base itself is a giant, eerie compound, and the sailors have got into some ferocious dust-ups with local gypsies, but in the 1986 NATO referendum this region turned out the highest 'yes' vote in Spain.

Puerto de Santa María

This is the traditional port of the sherry houses in Jerez, and it has quite a few bodegas of its own – Osborne, Terry and Duff Gordon among other famous names. The town has some interesting churches, mansions of the Anglo-Spanish sherry aristocracy, and the fine, restored 13th century Mudejár **castle of San Marcos**. The century-old **bullring** ranks up with those of Sevilla and Ronda in prestige. Puerto itself isn't a big resort, but there are some good beaches (**Puntilla** especially) on the edges of town.

Jerez de la Frontera

The name is synonymous with wine – by the English corruption of Jerez into sherry – but besides the finos, amontillados, olorosos and other varieties of that noble sauce, Jerez also ships out much of Spain's equally good brandy. Most of the well-known companies, whose advertising is plastered all over Spain, have their headquarters here, and they're quite accustomed to taking visitors – especially English ones – through the bodegas. Don't be shy. Most are open to visitors 9 am–1 pm Monday–Saturday – but not in August, or when they're busy with the *vendimia* harvest in September.

Business is good, and Jerez has been growing out in all directions. It couldn't be called an attractive town, but it has been around since Roman days, and there are a few lovely buildings for you to squint at after you've done the rounds of the bodegas.

La Colegiata, just off the central Plaza de los Reyes Católicos, is a curious pseudo-Gothic church built in 1706, with a separate bell-tower and Baroque staircase. Nearby, the 1575 **Ayuntamiento** is a lovely building with a small archaeology museum inside. There is a Moorish **Alcazar**, a tower and some remains of the baths. Outside town, on the road to Medina Sidonia, is the **Cartuja de la Defensión**, a 15th-century monastery with the best Baroque façade (added in 1667) in Andalucía. While in Jerez, look out for exhibitions scheduled at the **Escuela Andaluz del Arte Ecuestre** (School of Equestrian Art). Jerez's snooty wine aristocracy, an anthropological relic of this corner of Spain, takes horsemanship very seriously; they have some of the finest horses you're likely to see anywhere, and they know how to use them. Otherwise, you can see them all tarted up like Tio Pepe bottles at the annual **Horse Fair** in May. Another attraction for some is the recently opened **Museum of Flamenco-Flamencology**, a science you can delve into at Calle Quintos 1.

TOURIST INFORMATION

Jerez is planning a tourist office somewhere; it may be open by the time you get there. Puerto already has one, on C. Guadalete (Tel: 86 31 45). Check here for information on visiting the sherry bodegas.

WHERE TO STAY

No problem finding a place in any of the coastal resorts; especially in the high season, little old ladies meet the buses to drag you off to their *hostales,* and you'll probably do better negotiating with them in your pidgin Spanish than trying to find a place by yourself when it's busy.

A couple of places worth mentioning are the **Andalucía***, in Sanlucar (Gonzalez Montero 8, Tel: 36 01 40 doubles, 2420 pts with bath, 1815 pts without) and the **Paquita***, in Chipiona (Francisco Lara 11, Tel: 37 02 06, 1250–1850 pts doubles – no bath). Both are decent *hostales* near the beaches – but really typical of what you'll find in these modest resorts. **Del Sur**** in Chipiona is fancier, with a pool and garden, and still a bargain at the price (Av da. Sevilla 2, Tel: 37 03 50, 2700–3400 pts double). Rota is more of the same, but has a few classy modern resort hotels: **Playa dela Luz***** is one on the beach at Arroyo Hondo, a sports-oriented hotel (tennis, wind surfing, etc.) with a lovely pool and gardens (Tel: 82 05 00; doubles 4000–5750 pts). One place a lot like it in Puerto is the **Puertobahia*****, also on the beach (Av. de La Paz, Tel: 86 27 21, doubles 3670–4690 pts). Here the bargain choice is the **Bahia del Sol***, a little out of the way at Dunas de San Anton (Tel: 85 02 50, 1800 pts double with bath.)

In Jerez, there is no end of unremarkable hotels. The **Virt**** is a middle-range bargain with a decent air-conditioned rooms with bath for 3300 pts (C. Durán 20, Tel: 32 28 11). At **Las Palomas** nearby at C. Higueras 17, Tel: 34 37 73, a double with bath is only 1500 pts.

EATING OUT

Most of the restaurants in this area are open only during the summer, informal cafes where you can pick out the fish that catches your fancy. One of the best restaurants in the area, where you can try the local *manzanilla* with the day's catch, is **Casa Bigote** in Sanlucar (at Bajo Guia, 1600–2200 pts). In Rota the cuisine is heavily influenced by the presence of the naval base – pizza and Chinese restaurants alongside the usual seafood. Puerto has some expensive and well-known restaurants, but you may do just as well and have more fun with the simple cafes on the beach – grilled sardines the speciality, along with whatever else comes in that day.

Cádiz

If Cádiz were a tiny village, the government would immediately delcare it a National Monument and put up a sign. It's a big, busy seaport, though, and the tourist business generally leaves it alone. It's a pity, for Cádiz (if you pronounce it any other way but 'Cad-ee' no one will understand you) is one of the most distinctive Spanish cities, worth spending a few days in even if there are few 'sights'. The city is a small peninsula, built up tightly and pounded by the rough Atlantic on all sides whenever the wind's up. It comes in colours – 100 shades of off-white, bleached and faded by sun and spray into a soft patina, broken only by the golden dome of a rambling Baroque cathedral that would be a civic misfortune anywhere else, but seems inexplicably beautiful here.

History

Cádiz modestly claims to be the oldest city in Western Europe. It's hard to argue; the Phoenician city of *Gadir* has a documented foundation of 1100 BC, and while other cities have traces of older settlements, it would be difficult to find another city west of Greece with a continuous urban life of 3000 years. Gadir served as the port for shipping Spanish copper and tin, first to Tyre, and then to Carthage, and it was undoubtedly the station for the now-forgotten Phoenician trade routes with west Africa and England – and possibly even for explorations to America. Cádiz, however, prefers to consider Hercules its founder, and he appears on the arms of the city between his famous pillars.

Under Roman rule, **Gades** as it was called, was a favoured city, especially under Julius Caesar who held his first public office here. The city was out of the spotlight until the 16th century, when the American trade and Spain's growth as a naval power made a major port of it once again. Sir Francis Drake came here to 'singe the King of Spain's beard' in 1587, and later British admirals followed the custom for a century, calling every decade or so for a fish dinner and an afternoon's sacking and burning. The years after 1720 when Cádiz controlled the American market shaped its present character. Street names like Calle Conde O'Reilly (an Irish-born royal governor who did a lot for Cádiz) and a statue of one José MacPherson y Hemas testify to the contacts the city enjoyed with the outside world – uniquely so for Spain in those dark years. Being the city most exposed to outside influences, Cádiz became the most liberal and tolerant corner of Spain. Its shining hour came in 1812, when the Constitution was declared here, and the city became the capital of free Spain. In the 19th century Cádiz' carnival developed; some claim there is a strong Cuban influence behind its masquerades and crazy music. It says something about Cádiz that under the dictatorship, theirs was the only carnival Franco failed to suppress.

GETTING AROUND

Cádiz isn't the big passenger port it used to be, but you can still take the weekly ferries to Málaga–Almería, to Genoa, Italy, to Tenerife–Las Palmas–Arrecife in the Canary Islands, or to Palma de Mallorca with various stops along the way. They run a little more frequently in the summer. For all of them, see the Transmediterránea office on Av. Ramón de Carranza 26, Tel: 28 43 50. There's also a regular 20-minute ferry ride from the port to Puerto Santa María.

By train you can go only to Jerez (14 trains daily) and Sevilla (five trains) directly. The station is at the narrow landward end of the old city; just a few blocks from the Pl. San Juan de Dios (Tel: 23 43 01). Cádiz is served by two bus companies: Los Amarillos takes the route west to Rota and Sanlucar de Barrameda (Av. Ramón de Carranza 31 by the port) and Comes runs east to Tarifa and Algeciras (their terminal is on the Pl. de España). City bus 1 will take you from the Plaza de España to Cádiz's suburban beaches.

WHAT TO SEE

The approach to Cádiz is a dismal one, through marshes and salt pans cluttered with power lines and industrial junk. After this, you must pass through a long, narrow strip of land full of modern suburbs before arriving at the **Puerta de Tierra**, entrance to the old city on the peninsula. Almost everything about warfare in the 18th century had a certain decorum to it, and Cádiz' gates and formidable **land walls** (1757), all well-preserved, are among the most aesthetically pleasing structures in town.

The Cathedral

From the Puerta de Tierra, the Cuesta de las Calesas leads down to the port and rail station, then around the corner to **Plaza San Juan de Dios**, the lively, palm-shaded centre of Cádiz, with most of the restaurants and hotels on the surrounding streets. Two blocks away is the **Cathedral**, on a small plaza. A recent thorough restoration of this ungainly bulk has not destroyed its ingratiating charm. It was begun in 1722, at the height of Cádiz' prosperity (open daily 9.30 am–6.30 pm). Continuing eastwards, the Plaza Topete was named for a *tophet*, the Phoenician temple dedicated to that nasty habit of theirs of sacrificing first-born babies; remains of one were found here. Now this is Cádiz' almost excessively colourful **market district**, spread around a wonderful, dilapidated old market building.

The Constitution of 1812

A few more blocks east, the little church of **San Felipe Neri** on Calle Sacramonte is an unprepossessing shrine to the beginnings of Spanish liberty. On 29 March 1812, an assemblage of refugees from Napoleon's occupation of the rest of Spain gathered here and declared Spain an independent republic, guaranteeing full political and religious freedom. Though their Constitution, and their revolution, proved stillborn, it was a notable beginning for Spain's struggle towards democracy. Big marble plaques cover the church's façade, sent as tributes from cities and provinces all over Spain, many Latin-American countries, and the 'Casino Español de Puerto Rico'.

Around the corner, Cádiz's very good **Municipal Museum** has a huge Romantic-era mural depicting the event. In front of it, in the main hall, is the museum's star exhibit, a 15.4 m (50 ft) **scale model of Cádiz**, made entirely of mahogany and ivory by an unknown obsessive in 1779. Nearly every building is detailed – Cádiz hasn't changed much since. Among a collection of portraits of Spanish heroes is the Duke of Wellington, who in Spain carried the title of Duke of Ciudad Rodrigo. The best picture, though, also from that era, shows Hercules about to give Napoleon a good bashing with his club (open daily 9.30 am–1.30 pm, 5–9 pm, Sunday 10 am–2 pm).

Plaza de Mina

On this lovely square, in the north-western corner of the peninsula, you'll find the Tourist Information Office and the **Museum of Fine Arts and Archaeology** (open daily except Monday, 9 am–2 pm, 5–8 pm). The museum is currently undergoing a complete reconstruction, and only a few parts have been opened – including the best of their paintings; some Murillos and very good portraits of the Four Evangelists and John the Baptist by Zurbarán at his most Zurbaránish. The archaeology now open is mostly Phoenician and Roman sarcophagi and gravestones; among the statues there's a dumb-looking Emperor Trajan with a big Roman nose. On the top floor are unaffectedly charming puppets and stage sets from a Cádiz genre of marionette show called *Tia Norica*, still performed in these parts.

Circumnavigating Cádiz

It's a great city for exploring – streets as narrow as Toledo's, with mirrors on the corners so drivers can see around, and neither decaying nor prettified for the tourists. Keep an eye out for the little plaques – for the birthplace of Manuel de Falla, of Miranda, the first president of Venezuela, and others, reminders of what an important role this little city has often played. There are surprises, like the **Oratorio de Santo Cueva,** on Calle Rosario, with frescoes by Goya; note the houses, a style unique to Cádiz, with roof-terraces and little Moorish-looking turrets, from which the Gaditanos watch for ships coming in. In an hour or so you can walk entirely around Cádiz, on the coast road past parks like the pretty **Alameda de Apodara**, and forts and bastions of the 18th century, finally arriving on the southern shore for the famous view of the Cathedral rising just above the breaking waves of the Atlantic.

TOURIST INFORMATION
The office is on the Pl. de Mina (address C. Calderón de la Barca 1, Tel: 22 48 00).

WHERE TO STAY
Nothing very fancy in Cádiz, but a huge number of modest hotels in the area around Pl. San Juan de Dios. The **España** is a clean, pleasant hostel, though a little dear (C. Marquez de Cádiz 9, Tel: 28 55 00, 2000–2500 pts for a double with a bath, 1400–1600 pts without). Even better is the **Imares*** in a nice, well-kept old building at C. San Francisco 9, Tel: 21 22 57, doubles 2100–2600 pts with bath, 1500–1800 pts without). There will be no problem finding cheaper – lots of sailors pass through here. Few are really bad though; just look for the 'Camas' signs and take your pick.

EATING OUT
Dining, of course, means more fish. **El Faro**, at C. San Felix 15, is a place that takes it seriously, where you can get to know all of the amazingly wide range of seafood – things that we don't even have names for in English like *mojarras* and *urtas* – that come out of this part of the Atlantic (full-course dinners 1600–2100 pts). You don't have to go that high, though, for Cádiz is one of the best cities in Spain for memorable, cheap dining. Heading the list are two grim-looking, locally famous establishments next to each other on Pl. San Juan de Dios, the **Restaurante Economica** and the **El 9**; both have decent seafood, and will set you back about 600 pts for a full dinner. For seafood with a Basque touch, try the **Achuri**, on C. Plocia 15 (800–1200 pts). There are quite a few outdoor cafés and restaurants on the Plaza and adjacent Av. Ramón Carranza. Try the **Restaurant-Cafe Español** (around 1200–1500 pts), and find out what they mean by the sign 'We speak eight languages by hand signals.'

From Cádiz to Algeciras

The green, hilly countryside of this region looks a lot like the parts of Morocco just across the Straits; the hills force the main road away from the sea, leaving a few villages with fine beaches relatively unspoilt and good places to take time out from your overactive holiday; the problem is they're hard to reach unless you have a car.

GETTING AROUND
Buses from Cádiz to Algeciras (Comes station in Cádiz) are frequent enough, but service to the nascent resorts along the coast like Conil, Borbate and Zahara, is infrequent or nonexistent, which greatly decreases their allure unless you have a car or are willing to walk or hitch from the coastal highway where the bus stops are.

Algeciras' reason for being is its port, and there's no trouble getting a ferry either to Ceuta (at least six boats a day, nine in the summer) or Tangier (two at least, as many as seven daily in summer). Tangier is only 2½ hours away. Fares are reasonable, and rates are the same in any of the travel agencies around town that are official Transmediterránea agents. You'll need your passport for either destination, and you are advised to not do anything foolish on these well-policed borders. There's also a summer hydrofoil service from Tarifa to Tangier.

Algeciras' bus station is in the Hotel Octavo complex across from the train station; there are buses to La Linea about every half hour, and also connections to the Costa del Sol and Málaga. The trains go to Ronda, and from there to all points in eastern Andalucía; there is a daily *talgo* to Madrid and points north.

WHAT TO SEE

Beyond the marshland around Cádiz, you'll see the turnoffs first for **Santi Petri** with a castle by the beach, then **Conil**, **Caños de Meca** on Cape Trafalgar, **Barbate** and **Zahara de los Atunes** ('of the tunas'), all beach villages meeting the above description. The main attraction of this road is **Vejer de la Frontera**, whitest of the 'white villages' of Andalucía, strangely moulded around its hilltop site like a Greek island town, dominated by its castle and Gothic church.

Tarifa, at the southernmost top of Spain and of Europe, has the quality of looking either exotic and evocative, or merely dusty and drear, depending on the mood you're in and the hour of the day. It has miles of beaches around it, and a 10th-century Moorish castle, much rebuilt since; as every Spanish schoolboy knows, this is the site of the legend of Guzman el Bueno. In 1292, this Spanish knight was defending Tarifa against a force of Moors. Among them was the renegade Infante Don Juan, brother of King Sancho IV, who had Guzman's young son as a prisoner, and threatened to kill him if Guzman did not surrender. Guzman's response was to toss him a dagger. His son was killed, but Tarifa did not fall; the Nationalists recycled this legend for the siege of the Alcazar in 1936 (see Toledo) with the Republicans in the villain's role. Outside Tarifa, along the beaches east of the town, there are ruins of a once sizeable Roman town, **Bolonia** (visit by guided tour).

No matter what mood you're in, **Algeciras** is an awful place. Once a favoured resort (an international naval conference was held here in the 1920s), the last 30 years have seen it built up into a big port to counter British-held Gibraltar. As the main ferry port to Ceuta and Tangier, it does have a certain atmosphere; it is also the centre of one of the busiest drug-smuggling routes in the world, and every stevedore and cab driver will be whispering little propositions in your ear if you look the type.

With Africa so close – you can see Morocco's jagged, surreal peaks all along the coastal highway – the urge to jump on a boat may be irresistible.

Ceuta

The ferry here takes only an hour and a half, and leaves you in one of Spain's two remaining enclaves on the North African coast. Every time the Spanish make self-righteous noises about getting Gibraltar back, someone reminds them of these two colonial leftovers. Morocco's King Hussein (a good friend of Juan Carlos) mentions them every year in his New Year's speech; when he neglected to do so in 1986, suspicions were raised that somewhere a deal was being made. Lately Colonel Gaddafi has also been heard from on the issue. Ceuta has a mainly Spanish population; that is why it was excluded from the 1955 withdrawal from the Spanish Moroccan protectorate. They are the stumbling-block, and some way will have to be found to accommodate them before the inevitable transfer of sovereignity.

Ceuta is a pleasant enough town, but there's little reason to go there: only the impressive 16th-century **walls** and moat, and a **museum** dedicated to Spain's Foreign Legion (a band of cut-throats who became notorious during the Civil War under a one-armed, one-eyed commander named Millán Astray. Their slogan: 'Long live Death'. Like Andorra on the other end of Spain, Ceuta is a big duty-free supermarket, its main street peddling everything from whisky to telescopes. You can easily cross into Morocco from here, though it's better to take the ferry straight to Tangier.

TOURIST INFORMATION
Algeciras: by the port, Avda. de la Marina, Tel: 65 67 61.
Ceuta: C. Caliral 5, Tel: 51 13 39.

WHERE TO STAY
In Tarifa, the recently 'discovered' resort along this coast, rooms are surprisingly (and unnecessarily) expensive; the same is true of Conil. Still, you can find inexpensive *hostales* in both places with a little searching. Zahara and Barbate are a bit better; the **De Barbate**** on the central Adva. Generalisimo has rooms with bath for 1900–2100 pts (Tel: 43 00 50). In Algeciras there are rooms in modern buildings for all budgets in the street near the port. The hotel of Algeciras' bygone elegance is the **Reina Cristina****** on Paseo Conferencia (all the luxuries for 5995–7080 pts, Tel: 65 0061) where W. B. Yeats rested one winter, convalescing from some poetic dread disease.

Finding a place to sleep in Ceuta can be a problem as there are only a few hotels. The **Atlante**** is the best bet, a good bargain in the middle of town (Pso. de las Palmeras 1, Tel: 51 35 48; 2900–3700 pts double with bath, 2200–2350 pts without). More inexpensively, for 1500 pts (no bath) you can stay at the **Málaga*** (Isidro Merlivez 2, Tel: 51 18 50) or the **Oriente*** (Ten. Arribal 3, Tel: 51 11 15).

EATING OUT
The best restaurant in Ceuta is the **San Marco** with Italian food (and Italian owners). It's a way out from the centre on Crta. Playa Benlez 3 (1100–1400 pts). One place to meet the locals (and a strange bunch they are) is the **Restaurant Mar Chica** at Pso. Colon 7, with decent fish dinners from 450 pts up.

An Excursion to Morocco

The ferries run regularly enough for you to do this conveniently. If you do it from Ceuta, you'll have to take a cab or city bus (the one marked 'frontera') to the border; after some cacophanous border confusion, you wait for the infrequent bus or carefully negotiate a taxi trip to **Tetuan**, 30 km (18.8 miles) away. Tetuan is a decent town, full of gleaming white, Spanish colonial architecture; it has a famous market in its *medina*, a historical museum, and it's a good place to purchase Moroccan crafts.

Buses (there's no train) to Tangier are cheap and regular, run by a number of companies from the central bus station. They'll take you right to Tangier's port (on the way note how the Moroccans have turned Tangier's old Plaza de Toros into flats). Once in the big square outside the port entrance, you may take your chances with the inexpensive hotels in the surrounding streets, or take a cab to fancier spots in the newer, Europeanized districts. Tangier may not be as romantic as you expect; the wares in the markets of the *medina* are fun to look at, but the quarter itself is down-at-heel and dusty. You may not enter mosques in Morocco, but in the old governor's palace are two fine **museums** of archaeology and Moroccan art.

Unfortunately the real treasures of Morocco are all far to the south – Rabat, Fez, and Meknes – but you can still get quite a good look at Morocco from the admittedly international city of Tangier.

SOME MOROCCAN PRACTICALITIES

Wait until you get into Morocco to change money. Spanish travel agents will do it, often at a dishonestly low rate, and the rates at the border crossings aren't much better. The currency is the *dirham*, lately averaging about 12 to the pound, 8 to the dollar.

This corner of Morocco, being the fullest of tourists, is also full of English-speaking hustlers and creeps. We do not exaggerate: around the bus stations and ports they're thick as flies and 10 times as persistent, sometimes weaseling, sometimes menacing. Entertain no offers, especially of drugs or guided tours, and do your best to totally ignore the scum. The Moroccans don't like them either. Beyond that, you'll need your wits to bargain, with merchants, taxi drivers, and even hotel keepers. There's no reason why you can't do this firmly and gracefully. Also, crime is a problem after dark in these two cities.

On the good side, you'll have a chance to explore a fascinating society – and perhaps see a little reflection of the lost culture of Al-Andalus. Hotels, restaurants, and everything also will be almost half as expensive as in Spain. The food has an international reputation; national dishes like *couscous* and *harira* are superb. Don't judge Morocco by Tangier and Tetuan, and don't even judge those places by first impressions. A little side-trip to Morocco may not be an epiphany, but think how much you'll regret it if you pass up the chance.

Gibraltar

> '...a cosy smell of provincial groceries. I'd forgotten how much the atmosphere of home depended on white bread, soap and soup squares.'
>
> *Laurie Lee*

In three-and-half hours, you can experience the ultimate culture shock, sailing from the smoky souks of Tangier to Algeciras, Spain, with time for *churros* and chocolate before the bus takes you off to a mysterious enclave of red phone booths, warm beer and policemen in silly hats.

The Spanish bus will really take you only as far as **La Linea** ('the line', named for Gibraltar's old land walls), a lively, fun town that has built up dramatically since the reopening of the Gibraltar border in 1985. Prices in Gibraltar are outrageous by Spanish standards, and La Linea may be the best place to stay while you visit. It's just a short walk through the **neutral zone** (where presumably you may murder your travelling companions with impunity) into Gibraltar where immediately you'll be confronted with one of the Rock's curiosities. Nowhere else, perhaps, has a busy street crossing an airport runway; as you enter British territory you find yourself looking down the noses of 727s and Tridents. The airport, built on landfill perpendicular to the narrow peninsula, symbolizes British determination to hold on during the years Franco was putting the squeeze on Gibraltar, and also points up the enclave's biggest problem – lack of space.

History

Calpe, as the Greeks knew it, was of course one of the Pillars of Hercules, beyond which the jealous Phoenicians would permit no other nation's ships to trade. The other, less dramatic pillar is Mount Abyle in Morocco (visible across the straits on clear days). The Rock is full of caves, and can claim to be the oldest known inhabited spot in Spain – homes of Neanderthal man were found here even before the discovery at Neanderthal in Germany, but no one on Gibraltar knew how significant they were. The Rock's present name comes from its Moorish conqueror – *Jebel Tarik*, or 'mountain of Tarik ibn-Zayad'. Guzman el Bueno seized it for Castile in 1309, and in the centuries that followed it was one of the major battlegrounds of the Mediterranean. The Moors had it back for a while, and in 1540 Barbarossa's Turkish pirates briefly held the town.

The British arrived in 1704, taking Gibraltar in the name of Archduke Charles during the War of the Spanish Succession; after Charles' defeat they found the Rock such a convenient stepping-stone for their Mediterranean ambitions they decided to keep it. It was a crucial acquisition; Britain's imperial expansion across the Mediterranean and Middle East would have been almost inconceivable without it. In 1779–83, Gibraltar suffered its Great Siege, by a combined Spanish and French force and survived only by the tenacity of its defenders, and their presence of mind in tunnelling up into the rock to plant their guns on a commanding height halfway up. That was the beginning of modern Gibraltar's series of tunnels and galleries. Now there are about 48 km (30 miles) of them; Gibraltar is still very well defended.

GETTING AROUND

By Bus

Two companies serve La Linea, the town on the Spanish side of the border. Transportes Comes runs the service to Algeciras and points west, and the Portillo company to the Costa del Sol, Málaga and Madrid. Both have offices on Avda. de España, just off La Linea's central square, and from here it's a five-minute walk to the border. Gibraltar town buses and taxis do serve the frontier, about 0.8 km (0.5 mile) from the centre of town. The border has only recently been opened (Franco had closed it to try and choke Gibraltar's economy, and the reopening was delayed by Spanish pique over the Falklands war) but it's a good bet that some kind of direct bus service to Gibraltar – at least from the Costa del Sol – is not far away.

By Air
GB Airways has at least one daily flight to London (Gatwick) and to Tangier – which must be one of the shortest regularly scheduled flights in the world.

By Sea
The ferry to Tangier runs on Tuesday, Wednesday and Friday, more often in the summer. The fares are expensive (£15) like everything else in Gibraltar, and you'd be slightly better off doing it from Algeciras. In summer there's a hydrofoil to Algeciras and Tangier, daily except Sunday if the weather permits.

The Town

Despite all attempts to turn it into a perfect replica of an English seaside town, Gibraltar is still a fascinating place. The town is long and narrow, strung out along **Main Street** with most of the shops and pubs. The harbour is never more than a couple of blocks away, and the old gates, bastions and walls are fun to explore. You'll soon find that Gibraltar has a distinctive population – mostly Genoese, who have been around for centuries, along with Maltese, Indians, Spaniards, Jews and Moroccans, all as British as Trafalgar Square; when a referendum was held in the 1960s on joining Spain, they voted it down by 99.6 per cent.

Near the centre of town, on Lime Wall Road, you should spare a few minutes for the **Gibraltar Museum**, which offers a room-sized model of the Rock and a thorough schooling in its complicated history. It is built over the remains of a **Moorish bath**, with Roman and Visigothic capitals on its columns (Monday–Friday 10 am–1 pm, 3–6 pm, Sataurday 10 am–1 pm). Near the southern end of Main Street is the **Governor's Residence** in a 16th-century Franciscan convent (changing of the guard, Monday 10.20 am).

The Rock

The famous silhouette, surprisingly, does not hang over the seaward edge, but faces backwards towards La Linea; its entire eastern face is covered with the **Water Catchment System** that supplies Gibraltar's water, an engineering marvel as much as the tunnels. The only ways to get up on to the Rock, besides taking the taxi tour (£12 for a carload is the current official rate) are either to walk or to take the cable car up from the southern end of town. Halfway up, it stops at the **Apes' Den**. Gibraltar's best-known citizens are officially Barbary apes, a species of gregarious monkey much more common on the African side of the straits. They are unique in Europe, though, and there is an old saying that as long as they're here, the British will never leave Gibraltar. Understandably, they're well cared for, and have been since the days of their great benefactor, Winston Churchill. The Gibraltarians are fond of them, even though (as a local guidebook solemnly notes) they 'fail to share the same respect for private property' as the rest of us. Now that most of their feeding-grounds have been built over, they are on the dole, and it's fun to watch them when the official Keeper of the Apes comes round at feeding-time. Nearby are remains of a **Moorish wall**, and a short walk to the south, **St Michael's Cave**, a huge cavern of delicate stalactites now sometimes used as an auditorium (open daily 10 am–6.30 pm; sound-and-light shows at 11 am and 4 pm). On the northern end of the 'top of the Rock' facing Spain, the **Upper Galleries** are an extensive section of the original British tunnels open for visitors with wax dummies of 18th-century British soldiers digging and blowing up Spaniards. From here it's a short walk down to the **Moorish Castle**, with more dummies and some 13th-century towers and walls.

If you want to sit on a beach, Gibraltar has a few, but they're all on the eastern side, opposite from the town, and accessible by bus; **Catalan Bay** and **Sandy Bay** are both a little built up and crowded. **Eastern Beach** is better, though unfortunately it's next to the airport.

TOURIST INFORMATION

There's a booth right inside the frontier, another in the airport terminal a few hundred feet away, and a main office on John Mackintosh Square in the centre of town (Tel: 75 555). La Linea has a big new information centre just on the Spanish side of the border crossing (Tel: 76 99 50).

Note on currency: These days, most shops and restaurants in Gibraltar are perfectly happy to take British, Spanish or Gibraltar money. The enclave has its own currency and stamps – don't be stuck with any when you leave, as it's hard to get rid of anywhere else.

WHERE TO STAY

In La Linea, if you're on a budget. Prices in Gibraltar are twice to four times what they would be for comparable hotels in Spain. La Linea has only a few very inexpensive places at the moment, but now the border is open more are undoubtably on the way; those high-rise buildings under construction all along the shore certainly aren't new schools. In the meantime, heading the list is the **Hostal Sevilla***, Duque de Tetuan 4, Tel: 76 00 86, for no other reason than its flamboyant, crumbling glass-and-stone building and the nice old folks who run it (1000 pts for a double, no bath). Most of the others are in this area, around the Pl. de Iglesia. You can bed down with less panache but more comfort at the **Miramar**, Av. España 26 (Tel: 76 06 58; 1600–1800 pts double with bath, 1100–1300 pts without).

If you really want to stay in Gibraltar, consider the **Montarik Hotel**, on Main Street, Tel: 77 065, a good value by Gibraltar standards (£20–21 for a double with shower or bath, breakfast included). The **Rock Hotel**, a quality resort hotel of long standing, is up on the heights – about halfway up, under the cable car and near Gibraltar's casino. There's a pool, beautifully landscaped gardens and rooms with sea view and balconies (£45 for a double with balcony, £40 without; located on Europe Road, Tel: 73 000). If you need a beach the other resort hotel is the very modern **Caleta Palace** on Catalan Bay, Tel: 76 501 (£37–41 for a double, depending on the view). There is one opportunity for a cheap room in Gibraltar, the **Toc H Hostal** on Line Wall Rd near the harbour, Tel: 73 431, where they'll put you up for £1.90 per person. Understandably, they are usually full.

EATING OUT

This isn't such a problem in Gibraltar. Main Street is fairly lined with pubs, fish shops, and cafes, and there are plenty of little places around Catalan Bay and the other beaches. **Old Vic**'s on Main Street and the **Keystone Cafe** on Convent Lane are two popular, informal British-style joints. The **Wesley House**, at 299 Main Street is run by the Methodist Church, offering Methodist cuisine and the lack of atmosphere that reminds you of home (really, it's a good inexpensive restaurant, with a big menu and an average price of about £3). For anything fancier, stay in La Linea, where there are some good seafood restaurants along the Paseo Maritimo on the eastern shore, **La Marina** stands out; you can get an introduction there to one of the favourites of Spain's southern coasts; grilled sardines on a spit (1200–1600 pts).

Costa del Sol

At first glance, it doesn't seem the speculators and developers could have picked a more unlikely place to conjure up the Mediterranean's biggest holiday playground. The stretch of coast between Gibraltar and Málaga is devoid of beautiful or even attractive scenery, and its long beaches come in a uniformly dismal shade of grey. Spain's low prices are one explanation, and the greatest number of guaranteed sunny days in Europe another. The reason it happened here, though, is breathtakingly simple – cheap land. 40 years ago, all this coast had was fantastically poor fishing-villages and malaria, and it was one of the forgotten backwaters of Spain.

After a few decades of holiday intensity, though, this unlikely strip, all concrete and garish signboards, is beginning to develop a personality of its own. Any hype you hear or read about the Costa, anything that employs flowery prose and superlatives is utter nonsense; on the other hand, it has become almost fashionable to mock the Costa for its brash, *turismo* exuberance, and that is uncalled for. The Costa does attract people who don't expect much from their holiday (or retirement) except good-weather, like-minded companions, and places to play. Their presence, in such large numbers and from so many nations, has created a unique international community of everyday folks. It's easy to forget you're in Spain, but if you ever get homesick you can always take a break from Andalucía and have a noisy good time by the beach.

GETTING AROUND

The Portillo bus company has the franchise for this stretch of coast; and with the growth of tourism their service has become almost like a city bus-line, stopping every few hundred yards in the developed areas between Algeciras and Málaga. There's never too long a wait in either direction. San Pedro is where the buses branch off for Ronda, an easy destination from any town on the coast. You can also go directly to Sevilla or Madrid at least once daily from the bus station in Marbella.

Estepona and San Pedro

The first of the resort towns east of Gibraltar is also the quietest; the big developers haven't quite reached here yet; its biggest attraction is a nudist beach. If you're staying here, a worthwhile side-trip would be **Caceres**, 20 km (12.5 miles) north-west, up in the Sierra Bermeja, a typical white Andalucian village perched on a steep hill under the ruins of its castle. Nearby, outside the village of Manilva, there are ruins of a **Roman**

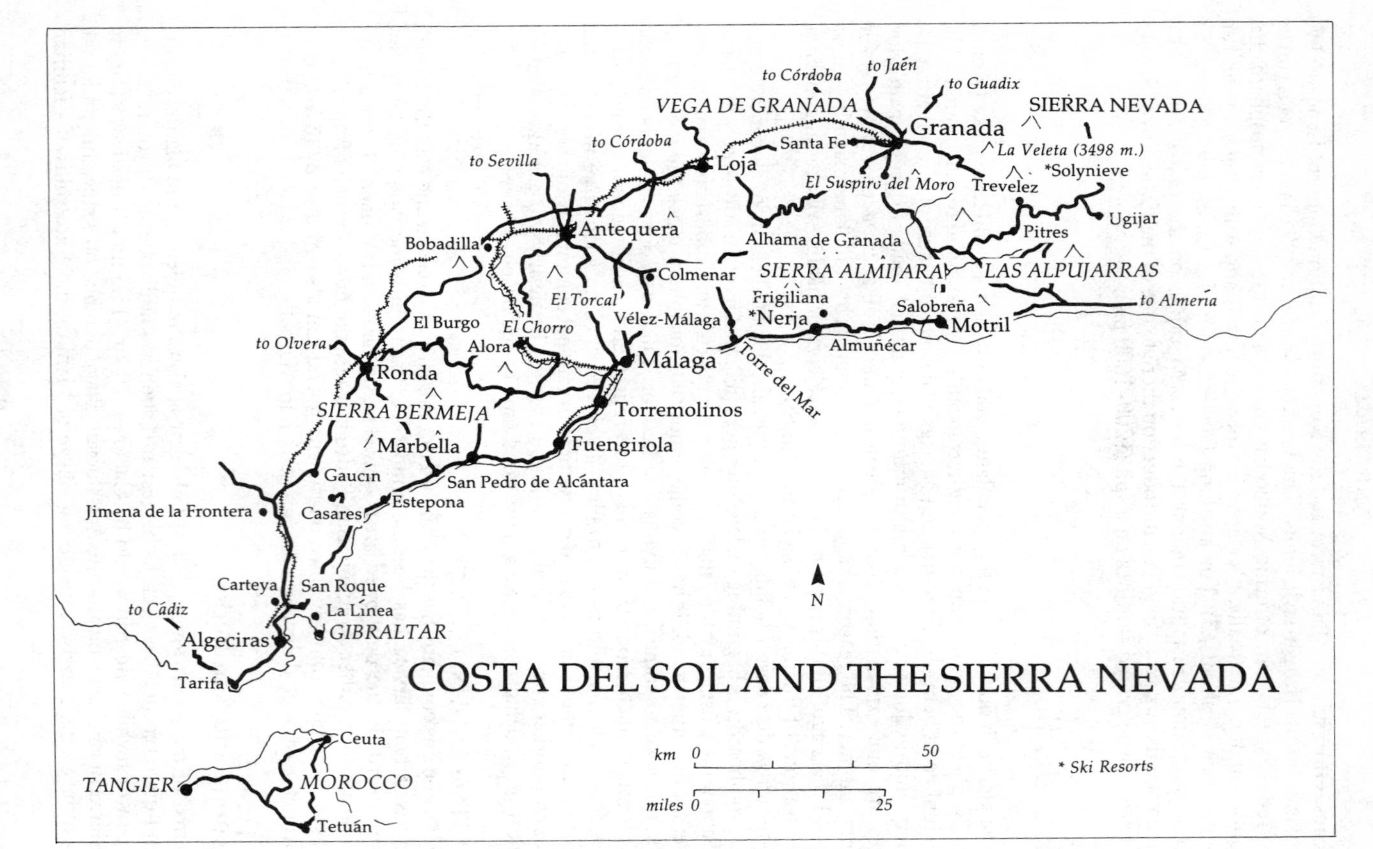
to Córdoba
to Jaén
to Guadix
VEGA DE GRANADA
SIERRA NEVADA
Granada
Santa Fe
La Veleta (3498 m.)
to Córdoba
Loja
to Sevilla
El Suspiro del Moro
Trevelez
*Solynieve
Ugijar
Antequera
Alhama de Granada
Pitres
Bobadilla
Colmenar
SIERRA ALMIJARA
LAS ALPUJARRAS
El Torcal
Frigiliana
Salobreña
to Almeria
El Burgo
El Chorro
Vélez-Málaga
*Nerja
Motril
to Olvera
Alora
Almuñécar
Málaga
Ronda
Torre del Mar
SIERRA BERMEJA
Torremolinos
Marbella
Fuengirola
Gaucin
San Pedro de Alcántara
Estepona
Jimena de la Frontera
Casares
N
Carteya
San Roque
to Cádiz
La Linea
Algeciras
GIBRALTAR
Tarifa
COSTA DEL SOL AND THE SIERRA NEVADA
Ceuta
km 0 50
* Ski Resorts
TANGIER
MOROCCO
miles 0 25
Tetuán

spa. The old spring still pours out strange, sulphurous water, and the locals drop in to bathe for what ails them.

San Pedro de Alcántara down the coast, is a little fancier, and probably the most attractive resort on the Costa del Sol – its developers get credit for learning at least a little from past mistakes. Most of the town is a good walk from the beaches. From here the only good road through the mountains will take you to Ronda (see page 451) and its surrounding villages – the best excursion you can make from the Costa.

Marbella

This is the poshest and most expensive resort in Spain. When you arrive, you'll find yourself asking why; Marbella has no visible attraction whatsoever. Its recently trendy old village, with a square full of orange trees, has been swallowed up by look-alike developments, nothing more than a high-rise suburb by the sea. The answer is simple: rich people come here because other rich people do. It's just a fashion, and in such an unpromising spot it can't last. Meanwhile, the prices are a joke, and Marbella is the last place in the world to spend your time. The top crust have already largely forsaken it for **Puerto Banus**, a new development 6 km (3.8 miles) to the west with a yacht harbour full of real dreadnoughts.

TOURIST INFORMATION

Estepona: Paseo Maritimo, Tel: 88 09 13
Marbella: C. Miguel Cano 1, Tel: 77 14 42.

WHERE TO STAY

In Estepona, there are more real bargains to be found than elsewhere on the coast. For a modicum of concrete splendour near the beach, the **Buenavista****, is the best bet (on the Pso Maritimo, Tel: 80 01 37, 2500–3000 pts doubles). Estepona isn't a place to spend money, though; there are plenty of inexpensive hostels (like **El Pilar***, Pl. José Antonio 22, Tel: 80 00 18, 1500–1700 pts a double, in a pretty setting) both in the town and on the beach.

San Pedro doesn't yet have a wide choice. **El Pueblo Andaluz** is one of the outstanding bargains on the coast, a pretty place near the beach built around an old Andalucían home with a pool, playground, restaurant and garden (on the coastal highway Tel: 81 16 42, 3800 pts for a double). There are some *hostales* in the town, all about 2000 pts for a double. Marbella is another place not to spend money; you can drop 12,000 pts here and get little to show for it. Surprisingly, there is a wide selection of *hostales* in the 2000 pts range, most of them in the old town like the pleasant **Hotel Paco**** (C. Peral 16, Tel: 77 12 00, doubles 1900–2100 pts with bath) and a dozen other places in the 1100–1500 pts range around C. Peral, C. San Francisco and other nearby streets in the old town. If you do want to splurge here, the best buys among the luxury hotels will be found on the less-crowded beaches outside the town, like **Las Chapas*****, a nearly self-sufficient holiday complex with opportunities for tennis, golf and water sports – it's right on the beach (on the coastal highway, 8 km (5 miles) to the east, Tel: 83 13 75; 5404–5780 pts for a double). Don't count on finding a room at any price during the season; package tours have taken over just as in the resorts to the east, and most places are booked pretty solid.

EATING OUT

Dining in Marbella can also empty your pockets quickly enough. Some of the more reasonable quality places can also be found near Las Chapas beach. **Los Papagayos** serves international cuisine (duck à l'orange is very good) and seafood (full-course dinner 2000–2500 pts). In town, on the Pl. de los Naranjos, the **Creperia Marbella** offers crepes with nearly anything inside and a wide choice of other dishes (1300–2000 pts). Many less expensive places, mostly specializing in seafood, can be found in the same area around C. Aduar as the cheaper *hostals*. If you really want to treat yourself to the best the Costa can offer, **La Hacienda** in Las Chapas offers unforgettable views in the lovely setting, delicious combinations of French cuisine and fresh Andalucian ingredients, and one of the longest wine lists in Spain. A truly elegant night out – from 4000 pts and up.

In Estepona, the best bet when you're tired of seafood is to try the Moroccan couscous at the **Restaurant del Paseo** on the coastal highway (1000–1500 pts).

Fuengirola

30 years ago, Fuengirola was a typical whitewashed, Spanish fishing-village. It's still white, but hardly typical, and even less Spanish. With the miles of speculative *urbanizacíones* that surround it, it would be easy to be unkind to Fuengirola except that everyone there seems to be having such a good time. The town, and its adjacent community of **Los Boliches** may be the only place in Spain where you'll see a sign in a shop-window reading *'Se habla Español'*; this laid-back international community appreciates a good joke. The shops of the old village have been transformed into pubs, English bookshops, travel agencies and Swiss–Chinese–Belgian–Italian–Moroccan, and even Spanish restaurants, but there's something genuine in the small-town atmosphere of this casual European village, where most of the permanent residents seem to know each other already.

GETTING AROUND

Besides the Portillo buses that ply the coastal highway towards Málaga and Marbella, there's also a suburban railway regularly connecting Fuengirola and Málaga. It stops at most points in between, and it's the best way to get in and out of Málaga airport.

WHAT TO SEE

Fuengirola's weekly event is the Tuesday outdoor **market**, the best place to observe this curious community. Unlike other resorts on the Costa, there are some things to see – the Moorish **Sohail Castle** above town, a bullring, even the brand new façade of a **Roman temple**. In Roman times there were important marble quarries in the mountains here, and recently divers discovered a wreck off the coast with these stones, bound for somewhere else; they've been salvaged and assembled on a spot near the beach. Visitors from Fuengirola have totally overwhelmed the village of **Mijas**, 3 km (1.9 miles) up in the hills above town. It's still a pretty place with a promenade offering a view out to sea, lots of pine woods and 'officially licensed burro taxis' to take you around.

Torremolinos

About Torremolinos, one of the oldest and biggest resort towns on the Costa, all sources agree; it is a ghastly, hyperactive, unsightly holiday inferno. In other words, it has character. Torremolinos isn't at all interested in our opinion, though, or yours either; it's doing quite well with its endless screaming blocks of bars, shopping centres and concrete hotels. For those who want to spend their holiday in the fast lane, in a raucous, international, entirely synthetic environment, this is the place.

Part of Torremolinos' character arises from its status as capital of what the newspapers like to call the 'Costa del Crime'. Literally thousands of clever bank-heisters, cons and embezzlers, mostly from Britain, add to the local colour, courtesy of Spain's traditional unwillingness to conclude extradition treaties with other nations. At the time of writing, an agreement with Britain has finally been reached, and the crooks will have to move along when their visas run out. There will still be plenty of other types left – smooth operators of uncertain nationality, religious cult agents, hedonists of all shapes and sizes, and other European detritus. They're only the surface though, the most noticeable segment of an enormous permanent and transient population, made up of gawking sun-seekers from every corner of Europe. The welcome signs on the outskirts of town proclaim 'City of Tourists'.

Torremolinos offers the greatest range of choices for hotels, dining and carousing of any resort on the Costa; the interesting part is **Carihela**, the old fishing-village on the edge of the new town that has been transformed into the sharpest quarter for restaurants and night spots.

TOURIST INFORMATION

Fuengirola: Ayuntamiento, town square, Tel: 47 61 66.
Torremolinos: C. Guetaria Tel: 38 15 78.

WHERE TO STAY

You really should come on a package tour if you find these places to your taste. That's what Fuengirola and Torremolinos are for, and you would get a better deal. If you're just passing though and want to rest in holiday anonymity by the beach, there are some possibilities.

It's always monumentally difficult to tell one new holiday hotel from the next, but two places do stand out as the best deals in Fuengirola: the **Florida**** in town on the Pso. Maritimo (Tel: 47 61 00; 3350–4250 pts, for a double), pool and gardens, though not luxurious it's still a comfortable enough place, and the **Cendrillon****, just outside town on the coastal highway, much the same as the Florida, only with tennis courts for 2000–3550 pts a double. Both are on the beach and popular with families. There are also plenty of inexpensive hostels around the centre of Fuengirola, and especially in its suburb of Los Boliches on the eastern end.

At Torremolinos and its neighbouring stretch of tourist sprawl at Benalmadena Costa, the possibilities are endless, though these, too, will probably be packed with package tours. They come in all price ranges, from about 9000 pts to rock bottom *hostals*. There are several golf hotels on the Costa, but the one that stands out is the **Parador del Golf****** on the road to Málaga, Tel: 38 12 55, with tennis, a pool, and right on the beach, definitely attracting an active crowd to some of the best rooms in Torremolinos. The price is average for a parador, 6500–8500 pts. One of the finest of the beach hotels (though it's hard to tell from the outside) is the **Don Pablo****** in the centre of the action, on the Pso. Maritimo, Tel: 38 38 88, 5300–7600 pts: nice beds, fancy salons, even a billiards room. Some of the good bargains can be found out towards Carihuela, along Avda Carlota Alexandre. The **Carihuela Palace-Park** offers many of the amenities of the larger hotels for a nicer price, 3000–4500 pts. One of its advantages is that it doesn't have a restaurant, in a town where tourists are often dragooned into full pension during the busy season (Avda Alexandre 27, Tel: 38 02 00). The **Miami**** is special, built around an old mansion and beautifully furnished (C. Aladino in Carihuela, Tel: 38 52 55, doubles 2475–3200 pts; you'll need to book). Carihuela is also the place to look for inexpensive accommodation, such as the spartan but acceptable **Hostal Pedro*** C. Bulto 1, Tel: 38 05 36, 1000 pts a double.

EATING OUT

Dining in Fuengirola is an experience; you can choose from any sort of restaurant from Indonesian to Belgian without going broke. One of the most exotic possibilities, **La Brava** is also one of the best, with Persian specialities and steaks in an outdoor patio (Avda Ramoń y Cajal, 2500 pts). The **Acropolis** is a very popular Greek restaurant at C. Salvador Rueda 73 in Los Boliches; try the stuffed chicken breast (2200 pts). If you've ever tried an Indonesian *rijstafel* in the Netherlands, you'll be glad to know there are plenty of such places on the Costa; the Dutch wouldn't live without it. One good one is **Djakarta**, also in Los Boliches at Trinidad 4 (2300 pts).

Dining in Torremolinos is much like Fuengirola – a choice of whatever you could possibly imagine. For fine Moroccan cuisine and charmingly garish decor, try the **Restaurant Marrakesh** (Ctra. de Benalmadena 1, in Torremolinos, 1500–2100 pts for a big full-course dinner, or if you've never had the Vietnamese variations on Chinese cuisine so popular in France, try **Vietnam del Sur** (at Playana, 'bloque 9' 800–1200 pts). The best seafood restaurants are in Carihuela, and one is very good indeed, the **Casa Guaquin** (C. Carmen 37, 900–1300 pts, a real bargain) where you can try such specialities of the Costa as 'fish baked in salt'. It's better than it sounds. Torremolinos' outstanding bargain is probably the all-you-can-eat at **Annabelle's**, on the Paisaje Pizarro, for almost 600 pts.

ACTIVITIES ON THE COSTA DEL SOL

Of course, part of the tourist industry is to find something for all those folks to do when they're fully browned from the beach. A quick look through the local publications (*Lookout*, a slick monthly magazine for the large British population of the Costa, a weekly English edition of Málaga's newspaper *Sur*, and various local entertainment guides) will show you all sorts of chances.

There are *bullrings* in Marbella, Fuengirola, Estepona, Mijas (a square one!) and Benalmadena Costa, though *corridas* are infrequent and the really serious action occurs in the big ring in Málaga; occasionally interesting **concerts** at the Casa de Cultura and

Salón Varieties in Fuengirola and the Mijas Arts Centre, among others; art exhibits and guitar and dance courses; and plenty of movies in English at the Cine Puerto Banus and the Cine Sohail, in Fuengirola.

For sports, there are no fewer than 14 golf courses on the Costa (green fees a little dear, 3000 pts and up); tennis at many of the hotels, most open to the public, even snooker clubs (in Fuengirola). Of course all the water sports are popular; you can always make arrangements for equipment or instruction through your hotel. There are **casinos** at Benalmadena Costa (the Torrequebrada, on the coastal highway) and quite a bit higher stakes, at Puerto Banus (the Casino de Marbella, at Torre del Duque).

Go ahead, and take the kids; there's a Disneyland-style amusement park at Benalmadena called **Tivoli World** with a Wild West, Chinese pagodas, Cinerama (that's right, Cinerama) and flamenco can-can shows. Also a small **Zoo** in Fuengirola, the Super Bonanza cruise boats for leisurely excursions between Torremolinos and Puerto Bonus, and horseback riding from the El Castillo Salvador stables outside Fuengirola (1000 pts per hour). For something out of the ordinary, get in touch with the Viajes CHAT travel agency in Torremolinos (Tel: 38 71 86) and they'll make arrangements for a hot-air-balloon ride over the Costa, champagne included.

Málaga

The Costa del Sol would not have been possible without the presence of this city, its resources and its airport. Most of the Costa's visitors pass through here on their way to the beaches, but few bother to stop. There's little reason to; Málaga can be challenged only by Valladolid for the honour of being the most hideous and sleazy of Spanish cities. Valladolid, though, is prosperous; Málaga's claims to fame are Spain's highest unemployment and crime rates.

If you prefer, you can visit the city without feeling too oppressed. In truth there are two Málagas: the grand boulevard (called the **Alameda** on its west end, **Paseo del Parque** to the east) which is really quite beautiful, and the rest of town, which is a desolation.

GETTING AROUND

As the main port of entry to the Costa del Sol and southern Adalucía, you'll probably pass through Málaga either coming or going.

By Air

Málaga's often frenetic airport connects the city to Madrid, Valencia, Almería, Sevilla, Melilla and Tangier, besides being the charter-flight gateway to the Costa. The easiest way to get into the city, or to Torremolinos or Fuengirola, is the suburban railway line (separate stops at the airport for the regular and charter terminals).

By Train

There's a daily *talgo* to Valencia and Barcelona, and at least four trains to Madrid. Direct connections also to Sevilla and Córdoba; for all other destinations in Andalucía you'll have to make a change at that inescapable Bobadilla Junction. The station is on C. Cuarteles (city office C. Strachen 2, Tel: 21 31 22 for information).

By Bus

There's no central station. **Portillo** buses for the Costa, Sevilla, Ronda and Algeciras, leave from C. Córdoba 7 off the Alameda (Tel: 22 73 00: Costa buses also stop at the Málaga RENFE station). **Bacoma** buses to Alora and Ronda from the RENFE station (Tel: 32 12 62). **Los Amarillos** for Antequera, Alameda 31 (Tel: 21 35 29).

Alsina Graells for Granada and Nerja, from C. Plaza de Toros Vieja 2, between the RENFE station and the Guadalmedina (Tel: 31 04 00) and also Alsina Graells for Almería, Alicante and Barcelona, departing from Plaza Europa (same telephone number).

By Boat

There are daily ferries to Melilla (a 7½-hour trip) and also one a week to Genoa, Italy via Almería, and another to the Canaries via Cádiz (both generally leave on Fridays).

WHAT TO SEE

Just off the Paseo del Parque, the steps lead up to the Moorish **Alcazaba**. Under the Moors, Málaga was the most important port of Al-Andalus, and from contemporary references it seems to have also been one of its most beautiful cities. King Ferdinand thoroughly ruined it in the conquest of 1487, and after the expulsion of the Moors in 1568, little remained of its ancient distinction. Little enough remains of the Alcazaba (fortress) except a few Moorish gates, but the site has been restored to a lovely series of terraced gardens with an **Archaeological Museum** at the top, containing relics from the Phoenician necropolis found on the site, and lists of Moorish architectural decoration salvaged from the ruins. The top of the Alcazaba also affords fine views over Málaga: it looks better from up here. There is a half-ruined **Roman theatre**, recently excavated on the lower slopes of the hill, and from the Alcazaba you may climb a little more to the **Gibralfaro**, the ruined Moorish castle that dominates the city (open summer 11 am–2 pm and 5–8 pm; winter 10 am–1 pm and 4–7 pm, Sunday 10 am–2 pm).

Back on the Paseo, note the chunky art nouveau **Ayuntamiento**, one of the more unusual buildings in Málaga. On the opposite side of the Alcazaba, on Calle Alcazabilla, is Málaga's **Museo de Belles Artes**, in a restored 16th-century palace (open summer 10 am–1.30 pm and 5–8 pm; winter 10 am–1 pm, 4–7 pm, closed Monday). It's worth a look for some good medieval polychrome icons, two strange paintings by Luis de Morales (c. 1580) and a small collection of Picassos on the first floor. Picasso was a native of Málaga, though once he left it at the age of 14, he never returned. Much of the museum is given over to the works of other late 19th-century Malagueño painters who make up in eccentricity for what they lack in genius; one of them, Muñoz Degrain, was Picasso's first teacher. Málaga's **cathedral** is a few blocks away on Calle Molina Lario. It's an ugly, unfinished 16th-century work, immense and mouldering; the only interesting feature is the faded, gaudy façade of the **Sacristy**, left over from an earlier Isabelline Gothic church that once stood here.

Melilla

Nobody ever goes to Melilla, the more obscure of Spain's two remaining *presidios* on the North African coast. It's a long boat ride from Málaga, or a slightly shorter one from

Almería, and onward destinations are severely limited. Morocco's big towns are far away, though you may consider Melilla as a quieter, less exasperating way to slip into Morocco than Tangier or Tetuan with their hustlers and aggravations. The town itself is prettier than Ceuta, hiding behind stern-looking fortifications over the water's edge, and a 1.6 km (1 mile) long beach spreads awkwardly from the walls. Melilla has had its problems lately; the Spanish papers regularly report the local police bullying the Moroccan minority during protests over discrimination and citizenship.

TOURIST INFORMATION

Málaga: C. Larios 5, just north of the Alameda (Tel: 21 34 45) and also at the airport (Tel: 31 20 44).
Melilla: C. General Aizpura (Tel: 68 42 04).

WHERE TO STAY AND EAT

Málaga looks deceptively good from the **Parador de Gibralfaro*****, up in the old Moorish castle over the city; the small hotel offers few luxuries (there are only 12 rooms), but the quality and the view make it a better bet than the more expensive modern hotels around the port (Tel: 22 19 02, doubles 5500–7500 pts).

Málaga is no resort, but if you're forced to stay overnight there are some acceptable middle-range and inexpensive places: the **Avenida**** at Alameda 5, Tel: 21 77 29, 2000–2500 pts double with bath). The **Castilla*** (1800 pts a double with bath; Tel: 22 86 37) and the **Guerrero*** (same price, Tel: 21 86 35) are well-run establishments in the same building at C. Cordoba 5, south of the Alameda. Any place on or around the Alameda will be decent, but avoid the cheap dives around the train station.

In Melilla, the **Anfora**** is a reliable, unremarkable hotel (C. Vallesca 8, Tel: 68 33 40, 3230–3720 pts) and there are quite a few modest *hostales* scattered all over.

EATING OUT

For a city that once had a reputation for seafood, Málaga today has few if any outstanding restaurants. There are plenty of fish places along the Paseo Maritimo on the shore east of the Alcazaba. **El Cabra** is a popular one (1400–2100 pts; C. Copa 21) but **El Lirio** next door is a little better (same average prices, C. Copa 15; good *sopa de pescados*). In the centre of town on C. Bolsa, **Restaurant Tiburon** has better-than-average combination plates for 600 pts.

East of Málaga

For some reason the tourist industry has neglected the areas east of the city. There are a few resorts strung out along the coastal highway, notably **Torre del Mar**, but they are all grim-looking places, little bits of Málaga that escaped to the beach. From Torre del Mar you can make a short detour inland to **Velez Málaga**, a pretty town on the edge of the mountains under a crumbling Moorish castle. Nearby are some scanty remains of a Greek-Phoenician settlement called Manaihe.

GETTING AROUND
The Alsina Graells buses from Málaga or Motril serve Nerja, Almuñecar and Salobreña (but the long-distance buses along the coast do not usually stop at these towns).

Nerja

Approaching this town, the scenery becomes impressive as the mountains grow closer to the sea. Nerja itself is pleasant and quiet for a Costa resort; tourism has made advances without yet ruining it. Its attractions are the **Balcon de Europa**, a promenade with a fountain overlooking the sea, and a series of secluded beaches under the cliffs – the best are a good walk away on either side of the town. A few kilometres east, the **Cueva de Nerja** is one of Spain's fabled grottos, with needle-thin stalactites – one, they claim, is the longest in the world – full of Gaudiesque formations. The caves were discovered only in 1959, just in time for the tourist boom, and they have been fitted out with lights and music, with photographers lurking in the shadow who'll try to sell you a picture of yourself when you leave. The caves were popular with Cro-Magnon man, and there are some paleolithic artworks (not open to visitors at this time). Occasionally, this perfect setting is used for ballet and concerts.

Almuñecar and Salobreña

The coastal road east of Nerja, bobbing in and out of the hills and cliffs is the best part of the Costa; the next resort however, **Almuñecar** is better left alone, a nest of dreary high-rises around a beleaguered village that has little of the character or quality of Nerja. **Salobreña** is much better, though it may not stay that way long. The village's dramatic setting, slung down a steep, lone peak overlooking the sea, is the most stunning of any on the coast, and helps to insulate it just a little from the tourist industry. The beaches, just starting to become built up, are about 2 km (1.3 miles) away.

From here, the next town is **Motril**, a large settlement set back from the sea with little to attract visitors. There isn't much Costa left further east, and the only real choice for a destination is the spectacular mountain road through the Sierra Nevada towards Granada.

TOURIST INFORMATION
Nerja: Puerto de Mar 1, Tel: 52 15 37.

WHERE TO STAY
Nerja has two fine hotels: the **Parador Nacional de Nerja****** (just outside town at El Tablazo; Tel: 52 00 50, 6500–8500 pts double) and the **Balcón de Europa***** (Pl. Balcón de Europa, Tel: 52 08 00, 3700–5350 pts. doubles) the latter is probably the better bet, though not quite as luxurious as the *parador*; the beautiful location on the 'balcony of Europe' in the town centre and the reasonable rates make the difference. Both hotels have lifts down to the beaches under Nerja's cliffs. Another good bargain on the beach is the **Portofino*** (Puerta del Mar 2, Tel: 52 01 50, 3000 pts a double with bath). There are a few more inexpensive places about town, notably the **Florida*** (C. San Miguel 35, Tel: 52 07 43; 1800 pts a double with bath, 1500 pts without) but Nerja

is notoriously tight during the high season. You have have serious trouble finding a place without a reservation.

In Salobreña, you have a choice between the **Salobreña*****, outside the town on the coastal highway (Tel: 61 02 61, 3540–3900 pts doubles, both beach and pool and a garden) and a number of *hostales* both on the beach and in the alleys.

EATING OUT

A popular restaurant in Nerja is the **Rey Alfonso** – nothing special about the cuisine but the view is superb, built over the cliffs directly under the Balcón de Europa (1600–2200 pts). For something different, at about the same prices, try the good German cuisine and innovative surprises (like zucchini flowers stuffed with ham) at **Udo Heimer's**, Pueblo Andaluz 27.

East of Motril to Almería

The coastal road cuts between the sea and plastic, in this case not coastal development, but agricultural plastic covering a good percentage of Europe's winter vegetables. At **Adra** you enter the province of Almería, the sunniest, driest and hottest little corner of all Europe. What they call winter here lasts from the end of November to March; scores of films (most famously *Lawrence of Arabia*) have been shot here, taking advantage of the light and the natural African/Western cowboy sets. Until the 1970s the **Costa de Almería**, difficult of access and bereft of utilities and water, was a package tourism virgin, charter flights now drop in from northern Europe, hotels are sprouting up here and there – but compared to what's come before, it's pleasantly underwhelming.

Adra was an ancient Phoenician town, and it was the last spot of Spain surrendered by the Moors, at the moment Boabdil sailed from here to Africa. Though it's still basically a fishing-agricultural village, it has spawned **Almerimar**, a large new development of mostly villas and flats, with a new marina and one of Spain's best new golf courses. From here you can dip into the eastern Alpujarras to the pretty 'city' of **Berja**, with its palatial country homes or **Canjáyar**, origin of most of northern Europe's Christmas grapes. The resorts at **Roquetas de Mar** (more golfing) and **Aguadulce** (oldest and biggest on the Almería coast) are easily reached from Almería capital by bus.

GETTING AROUND

Almería's airport is 8 km (5 miles) from the city on the road to Níjar, Tel: 22 19 54. Besides charters from London, Iberia has regular connections with Madrid, Barcelona and Melilla – its offices are at Pso. de Almería 42, Tel: 23 84 11. Transmediterránea runs car ferries from Almería to Melilla on the North African coast three days a week at 2 pm every Tuesday, Thursday, and Saturday; the voyage takes 6½ hours. Ticket office is at Parque Nicolás Salmerón 28, Tel: 23 67 56. Almería's RENFE station is a block from the bus station, on Ctra. Ronda, easy walking distance from the centre, Tel: 25 11 35 – there's an office as well at C. Alcalde Muños 1, Tel: 23 12 07. There are daily trains and *talgos* to Madrid, Barcelona and Valencia; you can also go to Granada twice a day, and daily at 11 pm take an all-night journey across Andalucía, arriving at

Córdoba at 7 am, or Sevilla at 8.30 am. The bus station, in the new part of town on the Pl. Barcelona, Tel: 22 10 11, has a daily service to the major cities of the Levante up to Barcelona; also to Madrid, Granada, Sevilla, Cádiz, Málaga and Cartagena. There are seven buses daily to Adra, hourly connections to Aguadulce and Roquetas, five to Berja, two each to Cabo de Gata, Mojacár, Nijár and Tabernas.

Almería

Almería has been a genial, dusty little port since its founding by the Phoenicians, though in the 11th century, dominating Al Andalus for a few decades after the fall of the Caliphate, it rivalled Córdoba in splendour. The upper city, with its narrow streets, tiny pastel houses and whitewashed cave dwellings hugging the looming walls of the **Alcazaba**, has retained a fine Moorish feel to this day. Built by the Caliph Abderrahman II in the 10th century, the Alcazaba is the most powerful Moorish fortress in Spain, though its great curtain-walls and towers defend mostly market- and flower-gardens – nothing remains of the once splendid palace. It has recently been restored (open 10 am – 2 pm and 4–9 pm). Behind the fortress, by the wall of Jayrán, you can visit the **Centre of Rescue of Animals of the Sahara**: before going up, get permission from the centre's headquarters near the tourist office – they'll give you a note letting you wander through the cages and enclosures of a wide variety of endangered animals and bird species brought up from the Sahara for research and breeding purposes, in an environment that must feel just like home.

Almería's **cathedral**, begun in 1524, was seemingly built for defence with its four mighty towers; prettier, and boasting a fine carving of St James Matamoros and a minaret-like tower, is **Santiago El Viejo**, just off the Puerta Purchena, near the top of the Paseo de Almería. It's a bit unusual to find a pilgrimage-style church, complete with cockleshells, so far off the main routes, but even more incongruous in the very heart of this hot town of swaying palms there's a huge Basque-style Alpine chalet.

East of Almería

The **Sierra Alhamilla** – one of the driest, most rugged and lunar of Spanish sierras – occupies this south-eastern most corner of Spain. The coastal road struggles out to the **Cabo de Gata**, with a pretty beach, solitary lighthouse and crystal-clear waters, popular with divers. Inland, the white village of **Níjar** is a charming oasis in an arid setting where potters actively carry on a craft introduced by the Phoenicians. Lorca's play *Blood Wedding* was based on incidents that occurred here around the turn of the century.

The main road east winds through the northern flanks of the sierra, passing through a lush huerta of country estates before rising into a weirdly beautiful but perfectly desolate region, where even in the springtime green is a foreign colour. Here in **Tabernas** are a couple of spaghetti western sets: at **Mini Hollywood** the town built by Sergio Leone for such classics as Clint Eastwood's first vehicle, *A Fistful of Dollars*, cowboy shoot'em ups and bank robberies are staged for the benefit of visitors. **Sorbas**, with its hanging houses, is most impressively seen from the highway; between the two, the government has decided to exploit the province's greatest natural resources – sunlight – with the country's largest solar energy installation.

Mojacár

Isolated amidst the rugged mountains, on a hill 2 km (1.3 miles) from the beach, trendy Mojacár has often been compared to a pile of sugar cubes. No town in Spain wears such a Moorish face – its little, flat-roofed, white houses stacked almost on top of one another. Before the equally white hotels were added to the scene a couple of decades ago, the women covered their faces with their veils when passing a stranger; a plaque by the fountain tells how the townspeople valiantly defended themselves against the army of the Catholic Kings. Most unusually, the old women in the village would paint a symbol known as the *indalo* (a stick figure with outstretched arms, holding up an arc) on their doors as a charm against the evil eye and thunderbolts. No one knows how long they've been doing it, though in the nearby caves of Vélez-Blanco, Neolithic drawings of *indalos* dating from 3000 BC have led anthropologists to the conclusion that this is one of the few, if only, cases anywhere of a prehistoric symbol handed down in one place for thousands of years.

TOURIST INFORMATION

Almería: C. Hermanos Machado 4, in the big ministries building; Tel: 23 47 05. Post office: Pl. de Ecuador.

WHERE TO STAY

When on location in Almería, Hollywood denizens have traditionally checked into the **Gran Hotel Almería******, in town at Avda. Reina Regente 8, Tel: 23 80 11 – here and there you can still see mementoes of the hotel's heyday. Rooms are plush and air-conditioned, and among the available diversions are a pool and bingo hall; breakfast only (doubles 6300–6900 pts). On the beach similar smart lodgings are available at **La Parra******, Bahia del Palmer, Tel: 34 05 04, located in a lovely setting, and offering golf, tennis, sauna, pool and children's facilities – and an indoor pool as well on those rare days when the Almerían sun fails to shine (open all year; doubles 7070 pts). Another comfortable and air-conditioned choice in town is the **Torreluz****, Pl. de Flores 6, Tel: 23 47 99 with doubles for 3095–3715 pts. There are a number of inexpensive hostels: the **Maribel*** is in easy walking distance of the bus and train stations on Avda. Lorca 115, Tel: 23 51 73, offering simple but adequate doubles for 1500–1700 pts with bath, or 1400–1550 pts without.

In Adra you can spend an economy beach holiday at the **Delfin***, Natalio Rivas 106, Tel: 40 00 50, with doubles with bath for 1900–2100 pts, or splurge and golf nearby at the **Golf Hotel Almerimar******, Tel: 48 09 50, a plush 38-room refuge, with tennis courts, pool, recreational activities in an attractive setting (open all year, doubles 6000–8000 pts). If you'd prefer peace and quiet to comfort and facilities, try the little **Isleta del Moro***, a telephone-less hostel on a quiet beach near Nijár, with a simple restaurant and rooms with bath for 1400 pts; open all year.

In Mojacár there's the modern beach-side **Parador Reyes Católicos******, Tel: 47 82 50, with a pool and air-conditioning; doubles 5500–7500 pts. In the village there are a couple of new, trendy hotels at lovely Mirador de la Puntica; **El Moresco***** has the advantage of being open all year, and indoor, outdoor and children's swimming pools (4995–5927 pts). There's little in the budget category; you'll spend less at **El Puntazo** on the beach (Tel: 47 82 29), where a nondescript double will set you back 1840–2070 pts with bath (open all year).

EATING OUT

The locals will all tell you the best restaurant in Almería is the **Anfora**, G. Garbín 25 (closed Sundays), specializing in the freshest of local ingredients – vegetables and seafood (1600 pts). This is off the Pl. S. Sebastian, near the Puerta de Purchena and another good seafood restaurant, **Imperial** (1700 pts). On the seafront, facing the gardens are a couple of inexpensive choices, **La Cartuja** and the **Canoe**, the latter with a 550 pts set menu.

In Mojacár seafood and couscous on Fridays are served at **Mamabel's** on Embajadores – open only in the evening (1500 pts); less expensive and overlooking the sea, **Mediterráneo** at Cueva del Lobo has more seafood for 800–1000 pts.

Between the Guadalquivir and the Coast: the Andalucian Interior

For some, this is the best of Andalucía. It doesn't have beaches, and it doesn't have famous buildings or museums. Tourists are in short supply too – mostly young Germans and British with backpacks, along with day-trippers from the Costa and a few examples of that beloved but endangered species, the serious British traveller, with nose in a Latin chronicle or a bird-watcher's guide. What this region does have is a chain of peaceful white villages, draped along hillsides under their castles, their steep streets lined with pots of geraniums. Some are prosperous, some quite poor; some have a reputation for friendliness, others can seem silent introverts. None of them are really different from the others – except to their natives, of course – and they all share some of southern Spain's most delightful scenery. It is a region of rolling hills broken by patches of grey mountains, well-tended lands devoted to the traditional Mediterranean staples of wheat, vines, and olives, coloured in the spring by orange and almond blossom in the lower areas. The big town of Ronda, and the curiosities around Antequera are the big attractions, but if you're like many of the travellers who come here you won't worry too much about destinations, but lazily pick your way from one pretty village to the next, get to know the land and its people and look for the little surprises that make the trip worthwhile.

GETTING AROUND

In this region, you'll be depending on buses. Arcos de la Frontera has regular connections to Jerez, Cádiz and Ronda; less frequently to Sevilla. From Ronda you can go directly to Jerez, Cádiz, Málaga, and most of the towns along the Costa del Sol; there are also four daily buses to and from Sevilla. Arcos and Ronda have connections to the villages in their hinterlands – usually only once a day, so if you're day-tripping, make sure there's a return. Ronda's new bus station is in the new town, on the Paseo de Andalucía.

Ronda has trains, too; the station is just a few blocks down Paseo de Andalucíate (Tel: 87 16 73 for information). There are at least three a day for Algeciras and Málaga, with connections at Bobadilla Junction for Madrid and the other cities of Andalucía. Some trains stop at Gaucin and Setenil.

Arcos de la Frontera

Starting from the west, near Jerez, **Arcos de la Frontera** is the first and one of the most spectacular of the towns, hung on a steep rock with wonderful views down to the valley of the Guadalete from the mirador near the Plaza del Ayuntamiento. The older sections of town under the castle (now a parador) contain some old palaces and the Isabelline Gothic **Santa María de la Asunción**. Arcos was an important fortress for the Moors, a seemingly impregnable eyrie that Alfonso the Wise was smart enough to take in 1264.

Further east, **Grazalema** is a lovely village, full of flowers and surrounded by pine woods. It has been famous for hand-woven blankets since Moorish times, and they still make them here on big old wooden looms. Nearby is **Setenil**, an odd village with some of its few streets lining the walls of a gorge. The houses are tucked under the overhanging rock, and their front doors overlook a stream. **Olvera** and **Zahara** have memorable silhouettes, their castles and churches sticking bravely up over the whitewashed houses.

Ronda

The Serrania de Ronda is a region of difficult topography, and it made life difficult for most would-be conquerors. A band of southern Celts gave the Romans fits in these mountains; various Christian chieftains held out for centuries against the Moors, and to return the favour the Moors kept Castile at bay here until 1485, just seven years before the conquest of Granada. **Ronda**, the only city in the Serrania, is a beautiful place, blessed with a perfect postcard shot of its lofty bridge over the steep gorge that divides the old and new towns. Because of its proximity to the Costa del Sol, it has lately become the only really tourist-ridden corner of the interior. Its monuments are few; what Ferdinand the Catholic didn't wreck in 1485, the French finished off in 1809. Ronda saw plenty of trouble in the Civil War, with hundreds of bodies being tossed into the gorge (the exact numbers, and who was doing the tossing, depend on who is telling you the story).

Don't be discouraged, though; the views alone are worth the trip. One of the best places to enjoy them is the **Alameda del Tajo**, a park on the edge of the **Mercadillo**, as the new town is called. Next to it, Ronda has one of Spain's oldest and most picturesque bullrings. The 1785 **Plaza de Toros**, the 'cathedral of bullfighting', gets only about three *corridas* a year, but it still has great prestige; the art of bullfighting was developed here. There's a small museum inside. The **Puente Nuevo**, as the bridge to the *Ciudad* (old town) is called, was built on the second try in 1740 – the first one immediately collapsed. The bridge's two thick piers descend almost 92 m (300 ft) into the bottom of the narrow gorge.

In the *Ciudad*

From the bridge, a steep path heads downwards to two 18th-century palaces: the **Palacio de Salvatierra** and the **Casa del Rey Moro**, built over Moorish foundations. From its garden there is a stairway – 365 steps cut out of the rock, called the **Mina** – that takes you down to the bottom of the gorge. Here there's a Moorish bridge and well-preserved remains of a **Moorish bath**. Back on top, if you survive the climb back up, there is the town's main church, **Santa María La Mayor**, still retaining the mihrab and minaret of the mosque it replaced, and the ruins of the **Alcazar**, blown up by the French.

Besides the opportunities for walks in and around the valleys under Ronda an interesting excursion can be made to an area of curiosities 15–20 km (9–12 miles) west of town. The hills around the hamlet of Montejague are full of caves. Two, the **Cueva del Gato** and **Cueva del Hundidero**, both full of stalactites and odd formations, are connected. The little stream called the Gaduares disappears in one and comes out in the other. 5 km (3.1 miles) south, past the village of Benaoján, the **Cueva de la Pileta** has some 25,000 year old art – simple drawings in black of animals and magic symbols (the caretaker lives in the farmhouse near the entrance if no one's around). 12 km (7.5 miles) west of Ronda, off the road to Grazalema, are the Roman ruins of **Acinpo** known locally as 'Ronda la Vieja', with a theatre and stage building like Mérida's. And finally, from the ancient isolated village of **Gaucin**, 25 km (15.6 miles) south-west of Ronda, you can see Gibraltar and the African coast over the peaks of the Serrania.

TOURIST INFORMATION

Ronda: Pl. de España, by the bridge (Tel: 87 12 72).

WHERE TO STAY

The **Parador Nacional Casa del Corregidor***** in Arcos has recently been reopened after a thorough restoration of the old palace that houses it; it's a lovely place, and quite popular, so book ahead (Pl. de España, Tel: 70 05 00, doubles 6500–7500 pts). Apart from that, in Arcos and the other 'white villages' there are only the simplest of places to stay and restaurants.

Ronda has a wider choice. The **Reina Victoria****** is a fine old hotel, built by the British around the turn of the century, with lovely views over the cliffs. The German poet, Rainer Maria Rilke, stayed here for a season and wrote some of his best-known works (C. Jerez, Tel: 87 12 40, doubles 6000–6600 pts). Less expensive, near the old town, the **Royal***** (C. Virgen de la Paz, near the bullring, Tel: 87 11 41, doubles 3000 pts). There are dozens of small *hostales* and *camas* over bars – most of them quite agreeable – in the Mercadillo (new town) on all the side streets of C. Jerez.

EATING OUT

The best meals Ronda can offer, with a view to match, are at the **Don Miguel**, overlooking the gorge next to the famous bridge; they also have a bar built into the bridge itself (1600–2800 pts for a full-course dinner). Otherwise, stick to the restaurants in the Mercadillo like the **Mesón Santiago** on C. Marina or the **Cafe Doña Pepa** next door. Quite a few really inferior tourist restaurants have been opening in conspicuous places to take advantage of day-trippers from the Costa: watch out.

El Chorro Gorge and Antequera

GETTING AROUND

Antequera is on the rail line from Algeciras to Granada, and there are easy connections to all points from nearby Bobadilla Junction (station on Av. de la Estación, Tel: 84 23 30). The bus station is on C. Alameda, with lots of buses to Málaga and Sevilla, less frequently to Granada and Córdoba, as well as Olvera, Osuna and the other villages of the region.

WHAT TO SEE

Heading east from Ronda, turn north at the town of Alora and in about 15 km (9.3 miles) you'll come to one of Andalucía's natural wonders, **El Chorro Gorge**, in the deep rugged canyon of the Río Guadalhorce, with sheer walls of limestone tossed about at crazy angles. Thrill-seekers can cirumnavigate it on an old concrete catwalk called **El Camino del Rey**, gradually crumbling into a ruin though, amazingly, they still keep it open. It's definitely worth the walk if you're nimble and not subject to vertigo, and it's easy to reach. El Chorro has its own rail station on the Antequera-Málaga line. If you're not up to stopping, the views from the train as it weaves in and out of tunnels around the gorge are great, too.

If, on the other hand, you have time to explore this region, around three separate artificial lakes of a big government hydroelectric scheme, seek out the **Church of Bobastro**, just west of El Chorro on the little road north from Alora. Bobastro is a 9th-century basilica cut out of bare rock that supposedly contains the tomb of Omar Ben Hafsun, a Christian emir who founded a short-lived independent state in the mountains. Some remains of the city and fortress he built can be seen on the heights nearby. To the west, 13 km (8.1 miles) from Antequera, **El Torcal** is a tall but hikeable mountain with unusual, eroded red limestone formations around it. Several paths are marked out. And some 30 km (18.8 miles) west of Antequera, off the road to Sevilla, the **Laguna de Fuente de Piedra** is one of Europe's largest breeding grounds for flamingos. You can see them from March to September; the rest of the year you'll have to look them up in Senegal.

Antequera

This is not an especially interesting city, though it's as large as Ronda. Some 5 km (3.1 miles) north of the town, the Neolithic monuments known as the **Cuevas de Menga** have been called the 'first real architecture in Spain'. They are nothing to compare with the *talayots* and *taulas* of the island of Menorca, but there's nothing like them in mainland Spain. There are three, all from about 2500 BC. The two largest, the Menga and Viera dolmens, are chambers about 21.5 m (70 ft) long, roughly elliptical and lined with huge, flat stones; other monoliths support the roof-like pillars. At El Romeral nearby, in the grounds of a sugar factory, the third of these temples has a domed ceiling. All have some etchings of figures and symbols around their walls.

North of Antequera

In the gentler hills to the north, approaching the valley of the Guadalquivir, a few more towns are worth mentioning if you're passing that way. **Osuna** was an important Roman military centre for the south of Spain, and survives as an attractive little city of white houses with characteristic *rejas* (grilles) over every window. Osuna was an aristocratic town after the Reconquista, home of the objectionable Dukes of Osuna who lorded it over much of Andalucía. Their 'pantheon' of tombs may be seen in the fine Renaissance **Colegiata Church** on a hill on the west side of town. Several decorative façades of 16th-century mansions can be seen along the **Calle San Pedro**. Osuna has a little **archaeology museum** in the **Torre del Agua**, part of the old fortifications, and a museum of dubious art in **La Encarnación** convent, a Baroque work of the late 18th century (both open daily except Monday, 10 am – 1.30 pm and 4–7.30 pm). Further east there's little to see; at **Puente Genil** an old Moorish-style mill still turns in a pretty setting along the Río Genil. **Montilla** and **Lucena** are centres of a great wine-growing region. **Priego de Córdoba** has a famous ensemble of Baroque churches, monasteries and fountains; the best is the **Asunción** Church with a beautiful dome over its Sagrario chapel.

TOURIST INFORMATION
Antequera: Pl. Coso Viejo, Tel: 84 18 27.

WHERE TO STAY AND EAT
The **Parador de Antequera******* is a plain, modern building but the only first-class hotel in the region (air-conditioning and pool, doubles 5000–6500 pts; C. Garcia del Olmo, Tel: 84 00 61). In the town centre, the best choice is the **Manzanito***, nine rooms in a pretty location on C. Calvo Sotelo (Tel: 84 10 23); doubles with bath 1700–1870 pts). The management also runs a good restaurant (500–800 pts) next door. Alora's only hotel, the **Alondra***, has only four rooms (C. Mola 56, 2400 pts with bath, 1000 pts without) and it is typical of the small *hostales* around these villages. In Osuna, the best is the **Cinco Puertas*** (also the only one with heating; doubles 1500 pts with bath, 1200 pts without; C. Franco 79, Tel: 81 12 43).

Granada and the Sierra Nevada

GRANADA

The first thing to do upon arrival is to pick up a copy of Washington Irving's *Tales of the Alhambra.* Every bookshop in town can sell you one in just about any language; it was Irving who put Granada on the map, and established the Alhambra as the necessary romantic pilgrimage of Spain. His style may seem flowery to some, and an outright irritation to the rest, but Irving was a master storyteller, and his little book of embellished legends will provide the best evening's entertainment in the only big city in Spain that shuts down at midnight.

Granada, in fact, might seem a disappointment without Irving. The modern city underneath the Alhambra is a stolid, remarkably unmagical place, with little to show for the 500 years since the Catholic Kings put an end to its ancient glory. As the Moors were expelled, the Spanish Crown replaced them with Castilians and Galicians from up north, and even today Granadinos are thought of as a bit foreign by other Andalucians. Their Granada has never been a happy place. Particularly in the last 100 years it has been full of political troubles. Around the turn of the century even the Holy Week processions had to be called off for a few years because of disruptions from the leftists, and at the start of the Civil War the reactionaries who always controlled Granada made one of the first big massacres of Republicans.

One of their victims was Federico Garcia Lorca, the Granadino who, in the decades since his death, has come to be recognized as the greatest Spanish dramatist and poet since the 'golden age'. If Irving's fairy tales aren't to your taste, consider the works of Lorca, in which Granada and its sweet melancholy are recurring themes. Few poets have ever kept such an intimate relationship with their home towns, even though Lorca once wrote that he remembered Granada 'as one should remember a sweetheart who has died'.

The Nasrid Kingdom of Karnattah

First Iberian *Elibyrge*, then Roman *Illiberis*, the town did not make a name for itself until the 1230s. In that decade, while the Castilians were seizing Córdoba and preparing to polish off the rest of the Almoravid states of Al-Andalus, an Arab chieftain named Muhammad ibn-Yusuf ibn-Nasr established a little state for himself around Jaen. When that town fell to the Castilians in 1235, he moved his capital to the town the Moors called *Karnattah*. Ibn Nasr (or Muhammad I, as he is generally known) and his descendants in the Nasrid dynasty enjoyed great success at first in extending their domains. By 1300 this last Moorish state of Spain extended from Gibraltar to Almería, but this accomplishment was possible only by a policy of cooperation with Castile, and it came entirely at the expense of other Moors. Muhammad and his successors were in fact vassals of the Kings of Castile, and aided them in campaigns more often than they fought them. The Nasrid Kingdom's mountainous terrain gave it a certain amount of security against the Castilians, and behind a wall of nearly impregnable fortresses – Gibraltar, Ronda, and Karnattah itself – it was able to survive and prosper for over two centuries. Karnattah at this time had a population of some 200,000 people – as many as it has now – and both its arts and industries were strengthened by refugees from the fallen towns of Al-Andalus.

This state of affairs lasted until the coming of the Catholic Kings. Isabel's religious fanaticism made the completion of the Reconquista the supreme goal of her reign; she sent Ferdinand out in 1484 to do the job, which he accomplished in eight years by a breathtakingly brilliant combination of force and diplomacy. Karnattah at the time was suffering the usual curse of Al-Andalus states – disunity founded on the egotism of princes. In this fatal feud, the main actors were Mulay Hassan, King of Karnattah, his brother El Zagal ('the valiant') and the king's rebellious son, Abn abd-Allah, better known to posterity as Boabdil el Chico. His seizure of the throne in 1482 started a period of civil war at the worst possible time. Ferdinand was clever enough to take advantage of the divisions; he captured Boabdil twice, and turned him into a tool of Castilian designs. Playing one side against the other, Ferdinand was able to snatch away one Nasrid province after another with few losses. When the unfortunate Boabdil, after renouncing his kingship in favour of the Castilians, finally changed his mind and decided to fight for the remnants of Karnattah (by then little more than the city itself and the Sierra Nevada), Ferdinand had the excuse he needed to mount his final attack. Karnattah was besieged, and after two years, Boabdil agreed to surrender under terms that guaranteed his people the use of their religion and customs. When the keys of the city were handed over on 2 January 1492, the Reconquista was complete.

At first the new dispensation went well in the city, both economically and in religious affairs. When Cardinal Cisneros arrived in 1499, however, he found the climate of tolerance intolerable, and soon forced the government into breaking its agreement with a policy of forced conversion, a policy cleverly designed to justify itself by causing a revolt. The First Revolt of the Alpujarras (1498), the string of villages near the city in the Sierra Nevada, resulted in the expulsion of all Muslims who failed to convert – the majority of the population had already fled – as well as decrees prohibiting Moorish dress and customs such as public bathhouses.

Beyond that, the Castilians followed a policy of purposely impoverishing the region, ruining its agriculture and bankrupting the important silk industry with confiscatory taxes and a ban on exports. The Inquisition enriched the Church's coffers here more than anywhere in Spain, by attaching the entire property of any converted Muslims who could be found guilty of backsliding in the faith. Not surprisingly, a second revolt in the Alpujarras occurred in 1568, after which Philip II ordered the dispersal of the remaining Moorish population throughout the towns and cities of Castile.

Such a history does not easily wear away, even after so many centuries. The Castilians corrupted Karnattah to *Granada*; just by coincidence that means 'pomegranite' in Spanish, and the pomegranite has come to be the symbol of the city. With its associations with the myth of Persephone, with the mysteries of death and loss, no symbol could be more suitable for this capital of melancholy.

GETTING AROUND

By train, Granada has connections to Guadix and Almería (three daily) to Algeciras, Sevilla, and Córdoba by way of Bobadilla Junction (they are sometimes complicated) and three daily to Madrid including one *talgo*. The station is on the northern end of town, about a mile from the centre, on Av. de los Andaluces (city ticket office is on C. Reyes Católicos, off Pl. Nueva, Tel: 22 34 97 for information). The main bus station, run by the Alsina Graells company, is equally inconveniently located on the Camino de Ronda (Tel: 25 12 58) with service to Madrid, all points in Andalucía. For Murcia, Alicante, Valencia and Barcelona, the service is run by the Bacoma line, in front of the train station at Av. Andaluces 12 (Tel: 23 18 83).

In the city, one very useful bus to know is the no. 11, a route that passes the train and bus stations, the Gran Vía and C. Reyes Católicos (take it in either direction since it's circular). A good way to see the Albaicín is to take the no. 7 bus from C. Reyes Católicos to the top of the hill (get off at C. Pages) and walk down. And the no. 2 from the Pl. Nueva will save you the trouble of climbing up to the Alhambra.

A Sentimental Orientation

In spite of everything, more of the lost world of Al-Andalus can be seen in Granada than even in Córdoba. Granada stands where the foothills of the Sierra Nevada meet the fertile 'Vega de Granada' the greenest and best stretch of farmland in Andalucía. Two of those hills extend into the city itself. One bears the **Alhambra**, the fortified palace of the Nasrid kings, and the other the **Albaicín** the most evocative of the 'Moorish' neighbourhoods of Andalucian cities. Parts of old Karnattah extended down into the plain, but they have been largely submerged into the new city. How much you enjoy Granada will depend largely on how successful you are in ignoring the new districts. In particular, three barbarically ugly streets that form the main automobile route through Granada are most deserving of your disdain: The **Gran Vía Colón** chopped through the centre of town in the 19th century, the **Calle Reyes Católicos** and the **Acera del Darro**. The latter two are paved over the course of the Río Darro, the little stream that ran picturesquely through the city until the 1880s. If you can manage to pretend these streets do not exist, you may see Granada as it deserves to be seen.

WHAT TO SEE

Before the three streets referred to above were built, the centre of Granada was the **Plaza Nueva**, a square that is also partly built over the Darro. The handsome building that gives it its character is the 1584 **Audiencia**, built by Philip II for the royal officials and judges. **Santa Ana church**, across the plaza, was built in 1537 by Diego de Siloée, one of the architects of Granada's cathedral. From this plaza the ascent to the Alhambra begins, up a narrow street called the **Cuesta de Gomerez**, past guitar-makers' shops, gypsies and vast displays of tourist trinkets, ending abruptly at the **Puerta de las Granadas**, a monumental gateway erected by Charles V.

The Alhambra

The grounds of the Alhambra begin here with a bit of the unexpected. Instead of the walls and towers, not yet even in view, there is a lovely grove of great elms, the **Alameda**; even more unexpectedly, they are the contribution of the Duke of Wellington, who took time off from chasing the French to plant them during the Peninsular War. Take the path to the left – it's a stiff climb – and in a few minutes you'll arrive at the **Gate of Justice**, entrance of the Alhambra. The orange tint of the fortress walls explains the name *Al-hamra*: 'the vermilion' and the unusual style of the carving on the gate is the first clue that here is something very different. The two devices, a hand and a key, carved on the inner and outer arches, are famous. According to one of Irving's tales, the hand will one day reach down and grasp the key; then the Alhambra will fall into ruins, the earth will open, and the hidden treasures of the Moors be revealed.

From the gate, a path leads up to a broad square, here are the **Puerta del Vino**, so called from a long-ago Spanish custom of doling out free wine here to the inhabitants of the Alhambra, and also the ticket booth. To the left you'll see the walls of the **Alcazaba**, the fort at the tip of the Alhambra's narrow promontory, and to the right the huge

GRANADA
N
AV. CALVO
AV. ANDALUCÍA
SOTELO
C. MARMOLILLOS
2
Jardines del Triunfo
C. SEVERO OCHOA
University
C. STA BARBARA
C. HOSPITAL
AV. FUENTENUEVA
RECTOR LÓPEZ AGUSTA
VENTANILLA
C. S. JUAN DE DIOS
19
ACERA S. ILDEFONSO
S. ILDEFONSO
PERNALEROS
20
Moorish Walls
to Murcia
C. ALCAHABA
CARRETERA DE MURCIA
S. CRISTÓBAL
MELCHOR ALMAGRO
22
23
LOS ARANDAS
GRAN VÍA COLÓN
C. ZENETE
LONA
18
ISABEL LA REAL
C. MARÍA LE MIEL
17
S. AGOSTÍN
C. PAN ADEROS
C. S. LUIS
16
C. DEL GRAN CAPITÁN
DUQUESA
24
TENDILLAS
NEGROS
C. TINA
ALMIRANTE
S. NICOLÁS
CAMINO DE RONDA
C. PICÓN
Pl. de los Lobos
HORNO DE ABAD
S. AGUSTÍN
PERRO ALTA
SAN JOSÉ
ALBAICIN
TRILLO
C. GUINEA
SACROMONTE
OBISPO HURTADO
TABLAS
Pl. Trinidad
S. JUAN DE LOS REYES
14
13
12
Cathedral
25
CALDERÍA
6
CARRETERA DEL DARRO
15

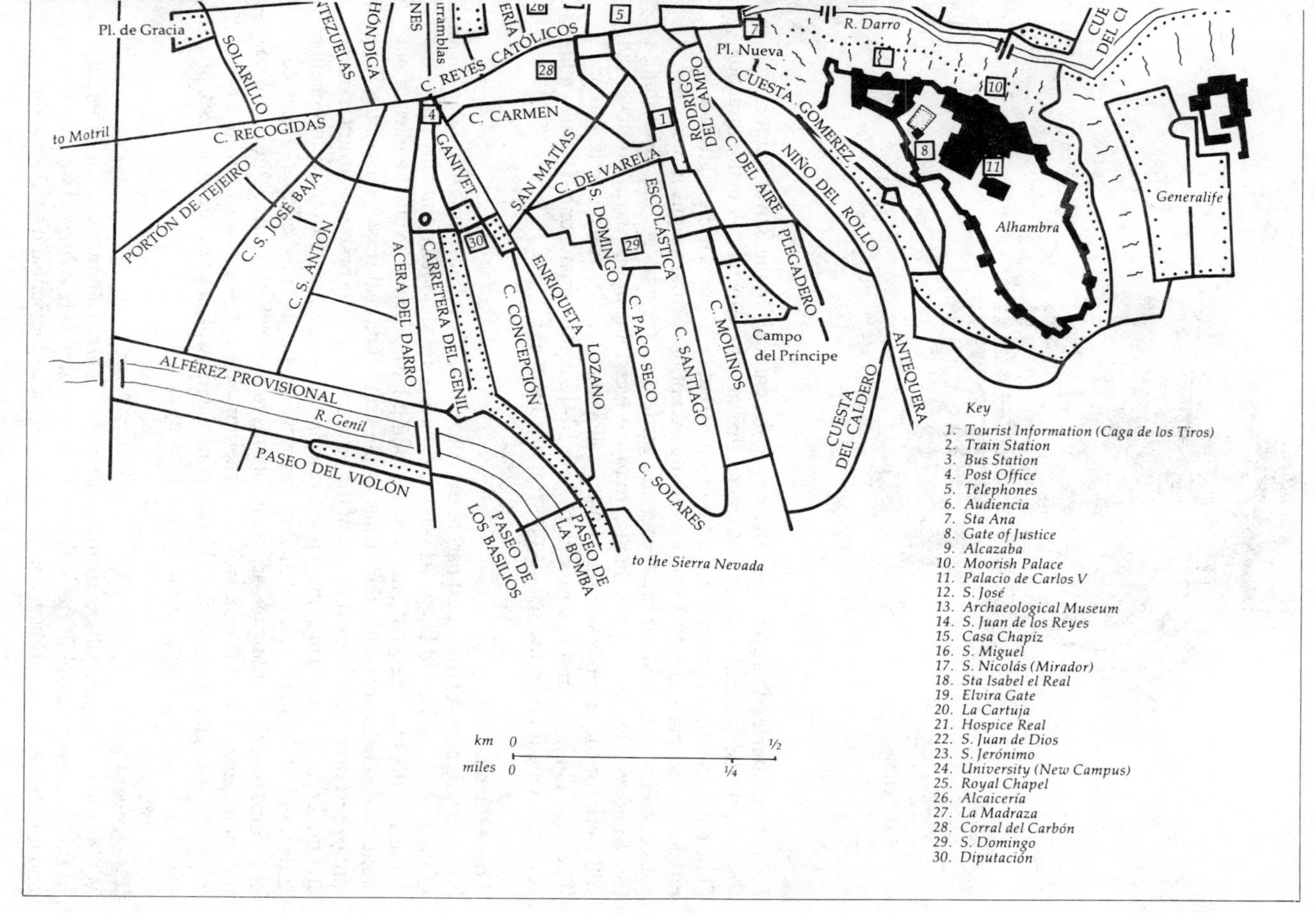
Pl. de Gracia
SOLARILLO
C. REYES CATÓLICOS
R. Darro
Pl. Nueva
CUESTA GOMEREZ
RODRIGO DEL CAMPO
C. CARMEN
to Motril
C. RECOGIDAS
PORTÓN DE TEJEIRO
C. S. JOSÉ BAJA
C. S. ANTÓN
ACERA DEL DARRO
CARRETERA DEL GENIL
GANIVET
SAN MATÍAS
C. DE VARELA
S. DOMINGO
ESCOLÁSTICA
C. DEL AIRE
NIÑO DEL ROLLO
PLEGADERO
Alhambra
Generalife
C. CONCEPCIÓN
ENRIQUETA
LOZANO
C. PACO SECO
C. SANTIAGO
C. MOLINOS
Campo del Príncipe
ANTEQUERA
CUESTA DEL CALDERO
ALFÉREZ PROVISIONAL
R. Genil
PASEO DEL VIOLÓN
PASEO DE LOS BASILIOS
PASEO DE LA BOMBA
C. SOLARES
to the Sierra Nevada
km 0 ½
miles 0 ¼
Key
1. Tourist Information (Caga de los Tiros)
2. Train Station
3. Bus Station
4. Post Office
5. Telephones
6. Audiencia
7. Sta Ana
8. Gate of Justice
9. Alcazaba
10. Moorish Palace
11. Palacio de Carlos V
12. S. José
13. Archaeological Museum
14. S. Juan de los Reyes
15. Casa Chapiz
16. S. Miguel
17. S. Nicolás (Mirador)
18. Sta Isabel el Real
19. Elvira Gate
20. La Cartuja
21. Hospice Real
22. S. Juan de Dios
23. S. Jerónimo
24. University (New Campus)
25. Royal Chapel
26. Alcaicería
27. La Madraza
28. Corral del Carbón
29. S. Domingo
30. Diputación

The Alhambra, Granada

Palace of Charles V; signs point your way to the entrance of the **Royal Palace** (Casa Real), with its splendidly decorated rooms that are the Alhambra's main attraction. (The entire complex is open daily 10 am–6 pm, 10 am–5.30 pm in winter. The steep admission – 350 pts – gets you into everything except the two museums in Charles V's palace, and is also good for the Generalife gardens on the adjacent hill. Everything's free Sundays after 2.30. If you don't care to see everything in one day, your ticket will still work for the sections you miss on the following day. The Alhambra is also open Tuesday, Thursday, and Saturday night from 10–12 in the summer or 8–10 pm in mid-season; seeing it under the stars is the treat of a lifetime.

The Alcazaba

Not much remains of the oldest part of the Alhambra. This citadel probably dates back to the first of the Nasrid kings. Its walls and towers are still intact, but only the foundations of the buildings that once stood within it have survived. Note the piles of old stone cannonballs set within the niches of the walls. The real reason for visiting is to climb the **Torre de la Vela** at the tip of the promontory for the best views over Granada and the Vega. The big bell at the top was rung in the old days to signal the daily opening and closing of the water gates of the Vega's irrigation system, and the Moors also used it as a signal post for sending messages and alarms to the furthest points of the surrounding mountains. The Albaicín, visible on the opposite hill, is a revelation: its rows of white, flat-roofed houses on the hillside, punctuated by palm trees and cypresses, provide one of Europe's most exotic urban landscapes

The Royal Palace

Words will not do, nor will exhaustive descriptions help to communicate the experience of this greatest treasure of Al-Andalus. This is what people come to Granada to see, and it is the surest, most accessible window into the refinement and subtlety of the culture of Moorish Spain. Words fail because the essence of this art is simplicity. The repetitious floral and geometric decoration of the palace's plasterwork and *azulejo* tiles can hardly be discussed as art in terms familiar to us, and the asymmetrical, indeed apparently random arrangement of chambers and patios would be hard to talk about as architecture. But despite this, this building can achieve in its handful of rooms what a work like Madrid's Royal Palace cannot even approach with its 2800.

It probably never occurs to most visitors, but one of the most unusual features of this palace is its modesty. What you see is what the Nasrid kings saw, and your imagination need add only a few carpets and tapestries, some well-crafted furniture of wood inlaid with ivory, and big round braziers of brass for heat or incense, to make the picture complete. Most of the actual building is wood and plaster, cheap and perishable, like a world's fair pavilion; no good Muslim monarch would offend Allah's sense of propriety by pretending that these wordly splendours were anything more than the pleasures of a moment (much of the plaster, wood, and all of the tiles, are in fact the products of careful restorations over the last 100 years).

The art of the Nasrids was an introspective, conservative style, the work of a small, isolated kingdom constantly on the defensive, yet with the burden of a great artistic heritage to maintain. There are few innovations, few elements of their style not already seen in the days of the Ommiad Caliphate. It has often been said, though, that their achievement was to bring these elements to perfection, in the incomparable setting of the Alhambra's hill. Most of this palace was built in the last half of the 14th century, the heyday of the Nasrid kingdom. Among the thousands of refugees who settled here from the lost provinces were nearly all the artists of Al-Andalus; together they created the greatest achievement of Moorish art, and also the last.

Like so many old royal palaces (those of the Romans, Byzantines or the Ottoman Turks, for example), this one is divided into three sections, one for everyday business of the palace and government; the next, more secluded, for the state rooms and official entertainments of the kings; and the third, where few outsiders ever reached, with the private apartments of the king and his household. Of the first, much was demolished by Charles V to make room for his palace. The small **Mexuar** where the kings would hold their public audiences, survives near the present-day entrance to the palace complex. The adjacent **Patio of the Mexuar**, though much restored, is one of the finest rooms of the Alhambra. Nowhere is the meditative serenity of the palace more apparent (unless you arrive when all the tour groups do) and the small fountain in the centre provides an introduction to an important element of the architecture – water. Pools, fountains and channels cut into the floors run everywhere in the palace's patios and gardens, and water is as much a part of the design as the wood, tile, and stone

COURT OF THE MYRTLES

If you have trouble finding your way around, remember the elaborately decorated portals never really lead anywhere; the door you want will always be tucked unobtrusively to the side; here, as in Sevilla's Alcazar, the principle is to heighten the sense of surprise. The entrance to the grand Court of the Myrtles, with its long goldfish pond and lovely arcades, is one of these. This was the centre of the second, state section of the palace; directly off it, you pass through the **Hall of the Boat**, so called from its hull-shaped wooden ceiling (don't fail to look up for beautiful wooden *artesonado* and plaster 'stalactite' ceilings everywhere in the palace) and into the **Hall of the Ambassadors**, where the kings presided over all important state business. Here again, the views over the Albaicín are priceless, and the decoration is some of the Alhambra's best.

In some of the smaller chambers off the Court of the Myrtles, you can peek out over the domed roofs of the baths one floor below; opposite the Hall of the Ambassadors is a small entrance into the dark, empty **crypt** of Charles V's palace, with curious echo effects

COURT OF THE LIONS

Another half-hidden doorway leads you into the third section, the king's residence, built around the spectacular **Court of the Lions**. As in much of Moorish architecture, the almost overripe arabesques of this patio conceal a subtle symbolism. The 'enclosed garden' that can stand for the attainment of truth, or paradise, or for the cosmos, is a recurring theme in Islamic mystical poetry, Here you may take the 12 endearingly preposterous lions who support the fountain in the centre as the months, or signs of the zodiac, and the four channels that flow out from the fountains as the four corners of the cosmos, the cardinal points, or on a different level the four rivers of paradise. The poetry and Koranic passages in the calligraphy around the walls carries these themes further.

Many of the rooms around the patio have exquisite decorations: the **Hall of the Abencerrajes**, the **Hall of the Two Sisters**, and other retreats of the harem apartments, and also the **Patio of the Lindaraja** (or Daraxa), Washington Irving's favourite spot in the Alhambra. The **Sala de los Reyes** is unique for the fragments of frescoes on its ceiling, paintings of court scenes that would not be too out of place in any Christian palace of medieval Europe.

Palace of Charles V and the Museums

Anywhere else, this elegant Renaissance building would be an attraction in itself. Here it seems only pompous and oversized, and our appreciation for it is lessened by the mind-numbing thought of this Emperor, with a good half of Europe to build palaces in, having to plop it down here – ruining much of the Alhambra in the process. Once Charles had smashed up the place, he lost interest, and most of the still unfinished palace was not built until 1616. The best parts are beautifully detailed sculptural **reliefs** around the portals, showing scenes from Charles' campaigns, and the circular **patio** inside, where bullfights and mock-tournaments were once held.

On its top floor has been installed Granada's **Museo de Bellas Artes** (open daily 10 am – 3 pm) a largely forgettable collection of religious paintings and polychromes, many from Granada churches. Downstairs, the **Museo Nacional de Art Hispano-Musulman** contains perhaps Spain's best collection of Moorish art, including some of the original paintings, *azulejo* tiles and plaster arabesques from the Alhambra palace, and some exceedingly fine wooden panels and screens. There is a collection of ceramic ware with fanciful figurative decoration – elephants and lady musicians – and a few curiosities, such as a star globe with no stars on it. The Koranic injunction against imagery extended even to the heavens, and Muslim astronomers had to be content with the names of regions and constellations on their charts and globes. Tucked in a corner of the museum are four big copper balls stacked on a pole, an ornament that once stood atop a Granada minaret. These were a typical feature of Andalucían minarets (as on La Giralda in Sevilla) and similar ones can be seen in Morocco today.

Behind Charles' palace a street leads into the remnants of the town that once filled much of the space within the Alhambra's walls, now reduced to a small collection of restaurants and souvenir stands. In Moorish times the Alhambra held a population of some 40,000, and even under the Spaniards it long retained the status of a separate municipality. At one end of the street, the 1581 **church of Santa María**, designed by Herrera, occupies the site of the Alhambra's mosque; at the other, the first Christian building on the Alhambra, the 1495 **Convento de San Francisco**, has been converted into a Parador.

The Generalife

Many of the trillions of visitors the Alhambra receives each year have never heard of it, and pass up a chance to see the finest garden in Spain. The Generalife was the summer palace of the Nasrid kings, built on the height the Moors called the 'mountain of the Sun'. To get there, it's about a five-minute walk from the Alhambra along a lovely avenue of tall cypresses.

The buildings, currently under restoration, are nothing special if you've just come from the Alhambra. They are in fact older than most of the Royal Palace, probably begun around 1260. The gardens and the view over the Alhambra and Albaicín are transcendent. They are built on terraces, on several levels along the hillside; in the centre, a long pool under sprays of water passes through beds of roses and an infinite variety of other blooms. A lower level, with a promenade on the hill's edge, is broken up into secluded bowers by cypress bushes cut into angular shapes of walls and gateways.

If you're walking down from the Alhambra, you might consider a different route, across the Alameda and down through the picturesque streets below the **Torres Bermejas**, an outwork of the Alhambra's fortifications built on foundations that may be as old as the Romans. The winding lanes and stairways around Calle del Aire and Calle Niño del Rollo, one of the most beautiful quarters of Granada, will eventually lead you back down near the Plaza Nueva.

Albaicín

Even more than the old quarters of Córdoba, this hilltop neighbourhood has successfully preserved some of the atmosphere of Al-Andalus. Its difficult site and the fact that it was long the district of Granada's poor, explains the lack of change, but today the Albaicín seems to be becoming fashionable again.

From the Plaza Nueva, a narrow street called the **Carretera del Darro** leads up the valley of the Darro between the Alhambra and Albaicín hills; here the little stream has not been covered over, and you can get an idea of how the centre of Granada looked in the old days. On the Alhambra side, old stone bridges lead up to a few half-forgotten streets hidden among the forested slopes; here you'll see some 17th-century Spanish houses with curious painted *esgrafiado* façades. Nearby, traces of a horseshoe arch can be seen where a Moorish wall once crossed the river; in the corner of Calle Baruelo there are well preserved **Moorish baths**. Even more curious is the façade of the **Castril House** on the Darro, a flamboyant 16th-century mansion with a portal carved with a phoenix, winged scallop shells and other odd devices that have been interpreted as elements in a complex mystical symbolism. Over the big corner window is an inscription 'Waiting for her from the heavens'. The house's owner, Bernando de Zafra, was once a secretary to Ferdinand and Isabel, and he seems to have got into some trouble with the Inquisition.

Castril House has been restored as Granada's **Archaeological Museum** (open daily except Monday, 10 am–2 pm) with a small collection of artefacts from the huge number of caves in Granada province, many inhabited since Paleolithic times, and a few Iberian settlements. There is a Moorish room, with some lovely works of art, and finally, an even greater oddity than Castril House itself, one room of the museum is filled with a collection of beautiful alabaster burial urns – made in Egypt, but found in a Phoenician-style necropolis near Almuñecar. Nothing like them has ever been discovered elsewhere in Spain, and the Egyptian hieroglyphic inscriptions on them are provocative in the extreme (translations given in Spanish), telling how the deceased travelled here in search of some mysterious primordial deity.

Further up the Darro, there's a small park with a view up to the Alhambra; after that you'll have to do some climbing, but the higher you go the prettier the Albaicín is, and the better the views. Among the white houses and white walls are some of the oldest Christian churches in Granada. As in Córdoba, they are tidy and extremely plain, built to avoid alienating a recently converted population unused to religious imagery. **San Juan de los Reyes** (1520) on Calle Zafra and **San José** (1525) are the oldest; both retain the plain minarets of the mosques they replaced. Quite a few Moorish houses survive in the Albaicín, and some can be seen on **Calle Horno de Oro**, just off the Darro, and **Calle Daralhorra** at the top of the Albaicín, the remains of a Nasrid palace that was largely destroyed for Isabel's **Convento de Santa Isabel la Real** (1501).

Here, running parallel to Calle Alcahaba is a long surviving stretch of Moorish wall. There are probably a few miles of walls left, visible around the hillsides over Granada; the location of the city made a very complex set of fortifications necessary. In this one, about halfway up, you may pass through at **Las Pesas Gate**, with its horseshoe arches. The heart of the Albaicín is here, around the pretty, animated **Plaza Larga**; only a few blocks away the **Mirador de San Nicolas** in front of the church of that name, offers the most romantic postcard view imaginable of the Alhambra with the snow-capped peaks of the Sierra Nevada behind it. Note the brick, barrel-vaulted fountain on the mirador, a typical Moorish survival; fountains like this can be seen throughout the Albaicín and most are still in use. Granada today has a small but growing Muslim community, and they have ground cleared just off the mirador to build a mosque. Construction hasn't started yet; apparently they are facing some difficulties with the city government.

On your way back from the Albaicín you might take a different route, down a maze of back streets to the **Elvira Gate**; this area is one of the most picturesque corners of the neighbourhood.

Sacromonte

For something completely different, you might strike out beyond the Albaicín hill to the **Gypsy Caves of Sacromonte**. Granada has had a substantial gypsy population for several centuries now. Some have become settled and respectable, others live in trailers on vacant land around town. The most visible are those who prey on the tourists around the Alhambra and the Capilla Real, handing out carnations with a smile and then attempting to extort huge sums out of anyone dumb enough to take one (of course, they'll tell your fortune, too). The biggest part of the gypsy community, however, still lives around Sacromonte in streets of some quite well-appointed cave homes, where they wait to lure you in for a little display of flamenco. For 100 years or so, the consensus of opinion has been that the music and dancing are usually indifferent, and the gypsies' eventually successful attempts to shake out your last peseta make it an unpleasantly unforgettable affair. Nevertheless, if you care to match wits with the experts, proceed up the Cuesta del Chapiz from the Rio Darro, turn right at the **Casa del Chapiz**, a big 16th-century palace that now houses a school of Arab studies, and keep going until some gypsy child drags you home with him. Serious flamenco fans will probably not fare better elsewhere in Granada except during the festivals, though there are some touristy flamenco night spots – the **Reina Mora** by Mirador San Cristobel is the best of them. On the third Sunday of each month, though, you can hear a **flamenco mass** performed in the San Pedro Church on the Carretera del Darro at 9 am.

Central Granada

The old city wall swung in a broad arc from Elvira Gate to the 'Puerta Real', now a small plaza full of traffic where Calle Reyes Catolicos meets the Acero del Darro. Just a few blocks north of here, in a web of narrow pedestrian streets that make up modern Granada's shopping district, is the pretty **Plaza Bibarrambla**, full of flower stands and toy shops, with an unusual fountain supported by leering giants at its centre. The narrow streets leading off to the east are the **Alcaiceria**. This was the Moorish silk exchange, but the buildings you see now, full of tourist souvenir shops, are not original; the Alcaiceria was burned down in the 1840s and was rebuilt in more-or-less the same fashion with Moorish arches and columns.

Cathedral and Capilla Real

The best way to see Granada's **cathedral** is to approach it from Calle Marques, just north of the Plaza Bibarrambla; the unique façade, with its three tall, recessed arches, is a striking sight, designed by the painter Alonso Cano. On the central arch, the big plaque bearing the words 'Ave Maria' commemorates the exploit of the Spanish captain who sneaked into the city one night in 1490 and nailed this message up on the door of the great mosque this cathedral has replaced.

Unfortunately, the rest of the cathedral (1521–1714) isn't up to the standard of its façade, and there's little reason to go in and explore its cavernous interior or dreary museum. Adjacent to it, however, you can pay your respects to that remarkable couple, Ferdinand and Isabel, in the **Capilla Real** (open daily 11 am–1 pm and 4–7 pm, Sunday 11am–1 pm). Los Reyes Católicos had already built a mausoleum in Toledo, but after the capture of Granada they decided to plant themselves here. Even in the shadow of the bulky cathedral, the Chapel reveals itself as an important work of the Isabelline style, with its characteristic roofline of Gothic traceries and pinnacles.

Inside, the Catholic kings are buried under a pair of marble sarcophagi with their recumbent figures, elegantly carved though not necessarily flattering to either of them.

The little staircase behind them leads down to the crypt, where you can peek in at their plain, lead coffins and those of their unfortunate daughter Juana the Mad and her husband Philip the Handsome, whose effigies lie next to the older couple above. The interior of the chapel is sumptuously decorated – it should be, considering the huge proportion of the crown revenues that were expended on it. The iron reja by Master Bartolomé and the retablo are especially fine. In the chapel's sacristy you can see most of Isabel's personal art collection – works by Van der Weyden, Berruguete, Botticelli and others, mostly in need of some restoration – as well as her crown and sceptre, and Ferdinand's sword.

Across the narrow street from the Capilla Real, a charmingly garish, painted Baroque façade hides **La Madraza**, a building of the Moorish university ('medrese'); though one of the best Moorish works surviving in Granada, it is hardly ever open to visitors. The Christians converted it to a town hall, whence its other name, the Casa del Cabildo.

Across Calle Reyes Católicos

Even though this part of the city is as old as the Albaicín, most of it was rebuilt after 1492, and its age doesn't show. The only Moorish building remaining is also the only example left in Spain of a *khan* or caravanserai, the type of merchants' hotel common throughout the Muslim world. The 14th-century **Corral del Carbón**, just off Reyes Católicos, takes its name from the time, a century ago, when it was used as a coal warehouse. Under the Spaniards it also served time as a theatre; its interior courtyard with balconies lends itself admirably to the purpose, being about the same size and shape as a Spanish theatre of the classic age, like the one in Almagro. Today it houses a government handicrafts outlet, and much of the building is under restoration.

The neighbourhood of quiet streets and squares behind it is the best part of Spanish Granada and worth a walk if you have the time. Here you'll see the **Casa de los Tiros**, a mansion built in 1505 on Calle Pavaneras, with strange figures carved on its façade. It presently houses the tourist information office and a **museum** of the city's history, closed indefinitely for restorations. **Santo Domingo** (1512), the finest of Granada's early churches, is just a few blocks to the south. Ferdinand and Isabel endowed it, and their monograms figure prominently on the lovely façade. This neighbourhood is bounded on the west by the Acera del Darro, the noisy heart of modern Granada, with most of the big hotels. It's a little discouraging, but as compensation, just a block away the city has adorned itself with a beautiful string of wide boulevards very like the Ramblas of Barcelona, a wonderful spot for a stroll. The **Carretera del Genil** usually has some sort of open-air market on it, and further down, the **Paseo del Salon** and **Paseo de la Bomba** are quieter and more park-like, joining the pretty banks of the Rio Genil.

Northern Granada

From the little square just north of the Cathedral, Calle San Jeronimo skirts the edge of Granada's market district and leads you towards the old **University** district. Even though much of the university has relocated to a new campus less than a kilometre to the north, this is still one of the livelier spots of town, and the colleges themselves occupy some fine, well-restored Baroque structures. The long yellow College of Law is one of the best, occupying a building put up in 1769 for the Jesuits; a small botanical garden is adjacent. Calle San Jeronimo ends at the Calle del Gran Capitan, where the landmark is the church of **San Juan de Dios**, with a Baroque façade and a big green-and-white tiled dome. **San Jeronimo**, a block west, is another of the oldest Granada churches (1520); it contains the tomb of Gonzolo de Córdoba, the 'Gran Capitan' who won so many victories in Italy for the Catholic kings.

Here you're not far from the Elvira Gate, in an area where old Granada fades into anonymous suburbs to the north. The big park at the end of the Gran Via is the **Jardines del Triumfo**, with coloured, illuminated fountains the city never seems to want to turn on. Behind them is the Renaissance **Hospice Real**, designed by Enrique de Egas. A few blocks south-west, climbing up towards the Albaicín, your senses will be assaulted by the gaudiest Baroque chapel in Spain, in the **Cartuja**, or Carthusian monastery on Calle Real de Cartuja (open daily except Monday, 10 am–1 pm and 4–7 pm). The 18th-century chapel and its sacristy, done in the richest marble, gold and silver, and painted plaster, fairly oozes with a froth of twisted spiral columns, rosettes and curlicues. It has often been described as a Christian attempt to upstage the Alhambra, but the inspiration more likely comes from the Aztecs, via the extravagant Mexican Baroque.

Lorca

Under Franco, any mention of Spain's greatest modern poet was forbidden (understandably so, since it was Franco's men who shot him). Today the Granadinos are coming to terms with Lorca, and seem determined to make up for the past. Lorca fans may pay their respects at two country-houses, now become museums, where the poet spent much of his early years, the **Huerta de San Vincente**, on the outskirts of town at Virgen Blanca, and the **Museo Lorca** at Fuente Vaqueros, a village just to the west on the Córdoba road (both open for guided tours every hour, 10 am–1 pm and 6–8 pm, daily except Monday).

TOURIST INFORMATION

The provincial tourist office in the Casa de Los Tiros, Calle Pavanera, has everything you need to know tacked up on the walls in amusing collages; they're also the best source for information on the Sierra Nevada and Alpujarras (Tel: 22 10 11). In addition, there's a Muncipal Tourist office near the Cathedral on C. Libreros.

WHERE TO STAY

The city centre, around the Acera del Darro, is full of hotels, and there are lots of inexpensive *hostales* around the Gran Vía – but the less you see of these areas the better. Fortunately, you can choose from a wide range around the Alhambra and in the older parts of town if you spend the time to look. Right in the Alhambra itself, the **Parador Nacional de San Francisco****** is perhaps the most famous of all paradors, housed in a convent where Queen Isabel was originally interred. It's beautiful, expensive, and small – you'll always need to book well in advance (doubles 9000–9500 pts, Tel: 22 14 93). Alternative choices very near the Alhambra would be the outrageously florid, neo-Moorish **Alhambra Palace******, where most rooms have terrific views over the city (C.

Peña Portida 2, Tel: 22 14 68, doubles with TV, air-conditioning 8300 pts) or the old **Washington Irving*****, a little faded but still classy (Paseo del Generalife 2, Tel: 22 75 50, doubles 6250 pts). On the slopes below the Alhambra, the **Kenia***** is a nice hotel recently installed in an old mansion with a garden (in a very quiet area, C. Molinos 65, Tel: 22 75 06, doubles 4200 pts). In the same area you can get a pool and air-conditioning at the **Los Angeles***** (Cuesta Escoriaza 4, Tel: 22 14 24, doubles 4410 pts).

There's one other hotel in the Alhambra, the **Hostal America*****, with simple, pretty rooms for 3900 pts, but like the *parador*, book well in advance (Tel: 22 74 71). For inexpensive *hostales*, the first place to look is the Cuesta de Gomerez, the street leading up to the Alhambra from Plaza Nueva. Besides the **Britz*** (at no. 1, 1800 pts with bath, 1275 pts without, Tel: 22 36 52) and the **Gomerez*** (at no. 10, 1000 pts no bath), both nice, there are plenty of other spots nearby if they're full. Just a few blocks north of the Plaza Nueva, with the prettiest location in Granada, overlooking the Río Darro, is the **Huespedes Sana Ana** (1200 pts, no bath, on C. Puente de Espiñosa, across the river). Off C. San Juan de Dios, in the university area, there are dozens of small *hostales* used to accommodating students. The **San Joaquin*** is one, with a pretty patio (Tel: 28 28 79, on C. Lavadero de la Cruz; 1600 pts double with bath, 1400 pts without) and there are others nearby on C. Lucena.

EATING OUT

Granada isn't known for its cuisine. There is an infinity of touristic places around the Plaza Nueva, with little to distinguish between them. Two fine old places popular with the locals are the **Cunini**, on C. Pescaderia, with seafood specialities and the **Sevilla**, on C. Oficios, a traditional Andalucían spot with dishes like *rabo de toro* on the menu. Both are near the cathedral, and both will set you back 1400–2000 pts. One of the touristy places, the **Abenhamar** on C. Abenhamar off C. Reyes Catolicos, has good *paella* and a decent 700 pts *menú del día.* In inexpensive restaurants the city fares somewhat better. There are a few on the Cuesta de Gomerez, notably the 550–800 pts combination plates at the **Restaurant Gomerez**, but you should try to get up to the Albaicín for dinner on at least one night. **El Ladrillo**, on C. Pages on the northern end of the hill, fills a whole plaza with tables and serves up vast quantities of fish and beer at bargain rates – this place is the most popular in the area. On the Plaza Larga, seafood and gazpacho are the standbys at the **Cocetin de la Parron**, an informal, somewhat trendy place (average 1200 pts). That rarest of finds in Spain, a decent pizza, can be had at the **Verona**, another very popular hole in the wall near the northern end of C. Elvira (pizzas about 500 pts). It may be a comment on local cooking that Granada has more Chinese restaurants than anywhere in Andalucía; one quite good and inexpensive one is the **Hong Kong**, on Av. Oloriz, three blocks east of the train station (full-course dinner around 900–1000 pts). Everyone's favourite rock-bottom, filling 300 pts menu is served up at the tiny **Cepillo** on C. Pescaderia, near the Cunini – order fish or squid

Sierra Nevada and the Alpujarras

From everywhere in Granada, the mountains peer over the tops of buildings, providing a constant temptation to the visitor. Fortunately, Spain's loftiest peaks are also its most accessible; from the city centre you can be riding on Europe's highest mountain road in a little more than an hour. Even if you're without a car, there's a daily bus from town that makes the Sierra Nevada an easy day-trip.

Dress warmly, though. As the name implies, the Sierra Nevada are snowbound nearly all year, and even in late July and August, when the road is clear and you can travel right over the mountains to the valley of the Alpujarras, it's as chilly and windy as you would expect it to be, some 3390 m (11,000 ft) above sea level. These mountains, a geological curiosity of sorts, are just an oversized chunk of the Penibetic System, the chain that stretches from Arcos de la Frontera almost to Murcia. Their highest peak, **Mulhacen**, is less than 40 km (25 miles) from the coast. You can see nearly all of the Sierra from Granada, a jagged snowy wall without really distinctive peaks. The highest expanses are barren and drear, but on a clear day they offer a view over most of Andalucía's provinces and parts of Morocco. Mulhacen and especially its sister peak **Veleta** can be climbed without too much exertion in August. The road goes right by Veleta, and in August you can even drive to the top.

GETTING AROUND

For the Sierra Nevada, there is a daily bus (Empresa Bonal, Tel. 27 31 11) from the Acera del Darro, near the big fountain in Granada, to the Albergue Universitario some 12 km (7.5 miles) from the peak of Veleta. Departures are at 9 am, and the return trip at 5 pm. If you're driving, call 48 01 53 for road reports in Spanish and English. For the Alpujarras: some buses on the Granada–Motril route stop in Lanjarón, but to penetrate the more isolated sections of the valley, you'll have to take a bus from Granada to Orgiva, the base for connecting buses to the other villages. The weekly Alpujarras tour bus from Granada on Sundays at 8 am also departs from the Acera del Darro.

Daily buses from Granada to Murcia and Alicante stop in Guadix (Bacoma line, from Av. de los Andaluces, in front of the train station)

WHAT TO SEE

Some 20 km (12.5 miles) before you reach Veleta, you'll enter the **Solynieve** ski area, beginning at its main resort, Prado Llano, and continuing up to Veleta. From Prado Llano there are cable cars up to the peak itself.

If you're adventurous and the road is clear – not much of a road, really, though, there are plans to upgrade it – you can continue onwards from Veleta down into the **Alpujarras**, a string of white villages along the valley of the Rio Guadalfeo, between the Sierra Nevada and the little Contraviesa chain along the sea-coast. In Moorish times this was a densely populated region, full of vines and orchards. Much of its population was made up of refugees from the Reconquista, coming mainly from Sevilla. After 1492, the region was granted as a fief to Boabdil el Chico, but with forced Christianization and the resulting revolts, the entire population was expelled and replaced by settlers from the north.

Though often described as one of the most inaccessible corners of Spain, far from the beaten track, you won't be alone if you visit the Alpujarras. With their often spectacular scenery these villages have attracted their share of tourists detouring from Granada and the Costa del Sol – there's even a weekly coach tour from Granada. Nevertheless, they're hardly spoiled; with the villages relatively close to each other, and plenty of wild country on either side, it's a great spot for hiking or just finding some well-decorated peace and quiet.

Most visitors don't chance the Sierra Nevada route to Capileira, but use the Alpujarras' front door, off the main road from Granada to Motril. On the way, just outside the city, you'll pass the spot called **Suspiro de Moro**, where poor Boabdil sighed as he took his last look back over Granada. The last 33 km (20.6 miles) of this route, where the road joins the Guadalfeo valley down to Motril, is one of the most scenic in Spain, but if you want to see the Alpujarras, you'll have to take the turnoff for **Lanjarón**, the only real tourist centre of the region – with almost as many hotel rooms as it has population. Lanjarón has long attracted visitors as a spa, and today it ships out most of the mineral water drunk in Spain. At **Orgiva**, the biggest town of the Alpujarras, you'll have a choice of keeping to the main road for **Ugijar**, or heading north through the highest and loveliest part of the region, with typical white villages climbing the hillsides under terraced fields. **Soportújar**, the first, has one of the Alpujarras' surviving primeval oak groves behind it; oaks and chestnuts, both rare elsewhere in Andalucía, are among the most common trees here. Next come **Pampaneira, Bubion** and **Capileira**, all within sight of each other on a short detour along the edge of the beautiful (but walkable) ravine called **Barranco de Poqueira**. Capileira, the last village on the mountain pass route over Mulhacen and Veleta, sees more tourists than most Alpujarras villages.

Trevelez, on the slopes of Mulhacen, likes to claim it's the highest village in Europe. It's also famous in Andalucía for its snow-cured hams. From there the road slopes back downwards to Juviles and **Berchules**, one of the villages where the traditional art of carpet weaving has been maintained since Moorish times. **Yegen**, some 10 km (6.3 miles) further, became temporarily famous as the long-time home of British writer Gerald Brenan. After that come more intensively farmed areas on the lower slopes, with oranges, vineyards and almonds; you can either hit Ugijar and the main roads to the coast and Almería, or detour to the little visited villages of **Laroles** and **Mairena** on the slopes of La Ragua, one of the last high peaks of the Sierra Nevada

East from Granada

It's a better road for coming to Granada than leaving it. Between that city and Murcia are some of emptiest, bleakest landscapes in Spain. For the first 70 km (12.5 miles) or so, the mountain scenery of the Sierra Nevada foothills outside Granada is fine, but as the land gradually flattens out, the first village you pass through is **Purullena**, long famous for its pretty ceramic ware. The town still makes its living from this, and the entire stretch of highway through it is lined with enormous stands and displays. The poverty of this region has long condemned many of its inhabitants to life in caves, nowhere more so than in **Guadix**. Times aren't so bad now, but several thousand of this city's population still choose to be troglodytes; their homes, complete with whitewashed façades built into the hillsides, and chimneys and television aerials sticking out of the top, can be seen in the **Barrio de Santiago** near the centre of town. The cave dwellings have their advantages. They're warmer in the winter and cooler in summer than most Andalucian homes, relatively spacious and well-ventilated – and when the time comes to build a new room, all you need is a shovel. The centre of Guadix is dominated by a

Moorish **alcazaba**, largely rebuilt in the 16th century, and a huge **Cathedral** begun by Diego de Siloé, builder of Granada's cathedral, and completed in the Baroque era. The great church and castle appearing together out of the empty hills make a striking sight.

There's not much else to distract you in this corner of Spain. If you're headed for Almería and the coast, you'll pass through **Calahorra**, with an unusual Renaissance castle with domed turrets, and **Gergal**, whose equally singular, perfectly preserved castle was built by the Moors. They claim you can see the stars more clearly here than anywhere in Europe, and Spain has built its national observatory outside town. The road from Guadix to Murcia is even lonelier; here the surprisingly elegant, little white-washed villages of **Vélez Blanco** and **Vélez Rubio** will provide a pleasant break in your travels. There are several caves in the neighbourhood where a wealth of 4000-year-old rock paintings of abstract patterns and symbols have been found.

WHERE TO STAY AND EAT

In the Sierra Nevada, most of the ski hotels close from June to December. Ask at the tourist office in Granada for what's available. An exception, staying open year round, is the **Parador Nacional Sierra Nevada***** (on the main highway, Tel: 48 02 00; doubles 5500–6500 pts), one of the smaller and newer *paradores*. Among the five modern hotels in the ski resort of Prado Llano, none particularly stands out; cheaper accommodation can be had at Peñones de San Francisco, at the end of the bus route. The **Albergue Universitario** there has rooms for 2000 pts half-board (Tel: 48 01 22). In the Alpujarras, Lanjarón has most of the rooms; a score of good bargains in the 2000–3000 pts range on or near the central C. Generalísimo Franco. Elsewhere, you'll find minimal though acceptable accommodation and food in Orgiva, Pampaneira, Capileira, Portugos (the **Mirador de Portugos***, Tel: 76 60 14, 2000 pts doubles with bath, 1600 pts without) and Ugijar.

EATING OUT

Most restaurants are open only in the ski season as well, and most are a little pretentious; **Rincón de Pepe Reyes** in Prado Llano has good Andalucian cooking for 1100–1600 pts.

ARCHITECTURAL TERMS

Historical and Architectural Terms

Ajimez: in Moorish architecture, an arched double window
Alameda: a park or promenade
Alcazaba: a Moorish fortress
Alcazar: a Moorish fortified palace
Ambulatory: a semicircular aisle around the high altar of a church
Arrabal: quarter of a Moorish city
Artesonado: Mudejár-style carved wooden ceilings, panels or screens
Ayuntamiento: city hall
Azulejo: painted glazed tiles, popular in Mudejár work and later architecutre, especially in Andalucía and Valencia
Baldachin: canopy on posts over an altar or throne
Barrio: city quarter or neighbourhood (Barrí in Catalan)
Boveda: vault
Calvario: calvary, or outdoor Stations of the Cross
Call: Jewish quarter in Catalunya
Capilla Mayor: seat of the high altar in a cathedral
Cartuja: a Carthusian monastery
Caserio: Basque country house or chalet
Castizo: anything essentially Spanish (from the Castilian point of view)
Castro: Celtic or Iberian fortress settlement
Castrum: Roman military camp
Churrigueresque: florid Baroque style of the late 17th and early 18th centuries in the style of José Churriguera (1650–1725) Spanish architect and sculptor
Cimborio: a cupola, or a cylindrical dome, as at Zamora cathedral
Citania: a *castro* (see above)
Ciudadela: a citadel
Converso: Jew who converted to Christianity
Corregidor: royal magistrate
Cortes: Parliament
Cortijo: Andalucian country house
Cromlech: circular ring of stones
Coro: the walled-in choir in the centre of a Spanish cathedral
Diputación: seat of provincial government
Embalse: reservoir
Ermita: hermitage
Esgrafiado: style of painting, or etching designs in stucco, on a façade
Estilo Desornamentado (or *Herreran*): austere, heavy Renaissance style inaugurated by Juan de Herrera

Fuero: exemptions, or privileges of a town or region under medieval Spanish law
Generalitat: Catalan parliament or autonomous government
Grandee: a select member of Spain's highest nobility
Granja: farm or farmhouse
Hermandad: 'Brotherhood', or specifically the national posse set up by Ferdinand and Isabel as a police force.
Hidalgo: literally 'son of somebody' – the lowest level of the nobility, just good enough for a coat-of-arms
Homage tower: the tallest tower of a fortification, sometimes detached from the wall
Horréo: Asturian or Galician granary or corn crib
Isabelline Gothic: late 15th-century style, roughly corresponding to the English perpendicular
Judería: Jewish quarter
Lonja: a merchants' exchange
Medina: walled centre of a Moorish city
Mesta: the sheep-raising cooperative of medieval Castile
Mezquita: a mosque
Mihrab: prayer niche in a mosque, facing Mecca
Mirador: a scenic overlook or belvedere
Modernista: Catalan art nouveau
Morisco: Muslims who submitted to Christianization to remain in Al-Andalus after the Reconquista
Mozaráb: Christians under Muslim rule in Moorish Spain
Mudejár: Moorish-influenced architecture; Spain's 'National style' in the 12th–16th centuries
Ojival: pointed (arches)
Patio: central courtyard of a house or public building
Pallazo: circular, conical-roofed shepherd's hut in Asturias and Galicia
Pazo: Galician manor house
Plateresque: 16th-century style; heavily ornamented Gothic
Plaza: a town square
Plaza de Toros: bullring
Plaza Mayor: square at the centre of many Spanish cities, often totally enclosed and arcaded
Posada: inn
Praetorium: palace of a Roman governor
Pronunciamento: a military coup
Puerta: gate or portal
Reja: iron grilles, either decorative ones in churches or those covering the exterior windows of buildings
Retablo: carved or painted altarpiece
Sala Capitular: chapterhouse
Seo: 'Cathedral' in Aragón or Catalunya
Solar: a town mansion
Transitional: in northern Spanish churches, referring to the transition between Romanesque and Gothic

LANGUAGE

Castellano, as Spanish is properly called, was the first modern language to have a grammar written for it. When a copy was presented to Queen Isabel in 1492, she quite understandably asked what it was for. 'Your majesty,' replied a perceptive bishop: 'Language is the perfect instrument of empire.' In the centuries to come, this concise, flexible and expressive language would prove just that, an instrument that would contribute more to Spanish unity than any laws or institutions, while spreading itself effortlessly over much of the New World.

Among other European languages, Spanish is closest to Portuguese and Italian – and of course, Catalán and Gallego. Spanish, however, may have the simplest grammar of any Romance language, and if you know a little of any Romance language you will find much of the vocabulary looks familiar. It's quite easy to pick up a working knowledge of Spanish; but Spaniards speak colloquially and fast, and in Andalucía they do it with a pronounced accent, leaving out half the consonants and adding some strange sounds all their own. Expressing yourself may prove a little easier than understanding the replies. Spaniards will appreciate your efforts, and when they correct you they aren't being snooty; they simply feel it's their duty to help you learn. There are dozens of language books and tapes on the market; one particularly good one is *Teach Yourself Spanish*, by Juan Kattán-Ibarra (Hodder & Stoughton 1984). If you already speak Spanish, note the Spaniards increasingly use the familiar 'tu' instead of 'usted' when addressing even complete strangers.

Pronunciation is phonetic but somewhat difficult for English speakers:

Vowels

a – short a as in father
e – short e as in set
i – long e as in complete
o – long o as in note
u – long u as in flute
ie – both vowels pronounced separately
ue – short e, the u is silent
üe – we, as in dwell

Consonants

b – in the middle of a word, often pronounced as v
c – before the vowels i and e, it is a Castilian affectation to pronounce it as *th*; many Spaniards and all Latin Americans pronounce it in this case as an *s*.
g – before i or e, pronounced as a hard H
h – usually silent
j – hard H
ll – ly or y
ñ – ny as in canyon (the ˜ is called a *tilde*)
q – k
r – usually rolled, which takes practice
z – th

Stress is on the penultimate syllable if the word ends in a vowel, on the last syllable if the word ends in consonant; exceptions are marked with an accent (´). If all this seems difficult, consider that English pronunciation is even worse for Spaniards. Young people in Spain seem to be all madly learning English these days; if your Spanish friends giggle at your pronunciation, get them to try to say *squirrel.*

Practise on some of the place names:

Madrid (ma-DREED)	León (lay-OHN)
Sevilla (se-VEE-ah)	Cáceres (CAH-ther-es)
Cuenca (KWAYN-kah)	Jaén (ha-AIN)
Sigüenza (sig-WAYN-zah)	Trujillo (troo-HEE-oh)
Jerez (her-ETH)	Badajóz (ba-da-HOTH)
Málaga (MAHL-ah-gah)	Alcazar (ahl-CATH-ar)
Valladolid (vy-ah-dol-EED)	Arévalo (ahr-EV-vah-lo)

Notices and street signs in Catalán or Basque are bound to be confusing. Today's federal Spain has five or six official languages, but nearly everyone understands **Castellano.**

Useful words and phrases

yes	sí	What is that?	¿Qué es eso?
no	no	what	qué
I don't know	No sé	who	quien
I don't understand (Spanish)	No comprendo (Español)	where	dónde
		when	cuando
Does someone here speak English?	¿Hay alguien que hable inglés?	why	por qué
		how	cómo
Speak slowly	Hable despacio	how much	cuánto
Can you assist me?	¿Puede usted ayudarme?	how many	cuántas
help!	¡Soccoro!		
		I am lost	Me he perdido
please	por favor	I am hungry	Tengo hambre
thank you (very much)	(muchas) gracias	I am thirsty	Tengo sed
you're welcome	de nada	I am sorry	Lo siento
It doesn't matter	no importa	I am tired	Estoy cansado
all right	está bien	I am sleepy	Tengo sueño
excuse me	perdóneme	I am ill	No siento bien
be careful!	¡Tenga cuidado!	Leave me alone	Déjeme en paz
maybe	quizás	good	bueno/buena
nothing	nada	bad	mal/malo
It is urgent!	¡Es urgente!	it's all the same	es igual
How do you do?	¿Cómo está usted?	slow	despacio
Well, and you?	¿Bien, y usted?	fast	rápido
What is your name?	¿Como se llama?	big	grande
hello	¡Ola!	small	pequeño
goodbye	Adios/Hasta luego	hot	caliente
good morning	Buenos dias	cold	frío
good afternoon	Buenas tardes	up	arriba
good evening	Buenas noches	down	abajo

SHOPPING, SERVICE, SIGHTSEEING

I would like...	Quisiera...	closed	cerrado
Where is/are...	Dónde está/están...	cheap/expensive	barato/caro
How much is it?	¿Cuánto vale eso?	bank	banco
open	abierto	beach	playa
		bed	cama

church	iglesia
hospital	hospital
money	dinero
museum	museo
newspaper (foreign)	periódico (extranjero)
pharmacy	farmacía
police station	comisaría
policeman	policía
post office	correos
sea	mar
shop	tienda
telephone	teléfono
tobacco shop (subpost office)	el estanco
toilet/toilets	servicios/aseos
men	Señores/Hombres/ Caballeros
women	Señoras/Damas

TIME

What time is it?	Qué hora es?
month	mes
week	semana
day	día
morning	mañana
afternoon	tarde
evening	noche
today	hoy
yesterday	ayer
soon	pronto
tomorrow	mañana
now	ahora
later	despues
it is early	Está presto
it is late	Está tarde

DAYS

Monday	lunes
Tuesday	martes
Wednesday	miércoles
Thursday	jueves
Friday	viernes
Saturday	sábado
Sunday	domingo

NUMBERS

one	uno/una
two	dos
three	tres
four	cuatro
five	cinco
six	seis
seven	siete
eight	ocho
nine	nueve
ten	diez
eleven	once
twelve	doce
thirteen	trece
fourteen	catorce
fifteen	quince
sixteen	dieciséis
seventeen	diecisiete
eighteen	dieciocho
nineteen	diecinueve
twenty	veinte
twenty one	veintiuno
thirty	treinta
forty	cuarenta
fifty	cincuenta
sixty	sesenta
seventy	setenta
eighty	ochenta
ninety	noventa
one hundred	cien
one hundred and one	ciento-uno
five hundred	quinientos
one thousand	mil

TRANSPORT

airport	aeropuerto
bus stop	parada
bus/coach	autobús/autocar
railway station	estación ferroviario
train	tren
port	puerto
port station	estación maritimo
ship	buque/barca/ embarcadero
automobile	coche
ticket	billete
customs	aduana
seat	asiento

TRAVEL DIRECTIONS

I want to go to...	Deseo ir a...
How can I get to...?	¿Como puedo llegar a...?
Do you stop at...?	¿Para en...?
Where is...?	¿Donde está...?
When is the next...?	¿Cuándo sale el próximo...?
From which stop does it leave?	¿De donde sale?

How long does the trip take?	¿Cuánto tiempo dura el viaje?
How much is the fare?	¿Cuánto vale el billete?
good trip!	¡Buen viaje!
here	aquí
there	allí
close	cerca
far	lejos
full	lleno
left	izquierda
right	derecha
forward	adelante
backward	atrasada
north	norte/septentrional
south	sud/sur/meridional
east	este/oriente
west	oeste/occidental
corner	esqina
square	plaza

DRIVING

rent	aquilar
car	coche
motorbike/moped	scooter/mobylette
bicycle	bicicleta
petrol?	gasolina
garage?	garaje?
This doesn't work	Esto no funciona
mechanic	mecánico
map	mapa
Where is the road to?	¿Dónde está el camino a...?
Is the road good?	¿Es buena la carretera?
breakdown	avería
(international) Driver's licenc	carnet de conducir (internacional)
driver	conductor, chófer
speed	velocidad
exit	salida
entrance	entrada
danger	peligro
no parking	estacionamento prohibido
narrow	estrecha
yield	ceda el paso

(Most signs will be in international pictographs)

Spanish menu and restaurant vocabulary

Entremesas y Huevos	**Hors d'oeuvres and Eggs**
alcachofas con mahonese	artichokes with mayonnaise
ancas de rana	frog legs
aceitunas	olives
caldo	broth
entremeses variados	assorted hors d'oeuvres
huevos de flamenco	baked eggs in tomato sauce
gazpacho	cold soup
huevos al plato	fried eggs
huevos revueltos	scrambled eggs
sopa de arroz	rice soup
sopa de espárragos	asparagus soup
sopa de ajo	garlic soup
sopa de fideos	noodle soup
sopa de garbanzos	chick pea soup
sopa de lentejas	lentil soup
sopa de verduras	vegetable soup
tortilla	Spanish omelette (with potatoes)
tortilla a la francésca	French omelette

Pescados	**Fish**
anchoas	anchovies
anguilas	eels
angulas	baby eels
almejas	clams
atún	tuna fish
bacalao	codfish (usually dried)
besugo	sea bream
bonito	tunny
boquerones	fresh anchovies
caballa	mackerel
calamares (or chiperones)	squid (*en su tinta*, in its own ink)
cangrejo	crab
ástaco	crayfish
centollo	spider crab
chirlas	baby clams
dorada, lubina	sea bass
escabeche	pickled or marinated fish
gambas	prawns
langosta	lobster
langostina	giant prawns
lenguado	sole
mariscos	shellfish
mejillones	mussels
merluzo	hake
mero	halibut
ostras	oysters
percebes	barnacles
pescadilla	whiting
pez espada	swordfish
platija	plaice
pulpo	octopus
rodaballo	turbot
rape	monkfish
raya	skate

salmon	salmon	trucha	trout
salmonete	red mullet	veneras	scallops
sardinas	sardines	zarzuela	fish stew

Carnes y Aves	**Meats and Fowl**		
albóndigas	meatballs	jabalí	wild boar
asada	roast	jamón serrano	smoked ham
bistek	beefsteak	jamón de York	baked ham
callos	tripe	lengua	tongue
cerdo	pork	lomo	pork loin
chorizo	sausage	morcilla	blood sausage
chuletas	chops	paloma	squab
cochinillo	suckling pig	pato	duck
corazón	heart	pavo	turkey
conejo	rabbit	perdiz	partridge
cordero	lamb	pollo	chicken
faison	pheasant	riñones	kidneys
filete	fillet	salchicha	sausage
fiambres	cold meats	sesos	brains
hígado	liver	ternera	beef

*Note that *potajes, cocidos, quisadas, estofados, fabadas* and *cazelas* are various kinds of stews.

Verduras Legumbres	**Vegetables**		
alcachofas	artichokes	guisantes	green peas
apio	celery	judías	French beans
arroz	rice	lechuga	lettuce
berenjena	aubergine (eggplant)	lentejas	lentils
cebolla	onion	patatas	potatoes
champiñones	mushrooms	patatas fritas	fried potatoes
col, repollo	cabbage	patatas salteados	baked potatoes
coliflor	cauliflower	pepino	cucumber
endivias	endives	pimento	pepper
ensalada	salad	puerros	leeks
espárragos	asparagus	remolachas	beetroots (beets)
espinacas	spinach	setas	Spanish mushrooms
garbanzos	chickpeas	zanahorias	carrots

Frutas y postres	**Fruits and desserts**		
albaricoque	apricot	helados	ice creams
almendras	almonds	higos	figs
arroz con leche	rice pudding	manzana	apple
bizcocho, pastel, torta	cake	melocotón	peach
		melón	melon
blanco y negro	ice cream and coffee float	naranja	orange
		pajama	flan with ice cream
cerezas	cherries	pasteles	pastries
ciruelas	plums	pera	pear
ciruela pasa	prune	piña	pineapple
flan	custard (creme caramel)	plátano	banana
		queso	cheese
frambuesas	raspberries	requesón	soft white cheese
fresas (con nata)	strawberries (with cream)	sandía	watermelon
		tarta	pie
galletas	biscuits (cookies)	torta	shortcake
granizado	slush, iced squash	turrón	nougat
		uvas	grapes

Bebidas	**Beverages**		
agua mineral (sin/con gaz)	mineral water (without/with fizz)	chocolate	chocolate
cerveza	beer	leche	milk
café (con leche)	coffee (with milk)	batido de leche	milkshake
cava	Spanish champagne	té (con limón)	tea (with lemon)
		vino (tinto, rosado, blanco)	wine (red, rosé, white)

Other words			
aceite (de oliva)	(olive) oil	mermelada	marmalade
ajo	garlic	mesa	table
almuerzo/comida	lunch	miel	honey
azúcar	sugar	pan	bread
bocadillo	sandwich	panecillo	roll
cambio	change	pimentón	ground pepper
camerero	waiter	pomelo	grapefruit
carta	menu	plata	plate
cena	dinner	sal	salt
cuchara	knife	salsa	sauce
cuchillo	spoon	servilleta	napkin
cuenta	bill	taza	cup
desayuno	breakfast	tenedor	fork
empañados	meat pie	tostada	toast
hielo	ice	vaso	glass
limón	lemon	vinegre	vinegar
mantequilla	butter		

FURTHER READING

General and Travel

Borrow, George, *The Bible in Spain* (various editions, first written in 1843). A jolly travel account by a preposterous Protestant Bible salesman in 19th-century Spain.

Ford, Richard, *Gatherings from Spain* (Everyman). A boiled-down version of the all-time classic travel-book *A Handbook for Travellers in Spain*, written in 1845. Hard to find but worth the trouble.

Hooper, John, *The Spaniards* (Viking 1986). New on the market, a comprehensive account of contemporary Spanish life and politics. Well done.

Lee, Laurie, *As I Walked Out One Midsummer Morning* and *A Rose for Winter*. Very well-written adventures of a young man in Spain in 1936, and his return 20 years later.

Michener, James A., *Iberia* (Fawcett, 1984). 950 pages of windy bosh, but full of fascinating sidelights just the same.

Morris, Jan, *Spain* (Penguin, 1982). A little disappointing considering the author; careless generalizations and dubious ideas sustained by crystalline prose.

History

Brenan, Gerald, *Spanish Labyrinth* (Cambridge, 1943). Origins of the Civil War.

Carr, Raymond, *Modern Spain 1875–1980* (Oxford, 1985). A confusing period, confusingly rendered.

Castro, Americo, *The Structure of Spanish History* (E. L. King, 1954). A remarkable interpretation of Spain's history, published in exile during the Franco years.

Elliot, H. H., *Imperial Spain 1469–1714* (Pelican, 1983). Elegant proof that much of the best writing these days is in the field of history.

Gibson, Ian, *The Assassination of Federico Garcia Lorca* (Penguin 1984).

Kanen, Henry, *The Spanish Inquisition* (out of print). The definitive history.

Mitchell, David, *The Spanish Civil War* (Granda 1982). Anecdotal; wonderful photographs.

Orwell, George, *Homage to Catalonia* (Penguin, 1982).

Thomas, High, *The Spanish Civil War* (Penguin, 1977). The best general work.

Watt, W. H., and Cachia, Pierre, *A History of Islamic Spain* (Edinburgh University Press, 1977).

Art and Literature

Brenan, Gerald, *The Literature of the Spanish People* (Cambridge, 1951).

Burkhardt, Titus, *Moorish Culture in Spain* (Allen and Unwin). Indispensable for understanding the world of Al-Andalus.

Cervantes, Miguel de, *Don Quixote* (Penguin and various editions).

Ellis, Havelock, *The Soul of Spain* (Constable, London 1937, out of print). An old-fashioned aesthete takes on Spain; good on art and discussing Spanish womens' erotic responses.

Garcia Lorca, Federico, *Three Tragedies* and *Five Plays: Comedies and Tragicomedies* (Penguin).

Hemingway, Ernest, *The Sun Also Rises, For Whom the Bell Tolls*, and *Death in the Afternoon* (various editions). The latter is Hemingway's book on bullfighting.

Irving, Washington, *Tales of the Alhambra* (various editions) and *The Conquest of Granada.*

Moorish Poetry, translated by A. J. Arberry (Cambridge, 1953). A translation of a 13th century anthology, mostly of Andalucian poets.

The Poem of the Cid, translated by R. Hamilton and Janet Perry (Penguin).

INDEX